TERRITORY AND POWER IN CONSTITUTIONAL TRANSITIONS

Territory and Power in Constitutional Transitions

Edited by
GEORGE ANDERSON
and
SUJIT CHOUDHRY

OXFORD
UNIVERSITY PRESS

OXFORD
UNIVERSITY PRESS

Great Clarendon Street, Oxford, OX2 6DP,
United Kingdom

Oxford University Press is a department of the University of Oxford.
It furthers the University's objective of excellence in research, scholarship,
and education by publishing worldwide. Oxford is a registered trade mark of
Oxford University Press in the UK and in certain other countries

First Edition published in 2019
Impression: 1

Published in the United States of America by Oxford University Press
198 Madison Avenue, New York, NY 10016, United States of America

British Library Cataloguing in Publication Data
Data available

Library of Congress Control Number: 2018957216

ISBN 978–0–19–883654–4

Printed and bound by
CPI Group (UK) Ltd, Croydon, CR0 4YY

Acknowledgments

We have accumulated many debts in the preparation of this volume. This project arises from a close partnership between the worlds of scholarship and practice—as is reflected in our own backgrounds, as a practitioner-scholar and a scholar-practitioner. George Anderson developed the initial idea for this project while a Senior Global Fellow from Practice & Government with the Global Fellows Program at the NYU School of Law, and a Visiting Fellow at the Center for Constitutional Transitions (then at the NYU School of Law) during the 2013/14 academic year, when Sujit Choudhry was the Cecelia Goetz Professor of Law at NYU. We are grateful to two great Deans—Trevor Morrison and Ricky Revesz—for making Anderson's year at NYU possible, and for providing generous financial support to the Center for Constitutional Transitions.

When we approached Sumit Bisarya, Head of Constitution Building at the International Institute for Democracy and Electoral Assistance (International IDEA), and Rupak Chattopadhyay, President and CEO of the Forum of Federations, to partner with us on this project, they enthusiastically agreed. Together, we refined the concept note and research questions, developed the work plan, and recruited a global network of scholars and practitioners to join our project. In addition to their intellectual contributions, they devoted considerable financial resources, and have been steadfast in their support and extremely patient as we brought this work to a conclusion. We are most grateful to them. We also thank Asanga Welikala, who was instrumental in the preliminary stages of the project.

Our first meeting of project authors—at which the authors presented outlines to allow for early feedback, and the refinement of the concept note—was generously hosted by the Gimnez Abad Foundation, in April 2014 in Zaragoza, Spain in the magnificent and historical Cortes de Aragón, Aljafería Palace, a particularly appropriate setting. José Tudela and Mario Kölling deserve our deepest thanks for making this event possible, which the Abad Foundation co-sponsored with the Center for Constitutional Transitions, the Forum of Federations, International IDEA, and the United Nations Department of Political Affairs (through the good offices of Jason Gluck, now with the United Nations Development Programme).

We presented the preliminary drafts of the chapters at a two-day international meeting in Brussels in October 2015, in cooperation with the European Union External Action Service and hosted by the European Union Committee of Regions. In addition to the project experts, this meeting was attended by nearly 100 representatives of multilateral organizations, regional organizations, ministries of foreign affairs, overseas development authorities, nongovernmental organizations, and technical advisors. We received valuable feedback and input from the meeting participants, which helped to further refine the parameters of the project and the chapters.

We were fortunate to recruit to this project some of the world's leading experts on constitutional transitions and territorial cleavages: Zaid Al-Ali, Jacques Bertrand, Harihar Bhattacharyya, César Colino, Jill Cottrell, Assefa Fiseha, Yash Ghai, Tom Ginsburg, Angustias Hombrado, Bryony Lau, Neophytos Loizides, Mara Malagodi, John McGarry, George Gray Molina, Gustavo Bonifaz Moreno, Luis Moreno, Cheryl Saunders, Nico Steytler, Rotimi Suberu, Stephen Tierney, Lucan Ahmad Way, Asanga Welikala, and Marie-Joelle Zahar. We have learned so much from them, both during our in-person meetings, and also during the lengthy editorial process, as they responded with good humor to several rounds of editorial comments.

During the 2017–18 academic year, Sujit Choudhry was in residence at the Center for Global Constitutionalism at the WZB Social Science Center, where its vibrant and interdisciplinary intellectual life provided an ideal environment for working on this project. He thanks Mattias Kumm for his generous hospitality.

As we reached the final stages of the project, we could not have completed this manuscript without the superb support of George Stairs at the Forum of Federations, who undertook the onerous task of ensuring proper formatting and completion of references. Finally, we would like to thank Jamie Berezin, Alex Flach, and John Louth at Oxford University Press for agreeing to enter into a unique arrangement whereby pre-publication versions of the chapters are available online to ensure their availability to as broad a global audience as possible.

A discussion paper setting out our preliminary reflections on the project results was published by International IDEA in 2015. A policy manual based on the completed project was published in 2018, jointly by the Center for Constitutional Transitions, the Forum of Federations, and International IDEA, and is available online.

Contents

Table of Legal Cases ix
List of Contributors xi
Introduction xv

1. Territorial Cleavages and the Bolivian Constitutional Transition 1
Gustavo Bonifaz Moreno and George Gray Molina
2. When the Total is Less than the Sum of the Parts: The Lessons of Bosnia and Herzegovina 22
Marie-Joëlle Zahar
3. The 2002–2004 Annan Plan in Cyprus: An Attempted UN-Mediated Constitutional Transition 43
Neophytos Loizides and John McGarry
4. Emergence and Transformation of Territorially Based Cleavages and Constitutional Responses in Ethiopia 60
Assefa Fiseha
5. States Reorganization and Accommodation of Ethno-Territorial Cleavages in India 81
Harihar Bhattacharyya
6. Dealing with Territorial Cleavages in Constitutional Transitions in Iraq 99
Zaid Al-Ali
7. Indonesia: "Special Autonomy" for Aceh and Papua 119
Jacques Bertrand
8. Constitutional Transitions and Territorial Cleavages: The Kenyan Case 140
Yash Ghai and Jill Cottrell
9. "Godot Has Arrived!": Federal Restructuring in Nepal 161
Mara Malagodi
10. Nigeria's Permanent Constitutional Transition: Military Rule, Civilian Instability, and the Unending Search for Democratic "True Federalism" in a Deeply Divided Society 181
Rotimi Suberu
11. The Philippines: Peace Talks and Autonomy in Mindanao 202
Bryony Lau
12. The Withering Away of Politically Salient Territorial Cleavages in South Africa and the Emergence of Watermark Ethnic Federalism 219
Nico Steytler
13. Spain: Constitutional Transition through the Gradual Accommodation of Territories 237
Luis Moreno, César Colino, and Angustias Hombrado
14. Sri Lanka's Failed Peace Process and the Continuing Challenge of Ethno-Territorial Cleavages 255
Asanga Welikala

15. After the Scottish Independence Referendum: Toward a Federal Moment for the United Kingdom? 275
Stephen Tierney

16. Dealing with Territorial Cleavages: The Rise and Fall of Ukraine's Faustian Bargain 292
Lucan Ahmad Way

17. Yemen's Failed Constitutional Transition 312
George Anderson

18. Processes of Constitutional Transitions in the Face of Territorial Cleavages 330
Cheryl Saunders

19. Constitutional Design and Territorial Cleavages 352
Tom Ginsburg

20. Territorial Cleavages and Constitutional Transitions: Political Mobilization, Constitution-Making Processes, and Constitutional Design 374
George Anderson and Sujit Choudhry

Index 429

Table of Legal Cases

UNITED KINGDOM CASES

MacCormick v Lord Advocate [1953] UKSC 396, at 411 278–79

EUROPEAN UNION CASES

Demopoulos and others v Turkey App No 46113/99, 3843/02, 13751/02, 13466/03, 10200/04, 14163/04, 19993/04, 21819/04 (ECtHR, March 1, 2010) 47
Sejdić & Finci v Bosnia and Herzegovina. App. Nos 27996/06 and 34836/06 (ECtHR, December, 2009). 35, 372

INTERNATIONAL CASES

AG Federation v AG Abia & Ors, [2002] 28/2001 NSC 199
Re Certification of the Amended Text of the Constitution of the Republic of South Africa, 1996, [1997] (1) BLCR 1 (CC) 230–31
Re Certification of the Constitution of the Province of KwaZulu-Natal, 1996, [1996] (11) BCLR 1419 (CC) 230
Re Certification of the Constitutional Text 1996, [1996] (10) BCLR 1253 (CC). 230–31
Re Certification of the Constitution of the Western Cape, [1997] (9) BCLR 1167 (CC) 230
Job Nyasimi Momanyi v Attorney-General, [2009] HCK 68, (2009) eKLR 1 154
Martin Nyaga Wambora v County Assembly of Embu, [2015] HCK 194 (2015) eKLR. 155–56
New State Ice Co v Liebmann, [1932] 285 USSC 262. 355–56
Njoya v Attorney-General Miscellaneous Civil Application No. 82 of 2004 (OS), [2004] eKLR (2008) KLR (EP) 658 . . . . 146–47, 153
Onyango v Attorney General, [2005] KHC 677 153
The Province of North Cotabato v The Government of the Republic of the Philippines Peace Panel on Ancestral Domain, En Banc, GR No. 183591, October 14, 2008. 209
Re Secession of Quebec, [1998] 2 SCR 217. 369
Wimal Weerawansa and Others v The Attorney General and the Minister for Relief and Rehabilitation, (2005) SCFR App Nos 228/05, 229/05 & 230/05, SCM 15.07.2005 268

List of Contributors

Zaid Al-Ali is the Senior Adviser for Constitution-building in the Arab region for International IDEA. In 2015–16, he was a Law and Public Affairs Fellow at Princeton University.

George Anderson was a deputy minister (permanent secretary) in the Canadian government and subsequently CEO of the Forum of Federations and a member of the Standby Team of Experts in the UN's Department of Political Affairs. His *Federalism: An Introduction* (OUP 2009) is in 23 languages with over 100,000 copies in print and his *Fiscal Federalism: A Comparative Introduction* (OUP 2010) is also widely translated. He has edited books on federalism and oil and gas, internal markets in federations, and rivers in federal systems. He is a fellow at the Centre for Democracy and Diversity at Queen's University, Kingston, Canada, and had earlier resident fellowships at Harvard and New York universities.

Jacques Bertrand is Professor and Associate Chair of Political Science (graduate studies), as well as Director of the Collaborative Master's Specialization in Contemporary East and Southeast Asian Studies (Asian Institute, Munk School of Global Affairs and Public Policy) at the University of Toronto (Canada).

Harihar Bhattacharyya is Professor of Political Science at the University of Burdwan (India). He has previously taught at the universities of Heidelberg (Germany), Hull (UK), Fribourg (Switzerland), and Delhi University. He was associated with the Burundi and Sri Lankan Peace processes and facilitated Constitution-making for Nepal.

Sujit Choudhry is an internationally recognized authority on comparative constitutional law, and has been an advisor to constitution building, governance, and rule of law processes for over 20 years, including in Egypt, Jordan, Libya, Myanmar, Nepal, South Africa, Sri Lanka, Tunisia, Ukraine, and Yemen. He founded and directs the Center for Constitutional Transitions (CT), and has published over 100 articles, book chapters, policy manuals, reports, and working papers. His edited volumes include *The Oxford Handbook of the Indian Constitution* (Oxford 2016), *Constitution-Making* (Elgar 2016), *Constitutional Design for Divided Societies* (Oxford 2008), and *The Migration of Constitutional Ideas* (Cambridge 2005). Choudhry sits on the Board of Editors of the *International Journal of Constitutional Law* (ICON).

César Colino is Associate Professor at the Department of Political Science at the Spanish National Distance-Learning University (UNED) in Madrid. His recent research and publications have revolved around comparative federalism.

Assefa Fiseha is an Associate Professor at the Centre for Federalism and Governance Studies at Addis Ababa University.

Jill Cottrell Ghai has taught law at universities in Nigeria, and at the University of Warwick and the University of Hong Kong. She has acted as an advisor for several constitutional processes and is currently working with the Katiba Institute in Nairobi on the 2010 Constitution of Kenya.

Yash Ghai received his legal education at Oxford and Harvard. He has taught at the law school in Dar es Salaam, and the universities of Warwick and Hong Kong. He has been involved in the making of around twenty Constitutions and acted as chair for a section of the Kenyan process. He is currently working to promote the Kenyan Constitution alongside his other research activities.

Tom Ginsburg is the Leo Spitz Professor of International Law at the University of Chicago. He holds BA, JD, and PhD degrees from the University of California at Berkeley. He currently serves as a Senior Technical Advisor to the Constitution Building Program of International IDEA.

Angustias Hombrado is Assistant Professor at the Department of Political Science at the Spanish National Distance-Learning University (UNED) in Madrid. She has published on the Spanish federal system and on decentralization, asymmetry, and territorial accommodation in comparative perspective, especially about the cases of Spain, Canada, and the United Kingdom.

Bryony Lau is an expert in conflict prevention, peace processes, and humanitarian aid in Southeast Asia. Over the past decade, she has worked for the International Crisis Group, including as lead researcher on the Philippines, as well as in regional roles for the International Development Research Centre and the Asia Foundation. She is currently working for *Medecins Sans Frontieres* in Myanmar. She holds degrees in politics and history from the University of Toronto and the University of Oxford, which she attended as a Rhodes Scholar.

Neophytos Loizides is Professor in International Conflict Analysis at the University of Kent. Neophytos has also served as a consultant to various governments and international organizations, including the Council of Europe.

Mara Malagodi is a Senior Lecturer in Law at City Law School, University of London. She earned her PhD and other degrees from SOAS, London, and BA and MA in International Relations & Diplomacy from Trieste. She is a scholar of the Middle Temple and a non-practicing barrister.

John McGarry is Canada Research Chair in Nationalism and Democracy at the Department of Political Studies, Queen's University (Canada). He is a Fellow of the Royal Society of Canada and an Officer of the Order of Canada.

George Gray Molina is Economic Advisor for Latin America and the Caribbean with the United Nations Development Programme. In his home country, Bolivia, he was Director of the Bolivian Ministry of the Presidency's economic think tank, UDAPE (*Unidad de Análisis de Políticas Sociales y Económicas*), and was also coordinator of the Bolivian Human Development Report Office. He has taught public policy at Columbia University's School of International and Public Affairs, and was a post-doctoral Global Leaders Fellow at University College, Oxford and Princeton's Woodrow Wilson School of Public and International Affairs. He is a graduate of Cornell and Harvard and holds a D Phil from Oxford.

Gustavo Bonifaz Moreno holds a PhD in Political Science from the London School of Economics and Political Science. His thesis, "The Gap between Legality and Legitimacy: the Bolivian State Crisis (2000–2008) in Historical and Regional Perspective," focuses on the shifting salience of social cleavages in Bolivia's history and its impact on the country's constitutional change.

Luis Moreno is a Research Professor at the Spanish National Research Council (CSIC) in Madrid (Spain).

Cheryl Saunders is a Laureate Professor Emeritus at Melbourne Law School, Co-convenor of the Constitution Transformation Network, and a Senior Technical Advisor to the Constitution Building Program of International IDEA. She has written widely on comparative constitutional law, comparative constitutional theory, and method and the application of comparative constitutional law and method in the field of Constitution-building.

Nico Steytler is the South African Research Chair in Multilevel Government, Law and Policy at the Dullah Omar Institute of Constitutional Law, Governance and Human Rights at the University of Western Cape. He researches multilevel government in South Africa, elsewhere in Africa, and further afield.

Rotimi Suberu is Professor of Politics and International Relations at Bennington College, Vermont, USA. Previously, he taught political science at the University of Ibadan, Nigeria.

Stephen Tierney is Professor of Constitutional Theory in the School of Law at the University of Edinburgh. He serves as a legal adviser to the House of Lords Constitution Committee.

Lucan Ahmad Way is Professor of Political Science at the University of Toronto. He is co-director of the Petro Jacyk Program for the Study of Ukraine and co-chair of the Editorial Board of *The Journal of Democracy*.

Asanga Welikala is a Lecturer in Public Law and the Director of the Edinburgh Centre for Constitutional Law at the University of Edinburgh. He is a Research Associate at the Institute of Commonwealth Studies, University of London, a Research Fellow at the Centre for Policy Alternatives (CPA), Sri Lanka, and a member of the Inclusive Transitions Practice Group of the Institute for Inclusive Transitions (IFIT), Spain. His research and teaching interests include comparative constitutional law, applied constitutional theory, and Commonwealth constitutional history. He co-convenes the Arthur Berriedale Keith Forum on Commonwealth Constitutionalism, an interdisciplinary research network of law, politics, and history at Edinburgh.

Marie-Joëlle Zahar is Professor of Political Science and Director of the Research Network on Peace Operations at the University of Montreal. A Senior Non-resident Fellow with the International Peace Institute and a former member of the United Nations Standby Team of mediation experts, her research focuses on the uses of violence by non-state armed groups and the uses and misuses of power-sharing as an institutional mode of conflict resolution.

Introduction

This volume looks at Constitution-making and constitutional design in societies in which territorial cleavages have been politically salient. It brings together analysis of political mobilization, Constitution-making processes, and constitutional design in societies that have very different structures of territorial cleavages and that have opted for very different constitutional designs—including both countries that have opted to accommodate territorial cleavages in their constitutional design and those that have not, even after a long constitutional debate. The book is original both in bringing together the three themes of political mobilization, Constitution-making processes, and constitutional design and in its wide variety of countries, which includes cases that resulted in constitutional arrangements that are federal or quasi-federal, special autonomy for certain territories, and unitary.

The volume is the product of a multi-year collaborative project that was centered on case studies of seventeen territorially divided countries that had gone through significant "constitutional moments." There is a degree of arbitrariness in the definition of these periods of constitutional transition: some were relatively brief while others spread over years; some brought significant change that may prove enduring; while others changed little or sometimes nothing in the formal constitutional arrangements. Even when change is significant, a country's constitutional issue may not be "settled" in any definitive sense, so that there will be further rounds of engagement over future changes. The seventeen constitutional moments examined in this volume were all periods of significant, heightened political engagement around potential constitutional change. They provide material for rich comparative analysis.

The project brought its participants together twice. First, for a planning meeting hosted by the Fundacion Manuel Gimenez Abad in Zaragoza, Spain, where case-study authors made initial presentations of their cases and the proposed methodology of the project was reviewed. It was agreed that three central thematic issues should be addressed in each case study: political mobilization, the Constitution-making process, and the constitutional design options and outcome. Each case-study chapter would have a similar structure so as to facilitate comparisons. In addition to the case studies, there were initial presentations on the three thematic issues, two of which—Constitution-making processes and constitutional design—are the subjects of separate, comparative chapters, drawing on insights and lessons in the case studies. It was also understood that the two general editors would write a brief introductory chapter as well as a concluding synthetic chapter. The Zaragoza meeting was followed a year later by a meeting of all participants in Brussels hosted by International IDEA and the European Union Committee of Regions in cooperation with the European Union External Action Service, which permitted more substantive case reviews and further refinement of the common approach. In addition to International IDEA, the other sponsors of our project were the Center for Constitutional Transitions (then at the law school of New York University), and the Forum of Federations. Given the interest of practitioners in the project, this volume will be accompanied by a policy manual that will be published by the Center for Constitutional Transitions, International IDEA, and the Forum of Federations.

The cases chosen were all relatively recent examples of constitutional transitions and they were highly varied in what might be called the political geometry or configurations of territorial and other cleavages around which politics was mobilized. A "highly territorialized" region is one politically mobilized around a strong sense of territorial (national, ethnic, linguistic, religious, economic) identity as well as devolutionary demands. The cases included:

- Five countries with *several highly territorialized regions*: Ethiopia, India, Nigeria, Spain, and Yemen.
- Two countries with *two or three highly territorialized regions*: Cyprus and Bosnia-Herzegovina.
- Five countries with relatively low levels of territorialization, but with *one or more highly territorialized peripheral regions*: Indonesia, Philippines, Sri Lanka, Ukraine, and the United Kingdom.
- Four countries with *relatively low levels of territorialization*, though with major identity cleavages and where the territorial issue was important in the constitutional transition: Bolivia, Kenya, Nepal, and South Africa.

As will become apparent in the case studies and the final chapter, the allocation of countries to these different types is approximate, in that some countries seem to straddle two types, but we believe even a rough classification helps illuminate dynamics.

In addition to differing in the territorial structure of their cleavages, the cases differ in the other characteristics of their political cleavages (ethnic, linguistic, religious, economic), histories of intergroup relations, experiences of conflict, violence and democracy, levels of economic development, and geopolitical situations and influences. Not surprisingly, they vary too in the *processes of Constitution-making* chosen and in the actual outcomes, which this volume explores in depth. Some of the processes were heavily top-down and imposed unilaterally by a strong leadership, others were top-down but negotiated by elites, while others were quite broadly participatory and subject to majoritarian or super-majoritarian decision-making rules. These processes must all deal with such issues as who participates at different stages, agenda-setting, the decision-making rules, and implementation; the sequencing of these can be messy and iterative and in any case is not determined by a society's stage of development.

A critical issue can be whether the process takes place in a context of constitutional continuity, where key rules are determined, or constitutional rupture, where key rules are decided by elites. This choice between continuity and rupture can be related to a country's history in the period leading up to the constitutional moment, whether it was violent combat or more peaceful, pluralistic politics. As for the outcomes in terms of *constitutional design*, these range in our case studies from fundamental constitutional reform to little or no change in the constitutional status quo (which is not necessarily equivalent to the political status quo), and the actual designs vary both in terms of the territorial allocations of power (devolved or not; symmetric or not) and in terms of arrangements for power-sharing and rights protections, whether in central institutions or territorial units. It is hoped that the great variety of these cases will help to recast the debate around constitutional processes, design, and territorial cleavages so that it moves toward more integrated consideration of how political mobilization, Constitution-making processes, and constitutional design interrelate.

It is a theme of this volume that constitutional transitions dealing with significant territorial cleavages face political dynamics and challenges that are quite distinct from such transitions where such cleavages are absent. They can involve different Constitution-making processes and very different constitutional design options from those in countries in which territorial cleavages have little political salience. Federalism or some form of devolution, sometimes with asymmetric arrangements for certain territories and other times with power-sharing within central institutions, are the types of constitutional options that arise in contexts of highly salient territorial cleavages.

Despite all the uncertainties, the comparative analysis of cases such as we undertake in this volume can enrich the study of Constitution-making processes and constitutional design, and help illuminate some tendencies or patterns associated with constitutional transitions in which territorial cleavages are significant. We hope it might also help narrow some of the many disagreements that characterize work in this field. With this goal in mind, the thematic chapters on Constitution-making processes and constitutional design along with the concluding chapter attempt to pull together some general conclusions and certain lessons.

In keeping with the idea that agency matters—we hope that the explicit or implicit lessons in this study may prove of potential use for principals, advisors, or analysts involved in similar situations in the future, as well as stimulating for students of the subject.

1

Territorial Cleavages and the Bolivian Constitutional Transition

Gustavo Bonifaz Moreno and George Gray Molina

Overview

Since the National Revolution of 1952, Bolivia's historical pendulum has regularly moved between periods of constitutional, legal, and policy reform and periods of social unrest, political mobilization, and popular revolt.[1] In the country's very recent past, this alternation was further tested when longstanding ethnic and territorial cleavages erupted at the very moment a twenty-year-long political coalition unraveled. The December 2005 landslide presidential election of Evo Morales set the stage for a protracted constitutional transition that is still playing out.

This chapter describes the historical dynamics behind the 2006–08 constitutional transition and the political process during that period. Our focus is on territorial dynamics, in a country divided from east to west by a decades-long political, ethnocultural, and economic divide. For a relatively weak state with multiple political accommodation mechanisms, the key tension ran deep, beyond the formalities of legal, electoral, and constitutional reform.

We maintain that the Bolivian transition cannot be explained merely by the innerworkings of the constitutional process itself, but by the broader political dynamics, which broadened territorial support for the *Movimiento al Socialismo—Instrumento Político por la Soberanía de los Pueblos* (MAS-IPSP or MAS) from western enclaves to the eastern lowlands over a five-year period. The constituent process took place simultaneously in different arenas: the formal institutions of Parliament and the Assembly, popular mobilization in the streets, and electoral competition between the blocs in conflict. This political shift was buttressed by two key institutions: an impartial electoral court and a functioning constitutional tribunal. These "second-tier" institutions secured the broad legitimacy for constitutional reform. They were helped by the conciliatory support of South American heads of state (through UNASUR), during a polarizing episode of political violence in Pando in September of 2008.

The new constitution, approved in a referendum in 2009, secured long-lasting social and collective rights achievements and launched a new period of political stability in Bolivia. However, the process was highly polarizing and kept the political situation on edge. Many important issues—unresolved tensions from the past—were kicked forward, including key territorial issues, such as fiscal decentralization and the legal status of indigenous, regional, and departmental autonomies.

[1] John Crabtree and Laurence Whitehead (eds), *Unresolved Tensions: Bolivia Past and Present* (Pittsburgh University Press 2008); Raúl L Madrid, *The Rise of Ethnic Politics in Latin America* (Cambridge University Press 2012).

Territory and Power in Constitutional Transitions. First Edition. Edited by Michael Anderson and Sujit Choudhry. Territorial Cleavages and the Bolivian Constitutional Transition © Gustavo Bonifaz Moreno and George Gray Molina 2019. Published 2019 by Oxford University Press.

Background

Bolivian society has been historically marked by deep-rooted class, ethnic, and regional cleavages. The political salience of these divisions has shifted in response to the different waves of modernization and the shifting balance of powers between regions, ethnic groups, and social classes. At critical junctures, the state and its institutions have become the focus of the struggle to establish political order, with periodic crises crystallizing in violent conflicts that acquired territorial overtones, which were addressed through constitutional changes.

The Revolution of 1952 was a struggle between the economic elites monopolizing political power and a coalition of middle classes and workers led by the miners. Out of this critical juncture ethnicity and regionalism were displaced by class as the driving force shaping the evolution of the Bolivian Constitution. The MNR (*Movimiento Nacionalista Revolucionario*), the party that led the revolution, adopted a very centralist approach to the state's bureaucracy, with a shift from territorial or clientelistic relations to functional or corporatist ones. Nevertheless, because the party wanted to promote state-led development in many hitherto neglected regions in the eastern lowlands,[2] the MNR invested major resources in building a road connecting the Andean regions to the city of Santa Cruz. Furthermore, the military governments that replaced the MNR after 1964 invested yet more resources in the creation of an agro-industrial hub in Santa Cruz. While in 1950 the capital of Santa Cruz department was a small town of 40,000 people living without electricity, running water, or paved streets, by 1976 the departments of the eastern lowlands and the southern department of Tarija were ahead of the rest of the country in human development, with Santa Cruz progressively becoming the richest department of Bolivia (Figure 1.1).

In 1996, after the Sánchez de Lozada administration approved a new market-friendly hydrocarbons law, foreign investment soon started to flow to the sector, and the dormant project of building a pipeline to Brazil came alive in 1999. From there on, Bolivia started a transition from an economy based on mining to a gas producer. Furthermore, through the pipeline to Brazil and the re-inauguration of the pipeline to Argentina in 2004, Bolivia became an important geo-political player in the energy market of the southern cone. These waves of policy reform adopted since 1952 transformed the economic geography of the country. Santa Cruz, and to a lesser extent Tarija, passed from being peripheral to the country's development to being its main drivers. This process, in turn, created the conditions for the politicization of the historical tensions between the Andes and the eastern lowlands.

By 2010, Bolivian exports reached 7 billion dollars, of which 77 percent came from the mining and hydrocarbons sectors. Bolivia's new wealth led to redistributive struggles, notably between the elites of the producing departments of Santa Cruz and Tarija and a popular-indigenous bloc of social movements, which sought a bigger share for the state for redistribution among the most vulnerable populations, especially in the highlands.

[2] The notion of eastern lowlands is a geographic reference to the departments of Pando, Santa Cruz, and Beni, which are located in a tropical zone outside the Andes. On the other hand, the notion of the *half moon* is a political reference to the eastern lowlands plus the department of Tarija, located in the southern valleys of the country. Civil society in the half moon has been historically associated with the demand for departmental decentralization.

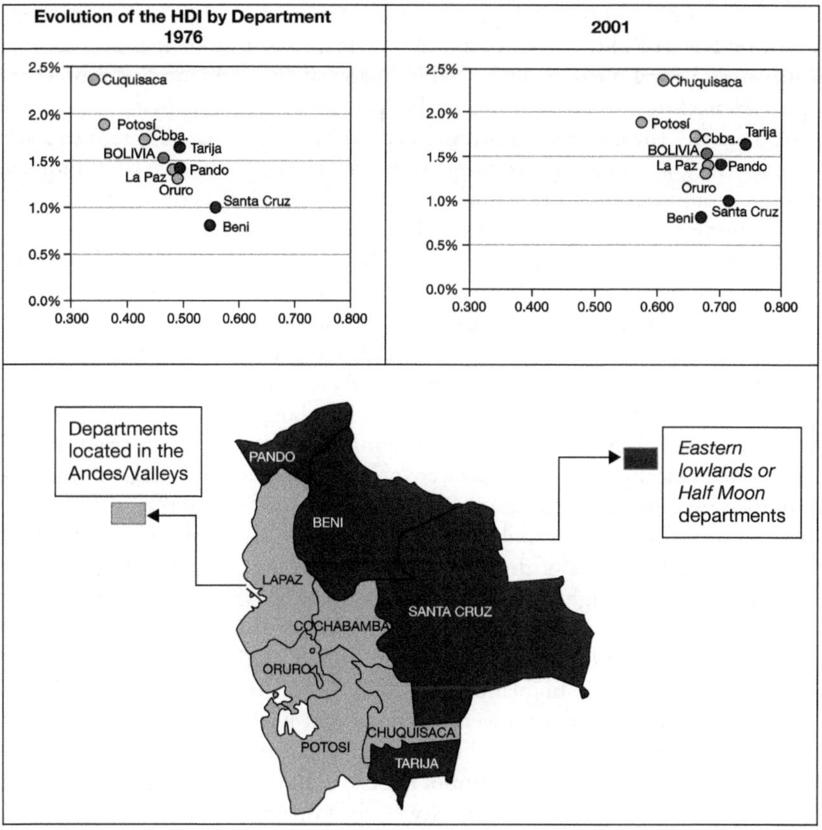

Figure 1.1 The Geography of Development 1976–2001

It was thus among the elites and civil society organizations of Santa Cruz that the demand for a territorial decentralization of power re-emerged, politicizing the east–west territorial cleavage. When democracy returned in the early 1980s, these groups, gathered around the *Civic Committee of Santa Cruz*, demanded political decentralization and the democratic election of departmental governments. Soon after, Civic Committees raising similar demands emerged in all departments.

After 1952, relations between the state and indigenous communities had been rendered in class terms, with the indigenous re-labeled as peasants and the key issue regarding their betterment being the distribution of land. However, with the return to multiparty democracy during the 1980s and 1990s, ethnicity re-emerged as a relevant cleavage for the constitutional debate. Furthermore, ethnicity acquired territorial overtones because the newly created indigenous organizations demanded the transition toward a plurinational state, in which their collective rights to land and ancestral territories should be reconstituted.

The main parties that led the transition to democracy in the 1980s, as well as the constitution, were products of the ideological framework of the revolution of 1952. Hence, the demands for decentralization and a plurinational state were at odds with the leading parties and spirit of the constitution. Suddenly, in a radical departure from its post-revolutionary tradition, Bolivia adopted, in April 1994, one of the most ambitious decentralization policies in the region[3] when Congress passed the Popular Participation Law (PPL) that territorialized Bolivia into 311 municipalities, embracing both urban and rural areas, many of which had barely experienced the presence of the state. Henceforth, councilors would be directly elected and in turn they would elect the mayors.[4] The law created oversight committees (*Comites de Vigilancia*), which represented the grassroots organizations from urban neighborhoods, rural indigenous communities, and peasant trade unions. It also allocated 20 percent of the national budget to municipalities, according to their population.

The MNR's switch from its centralist outlook was in response to demands for a radical decentralization of the state that were affecting the party's legitimacy in rural Bolivia and the eastern lowlands. Thus, President Gonzalo Sánchez de Lozada decided to decentralize Bolivia, but not under the terms demanded by elites of the *half moon* or by the indigenous peasantry of the western highlands. As a consequence, the actors pushing for devolution were not entirely satisfied by the PPL, though they used the institutional and electoral power of the new autonomous municipalities as platforms to advance their demands. Paradoxically, their demands were propelled by the very success of the PPL in terms of the provision of public goods, especially in the poorer rural areas.[5]

While trust in Congress and political parties increased nationally and in the Andean region during the first years of devolution, the Asian financial crisis of the late 1990s hit Bolivia hard and brought on a legitimacy crisis of the traditional political parties, whose support in the Andean region collapsed between 1997 and 2002. Between the national elections of 1997 and 2002, the traditional parties (the MNR, MIR, and ADN[6]) lost support in the highlands while still dominating in the eastern lowlands and Tarija. The traditional parties were more resilient in the eastern lowlands because they benefitted more from neo-liberalism. This disjuncture would be important for the explanation of the further development of the crisis. In the national elections of 1997, the ADN and MIR obtained the majority of the votes nationwide but in 2002 two parties, the ADN and CONDEPA (*Conciencia de Patria*), disappeared as the system became polarized. At one extreme was the MAS, supported by a network of peasant organizations and urban popular sectors, and the indigenous Aymara nationalist MIP (*Movimiento Indigena Pachakuti*), which won surprising victories in the Aymara regions surrounding Titicaca Lake; these two parties captured one-third of Congress and formed an anti-systemic alliance. Their strongholds were the rural western highlands and the poorer urban outskirts, and they were far from classic political parties, having been founded by networks of urban and rural trade unions, grassroots organizations, and social movements that practiced the politics of mobilization in the streets with the aim of opposing neo-liberal policies and pushing for the collective rights of indigenous groups. They demanded that the state be central in the appropriation and redistribution of revenues from the export of natural resources, particularly natural gas. They wanted to refound Bolivia under the principles of plurinationalism, by which the

[3] Jean-Paul Faguet, *Decentralization and Popular Democracy: Governance from Below in Bolivia* (University of Michigan Press 2012); Kathleen M O'Neill, "Decentralization in Bolivia: Electoral Incentives Outcomes" in Alfred P Montero and David Samuels (eds), *Decentralization and Democracy in Latin America* (University of Michigan Press 2004).

[4] René A Mayorga, "Procesos electorales, reforma política y sistema político en Bolivia (1992–1996)" [1996] Elecciones Y Democracia, UNAM, 327.

[5] Faguet (n 3).

[6] MIR: *Movimiento de Izquierda Revolucionaria [The Revolutionary Movement of the Left]*; ADN: *Accion Democratica Nacionalista [Democratic Nationalist Action]*.

indigenous peoples would gain territorial and cultural autonomy as well as political voice inside government. They called for a Constituent Assembly (CA) to achieve this.

In 2003, a massive protest inspired by these demands triggered a violent state response by the coalition in government. This event prompted further mobilization, with new protests from different areas moving toward La Paz. The middle classes, furthermore, turned their back to President Sánchez de Lozada, by organizing hunger strikes demanding his resignation. Finally, the President resigned in October of 2003, giving way to the succession of the Vice-President, Carlos Mesa, who, in his first address to the Congress, committed to paving the way for a CA and a binding referendum on the country's hydrocarbons policy. His proposals became known as the *October Agenda*.

The cycle of instability and mobilization to this point was mostly located in the western highlands. Civil society in the eastern lowlands, particularly in the city of Santa Cruz, had followed the events in the Andes with suspicious indifference. However, after the upheavals of 2003, the elites of Santa Cruz started to feel threatened by the rise of the socio-political bloc that toppled the Sánchez de Lozada regime. In October, the *Civic Committee of Santa Cruz* issued a communiqué, *Enough!*, which identified the roots of the crisis in "the frustration produced by the existence of a centralist, corrupt and inefficient system of government that could be traced back to the foundation of the Republic,"[7] while shorter-term causes lay in the closed character of the political system, which needed to "open to the demands of civil society for the re-foundation of the country based on a new economic, political and administrative structure."[8] Ominously, the Civic Committee warned:

> If [the above mentioned changes do not take place] we put in doubt the permanence of Santa Cruz in the current structure of the country . . . we just recognise the legality and legitimacy of a political system to the extent that we can exercise the right to decide on our own destiny under the inalienable principle of self-determination, to which all peoples of the world are entitled.[9]

In the days that followed, the Committee met with other institutions and organizations under the umbrella of the Assembly of Santa Cruz and with the Civic Committees of the southern Department of Tarija and the northern Pando. The Assembly of Santa Cruz reaffirmed its "unwavering will for the re-foundation of Bolivia on the basis of regional autonomies to be incorporated in the Constitution"[10] and it "ratified the decision to export natural gas to new markets, without any type of subordination to a national referendum and the right of producing departments to promote their own development . . . [through an increase in departmental royalties]."[11]

President Mesa followed his commitment to the October Agenda by rallying his popular support and a loose alliance with anti-systemic forces within parliament, to pass a constitutional amendment in February 2004 that created the possibility of calling a CA. This would be able to pass a new constitution with the approval of two-thirds of its members; it also provided for participatory institutions, notably a referendum on the country's hydrocarbons policy, demanded by those who protested against Sánchez de Lozada. Furthermore, the reform also opened the space for citizen organizations and indigenous peoples to participate in local and national elections. Until then, candidates had had to belong to a legally recognized political party even for municipal elections, and such parties had to meet a minimum threshold of national

[7] Press release from the Civic Committee of Santa Cruz, October 17, 2003, downloaded from PIEB, Virtual archives, *Programa de Investigación Estratégica en Bolivia* (PIEB*), Periódico digital de investigación sobre Bolivia*, available at: www.pieb.com.bo/index.php.

[8] ibid. [9] ibid, emphasis added. [10] ibid. [11] ibid.

voter support. The 2004 reform liberalized the minimum thresholds by differentiating between the territorial scales of electoral contests, so that a political party, *citizen organization*, or *indigenous people* could participate exclusively at the local level. This led to the emergence of differentiated and semi-autonomous sub-national party systems.

While Sánchez de Lozada had suffered bitter opposition concentrated in the western highlands, Mesa now faced similar opposition from the civic movements of the eastern lowlands. By June 2004, the demand for departmental autonomy, endorsed by the civic committees of Beni, Tarija, and Pando, was ratified by hundreds of thousands of people gathered in a summit known as *cabildo*, in the city of Santa Cruz. In January of 2005, hundreds of thousands gathered again in Santa Cruz to demand autonomy and direct election of departmental governors. The demands coming from these popular demonstrations became known as the January Agenda. The Mesa administration felt compelled to respond and by June of 2005 it called for the direct *selection*[12] of prefects, by popular vote; however, the radicalization of the civic movement also led Mesa to resign and new elections were called.

While the traditional parties had held on to their hegemony in the eastern lowlands in 2002, the 2005 elections led to the complete collapse of the party system installed in 1985. Evo Morales was elected president in a political system that had become highly polarized along territorial lines. While the MAS-IPSP became the most important political organization of the entire country, in the eastern lowlands a new political movement called PODEMOS (*Poder Democrático y Social*) emerged in opposition to MAS; it was decentralized and worked more as a confederation of local and departmental organizations than as a classic political party. Some of its members came from the collapsed traditional parties, while others emerged from a new generation of businessmen and regionalist activists, endorsing the pro-autonomist agenda.[13] In sum, between 2002 and 2005 the political system imploded, a collapse only resisted by the flexible structure of the MAS.[14] The elections of 2005 saw a major realignment in which the previous fragmentation gave way to a political system polarized along territorial lines: MAS won 53.7 percent of the vote nationally and dominated in the western highlands, while PODEMOS won 28.6 percent nationally, but swept the eastern lowlands.

These two forces were highly polarized in regards to their decentralization proposals. The *January Agenda* called for a highly decentralized—and probably asymmetric—regime built upon the foundations of departments. The October Agenda, on the other hand, called for a plurinational state that would be quite centralized in terms of economic policy but built upon the reconstitution of many of the pre-colonial territories inhabited by the indigenous peoples.

The Period of Constitutional Engagement

December 18, 2005, was doubly important historically, both because of Evo Morales's victory and because departmental prefects were democratically elected for the first time. The institutional reforms of 2004 broke the monopoly of representation of traditional

[12] For the first time, prefects—namely the main executive authorities in the departments—would be elected by the popular vote. To maintain a sense of legality, though, this exercise was named selection of prefects, because the president should endorse the outcome of the electoral process. He would appoint as prefects those who won the election in each department.

[13] Such as Oscar Ortiz, former President of the Chamber of Commerce and Industry of Santa Cruz.

[14] Santiago Anria, "Social Movements, Party Organization and Populism: Insights from the Bolivian MAS" (2013) 55 (3) Latin American Politics and Society 19.

political parties, with important effects in these newly departmental political systems and their relationships with the center. While the MAS won 54 percent of the vote nationally and led in five departments, it got only 33 percent in the prefectural elections and led in only three. PODEMOS, for its part, won 29 percent of the vote nationally and led in four departments, but dropped to 20 percent in the prefectural elections and led in only three. Different local political organizations, some with clear pro-autonomy agendas, successfully challenged the hegemony of the MAS-IPSP. In sum, forces with increasingly contradictory agendas for reforming the state and the territorial distribution of power prevailed in the national and departmental elections.

Six of the nine newly elected prefects opposed the central government of Morales. At the same time, the reform providing for the election of prefects was not matched by any changes in the distribution of powers or for the resolution of conflicts between the president and a prefect. Whereas before 2005, the president could remove a prefect with whom he was in conflict, the prefects were now secure in office so in the event of conflict with the president they could try to mobilize support in the streets and at the ballot box.

Nationally, Morales and the MAS controlled 55 percent of the lower chamber of Congress, but just 44 percent of the Senate, where PODEMOS held the presidency. Thus, it became very difficult for the MAS to pass the laws promised in its *agenda for change*. In this context of divided government, Congress faced competing proposals for calling a Constituent Assembly and for a referendum on departmental autonomy. Calling for such an assembly was the first concern of both the MAS and PODEMOS. The latter had presented a complete project for a new Constitution in its 2005 campaign, whereas the MAS envisaged the CA "as a plural, peaceful and inclusive scenario for the construction of a multinational and pluricultural state."[15] Soon after Morales assumed the presidency, he made his priority to call for a CA under the most favorable conditions for the new majority in the lower house and the social forces backing it. These forces had come together in November 2003 under the umbrella of the *Unity Pact* (UP), which was a coalition of social and indigenous movements formed in the wake of the violent suppression of demonstrations; it was closely connected to the MAS-IPSP, and it supported a platform for popular constitutional reforms. However, the MAS-IPSP was weakened in not having the two-thirds majority in both houses required for constitutional amendments. Nevertheless, in February of 2006 Morales sent to Congress a proposed Law Calling for a Constituent Assembly (LCCA), which would have 210 members, with three members elected in each of the seventy districts, with a political organization obtaining a simple majority getting all three seats.

This was immediately rejected by PODEMOS, but it was divided internally and could not agree on a counter-proposal. The civic committees of Santa Cruz and Tarija took the initiative to propose an assembly of five members per department, plus one each from the seventy districts, and this idea was later refined and adopted by PODEMOS. Furthermore, the civic committees of the *half moon* pressured their opposition congressmen to condition their approval of the law calling for a CA on a law calling for a binding referendum on departmental autonomy.[16] The opposition also demanded that the CA require a two-thirds majority to approve a new Constitution.

Morales objected to a binding referendum on departmental autonomies. This led the civic committees of the *half moon* and its prefects to declare a state of alert and call

[15] Gustavo Rodriguez Ostria, "Historical Framework of the Constituent Assembly," in: Historical and Documented Encyclopaedia of the Bolivian Constituent Process, Vice-Presidency of the Plurinational State of Bolivia, La Paz-Bolivia (2011), quoting the MAS-IPSP 2005 electoral program.

[16] ibid.

for mobilization in their regions, while the UP declared it would besiege Congress to ensure approval of a favorable law on a CA. Thus, determining the rules of the CA and around a referendum accentuated the process of polarization. Neither the MAS-IPSP nor PODEMOS could achieve the two-thirds majority needed to approve a new constitution or even to call for a CA. Therefore, the MAS-IPSP resorted to a strategy of trying to craft an electoral formula that would permit it to win the two-thirds of the CA—or, failing that, to reduce the requirement for a two-thirds majority. PODEMOS considered it vital to resist both possibilities, while the civic committees and the newly elected prefects of the *half moon* focused on getting a referendum on departmental autonomies, whose results would be determined on a departmental, not an aggregated level, and would bind the CA.

After months of conflict, Congress managed to agree, unanimously, on a framework stable enough to channel the *October* and *January* agendas toward the creation of a CA. First, Congress approved a law that provided for a CA of 255 members; 210 would be elected in the 70 districts on the basis of two members going to the party or organization with the largest vote and one to that with the second largest vote. The other forty-five members would be elected in the nine departments, with five per department; two would go to the party or organization with the largest vote and one each to those with next three largest votes (so long as at least 5 percent of the vote and, if not, the balance would be assigned among the first and second on a proportional basis). This agreement was a successful postponement strategy on the larger issue of the new Constitution, which avoided violence. The CA was to meet in Sucre, Capital of the Republic, and would work for six to twelve months beginning in August 2006. The proposed new constitution was to be approved by a two-thirds majority in the CA and then submitted to a national referendum, where a simple majority could approve.

In a second stage, Congress approved a law for a referendum on departmental autonomy that would be:

> a direct and sovereign manifestation of the popular will, [and] shall constitute a binding mandate for the members of the Constituent Assembly. Those Departments which, through the present Referendum, adopt the decision, by a simple majority of votes, will access to the regime of departmental autonomy immediately after the approval of the new Constitution.[17]

The referendum would be held on the same day as the election of the constituent members of the CA. Voters would be asked:

> Do you agree, within the framework of national unity, to give the Constituent Assembly the binding mandate to establish a regime of departmental autonomy, immediately applicable after the approval of the new Constitution in the departments in which this Referendum obtains a majority, so that the citizens of these departments can directly elect their authorities and receive executive powers, normative and administrative attributions and economic and financial resources from the central Government, assigned to them by the new Constitution and the Law?[18]

On July 2, 2006, Bolivians voted to elect the CA and decide if they wanted to advance toward a regime of departmental autonomy. The balance of powers resulting from the 2005 general elections held relatively stable for the election of members of the CA, with the MAS remaining the most important political force nationally, with PODEMOS in second place. However, PODEMOS lost some momentum because of conflict between its national leadership and the emerging pro-autonomy forces; in

[17] Law 3365 *ley de convocatoria a referendum nacional vinculante a la asamblea constituyente para las autonomias departamentales* 2006 (Bolivia).

[18] ibid.

Santa Cruz, for example, the recently elected prefect, Ruben Costas, with his former civic committee, presented their own candidates under the banner *Autonomia para Bolivia* (APB), which advocated a more extreme version of departmental autonomy. Thus the CA ended up with 54 percent of its members from the MAS, 24 percent from PODEMOS, and the remainder divided among fourteen formations, with one to eight members each, none of which had more than 4 percent of the vote.

The design for its election produced gridlock within the CA. The MAS-IPSP got the majority of seats but less than the two-thirds needed to approve its own project. The gridlock was reinforced by the outcome of the referendum on autonomies, in which the four *half-moon* departments of the eastern lowlands opted for departmental autonomies. This pitted them both against President Morales, who had stated that he would vote no in the referendum because he "didn't want autonomies for the oligarchies"[19] and against voters in the highland regions who voted no by large majorities. The law governing this referendum had established that the results would bind the CA to implement this change in the departments favoring autonomy, but the CA was deeply polarized on the issue.

From the outset, the CA faced procedural paradoxes. Congress had approved unanimously the LCCA, which had reaffirmed the two-thirds majority rule for the approval of the constitution by the CA. Nevertheless, there was an unresolved issue related to the proper nature of the CA as the source of the new legal order: could a law approved by the legislature have paramountcy over a CA charged with drafting a new Constitution? Or, could the CA, drawing on its popular mandate, establish its own internal rules for approving a draft Constitution and thus override article 25 of the LCCA. The MAS-IPSP argued that the CA was plenipotentiary, so that their majority within the CA had the legitimacy to approve a draft by simple majority. The opposition fiercely resisted this as illegal and contrary to the LCCA. To complicate things even further, the representatives of the *half moon* argued that the agenda for autonomy for their departments had superior legitimacy and legality because of the popular mandate expressed in the referendum, which followed the legal procedures embedded in the law on referendums on departmental autonomy. After intense internal debates within the coalition of the MAS-IPSP and the UP, the majority in the coalition decided that a draft Constitution should be approved by absolute majority. This was forced through, mostly by members of the MAS, and the opposition forces reacted by abandoning the CA and returning to the streets.

PODEMOS, along with the prefects, the civic committees, and the parliamentary brigades of the *half moon* organized protests in early September 2006. The UP responded with a massive gathering in which they hardened their position, declaring the CA as foundational and plenipotentiary. The *half-moon* forces responded by calling for departmental strikes. After a couple of weeks, the MAS and the UP stepped back a little with a revised proposal for approving each article by majority, while the text as a whole would be approved by two-thirds. Once again, the opposition rejected the offer. Finally, the MAS used its majority to impose its proposal, whereupon eighty-nine members of the opposition started a hunger strike in early December of 2006. In Santa Cruz, the prefect, other authorities, and the civic committee called for a third massive demonstration or *Cabildo*, in which allegedly a million people gave the departmental government a mandate to draft an autonomous charter or *Estatuto Autonomico*, which had to be approved in a future departmental referendum.

[19] Rodriguez Ostria (n 15).

These events led to a growing sense of uncertainty within the general population. A study of public opinion by UNDP during December of 2006, based on a survey in the cities of Santa Cruz, Cochabamba, La Paz, Tarija, and El Alto, showed high levels of uncertainty and fear about the conflict within the country, its territorial integrity, and the future of democracy among the urban population, especially in Santa Cruz and Tarija; this would prove important for the final outcome of the crisis.[20] With the CA in gridlock, the issue of autonomy became more polemic and contentious. According to the interviewees, departmental autonomies were mostly imagined as a potential trigger for further "disunion, separatism . . . conflict and confrontation in the Eastern highlands. Highlanders held this negative view of autonomies because of the unfairness and inequality that (the autonomous departments) would generate between them and the poorest departments of the country."[21] For lowlanders: on the contrary, autonomy basically meant "to own what we produce."[22]

Following the developments in the *half moon*, in early December 2006, Manafred Reyes Villa, the prefect of Cochabamba, a largely indigenous department in the highlands, decided his department should reverse the 63 percent vote it had delivered against autonomy in the referendum, so he called for a new departmental referendum. A month later in January 2007, thousands of coca growers, peasants, and groups from the city's outskirts marched on its center, where they burned the prefectural building and called for a stop to the referendum and the resignation of Reyes Villa. In response, parts of the urban population confronted the peasantry with sticks and stones. The police were overwhelmed and the confrontation resulted in three dead and 450 injured.[23]

This episode was a turning point in which the conflict shifted from a state-society dynamic toward a direct confrontation among social groups. Since 2000, social protest and conflict had increased in a sustained manner, largely directed toward the central or the departmental governments. The conflict in January 2007 was the first in which peasant sectors, initially mobilized against the prefect, soon clashed directly with the urban population. After years of being concentrated in the political center of La Paz, social conflicts and protests progressively spread in a decentralized pattern.

After the violence in Cochabamba, the MAS-IPSP proposed a new formula to solve the impasse surrounding the two-thirds issue. This led to an agreement that the thematic commissions of the CA would approve their final drafts by majority, as would the plenary for a draft Constitution; however, each article would be passed by a two-thirds majority of the plenary and, in the event of an impasse, the disputed articles should be subject to a national referendum where they would be decided by absolute majority. However, the shifting positions of the MAS had made the opposition skeptical about achieving a credible commitment with the majority, and so it started to behave less as a party upholding a veto power within the CA, and more as a pressure group interested in boycotting the CA. One final blow to the CA would polarize Bolivian society even further; namely, the status of Sucre.

[20] The UNDP study took place when the CA was in a stalemate related to the two-thirds issue.

[21] United Nations Development Program, "Informe Nacional sobre Desarrollo Humano 2007: El estado del Estado en Bolivia" (UNDP 2007) <www.bo.undp.org/content/bolivia/es/home/library/mdg/informe-de-desarrollo-humano-2007.html>.

[22] ibid.

[23] See Maria Lohman and José Luis Gareca, "¿Como entender los conflictos del 11 de Enero?" (Somos Sur March 2006) <www.somossur.net/documentos/11_de_enero.pdf>; *BBC Mundo: Enfrentamientos en Bolivia*, January 12, 2007, http://news.bbc.co.uk/hi/spanish/latin_america/newsid_6254000/6254243.stm

As a result of the civil war of 1899 between La Paz and Sucre, La Paz became the permanent site of the executive and legislative branches of government even though Sucre remained technically the capital. Because the CA of 2006 took place in Sucre, many groups within civil society and Sucre's mayor organized an *Interinstitutional Committee* to lobby the CA on the possible return of the legislature and executive to Sucre. This committee crafted an alliance with the leadership of the *half moon*, including its civic committees, mayors, MPs, and supporters of PODEMOS. In March 2007, a representative from Santa Cruz, Ruben Dario Cuellar of PODEMOS, introduced a demand in the CA for the return of the legislative and executive branches to Sucre, and this quickly mobilized the populations of both La Paz and Sucre, where demonstrators took to the streets. By July, the mayors of La Paz and El Alto, along with the representatives of La Paz in the CA, including many from PODEMOS, and different civic organizations of both cities called for a massive demonstration or *cabildo*, aimed at dwarfing the *Cabildo del Millon* that had taken place in Santa Cruz. Its motto was "*La Sede no se Mueve*" (the site [of government] shall not move). Two million people gathered in the city of El Alto to call for the withdrawal of the issue of the capital from the CA debates. In response, Sucre held its own *cabildo* days later, attended by the prefects and civic committees of the *half moon*. It was clear that under such conditions, a new Constitution would not be ready in August, the deadline established by the LCCA, so Congress extended the deadline to December 2007.

Caught between the conflicting forces of La Paz and Sucre on the issue of the capital, the MAS came down on the side of its territorial power base; namely, La Paz and El Alto. In August, using its majority, the MAS struck the issue of the capital from the agenda of the CA. Soon after, the CA was literally besieged by the local population in Sucre. Vice President Garcia Linera made a final attempt to gather consensus within the CA, and called for the formation of a supra party commission to save it. But in a meeting between Garcia Linera and the President of the Civic Committee of Santa Cruz, Branko Marinkovic, the latter expressed "his rejection of the [continuation] of the CA [or] the idea of calling for a new one . . . according to him because the road would be *too complicated*, with *too many changes and uncertainties*."[24]

Given the impasse, the executive intervened and, in coordination with the UP, prepared its own draft constitution outside the CA, which it expected to get fast approval by the MAS' majority in the CA. Garcia Linera called for the social movements to defend the CA; "Let's not leave it [the CA] to be kidnapped by a political minority . . . It is the people with their mobilisation who shall defend this democratic conquest, the most important in the last fifty years."[25] Leaders of the *half moon* announced that if the CA did not deliver a full regime of autonomies, they would start to apply it *de facto*. The population of Sucre, for its part, gathered outside the building where the CA was meeting to stop the proceedings until the issue of the capital was reinstalled in the debate. The MAS-IPSP and executive branch then instructed their constituent members to reinstall the CA in the *Glorieta Palace*, which was a military precinct. The members of PODEMOS, the MNR, and part of the UN boycotted the session.

Thousands gathered outside *La Glorieta* trying to block the plenary session, military units blocked their way, and three protesters died. Under these conditions the CA, by now mostly made up of representatives of the MAS, approved a draft Constitution without debating a single article. And on November 27 the Congress, in the absence of the opposition and surrounded by social movements, approved the possibility for

[24] Rodriguez Ostria (n 15).

[25] Garcia Linera quoted in a report from *Los Tiempos* (Cochabamba November 9, 2007).

the CA to meet anywhere in the country, after which it moved to Oruro, one of the strongholds of the MAS. Finally, on December 9, 164 members out of 255 (less than two-thirds) approved a new draft constitution of 411 articles. The opposition withdrew to the *half moon*. Five days later President Morales signed the draft Constitution to be approved in a future referendum and there was a massive celebration in La Paz. On the same day, the so-called provisional autonomous commission of Santa Cruz stated that its draft *Autonomous Charter* was ready for approval in a future referendum, a move that was followed by the other three departments of the *half moon*, during the following weeks.

By January 2008, the blocs in conflict had broadened their organizational bases. The UP and the MAS-IPSP gathered around an organization called the National Council for Change (CONALCAM),[26] which pushed for an immediate approval of the so-called Oruro Constitution. On the other side, the civic-committees of the *half moon* and its prefects formed an organization called the Democratic National Council (CONALDE),[27] advocating a regime of departmental autonomies. The relation of CONALDE and PODEMOS was not clear and became competitive over time. Later on, the *Interinstitutional Committee* of Sucre and its prefect,[28] as well as the prefect of Cochabamba and its mainly urban-based civic committee, joined CONALDE.

Each department of the *half moon* called for a referendum to approve its constitutive statute between May and June 2008. The MAS-IPSP called for the population of these departments to de-legitimize them by mobilizing in the streets and boycotting them.[29] The referendums in the four departments (Beni, Pando, Santa Cruz, and Tarija) represented a victory for CONALDE, which won from 79 to 86 percent for the yes. Despite some important pockets of resistance within the *half moon*, CONALDE was emboldened by these results and felt strong enough to send a letter to President Morales calling for a dialogue on the basis of the autonomic statutes. It claimed: ". . . with [our] victory in Tarija, we are four departments that have consolidated their autonomy . . . and soon we will be five, six and later nine . . ."[30] If Morales didn't agree on these terms, it proposed to call early elections in order for "the people to settle this contradiction."[31]

The national leadership of PODEMOS, which had been absent in the struggle for the autonomous statutes, began to see the rise of CONALDE as a threat to its claim of representing the opposition. In a tactic designed to reassert its leadership, the top ranks opted to refloat a draft law that had been presented by the MAS in December 2007, by which the President and prefects would measure their popular support in a recall referendum. At the time, PODEMOS had blocked the project because a recall referendum was not a legally recognized instrument. But in the new circumstances, PODEMOS assumed that a weakened government would reject the idea. However, after a moment of hesitation, Morales decided to take the challenge.

[26] *Consejo Nacional para el Cambio [National Coordinator for Change].*

[27] *Consejo Nacional Democratico [National Democratic Council].*

[28] Savina Cuellar, a peasant leader who was former member of the MAS-IPSP and switched sides after the conflict over the capital.

[29] International Crisis Group, "Bolivia: Rescuing the New Constitution and Democratic Stability" (Latin America Briefing No 18, International Crisis Group June 19, 2008) <www.crisisgroup.org/latin-america-caribbean/andes/bolivia/bolivia-rescuing-new-constitution-and-democratic-stability>.

[30] Boris Miranda, *La Mañana después de la guerra* (El Cuervo Editorial 2012) 114, quoting the letter from CONALDE to President Morales (June 2008), after the referendum on the autonomous statute of Tarija.

[31] ibid.

The recall referendum of August 10 delivered a 67 percent vote for Morales nationally, though he lost in three of the *half-moon* departments. Many people voted to ratify both Morales and their respective prefects, including key opposition prefects[32] such as Ruben Costas from Santa Cruz, who was ratified with a 66 percent vote. Nevertheless, it was clear that Morales was the most legitimate political actor at the national level. Morales addressed the nation in a conciliatory tone offering to harmonize the constitution and the statutes. In contrast, the tone of Costas's speech was highly confrontational, accusing Morales of the main responsibility for the political crisis.[33] Costas did not attend the meeting then held by Morales in La Paz, and soon after it started, the other prefects of the *half moon* abandoned it. Thus, instead of settling the crisis, the recall referendum intensified tensions between the contending forces.

Emboldened by its nationwide electoral support, the government, in coordination with CONALCAM, advanced the idea of a referendum on the *Oruro Constitution*, which would be done by presidential decree, contrary to the 2004 Constitution and the LCCA. Vice President Garcia Linera declared: "Bolivia has given us the mandate to continue with this process," and he declared the dialogue on a new Constitution and departmental statutes closed.[34] He offered "to regulate departmental autonomies through a law in a future dialogue . . . the day after the new Constitution was approved."[35] In reaction, the prefect of Tarija called for elections to form a "Departmental Parliament [as was] established in the Autonomic Statute of Tarija."[36] The National Electoral Court managed to temper the escalation by stating that it would not administer any electoral process called by either the government or the prefects if it was not approved by Congress.[37]

September 2008 marked the turning point when the crisis reached its highest peaks of violence. On September 2, CONALDE called for a region-wide mobilization and the blockade of roads until they reach their objectives of recovering their share of the tax on hydrocarbons, achieving rejection of the referendum on the new constitution called by the MAS, and getting recognition of the departmental autonomies.[38] The Executive took a step back and agreed to call for a referendum through a law approved by Congress, but the next day CONALDE upped the stakes and called for the ". . . the application of the autonomic statutes . . . and the formation of a broad front of citizens, organisations and institutions to defend democracy."[39] CONALCAM, as a response, called for a "siege to Congress until they approve, by two thirds, a law calling for a Constitutional referendum."[40]

CONALDE initiated protests, hunger strikes, and road blockades in the eastern lowlands. The immediate aim was to force Morales to compromise by including key aspects of the autonomous statutes, as drafted in the regions, in the new Constitution.[41] Soon after, all major roads in the eastern lowlands and Tarija were blocked and the major offices of the central government in the *half moon* were stormed and taken by

[32] Though the prefects of Cochabamba and La Paz, strongholds of the MAS, were recalled, creating a clear divide between the eastern lowlands and the western highlands of the country.

[33] Miranda (n 30); Rodriguez Ostria (n 15); Gustavo Bonifaz Moreno, "Causas y consecuencias geopolíticas de la brecha entre legalidad y legitimidad en Bolivia. El caso de la violencia en Pando en septiembre de 2008" (2011) 33 Friedrich Ebert Stiftung-Colombia Programa de Cooperación en Seguridad Regional Policy Paper 1.

[34] Rodriguez Ostria (n 15) ch. 3, 17. [35] ibid 19 (emphasis added). [36] ibid 20.

[37] ibid. [38] ibid. [39] ibid. [40] ibid.

[41] Raúl Peñaranda, Carlos Bohort Irahola, and Carlos Romero (eds), "*Del conflicto al dialogo: Memorias de un acuerdo constituciona*" (Friedrich Ebert Stiftung, Netherlands Institute for Multiparty Democracy and Bolivian Foundation for Multiparty Democracy 2009).

the autonomist movement. In three days, seventy-five of these buildings were taken as part of a campaign, later on, to "nominate new authorities by the opposition prefects . . . aiming at the creation of a parallel legal order."[42] By September 5, civic committee supporters in Pando had taken over the regional airport. President Morales accused the civic committees and the prefects of initiating a *civic-prefectural coup d'état*. By September 11, the situation deteriorated to the point that a gas pipeline supplying Brazil was blown up.[43] Over the following hours, street battles took place between supporters of CONALCAM and CONALDE in Tarija, in the south of Bolivia.

In Pando, at the other end of the country, rural peasant unions decided to start a march toward the departmental capital, Cobija, in order to re-take the land reform offices and overthrow the opposition prefect, Leopoldo Fernandez. This was part of a nationwide initiative of counter-mobilization organized by CONALCAM, in coordination with the MAS-IPSP. On September 9, Fidel Surco, leader of CONALCAM, declared that this was going to be a nationwide siege, adding: "we will teach them [CONALDE] how to do roadblocks."[44] In sum, the entire country was engulfed in a dynamic of mobilization and counter-mobilization, drifting toward civil war.

Peasants from Pando started the mobilization. The mayor of a small municipality controlled by the MAS provided them with trucks[45] and they joined a second column of peasants before heading to Cobija. They encountered pro-autonomist activists and took six of them as hostages.[46] By noon, a small police unit of fifty men was the only obstacle separating the parts. The police negotiated the release of the hostages but could not disarm the factions. After the hostages were released, civic committee supporters opened fire. Over the next few minutes, at least eleven peasants and one additional civic committee supporter were killed, raising the death toll to thirteen. According to a UN report, 593 Bolivians crossed the border to seek refuge in Brazil.[47] In the following days, the government declared a state of emergency in Pando and imprisoned the prefect, Leopoldo Fernandez. Nevertheless, violence showed no signs of ending, since thousands of members of CONALCAM, many armed, were advancing toward the city of Santa Cruz. Only after the international community offered to mediate, did the violence cease, just before the CONALCAM armed march reach Santa Cruz.

The intervention that stopped further violence came from outside Bolivia, from an emergency meeting of UNASUR[48] on September 15, 2008.[49] The UNASUR initiative had followed the mission led by the OAS[50] in April 2008.[51] The OAS, through its Secretary of Political Affairs, Dante Caputto, was given the mandate to mediate between the government on the one hand and the opposition in the legislature and the prefects on the other hand. UNASUR, through its pro-tempore chair, President Michelle Bachelet, issued a communiqué expressing strong support for government: "the [UNASUR] governments emphatically reject and will not recognise any

[42] Miranda (n 30) 48. [43] Bonifaz Moreno (n 33); Rodriguez Ostria (n 15).
[44] *La Razon* (La Paz September 9, 2008). [45] Bonifaz Moreno (n 33). [46] ibid.
[47] ibid.
[48] *Union de Naciones Suramericanas* is a political integration project formed by all the Spanish-speaking countries of South America.
[49] Peñaranda, Irahola, and Romero (n 41). [50] Organization of American States.
[51] Interview with Rodrigo Zubieta, 2013 (Via Skype from Washington D.C.). Zubieta is the former advisor to Dante Caputto, Secretary for Political Affairs of OAS in 2008. Zubieta is the current Head of Special Missions at the OAS.

situation that attempts a civil coup or a rupture of the established institutional order, compromising the territorial unity of Bolivia."[52]

The first meetings after the violent confrontations were held in the city of Cochabamba from September 18 to October 5. The negotiations bogged down, however, over a lack of compromise regarding the opposition demand to reinstate hydrocarbon revenues in favor of the departments. The talks moved from open-door meetings in Cochabamba, to closed-door meetings in La Paz, between leaders of the congressional majority and minority.

Three issues sealed the compromise agreement. First, the government agreed to seek a single re-election period for President Morales under the new Constitution. This meant forfeiting the possibility of a serial re-election, or at least two consecutive re-elections. Second, the opposition agreed to scale down their demands in the autonomy chapter of the Constitution and to give a new Congress the authority to prepare a future law on decentralization. Third, both sides agreed to an electoral roadmap which would see a ratification referendum on the new Constitution in the following months and general elections the following year. Finally, after changing 144 Articles, Congress approved the new draft Constitution on October 20, 2008. In January 2009, the constitutional referendum saw more than 60 percent of the electorate voting for the new Constitution, though it was opposed in the four departments of the *half moon*, whose civic leaders and prefects had campaigned against it.

Outcome

In early 2009 general elections took place, in accordance with the roadmap negotiated by the parties. Their outcome gave the MAS the upper hand in defining the future process of decentralization. This happened because PODEMOS disappeared. The opposition became much more fragmented and volatile, whereas the MAS won two-thirds of the seats in Congress. This gave the party the chance to shape the Framework Law on Autonomies and Decentralization (FLAD) that was approved in 2010.

Before the adoption of the Constitution of 2009, Bolivia was politically decentralized only at the municipal level. Thus, Bolivia was a two-tier model of decentralization. The central government was the only level in the system that had its political legitimacy provided by competitive elections and it made most major decisions up until 1994. After 1994 local governments were also elected by popular vote and they administered, with autonomy in terms of planning and budgeting, the provision of education and health services, infrastructure, irrigation, roads, sport, and cultural programs. However, the departmental prefects were appointed by the President until 2005 and did not have political autonomy, but merely executed infrastructure projects within a decentralized administrative scheme of the central government.

After 2009, under the new Constitution and as result of the politicization of territorial cleavages that had occurred, the system and its functioning became much more complex. The central government shared many areas of responsibility with the departmental, municipal, and indigenous or peasant levels. The departments, with elected governors and assemblies, administered, exclusively or jointly with other levels, the planning and provision of public services, while the municipal level kept the powers

[52] The Union of South American Nations (USAN; Spanish: *Unión de Naciones Suramericanas*, UNASUR), "Informe de la Comision de UNASUR cobre los sucesos de Pando: hacia un alba de justicia para Bolivia" (UNASUR 2008) 1.

obtained after 1994. The indigenous authorities, now elected according to their customary rules and practices, obtained significant territorial autonomy through the FLAD[53] of 2010. Thus the constitutional settlement had addressed the tensions between the *half moon* and the Andes and between indigenous and non-indigenous sectors of society by creating a complex multilayer structure of government, while leaving important issues regarding the fiscal structure and the extent of autonomy of indigenous systems of justice postponed for further legislation.

In December 2010 Congress approved the Law of Jurisdictional Demarcation (LJD)[54] which decided the scope of indigenous law within the framework of the new legal system. Following the re-definition of the Bolivian state as a plurinational state, the legal system is based on the principle of legal pluralism, by which the ordinary, namely *Western*, legal system is joined, in equal hierarchy, by the indigenous system of law and jurisdiction as well as a third jurisdiction for environmental and agrarian laws and regulations based on mutual cooperation and coordination. Disputes between these systems will be settled by the new Plurinational Constitutional Tribunal. Thus a majority of Bolivia's population decided, via referendum, to recognize the collective right to self-government for the indigenous population along with their institutions and customary norms within a framework of balance with the ordinary legal system.

Despite the fact that many indigenous organizations were not satisfied with the outcome, the new framework establishes that for a matter to fully fall into the jurisdiction of the indigenous legal system, especially regarding criminal law, there must be a material, personal, and territorial concurrence or identity. In other words, indigenous laws will be applied to members of a particular indigenous people, to facts, relations, and conflicts originated or whose effects take place within the territory of the indigenous autonomy, and regarding facts, relations, or conflicts historically regulated by the indigenous norms and procedures of the group. Indigenous norms have to respect the individual rights, the rights of women and young persons recognized in the Bolivian constitutional and in international law. As of 2016, eleven indigenous territories have decided to become indigenous autonomies though the full exercise of their normative powers awaits the approval of their autonomic charters. In June 2015 five indigenous autonomies held referendums in which three approved their charters and two rejected them. In any case, it is too early to make a thorough analysis of the workings of legal pluralism within the indigenous autonomies and the overall legal system of the country. It is foreseeable though that the implementation of such a complex legal-institutional design will lead to tensions.

Another issue that was postponed remains unresolved. The MAS won over two-thirds of the seats in parliament in the elections of 2009 and 2014, and the opposition has remained divided and volatile. There was to have been a *fiscal pact* to determine the allocation of tax powers to the decentralized entities, but this did not happen in the new law on decentralization (FLAD) in 2010 and was pushed into the future, because the central government did not see a pact as being in its interest. Regional opposition parties control Santa Cruz and Tarija, but in the absence of a national opposition able to counterbalance the hegemony of the MAS, they lack the political weight to force a real negotiation of a fiscal pact. This situation will probably extend well into the future, at least until the elections of 2019. The fiscal pact is important for the politics of territorial cleavages in Bolivia because both the central government and the departments

[53] Law 031 *Ley Marco de Autonomias y Descentralizacion Andres Ibanez* 2010 (Bolivia).
[54] Law 073 *de Deslinde Jurisdiccional* 2010 (Bolivia).

rely heavily on the income obtained by the country for its exports of oil and, more importantly, natural gas.

The taxation of hydrocarbons and its relationship to the funding of subnational territorial entities has gone through several phases. From 1957 to 1996, the Bolivian state imposed a 50 percent take of oil and gas revenues, of which 11 percent went to the producing departments. The Popular Participation Law of 1993, analyzed in the background section, created the new municipal structure of Bolivia and established the principle of fiscal co-participation, according to which municipalities and universities respectively received shares of 20 percent and 5 percent of total national revenue.[55] Municipalities received these funds according to their population size, though the poorest municipalities, often with small populations, received further resources under a pro-poor formula for the distribution of funds that Bolivia received under the World Bank's HIPC II initiative[56] as of 2000. Hence, up until 2005, municipalities did not receive funds from royalties or taxes on hydrocarbons.

In 1996, a neo-liberal reform of the Hydrocarbons Code dropped the government's take from 50 to 18 percent with a view to encouraging development, while maintaining the 11 percent royalty that went to producing departments. The same year, a new Administrative Decentralization Law devolved administrative responsibilities to the intermediate level (departments), but it was less ambitious than the municipalization reform of 1993 in that it did not advance democratic legitimacy at the departmental level or provide them with further resources. These reforms were clearly aimed at weakening the regional elites of the departments of the eastern and southern lowlands, who were perceived by President Sánchez de Lozada as threatening the central authority of the state.

As discussed in the section on constitutional engagement, these elites would reemerge as key actors demanding an ambitious territorial autonomy and more revenues for their departments. In response, in 2005, the Mesa government returned to a 50 percent take. Out of the extra 32 percent captured under the new tax, 4 percent went to each producing department, bringing their total share of production revenues to 16 percent. However, the 4 percent for the four producing departments allocated 2.7 percent to municipalities and 0.3 percent to universities, so the departmental governments got only an additional 1 percent. Each non-producing department received 2 percent for a total of 10 percent for the five of them, with the same scheme for proportional allocation within departments to municipalities, universities, and departmental governments. The remaining lion's share of the enhanced take was collected by the central government and redistributed to universities, the armed forces, the elderly, and an indigenous development fund.[57] By assigning these revenues to municipal governments and indigenous sectors, the MAS-IPSP tried to counterbalance the pro-autonomy segments of the *half moon* notably at the departmental level while empowering its rural and indigenous constituency.

Hence, the formula by which these percentages were assigned to different territorial levels was not the result of a rational exercise in terms of efficiency or equity; rather, it was the result of a highly political conflict among producing and non-producing

[55] Maria Lasa Aresti, "Oil and Gas Revenue Sharing in Bolivia" (Natural Resource Governance Institute, Revenue Sharing Case Study, April 2016).

[56] The HIPC initiative was an IMF–WB joint effort launched in 1996 and reviewed in 1999 to benefit highly indebted poor countries, enabling debt relief and strengthening the links between debt relief, poverty reduction, and social policies. https://www.imf.org/en/About/Factsheets/Sheets/2016/08/01/16/11/Debt-Relief-Under-the-Heavily-Indebted-Poor-Countries-Initiative

[57] Lasa Aresti (n 56).

departments, municipalities, indigenous organizations, and private interests over their respective shares. As the traditional party system collapsed between 2003 and 2005, Congress experienced a legitimacy crisis over the distribution of gas revenues, notably driven by the lobby of the pro-autonomist departments, particularly Santa Cruz and Tarija, as well as by the indigenous and peasant organizations that constituted the MAS. Carlos Mesa, an outsider who had come into politics as Sánchez de Lozada's Vice-Presidential Candidate in 2002, became President in 2003 following Sanchez's resignation, but he had no parliamentary support to counterbalance the centrifugal struggle over the allocation of oil and gas rents.

In 2005, Morales won the presidency and was determined to implement the MAS's view of the role of the state. He nationalized the petroleum sector in 2006 and increased the governmental take to 82 percent of total revenues in the case of the so-called *megafields*—those with production greater than 100 million cubic feet per day.[58] Morales favored greater central control of revenues, notably to fund payments to the elderly, so in 2008 he reduced the share going to producing departments by 30 percent. This led to demonstrations and violence in the producing regions and finally to the international mediation that led to the negotiations on a new Constitution. Indeed, one of the key issues that led to the final agreement was a commitment by the government to abstain from further cuts in the departments' share of these revenues. So while the opposition at the national level remains weakened and fragmented, the government has been cautious in this regard, recognizing that a change in policy could trigger renewed tensions between the central government and the departments that constituted the *half moon*.

The distributive struggle surrounding the gas rents was particularly sensitive in the last decade because, propelled by the high commodity prices registered in those years; Bolivia has been experiencing its highest ratios of economic growth ever. By 2010, the revenues obtained by the Bolivian state due to its exports of hydrocarbons constituted 6 percent of its GDP.[59] In sum, the struggle over sharing petroleum revenues has been a key driver of the country's territorial cleavages. However, because the political struggle over revenue allocation was essentially cast in territorial terms—the shares for departments, municipalities, indigenous territories, provinces—the outcome has been an extremely unequal allocation of resources in per-capita terms. For example, by 2012, when governmental revenues from oil and gas averaged $93 per capita across the whole country, the department of Tarija—which contains less than 5 percent of the population—received $953 per capita while the department La Paz—containing almost a third of the Bolivian population—received less than $10 per capita.[60] Decades of pressure exercised by the highly organized and politicized regional movements, and re-activated during the period of constitutional engagement, explains this outcome, which Morales, despite his political victories, was not able to overturn.

The dramatic decrease in the international prices of oil and gas since 2014 have affected the shares going to different governments in Bolivia and create further pressure for negotiation of a new fiscal pact. During the negotiations to approve the new Constitution, and on decentralization in the FLAD of 2010, the producing departments obtained tax powers whose implementation was postponed, because with

[58] Currently, there are two megafields operating in Bolivia—San Alberto and Sábalo—both located in the department of Tarija.

[59] Gonzalo Chavez, "Ingresos fiscales por la explotacion de hidrocarburos en Bolivia" (Inter-American Development Bank Policy Briefing 2013).

[60] Lasa Aresti (n 56).

their fiscal share and high revenues at the time, they didn't see the need to use these powers. However, the prospect of much lower petroleum revenues could lead the gas-producing departments to become much more assertive on petroleum revenue sharing. Probably as a preemptive mechanism, the government has adopted new centralizing strategies. The president controls the Ministry of Autonomies and Decentralization, created under the 2009 Constitution, and later demoted and absorbed into the Ministry of the Presidency in 2017. Since 2009, the central government has resorted to judicial prosecutions in its conflict with the prefects of the *half moon*. After a trial lasting eight years, the prefect of Pando was sentenced to fifteen years in prison for the violence of 2008. The prefect of Tarija was granted political asylum in Paraguay in 2011. The former prefect of Beni is now in jail awaiting trial on charges of corruption. Finally, the only prefect still in charge, namely Ruben Costas of Santa Cruz, is also accused of corruption but is free on bail while awaiting trial.

Another important issue for reaching a constitutional deal in 2008 was the MAS's commitment to limit President Morales to two consecutive terms. However, since the opposition has lost ground in the subsequent elections of 2009 and 2014, leaving the MAS in full control of the legislative agenda and the selection of the members of the Constitutional Tribunal, the MAS has been trying to undo the constitutional agreement of 2008 in regard to the issue of the reelection of Morales. In 2014 the Constitutional Tribunal ruled that Morales's terms in office should be counted from the approval of the new Constitution and not from when he was first elected president. Furthermore, the MAS used its two-thirds majority in parliament to approve a draft amendment to the Constitution that would permit Morales to be re-elected in 2019.[61] However, the majority of voters surprisingly rejected the amendment in a referendum in February 2016. This result was probably influenced by the economic effects of the fall in commodity prices and by corruption allegations against important indigenous leaders in charge of the indigenous fund, but especially by a scandal implicating the former domestic partner of Morales in influence peddling to facilitate contracts between the government and a Chinese construction company.

Morales and the MAS did not accept the results and the issue of his re-election was refloated in November 2017. The Constitutional Tribunal, answering to a constitutional consultation by parliamentarians from the MAS, agreed to allow Morales for a new re-election, based on the argument that the prohibition to elect the president for consecutive terms violates his political rights and the rights rest of the authorities elected by popular vote in Bolivia, allegedly contradicting Inter-American Convention on Human Rights. According to the Bolivian Constitution, international treaties on human rights must be applied with preference to the Constitution. After ten years of relative calm, massive protests have taken place in Santa Cruz against this decision in December 2017 and February 2018.

Lessons Learned

Was the Bolivian constitutional transition mostly a story of enlightened institutional design or deft political accommodation? Structure or agency? As the constituent assembly met, most academic attention focused on the inner-workings of the assembly and the contents of the constitutional text itself. Years after the approval of the new

[61] *La Razon* (La Paz November 7, 2016) 7.

Bolivian Constitution, a new appreciation for the politics of approval comes into clearer focus. We believe the Constitution approved in 2009 reflects the balance of powers crystallized at the moment. The MAS successfully imposed the general framework of the Constitution but at the same time it had to accept the inclusion of significant departmental autonomies, to a large extent as proposed by the *half moon* early on. The Constitution and other legislation have actually adopted many parts of the institutional design envisaged in the autonomic charters approved in 2008. This is why the Constitution defines Bolivia as a plurinational state with autonomies.

A central question is why so much political energy was focused on constitutional reform, given Bolivia's historically weak state and very strong societal dynamic. Political dividends would appear to have been higher for incremental changes that sustained the reigning political coalition. We suggest these general conclusions:

- Bolivia's constitutional agreement was possible in a weak state/strong society context because of two contextual factors. First, Bolivia had key procedural rules —institutions such as the Bolivian electoral court and the constitutional tribunal—to guide its turbulent and polarized constitutional process. Without a strong electoral court, in particular, the process and substance of constitutional reform would have been tainted by a polarized political environment. The electoral court was very important in redirecting the approval of the new Constitution toward Congress when it declared that it would not administer any referendum on the Constitution or departmental autonomy if it was not sanctioned by law. Second, agreement was helped by the permeable and shifting political coalitions and re-alignments, in which neither ethnic nor territorial cleavages were fixed or absolute. The political gains of the MAS in the eastern lowlands and southern gas-producing departments set the stage for a national accommodation that had not been seen since the early political momentum of the 1952 National Revolution itself.
- The constitutional reform process followed a unique window of opportunity—the collapse of an historic political party alignment and the emergence of strong, alternative political coalitions, with one party becoming dominant. The MAS geared its political messaging and coalition-building toward the urban middle and popular classes as well as the informal sector of small businesses. This deliberate strategy of broadening its political tent—beyond its traditional ethnic and territorial reach in the Andes—paid off very well. The lesson is that in critical junctures competitive and open electoral politics can create incentives for bridging the territorial cleavages if the system contains parties and electoral laws conducive to the formation of crosscutting coalitions. However, the success of electoral competition—rather than mobilization in the streets—requires an impartial electoral authority respected by all the contending forces.
- Finally, the Bolivian constitutional transition set a floor for further social and political reforms—the beginning rather than the end of an ongoing political process. Although the rhetoric behind the constitutional reform was of comprehensive and systemic change, the new Constitution is a negotiated and incremental text. It combines republican, liberal, and democratic features along with newer collective indigenous rights and a more robust treatment of social and economic rights. It has by no means achieved closure. Many issues not included in the constitutional reform continue to define the policy agenda in Bolivia today —from fiscal redistribution and justice-sector reform to term limits on the presidency, the

judicialization of the relations between the central government and subnational governments controlled by the opposition, and the implementation, in practice, of the principle of plurinationalism. Despite the political dominance of Morales in national politics and his attempts to re-centralize political power, he has had to reach some degree of accommodation on fiscal matters with the *half moon*, which continues to derive significant advantage from its natural gas resources. However, Morales' push to change and ultimately bypass the constitutional consensus of 2008, in his pursuit of re-election, has driven recent political instability and the potential reactivation of longstanding cleavages, including the regional divide, which is the subject of this chapter.

The Bolivian case shows both the potential scope and limitations of democratic constitutional transitions in weak states. The territorial dimensions of this process continue to play out today. Fragile and contingent agreements create the basis for robust institution-building over time. They also put more pressure on key political actors and institutions. As with many challenges in Bolivian democracy, constitutional change continues to be an open and evolving challenge.

2

When the Total is Less than the Sum of the Parts

The Lessons of Bosnia and Herzegovina

Marie-Joëlle Zahar

Overview

The territorial reorganization of Bosnia and Herzegovina (BiH) is one of the key outcomes of the Dayton Peace Agreement (DPA), the US-brokered agreement that brought the conflict in Bosnia and Herzegovina to an end. As they sought to silence the guns, the mediators behind the DPA struggled with the need not to reward the ethnic cleansing that harkened back to Europe's darkest hours while having to acknowledge that ethnic cleansing had, in fact, profoundly affected the demography of the country. The result was a complicated structure. Bosnia was reorganized as a consociational federation comprising two entities: Republika Srpska (RS) and the Federation of Bosnia and Herzegovina (FBiH).

In many ways, the territorial restructuring agreed at Dayton could be perceived as "ground zero" for many of the other cases in this volume. This chapter analyzes the impact of territorial restructuring in BiH and the context in which it took place. The restructuring of Bosnia was decided behind closed doors and under international pressure. The process was brief and backward (rather than forward) looking in the sense that it was primarily driven by the imperative to end the war. The Bosnian case study thus serves as a harbinger of the unintended and detrimental consequences that follow from poor process. It tells the tale of a territorial restructuring driven by strategic considerations that resulted in the hardening of contentious ethnic identities, the capture of the state by ethnic entrepreneurs, and the subsequent inefficiency, instability, yet unexpected resiliency of the BiH.

Background

Volumes have been written about the context that accompanied the breakup of the Socialist Federal Republic of Yugoslavia.[1] While this is not the place to recount this history in detail, suffice it to highlight that, in the decade preceding its disintegration, the country met multiple challenges. Faced with nationalist stirrings in the 1970s, Tito introduced a new Constitution in 1974 which gave greater autonomy to the Republics, recognized the autonomous status of the two provinces of Kosovo and Vojvodina, and

[1] Laura Silber and Alan Little, *Yugoslavia: Death of a Nation* (Penguin Books 1997); Misha Glenny, *The Fall of Yugoslavia: The Third Balkan War* (3rd edn, Penguin Books 1996); Susan L Woodward, *Balkan Tragedy: Chaos and Dissolution After the Cold War* (Brookings Institution Press 1995).

Territory and Power in Constitutional Transitions. First Edition. Edited by Michael Anderson and Sujit Choudhry. When the Total is Less than the Sum of the Parts: The Lessons of Bosnia and Herzegovina © Marie-Joëlle Zahar 2019. Published 2019 by Oxford University Press.

promoted Macedonians and Montenegrins to nationalities. The 1974 Constitution ushered in a period of economic growth but it left the Serbs, one of the two founding constituent peoples of the SFRY, deeply dissatisfied. They perceived the granting of autonomy to Kosovo and Vojvodina, both of which are located in Serbia, and the recognition of Macedonians and Montenegrins as nationalities as attempts to weaken them relative to Croats, the group from which President Tito hailed.[2] Indeed, "ever since the founding of Yugoslavia, two distinct nationalist policies have struggled for primacy in the debate over the country's political future: Croatian separatism striving for an independent state and Serbian centralism striving to preserve the common Yugoslav state under its dominion."[3] Following Tito's death in 1980, mounting debt and the end of the Cold War exerted further pressure on the SFRY. The country had benefited from its unique position during the Cold War to navigate the international system and extract concessions from East and West. When this ended, richer republics resented having to pay interest on the debt of poorer ones and the decision to exit the Federation gained increasing support among elites and in the population, particularly in Slovenia.[4]

With the departure of Slovenia, then Croatia, both of which declared independence in 1991, the disintegration of the SFRY exerted particularly intense pressure on Bosnia and Herzegovina (BiH). One of the most diverse SFRY republics, Bosnia had to contend with large Serb and Croat communities. According to the 1991 Yugoslav census, the republic had 4,377,053 inhabitants including 1,902,956 Muslims (43.47 percent), 1,366,104 Serbs (31.21 percent), and 760,872 Croats (17.38 percent). Approximately 5.54 percent of the population, or 242,682 persons, defined themselves as Yugoslavs while 104,439 persons (2.40 percent) belonged to other minority groups.[5] Elections in 1990 yielded a Bosnian parliament divided between three nationalist parties, the Stranka Demokratske Akcije (SDA, Party of Democratic Action—Bosniac[6]), the Hrvatska Demokratska Zajednica (HDZ, Croatian Democratic Union), and the Srpska Demoktraska Stranka (SDS, Serb Democratic Party). Initially governing as an inter-ethnic coalition, the three parties quickly differed over whether to stay within the rump SFRY (favored by the SDS) or become independent (favored mostly by the SDA). Amid a deepening split, the war in neighboring Croatia stoked up fears that the Yugoslav National Army (JNA, Jugoslavenska Narodna Armija) was implementing a plan to arm Serbs in the remaining Yugoslav republics in an attempt to thwart decisions to declare independence.[7] In reaction, the BiH parliament declared sovereignty on October 15, 1991 and announced its plan to hold a referendum on independence

[2] Steven L Burg, "Ethnic Conflict and the Federalization of Socialist Yugoslavia: The Serbo-Croat Conflict" (1977) 7 (4) Publius 119; Doris Gödl, "Challenging the Past: Serbian and Croatian Aggressor-Victim Narratives" (2007) 37 (1) International Journal of Sociology 43; Michael Sorenson, "Major Causes of the Hatred Between Serbs and Croats" (1993) 34 (1) Balkan Studies 119.

[3] Vesna Pesic, "Serbian Nationalism and the Origins of the Yugoslav Crisis" (Peaceworks No 8, United States Institute of Peace 1996) <www.usip.org/publications/1996/04/serbian-nationalism-and-origins-yugoslav-crisis>.

[4] See notably Woodward (n 1).

[5] Department of Statistics Bosnia and Herzegovina, "Zavod za statistiku Bosne i Hercegovine Bilten no 234 (Department of Statistics Bosnia and Herzegovina Bulletin No 234)" (Government of the Socialist Republic of Bosnia and Herzegovina 1991). It is worth noting that the last Yugoslav census was conducted at a time of tension between the communities, something that may have biased the results particularly as regards the definition of nationality, language, and religious conviction. See Snjezana Mrdjen, "Le dernier recensement de la Yougoslavie" (1991) 263 Populations et Sociétés 3, 3–4.

[6] The term Bošniak has come to be used to refer to Bosnian Muslims.

[7] On the Yugoslav support to the Serbs of Bosnia see Veljko Vujačić, "Elites, Narratives, and Nationalist Mobilization in the Former Yugoslavia" (2007) 40 (1) Comparative Politics 103; Branimir Anzulovic, *Heavenly Serbia: From Myth to Genocide* (New York University Press 1999); VP Gagnon,

on February 29 and March 1, 1992. On October 24, Serb members of parliament walked out and formed the Assembly of the Serb People of Bosnia and Herzegovina which established the Serbian Republic of Bosnia and Herzegovina in January 1992.[8] On November 18, 1991, it was the turn of the HDZ to proclaim the existence of the Croatian Community of Herzeg Bosna. The 1992 referendum was boycotted by a majority of Serbs but with a turnout of 63.4 percent of voters of whom 99.7 percent voted yes, BiH declared independence on March 3, 1992.

Academics have hotly debated whether the conflict that ensued was an ethnic war or not.[9] While ethnicity was clearly instrumentalized by leaders vying for power, at the outset of the Bosnian war there were also genuine fears among Serbs regarding their status in an independent BiH. These fears were stoked by two interrelated external factors—newly independent Croatia's failure to provide adequate minority rights guarantees to its own Serb minority and the conclusions of the Arbitration Commission of the Conference on Yugoslavia. Croatian Serbs reacted very strongly to Zagreb's failure to provide them with acceptable minority rights guarantees. With the support of Belgrade, they proceeded to arm themselves prompting the new Croatian government to assert control over police stations in Serb-majority areas. The Milosevic government in Belgrade poured oil on the fire suggesting that this state of affairs would inevitably lead to a repetition of the pro-Nazi Croat Ustashe regime's genocide against the Serbs in World War II. Supported by the JNA, fearful Croatian Serbs escalated the conflict between them and the Croatian government.

Meanwhile, the rights of constituent peoples were being examined by the Arbitration Commission of the Conference on Yugoslavia (commonly known as the Badinter Arbitration Committee) that had been set up by the European Economic Community to provide the International Peace Conference on Yugoslavia chaired by Lord Carrington with legal advice. Asked to consider whether the Serbian population in Croatia and Bosnia and Herzegovina, as one of the constituent peoples of Yugoslavia, had the right to self-determination, the commission concluded on January 11, 1992 that the Serbs of Croatia and BiH were entitled to "all the rights concerned to minorities and ethnic groups [. . .]" and "that the Republics must afford the members of those minorities and ethnic groups all the human rights and fundamental freedoms recognized in international law, including, where appropriate, the right to choose their nationality."[10] Scholars have suggested that the conclusions of the Badinter Arbitration Committee provided some of the justification for the ethnic cleansing that the Vojska Republike Srpske (Army of Republika Srpska) carried out from 1992 until 1995.[11] Serb leaders interpreted these conclusions as proof that their community would be demoted from a constituent people to a mere national minority

"Serbia's Road to War" (1994) 5 (2) Journal of Democracy 117; Tim Judah, *The Serbs: History, Myth, and the Destruction of Yugoslavia* (Yale University Press 1997).

[8] This would become the *Republika Srpska* in August 1992.

[9] Steven Majstorovic, "Ancient Hatreds or Elite Manipulation? Memory and Politics in the Former Yugoslavia" (1997) 159 World Affairs 170; Woodward (n 1); Bogdan Denis Denitch, *Ethnic Nationalism: The Tragic Death of Yugoslavia* (University of Minnesota Press 1996); Anthony Oberschall, "The Manipulation of Ethnicity: From Ethnic Cooperation to Violence and War in Yugoslavia" (2000) 23 (6) Ethnic and Racial Studies 982; VP Gagnon, *The Myth of Ethnic War: Serbia and Croatia in the 1990s* (Cornell University Press 2004); Silber and Little (n 1).

[10] Allain Pellet, "The Opinions of the Badinter Arbitration Committee: A Second Breath for the Self-Determination of Peoples" (1992) 3 (1) European Journal of International Law 1178.

[11] Jennifer Jackson Peerce, "Ethnic Cleansing as an Instrument of Nation-State Creation: Changing State Practices and Evolving Legal Norms" (1998) 20 (4) Human Rights Quarterly 817; Robert M Hayden, "Imagined Communities and Real Victims: Self-Determination and Ethnic Cleansing in

in an independent BiH. For the community to be entitled to join the rump Federal Republic of Yugoslavia (FRY, composed of Serbia including Kosovo and Vojvodina, Macedonia, and Montenegro), Serbs needed to establish majority control over territory and to hold a referendum on secession. Thus was born the decision to compel Bosnian Muslims to leave the territory of the Republika Srpska.[12] From there to physically eliminating those who would not comply, there were only too few steps.

The war in BiH began with the siege of Sarajevo in April 1992. It would last until August 1995 when BiH President and SDA Party leader Alija Izetbegović, FRY President Slobodan Milošević, and Croatian President Franjo Tudjman agreed on the terms of the General Framework Agreement for Peace (GFAP also known as Dayton Peace Accords or DPA). The manner in which the DPA addressed the territorial dimension of the conflict would structure the politics of BiH for years to come.

The Period of Constitutional Engagement

Looking back on the manner in which the DPA dealt with the enactment of the BiH Constitution, two major issues deserve mention: the process (or lack thereof) of constitutional change and the centrality of territory. Both would determine in great part the structure of present day Bosnian politics.

Constitutional process, what process?

In the words of its architect, US diplomat Richard Holbrooke, the word Dayton has "entered the language as a shorthand for a certain type of diplomacy—the Big Bang approach to negotiations: lock everyone up until they reach agreement."[13] In twenty days of November 1995, a process of mostly proximity talks at Wright-Patterson air base in Dayton, Ohio, saw Bosnia emerge with a peace agreement, of which the country's new Constitution was an annex. The talks were held between President Izetbegović and Prime Minister Haris Silajdžić representing the Bosniacs, FRY President Slobodan Milošević representing the interests of Serbia and of the Bosnian Serbs, and President Franjo Tudjman of Croatia representing his country and speaking for the Bosnian Croats. The interests of the Yugoslav and Croat presidents did not always coincide with those of their ethnic kin in Bosnia.[14] Milošević wanted sanctions on the FRY lifted and he was therefore interested in forcing the Bosnian Serbs to compromise. In fact, at a key point in the talks, he broke ranks with the Bosnian Serbs over the fate of Sarajevo. He agreed to hand the capital city to the Bosniacs in what Holbrooke and his team could only explain as a move to weaken the radical SDS leadership based in Pale and which, in Milošević's opinion, had become an "impediment."[15] As for Tudjman, he was mostly interested in a settlement of the Eastern Slavonia conflict, the conflict that opposed his government to Croatian Serbs in the Krajina.

Yugoslavia" (1996) 23 (4) American Ethnologist 783; Ralph K White, "Why the Serbs Fought: Motives and Misperceptions" (1996) 2 (2) Peace and Conflict: Journal of Peace Psychology 109.

[12] See also Marie-Joëlle Zahar, "Republika Srpska" in Tozun Bahcheli, Barry Bartmann, and Henry Srebrnik (eds), *De Facto States: The Quest for Sovereignty* (Routledge 2004).

[13] Richard Holbrooke, *To End a War* (Random House 1998) 212.

[14] Nina Caspersen, "Between Puppets and Independent Actors: Kin-State Involvement in the Conflicts in Bosnia, Croatia and Nagorno Karabakh" (2008) 7 (4) Ethnopolitics 357.

[15] Holbrooke (n 13) 293.

It is worth reiterating what many have since highlighted: two of the protagonists of the conflict, the Bosnian Serbs and the Bosnian Croats, were not directly involved in the talks. Truth be told, there were senior Bosnian Serb officials in Milošević's delegation. Momcilo Krajišnik, then a member of the collective presidency of Republika Srpska, Nikola Koljević, who had been the Serb member of the collective presidency of Bosnia following the 1990 elections before becoming vice-president of the RS, and General Zdravko Tolimir, a deputy of VRS commander Ratko Mladić, were present at Dayton. But, as Holbrooke recalls, they were "relegated to the second floor of the two-story Serb quarters, and treated [by Milošević] with open contempt."[16] After an incident on day eight of the talks, during which Krajišnik was particularly uncompromising on the fate of Sarajevo, he and his Bosnian Serb colleagues "were truly nonpersons at Dayton."[17] For their part, Bosnian Croat officials were included in the Bosnian delegation but Holbrooke's account of the talks makes it clear that their involvement was marginal. Nor was there any consideration of the opinion of ordinary citizens of BiH in the process.

The centrality of territory

While there was no constitutional process to speak of during the negotiations that led to the signing of the DPA, territory was central to the talks. To appreciate the role that territory played at Dayton requires us first to review the manner in which territorial divisions were dealt with in previous attempts at bringing Bosnia and Herzegovina's war to an end. This review will set the stage for better appreciation of the territorial issues as they played out at the Dayton peace talks.

The DPA has often been hailed as the agreement that managed to end the war while restoring a single, multiethnic Bosnia.[18] While the USA did not oppose voluntary changes that would either modify the international boundaries of the country or divide it into more than one country,[19] Washington was intent not to reward ethnic cleansing nor to go along with partition plans that presidents Milošević and Tudjman were said to have hatched in 1991.[20] In so doing, Dayton and its architects were attempting to depart from a trend, begun even before the war erupted in Bosnia, to equate nation with ethnicity and to allocate separate territories to different nationalities in a stark illustration of the logic expounded by Chaim Kaufman when he argued that the only solution to the security dilemma triggered by ethnic civil war was the partition of countries along communal lines.[21]

Ever since the "Statement of Principles for New Constitutional Arrangements for Bosnia and Herzegovina,"[22] the assumption had been that, even as Bosnia would become an independent state, it would be partitioned into ethnic cantons. Meeting in Lisbon under the chairmanship of the then-foreign minister of Portugal, José Cutileiro, the European Community Conference on the Former Yugoslavia's working group on Bosnia "established the cartographic and statistical criteria for the division of Bosnia."[23]

[16] ibid 243. [17] ibid 256. [18] ibid 335. [19] ibid 363–4.

[20] Mladen Klemenčić, "The Boundaries, Internal Order and Identities of Bosnia and Herzegovina" (2000–2001) 8 (4) IBRU Boundary and Security Bulletin 63.

[21] Chaim Kaufmann, "Possible and Impossible Solutions to Ethnic Civil Wars" (1996) 20 (4) International Security 136.

[22] Developed by the European Community Conference on the Former Yugoslavia which was established in 1991 and chaired by Lord Carrington.

[23] David Campbell, "Apartheid Cartography: The Political Anthropology and Spatial Effects of International Diplomacy in Bosnia" (1999) 18 (4) Political Geography 395, 406.

The map was based on the 1991 Yugoslav national census and on a crude evaluation of the national absolute or relative majority in each municipality. As David Campbell rightfully remarks, not only did such a territorial division fail to "achieve the perfect alignment between identity and territory necessary to satisfy the nationalists," it also reflected an underlying tension between the professed support of outsiders for the independence and integrity of BiH and their efforts to redraw internal boundaries according to a "separatist logic hostile to any notion of overarching authority."[24]

With the Bosnian war in full swing and ethnic cleansing underway, the EC and the UN launched a new initiative, the International Conference on the Former Socialist Federal Republic of Yugoslavia (ICFY). Meeting at its first session in London, on August 27, 1992, the ICFY reasserted "the priority of individual rights and the importance of sovereignty, independence and territorial integrity."[25] Among the principles that participants adopted as the basis for a future negotiated settlement was the "non-recognition of all advantages gained by force or fait accompli or of any legal consequences thereof." However, the ICFY acknowledged that a Bosnian unitary state would be rejected by at least two communities; furthermore, it accepted the need to protect minorities and the right to self-determination. In attempting to reconcile all these principles, ICFY co-chairmen Cyrus Vance and Lord Owen proposed a decentralized state structure consisting of nine provinces and a capital district. Vance and Owen argued that only such a solution would "not acquiesce in already accomplished ethnic cleansing, and in further internationally unacceptable practices."[26] According to their proposal, each of the three communities would constitute the majority in three of the nine provinces. In January 1993, the Vance-Owen Peace Plan (VOPP) was presented to the parties. Bosnian Croats accepted it, in great part because the map it drew was particularly favorable to them. Bosnian Muslims reluctantly went along. However, the Bosnian Serb Assembly rejected the plan thus bringing this particular peace effort to an end.[27]

With Cyrus Vance replaced by Thorvald Stoltenberg, the ICFY resumed its efforts to seek acceptable terms for the conclusion of a peace agreement. In the meantime, Serbs and Croats had hardened their positions. They now sought a confederal solution with three separate republics.[28] The map that Owen and Stoltenberg negotiated gave approximately 53 percent of the territory to the Bosnian Serbs, 30 percent to the Bosniacs, and 17 percent to the Croats. It included complex arrangements for protected routes that would connect the Bosniac-majority towns of Žepa and Goražde to the Bosniac Republic through Serb territory. A new set of constitutional principles were also agreed whereby the loose confederation thus formed would be ruled by a nine-member council with three members representing each group. Key positions such as those of Prime Minister and Foreign Minister would rotate among the groups and the three republics would be allowed to enter into agreements with neighboring states only if these agreements did not damage the interests of the other republics.[29] This

[24] ibid 408. [25] ibid.

[26] "United Nations: Secretary-General Report on the International Conference on the Former Yugoslavia" (1992) 31(6) International Legal Materials 1549.

[27] Paul C Szasz, "The Quest for a Bosnian Constitution: Legal Aspects of Constitutional Proposals Relating to Bosnia" (1995) 19 (2) Fordham International Law Journal 368.

[28] David Owen, *Balkan Odyssey* (Harcourt Brace and Co 1995).

[29] Mladen Klemenčić, *Territorial Proposals for the Settlement of the War in Bosnia and Herzegovina* (Martin Pratt and Schofield eds, Boundary and Territory Briefing vol. 1 no. 3, International Boundaries Research Unit 1994) 53.

plan would ultimately be rejected by the Bosniacs who wanted more territory than they could get at the negotiating table and who, strong of the support of the USA, believed that their military fortunes could still improve to create a context in which these demands would be met.[30]

A number of developments laid the ground for the next effort, which, unlike its predecessors, focused primarily on ending the conflict between Bosniacs and Croats. First came a challenge to the official Croat ethnic narrative by Ivo Komšić, a Croat-member of the Bosnian collective presidency and leader of the Croat Peasant Party. Komšić proposed a new map which, although it reaffirmed the principle of cantonization, starkly differed from international proposals in that it was not based on the principle of ethnic majority.[31] Then, following the February 1994 attack on the market in Sarajevo, the international community decided to take a firmer stance and the UN Protection Force (UNPROFOR) issued an ultimatum to the Serbs to withdraw from their positions around the city. This coincided with the US decision to assume leadership of the international community's efforts. To change the balance of forces on the ground, the USA worked on healing the rift that had developed between Bosniacs and Croats since 1993.

As Bosniacs and Croats came under pressure to renew their alliance, Bosnian Prime Minister Haris Silajdzić and Croatian Foreign Minister Mate Granic held a series of meetings in Frankfurt and in Washington in February 1994. These resulted in the announcement, on March 1, 1994 in Washington, of an agreement establishing the Federation of Bosnia and Herzegovina (FBiH), a Muslim–Croat federation[32] of BiH territories with Muslim and Croat majorities. The constitution of the newly established Federation was ratified by the Bosnian parliament on March 29 and 30.[33] The structure of the federation was a clear prelude to the DPA. The agreement described the Federation as the outcome of Bosniacs and Croats exercising their rights as constituent peoples to transform the internal structure of the territories where they were a majority; it also underlined that decisions on the constitutional status of Serb-majority territories would be made "in the course of negotiations toward a peaceful settlement and at the International Conference on the Former Yugoslavia."[34] The constitution of the new federation was part of the Framework Agreement signed by Bosniac and Croat representatives in Washington D.C. Pursuant to this constitution, the Federation of Bosnia and Herzegovina would be governed according to principles of proportional representation with a Bosniac and a Croat alternating at the helm as President and Vice-President, a government where all ministers would have deputies who would be from a different constituent people, a House of Representatives elected on a proportional basis, and a House of Peoples with equal numbers of Bosniac and Croat representatives as well as a number of delegates representing "Others."

[30] Owen (n 28).

[31] Klemenčić, *Territorial Proposals for the Settlement of the War in Bosnia and Herzegovina* (n 29) 66–70.

[32] The initial designation of Bošniaks was Muslim Bosnians.

[33] For this occasion, Muslim and Croat parliamentarians elected in 1990 were summoned.

[34] Framework Agreement for the Federation Peace Agreements (March 1, 1994) (Washington Agreement) <www.usip.org/sites/default/files/file/resources/collections/peace_agreements/washagree_03011994.pdf>.

Territorial issues and the Dayton Peace Agreement

Territory was as central to the DPA as it had been to other attempts at finding a solution to the war in BiH. This is nowhere clearer than in Richard Holbrooke's account of territorial negotiations that led to the signing of the DPA, from the status of BiH's capital city, Sarajevo, to discussions around the Posavina "pocket," the Posavina corridor and the towns of Brčko Goražde, Srebernica, Žepa, and Bosanski Novi. Rather than delve into the details of the answers to each of the above-mentioned territorial issues, the following discussion is intended to highlight the constitutional solutions that Dayton offered to the quandaries that stood in the way of earlier efforts at conflict resolution. The discussion will focus on (a) the legal continuity of Bosnia and Herzegovina, (b) the institutional structure of and division of powers in BiH or the relationship between the parts and the whole, and (c) the issue of citizenship. It is important to underline that this discussion refers to the Constitution of Bosnia and Herzegovina as spelled out in Annex 4 of the DPA. Since then, a number of amendments have been introduced that will be touched upon in the next section of this chapter.

The legal continuity of BiH

When BiH gained independence as a result of the 1992 referendum, the new state was immediately recognized by and granted membership in the United Nations. But the three communities that comprised the majority of its citizens fundamentally disagreed on its legitimacy and on the form it ought to take. Of the three, Bosniacs were the strongest proponents of a sovereign unitary state. While open to Bosnian sovereignty, Croats preferred cantonization. For their part, Serbs preferred for BiH to remain within the FRY; their second-best option revolved around the right of Serb areas to seek secession and rejoin the FRY.[35] Not only did the three communities broadly disagree, Serbs considered the birth of independent BiH illegal because of the fact that the referendum on independence had gone ahead in spite of the boycott of one of the constituent people.

The question as to whether the state that would emerge from peace negotiations would be a legal continuation of BiH or a completely new state was thus tabled as early as the Owen-Stoltenberg plan. The DPA resolved this issue in favor of continuity of the state and of its international legal personality. The decision was made on multiple grounds: because the issue represented an emotional charge for Bosniacs; because US negotiators did not want to grant *de facto* legitimacy to Republika Srspka—something that would have happened if a new state of BiH was created out of the union of the RS and the Federation; and because there were matters of international legal practicality regarding the action filed by BiH against the FRY before the International Court of Justice for abetting genocide.

The BiH constitution thus stated that the country "shall remain a Member State of the United Nations."[36] Continuity of Bosnia's international legal personality contrasted with the rupture in constitutional continuity that was the product of the Dayton agreement. The DPA provided that the constitution "shall enter into force upon signature of the General Framework Agreement as a constitutional act amending and superseding the Constitution of the Republic of Bosnia and Herzegovina."[37] However, Annex II

[35] Klemenčić, *Territorial Proposals for the Settlement of the War in Bosnia and Herzegovina* (n 29) 31–2.

[36] Bosnia and Herzegovina Constitution, art. I(1).

[37] ibid art. XII(1).

to the constitution on "Transitional Arrangements" did ensure the continuation of laws, regulations, judicial rules, pending judicial and administrative proceedings, as well as governmental bodies in force or existence within the territory of Bosnia and Herzegovina

Nevertheless, the manner in which the Constitution was written conforms with what Saunders in her chapter characterizes as a "revolutionary" legal rupture, in that the new Constitution was not made in conformity with the amending rules of its predecessor, but derives its legitimacy from an agreement of some kind, in this case the Dayton Peace Agreement, or from a diktat on high. In choosing this approach, however, little if any consideration was given to the democratic deficit inherent in the process: a Constitution negotiated as part of a peace agreement, under conditions where some of the key actors (particularly the Bosnian Serbs but also the Bosnian Croats to a certain extent) were not effectively at the table. Yet, as Paul Szasz astutely remarked, allowing the Constitution to enter into force in any other way, either by ratification by the respective legislatures or by referenda, would have implied a new start for the state.[38] For all the reasons expounded above, this was unacceptable.

BiH, greater than the sum of its parts?

Under the DPA, Bosnia and Herzegovina was reorganized as a state comprised of two Entities, the Federation of Bosnia and Herzegovina (FBiH comprising 51 percent of BiH territory) and Republika Srpska (RS with 49 percent of BiH territory).[39] Much as the stated objective was to restore a single multiethnic Bosnia, the federal structures reflect the ethno-territorial nature of the arrangement reached at Dayton.

The entities share a central legislature, the Parliamentary Assembly of Bosnia and Herzegovina consisting of a House of Representatives and a House of Peoples as well as a three-member collective Presidency. This central government is two-thirds Muslim and Croat and one-third Serb. The federal House of Peoples is comprised of fifteen delegates—two-thirds hailing from the Federation (five Croats and five Bosniacs), one-third (five Serbs) from Republika Srpska (RS).[40] The BiH House of Representatives is composed of forty-two members, two-thirds elected from the FBiH and one-third from the RS. Members of the Presidency (one representative from each constituent people) are directly elected from the FBiH (Bosniac and Croat members) and from the RS (Serb member). A proposed decision of the Parliamentary Assembly may be declared "destructive to a vital interest of the Bosniac, Croat, or Serb people."[41] This constitutional provision provides members of each constituent people with veto power over contested legislation. In such instances, a joint committee including three members of each community reviews the legislation; if they fail to reach agreement, the matter is forwarded to the Constitutional Court.[42] A similar veto exists within the presidency.[43]

Not only is the structure of BiH complicated and premised upon a delicate balancing act between Bosniacs, Croats, and Serbs, but also the powers of the central government

[38] Szasz (n 27) 378.

[39] The description of the structure of BiH draws in great part on Marie-Joëlle Zahar, "Bosnia and Herzegovina" in Ann L Griffiths (ed.), *Handbook of Federal Countries* (2nd edn, McGill-Queens University Press and the Forum of Federations 2005) 73–89.

[40] Croat and Bosniac delegates are elected respectively by the Croat and Bosniac delegates to the House of Peoples of the Federation of Bosnia and Herzegovina. The National Assembly of Republika Srpska selects the Serb delegates to the federal House of Peoples.

[41] Bosnia and Herzegovina Constitution, art. V(2)(e).

[42] ibid art. IV(3)(f).

[43] ibid art. V(2)(d).

are weak relative to the Entities. BiH institutions are responsible for foreign policy and trade; customs; monetary policy; finances of the institutions and international obligations of Bosnia and Herzegovina; immigration, refugee, and asylum policy and regulation; international and inter-entity criminal law enforcement; the establishment and operation of common and international communications facilities; regulation of inter-Entity transportation; and air traffic control. However, residual powers are the preserve of the Entities which also control the all-important power of taxation.[44] In some instances, the Entities even appear to "intrude into the jurisdiction of the central government."[45] Thus, while foreign policy is a responsibility of the central government, the Entities can establish special parallel relationships with neighboring states.[46] They can also enter agreements with foreign states and international organizations with the consent of the federal Parliamentary Assembly. Last but not least, national defense is conveniently and conspicuously missing from the list of exclusive powers of the central government. This reflected two realities: the profound mistrust of the parties and their unwillingness to disarm or join forces in a common national army and the fact that the FBiH constitution, negotiated before the DPA, had assigned to the Federation exclusive responsibility for "[o]rganizing and conducting the defense of the Federation and protecting its borders, including establishing a joint command of all military forces in the Federation."[47]

The thorny issue of citizenship

BiH was born of an arranged marriage buttressed by a change in the balance of power on the ground in the summer of 1995. Indeed, the DPA was signed against the background of territorial gains by the FBiH forces and of NATO air strikes on Bosnian Serb military positions. But this was a marriage in which at least one of the parties was an unwilling partner. As discussed earlier in this chapter, Bosnian Serbs did not want to see an independent Bosnia and Herzegovina, preferring to remain within the Former Yugoslavia and resorting to ethnic cleansing, in part, to be able to justify the legality of a referendum that would allow them to secede from Bosnia. How the new Constitution dealt with this fact and the extent to which it was able to create the framework for a BiH citizenship are therefore important issues for consideration.

Much as the Constitution stipulated that BiH should "ensure the highest level of internationally recognized human rights and basic freedoms" to its citizens, "without discrimination on any basis, including gender, race, skin, color, language, religion, political or other opinions, national and social origin, belonging to a national minority, [and] financial status that is acquired by birth,"[48] the ethno-territorial foundations of the state prevented this aspiration from being translated into reality. In fact, citizenship

[44] The federal Parliamentary Assembly has responsibility for "deciding upon the sources and amounts of revenues for the operations of the institutions . . . and international obligations of Bosnia and Herzegovina" (BiH Constitution IV(4)(b)). The FBiH provides two-thirds and the RS one-third of the revenues required by the federal budget, "except insofar as revenues are raised as specified by the Parliamentary Assembly" (BiH Constitution VIII(3)). Under Article III(2)(b) the Entities are also expected to provide "all necessary assistance" to the central government in order to enable it to honor its international obligations.

[45] Zahar, "Bosnia and Herzegovina" (n 39).

[46] This was deemed consistent with the Constitution, including with provisions concerning the sovereignty and territorial integrity of BiH.

[47] Bosnia and Herzegovina Constitution, art. III(1)(b).

[48] Srdjan Dizdarevic, "The Need to Change the Constitution of Bosnia and Herzegovina" (2005) 1 (4–5) Südosteuropa Mitteilungen 90, 91.

of BiH is based on the notion of constituent peoples. Article 1.7(a) stipulates that all citizens of the two Entities are citizens of Bosnia and Herzegovina. However, rather than transcending the ethnic divisions of the war, the Constitution institutionalized them and gave privileged political status to Bosniacs, Croats, and Serbs, and, while mentioning them in the Preamble, it left "Others" "out of the reach of the constitutional regulative."[49] In so doing, the Constitution jeopardized the notion of equal citizenship and the principle of non-discrimination as regards access to state functions. The fifteen or so other peoples identified as living in Bosnia by the 1991 census were thus excluded from seeking political office.

Furthermore, in spite of all the talk of reversing ethnic cleansing, the Constitution disallowed Serbs living in the FBiH and Bosniacs and Croats living in RS "the possibility of using the passive election right for seats in the Presidency of BiH and the House of Peoples of the Parliamentary Assembly of BiH."[50] Last, but not least, the Constitution also allowed citizens of Bosnia to hold citizenship of another state.[51] Thus, not only did the Constitution institutionalize a situation whereby citizenship of BiH was mediated by citizenship of the Entities, it also provided arrangements for those Entities and communities that did not want to see an independent Bosnia to maintain citizenship ties with the FRY and with Croatia.

Outcome of the Process

In the twenty years since the DPA was negotiated, the outcome of the decisions summarized above has been abundantly discussed and commented upon. "[Dayton] created a complex institutional structure, composed of one state, two entities, three peoples, an estimated 3.9 million citizens, and five layers of governance led by 14 prime ministers and governments, making Bosnia the state with the highest number of presidents, prime ministers, and ministers per capita in the entire world."[52] It has contributed to creating political paralysis, institutionalizing ethnicity, and perpetuating corruption and inefficiency at both Entity and BiH level institutions.[53]

[49] ibid. [50] ibid 92.

[51] Provided that there is a bilateral agreement, approved by the Parliamentary Assembly between Bosnia and Herzegovina and that state governing this matter. See Bosnia and Herzegovina Constitution, art. I(7)(d).

[52] Roberto Belloni, "Bosnia: Dayton Is Dead! Long Live Dayton!" (2009) 15 (3–4) Nationalism and Ethnic Politics 355, 359.

[53] For example, see David Chandler, *Bosnia: Faking Democracy After Dayton* (Pluto Press, 2000); Eldar Sarajlic, "Bosnian Elections and Recurring Ethnonationalisms: The Ghost of the Nation State" [2010] (2) Journal on Ethnopolitics and Minority Issues in Europe 66; Robert M Hayden, "'Democracy' without a Demos? The Bosnian Constitutional Experiment and the Intentional Construction of Nonfunctioning States" (2005) 19 (2) East European Politics & Societies 226; Dejan Guzina, "Dilemmas of Nation-Building and Citizenship in Dayton Bosnia" (2007) 9 (3) National Identities 217; Florian Bieber and Carsten Wieland, *Facing the Past, Facing the Future: Confronting Ethnicity and Conflict in Bosnia and Former Yugoslavia* (Longo 2005); Andrea Kathryn Talentino, "Intervention as Nation-Building: Illusion or Possibility?" (2002) 33 (1) Security Dialogue 27; Charles G Boyd, "Making Bosnia Work: A Report From the Field" (1998) 77 (1) Foreign Affairs 42; Ulrich Schneckener, "Making Power-Sharing Work: Lessons from Successes and Failures in Ethnic Conflict Regulation" (2002) 39 (2) Journal of Peace Research 203; Roberto Belloni, "Peacebuilding and Consociational Electoral Engineering in Bosnia and Herzegovina" (2004) 11(2) International Peacekeeping 334; Roberto Belloni, *State Building and International Intervention in Bosnia* (Routledge 2008); David Chandler, "The Problems of 'nation-building': Imposing Bureaucratic 'rule from Above'" (2004) 17 (3) Cambridge Review of International Affairs 577; Nils B Weidmann, "Violence and the Changing Ethnic Map: The Endogeneity of Territory and Conflict in Bosnia" (2009) Households in Conflict Network Working Paper 64, 2 <https://ideas.repec.org/p/hic/wpaper/64.html>; John W

Rather than dwell upon these outcomes again, I focus on whether and how change has been brought about. In so doing, I look at the role played by international engagement in the implementation of the DPA, the activism of BiH's Constitutional Court, and the impact of the European Union. I also put the focus squarely on only one instance in which each of these mechanisms sought to break the deadlock of Bosnian politics as a way of assessing the opportunities and the limits therein.

The international arbitration of Brčko

International engagement has been key in securing the implementation of the DPA. As early as 1997, the Peace Implementation Council representing all the international actors involved in the implementation of the DPA agreed, at a meeting in Bonn, to give its High Representative in Bosnia exceptional powers to ease implementation of the agreement and to remove from office any obstructionist Bosnian officials. These "Bonn Powers,"[54] as they came to be known, were instrumental at key moments such as when the High Representative unilaterally signed a law on citizenship in 1997 which allowed Serbs living in the FBiH and Bosniacs and Croats living in RS the right to vote for candidates and stand for election to the Presidency of BiH and the House of Peoples of the Parliamentary Assembly of BiH.

As regards territorial issues, however, international engagement is best illustrated by the international arbitration of Brčko, a Bosnian-majority strategic municipality, which is key to the territorial continuity of the RS as it divides the eastern and western parts of the Republic. The fate of Brčko, which according to the 1991 census was a microcosm of Bosnian ethnic heterogeneity, could serve as a harbinger of the future of Bosnia. Handed to the RS, it would seal the territorial dimension of ethnicity and the segregationist logic underlying it. Handed to the FBiH, it would signal the international community's intent to prevent RS from functioning as one. At Dayton and as neither party was willing to compromise, they ultimately agreed to have the territorial dispute settled by international arbitration. After placing the district under international supervision in 1997, the International Arbitral Tribunal for Brčko, led by Robert Owens a former legal advisor to the US State Department, issued a final award in 1999. It ruled that Brčko should become a democratic multiethnic unit of local government to be developed by the Office of High Representative (OHR) supervisory regime. The FBiH and RS would jointly hold the territory of the resulting Brčko District "in condominium."[55] This decision would yield a number of positive outcomes. Brčko saw a high rate of returns, its local institutions were multiethnic, its inhabitants could claim citizenship first in either and then in both BiH Entities.[56] Yet, Brčko is by no means free from some of the ills that plague BiH. While under international supervision, the supervisory authorities intervened repeatedly to transcend differences. Brčko's local institutions of governance have suffered the same corruption as the rest of the

Hulsey, "'Why Did They Vote for Those Guys Again?' Challenges and Contradictions in the Promotion of Political Moderation in Post-War Bosnia and Herzegovina" (2010) 17 (6) Democratization 1132.

[54] For a comprehensive analysis of the Bonn Powers see, Tim Banning, "The 'Bonn Powers' of the High Representative in Bosnia Herzegovina: Tracing a Legal Figment" (2014) 6 (2) Goettingen Journal of International Law 259.

[55] Peter C Farrand, "Lessons from Brcko: Necessary Components for Future Internationally Supervised Territories" (2001) 15 Emory International Law Review 229.

[56] Alex Jeffrey, "Building State Capacity in Post-Conflict Bosnia and Herzegovina: The Case of Brčko District" (2006) 25 (2) Political Geography 203.

country. As a result, promising signs of economic recovery soon became stunted and investments fled the District as they did the rest of BiH.[57]

The Constitutional Court and the Constituency of Peoples

If international activism is credited for breaking the paralysis of the Bosnian political system and forcing the implementation of the DPA, BiH's Constitutional Court played an equally important role in attempting to reverse the strict ethno-territorial logic of Dayton. Most significant in this respect was the Court's 2000 decision on the Constituency of Peoples. This decision resulted from proceedings, instigated in 1998 by the then Chairman of the BiH Presidency, Alija Izetbegović, who was seeking implementation of Art. XII.2 of the BiH Constitution according to which the Entities had to amend their respective constitutions to bring them in line with the BiH Constitution within three months of the latter's entry into force. Izetbegović argued that "the same provisions contained in the constitutions of entities, which violated the Constitution of BH and the overall Dayton Agreement, also discriminated against Bosnians and Croats in the Republic of Srpska (RS) and against Serbs in the Federation of Bosnia and Herzegovina (Federation of BH) by treating them as constituent peoples."[58]

In its ruling on the matter, the Court interpreted the Preamble of the BiH Constitution as affirming three normative principles[59]: (1) the multiethnicity of the state and the fact that "territorial delimitation does not have to lead to institutional segregation and national homogenization within the State institutions;"[60] (2) the collective equality of the constituent people of BiH which was interpreted as "effective political participation in decision-making processes not only through individual equality in respect of the electoral right but also through the collective ethnic representation of the three constituent peoples;"[61] and (3) the prohibition of discrimination *de jure* and *de facto* with retroactive effect.

This decision meant that Entities could not discriminate against any member of the three constituent peoples, particularly demographic minorities; nor could they grant special privileges to majorities. As a result, Serbs were included as constituent peoples in the FBiH while Bosniacs and Croats were recognized as constituent peoples in RS. The decision led to the reorganization of Entity institutions and to the introduction of "mandatory quotas of representation in all parts of government for all three constituent ethnic groups in both entities [as well as] the introduction of the language and script of other constituent ethnic groups as official language" in all parts of BiH.[62] Addressing the tension between individual and collective rights, the Court also ruled that the total exclusion of persons from the representative system gave rise to a violation of their individual political rights. This established the right of "Others" to be represented in parliaments and administrative bodies. It is, however, worth noting that it took two

[57] International Crisis Group, "Brčko Unsupervised" (Europe & Central Asia Briefing No 66, International Crisis Group December 8, 2011) <www.crisisgroup.org/europe-central-asia/balkans/bosnia-and-herzegovina/brcko-unsupervised> accessed November 16, 2015.

[58] Zlatan Begić and Zlatan Delić, "Constituency of Peoples in the Constitutional System of Bosnia and Herzegovina: Chasing Fair Solutions" (2013) 11 (2) International Journal of Constitutional Law 447, 450.

[59] For a detailed discussion of the interpretation of these principles see Saša Gavrić and Damir Banović, "Constitutional Reform in Bosnia and Herzegovina – Procedures, Challenges, Recommendations" (2010) 1 Südosteuropa Mitteilungen 60.

[60] ibid 66. [61] ibid. [62] ibid 60.

years and the intervention of the OHR to enforce the amendments to the Entities' constitutions and create the space for institutional reorganization.

The European Court of Human Rights: *Sejdić & Finci v. Bosnia and Herzegovina*

Notwithstanding the 2000 Constitutional Court decision on the Constituency of Peoples, it would take another legal challenge to address the status of "Others" in BiH. Indeed, in spite of the fact that, "as of 2002, seven seats out of 58 are reserved for 'others' in the Federation's House of Peoples, while in the case of RS, national minorities are guaranteed four seats out of 28 in the Council of Peoples,"[63] national minorities continued to be denied one of the basic citizenship rights at the federal level of the state: the right to compete for office. The definition of Bosnia as a country of constituent peoples bars members of national minorities from running for office at the state presidency level, or seeking election to the BiH House of Peoples.

In summer 2006, two BiH citizens, Dervo Sejdić and Jakob Finci, instituted proceedings before the European Court of Human Rights (ECtHR). They claimed that the Constitution and the Election law of BiH prevented them from running for Presidency and for the BiH House of Peoples solely on the ground of their Roma and Jewish origins. They relied on Articles 3 (prohibition of inhuman and degrading treatment), 13 (right to an effective remedy), and 14 (prohibition of discrimination) of the European Convention for the Protection of Human Rights and Fundamental Freedoms (ECHR), on Article 3 of Protocol No. 1 (right to free elections), and on Article 1 of Protocol No. 12 (general prohibition of discrimination) to the Convention.[64]

As it sided with the plaintiffs, the Court stated that "The nature of the conflict was such that the approval of the 'constituent peoples' (namely, the Bosniacs, Croats and Serbs) was necessary to ensure peace. This could explain, without necessarily justifying, the absence of representatives of the other communities (such as local Roma and Jewish communities) at the peace negotiations and the participants' preoccupation with effective equality between the 'constituent peoples' in the post-conflict society."[65] The Court highlighted that Bosnia and Herzegovina had undertaken to review and revise its electoral legislation according to EU standards when it became a member of the Council of Europe in 2002 and when it ratified the Stabilisation and Association Agreement with the European Union in 2008. Acknowledging that Sejdić and Finci had been victims of discrimination, the Court urged Bosnia to amend constitutional provisions regarding the election of the members of the House of Peoples and the Presidency. As I write, the twentieth anniversary of the DPA has just been celebrated. But the implementation of the peace agreement is still overseen by a High Representative and the country has not yet made sufficient progress to be admitted into the EU.

[63] Guzina (n 53) 227.

[64] Samo Bardutzky, "The Strasbourg Court on the Dayton Constitution: Judgment in the Case of *Sejdić and Finci v. Bosnia and Herzegovina*, 22 December 2009" (2010) 6 (2) European Constitutional Law Review 309, 317.

[65] Marko Milanovic, "Sejdić & Finci v. Bosnia and Herzegovina (Eur. Ct. H.R.), Introductory Note by Marko Milanović" (2010) 49 (2) International Legal Materials 281.

Lessons Learned

Negotiated at Dayton, the territorial restructuring of Bosnia was driven by strategic considerations. Its primary purpose was to square the circle between the reality of ethnic segregation on the ground and the desire to rebuild a multiethnic Bosnia to prevent those responsible for ethnic cleansing from reaping the political rewards of their violent actions. As the political agreement was institutionalized into a new Constitution, including a set of rules and norms regulating the relationships between the two Entities and the central government, the negotiators decided to make the Constitution into an annex of the peace agreement. The provisions of the Constitution were thus as much if not more backward than forward looking. They established an ethno-territorial system of governance that resulted in the hardening of contentious ethnic identities, the capture of the state by ethnic entrepreneurs, and the subsequent inefficiency, instability, yet unexpected resiliency of the BiH. In conclusion, I consider the lessons of Bosnia for the way in which territorial cleavages ought to be handled in constitutional processes. I focus on two lessons: state capture and citizen loyalties.

State capture

Commenting on the 2010 elections, long-term Bosnia observer Peter Lippman described the paradox of Bosnian politics as follows: "that while there is no reasonable alternative to peaceful change through electoral politics, the structural arrangements created by the Dayton constitution have created long-term paralysis. The primacy given by Dayton to ethnic categories, to the detriment of voters as citizens, lies at the root of this paralysis."[66] The DPA has, indeed, facilitated the capture of the Bosnian state by ethnic entrepreneurs. Nowhere is this clearer than in an overview of party politics and electoral outcomes since 1995.

The international community viewed continuous, free, and fair elections as the road to BiH's stability and recovery.[67] It spared no effort to ensure that elections in BiH, which involve a total of fifteen simultaneous races,[68] would live up to international standards. International custodians of the DPA have also sought to de-nationalize politics by supporting multiethnic and moderate mono-ethnic parties. These efforts involved a mix of carrots and sticks: successive High Representatives have used the Bonn powers to place funding and political constraints on ethnonationalist parties while providing incentives, including technical assistance and public support, to parties seen to be more moderate.

In spite of it all, twenty years later, "multiethnic parties have met with very limited electoral success and moderate mono-ethnic parties have found electoral success primarily by radicalizing their political discourse to match that of nationalist parties."[69]

[66] Peter Lippman, "Bosnia's Politics of Paralysis" (*Open Democracy*, October 19, 2010) <www.opendemocracy.net/bosnia%E2%80%99s-politics-of-paralysis/peter-lippman>.

[67] Commission on Security and Cooperation in Europe (United States Helsinki Commission), "Elections in Bosnia-Herzegovina, September 12–13, 1998" (105th Congress 2nd Session, CSCE 1998) <www.csce.gov/sites/helsinkicommission.house.gov/files/Bosnia1998elections.pdf>.

[68] The fifteen races are: the collective BiH presidency; the BiH House of Representatives; the presidency of the RS, the RS National Assembly; the Federation House of Representatives, and ten Federation cantonal races. In addition, there are municipal elections in which polls are organized in 145 municipalities.

[69] Hulsey, " 'Why did they vote for those guys again?' " (n 53).

This pattern has endured in spite of attempts to tweak electoral rules.[70] To account for this, now "classic case of party politics gone wrong," one must look at the impact of constitutional and electoral arrangements on party and voter behavior.[71]

By organizing politics around ethnicity, the DPA and the BiH Constitution created the conditions for the persistence of ethnonationalist parties. Bosnia observers acknowledge that while the country's party system is well consolidated and competitive, it is still largely based on ethnicity and competition takes place "between parties of one ethnicity, frequently within electoral constituencies that are ethnically homogeneous."[72] Although they vote in fifteen simultaneous races, many of these races do not pit parties or candidates belonging to the three constituent peoples against each other. This is what Hulsey describes as mono-ethnic non-competitive electoral competition; that is, "positions where a constituency either de facto or de jure represents only one ethnic group and in which elected representatives are not in direct competition for resources with elected representatives of other ethnic groups."[73] If nationalism is the result of either intense competition or a security dilemma pitting the three Bosnian constituent peoples against one another, mono-ethnic non-competitive constituencies should be best placed to produce non-nationalist parties as there are no ethnic "others" against whom to campaign.[74] In contrast, mono-ethnic competitive contexts are contexts where the constituency is mono-ethnic but where the elected representative "is in direct competition with representatives of other ethnic groups. For example, the members of the presidency are allocated to each ethnic group but sit on a presidential council and vote with the other two members of the presidency."[75] These contexts usually encourage outbidding as various parties try to win votes by positioning themselves as the true defenders of the community, the so-called "ethnic tribune" effect.[76] In other words, within each Entity, parties will run on the basis of political programs that address needs and wants; they position themselves against other parties representing the same constituent people. However, as they move onto the larger Bosnian political sphere, parties present themselves as champions of their own community's political project and become more ethnonationalist.

That this pattern exemplifies the logic of the system, which drives parties to adopt an ethnonationalist attitude to maintain themselves in power, is best illustrated by the trajectories of the Stranka Nezavisnih Socijal Demokrata (Alliance of Independent Social Democrats, SNSD) and the Stranka za Bosnu i Herzegovinu (Party for Bosnia and Herzegovina, SBiH). SNSD and SBiH were respectively the junior partners of the Serbian SDS and the Bosniac SDA; they fought the dominant ethnonationalist parties for community votes but also entered into coalitions with them. By the 2000 election,

[70] See Carrie Manning, "Elections and Political Change in Post-War Bosnia and Herzegovina" (2004) 11 (2) Democratization 60; John Hulsey, "Electoral Accountability in Bosnia and Herzegovina under the Dayton Framework Agreement" (2015) 22 (5) International Peacekeeping 511.

[71] Hulsey, "Electoral Accountability in Bosnia and Herzegovina under the Dayton Framework Agreement" (n 70).

[72] Hulsey, "'Why did they vote for those guys again?'" (n 53) 1138.

[73] Three electoral contexts coexist in Bosnia: mono-ethnic, non-competitive; mono-ethnic competitive; and multiethnic. "*Multi-ethnic constituencies* are those where the representation of any particular group is not fixed and is an open competition involving voters of more than one ethnic group" (italics added). See ibid 1141.

[74] John Garry, "Consociationalism and its Critics: Evidence from the Historic Northern Ireland Assembly Election 2007" (2009) 28 Electoral Studies 458, cited in Hulsey, "Why did they vote for those guys again?" (n 53) 1141.

[75] Hulsey, "Why did they vote for those guys again?" (n 53) 1141.

[76] Paul Mitchell, Geoffrey Evans, and Brendan O'Leary, "Extremist Outbidding in Ethnic Party Systems is Not Inevitable: Tribune Parties in Northern Ireland" (2009) 57 (2) Political Studies 397.

both parties had garnered sufficient electoral support and presented themselves as moderate nationalist alternatives to the SDS and SDA; they gained substantial international support and joined the "Alliance for Change." After a period during which their electoral fortunes fluctuated, both resurged in the 2006 elections, a resurgence which coincided with a nationalist turn in both parties.[77]

The DPA did not only produce an electoral system that favors ethnonationalist politics, it also provided parties that gain political power with access to the resources of the state and with a wide patronage network. Article 9(3) of the Constitution of Bosnia and Herzegovina mandates that government appointments be generally representative of the population of Bosnia and Herzegovina. This opens the doors for politicians to use the quota system to appoint their supporters to government positions. According to a 2014 International Crisis Group report, "party leaders are said to exercise power through subordinates in posts at all levels of government, who in turn have an array of tools for directing money and jobs to chosen targets. Regulatory authority can be used to open business opportunities, block competitors and increase or decrease real estate value."[78] Control over essential economic resources is another important tool of state capture. Bosnia's wartime ethnonationalist parties seized control of the "most lucrative assets in their respective territories, including utilities, transportation networks, and industrial enterprises."[79] And in spite of a transition to a market economy, "Government has retained large shares in a vast number of privatised firms, can name their executives and directors and influence hiring. This is especially true in the big-money areas: energy, telecommunications, infrastructure construction, banking and forestry."[80]

Says Peter Lippman, "the ethno-nationalist dimension is more a tool than an immutable reality. Many of Bosnia's voters and political observers alike understand that politics in Bosnia-Herzegovina is about power and profit rather than ethnic animosity. Indeed, few of Bosnia's post-war leaders have escaped being tarnished by some corruption scandal or abuse of authority."[81] In a country where unemployment reaches 40 percent, "politics is a cash cow and politicians are among the highest paid in Europe in comparison to the salaries of the rest of the population."[82] Politics does not only profit politicians financially; observers contend that, while Bosnia is consistently ranked near the bottom of international rankings on ease of doing business, "government officials circumvent regulations to operate the economy in a complex, informal system of patronage and corruption."[83]

Beyond electoral politics and control of the economy, the most telling sign of state capture may be the emergence of an extremely powerful informal institution, the Šestorka (sextet). This self-selecting informal coalition includes the leaders of the two

[77] Hulsey, "Why did they vote for those guys again?" (n 53) 1136. [78] ibid.

[79] International Crisis Group, "Bosnia's Future" (Europe Report No 232, International Crisis Group July 10, 2014) 13, <www.crisisgroup.org/europe-central-asia/balkans/bosnia-and-herzegovina/bosnia-s-future>.

[80] International Crisis Group, "Federation of Bosnia and Herzegovina – A Parallel Crisis" (Europe Report No 209, International Crisis Group September 28, 2010) 2–3, <www.crisisgroup.org/europe-central-asia/balkans/bosnia-and-herzegovina/federation-bosnia-and-herzegovina-parallel-crisis>.

[81] Lippman (n 66).

[82] Heather McRobie, "Breaking the Old Narratives of Bosnia" (*Precarious Europe*, September 20, 2014) <www.precariouseurope.com/power/breaking-narratives-bosnia>.

[83] "In 2013, Bosnia was 131st in the World Bank's Doing Business ranking, third worst in Europe. In such areas as 'Starting a Business' and 'Dealing with Construction Permits', it is among the world's worst, 174th and 175th respectively, and sinking (2014 rankings)." International Crisis Group, "Bosnia's Future" (n 79) 13.

major political parties of each community.[84] As these all-powerful men need not be office holders, their power is not matched with equivalent accountability. The Šestorka has become the major interlocutor of the international community and, according to some, the real government of Bosnia. Says the ICG, "When international officials want to negotiate an important issue with Bosnia's leadership, these are the men they call."[85] No decisions are taken without the Šestorka's approval. It has a say on the distribution of senior government posts and on the formation of governing coalitions; it controls election lists. However, "the Group's most important task may be dividing spheres of influence: control over public utilities, privatisation, concessions, state-owned banks, government tenders and other sources of revenue and patronage."[86]

Citizens' loyalties

"He who sows hunger reaps anger." Such was the graffiti one could find on the walls of Sarajevo in February 2014 as Bosnia witnessed a countrywide wave of popular protests against corruption and stagnation. Originating in the northern industrial city of Tuzla and quickly spreading to major cities and towns, the protests were met by police brutality. While the political elites sought to dismiss the movement as hooliganism, protesters who took part in this "Bosnian Spring" accused the elites of "pursuing their own interests and stirring ethno-nationalist tensions for political gain at the expense of providing essential services for all their citizens."[87]

The mobilization gave rise to a new phenomenon—"plenums" or public assemblies—in which citizens exercised direct democracy and articulated their demands. However, no sooner had the plenums begun to organize that the country was hit by severe flooding; this national emergency brought the protest movement to a halt. Both the short-lived timespan of the mobilization and the natural disaster that followed complicate the assessment of the movement and of its transformational potential. Citizens did score some successes as the prime ministers of cantonal governments in Sarajevo, Tuzla, and Zenica resigned. The protests and the plenums resurrected hopes for citizen-led reforms but they did not result in major changes. In fact, Lena Pasic makes the important point that, in spite of claims that the protests amounted to a sort of a "Bosnian spring," "Social unrest in February was mainly in the Federation, and although citizens and students in Republika Srpska also decided to voice their grievances, they were not connected with the citizens' groups in the other entity."[88]

On October 12, 2014, Bosnians voted in the country's sixth general election amid heightened expectations regarding political participation. After all, not only had the year witnessed the first wide-scale citizen mobilization movement, this was also the first election in which the post-war generation would have the right to vote. Nevertheless, "the statistics on voter turnout showed that civil mistrust of democratic institutions

[84] According to the ICG, the six leaders are Sulejman Tihić (SDA), Zlatko Lagumdžija (SDP), Milorad Dodik (SNSD), Mladen Bosić (SDS), Dragan Čović (HDZ), and Martin Raguž (HDZ 1990). At times, a third Bosnian patriot is a seventh Group member (making it a sedmorka). In 2006, Čović was convicted for wrongly exempting a company of import duty while FBiH finance minister. He was ultimately retried and acquitted of all charges. ibid 11.

[85] ibid. [86] ibid.

[87] McRobie (n 82); see also Chiara Milan, "Sow Hunger, Reap Anger" (*Roar Magazine*, February 9, 2014) <https://roarmag.org/essays/bosnia-protests-tuzla-workers/>.

[88] Lana Pasic, "Protests, Floods, Elections, Anniversaries, and Arrests: Reflecting on Bosnia's Main Events of 2014" (*Balkan Analysis*, January 14, 2015) <www.balkanalysis.com/bosnia/2015/01/14/protests-floods-elections-anniversaries-and-arrests-reflecting-on-bosnias-main-events-of-2014/>.

and the country's political representatives remain[ed] high – election turnout was only 54.14 percent, lower than during the 2010 elections."[89] True to the pattern established since the DPA, the October 2014 elections brought nationalist parties back into power, the only exception being the victory of Mladen Ivanic, from the opposition party in Republika Srpska, who won the Serbian seat in the Presidency.

It would thus seem that, not only does the system incentivize parties to adopt a nationalist rhetoric if they want to gain and maintain power, it also incentivizes voters to give preference to ethnonationalist parties over more moderate, nationalist, or mixed alternatives. To understand why voters keep going back, to paraphrase the title of John Hulsey's article, one must understand that voters usually cast votes in simultaneous mono-ethnic non-competitive, mono-ethnic competitive, and sometimes multiethnic races. "For example, a Bosniak voter from a canton with a majority Bosniak population in the Federation votes for the Bosniak member of the state-level presidency (a monoethnic, competitive context), the state-level parliament (multi-ethnic), the Federation parliament (multi-ethnic) and the Cantonal Assembly (monoethnic, non-competitive) all during the same visit to the ballot box."[90] In other words, the campaign that leaders wage in one specific race impacts voter decisions across races. And while voters do not necessarily like Bosnia's political parties, with only 17 percent expressing willingness to join one in a 2013 PRISM survey,[91] they understand that, in mono-ethnic competitive and multiethnic contexts, a vote for a non-ethnic or multiethnic party is construed as weakening one's ethnic community.

Yet, as discussed in the preceding section, it is precisely ethnonationalist parties that control access to employment. Furthermore, it is membership in a constituent people which, according to the terms of the DPA, entitles people to specific benefits and rights. Putting two and two together, "people continue to vote for nationalist parties, not necessarily because they wish to return to the politics of genocide and ethnic polarization, but because these parties can deliver the means of sustenance. As long as what happens at the ballot box does not shake the nationalist parties' influence in this area, they will remain strong."[92]

Dayton, a model or a cautionary tale?

It has been twenty-four years since the DPA was negotiated. The agreement dealt with territorial cleavages in a way that yielded a set of complicated institutional arrangements that allowed Bosnia's main political actors to pursue their political projects. Officially, Serbs, Croats, and Bosniacs are citizens of the same country; the reality is more complicated. The DPA may have ended the war; it did not solve the fundamental disagreement over the nature of the state. The RS leadership still intermittently threatens partition; Croat leaders have on occasion demanded their own entity; and some, though not all, Bosniac politicians have called for the total abolition of the Entities while others have adopted a clerical nationalism strongly supported by the Reis Mustafa *efendija* Ceric (head imam of Bosnia's Muslim community).[93] As Dayton forbids secession and as any

[89] ibid. [90] Hulsey, "Why did they vote for those guys again?" (n 53) 1141.

[91] "More than 87 per cent expressed little or no confidence in parties, with scant difference among regions or groups (though slightly greater Croat confidence). 86 percent blamed politicians for BiH problems. Croats, at 23.6 per cent, were most willing to join a party." PRISM Research survey, May 2013, cited in International Crisis Group, "Bosnia's Future" (n 79) 12.

[92] Julian Borger, "Bosnia's bitter, flawed peace deal, 20 years on" *The Guardian* (Bosnia-Herzegovina, November 10, 2015) <www.theguardian.com/global/2015/nov/10/bosnia-bitter-flawed-peace-deal-dayton-agreement-20-years-on>.

[93] Lippman (n 66).

change to the Entity system requires consensus among all three constituent peoples lest one of them use their veto right, none of these proposals is likely to see the light any time soon. The ongoing fundamental disagreement about the nature of the state is at the heart of Bosnia's paralysis. "For the past decade, the country has drifted. Bosnia currently has one of the highest youth unemployment rates in the world, according to World Bank statistics."

Yet, not only do nationalists consistently win at the polls, when asked in a recent survey, most Bosnians said they would vote for Dayton had there been a referendum for the DPA today. In fact, "across all ethnic groups a minority—only 28 percent—say they would have definitely or probably voted against Dayton in 2013. Bosnian Serbs [who were initially opposed to the agreement] are seven times more likely to say they would vote for the agreement than would oppose it."[94] It is, however, important not to interpret this support as an unreserved endorsement. In fact, two-thirds of the Serb respondents also said they would support Republika Srpska's full independence while the Bosnian Muslims are polarized "about whether or not Dayton's broader compromise was and is a good thing."

Academics are sharply divided on whether Bosnia is a model or a cautionary tale. Julian Borger quotes Marko Attila Hoare, a British historian of Bosnia, as saying "Thanks to Dayton, Karadžić's Serbs snatched a victory from the jaws of defeat, the Republika Srpska was consolidated and Bosnia was condemned to permanent dysfunction."[95] Borger himself argues that Dayton "spawned a political system that is a cash cow for politicians," a system that is both self-serving and self-perpetuating.[96] Edward Morgan-Jones and his co-authors acknowledge that, although the agreement did not just aim to secure the end of violence but also to protect human rights and cooperation, ethnic divisions and fragmentation prevented these goals. Yet, they conclude that "despite the caveats . . . Bosnia's citizens appear to have accepted Dayton as the best compromise available. And despite the common narrative of 'ancient ethnic hatreds,' perhaps Bosnia stands for the possibility that post-conflict societies needn't always be hostages to their past."[97]

However, Bosnia's most enduring lesson regards the potential for change once a system so complex and intricate is established. Twenty years of international efforts to manipulate carrots and sticks and weaken the hold of nationalist parties on power have failed to achieve their objective. The reason is the twin impact of Bosnia's constitutional and political context. The DPA sought to address Bosnia's *de facto* partition while at the same time ensuring the country's territorial integrity. The result was a complicated arrangement which profited nationalist parties. These parties have, in turn, perpetuated and exploited ethnically defined security dilemmas. By threatening partition or centralization, perpetuating uncertainty about the country's political and economic future, they have managed to "trump the incentives for change created by institutional and electoral reform."[98] As a consequence, Bosnia is as resilient and

[94] According to survey results, 42 percent of Bosnia's Serbs would definitely vote for Dayton, only 9 percent would vote against it. Croats are the least enthusiastic group with 37 percent not sure if they support the DPA and 22 percent who would either probably or definitely vote against it. Edward Morgan-Jones, Neophytos Loizides, and Djordje Stefanovic, "20 years later, this is what Bosnians think about the Dayton peace accords" *The Washington Post* (Monkey Cage, December 14, 2015) <www.washingtonpost.com/news/monkey-cage/wp/2015/12/14/20-years-later-this-is-what-bosnians-think-about-the-dayton-peace-accords/?utm_term=.71d3f7dce4d2>.

[95] Borger (n 92). [96] ibid. [97] Morgan-Jones, Loizides, and Stefanovic (n 94).

[98] Carrie Manning and Miljenko Antic, "The Limits of Electoral Engineering" (2003) 14 (3) Journal of Democracy 56.

stable as it is dysfunctional. Thus lies the paradox of Bosnian politics as aptly stated by Lippman: "that while there is no reasonable alternative to peaceful change through electoral politics, the structural arrangements created by the Dayton constitution have created long-term paralysis. The primacy given by Dayton to ethnic categories, to the detriment of voters as citizens, lies at the root of this paralysis."[99]

[99] Lippman (n 66).

3

The 2002–2004 Annan Plan in Cyprus

An Attempted UN-Mediated Constitutional Transition

Neophytos Loizides and John McGarry

Overview

This chapter focuses on the 2002–04 Annan Plan for Cyprus[1] and, more specifically, on the period leading to its fifth and final version. Although problematic in many of its provisions, the Annan Plan attempted to secure agreement on a reunited federal Cyprus within the European Union[2] and has been described as a major turning point in the recent history of the Cyprus problem.[3] The Plan's five successive iterations were widely debated, leading to a lengthy document submitted for popular ratification in each of the Greek Cypriot and Turkish Cypriot communities in April 2004. According to the UN Secretary General, most of its 9,000 pages were drafted by hundreds of Greek Cypriots and Turkish Cypriots whose extraordinary efforts produced one of the most comprehensive peace plans in the history of the United Nations.[4] Despite the UN's efforts to present a balanced document, the Plan was eventually rejected by the overwhelming majority (76 percent) of Greek Cypriots, although it was endorsed by 65 percent of Turkish Cypriots.[5] Regardless of the outcome, the Annan Plan for Cyprus is an interesting case of an attempted peace settlement/constitutional transition not just because of its substantive provisions, but also as we argue below its process; it is also relevant for the current peace talks in Cyprus and for other divided polities where

[1] The Plan is widely known as the Annan Plan, because of the personal involvement of the UN Secretary General, Kofi Annan in its making and promotion to the Cypriot public. Technically, the correct name of the plan is *The Comprehensive Settlement of the Cyprus Problem, 31 March 2004*. Although the plan is commonly attributed to Kofi Annan, Didier Pfirter, a Swiss diplomat then attached to the United Nations, is considered to be one of its main authors.

[2] The Annan Plan was introduced at the time of EU accession negotiations with Cyprus and another nine candidate states, leading to the largest enlargement ever in terms of people and number of countries. See Nathalie Tocci, *The EU and Conflict Resolution. Promoting Peace in the Backyard* (Routledge 2007); Thomas Diez, Albert Mathias, and Stetter Stephan, *The European Union and Border Conflicts: The Power of Integration and Association* (Cambridge University Press 2008).

[3] See, for instance, Chrysostomos Pericleous, *The Cyprus Referendum: A Divided Island and the Challenge of the Annan Plan* (IB Tauris 2009); Hubert Faustmann, "The Cyprus Question still Unsolved: Security Concerns and the Failure of the Annan Plan" (2004) 6 Südosteuropa Mitteilungen 44. Ahmet Sözen and Kudret Özersay, "The Annan Plan: State Succession or Continuity" (2007) 43 (1) Middle Eastern Studies 125.

[4] United Nations Secretary-General, "Secretary-General's Video Message to the Cypriot People" (*United Nations*, April 21, 2004) <www.un.org/sg/en/content/sg/statement/2004-04-21/secretary-generals-video-message-people-cyprus> accessed October 7, 2014.

[5] For survey-based interpretations of public attitudes following the Annan plan see Alexandros Lordos, Erol Kaymak, and Natalie Tocci, *A People's Peace in Cyprus: Testing Public Opinion on the Options for Comprehensive Settlement* (Centre for European Policy Studies 2009).

Territory and Power in Constitutional Transitions. First Edition. Edited by Michael Anderson and Sujit Choudhry. The 2002–2004 Annan Plan in Cyprus: An Attempted UN-Mediated Constitutional Transition Published 2019 by Oxford University Press.

international mediators seek to resolve protracted stalemates through comprehensive constitutional formulas.

The chapter argues the Annan Plan had predictable adoptability problems with its provisions on power-sharing, sovereignty, security, and human rights failing to include timely and credible incentives that would secure the support of elected political elites and undecided voters. The process was also handicapped by the design and timing of the referendums. Specifically, in what many impartial observers now see as a major diplomatic blunder, involving both the UN and the European Union, the referendums were held only after the accession of Cyprus (effectively the Greek-Cypriot controlled part) to the European Union had already been guaranteed. This removed the incentive of EU accession for the Greek Cypriots.

More broadly, the fate of the Plan raises a set of wider empirical and conceptual issues for the study of constitutional transitions particularly concerning how to ratify externally mediated peace agreements. Although the provision for twin Cypriot referendums seemed democratic, at the end it failed to legitimize the UN-endorsed constitutional transition. As this chapter demonstrates, the fear of an "imposed settlement" has been central to the narratives of the two communities, particularly Greek Cypriots. The 1960 Constitution was forced on the communities, especially the Greek Cypriots. According to one account, it resulted from deliberate blackmail against their leader, Archbishop Makarios.[6] The precedent of 1960 made any sort of "robust" UN intervention less likely to succeed among Greek Cypriots. Compounding matters, in an exercise of "extreme" international arbitration, the UN decided to proceed to the twin referendums without securing the support of elected representatives, including that of the Greek Cypriot leader and President of Cyprus, Tassos Papadopoulos. The referendum process undermined the role of elected leaders in Cyprus, thereby contradicting a key premise in the design of consociational arrangements.[7]

The chapter begins by sketching the background of the Cyprus problem. It addresses the period of constitutional negotiations around the Annan Plan and then discusses the unintended outcomes. It concludes by pointing to the broader lessons to be learned.

Background to the Cyprus Conflict

Cyprus gained its independence from the United Kingdom in 1960 following decades of Greek Cypriot opposition to colonial rule including the 1955–59 EOKA struggle for national liberation.[8] As the Greek Cypriot and Turkish Cypriot communities harbored conflicting views on the future of the island, resistance against British rule eventually produced intercommunal violence. The majority Greek Cypriots (80 percent)

[6] Historian Alan James argues British intelligence services blackmailed Makarios to accept the 1960 Constitution after showing him photos of his personal life. See Alan James, *Keeping the Peace in the Cyprus Crisis of 1963–64* (Palgrave 2002) 20.

[7] Lijphart defines consociational democracy as "government by elite cartel designed to turn a democracy with a fragmented political culture into a stable democracy." It is "based on the assumption that the elites understand the perils of political fragmentation" and requires that elites are committed "to the maintenance of the system." Arend Lijphart, "Consociational Democracy" (1969) 21 (2) World Politics 207, 216.

[8] EOKA (National Organization of Cypriot Fighters) fought against British rule between 1955 and 1959.

historically aspired for union (*enosis*) with Greece while the Turkish Cypriot community (18 percent) totally rejected this, aiming instead for the island's partition (*taksim*).[9]

To avoid broader conflict among NATO allies, the governments of the United Kingdom, Greece, and Turkey reached a compromise in 1959 on an independent Cyprus, with caveats. The new arrangement included significant constitutional, security, and other guarantees for the Turkish Cypriot community, reflecting the strength of Turkey in relation to Greece rather than Turkish Cypriots in relation to Greek Cypriots. It also envisaged separate electoral rolls for the two communities; Greek Cypriots were to elect the President of the Republic and Turkish Cypriots the Vice-President, although the two offices were arguably comparable in powers. Under the 1960 Treaty of Guarantee, the United Kingdom and the two "motherlands" (Greece and Turkey) gained the right to intervene in Cyprus through unilateral action but with the sole aim of re-establishing a balanced state of affairs.[10] In addition, under the 1960 Treaty of Establishment, the United Kingdom was allowed to retain two "sovereign" bases incorporating nearly 100 square miles of the island.

Inevitably, the 1960 Constitution contributed to a suspicion of outside imposition among Greek Cypriots that was to resonate in 2004. The power-sharing arrangements between Greek and Turkish Cypriots established in 1960 lasted for only three years. The 1960 Constitution aimed at addressing the difficulties associated with majoritarianism in the Cypriot context by installing a consociational system as a safeguard for the two communities. However, the Greek Cypriot side felt these constraints against majority rule constituted "a betrayal of their . . . rights."[11] Lack of political commitment to the new state, combined with ambiguous constitutional language on how to manage unfinished matters (e.g., regarding the establishment of separate municipalities) led to conflict and constitutional collapse.[12]

The new republic's presidential system, moreover, increased polarization and tensions. The presidential-style consociationalism of the Zürich–London Agreements contradicted many of the recommendations of consociational theorists.[13] The presidency was dual in nature, but it presented each of the two communities as political monoliths, preventing the sort of internal diversity that might have been possible in a parliamentary executive coalition and that might have opened up political alignments cutting across the two communities. The dual presidency delayed the emergence of political parties in both communities and resulted in every political clash taking place along communal lines.[14]

[9] For a comparison of the evolution of violence to other British colonies, see Chares Demetriou, "Political Radicalization and Political Violence in Palestine, Ireland and Cyprus" (2012) 36 (3) Social Science History 391.

[10] Stephen George Xydis, *Cyprus: Reluctant Republic* (Volume 11 of Near and Middle East Monographs, Mouton 1973); Zaim Necatigil, *The Cyprus Question and the Turkish Position in International Law* (Oxford University Press 1989); Tozun Bahcheli, *Greek–Turkish Relations since 1955* (Westview Press 1990).

[11] Oliver Richmond, "Ethno-nationalism, Sovereignty and Negotiating Positions in the Cyprus Conflict: Obstacles to a Settlement" (1999) 35 (3) Middle Eastern Studies 42, 50.

[12] Diana Weston Markides, *Cyprus 1957–1963: from Colonial Conflict to Constitutional Crisis: the Key Role of the Municipal Issue* (University of Minnesota 2001).

[13] Arend Lijphart, *Electoral Systems and Party Systems: A Study of Twenty-Seven Democracies 1945–1990* (Oxford University Press 1994); see also Juan J Linz, "The Perils of Presidentialism" (1990) 1 (1) Journal of Democracy 51; Scott Mainwaring and Matthew S Shugart, "Juan Linz, Presidentialism, and Democracy: A Critical Appraisal" (1997) 29 (4) Comparative Politics 449; John McGarry, "Is Presidentialism Necessarily Non-collegial?" (2013) 12 (1) Ethnopolitics 93.

[14] For a detailed analysis of this period see Christoforos Fokaides, "Reconciling Nation and State: Glafkos Clerides and Political Transformation in Cyprus" (PhD dissertation, University of Kent 2014).

Compounding the problem, in the 1960s Cyprus lacked neutral and effective security mechanisms while the two "motherlands," Greece and Turkey, played a negative role in exacerbating divisions. In 1963, President Makarios attempted to change the constitution in a majoritarian direction, putting forward a thirteen-point proposal for its amendment. Turkey and Turkish Cypriot leaders opposed the changes and fighting broke out between the two communities, ending Turkish Cypriot participation in the Cyprus government. In early 1964, the United Nations sent a peacekeeping force to the island, starting one of the longest operations in the organization's history. In 1967, another clash between the two communities caused a near-war crisis between Greece and Turkey. Throughout this period, the motherlands played major roles in instigating extremism in their respective communities either directly or via paramilitaries.[15]

On July 20, 1974, Turkey sent troops to Cyprus in response to a coup five days earlier by the Greek Junta against Makarios, and which Turkey saw as designed to unite Cyprus with Greece. Turkey's invasion (or intervention/peace operation as it is commonly described by Ankara and by Turkish Cypriots) led to the *de facto* division of Cyprus into two areas; a Turkish army controlled area in the north and the internationally recognized government controlled area in the south. The Republic of Cyprus lost control of about 37 percent of its territory and nearly 60 percent of its coastline. It also lost a number of large villages with predominantly Greek Cypriot populations, as well as the town of Morphou and the Greek sector of Famagusta (Varosha); the latter, at that point the most economically vibrant urban area in Cyprus, has remained an abandoned "ghost city" since 1974.

Approximately a third of the Greek Cypriot population of Cyprus (about 160,000 civilians) were forced by the Turkish military to flee their ancestral homes, while a similar proportion but smaller number of Turkish Cypriots (about 45,000) residing in the south opted (and in some cases were forced) to abandon their homes and leave for the northern part of the island.[16] The tragedy of July 20, 1974, is the equivalent for Greek Cypriots of Nakba Day for Palestinians, a day which commemorates that community's losses during the 1948 Palestine War (the War of Independence from the Israeli perspective).[17] For decades, Greek Cypriots have pointed to their displacement, missing persons, and suffering following the invasion, emphasizing the illegality of the Turkish army-controlled areas in the north.[18]

While Turkish Cypriots acquired a disproportional amount of territory in 1974, their legal jurisdiction over this territory has not been recognized by any state other than Turkey. Since 1964, when Turkish Cypriots were expelled from the government and forced into enclaves (in the Turkish Cypriot narrative) or abandoned their posts in the pursuit of *taksim* (in the Greek Cypriot narrative), Greek Cypriots have maintained control of the internationally recognized Republic of Cyprus. The republic's foreign policy has reflected longstanding Greek Cypriot positions on the injustice of 1974 and has aimed at preventing the *de jure* recognition of the new realities.[19] Perhaps

[15] See Drousiotis Makarios, *The First Partition, Cyprus 1963–1964* (Alfadi 2008).

[16] Nicholas Sambanis, "The United Nations Operation in Cyprus: A New Look at the Peacekeeping-Peacemaking Relationship" (1999) 6 (1) International Peacekeeping 79; Neophytos Loizides and Marcos A Antoniades, "Negotiating the Right of Return" (2009) 46 (5) Journal of Peace Research 611.

[17] Neophytos Loizides, *Designing Peace: Institutional Innovations in Cyprus and Divided Societies* (University of Pennsylvania Press 2016).

[18] For an analysis of the Greek Cypriot narratives and their politicization, see Rebecca Bryant, *The Past in Pieces: Belonging in the New Cyprus* (University of Pennsylvania Press 2010); see also Iosif Kovras, *Truth Recovery and Transitional Justice: Deferring Human Rights Issues* (Routledge 2014).

[19] James Ker-Lindsay, *The Foreign Policy of Counter Secession: Preventing the Recognition of Contested States* (Oxford University Press 2012).

understandably, the events of 1974 have caused Greek Cypriots to become fixated on justice and rights discourses while Turkish Cypriots have relied on the events of 1963–64 to justify the "new realities" on the ground. As in comparable situations elsewhere, "absolutist demands" on each side have made it difficult to reach a mutually beneficial settlement.

In addition to power-sharing, citizenship, and security questions, negotiations on the Cyprus problem have focused historically on the right of return for displaced persons to their properties on the one hand and the property rights of current users on the other. Greek Cypriots have demanded a right of return, citing international human rights law, European Court of Human Rights (ECtHR) decisions on the Greek Cypriot displaced and the need for a settlement to be perceived as just.[20] Turkish Cypriots, in contrast, have insisted on preserving their demographic presence in northern Cyprus, arguing that realities on the ground, security concerns and the principle of "bizonality" dictate that any right of return should be strictly limited.[21] Another thorny issue is the status of the populations transferred from Turkey to the northern part of the island after 1974, alternately described as settlers or immigrants in the rival accounts of the Cypriot conflict.

Greek and Turkish Cypriots also disagree on how to address the issue of sovereignty. Since 1974, the two sides have developed rival visions (still a central problem in negotiations), with Greek Cypriots defending the continuity of the Republic of Cyprus and insisting any federation must evolve from the Cypriot unitary state, while Turkish Cypriots aim for a federation comprised of two founding (constituent) states. In political science terms, this is the difference between what Stepan et al. call a "holding together" federation and a "coming together" federation.[22] The Greek Cypriots fear that a "coming together" federation would break up easily, as its two constituent parts would retain their sovereignty; indeed, many Greek Cypriots believe the Turkish Cypriot aim in negotiations is not to establish a joint Cyprus but to partition it, after a temporary union, but this time securing the recognition that has eluded them hitherto. During negotiations on the Annan Plan, the UN described the "breakdown of the new state of affairs followed by secession of a sovereign Turkish Cypriot state and the consequent partition of Cyprus" as "the Greek Cypriot nightmare."[23] In contrast, the Turkish Cypriot nightmare is that a "holding together" settlement would subject them to Greek Cypriot majority rule as in the pre-1974 period, with little hope of escape via secession. Not surprisingly, the UN considered sovereignty "as perhaps the most contentious conceptual issue" during the Annan Plan negotiations.[24]

In "High-Level" agreements in 1977 and 1979, the Greek Cypriot and Turkish Cypriot leaders accepted that Cyprus should be federalized (although they did not agree on the nature, institutional design, or meaning of federalism).[25] At the same

[20] United Nations Document S/2003/398. "Report of the Secretary-General on His Mission of Good Offices in Cyprus" (*United Nations*, April 1, 2003), 6.

[21] ibid; since 2010, the Turkish Cypriot side has relied on the Demopoulos case at the ECtHR to support the rights of new owners including settlers. For the Court, rehousing potentially large numbers of men, women and children even with the aim of vindicating the rights of past victims cannot be imposed as an unconditional obligation on a government. *Demopoulos and others v. Turkey* App nos 46113/99, 3843/02, 13751/02, 13466/03, 10200/04, 14163/04, 19993/04, 21819/04 (ECtHR, March 1, 2010).

[22] Alfred Stepan, Juan Linz, and Yogendra Yagav, *Crafting State-Nations: India and Other Multinational Democracies* (Johns Hopkins University Press 2011) 25–6.

[23] ibid 16. [24] UN Document S/2003/398 (n 20) 16.

[25] Tozun Bahcheli and Nicholas X Rizopoulos, "The Cyprus Impasse: What Next?" (1996) 13 (4) World Policy Journal 27; John McGarry, "Consociational Theory, Self-Determination Disputes and Territorial Pluralism: The Case of Cyprus" in Karlo Basta, John McGarry, and Richard Simeon (eds),

time, pro-settlement Cypriots combined a federalist vision with the prospect of Europeanization for the whole island.[26] In 1990, the Republic of Cyprus applied for membership in the European Union; three years later, the Commission confirmed its eligibility for membership, despite objections from Turkey and the Turkish Cypriot leadership.[27]

On December 13, 1997, at the Luxembourg European Council, the EU member states decided Cyprus could begin the formal process of negotiating the conditions of its membership but rejected Turkey's application.[28] Two years later, Greece lifted its veto of Turkey's EU candidacy at the European Council Meeting in Helsinki in December 1999, following the rapid improvement of relations with Turkey after the August 1999 earthquakes. The positive climate between Greece and Turkey, as well as the prospect of European enlargement in the eastern Mediterranean, were seen as potential catalysts for a political settlement in Cyprus.[29]

EU accession meant immediate benefits for both communities on the island, and progress toward it encouraged a re-alignment of political cleavages. On the Turkish Cypriot side, the peace process was opposed by right-wingers (veteran Turkish Cypriot leader, Rauf Denktaş, and the National Unity Party—UBP), who nonetheless found themselves under increasing pressure for sacrificing their community's place in Europe. Even though the left was historically a minority, Mehmet Ali Talat's Republican Turkish Party (CTP) led a successful pro-unification campaign and protested against Denktaş's policies in large pro-EU rallies in 2002–03. In December 2003, the CTP became the main coalition party in the north with the Democratic Party (DP) as the junior partner; the latter, although associated with Denktaş's legacy, significantly moderated its position. Greek Cypriot political parties were similarly divided. The center-right Democratic Rally (DISY), despite its conservative heritage and links to the Greek ethnonationalist tradition particularly the *enosis* movement, supported the peace process under the leadership of Nicos Anastasiades. Former President Clerides (1993–2003), founder of DISY, was committed to Europeanization and campaigned successfully among right-wing voters for a "federal Cyprus within a federal Europe."[30] While DISY represented about a third of Greek Cypriot voters in the late 1990s, the remaining voters were divided equally between the historically pro-settlement Progressive Party of Working People (AKEL) and two smaller parties, the Democratic Party (DIKO), and the Movement for Social Democracy (EDEK). DIKO and EDEK were hardline on the Cyprus question, yet in the period preceding EU accession, both moderated their positions. Perhaps surprisingly, given what transpired in 2004, the first version of the Annan Plan was endorsed in 2002 as a basis for negotiations by all Greek Cypriot parties. The DIKO leader, Tassos Papadopoulos, President of Cyprus

Territorial Pluralism: Managing Difference in Multinational States (University of British Columbia Press 2015).

[26] Joseph Joseph, *Cyprus: Ethnic Conflict and International Politics: from Independence to the Threshold of the European Union* (St. Martin's Press 1997).

[27] For a discussion of the main milestones leading to EU accession, see James Ker-Lindsay, "The Role of the EU as Conflict Manager in Cyprus" in Richard Whitman and Stefan Wolff (eds), *European Union as a Global Conflict Manager* (Routledge 2012).

[28] Doga Ulas Eralp and Nimet Beriker, "Assessing the Conflict Resolution Potential of the EU: The Cyprus Conflict and Accession Negotiations" (2005) 36 (2) Security Dialogue 175.

[29] Bahar Rumelili, "Transforming Conflicts on EU Borders: The Case of Greek-Turkish Relations" (2007) 45 (1) Journal of Common Market Studies 105; James Ker-Lindsay, *Crisis and Conciliation: A Year of Rapprochement Between Greece and Turkey* (IB Tauris 2007); Ziya Öniş and Şuhnaz Yilmaz, "Greek-Turkish Rapprochement: Rhetoric or Reality?" (2008) 123 (1) Political Science Quarterly 123.

[30] See Fokaides (n 14).

from 2003 to 2008, eventually came to lead the "no" campaign, while his main ally in government—the pro-settlement AKEL—rejected the Plan in a last-minute decision.[31]

The Period of Constitutional Engagement: The Promise of the Annan Plan

In November 2002, the UN Secretary General's Special Adviser on Cyprus, Alvaro de Soto, presented the first of five versions of a comprehensive plan for the resolution of the Cyprus problem. The plan was introduced only days after the victory of Recep Tayyip Erdoğan's Justice and Development Party (AKP) in elections in Turkey. The AKP initiated constructive diplomatic initiatives over Cyprus,[32] while Turkish-Cypriot civil society organizations mobilized to support a federal settlement within the next enlargement round of the European Union. In late 2003, Talat's pro-settlement CTP won the Turkish Cypriot parliamentary elections and entered a governing coalition with the Democratic Party. The main obstacle to a settlement on the Turkish Cypriot side remained the President of the TRNC, Rauf Denktaş, who, under the Turkish Cypriot's semi-presidential system, was their main negotiator. However, even Denktaş was pressured into lifting restrictions on travel across the so-called Green Line separating the two communities in April 2003. On the Greek Cypriot side, the picture was murkier. Pro-settlement elements in Greek Cypriot civil society failed to mobilize effectively in the 2002–04 period in part because their leaders had already taken moderate positions, possibly to prevent any obstacles to Cyprus's EU accession process, which was occurring alongside the peace process. Ominously, however, Greek Cypriot voters refused to renew the mandate of their moderate leader, Glafkos Clerides, in presidential elections in February of 2002, electing instead a hardliner, Tassos Papadopoulos, who had accused Clerides of selling out Greek Cypriot interests. By early 2004, the sides adopted an approach to mediation that was unusual in divided societies, and particularly surprising given the entrenched view in the Greek Cypriot community that Cyprus had been treated as a pawn by outsiders. They offered the UN Secretary General the role of arbiter: he was authorized to "fill in any gaps" in the negotiations that had not been agreed to by the respective negotiating teams and to submit the Plan directly to the public in parallel referendums without the prior consent of the two leaders.

The resulting Annan Plan was based on the premise that both communities would (and must) gain from the settlement. It was anticipated that Turkish Cypriots would gain autonomy under a decentralized and bizonal federal system, as well as power-sharing within federal institutions. Greek Cypriots were to gain territory, which would be transferred from the Turkish Cypriot region to the Greek Cypriot region (see proposed territorial adjustments in Figure 3.1 below). Greek Cypriot displaced persons would also be able to return to their properties in the newly acquired territory, as well as at least some properties in the territory that would remain under Turkish Cypriot administration, although not necessarily to the same extent in both cases. The reunited island was also to enjoy EU membership.[33]

[31] Nicos Trimikliniotis, "A Communist's Post-Modern Power Dilemma: One Step Back, Two Steps Forward, 'Soft No' and Hard Choices" (2006) 18 (1) The Cyprus Review 1.

[32] Morton Abramowitz and Henri Barkey, "Turkey's Transformers" (2009) 88 (6) Foreign Affairs 118.

[33] Claire Palley, *An International Relations Debacle: the UN Secretary-General's Mission of Good Offices in Cyprus 1999–2004* (Hart Publishing 2005); Ahmet Sözen and Kudret Özersay, "The Annan Plan: State Succession or Continuity" (2007) 43 (1) Middle Eastern Studies 125; Harry Anastasiou,

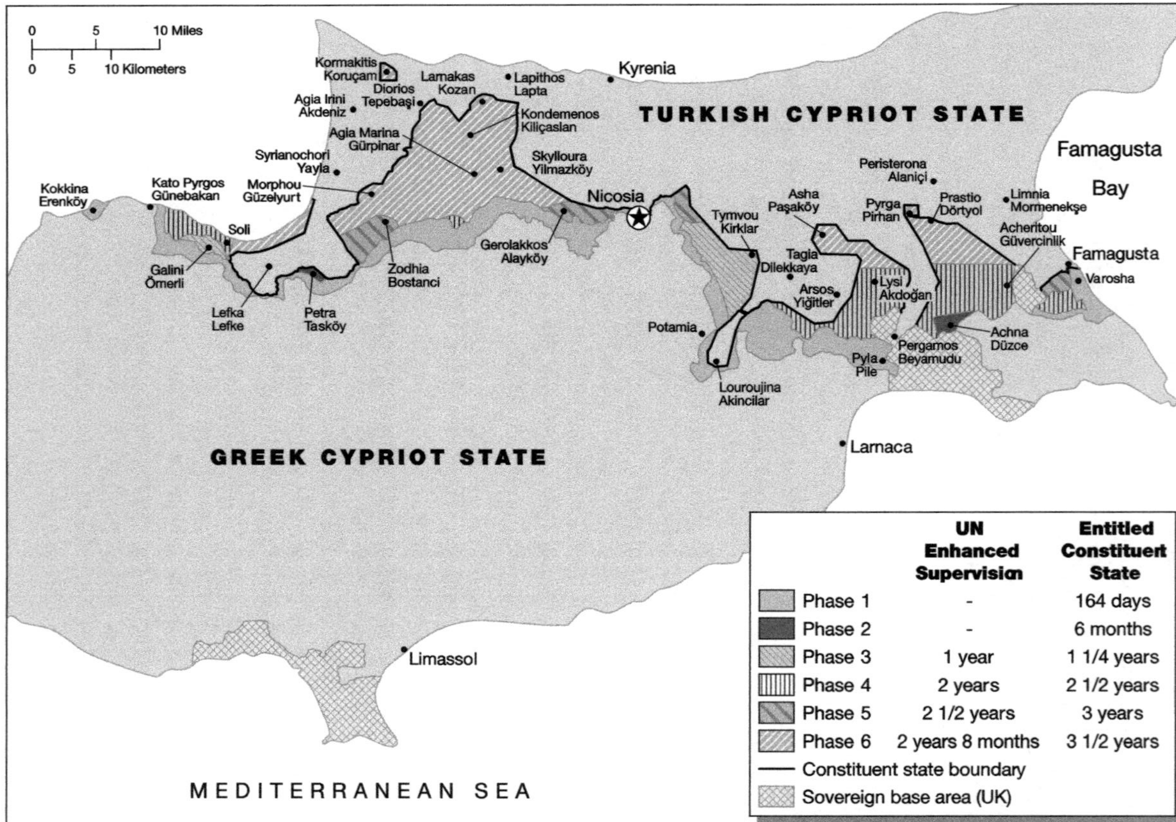

Figure 3.1 Territorial adjustments in the Annan Plan. UN Cartographic Section (see also Loizides, *Designing Peace* (n. 17), 107)

In the negotiations, the Greek Cypriot leadership emphasized the need for the settlement to be perceived as just by victims of displacement and it demanded maximum territorial concessions and restitution of property. In contrast, Turkish Cypriots argued that current realities on the ground had to be respected, and that only a minimum number of Turkish Cypriots could be resettled. As shown in the UN map, the proposed territorial adjustments included the Greek Cypriot part of Famagusta (Varosha), the town of Morphou/Guzelyurt, and a number of villages across the buffer zone (plus a Maronite enclave in Kormakitis). The UN sought to keep the number of Turkish Cypriots who would have to be resettled as low as possible, mainly resettling villages where the 2004 Turkish Cypriot population was relatively low compared to the pre-1974 Greek Cypriot population. This was the main reason, according to the drafters of the Plan, for a wiggly line instead of a straight one across the new territorial border.[34]

If the Annan Plan had been approved by Greek Cypriots, the reunited island would have had a Senate with a fifty-fifty composition (twenty-four Turkish Cypriot and twenty-four Greek Cypriot Senators) reflecting the principle of the "political equality" of the two communities. The Chamber of Deputies was also to have forty-eight members, based on population, but with no less than a quarter of the seats allocated to each of the two constituent states. According to all versions of the Plan, ordinary decisions in the Senate would have required a majority of the Senators to agree, including at least a quarter of the representatives from each community. On issues of vital interest, such as the election of the Presidential Council (an executive body similar to that in Switzerland), there was to be a provision for a "special majority" of at least two-fifths of the Senators from each side, plus approval by the Chamber of Deputies.[35]

The procedure for electing the Presidential Council differed significantly from the provisions for ministerial appointment in the 1960 Constitution, where the communally elected Greek Cypriot President and Turkish Cypriot Vice-President were each responsible for appointing their respective communities' share of the Council of Ministers. In the Annan Plan, the Presidential Council was to be elected on a "single list by special majority in the Senate and approved by majority in the Chamber of Deputies for a five-year term."[36] This provision was designed to facilitate a moderate Council, in line with the centripetalist thinking of Donald Horowitz,[37] but it introduced a potentially serious problem; namely, that there might be no federal government and no formal constitutional way to elect one. It is possible to guarantee

The Broken Olive Branch: Nationalism, Ethnic Conflict and the Quest for Peace in Cyprus, Vol. 1 The Impasse of Ethnonationalism (Syracuse University Press 2008).

[34] For instance, the map attached to the third plan affected about 47,000 people, of whom 11,000 were to be rehoused within their current city, Famagusta, with another 12,000 from Morphou/Guzelyurt going to another city as a community, leaving about 24,000 people from other affected locations to be relocated; see an interview in *Kibris TV* with one of the architects of the Plan and legal advisors to the UN mission in Cyprus, Didier Pfirter interviewed by *Editor in Chief of the KIBRIS Media Group* Suleyman Erguclu (unknown location March, 20 2003) available at http://www.erguclu.eu/mulakatlar/030320%20Didier%20Pfirter%20(turkce).htm accessed December 28, 2017.

[35] UN Document S/2003/398 (n 20) 19; United Nations Peacemaker, "The Comprehensive Settlement of the Cyprus Problem, 31 March" (*United Nations*, March 31, 2004) <https://peacemaker.un.org/node/2961> accessed January 19, 2005.

[36] UN Peacemaker (n 35) 10.

[37] For example, see Donald Horowitz, *A Democratic South Africa? Constitutional Engineering in a Divided Society* (University of California Press 1991); Donald Horowitz, *Ethnic Groups in Conflict* (University of California Press 2004); Horowitz has not endorsed cross-voting as a form of centripetalism despite overlaps, see John McGarry and Neophytos Loizides, "Power-Sharing in a Re-United Cyprus: Centripetal Coalitions vs. Proportional Sequential Coalitions" (2015) 13 (4) International Journal of Constitutional Law 847.

that one list will win a majority in the Senate in a two list run-off, but impossible to guarantee that any list will win two-fifths support from the representatives of two groups. Apparently, the negotiators sought to address this issue through an understanding that there would be a Belgian-style requirement for the previous government to stay in power if party negotiations failed to establish a new coalition. This would not have solved the problem of how to form the first government and could have led to long periods of unelected administrations as in the Belgian case. The Presidential Council was to be comprised of four members from the Greek Cypriot Constituent State and two members from the Turkish Cypriot Constituent State, and could not make decisions without at least one affirmative vote from each side. It was to elect two of its members "not hailing from the same constituent state" to a rotating presidency/vice-presidency, with the member from the larger (Greek Cypriot) constituent state holding the position of president for two-thirds of each term.[38]

The Plan envisaged a Supreme Court comprising an equal number of Cypriot judges from the two communities and an unspecified number of foreign judges appointed by the UN. This was similar to the Supreme Court established by the 1960 Constitution, where an external judge held the "swing vote," and to provisions in the 1995 Dayton Accords in Bosnia-Herzegovina, but it went against the grain of preferring domestic judges for domestic courts. The Court would have powers to settle disagreements over the new constitution, including the resolution of disputes within the federal level of government and between the federal and constituent state levels.

The issue of displaced persons was a central part of the plan. Turkish Cypriots viewed property rights within the confines of "bizonality," interpreted to mean a markedly restricted right of restitution for Greek Cypriot properties in the future Turkish Cypriot constituent state.[39] During the negotiations, the UN mediators argued that international norms since WWII favored a settlement based on respect for individual rights but also took into consideration that the main contentious events in Cyprus had occurred thirty to forty years previously; since then, roughly half of Turkish Cypriots and a third of Greek Cypriots had rebuilt their lives.[40] In general terms, the Plan offered displaced Greek Cypriots hailing from the future Turkish Cypriot state restitution of about a third of their property, with compensation for the rest. To further reduce Turkish Cypriot apprehensions about the resettlement of Greek Cypriots under Turkish Cypriot administration, the Plan de-linked political rights from residency. Unusually for federations,[41] the upper chamber (the Senate) was to be elected not by voters in the two regions but by voters in the two communities, voting separately. In addition, the franchise for the lower federal chamber (Chamber of Deputies) was to be based on "internal constituent state citizenship," a status regulated by each of the constituent states. Voting for constituent state and local institutions was to be based on "permanent residency," a status that was also, presumably, to be regulated by each of the constituent states, but subject to the European *acquis* with respect to nationals of other EU states.[42]

[38] United Nations Peacemaker (n 35), art. 5(2)(d).

[39] Ayla Gürel and Kudret Özersay, *The Politics of Property in Cyprus: Conflicting Appeals to "Bizonality" and "Human Rights" by the Two Cypriot Communities* (PRIO Report 3, International Peace Research Institute, Oslo (PRIO) 2006) <http://northcyprusfreepress.com/wp-content/uploads/2012/08/prio-cyprus-property-report.pdf> accessed October 20, 2013.

[40] UN Document S/2003/398 (n 20) 20–3.

[41] The Belgian Senate had some Senators directly elected from communal lists until 2014. All are now indirectly elected by the community and regional legislatures.

[42] UN Peacemaker (n 35) art. 3(3), 3(5), 3(7), 13.

The Plan was arguably most problematic, from the perspective of Greek Cypriots, with respect to Turkey. The Treaty of Guarantee, which allowed three guarantors (Turkey, Greece, and the UK) unilateral intervention rights in Cyprus, was to be retained, *mutatis mutandis*, in the first article of the new settlement. This was the treaty that Turkey had used to legitimize its invasion/intervention in Cyprus in 1974. The Plan also permitted the stationing of 3,000 Turkish (and Greek) troops in Cyprus for fourteen years or until Turkey entered the European Union, whichever came first, and envisaged a potentially permanent stationing of 650 Turkish troops and 950 Greek troops after that.[43] On the issue of the repatriation of the Turkish settlers who had been introduced to Cyprus after 1974, the plan was ambiguous.[44]

Greek Cypriots were also concerned about the Plan's power-sharing provisions. As a large majority, many of them resented the Plan's underlying principle of the "political equality" of two communities. Typically, Greek Cypriots instead favored an emphasis on individual equality with "minority" rights that fell far short of what Turkish Cypriots would accept. Another Greek Cypriot concern was that Turkish Cypriots would use the settlement to secure secession, but this time with recognition. This fear was focused on parts of the Plan that implied the Turkish Cypriots had retained sovereignty, and could act independently in negotiating treaties, both markers, according to Greek Cypriot nationalists, of confederations rather than federations. This concern was exacerbated by a nationalist argument that the continuity of the Republic of Cyprus was not assured, because it was not explicitly recognized.[45] From this perspective, the Greek Cypriots were in danger of losing their state, including succession rights within the European Union, at the same time as the Turkish Cypriots gained recognition. This was the background to Tassos Papadopoulos's famous comment during a TV broadcast aired during the referendum campaign: "I received an internationally recognised state and I cannot deliver a 'community' without a right of speech internationally and seeking a guardian, and all this with empty, deceiving expectations, with the unfounded illusion that Turkey will honour its commitments."[46]

Equally important to the Plan's substance was its timing in relation to accession to the European Union. As majorities on both sides entertained strong hopes of joining the EU, accession seemed to offer the catalyst for reunification. However, in arguable contrast to other parts of Europe in line for accession at the time, the incentives of EU accession failed to have a productive effect. This was for the simple reason that

[43] UN Peacemaker (n 35) art. 8(1)(b).

[44] On the issue of settlers, the ambiguity was partly due to the multiple routes toward naturalization or residency options provided for the settlers by the Plan. According to Pfirter "anybody who is married to a Cypriot will automatically get citizenship. A further 45,000 people will get citizenship in a certain order of priority, and we expect that anyone who has grown up in Cyprus are the first priority category in that. Or those who stayed here for a long time should be covered by that number. Another roughly 15,000 people, it will be 10 percent of the Turkish Cypriot population, will get permanent residency and they will be able to obtain citizenship after some more years, depending on how long they have already stayed in Cyprus. Students and academic staff will be allowed to stay in Cyprus in unlimited numbers," Pfirter (n 34).

[45] The Annan Plan did not specify the issue of continuity vs. succession in an attempt to avoid antagonizing the positions of the two sides. Instead it adopted the principle of "virgin birth" for the United Republic of Cyprus, which suggested the United Cyprus Republic, like Jesus, had no father and was born although he pre-existed. The virgin birth approach aimed at reconciling the views of the two sides that the new state was not the continuation of the Republic of Cyprus as in the Greek Cypriot view, or two separate states as in the Turkish Cypriot view.

[46] Tassos Papadopoulos, "Address to Cypriots by President Papadopoulos" (translated full text, *Cyprus New Agency*, April 8, 2004) <http://www.hri.org/news/cyprus/cna/2004/04-04-08.cna.html#01> accessed October 7, 2014.

de jure accession of the Republic of Cyprus (and *de facto* accession of the territory controlled by the Greek Cypriots) had already been secured at the European Council in Copenhagen in December 2002, before the election of Papadopoulos and before the referendums; therefore, Greek Cypriots had no EU-related incentive to vote "yes."

This demonstrates the criticality of the timing of EU incentives. The EU could have made a settlement of the Cyprus problem a precondition for the island's accession. Although this option was widely debated, Greece and the Greek Cypriot side argued convincingly that such a precondition would give the Turkish side (including Turkey, which had invaded the island) a veto over Cyprus's accession, forcing the Greek Cypriot community to pay the costs of possible Turkish intransigence. More importantly, Greece threatened to veto the entire EU Eastern enlargement if "unfair preconditions" were introduced for Cyprus's accession. Following this logic, in the Presidency Conclusions of December 1999, the European Council welcomed the launching of talks aiming at a comprehensive settlement of the Cyprus problem and expressed strong support for the UN Secretary-General's efforts to bring the process to a successful conclusion. More specifically, the European Council underlined that "a political settlement will facilitate the accession of Cyprus to the European Union. However, it noted that if no settlement has been reached by the completion of accession negotiations, the Council's decision on accession will be made without the above being a precondition."[47]

Outcome of the Process

The Annan Plan was rejected during the twin April 2004 referendums by a landslide majority of Greek Cypriots (76 percent), while a substantial majority of Turkish Cypriots (65 percent) approved it. Reunification did not take place, but in the following month Cyprus formally joined the EU as agreed at the European Council summit in Copenhagen in 2002. Since then, all of Cyprus has been in the EU, *de jure*, but the *acquis communautaire* (European body of law) does not apply to areas of the island outside the control of the Republic of Cyprus. Turkish Cypriots who have retained citizenship in the Republic of Cyprus are entitled to travel, study and work in EU countries, but the northern part of the island cannot initiate or receive direct flights, operate internationally recognized universities, or trade directly with the rest of Europe.

The outcome of the Annan Plan referendums has shaped the foreseeable future of Cyprus mediations. Following its overwhelming rejection, Greek Cypriots have been determined to change key aspects while Turkish Cypriots, particularly those on the left, have emphasized continuity. Turkish Cypriot right-wingers opposed the Plan and were glad it failed, particularly as Greek Cypriots took the blame. Following the referendums, Turkish Cypriots argued for further economic and political integration of the northern part of the island with the EU, but Greek Cypriots accommodated this demand only partly, linking any further progress to equal concessions from Turkey and

[47] Helsinki European Council, "Presidency Conclusions 10 and 11 December 1999" (*Helsinki European Council* December 10–11, 1999) <www.consilium.europa.eu/uedocs/cms_data/docs/pressdata/en/ec/ACFA4C.htm> accessed November 3, 2014. In 2003 the first author recommended that Greek Cypriots should unilaterally endorse the Annan Plan III as part of the accession package deal, building federal institutions in advance and leaving the door open for the Turkish Cypriots to join at a later time. This option could have potentially resolved the dilemma facing EU and UN mediators at the time; see Neophytos Loizides "After The Hague: Which Way to Turn in the Cyprus Negotiations" Cyprus Action (March 12, 2003) <https://works.bepress.com/neophytos_loizides/29/ > accessed December 28, 2017.

the Turkish Cypriots, including the return of the town of Varosha. Meanwhile, the EU decided to slow down Turkey's accession talks in December 2006, citing the country's reluctance to open its ports and extend trade privileges to the Republic of Cyprus.

In February 2008, the election of Demetris Christofias from the traditionally pro-settlement AKEL as President of the Republic of Cyprus brought new hope for a settlement. Christofias, however, failed to make the necessary groundbreaking decisions, despite some initial progress in the peace talks. For example, an alternative cross-voting (centripetal) arrangement to elect the presidency of a united Cyprus was agreed upon by Talat (elected as Turkish Cypriot leader in April 2005) and Christofias in 2010, a plan pioneered by Costa Carras and the Friends of Cyprus as early as the 1970s.[48] The 2010 compromise envisaged a direct election, unlike the indirect election of the Annan Plan. It proposed that the united Cyprus would be governed by a two-person collegial presidency, comprising a Greek Cypriot and Turkish Cypriot. Greek Cypriots and Turkish Cypriots were each to be given two votes, one for each position. Greek Cypriot votes cast for the Turkish Cypriot position were then to be "weighted" to constitute exactly the same proportion of votes cast for the Greek Cypriot position by Turkish Cypriots. As Turkish Cypriots are approximately 20 percent of the electorate, the effect of this would have been to give each community's voters an approximately 20 percent say in the election of the other community's candidate. For two-thirds of each term, the Greek Cypriot member of the presidency would serve as President and the Turkish Cypriot as Vice-President, with the two reversing positions for the remaining third.

Yet convincing hardliners to endorse a centripetal electoral formula that clearly threatens their political influence has proven impossible. Nationalist Turkish Cypriot political parties, such as the National Unity Party (UBP) and Democratic Party (DP), unsurprisingly, refused to endorse an electoral system that, in their view, was negotiated by moderate parties to keep moderate parties in power. The same logic has applied to a lesser degree to Greek Cypriot parties, other than AKEL. In the Turkish Cypriot community, opposition to this formula solidified right-wing opposition, leading to the election of hardliner Derviş Eroğlu as President of TRNC in April 2010 and the discarding of the moderates-privileging electoral system.

Following Eroğlu's election, progress in mediations slowed to non-existent, in spite of the election of Nicos Anastasiades, who had supported the Annan Plan, as President of the Republic of Cyprus in March 2013. New challenges emerged in the island as a result of the March 2013 bailout plan following the Eurozone debt crisis and disputes over natural gas. It was not until the election of the moderate Mustafa Akinci as Turkish Cypriot leader in March of 2015 that negotiations were substantively renewed. Akinci, a veteran peacemaker started his political career as the mayor of the Turkish Cypriot sector of divided Nicosia, and worked closely with his Greek Cypriot counterpart Lellos Demetriades to address the city's impending environmental disaster in the absence of a common sewer system. His election in 2015 and that of Anastasiades two years earlier demonstrated a remarkable fact. The Cypriot public came to question partition by electing two prominent pro-unification figures in the hope of addressing the island's long stalemate. What has been encouraging about Akıncı is how he was elected

[48] Cross-voting or weighted-voting has a long history in the island and is undeniably one of the most innovative ideas produced in bicommunal workshops in recent decades. Costa Carras and the London-based Friends of Cyprus association have both lobbied for such arrangements since the late 1970s. References to cross-voting were also included in the Greek Cypriot proposals of 1989 and even been proposed before 1974 by Glafcos Clerides. Neophytos Loizides, and Eser Keskiner, "The Aftermath of the Annan Plan Referendums: Cross-Voting Moderation for Cyprus" (2004) 5 (2–3) Southeast European Politics 158.

having campaigned openly in favor of returning the deserted suburb of Varosha to its Greek Cypriot inhabitants, and likewise how Anastasiades made a resounding comeback to politics despite his support for the Annan Plan in 2004.

But the efforts for a peace settlement in the past two years may have been hindered, ironically, by relying excessively on the Cypriot sides themselves to address complex constitutional issues. Unlike the Annan Plan, recent mediations have gone to the other extreme by restricting the role of the UN in proposing ideas or compromise packages for the consideration of the two sides, a common practice for decades in the Cyprus peace talks and mediations elsewhere. Even so, one should not underestimate the unique challenges leaders and mediators in Cyprus face. Breaking the Cypriot settlement will be the equivalent for the Eastern Mediterranean to the German reunification for Europe but in a more difficult setting of an ethnically divided society and a worsening regional environment.

Lessons Learned

Study of the Annan Plan and its aftermath is important not only for the current and any future peace process in Cyprus but also for the lessons it provides for mediation in other divided polities. An important innovation in conflict resolution associated with the Annan Plan was that both sides gave the UN permission to arbitrate on non-agreed matters before the April 2004 referendums. Putting a settlement to the people that had not been endorsed by leaders beforehand raised serious concerns about future implementation, not to mention the prospects for a positive vote. As noted elsewhere in this volume, referendums are always risky; introducing them without the explicit support and consent of elected leaders is not advisable.

Timing is equally critical. Turkish Cypriots approved the Plan in the referendum, suggesting Greek Cypriots may have done likewise had the UN pressed for an earlier vote, before the Republic of Cyprus (Greek Cypriots) secured EU accession in 2002 and lost their incentive. Winning public support for a yes vote among Greek Cypriots proved extremely difficult by 2004. Greek Cypriots voters had essentially "nothing to lose" in their accession process. Indeed, they were arguably handed an incentive to vote "no," as once within the EU and armed with a veto over Turkey's accession, as well as the *de facto* extension of the *acquis* to the Turkish Cypriot region, they would be in a much stronger position to negotiate a deal. This suggests that if the EU is to play a positive role in future mediations in Ukraine or Georgia, it should consider tying accession, or closer relations, to the achievement of a political settlement.

The Cypriot experience also demonstrates the limits of using the carrot of EU accession to secure one-sided concessions. Rather than softening their position after 2004, as Greek Cypriots anticipated, Turkish Cypriots elected a hardliner, Eroğlu, in 2010. They did so partly because of their disillusionment with Talat's failure to deliver a settlement, but also out of annoyance at the EU, which they felt had become pro-Greek Cypriot. Turkey's AKP government has shown little flexibility following Greek Cypriot threats to veto Turkey's accession, an inclination strengthened by its realization that powerful EU states do not want to admit a large Muslim country. Especially following Turkey's July 2016 coup and the subsequent anti-democratic backlash, even the strongest supporters of the country's accession seem to have lost hope. While the Greek Cypriot "no" vote may not have worked as Greek Cypriots intended, the latter faced near bankruptcy following the post-2008 sovereignty debt crisis. Although this crisis is not directly linked to the absence of a settlement, Greek Cypriots are unlikely to support a future settlement unless it includes a clear prospect for economic recovery. For its part, Greece has experienced almost a decade of financial and political meltdown with negative financial and political effects in Cyprus, including the election in the parliament of the far-right Elam, an extension of Greece's Golden Dawn.[49]

Inevitably, the EU's failures in Southern Europe have weakened its image and influence among applicant countries. Moreover, in addition to its new financial solvency, Turkey has developed a much more independent (for many observers hostile) foreign policy in recent years, frequently in direct opposition to the USA and the EU. Any foreign policy advantages Greek Cypriots have gained in the past decade have not been due to EU accession but to the mistakes and antagonistic behavior of Erdoğan's government, particularly toward Netanyahu's Israel and al-Sisi's Egypt, both of which have recognized Cyprus's EEZ over Ankara's strong objections. Additionally, Turkey's economic achievements in the first decade of AKP rule have been undermined since 2005. In the past couple of years the country has experienced an economic slowdown and unprecedented political instability that are threatening its immediate future. It would facilitate a return to normalization if Turkey could cooperate more closely with the EU, and this would benefit the EU also, not least in the management of the migration/refugee crisis that has accompanied the devastating civil war in Syria. A Cyprus settlement would facilitate a closer relationship between Turkey and the European Union; in the long term this may provide for renewed accession negotiations, add large fiscal benefits for Turkey within the EU, and potentially eliminate visa requirements for Turkish citizens traveling or working in Europe.

As noted here, revisiting past experiences is essential if the Cyprus problem is to be resolved. Accordingly, external mediators are no longer considering an imposed settlement (as in 1960) or an arbitrated settlement (as in 2004) but one that will require the prior and mutual assent of both leaderships and then the approval of both communities in simultaneous referendums. These steps have been endorsed by the leaders themselves, in the Anastasiades-Eroğlu Joint Declaration of February 11, 2014. It would also be helpful if, prior to a referendum, political parties with majority support in each community gave their explicit and formal support to the settlement agreement, and if Ankara and Athens similarly committed to accepting the plan and facilitating its implementation. These steps would replicate the "triple lock" requirement that was used in the Northern Ireland negotiations that produced the Belfast Agreement in 1998: it was stipulated that an agreement would have to accepted by the parties to the negotiations, Northern Ireland's voters in a referendum, and by the Westminster Parliament.

Besides these procedural steps, it is important that a future peace settlement differs in its substantial provisions from the Annan Plan. Following the anti-Annan Plan campaign of President Papadopoulos and his coalition partners, the Plan's key parameters continue to be seen as politically "toxic" by Greek Cypriots. A failed future referendum on a settlement similar to the Annan Plan would simply prolong the stalemate, or perhaps break it in a way that would not be positive. One challenge for future mediators

[49] Antonis Ellinas, "The Rise of Golden Dawn: The New Face of the Far Right in Greece" (2013) 18 (4) South European Society and Politics 543; Iosif Kovras and Neophytos Loizides "The Greek Debt Crisis and Southern Europe: Majoritarian Pitfalls?" (2014) 47 (1) Comparative Politics 1; Nikolaos Zahariadis, "Powering over Puzzling? Downsizing the Public Sector during the Greek Sovereign Debt Crisis" (2016) 18 (5) Journal of Comparative Policy Analysis: Research and Practice 464. See also most recent comparison of the politics in the two "motherlands" in Ioannis Grigoriadis, *Democratic Transition and the Rise of Populist Majoritarianism: Constitutional Reform in Greece and Turkey* (Palgrave 2018)

is to prove there are innovative win-win solutions beyond the Annan Plan, drawing on successful negotiations in divided societies.[50]

Opinion polls could minimize the risk of failure in a future peace referendum. Indeed, the use of polls could improve the prospects for a settlement by targeting specific constituencies to win their support. Critics argue that negotiations for the Annan Plan took place behind closed doors. While it is difficult to see how leaders could negotiate in public, polling public preferences and engaging a wider network of political and civic actors would be helpful. For example, comprehensive data including all displaced persons and property owners would be useful in resolving the property chapter in a voluntary manner. Having available data would bring certainty to all sides as to the benefits and obligations of a settlement and also allow mediators to know the extent to which monetary compensation (and how much) will be sufficient to entice the voluntary transfer of disputed properties. Given this is a time-consuming exercise, it could take place during stalemates or lulls in the talks to incentivize and facilitate the next round of negotiations.

The future peace process in Cyprus could also benefit from cross-learning from other divided places. Admittedly, the drafters of the Annan Plan drew on a significant number of comparable cases, including Belgium, Bosnia Herzegovina, El Salvador, and Switzerland.[51] And since 2004, new attempts to resolve conflicts have taken place across the world, all with relevant lessons for Cyprus. Accommodation mechanisms shown to be successful elsewhere are more likely to be endorsed by leaders; they will also minimize the fears of both Cypriot communities about the functionality of the settlement and its possible breakdown.

As an example of such cross-learning, we have elsewhere presented and defended an important innovation in consociational theory and practice from Northern Ireland: the proportional sequential (PS) coalition.[52] As argued earlier, the Annan Plan's provisions for a federal executive might have led to no government, creating a "new" Cyprus problem. More importantly, the Annan plan constitutional formula and the compromise of Christofias and Talat in 2010 had predictable adoptability problems; they created no incentives for rejectionist parties to get on board and, in fact, exacerbated the opposition of these parties by directly threatening their interests. By way of contrast, PS coalitions are automatically determined by election results and allocate portfolios on a proportionate and liberal basis amongst a divided place's main political parties. They provide for the broad inclusion of left- and right-wing parties from each community in a way that opens up possibilities for cross-cutting alignments on programmatic issues. A PS coalition would increase incentives for right wing parties in each community to reach, support, and operate a settlement.[53] Greek Cypriot fears that power-sharing executives are dysfunctional could be addressed by agreed deadlock-breaking mechanisms.

Finally, mediations in Cyprus aimed at power-sharing should be seen from the perspective of a "frozen" rather than an ongoing conflict. In frozen conflicts, it is wondered

[50] For a discussion of relevant lessons from other divided societies, see Loizides, *Designing Peace* (n 17).

[51] Alvaro De Soto and Graciana del Castillo, "Obstacles to Peacebuilding" (1994) 94 (Spring) Foreign Policy 69.

[52] McGarry and Loizides, "Power-Sharing in a Re-United Cyprus" (n 37).

[53] For example, Turkish Cypriot parties could win three cabinet seats (out of nine) but at the same time, decisions would require at least one Turkish Cypriot vote or two depending on the nature of an issue. Ideally, there could be informal rules encouraging the consent of all cabinet members, thus ensuring a wider consensus.

if the dispute will ever be solved through some form of consociational federation, with skeptics arguing that agreement on partition is easier to achieve. But an examination of the Greek Cypriot political discourse suggests a negotiated partition is not politically imaginable. The Greek Cypriot cleavage has traditionally been between federalists and unitarist hardliners. The latter led the campaign for the rejection of the Annan Plan in 2004 and won by arguing the settlement would lead to a constitutional breakdown and partition. Politically, it would be a surprise even for smaller Greek Cypriot political parties to support a negotiated partition as an option. However, if the next round of mediations fails, a tacit form of partition along current boundaries may become more likely through the silent continuation of the status quo. This would be a lose-lose situation, with Greek Cypriots gaining no territorial concessions and Turkish Cypriots continuing to face international legal constraints. A third option is the gradual settlement of the Cyprus problem in several smaller steps, each step representing a new set of agreements over a longer period of time. This approach has been advocated by Cypriot academics[54] and has been initially endorsed by Turkish Cypriot leader Mustafa Akinci not as a substitute to a comprehensive settlement but as a parallel process for ending the Cypriot partition.

In hot conflicts where there is violence, mediators are likely to seek quick solutions that prioritize the prevention of loss of life over legitimacy issues. In contrast, in frozen conflicts such as Cyprus, with over four decades of almost no violence, citizens are more likely to expect a democratically debated and approved peace settlement. They are also likely to want clarity on the obligations and benefits of such an arrangement. An important feature of the Annan Plan was the practice of constructive ambiguity, the postponement of solutions to certain issues, and the avoidance of direct conflict with the perceived interests and declarations of either side. Mediators are often tempted to leave such gaps in peace agreements to expedite a negotiated yet incomplete peace process, yet in Cyprus, they formed a rallying point in the 2004 "no" campaign. Judging from the experience of the Annan Plan, a future Cypriot peace settlement will require more precision in its legal, human rights, and security provisions, not to mention its explication of the benefits and obligations for each side. But with prospects looking less promising in 2018 at the time of writing, clearly, a Cypriot constitutional transition to a reunified republic remains an uphill task.

[54] For a nuanced analysis of the piecemeal approach to the settlement of the Cyprus problem, its merits, and potential risks, see Constantinos Adamides, Nicos Peristianis, Sertaç Sonan, and Yücel Vural, "Report on the Usefulness of the Piecemeal Model in the Case of Cyprus" (Politeia/Choice/Friedrich-Ebert-Stiftung 2014); see also discussion of the piecemeal approach at University of Kent, "Turkey and Cyprus Regional Peace and Stability Conference, Ankara, Turkey, 28 February 2015" (*University of Kent*, February 26, 2015) <http://blogs.kent.ac.uk/polir-news/2015/02/26/turkey-and-cyprus-regional-peace-stability-conference-ankara-turkey-28-february-2015/>.

4

Emergence and Transformation of Territorially Based Cleavages and Constitutional Responses in Ethiopia

Assefa Fiseha

Overview

On March 13, 2014, *Time* published an article entitled "Forget the BRICS and meet PINES," which reported on Ethiopia's socio-economic progress. In the last decade, Ethiopia has shown a continuous 10–11 percent annual economic growth, including improved access to education, health facilities, and the massive expansion of road, rail, and telecommunications infrastructure. Several hydroelectric dams are boosting its economy and it plans to be the energy giant of the Horn region, exporting electricity to neighboring countries. This chapter tells the story of Ethiopia's remarkable political transformation, which has underlay these successes but has important weaknesses as well.

Ethiopia has enormous diversity and a long history of independence. However, the modern Ethiopian state emerged toward the end of the nineteenth century after Emperor Menlik II (1889–1913) incorporated under his control previously quasi-autonomous kingdoms in the South, the Southwest, and the East. While central power in ancient Ethiopia was partly accessible to provincial and regional forces, with the emergence of centralized state, these forces were largely shut out. The newly centralized and homogenizing state, which incorporated the old provinces, was presided over by a narrow centralizing ruling elite. In reaction, there arose with the Ethiopian Student Movement a class and broadly based ethnonationalist political mobilization that put forward an alternative for state reform during the early 1970s. The then governing elite lost its momentum while the student movement inherited the burden of providing a political solution to the "question of nationalities" and in doing so it adopted a Marxist–Leninist interpretation to the nationality question, which was also a factor in radicalizing it.

Ethiopia's constitutional transformation resulted from the collapse of the socialist dictatorship and the victory of a coalition of ethnonationalist insurgent forces. The new rulers rejected the centralization and cultural homogenization of the past and designed a federal system that aims to empower ethno-national groups at regional state level. Ethiopia's case indicates that it is hardly possible to contain politically mobilized, territorially based ethnonationalist groups short of a federal arrangement that allows such groups to exercise some self-rule at a regional level while ensuring representation at the federal level. This institutional design has by ending the protracted civil war that brought the country to the brink of collapse in 1991, promoted relative peace and political stability to the country in an otherwise conflict prone region. Yet its functioning has been characterized by the strong dominance of the governing party

Territory and Power in Constitutional Transitions. First Edition. Edited by Michael Anderson and Sujit Choudhry. Emergence and Transformation of Territorially Based Cleavages and Constitutional Responses in Ethiopia Published 2019 by Oxford University Press.

coalition, which has limited state autonomy, political pluralism, and democratic rights. Its strong focus on ethnonationalist rights has also created problems for minorities and individual citizens within the regional states. But despite these political shortcomings, the new regime has proven able to *deliver* much-needed services and ensure equitable development throughout the country, accomplishments that are critical to its success and stability.

Background

The concept of "devolved autocracy" is often used in analyzing relations between the center and the provinces in historic Ethiopia, yet this fails to capture the essence of the relationship.[1] Ancient constitutional documents of the thirteenth century such as the *Kibra Nagast* (Glory of the Kings) and constitutional practices deeply rooted in the notion of *Niguse Negast* (King of Kings)[2] demonstrate the dual, if not multiple, centers of power in Ethiopia.[3] While the monarchy at the center served as a pillar of unity, various kinds of regional forces[4] representing diversity exercised important powers such as taxation, maintenance of local security, and regulation of trade.[5] The seat of Ethiopia's political capital was often called "wandering" as it shifted from one province to another with the change of emperors.

Direct central authority was hindered by the vastness of the state's territory, the topography with its absence of transportation and communications facilities, the demands of local nobilities for some autonomy, fiscal and manpower constraints, and ethnic, linguistic, and regional diversity and disparities. Thus regional forces enjoyed some autonomy, as kingdoms that merely acknowledged the existence of a distant emperor. The more powerful provincial kings—alone or in coalition with others—were sometimes contenders for the throne itself.[6]

The fact that the imperial power was open to potential contenders of power from the several provinces meant that state power was not highly ethnicized, at least before the emergence of the modern state under Menlik II. Greenfield wrote: "struggles and rivalry lay between regions, later perhaps provinces, and not between tribal groups . . . tribalism had no place in Ethiopian politics."[7]

The decentralized feudal state structure changed radically with the emergence of a strongly centralized unitary state toward the last quarter of the nineteenth century spearheaded by Emperor Menlik II (1889–1913). This was further consolidated during the absolute monarchy of Emperor Haile Selassie (1930–74)[8]. With the

[1] Christopher Clapham, "The Ethiopian Experience of Devolved Government" (2013) 1(1) *Ethiopian Journal of Federal Studies* 18.

[2] Haggai Erlich, *Ras Alula and the Scramble for Africa* (The Red Sea Press 1991) 2.

[3] This is not to deny that communities in the periphery remained largely subjects when it comes to their role in the center.

[4] On occasions the center lost dominance as in Yodit/Gudit's attack on the Christian Empire in the tenth century; the campaign of Imam Ahmed (1527–43), and the Age of Princes (*Zemene Mesafint* 1769–1855).

[5] Bahru Zewde, *A History of Modern Ethiopia 1855–1991* (first published 1991, 2nd edn, James Currey 2001).

[6] Donald Levine, *Wax and Gold: Tradition and Innovation in Ethiopian Culture* (The University of Chicago Press 1965) 154–5.

[7] Richard Greenfield, *Ethiopia: A New Political History* (first published 1965, Pall Mall Press 2013) 46.

[8] Revised Constitution of Ethiopia (Revised Constitution), art. 4.

emergence of the centralized unitary state, Addis Ababa became not only the capital of Showa, Menlik's home province, but also of Ethiopia. Showa then emerged as the epicenter of power and resources, with the homogenizing centrist state liquidating quasi-autonomous kingdoms. The new ruling elite designed a "nation building" strategy with the slogan "one language and one religion" where the elite's Amharic language[9] served as the only national language until 1991 and Christian religion (the religion of 44 percent of the population) which, despite the presence of 35 percent Muslims in the country, remained the official state religion until 1974.[10] Both language and religion served as twin tools for homogenization. The design of the "nation building" project was thus exclusive and narrowly based along the lines of the then ruling elite's identity that had little space for diversity. Central power was no longer accessible to various contenders: identity began to matter for inclusion or exclusion from power and in the process it began to be politicized. Thus at the heart of the reason for transformation from regional/provincial-based movement to ethno-nationalism remains the exclusionist and centrist state.

The process of centralization and homogenization was far from smooth. It faced serious challenges initially in the form of provincial rebellions headed by nobilities, various peasant protests, and later in a more radical form from university students. As political parties were banned in the country, the initial resistance against the process of centralization emerged in the form of peasant rebellions such as those from Tigray (1943), Gojjam (1968), Bale (1963/1970), Yejju (1948), and Gedeo (1960). Conflict in traditional Ethiopia manifested mainly in the form of provincial rebellion against the center and aimed at modest reforms without upsetting the whole system. Secession was also not in the agenda.[11] The opposition mainly looked for adjustment and restoration of violated rights like better administration, lower taxes, respect for local autonomy, and reduction of corruption.

The resistance against the regime was intensified during the early 1970s as most of the sources of discontent were articulated by the young, radical, and left-oriented university students. The Ethiopian Student Movement (ESM) emerged as an amorphous, ideologically and ethnically diverse university students' association. In due course it spawned many political parties and together these challenged imperial rule. This resistance not only called for state reform but also even at times challenged the state itself and the resistance brought new forms of leadership, social composition, and ideological orientations.[12] The student movement's slogans—"land to the tiller," "end to national oppression," "equality of religion," and "social justice"—were very popular in taking on the imperial regime.[13] The ESM argued that post-Menlik Ethiopia constituted a "prison house of nationalities"[14] and that the "nation building" project was a failure; the activists called for an end to "national oppression" through the grant of the right

[9] Revised Constitution, art. 125; 1987 Constitution of Ethiopia (1987 Constitution), art. 116.

[10] The 1955 Revised Constitution of Ethiopia (1955 Revised Constitution), art. 126.

[11] Gebru Tareke, *Ethiopia: Power and Protest: Peasant Revolts in the Twentieth Century* (Cambridge University Press 1991).

[12] Christopher Clapham, "Ethnicity and the National Question in Ethiopia" in Peter Woodward and Murray Forsyth (eds), *Conflict and Peace in the Horn of Africa: Federalism and its Alternatives* (Dartmouth 1994) 29.

[13] Kiflu Tadese, *The Generation Volume 1: The History of the Ethiopian People's Revolutionary Party* (Kiflu Tadesse Publishing 1993). This very controversial volume was translated and published in Amharic in 2014.

[14] ibid 121.

to self-determination to the nationalities.[15] Since then, the nationality question has remained a key issue for the political parties.

As leftist organizations, nearly all sympathized with the "nationality question." Yet, apart from sharing the view that the nationality question needed to be addressed, the exact *meaning* and *scope* of this vague concept and the strategy to address it, was far from clear. Depending on their proposed solution to the "nationality question" slowly many rival groups emerged. One camp constituted the Ethiopian Peoples Revolutionary Party (EPRP since 1972), while the other became the all Ethiopian Socialist Movement (nicknamed MEISON since 1968), which remained multi-ethnic while choosing to provide a solution to the nationality question by mass organization along class lines.[16]

The ESM became the gravedigger of the Emperor and major driving force behind the 1974 Revolution. The wide support accorded to the students and the failure to introduce even modest reform by the aging Emperor brought about the 1974 Revolution. As popular as the Revolution might have been, it was, however, hijacked by the Military Junta (1974–91), otherwise known as the *Derg*, a committee of 120 junior military officers, the only organized force at the time. The Revolution gave a mortal blow to the old monarchy but except for the change of source of political legitimacy from Solomonic genealogy[17] to Socialism as a new tool for building the "nation state," the centralist character of the state and its policy to the emerging demand by ethnonationalist groups remained intact and was even strengthened in its brutal form to a degree that far exceeded the imperial regime.

MEISON had sided with the military on the assumption that it would outsmart it and take control itself. The "socialist" regime (1974–91) gave rise to a protracted civil war and political instability that brought the country to the brink of collapse by 1991. Despite sharing same leftist ideology, rivalry between the EPRP and MEISON and the conflicts with the junta brought on the "Red Terror" and "White Terror" in the early 1970s, which consumed the lives of thousands of young Ethiopians from all sides. The story of multi-ethnic and class-based parties thus came to a tragic end. And this period of *militant political culture* left a legacy that continues to haunt Ethiopia as was seen following the 2005 elections.[18]

What transpired toward the end of the 1980s, when the state failed to address demands of ethnonationalist groups, was a failed "nation building" project[19] that politicized identity and created a privileged centrist political elite whose values and identity was equated with the state. As in many other failed "nation building" projects a privileged ruling elite's identity and language were used as a mask to impose the centrist ruling elite's identity, language, and religion on others. Identity and language became a means for *exclusion or inclusion*, a source of pride, or a source of social and psychological trauma. The bulk of the society were marginalized by the state and considered as secondary class *subjects*, not citizens. Their identity was viewed as inferior, stigmatized, and traumatized and this explains the passions and emotions associated with the protracted nature of intergroup conflicts. The conflict became nastier and protracted as ethnonationalist groups sought not only to gain shares in power and

[15] Bahru Zewde, *The Quest for Socialist Utopia: The Ethiopian Student Movement 1960–1974* (James Currey 2014) 218.

[16] ibid 261.

[17] John Markakis, *Ethiopia: Anatomy of Traditional Polity* (Clarendon Press 1974).

[18] Jon Abbink, "Discomfiture of Democracy? The 2005 Election Crisis in Ethiopia and its Aftermath" (2006) 105 (419) African Affairs 173.

[19] Greenfield (n 7) 88.

resources but also to reverse their inferior status and claim back their "collective self-esteem." While many actors and peace mediators often focus on power and resource inequalities, the non-material causes of conflict are often the core element of mobilization: the search for respected collective self-esteem, for psychological and emotive satisfaction.[20] The negative historical interaction among the political elite left deep-rooted mistrust in which selected history was and is used as a tool for mobilization in order to deal with real or perceived threats. As is often said "identity is the fruit of history"[21] but with a view to making sense of the present.

The EPRDF, made up of all the national liberation movements including the Tigray People Liberation Front (TPLF) which played a leading role, rejected the subjugation of ethnonationalism to class. It mobilized its supporters along ethnonationalist lines to end the oppression by the centrist and assimilating ruling elite of the socialist regime. This group held that a new and democratic Ethiopia could only be constructed through the voluntary and consensual association of its parts, the "nation, nationalities and the people."[22] The TPLF was one among many such groups that subscribed to this view and that posed a major threat to the military after February 1975.

Tigrayan-based ethnonationalism had deep historical and political resources for mobilization. The key foundations of the Ethiopian state— the *Geez* language and written script, the number (*Kutur*), the Ethiopian calendar and the state's Christian religion—and that defined it until 1974 were the result of Axumite invention and innovation.[23] This elite remained a key player in Ethiopia's political life until the end of the nineteenth century when it lost political influence with the emergence of the centrist elite. The Tigrayan elite, which attributed its alienation to a deliberate Showan design, had long envisioned strong regional autonomy along with loyalty to the overarching Ethiopian state as a possible way out of the state crisis; it held that sub-state identity can coexist with Ethiopian identity. Reflecting this context, the leader of the TPLF, Meles Zenawi, said "The Nile/Abay river has no life without its tributaries, there is as well no Ethiopia without its diversity."[24]

Thus, at the time, the TPLF had genuine political and economic grievances as well as rich historical material at its disposal to construct an ethnonationalist narrative and ideology.[25] This project as articulated by the TPLF made sense to all other marginalized groups in the country and became shared among the four coalitions that came together to form the Ethiopian Peoples' Revolutionary Democratic Front (EPRDF): the Oromo People's Democratic Organization (OPDO, 1989), the Southern Ethiopia People's Democratic Movement (SEPDM, 1992), and the Amhara National Democratic Movement (ANDM, 1980s). It was this coalition that defeated the junta in 1991 and remains the dominant force since then.

[20] William Zartman, "Dynamics and Constraints in Negotiations in Internal Conflicts" in I. William Zartman (ed.), *Elusive Peace: Negotiating an End to Civil Wars* (The Brookings Institution, 1995) 5.

[21] Nancy Bermeo, "Conclusion: The Merits of Federalism" in Ugo Amoretti and Nancy Mermeo (eds), *Federalism and Territorial Cleavages* (The Johns Hopkins University Press 2004) 461.

[22] Tareke (n 11) 202.

[23] Aregawi Berhe, "The Origins of the Tigray People's Liberation Front" (2004) 103 (413) African Affairs 569.

[24] Interview by the author with a senior party member of the Tigray People's Liberation Front, March 15, 2010, (Addis Ababa, Ethiopia, 2010).

[25] Alemseged Abay, "Diversity and State Building in Ethiopia" (2004) 103 (413) African Affairs 593.

The Period of Constitutional Engagement (1991–94)

Just as the emergence of the modern state under Menlik II represented an important event for centralization, the post-1991 period brought a fundamental shift in relations between state and society. Toward the end of 1980s the military representing the centrist political elite and its "nation building" project through socialism, was losing ground. The EPRDF had already succeeded in defeating the military in major battles. The military junta's downfall was being accelerated by economic stagnation and global changes, notably the end of the Cold War and the collapse of the former USSR, the junta's main ally. Nonetheless, there was a last attempt, held in London in May 1991, to bring a peaceful end to the raging civil war. The conference bought together the *Derg* and the opposition, represented mainly by the Eritrean People's Liberation Front (EPLF) and the TPLF. It was mediated by Herman Cohen, United States Assistant Secretary of State for African Affairs. But realizing the weakening of the *Derg*, its delegates lost interest in pursuing the peace process. On May 21, 1991, Mengistu Haile Mariam, the President and head of the *Derg*, left Addis Ababa by airplane, allegedly to visit a military camp in the south west of the country, but he flew to Nairobi, from where he went into exile in Zimbabwe.[26]

With the regime's military apparatus fast crumbling, the EPRDF and EPLF were ready to fill the emerging political vacuum by controlling Addis Ababa and Asmara respectively. They were later joined by the Oromo Liberation Front (OLF),[27] which was partly a product of the student movement of the 1970s, that had long supported the right to self-determination of the Oromos, the largest ethnic group in the country; however, it remained weakly connected to the very people it claimed to represent. These groups made a joint statement confirming the need to establish a broadly based Transitional Government of Ethiopia (TGE).[28] The OLF remained a key player during the early periods of the TGE. A national conference on transition was convened in Addis Ababa from July 1 to 5, 1991, with the attendance of some twenty-seven political parties, of which a number, including the OLF, had received support from representatives of the international community.

The conference resulted in the signing of the Charter, which served as an interim constitution from 1991 to 1994. It provided for the establishment of an eighty-seven-seat Council of Representatives (CoR) as the legislature during the interim period as well as for the establishment of the TGE, which was to have law-making, executive, and judicial powers until an elected government replaced it (as happened in 1995). While key positions such as the presidency, defense, and foreign affairs were reserved to the EPRDF, initially the TGE largely remained a coalition government in which several parties such as the OLF were granted seats both in the CoR and the newly established executive. During the early phase of the TGE, one could state firmly that the TGE was a more inclusive government as the country had had in its entire history. Although it was not elected, it was able to represent the then existing contending views and communities.[29]

[26] Sarah Vaughan, "Ethnicity and Power in Ethiopia" (PhD thesis, Edinburgh University 2003).

[27] For details on the OLF, see Merera Gudina, *Ethiopia: Competing Ethnic Nationalisms and the Quest for Democracy 1960–2002* (Shaker Publishing 2003) 102–5, 198; also Vaughan, "Ethnicity and Power in Ethiopia" (n 26).

[28] Sarah Vaughan, "The Addis Ababa Transitional Conference of July 1991: Its Origins, History and Significance" (1994) 51 Centre of African Studies, Edinburgh University, Occasional Paper Series.

[29] Leenco Lata, "The Making and Unmaking of Ethiopia's Transitional Charter" in Asafa Jalata (ed.), *Oromo Nationalism and the Ethiopian Discourse: The Search for Freedom and Democracy*

There was a strong commitment to peaceful competition for power and the renouncing of force as a condition for participation in the July conference. In the context of political uncertainty given the collapse of the military regime, there were some centrist political forces that opposed the agenda of the "National Liberation Fronts;" these forces established a new party under the umbrella of the Coalition of Ethiopian Democratic Forces, both at home and abroad, and condemned the peace process in London as well as the subsequent conference in Addis Ababa; they called for dissolution of the TGE. These radical and centrist groups, which included the former regime's party, the Workers Party of Ethiopia, were left out because of "their unwillingness to renounce violence as a means to achieve political ends." It was not clear if they were prepared to compete peacefully given the wide availability of small arms and ammunition in several parts of the country.[30]

In retrospect, one could say that the process of making the Charter, establishing the TGE and later the federation, would have been an uphill battle, possibly ending in a deadlock, if the centrist political elite and its army had engaged in the process in full force. As it happened, the military junta collapsed and the old centralizing political elite was either excluded or in disarray, so the victorious "National Liberation Fronts," which had forcefully dismantled the junta, had a relatively easy way in recasting the post-1991 Ethiopia.[31] Certainly, representatives from the University were not as active as the leaders of the liberation fronts, yet they aired views critical of the shift in favor of marginalized groups during the conference.

The process of constitutional design is as important as the final product in that it needs to be inclusive and open to representatives of various views. The legitimacy of the Charter, the eventual Constitution, as well as the institutions they establish, all derive from the character of the process. In this regard, the promising beginning at the time of the formation of the TGE did not end as intended. Following the reorganization of the state structure, with the national and regional governments, there was a serious disagreement over a regional election, which was scheduled for June 1992. While OLF and the centralizing All Amhara Peoples Organization asked for a postponement, alleging that they needed time to prepare and compete in the regions, the EPRDF insisted on proceeding as scheduled. Following this and other disagreements, the OLF, which had been one of the major actors during the making of the Charter, withdrew from the government and attempted—unsuccessfully—to re-launch a guerrilla insurgency. Since then, its leaders have gone into exile and many factions seem to be emerging within the Oromo community. The OLF's major source of contention with the EPRDF was that the latter had allied itself with another Oromo group, the OPDO, and this infuriated the OLF which saw itself as the only legitimate Oromo party. Other opposition groups also withdrew in 1993, which resulted in a TGE largely dominated by the EPRDF. There is a question whether the breakup of the TGE was merely over a logistical matter related to an election or over a something more substantive about the transition and next steps. The evidence is scanty but it seems that the breakup reflected the beginning of a *design* for a dominant party system under the

(The Red Sea Press 1998); Marina Ottaway, "The Ethiopian Transition: Democratization or New Authoritarianism?" (2005) 2 (3) Northeast African Studies 67, 73.

[30] Vaughan, "The Addis Ababa Transitional Conference of July 1991" (n 28).

[31] This is not to undermine the role of parties such as the Ethiopian Democratic Coalition led by the popular Nebiyu Samuel, the Ethiopian Democratic Union led by Mengesha Seyoum, and the Ethiopian National Democratic Organization led by the late Kifle Wodajo, who actively proposed mid-way solutions with little success.

EPRDF. While the conference that begun as inclusive of a range of political actors and established a fairly inclusive TGE, it was followed by the evolution of a less inclusive TGE toward the end of its term. It is hard to disagree with Marina Ottaway's apt observation of the last few years of the transition. "It is a formal process devoid of content. The spirit of the democratic transition was missing completely as democratization became a purely formal exercise, the major contenders of power from the opposition missing throughout."[32] As will be explained later, political pluralism has thus become a victim of the dominant party in Ethiopia. The sidelining of the political opposition as demonstrated in 2016 has begun to embolden hardliners.

The Charter (Articles 9–12) established the framework for the TGE and guaranteed nationalities the right to administer their own affairs within their defined territory, the right to participate in the central government based on fair and proper representation, and the right to self-determination including the right to secede that finally became Article 39 of the 1995 Constitution. Dominated by the ethnonationalist parties, the conference reflected a dramatic shift of political power from centralizing politicians to a new group from hitherto marginalized regions. Ethnicity became the basic principle for the political organization of the state and society and the centralized state was to be restructured into a federal system of government. This principle and restructuring were again anchored in the right to self-determination of ethnonational groups. The rationale for such a radical change was that this formula provided a decisive remedy for Ethiopia's long-standing "nationality question." Despite this rhetoric, the federal system created by the Charter was strongly centralist in that it was unequivocally clear that the states of the federation were subordinate to the transitional government in every respect.[33] Moreover, the states that were given political power over the internal affairs of the regions were made accountable not just to the people who elected them, but also to the CoR of the TGE, which meant that they did not have the autonomy normal for states in a federation.[34] In the exercise of their powers, the states were subject to the relevant general policies and laws of the central government.

Ethiopia's territorial and provincial arrangements had expanded and shrunk several times over the years. The reasons for such provincial restructuring varied over time.[35] In the twentieth century alone, nearly all the emperors and the military divided and subdivided provinces several times partly favoring or disfavoring the local dynasty's size of territory depending on relations with the center and partly to make sure that the groups remained subdivided into several provincial territories which could not become a threat to the center. The post-1991 redrawing of territories, by contrast, aimed at making them the basis for exercising self-rule by the larger ethnonationalist groups. This goal remained the main driving force in establishing the states both during the TGE and the making of the 1995 Constitution.

It is surprising how little debate there was during the preparation and adoption of the Charter on the process and principles that should guide the restructuring of the new states. This came later after the establishment of the TGE. The TGE established

[32] Ottaway (n 29) 73, 81–3.

[33] See the Transitional Period Charter of Ethiopia No. 1 *Negarit Gazeta* 50th year No. 1 Addis Ababa, July 22, 1991, hereinafter called the Charter art. 9.

[34] See the Charter, art. 3(5); Vaughan, "The Addis Ababa Transitional Conference of July 1991" (n 28) 48.

[35] See Daniel Gamachu, "A Nation in Perpetual Transition: The Politics of Changes in Administrative Divisions and Subdivisions in Ethiopia" in Harold Marcus and Grove Hudson (eds), *New Trends in Ethiopian Studies, Papers of the 12th International Conference of Ethiopian Studies* (The Red Sea Press 1994) 80–113.

a Boundary Commission in August 1991 composed of ten members representing six political parties.[36] Among the parties represented in the TGE, there was a consensus regarding the establishment of the Commission and its outcome. Based on the data available from the Institute for the Study of Ethiopian Nationalities (ISEN), an institution established by the military junta in 1983, and the Commission's own observations, the Commission submitted its proposals to the CoR. The Council debated the proposal and finally issued Proclamation Number 7/1992, which established fourteen new states largely based on language. It was provided that adjacent nations, nationalities, and peoples may by agreement combine any of the fourteen regions.[37] Accordingly, the original fourteen regional states were reduced to nine, when five regional states in the South amalgamated to form the Southern Nations, Nationalities and Peoples Regional State (SNNPRS) toward the end of the transition. Except for this merger and the decision that region fourteen, Addis Ababa, would become merely an autonomous federal capital accountable to the federal government and not a state, the 1995 Constitution largely inherited the regional states established during the TGE.

A major task of the TGE was to direct the process of Constitution-making and pave the way for a new national election based on the ratified Constitution. To facilitate the transition to a newly elected government, the TGE established a Constitutional Commission based on Proclamation Number 24/1992 in August 1992. The Commission was composed of twenty-nine members elected by CoR from among various sections of the population. Political organizations in the CoR had seven representatives, while trade unions, the Ethiopian Chamber of Commerce, and women had three representatives each. Lawyers, teachers, and health associations had two representatives each. Despite this effort at broad representation including political parties, the Commission was largely dominated by the EPRDF as many of the opposition forces withdrew from the transition. Yet a few opposition party representatives did choose to constructively engage in the drafting process. Notable in this regard was the late Kifle Wodajo, who acted as chair of the Commission.[38] The Commission's mandate included organizing debates across the country on various topics related to the Constitution. It also had a technical committee that helped prepare a draft Constitution.

The Constitutional Commission submitted its draft Constitution to the Constitutional Assembly along with the report on opinions gathered throughout the country, including the commentaries of the CoR. The Assembly had 543 members, who had been elected directly by the people in June 1994, in the first elections since the overthrow of the junta. Many opposition members of the TGE had withdrawn from the process and some, such as the OLF, even went to exile, so the electoral process was largely dominated by the EPRDF. Yet a few dozen members from some opposition parties such as the late Major Admasu Zeleke remained vocal members of the Assembly. In terms of mandate, the Assembly was free to accept, reject, or modify the draft Constitution. It debated the draft during November 1994. The most divisive issues were self-determination of nationalities, redrawing the boundaries of the regional states, the secession clause, and whether land should remain private or be owned by the state. Not surprisingly, the final Constitution largely reflected the views of the EPRDF.

[36] The parties represented in the Boundary Commission included EPRDF that had 3, OLF 2, Guraghe 1, Hadiya 1, Harari 1, Somali 1, Afar 1 representatives. See Vaughan "Ethnicity and Power in Ethiopia" (n 26) 33, 151.

[37] Proclamation Number 7 (1992), art. 3(2)(b).

[38] Vaughan, "Ethnicity and Power in Ethiopia" (n 26).

The Constitution was ratified by the Assembly on December 8, 1994 and came into effect on August 21, 1995. Ethiopia officially adopted a federal form of government as of this date. National elections were held in May 1995 for the regional and federal parliaments and the new federal parliament was inaugurated on August 21, thus bringing the TGE and the Charter to an end.

While the constitutional process proceeded expeditiously, there were serious debates and disagreements over the fundamental nature of the new regime, and these reflected differing historical narratives and conceptions of the future.

The first version represented the view of the *centralizing* political elite, aired through the representative from the University (the late surgeon Professor Asrat Woldeyesys who founded the All Amhara Peoples Organization—AAPO) during the TGE and later through the late Major Admasu Zeleke during the Constitutional Assembly.[39] Also called the "Greater Ethiopia" perspective, its core point was that the "nation building" (*hager maknat* in Amharic) project based on "one language and religion" is a normal process that aimed at integrating Ethiopia politically and culturally. This view held that it was hardly possible to combine self-rule by the nationalities with Ethiopian statehood because the identities of the nationalities are incompatible with an overarching Ethiopian state, which should command absolute loyalty—"Ethiopia first" as some called it. For this centralizing elite, any form of political mobilization based on ethnicity and sub-state identity should be banned.

The elite group had two factions in relation to federalism. Hard-line centralizers insisted on a unitary state with the sovereignty of the state indivisible and no right of self-determination for the nationalities. The more moderate faction, who may be called instrumentalists, did not fully rule out a federalism based on geography (possibly the historic provinces) so long as it was not based on ethnicity. This group insisted that ethnicity, like religion, should be left to the private sphere. They thought that if the over-concentration of political and economic resources at the center were properly reformed, ethnicity would have little role. For them, the main issue was political and economic deprivation and they argued that ethnonationalism would wither away if the state were democratized, rights respected, and needed services delivered.

Given that Ethiopia is a country of minorities, with no ethnonationalist group constituting a majority, subscription to an "ethnic free" federal structure or separation of state and ethnicity was, given the history of past ruling elites, a formula for imposing the elite's culture, language, and religion on others. The state can hardly be free of ethnic considerations when it comes to choosing a language for parliament, courts, education, and the media,[40] all of which have implications as well for the territorial organization of the state. This perspective was an unacceptable solution to significant ethnonationalist groups, which were strongly mobilized around demands for more than individual rights.[41]

There was a second group of more moderate centralizers, which was represented by the late Kifle Wodajo, a veteran diplomat and moderate opposition leader, who later became the chairman of the drafting committee for the 1995 Constitution. They acknowledged the relevance of federalism and the institutional response to the right of

[39] See programs of the AAPO and the former vocal and centrist opposition party, the Coalition for Unity and Democracy (CUD).

[40] Will Kymlicka, *Multicultural Odysseys: Navigating the New International Politics of Diversity* (Oxford University Press 2007).

[41] Coherent critique of the "ethnic free" individual rights-based alternative to group-based ethnonationalism; see ibid.

nationalities, including the right to self-rule, but they rejected the clause on secession.[42] Of late many of the centralizing political parties seem to be adopting this perspective partly in reaction to the interest many ethnonationalist groups have shown in "ethnic federalism," but the alternatives are yet to be articulated well or are dubious.[43]

A strongly contrasting view to those of the traditional elites was that of the EPRDF,[44] which considered itself to be the successor of the student movement of the 1970s and the main architect of the transition (1991–94) and the 1995 Constitution. It long argued that the Charter and the new Constitution should explicitly address the "question of nationalities," necessarily by granting the nationalities the right to self-determination, including secession. As a result, the key features of the federal Constitution are heavily influenced by the idea of "nations, nationalities and peoples" right to self-determination and self-rule as a solution to the "question of nationalities." Meles Zenawi, who was the chief ideologue of his party, stated, "If you don't open the doors and walls of a house (hence the right to secede), those confined within will break the doors and walls and run out to get fresh air. So leave the doors and windows open for the people to feel free and relax inside the house."[45] Meles echoed Lenin's claim that "the union of states must take place voluntarily . . . which is unthinkable without the freedom of separation."[46] This development seems to have been driven by political reality,[47] notably the mobilization and ideological commitment of ethnonationalist groups. However, some contend that the Marxist–Leninist response to the "nationality question" aimed to neutralize, not foster, ethnonationalism, in that the Leninist goal was to achieve "voluntary" integration and unity through the machinations of a vanguard party, democratic centralism, and universal values of socialist indoctrination.[48] Thus self-determination seems to be an interim right and yet is anchored as a constitutional right; there is a tension between granting such a right to an ethnonationalist group in its full sense versus constraining it through the party system, a point illustrated later in this chapter.

Outcome

What emerged as the final Constitution, at least formally, was a partly fictitious "coming together" type of federation. The Constitution is viewed as a political contract and the result of the "free will of nations, nationalities and peoples" that are politically mobilized, territorially grouped, and declared as sovereign (Article 8). It insists on the need for some congruence between the nation and nationalities and the territory of their regional states in order to ensure self-rule. Moreover, Article 39 stipulated: "every nation, nationality and people in Ethiopia has an unconditional

[42] See Minutes of the Constitutional Assembly v.3 (Addis Ababa, 1994). Unpublished, available with the author.

[43] See Lidetu Ayalew, *The Third Way* (Commercial Printing Press 2015, Amharic), which prescribes federalism but not on an ethnic basis.

[44] Vaughan "The Addis Ababa Transitional Conference of July 1991" (n 28).

[45] John Markakis, *Ethiopia: The Last Two Frontiers* (James Currey 2011) 232.

[46] V I Lenin, *Collected Works* (5th edn, Moscow Progress Publishers 1977) 84.

[47] Its inclusion in the constitution, apart from the fact that it was a long held view of the current ruling party owing to its leftist inclination, was justified as a means for bringing national liberation fronts' such as the Oromo and the Ogaden with the agenda of secession to the negotiation table. In reality it was impossible to bring such strongly secessionist parties to the TGE without the rights mentioned in Article 39.

[48] Vaughan, "Ethnicity and Power in Ethiopia" (n 26) 170–1.

right to self determination, including the right to secession" and "the right to speak, to write and to develop its own language; to express, to develop and to promote its culture and to preserve its history." Ethno-national groups have also "the right to full measure of self government which includes the right to establish institutions of government in the territory that it inhabits and to *equitable representation* in the state and federal governments . . ." The Charter and the Constitution provided that the constituent states be reorganized on "the basis of settlement patterns, language, identity and consent of the people concerned" (Article 46.2) and while it is not explicit that the states are organized along ethnic lines, it is clear that the key factor was language. Thus, the distinctive character of the Ethiopian Constitution lies very much in its empowering ethnonationalist groups who are considered to be founders of the federation.

Language, in particular, plays a key role for drawing internal political boundaries, not only for establishing the regional states but also in the establishment of local-level self-rule as in the SNNPRS. The SNNPRS during the transition was five separate states and it was later amalgamated into one, quite atypical, state. With a population of 17 million (20 percent nationally) and some fifty-six ethnic groups, it has extraordinary heterogeneity, with many relatively small ethno-linguistic groups in which *local* governments, not the regional state as in other states, are designed for ensuring self-rule to the various groups. In addition the various groups share power and resources in the regional state institutions, particularly within the executive and civil service. As such, the SNNPRS is a quasi-federation within a federation.

Over all the federal system is a design that combines an appropriate combination of "shared rule and self rule."[49] It divides power between the federal government and states and ensures ethnonationalist groups fair representation in federal institutions. Through their representation in federal institutions, ethnonationalist groups are given the opportunity to influence decision-making at the center. The logic of this form of federalism is that ethnonationalist groups can respect the institutions of governance and contribute positively to a stable federation only when they are granted a satisfactory combination of *influence* at the center and *meaningful autonomy* at sub-state level.[50] This somehow determines whether ethnonationalist groups will remain loyal to the overarching federation or will prefer to walk away from it. Here the second chamber, the House of the Federation, which currently has 153 members representing seventy-six nationalities indirectly elected by state legislatures, plays a critical role in the allocation of federal subsidy to the states and the resolution of disputes among states. In addition, there is a commitment to provide regional state representation in other federal institutions, as expressed in a constitutional principle (Article 39.3). In practice, there is every attempt to reflect the country's diversity in the establishment of the federal executive and senior party leadership within the ruling coalition. Of the thirty-one federal executive positions appointed in October 2015, the SNNPRS and Oromia each had eight minsters, the Amhara nine, Tigray four, and Afar and Somali each one.[51] Yet it is vital to note that executive power sharing is limited to the four

[49] Daniel Elazar, *Exploring Federalism* (Alabama University Press 1987).

[50] Arend Lijphart, "Consociationalism and Federalism: Conceptual and Empirical Links" (1979) 12 (3) Canadian Journal of Politics 499, 500.

[51] See All Africa, "Ethiopia: Hailemariam Forms New Administration" (*allAfrica.com*, October 6, 2015) <http://allafrica.com/stories/201510070627.html> accessed October 17, 2016. Of the 84.8 billion birr federal subsidy allocated to regional states by the House of Federation in 2015, Oromia received 27.5 billion birr, Amhara 19.7 billion birr, SNNPRS 17 billion birr, Somali 6.9 billion birr, Tigray 6 billion birr, Afar 2.6 billion birr, Benishangul Gumuz 1.8 billion birr, Gambella 1.3 birr, and Harari 849 million birr.

party groups of the ruling coalition, which govern the four major states and have affiliate parties that govern the remaining five states. Little effort is made to incorporate ministers from outside the ruling coalition's partners, as would happen in a broader power-sharing scheme, such as occurred during the TGE but was then abandoned.

A remarkably positive feature of the Ethiopian federal system has been the political will and commitment of the new leaders to enhance the political and administrative institutions of the units. When the federal process began in 1995, the regional states hardly had any serious administrative or political capacity owing to centuries of centralization by the national elite. Realizing this key challenge, the new leaders established institutional mechanisms specially geared to upgrade the capacity of the existing and newly recruited civil servants and political figures in the states. The size of the Ethiopian civil service went from 300,000 in 1991 to 1.2 million in 2014. The national budget rose from 9 billion birr in 1995 to 223 billion birr in 2015, the lion's share of which goes to infrastructure expansion nationwide and to improve access to education and health. The size of the federal subsidy to the states increased from 4.2 billion birr in 1995 to 88 billion birr in 2015. This dramatic expansion of state and local capacities and functions gave some real meaning to the Constitution's promise of self-rule—even if states operate largely within federally legislated policy frameworks—and it was instrumental in realizing the goals of equitable development.

The role of the ruling ethnonationalist based coalition also seems to have been transformed since it took power. The political leaders of post 1991 Ethiopia may have come to power as "leaders of National Liberation Fronts" but they were transformed by the exercise of state power. This can be seen with Meles Zenawi, who emerged as Ethiopia's uncontested, dominant figure in defining the pro-poor and pro-development ideology of his government and became a leading statesman in the Horn and Africa at large. The Flag Day celebrated every September brings together heads of the army and all the regional state figures to signal their loyalty to the country and its values in a way that would have been unimaginable in the early 1990s.

The over-emphasis on the rights of "nations, nationalities and peoples" is not without implications. It provides the rationale for various ethnonationalists groups to demand that regional state boundaries be reorganized and so boundaries of units can be unstable and face frequent claims for adjustment or even claims for establishing new regional states or local governments. As a result, it became clear that to physically demarcate geographical borders between the various ethnic groups was difficult and at times resulted in conflicts. Indeed, no official map showing the boundaries of the nine regional states exists to date. Critics have aired their concern stating that the Constitution emphasizes the politics of difference and is a high-risk strategy that may bring the country's disintegration.[52]

Minorities within the states and individual citizens can also suffer from the over-emphasis on the rights of nationalities in that they are at the mercy of the political elite in their state. The challenges minorities face differ from one regional state to another. In Tigray and Amhara states, the state constitutions acknowledge the existence of minorities, but minorities face language-based discrimination and are not represented in state institutions, particularly the executive. In some states such as Oromia, the state Constitution does not even acknowledge the existence of minorities, which are thus subject to legal, linguistic, and political discrimination. In states such as Benishangul Gumuz and Gambella, the state Constitutions clearly favor the majority communities

[52] Minase Haile, "The New Ethiopian Constitution: Its Impact upon Unity, Human Rights and Development" (1996) 20 (1) Suffolk Transitional Law Review 1.

and minorities are subject to legal and political discrimination. The rights of minorities in the states are vital because with increased foreign and domestic investment inter-regional migration is expected to rise, thus bringing more minorities into states. Yet it appears the federation has inherent tensions as it fails to strike a balance between the right to self-rule of various groups on one hand, and the need to promote free movement of labor and capital, on the other. Experience from other multi-ethnic federation shows cases where the right to self-rule of ethnonationalist groups was conditioned on a clear guarantee for minority and individual rights and there is the fear that once national minorities acquire self-governing power at sub-state level, they might use it to prosecute, dispossess, expel, or kill anyone who does not belong to their group.[53] As we have seen, in Ethiopia's case the process of empowering ethnonationalist groups at sub-state level was conducted without institutional and policy mechanisms to minimize this major risk. The generously listed human rights provisions in the Constitution are overshadowed by group rights and are not backed by strong enforcement mechanisms. Regular courts that are expected to enforce constitutionally guaranteed human rights have no mandate to interpret and enforce the supremacy clause of the Constitution as this power is assigned to the political body—the second chamber—the HoF.

In theory, the division of power envisaged in the Constitution (Articles 51 and 52) along with the right to self-rule allows the states to design their own socio-economic and development policies subject only to broad federal-wide standards set in the Constitution. However, a clearer picture of the operation of the federal system in Ethiopia can be drawn if one looks at the party system. Many critics point to the most obvious limitation of Ethiopia's federalism, particularly the paradox between generously granted constitutional powers to the states and a centralized federal system in practice, which arises from centralized party system. The EPRDF controls not only the federal government but also all the regional state governments either directly itself or through its member parties (the four coalitions each lead the four relatively influential states) or indirectly through affiliated parties that control the other five states.[54] As a result of this party structure, most policies and development projects that have implications for the federal and state governments are generated through the party's central apparatus.[55] Those policies then become the basis of five-year plans for both the federal and state governments. The nomination, election, and appointment of key political figures both at the federal and regional state level are made and effected through the centralized party structure, the role of federalism and the legislative bodies being reduced to serving as rubber stamps. Thus, the autonomy of the states is limited in practice, and the party structure *overshadows* the federal and regional government institutions. The party structure and its decision-making procedures undermine the federal division of power and subordinate the state governments to the center.[56] In this regard, Ethiopia is not as federal as promised by the Constitution.

Tensions over the lack of respect for the federal character of the country boiled over in 2016 with the development plan that proposed to "integrate" Addis Ababa and the surrounding Oromo territories.[57] The federal capital is geographically located within Oromia regional state and there has been an ongoing debate about the growing

[53] Kymlicka (n 40) 93–4. [54] Markakis, *Ethiopia: The Last Two Frontiers* (n 45) 8–9.

[55] See Assefa Fiseha, "Theory versus Practice in the Implementation of Ethiopia's Ethnic Federalism" in David Turton (ed.), *Ethnic Federalism: The Ethiopian Experience in Comparative Perspective* (James Currey 2006); Gudina (n 27) 119.

[56] Fiseha (n 55).

[57] What constitutes "integration" was far from clear but this measure was interpreted by the Oromo political elite as "annexation" of Oromo territory.

impacts of massive investments on the surrounding Oromo areas, which resulted in the eviction of Oromo peasants. Given the widespread sense among Oromos of their marginalization and the perception of the weakness and "illegitimacy" of the regional state party (OPDO), which followed from the Oromo Liberation Front walking out of the victorious coalition in 1992 and subsequently being disbanded, the plan sparked extensive riots and caused several hundred deaths. Article 49(3) of the constitution stipulates that the special interest of the Oromia regional state in Addis Ababa shall be respected, but two decades after the Constitution came into force "the special interest" clause has not been enforced. The relevant stakeholders have not reached consensus on the "integrated development plan." "We want genuine self- rule"[58] was one of the popular slogans during the widespread protests in Oromia in the early 2016.

On the positive side, given Ethiopia's diverse society, a coherent and disciplined party in the federal and state arenas appears to be an asset, compared, for example, with what happened in Nigeria during the 1960s and what transpired in Mwai Kibaki's government in Kenya after Daniel arap Moi stepped down as president in December 2002.[59] It is also this force that counterbalances the centrifugal tendencies and serves as glue holding the different groups together. However, the ruling party in Ethiopia seems to be exceeding acceptable limits and is contradicting the constitutionally proclaimed principles of self-rule and state autonomy by practicing democratic centralism. More critically, its impact on the institutions of the federal government and the states remains serious in that these institutions have not evolved separate from and autonomously from the party. Any crisis within the party can affect regional state institutions, which makes their political life less predictable.[60]

This partisan context is reinforced by an incomplete process of transition and a political culture characterized by hierarchy and authoritarianism with their emphasis on obedience to the higher level within the political elite, both of which affect the federal experiment.[61]

The opposition, which has been very diverse ever since 1991–92, long preferred to withdraw from the process claiming that the transition was not open and inclusive enough, thereby hoping to undermine its legitimacy. A section of the opposition has also been accused of failing to remain loyal to the rules of the game set in the Constitution in that it shows some tendencies to try to come to power by force or by applying authoritarian methods during elections. Hence the challenge of democratization in Ethiopia is a much more complicated matter than the culture of the dominant party. When the opposition's strategies of withdrawal from the constitutional process and boycotting of elections did not succeed in delegitimizing the transition and new Constitution, the opposition resorted to a limited engagement whose purpose was only to expose electoral manipulations within the ruling party and not to engage in the process genuinely.

The incomplete process of transition resulting from the disengagement of a section of the opposition, shrinkage in the political space by the regime,[62] and the divergent

[58] René Lefort, "Unrest in Ethiopia: the ultimate warning shot?" (*Open Democracy*, February 2, 2016) <www.opendemocracy.net/ren-lefort/unrest-in-ethiopia-ultimate-warning-shot> accessed April 18, 2016.

[59] Joel Barkan, "Kenya After Moi" (2004) 83 (1) Foreign Affairs 87.

[60] Some have already hinted that "while federalism may survive the EPRDF, the present political framework is so dependent on the regime that created it and its survival is unlikely" quoted from Christopher Clapham, "Post War Ethiopia: The Trajectories of Crisis" (2009) 36 (120) Review of African Political Economy 191.

[61] Ottaway (n 29) 73, 81–3; Abbink (n 18).

[62] Abbink (n 18).

perspectives with little political accommodation has made the transition to democracy more challenging and protracted. In the five national elections held so far, the opposition had only a dozen seats in the 547-seat parliament. Only in the third term (2005–10), following the relatively open and democratic election, did the opposition gain 171 seats in parliament, as well as all seats of the Addis Ababa city Council. But disagreements among the opposition itself and with the EPRDF led to violent demonstrations in June and November 2005, with losses of life and destruction of property. Two groups within the opposition are worth mentioning. One is the Coalition for Unity and Democracy (CUD), a right-wing centralizing elite largely opposed to federalism and "ethnic" federalism in particular. This group decided not only to boycott the parliament in October 2005 and its seats in Addis Ababa Council but it also claimed it won the 2005 election and therefore called for a "color revolution" similar to Ukraine's Orange Revolution and Georgia's Rose Revolution to unseat the EPRDF. This played into the ruling party's accusation that the opposition is not ready to play by the rules of the game. The second group was an ethnic-based coalition popularly known as *Medrek* (Forum), which supports the fundamental principles in the constitution but differs from the ruling party on two counts: it opposes the right to secession and rejects the centralizing tendencies in federal practice. *Medrek* decided to take its seats in parliament and continued to engage the ruling party. Overall, the opposition often operates in major cities but lacks roots in the more populous rural areas compared with the ruling party. While it may win some seats in the federal parliament, it is unlikely that it will control of any states in the short term.

The EPRDF was badly shaken by the 2005 election crisis and moved aggressively to reassert control and constrain the opposition. Its policy of "controlled freedom" meant that the opposition won only one seat in the 2010 election (and another went to an independent). In the May 2015 elections, despite winning 30–35 percent of the vote, the opposition failed to win a single seat because of the first-past-the-post electoral system and divisions among opposition parties. As a result, effective participation in political life is restricted to the members of the ruling party and its allies,[63] leaving a large section of society unrepresented and in disarray.[64] The ruling party is also engaged in ideological campaigns related to the developmental state, strengthened its organization down to the grass roots, and (more positively) improved service delivery. As a result, some have gone to the extent of concluding that the multiparty system in Ethiopia has given way to one party state.[65] This scenario certainly hints where Ethiopia's democratization process is heading. Human rights monitoring institutions point to extensive, restrictions on rights, and restricted access to state media (which is minimally open only during elections). In essence, elections are becoming a formal process without competitive options for voters and a very biased playing field favoring the governing parties. Opposition parties are only just tolerated and provided *controlled freedom*[66] so

[63] Leonardo Arriola and Terrence Lyons, "Ethiopia: The 100% Election" (2016) 27 (1) Journal of Democracy 76.

[64] The ruling party has an estimated 6.5 million members. But because there is no separation between party and government institutions, the government seems to be captured by its members and is not as such in the service of the estimated one hundred million population of the country.

[65] See Kjetil Tronvoll, "The Ethiopian 2010 Federal and Regional Elections: Re-establishing One Party State" (2010) 110 (438) African Affairs 121.

[66] This was a common expression used by the ruling party following the aftermath of the 2005 election crisis telling the opposition that their freedom is symbolized by a "chicken with a long rope" where its freedom is limited by the length of the rope to which it is tied.

long as they do not pose a major threat to the ruling party. The situation is close to what some call elections with little democracy.[67]

The EPDRF's omnipotence has weakened moderates in the opposition and led to widespread social movements and street protests emboldening hardliners. As some argue "In Ethiopia, an election victory of 100 percent of parliamentary seats sends the message to potential rebels that there is only one game in town and that to imagine otherwise would be futile."[68] This is exactly what transpired in 2016. When the political opposition was weakened and lost political space in parliament, the discontented section of society was left with little option than the social media and outlawed parties outside of the country. During the protests in Oromia and the Amhara region, it was all clandestine and as *The Reporter* rightly wrote, "it was a revolution without leaders,"[69] without leaders in the sense that the leaders were not the traditional loyal opposition figures but clandestine and new ones using social media as an outlet. It is not common to witness a discontent of this magnitude immediately after a "100 percent" win in election. There is a need to open space for accommodation of political dissent and reach out to the silent majority to engage in public affairs.

The developments following the latest protests indicate that post-Meles transition is not yet over. The federal system under Meles operated under three major unwritten frameworks: a big man (Meles, nicknamed by Clapham "the philosopher-king of the EPRDF"),[70] democratic centralism (his main tool), and the vanguard party. After Meles's death, the collegial central government that emerged permitted regional states to exercise meaningful self-rule and influence decisions at federal level. This has given rise to a perception of a weak center and fragmentation of the vanguard party while ethnonationalism is growing.[71] Some regional states have declared an "economic revolution" of an ethnonationalist character, which is designed to address increasing youth unemployment but may discourage international and domestic investments.[72] Some believe that "since the death of Meles Zenawi, the top part of the power structure has exploded into a multiplicity of competing centres . . . Ethiopia at present is like a ship without a skipper, with respectful but passive crew and a faltering engine"[73] or lately "the federal centre is disintegrating."[74] With the center weakening,[75]emboldened

[67] Steven Levitsky and Lucan A Way, "Elections without Democracy: The Rise of Competitive Authoritarianism" (2002) 13 (2) Journal of Democracy 51.

[68] Arriola and Lyons (n 63) 86.

[69] See Solomon Goshu, "Rebellion without leaders: Where is Ethiopia Heading?" *The Reporter* (Amharic) (Addis Ababa, v. 21 n. 1702 *Nehase* 15, 2008 E. C. (August 21, 2016)).

[70] Meles's former ally and close friend Alex De Waal wrote "Meles's political praxis became detached from the collective leadership and party apparatus, and he was increasingly running party and government as a one man show." See Alex De Waal, *The Real Politics of the Horn of Africa: Money, War and the Business of Power* (Polity Press, Cambridge, 2015) 163; Christopher Clapham, *The Horn of Africa: State Formation and Decay* (Hurst and Company, London, 2017) 69.

[71] The slogan of the ruling party was that its struggle was "class in content but ethno-nationalist in form." Current realities show ethno-nationalism has trumped class.

[72] For example, Dangote's cement factory operating in Oromia regional state was required to outsource the supply of materials such as quarry and other raw materials to youth from Oromia regional state. See Fasika Tadesse, "Authorities in the Dark Over Dangote's Threat to Cease Ethiopian Operation" *Fortune* (English weekly newspaper) 18: 896, June 26, 2017; see also Kaleyesus Bekele, "Dangote partly suspends its operations in Oromia" *The Reporter (Amharaic)* 2: 1802 *Hamle* 30, 2009 E.C.

[73] Rene Lefort, (n 58) 391.

[74] Rene Lefort, "Ethnic clashes" in Ethiopia: Setting the record straight *Open Democracy* https://www.opendemocracy.net/ren-lefort/ethnic-clashes-in-ethiopia-setting-record-straight accessed October 22, 2017.

[75] The major crisis between the regional states of Oromia and Ethio Somali displaced hundreds of thousands with massive eviction of minorities in different regional states. The federal government

ethnonationalist leaders with competing and often conflicting interests are emerging as default leaders at the regional state level. With many of the political issues unresolved and protests in Oromia and Amhara mounting, Prime Minister Haile Mariam Desalegn resigned in February 2018. His six years in office (2012–18) was the weakest government in Ethiopia's modern history, with indecisiveness and anarchy reminiscent of the Era of the Princess.

Ethiopia entered into a third political era with the coming to power[76] of a charismatic, young, and populist new PM, Dr. Abiy Ahmed in April 2018. He delivered compelling and uplifting speeches, emphasizing love, reconciliation, and forgiveness. His narrative of federalism is different from his predecessors, but it is not yet clear whether he will accept real diversity or return to the narrative of the centrist elite "Ethiopia *Tikdem*."[77] He comes from the Oromo wing of the ruling coalition and has appointed more Oromos to key federal positions.[78] He released thousands of prisoners, including key opposition figures, ended the state of emergency, called for dialogue with political parties in the diaspora, and initiated several reforms, giving Ethiopia some sense of hope and optimism for a democratic opening.

With formerly "terrorist" factions of the OLF, Patriotic *Ginbot-7*, and different opposition groups invited to operate peacefully, the next challenge is dialogue and negotiation to bring about the necessary reforms and a renewal of democratization. Success will have risks and some have drawn parallels with the USSR in the early 1990s.[79] The critical issue is whether Abiy can democratize Ethiopia without risking disintegration, given the impetus toward secession in several regional states. Abiy's daring decision to engage all issues at once risks opening Pandora's Box when it is unsure whether the *party machinery has the capacity, the willingness, and, more importantly, the consensus to manage* accumulated complex issues that need urgent reform. There are differences around process (an inclusive transition or more piecemeal reforms by bilateral dialogue—with Abiy favoring the latter) and around the future of "ethnic federalism." Opening so many issues at once and the return risks shaking the already fragile coalition and political system, when a more focused and consensual approach might be better. Many of Abiy's decisions of the PM by-pass existing institutions, which has created resentment among senior party and government figures.[80] The party itself seems in disarray. The Prime Minister, behaving more like a president, is broadening his social base outside the party in what appears to be a deliberate dismantling

proved unable to address the crisis through political reform. Regional state parties instructed their MPs how to vote or to boycott in the federal parliament as if it were a confederation, leading the council of Ministers to adopt an emergency law by decree on March 1, 2018. When this failed to ensure law and order and to protect the mobility of people and goods, the government had to issue a second emergency law.

[76] This is the first Prime Minister elected despite sizable dissent (108 votes in favor from the 171 votes) from within his party in the history of the ruling party.

[77] "*Sinnore Ethiopiawian, sinmote Ethiopia*" ["we are Ethiopians while alive and we become Ethiopia when we die"] was what he coined in his acceptance speech to parliament in April 2018.

[78] Among others, the position of the Prime Minister, Foreign Affairs, Attorney General, Ministry of Defense, the Presidency, Revenue Authority, and Mayor of Addis are now controlled by the OPDO. The PM also restructured the military and security apparatus, which was perceived as TPLF's domain, bringing in more actors to this sector from the other coalitions of the ruling party.

[79] See Alemayehu Woldemariam, "Ethiopia's Charismatic Leader: Riding the Wave of Populism or Reforming Ethnic Federalism?" *Ethiopia Observer* at https://www.ethiopiaobserver.com/2018/07/04/ethiopias-charismatic-leader-riding-the-wave-of-populism-or-reforming-ethnic-federalism/ accessed July 4, 2018.

[80] The TPLF and some retired figures from the ANDM already issued a press release accusing the PM of acting without proper consultations and for infesting the party with "alien ideology."

of the party apparatus perhaps with the anticipation that it needs to break apart.[81] This is risky as the ruling party was the flag bearer of federalism (with all its limits) and it is difficult to anticipate a successor given the fragmented opposition and Ethiopia's political culture. Despite all the odds, the EPRDF was able to elect Abiy peacefully in the midst of crisis: a rare phenomenon in Ethiopia's recent political history. The EPRDF has been a formidable force and its breakup could cost Ethiopia dearly. As noted by *Fortune*: "His popular rhetoric may have pleased a large number of the public, but his accountability lies with the 180-member EPRDF Council that has elected him . . ."[82] It is too early to tell how Abiy will balance personal ambition, popular support, and his internal party constituency, so the third phase of EPRDF rule is highly uncertain—both hopeful and risky at the same time.

Lessons Learned

The territorially based, ethnonationalist forces behind Ethiopia's political transition naturally favored a federal constitutional structure. Their arrival in power represented a decisive break from the former ruling elites—whether imperial or socialist—which were highly centralizing and advocates of a homogenized identity, which necessarily marginalized most parts of the population. Contrary to previous regimes' policies on diversity, the post-1991 regime in Ethiopia not only officially recognizes diversity but also accommodates it constitutionally through the design of its federal institutions. With the end of the military junta in May 1991, Ethiopia was on the brink of collapse when ethnonationalist political groups took control. Two decades later, the federal option can be seen to have brought relative peace and political stability to a fragile region, otherwise known as the "Horn of Conflicts."

However, a key lesson is that Ethiopia's formal federal structure, necessary as it may have been, has functioned through the dominance of one party. Dominant party politics has in important ways trumped political federalism. It is true that the EPDRF is itself a coalition of four major ethnonationalist groups, so there have been elements of power sharing within the party. But the party constrained real political competition and thus the democratic nature of federalism. Moreover, the party system restrained autonomy and policy diversity at state level and the party largely prevailed over the constitutionally designed autonomy of the states and their institutions.

A second lesson is that despite the political dominance of one party, Ethiopia has in important ways been federalized. It has made major strides in creating structures and capacity within the regions, so that at the administrative level the country truly has a federal structure. The new leaders moved aggressively to upgrade the capacity of state and local governments, staffed by local people and using local languages. This shifting of government into the regions succeeded in realizing at least some of the Constitution's promise of self-rule for ethnonationalist populations. Officially proclaiming itself as a "developmental state," government in Ethiopia has made great strides in delivering security and services. Some of this reflects the close links between party and government: compared with many other African countries, where

[81] One rumor is that the some Western countries wish to see the end of the EPRDF as it had strong ties with China and insisted on the ideology of the developmental state.

[82] "Fine Line," *Fortune* v.19 no. 947 June 19, 2018 https://addisfortune.net/columns/the-speed-at-which-abiy-ahmed-takes-things-has-begun-to-unnerve-many/ accessed July 15, 2018.

government institutions remain soft, the EPRDF has shown commitment and has a strong structure all the way down to the family level, which gives it a huge potential for mobilizing resources and the people for achieving its developmental objectives. For Ethiopia, and probably many other developing diverse countries, the state's ability to deliver much-needed services on an equitable basis can be fundamental in undermining secessionist movements.

There is perhaps little that federalism or decentralization alone can do to contain political conflict if government fails to promote development and improve the quality of services for the population. Thus economic growth and delivery of services can be seen both as an end and a means to an end in a highly diverse, underdeveloped country. With improved living standards and good government administration, there may be a moderation of ethnonationalism and the emergence of alternative forms of social and political mobilization, along the lines of class and ideology, and with an active civil society. However, the recent political turmoil in Ethiopia has seen a strengthening of ethnonationalism, which, if not successfully managed, poses fundamental risks.

There may also be lessons from Ethiopia's "ethnic federalism." There are critical challenges associated with the over-emphasis on the rights of "nations, nationalities, and peoples" reflected in several sections of the Constitution. The fact that the individual *citizen* is not expressly mentioned as a founder of the Constitution is revealing about their being left out of the process of establishing the federation. In particular, minorities and individuals within the states are at the mercy of the local elite and ethnic majorities. This is critical because inter-regional migration will rise with economic development and the free movement of labor is both a principle and an economic necessity. Commitment to rule of law and strong judicial protection of constitutionally entrenched rights are supposed to be the cure, but they are far from realized in Ethiopia.

The challenge related to political pluralism is even more serious. The federation has operated under a dominant party that has remained fairly accommodative to ethnonationalist groups, especially within its governing coalition, but it has been less tolerant of political pluralism or opposition until very recently. It is hardly possible to maintain a truly federal system without democratic practices and it is this challenge that makes political life in Ethiopia less predictable, especially with the current reforms. Some hope that with a more accommodative federal institutional arrangement and material betterment, there would be the emergence of "other forms of mobilization," such as class, that cross-cut and prevail over ethnonationalist mobilization.[83] Ethno-linguistic and cultural diversity are supposed to give more space for cosmopolitan citizenship and political pluralism. Yet for now ethnonationalist political mobilization in Ethiopia appears predominant, with little indication that it will give way to more class or ideologically based mobilization. Indeed, we still have to find a rational explanation as to why class-based parties of the 1970s failed to prevail or why ethnonationalist-based organizations proved more effective. Nevertheless, the claim that there is a need to nurture political pluralism of a form different from ethnonationalist diversity is timely, especially given the current political opening. Since 1995, Ethiopia did not do well in terms of accommodating political pluralism, with the exception of the 2005–10 third parliamentary term when the political

[83] Andreas Eshete, "Coming to Terms with Diversity: The Ethiopian Experience" (Federalism for Peace, Democracy and Development: Experience Exchange on Federalism and Decentralization in the East Africa Region conference, Addis Ababa, Ethiopia, February 25–7, 2013).

opposition gained a significant number of seats in parliament. However, the protests during the term of Haile Mariam Desalegn and the coming to power of Abiy Ahmed have seen a remarkable transformation of the political space. Whether this opening gives life to an effective federalism and political pluralism or leads to deeper fractures is now the central issue of Ethiopian politics.

5

States Reorganization and Accommodation of Ethno-Territorial Cleavages in India

Harihar Bhattacharyya

Overview

What holds India, a vast multi-ethnic country, together in the midst of so many odds? The question is particularly significant because India's unity and integrity has been possible despite democracy. The key to the above success lies in a mode of federation building that sought to continuously "right-size" the territory of India. The method followed in doing so is called "states reorganization" in India as a result of which ethno-territorial cleavages have been accommodated and regulated. The result has been durable ethnic peace and political stability. At independence (August 15, 1947), India inherited nine provinces and more than 560 princely states from the old colonial arrangements. An interim state structure was put in place, but it was recognized that a fundamental restructuring would be required in due course. The process was complex and painstaking, but managed to create sub-national units called "states,, mostly on the basis of language; subsequently non-linguistic ethnic factors were also taken into consideration. This chapter focuses on the process of "states reorganization" during the 1950s and 1960s, with some discussion of the subsequent processes notably of the strategically important North-East, which has seen various insurgencies. It provides brief "background" to the process by highlighting the key constitutional and political issues before moving to the main core of the process and constitutional changes associated with the various reorganizations. It seeks to show in particular the nature of institutional responses of the Indian state to ethno-linguistic cleavages with particular attention to the States Reorganization Commission. The chapter also examines the outcome of these exercises, and shows how "subnational autonomy" became major incentives for the regional political elites. The linguistic "right-sizing" of the subnational units, coupled with considerations of economic viability and administrative convenience, removed very early on a major source of ethnic conflicts in India. The chapter also examines the comparative lessons learned, and concludes with particular reference to the effects of India's ongoing neo-liberal reforms (post-1991) that have offered newer challenges for state autonomy and future territorial changes.

Background

India's defining constitutional moment was 1946–49 when the main elements of India's constitutional structure were determined, but unusually the territorial structure of the state was not settled beyond the general idea of a quasi-federal structure. In the event, India's territorial restructuring took place in several phases over many years.

Territory and Power in Constitutional Transitions. First Edion. Edited by Michael Anderson and Sujit Choudhry. States Reorganization and Accommodation of Ethno-Territorial Cleavages in India

The drafting of the Constitution was assigned to the Constituent Assembly, which was formed by indirect elections in 1946 before independence and following the major holocaust between Hindus and Muslims (the "Great Calcutta Killing of 1946") and the Partition between Pakistan and India. The territorial issues were most perplexing during the constitutional drafting, not simply because India was vast and complex, but more importantly, because territorial issues had factored into the mainstream anti-British nationalist politics led by the Congress since the beginning of the twentieth century, if not earlier. It was recognized that state reorganization along linguistic lines was probably inevitable, but given the recent traumas as well as the concern of the Congress Party to focus on building the Union first, the issue was put off. Language has long been politically salient in India, which today has twenty-two officially recognized languages—most territorially rooted with millions of speakers—and as many as 1,549 distinct mother tongues,[1] about 10 percent of the population belong to territorially concentrated aboriginal peoples speaking various dialects; only in the state of Jammu and Kashmir are Muslims in a majority.

With the rise of Mahatma Gandhi and anti-British nationalist movements, territorially based ethno-linguistic identities came to be utilized by Congress for building mass bases. From the beginning of the twentieth century (the India National Congress was formed in 1885), Congress's organizational set-up came to reflect ethno-linguistic territorial cleavages. By 1918, the Congress had formed twenty-one Provincial Congress Committees, which were all "vernacular units" and territorially concentrated.[2] At its Nagpur session in 1920, Congress formally committed itself to reorganizing India after independence into a federation based on linguistically based units.[3] The Motilal Nehru Report of 1928 reiterated this commitment.[4]

Ethnic issues were never given much weight by the British colonial regime in India, whether by the East India Company until 1857 or directly by the Crown after 1858. First, the administrative boundaries of the eleven provinces that were directly governed by the British (under three presidencies of Calcutta, Madras, and Bombay), were not drawn in keeping with ethnic boundaries, so there were ethno-linguistic resentments and conflicts, which very often took the form of regional-national self-determination advocacy by regional elites against those in power, who did not necessarily represent the majority.[5] For example, in the Madras Presidency, the elite was largely western-educated Tamils who were dominant over others, such as the Telugus. This was so even though the colonial authorities as such did not include many Indians in administration

[1] Bipan Chandra, Aditya Mukherjee, and Mridula Mukherjee, *India After Independence* (Penguin Books 2008) 107.

[2] As I have shown elsewhere (Bhattacharyya 2010), the INC had been cultivating such cleavages from the late nineteenth century. This was highlighted not only at the all-India fora of the INC, but also, more strongly, by the regional level leaders of importance. See Harihar Bhattacharyya, *Federalism in Asia: India, Pakistan, and Malaysia* (Routledge 2010) 60–5; and Harihar Bhattacharyya, "Ethnic and Civic Nationhood in India: Concept, History, Institutional Innovations and Contemporary Challenges" in Santosh C Saha (ed.), *Ethnicity and Socio-Political Change in Africa and Other Developing Countries: A Constructive Discourse in State Building* (Lexington Book 2008) 181–3.

[3] It should be recorded that the even the British authorities were not insensitive to the linguistic factors in governing the provinces. The first two linguistic States, namely Orissa (now Odisha) and Sindh were created by them in 1936. Even before that, the Mantagu-Chelmsford Report of 1918 recognized the issue when it said the "business of government would be simplified if administrative units were both smaller and homogenous."

[4] See Bhattacharyya, "Ethnic and Civic Nationhood in India" (n 2) 181–2.

[5] AR Desai, *Social background of Indian Nationalism* (Popular Prakashan 1948); for a detailed examination of Tripuri nationalism, constructed in the vernacular Bengali, see Harihar Bhattacharyya, "The Emergence of Tripura Nationalism, 1948–50" (1989) 9 (1) South Asia Research 54.

and justice. Some ethnic groups, which had received English education, had greater chances of inclusion at the lower levels of administration and justice. This was notably the case for the Bengalis, especially the *Bhadralok* (three top caste groups of Brahmins, Kayasthas, and Baidyas),[6] and higher-caste Tamils, and this subsequently became a matter of much discontent among other ethnic groups in both presidencies, which were ethnically heterogeneous. In reaction, Congress, as the main party of the anti-colonial liberation movements, in the initial years sought more Indianization of the administration and justice. And the discrimination led to self-determination movements of territorially rooted ethnic-minority groups. Historical studies show that from its very birth Congress was an interregional coalition seeking to craft a composite national entity.[7] Congress's national ideology was at variance with its continuing cultivation of ethnic aspirations, including by its regional units working to build mass bases. Nationally, Congress's so-called "composite nationalism" approach coexisted with the rise of ethno-regional nationalities in different regions of India, such as Assam, Tripura, Gujarat, and Andhra Pradesh, which Congress promised to accommodate within the future federation of India.[8] Thus, the political elites—most notably, Jawaharlal Nehru, following a long intellectual trajectory built by Rabindra Nath Tagore and before him Bhudev Mukhopadhyay[9]—forged unity out of diversity.

India thus inherited from the imperial British different types of cleavages calling for solution. In imperial India, the major cleavage was of course the religious conflict between Hindus and Muslims, which led to Partition on August 14, 1947. However, the religious cleavage still remains in India, which has more Muslims than Pakistan, and where Muslims, aside from Kashmir and a few districts elsewhere, are not territorially concentrated. Neither the Hindus nor the Muslims are homogenous. The main political cleavage at independence was between the 560 princely states versus the directly ruled provinces. The ethno-linguistic cleavages were primarily linguistic in character but they also included tribal affiliations, particularly in the North-East of India. The princely states were of different sizes and socio-cultural complexion and were interspersed between India's provinces. During the colonial period, they enjoyed varying degrees of "independence" under indirect rule of the British, though the colonial authorities made sure their Political Residents in the princely states keep a constant vigil on the affairs of the kingdoms.

Ethno-territorial cleavages were particularly acute in Madras and Bombay Presidencies, and central and northern India. In1931 there were 17.7 million Telugus, 4 million Oriyas, 3.7 million Malayalam, and 1.7 million Kannada speakers in Madras Presidency and the minority language speakers were territorially concentrated, while in the Bombay Presidency, there were 3.4 million Guajarati, 3.1 million Sindhi, and 2.6 million Kannada-speaking people. The picture was no less complex in northern and central India.[10] But the cleavages in Madras and Bombay Presidencies were particularly urgent and a hard task for state reorganization.

[6] For details, see JH Broomfield, *Elite Conflict in a Plural Society: Twentieth-Century Bengal* (University of California Press 1968).

[7] John R McLane, *Indian Nationalism and the Early Congress* (Princeton University Press 1977).

[8] Desai (n 5).

[9] Harihar Bhattacharyya 2011, "Sensing and Acknowledging India's Cultural Diversity for Nationhood: Bhudev Mukhopadhya and Ranindra Nath Tagore," *The Calcutta Review*, Vol. XlII Nos. 1 & 2, 102–19); Jawaharlal Nehru, *The Discovery of India* (The Signet Press 1946) 61–2.

[10] Bhattacharyya 2011, 102–19.

The Period of Constitutional Engagement

During India's major Constitution-making process from 1946 to 1949, the Constitution-makers were preoccupied with the pressing problems of "national" unity and solidarity in the aftermath of Partition, as well as the vexed problem of "integration" of the princely states. While the issue of the longer-term territorial structure of the country was considered and pushed actively by some elements, in the end, the Constituent Assembly chose not to deal with it substantively, though it did ensure that a powerful procedure was designed that would permit such a restructuring in due course.

The Constitution was made by Indians through a constituent assembly elected indirectly by the provincial legislatures elected in 1946. The Constituent Assembly, formed on July 11–22, 1946, owed its origin to the British Cabinet Mission Plan (1946) for a constitutional solution to India's problems of unity between the Hindus and the Muslims and other communities and the princely states. Congress did not accept the whole of the Plan, but the Muslim League led by MA Jinnah did, on the assumption that eventually it would produce a separate state of Pakistan for the Muslims.[11] Earlier, the Government of India Act 1935 had, for the first time, provided for a federation for India, and this was partially implemented in the directly ruled provinces; in 1937 different political parties, particularly Congress and the League, took part in elections and formed provincial governments.[12] However, the Cabinet Mission Plan for a federal solution to India's communal problems did not work, notably in relation to the religious cleavage, and India was partitioned on August 14, 1947. The next day, August 15, 1947, Pakistan and India won independence as two sovereign states.

India's Constituent Assembly met for the first time on December 9, 1946, with British concurrence, but the League members boycotted it, which meant about 100 million Muslims were not represented.[13] With the Partition of the country and the rise of Pakistan, the Assembly became virtually a Congress body, in which the party had a built-in majority of 82 percent.[14] The Assembly originally had 385 members, including ninety-three members nominated by the princely rulers. As Granville Austin famously wrote: "The Constituent Assembly was a one-party body in an essentially one-party country. The Assembly was the Congress and the Congress was India."[15] The Constituent Assembly was playing a dual role: drafting the constitution, and acting as a Legislature for the Interim Government (1946–49), headed effectively by Jawaharlal Nehru (as Vice-President of the Viceroy's Executive Council). What remained of the League in India joined the government after some hesitation with the purpose of "wrecking."[16] Ministers of the Union government had to be members of the Assembly, and they participated in Constitution-making. Although top leaders of the liberation struggle (Nehru, Azad, Ambedkar, and Prasad) constituted an oligarchy over the Assembly, its internal processes and eight committees appeared to be democratic.[17] Since the leaders in making the Constitution were also practitioners in government, the practical insight of governance could be brought to bear upon Constitution-making. According to Austin,[18] "[The] shadow of the Oligarchy covered the Assembly Party (of Congress), yet it did not dominate."

[11] Granville Austin, *The Indian Constitution: Cornerstone of a Nation* (Oxford University Press 1999) 5.

[12] Bhattacharyya, *Federalism in Asia* (n 2) 55–7. [13] Austin 1999 (n 11) 7.

[14] ibid 10. [15] ibid 8–9. [16] ibid 6. [17] ibid 18–21. [18] ibid 22.

The ethno-territorial issue kept members of the Constituent Assembly (CA) preoccupied for two consecutive days, November 17–18, 1948, in search of institutional solutions in building the Union.[19] The issue came up frequently in the debates of the CA for three years but the Assembly did not resolve the problem. The members with strong ethnic roots from areas such as Madras (now Tamil Nadu) and the Punjab were vociferous in highlighting the self-determination rights of those communities.

At that time, the issue of territorial reorganization of India meant largely[20] the formation of linguistic provinces or sub-national units, to which Congress had committed itself formally since 1920. Pattabhi Sitaramayya, a leading member of the CA, and Congress Party President in 1948, insisted upon solving the problem of formation of linguistic provinces as "the first and foremost problem."[21] The supporters of linguistic provinces even held a conference in New Delhi on December 8, 1946 before the inaugural meeting of the Assembly, and these included such important Congress leaders as the Deputy Speaker of the CA, and a member of the Drafting Committee.[22] The records of the meeting of the Congress in early 1947 show clearly that within the party pressure for linguistic provinces was alive. A meeting on June 12, 1947 even considered the creation of Andhra, Karnataka, Maharashtra, and other states. The Constituent Assembly formed the advisory Dar Commission (Linguistic Provinces Commission) on June 17, 1948, which was broadly sympathetic to the cause but cautioned against forming units solely on the basis of language.[23] Congress formed its own high-powered committee to take a second look at the problem. The JVP committee (of Jawaharlal Nehru, Vallabbhai Patel, and Pattabhi Sitaramayya) also came to the conclusion: "We feel that the present is not an opportune moment for the formation of linguistic provinces."[24]

The Assembly finally came up with a quasi-federal centralized constitution with two tiers of government whose powers were determined in detail by means of three lists (Union, State, and Concurrent). The Union government was made very powerful but the states were given their own jurisdiction and the Constitution made the federation administratively decentralized,[25] because the central government was to be "all staff but no line," which meant that the states were not only to implement their own laws, but also to take care of many central government laws particularly those relating to development, and tax collection. The states' taxing powers were limited but there was provision for a Finance Commission every five years which would recommend a formula for distributing the divisible pool of central taxes amongst the Union and all the state governments. On the more vexed territorial issues, the outcome of the Assembly's deliberations was to provide for four types of states, with different powers and status, on a basis that was, according to Basu, historical and political.[26] When the Constitution was inaugurated on January 26, 1950, India had twenty-seven states of different types, powers, and status: the nine directly ruled former provinces were made category A states; the 226 princely states (geographically contiguous to the provinces) were merged to form the category B states; sixty-one relatively small states were converted into the category C states, and the rest were merged into the category A states.[27]

[19] Government of India Constituent Debates Records, "Constituent Assembly Debates on 17 November, 1948" (*IndianKanoon.org*, 17 November 1948) <https://indiankanoon.org/doc/1437986/> accessed 18 December 2017 and 16556911 .

[20] The other part of reorganization entailed integration of some 500-odd princely states of different sizes and complexion. Austin commented: " . . . the integration of the States apparently presented the Assembly with the federal problem in its most familiar forms," see Austin (n 11).

[21] ibid 241. [22] ibid. [23] ibid 242. [24] As quoted in ibid.

[25] Ronald L Watts, *Comparing Federal Systems* (3rd edn, McGill-Queen's University Press 2008).

[26] Durga Das Basu, *Introduction to the Constitution of India* (Prentice-Hall of India 1997) 69.

[27] Bhattacharyya, *Federalism in Asia* (n 2) 89.

The Andaman and Nicobar Islands and Acquired Territory, if any, were placed under category D. Despite this territorial recasting and merging, the Assembly chose not to resolve the ethno-territorial cleavages at that time. However, it kept the issue alive in Articles 2 and 3 of the Constitution, which gave the Union Parliament virtually unilateral power to create new states, alter the boundaries of the states, change the name of the states, and so on.[28] It could do this by a simple majority vote in Parliament. The only protection for existing states was that the legislatures of directly affected states were to be consulted before the Union Parliament decided. This provision is extraordinary in a federal context and is one of the reasons why the Indian Constitution is sometimes referred to as quasi-federal.

The rights to religion and language (including script and minority culture) were made fundamental and placed under Part III of the Constitution ("Fundamental Rights"), which was an important symbolic, non-territorial recognition of identity. The 8th Schedule contains provisions for official recognition of languages. While any territorial claim on the basis of religion was ruled out,[29] there was provision for both non-territorial and territorial recognition and accommodation of languages. Thus, the Constitution provided for a federal structure with various types asymmetry for accommodation of ethnic identity, while the guiding political goal remained "unity-in-diversity."

Political mobilizations and constitutional changes were interlinked. As indicated above, Congress had conceded to language-based territorial claims of statehood from the beginning of the twentieth century and had recast its own provincial units accordingly. Although Congress had committed itself to the principle at its Nagpur Secession in 1920, after independence, for a variety of reasons (the memories of the religion-based Partition in 1947 following the "great" communal riots in 1946 and the consequent dislocation), Congress rulers at the Center showed reluctance on the issue, but not for long, as its various language-based units were at the forefront of the movements for territorial recasting.

There was a "chorus of calls"[30] for a new language-based political map of India almost immediately after independence. In each of the linguistically distinct regions, different constellations of forces mobilized around the issue, but the local units of Congress always favored creating a linguistic state.[31] The leaders within Congress—more specifically leaders of its Provincial Committees—were the main actors fighting for linguistic units. But there were also regionally based parties and groups, including associations, formed specifically to demand a linguistic state.

One of the strongest movements was on the part of the Telugus, whose demand for a linguistic state dated from 1916.[32] The fast unto death, on December 15, 1952, of Sri Potti Ramalu, a committed Gandhian who demanded a Telugu-speaking state of

[28] These two articles, particularly Article 3, on the face of it, are anti-federal because they compromise with the territorial integrity of the federal units. In effect, however, they proved to most effective in India's federation building since the early 1950s, see Harihar Bhattacharyya "India creates three new states" (2001) Federations: What is New in Federalism worldwide (Vol. 1, No. 1).

[29] Articles 25–30 of the Indian Constitution dealing with the freedom of religion and associated matters do not allow any scope for statehood demand on the basis of religion.

[30] Joseph E Schwartzberg, "Factors in the Linguistic Reorganization of Indian States" in Paul Wallace (ed.), *Region and Nation in India* (Oxford University Press 1985) 161.

[31] Even the Communist Party supported it in order to identity itself with the "regional nationalism of the Telugu people," as a means of building a mass base for the party. For details, see Mohan Ram, "The Communist Movement in Andhra Pradesh" in Paul R. Brass and Marcus F Franda (eds), *Radical Politics in South Asia* (MIT Press 1973) 291.

[32] ibid.

Andhra Pradesh,[33] triggered large-scale violence in the region. The state of Andhra was then carved out of Madras on October 1, 1953, thus forcing the larger issue of state reorganization to the fore.

Despite initial reluctance and hesitancy,[34] the central government headed by Nehru could no longer ignore the issue. Nehru announced in Parliament on December 22, 1953 that a Commission would be appointed to examine "objectively and dispassionately" the question of the reorganization of the states of the Indian Union. A State Reorganization Commission (SRC) was formed on December 29, 1953, headed by S. Fazl Ali (a former judge), with two others commissioners, H.N. Kunzru (a Kashmiri *Pandit* and scholar and legislator of long-standing) and K.M. Panikkar (a noted historian). The Commission was to report by June 30, 1955 and submitted its report (after an extension) on September 30, 1955. Its mandate was as follows:

> The Commission will investigate the conditions of the problem, the historical background, the existing situation, and the bearing of all important and relevant factors thereon. They will be free to consider any proposal relating to such reorganization. The Government expect that the Commission would in the first instance, not be going to the details, but make recommendations in regard to the broad principles[35]

The government deliberately avoided any special mention of the linguistic principle in this mandate. This was in tune with the previous positions of the Dar Commission (1948) and the JVP Report (1948) of the Constituent Assembly, but at variance with Congress's direct espousal of the linguistic principle during the struggle for freedom at least from 1920.

The SRC invited submissions from the public and other parties and received a total of 152,250 of which 2,000 were considered as "well-considered."[36] It toured the country for one year, visiting 104 places and interviewing some 9,000 people of all walks of life. It was mandated to consider all factors, but the main criterion remained language. In estimating mother tongue populations, the SRC depended on the 1,951 Census Reports, which did not go below the "taluk" or "tehsil" (block level administration-revenue units) level, so that village level data could not be estimated.

The SRC's report made clear that its criteria went beyond, language: "[A]fter full consideration of the problem in all aspects, we have come to the conclusion that it is neither possible nor desirable to reorganize States on the basis of the single test either of language or culture, but that a balanced approach to the whole problem is necessary in the interests of our national unity."[37] The SRC's so-called "balanced approach" entailed recognizing "linguistic homogeneity as an important factor conducive to administrative convenience and efficiency," while repudiating the "home land concept" of "one language one state."[38] It commented that the creation of Andhra Pradesh included factors such as cultural affinity, administrative convenience, and economic well-being, along with language.[39] Moreover, the solution to ethno-linguistic cleavages entailed a lot of territorial adjustment to give a manageable shape to a new state.

[33] For details on the movement for Andhra Pradesh, see Ram 1973 281–325.

[34] As Roger King points out that Nehru had some reservations about the outcome of the language-based movements for territorial recasting because he thought it would benefit only some dominant castes behind those movements. Roger King, *Nehru and the Language Politics in India* (Oxford University Press 1997).

[35] *State Reorganization Commission Reports, 1955*, Preface.

[36] Schwartzberg (n 30) 164.

[37] *State Reorganization Commission Reports, 1955 (Government of India) Vol. 1*, ch. 3, 45. The so-called "balanced approach" is reiterated in SRC Report Vol. 4, 254.

[38] ibid 45–6. [39] ibid SRC Vol. 4, 254.

In brief, the Commission recommended the creation of sixteen states, linguistically as homogenous as possible, by means of transfer of some territories up to the block level from one to the other, merger of some linguistically dominant territories into one state (such as Kerala), bifurcation of some states into two, keeping as is such Hindi-speaking states as Bihar, Uttar Pradesh, and Rajasthan (with minor territorial adjustments) but recommending the creation of the only new Hindi-speaking state of Madhya Pradesh. Orissa (now Odisha) and Jammu and Kashmir were recommended for no change. Telangana was not recognized as a separate state but recommended for inclusion in Hyderabad.

Thus, the Commission was trying to make states linguistically as homogeneous as possible, by cutting and pasting, mutual transfer, and merger. Nonetheless, the question of linguistic minorities was unavoidable which is why the SRC reiterated the constitutional safeguards (under Article 347) for minority languages to have instruction in the mother-tongue at the primary school level and suggested that the domicile tests in place in many states be liberalized and simplified for the advantages of the linguistic minorities (under Article 16(c)).

Parliament passed the States Reorganization Act 1956, doing away with the three categories of states in the 1950 Constitution and putting all states on an equal footing in terms of powers and authority (except Jammu and Kashmir whose accession to India took place under very "special" circumstances about which, interestingly, the SRC made no recommendations). The government accepted most of the SRC's recommendations, but made some modifications in the States Reorganization Act:[40]

1. Andhra Pradesh, (Andhra, restyled) was enlarged with the addition of the Telugu-speaking people from the Telengana region of Hyderabad (the largest former princely state ruled by a Muslim dynasty).[41]
2. Mysore, a former princely state, already integrated to India, was enlarged by absorbing the Kannada speaking areas of Hyderabad, Bombay, and Madras.[42]
3. Bombay was made a bilingual state (Marathi and Gujarati) by adding of Maratha-speaking areas of Hyderabad, Central Provinces, and Berar, and the Guajarati-speaking areas of Saurashtra and Kutch.
4. Central Provinces was renamed Madhya Pradesh, though diminished in the south by the loss of associated areas of Berar but enlarged by the merger of three other Hindi-speaking areas of Madhya Bharat, Vindhya Pradesh, and Bhopal.[43]
5. Punjab was enlarged by the merger of the Punjab and East Patiala States Union (PEPSU) to form the second bilingual state where the Hindi speakers were dominant in the South and the Punjabi speakers in the North.
6. Kerala was created by enlarging Travancore-Cochin by absorbing a portion of the Malabar Coast of Madras to form the Malayali-speaking state. In this case the SRC recommendations were mostly followed.

Thus, as a result of the implementation of the States Reorganization 1956, fourteen new or revised states with equal powers and status emerged, largely respecting the SRC

[40] Schwartzberg (n 30) 165.

[41] The SRC's recommendation was that the Andhra Pradesh should continue for the time being as it is except some minor adjustments. *State Reorganization Commission Reports, 1955, Vol. 4, section VI "Proposals for Reorganization,"* 257.

[42] The SRC recommendation was to form Karnataka including Mysore and other Kannada-speaking areas of Madras, Bombay, Hyderabad, and others (*State Reorganization Commission Reports, 1955*, 257). The Mysore State became Karnataka on November 1, 1973 with the *Mysore State (Alteration of Name) Act, 1973* (India). Also see, PM Bakshi, *The Constitutions of India* (Delhi Law House 2014) 349.

[43] In this case also, the SRC recommendations were mostly followed.

proposals. The other minor changes in respect of Bihar and West Bengal were adhered to. However, Tripura was not merged in Assam.

The SRC's proposals and new state creation did not satisfy all stakeholders. For example, the creation of a bilingual (Marathi and Gujarati) state of Bombay was strongly opposed by groups among both the Marathi and the Gujrati people. The leadership of this opposition was provided by Samjuka Maharasthra Samity (a united front with the Communists and other left parties such as the Praja Socialist Party) in Maharashtra[44] and the Maha Gujarat Janata Parishad in Gujarat. Anti-Congress opposition parties in Gujarat supported by students, farmers, workers, artisans, and businessmen organized a powerful protest, which resulted in eighty deaths in 1956 due to riots that broke out in Bombay.[45] The whole situation went to such an impasse that a respected Congress leader, CD Desmukh, then Finance Minister in the Central Cabinet, resigned. On the other hand, a large section of Congressmen also joined the movement for a United Maharashtra.[46] The strong movement for a United Maharashtra was linked with the fate of the Gujaratis, who were deeply concerned that they would be a minority in the new state of Maharashtra. Violence and arson spread to Ahmadabad and other parts of Gujarat, with sixteen people killed and 200 injured in police shootings.[47]

Thus the first major phase of state reorganization in India was not entirely a peaceful process and important ethno-linguistic issues were left unresolved. The question of the most linguistic minorities could not be avoided, but only minimized to a large extent. States reorganization ensured that the combined percentage of all linguistic minorities in a state should not be more than half of the population, but there were several cases where linguistic minorities totaled more than 40 percent of the population: in descending order, they were Jammu and Kashmir; Rajasthan, Punjab, and Assam.[48] Mysore had a diversity of languages but the total minority did not exceed about one-third. In the rest of the cases, the figure was about 22 percent.[49] These remaining numerous minorities were thus significant, but reorganization had, remarkably, reduced the combined linguistic minorities nationally from more than 50 percent of the total population before 1956.

In the 1960s there was a round of reorganization along mostly linguistic lines in respect of bilingual Bombay and Punjab. After the major disturbances and movements in Bombay, the Bombay Reorganization Act 1960 gave birth to two linguistically more homogenous states of Maharashtra (with the majority Marathi-speaking people) and Gujarat (with the overwhelmingly Gujarati-speaking people). Bilingual Bombay had had linguistic minorities that constituted as much as 49 percent, mainly Guajarati along with tribal peoples and migrants. No wonder, the Gujaratis demanded and got their State of Gujarat in 1960, which even today is the most linguistically homogenous state in India.

Punjab's reorganization was perhaps the most complex in the 1960s, and it underwent two stages—1956 and 1966—before it was resolved. It is the lone case in India where the religious factor weighed along with the linguistic one. The SRC had rejected demands, largely from the Sikh-supported Shiromani Akali Dal, for a Punjabi-speaking state to be called Punjabi Suba. The Commission found that Punjabi was not sufficiently grammatically distinct from Hindi to quality as a language; however, the situation was complicated because the religion was as at least as much a factor as

[44] Ram Joshi, "Maharashtra" in Myron Weiner (ed.) *State Politics in India* (Princeton University Press 1967) 197–8.
[45] Chandra, Mukherjee, and Mukherjee (2008) (n 1)128–9. [46] ibid 129.
[47] ibid. [48] Schwartzberg (n 30) 165. [49] ibid.

language. The Hindu-based Jan Sangh (renamed the BJP in 1980) opposed creating this state on the ground that it reflected a "communal demand."[50] Congress was also opposed. For many "the linguistic argument (was) considered to be merely a camouflage for the eventual creation of a theocratic state."[51] The SRC 1955 did not recommend the division of Punjab; on the contrary, it proposed to merge the PEPSU (a state created in 1948 combining eight princely states) and Himachal Pradesh with Punjab.[52] But the Government of India's 1956 reorganization did not adopt a "united Punjab," deciding to merge only the PEPSU with Punjab, keeping Himachal Pradesh as a separate entity.[53] This arrangement gained some territories (the PEPSU; twenty districts) for Punjab, with Hindus remaining a large majority (63.7 percent) and the Sikhs a clear minority (33.3 percent).[54] But things changed with the very adamant Punjabi Suba movement, Lalbahadur Shastri as the new Prime Minister after the death of Nehru, and unsettling international factors (the Chinese invasion of India in 1962 and the Indo-Pak war in 1965), so the Center gave in and decided to partition Punjab into three states: the south-east Hindi-speaking area was formed into a new state of Haryana; the Punjabi-speaking but Hindu-populated areas of the Himalayan territory were attached to Himachal Pradesh; and the rest of the truncated (with one-fifth of the territory of pre-independence Punjab) Punjabi-speaking areas were delineated as Punjab.[55] The city of Chandigarh, with a Union Territory status in the Indian Constitution, remains the joint capital for Punjab and Haryana. But the creation of Punjab, truncated though it was, became a state in which the Sikhs became a majority for the first time with about 55 percent of the population, the rest being the Hindus and others.

By 1966, the government had achieved major reorganization of the states within mainland India, but had not addressed the complex issues in the North-East. The region, connected by a narrow strip of land to mainland India and surrounded on three sides by international borders (China, Bhutan, Myanmar, and Bangladesh) is India's most sensitive strategically and a major security concern. It is also known as India's "insurgent country." The North-East is very distinct from the rest of India in terms of history, demography, and political institutions. During British colonial rule, it was largely kept isolated from the mainland. It was divided into the North East Frontier Province, Assam (a directly governed British Chief Commissioner's province), and Manipur and Tripura as two ancient princely states. (Sikkim formerly a kingdom and inhabited by people mostly speaking Nepali joined the Indian Union in 1974 as an "Associate State" to be promoted to a (full) state in 1975.) Historically, the region had different, often tortuous, trajectories of being incorporated into the British Empire.[56]

[50] Chandra, Mukherjee, and Mukherjee (2008) (n 1) 129.

[51] Baldev Raj Nayar, *Minority Politics in the Punjab* (Princeton University Press 1966) 322–3.

[52] *State Reorganization Commission Reports, 1955, Vol. 4*, 258.

[53] Nayar (n 51) 444.

[54] ibid.

[55] Gurharpal Singh, *Communism in Punjab: A Study of the Movement Up to 1967* (Ajanta Books International 1994) 30.

[56] See Sanjib Baruah, *India Against Itself: Assam and the Politics of Nationality* (University of Pennsylvania Press 2005); Sanjib Baruah, *Durable Disorder: Understanding the Politics of Northeast* India (Oxford University Press 2005); Shibani Kinkar Chaube, *Hill Politics in Northeast India* (Orient Longman 1973); Harihar Bhattacharyya, *Communism in Tripura* (Ajanta Books International 1999); Subrata K Mitra and Harihar Bhattacharyya, "The Multicultural Challenge: The Post-Colonial State and Subnational Movements in India's North-East" in L Basta-Fleiner and others (eds), *Rule of Law and Organization of the State in Asia: The Multicultural Challenge* (Fribourg: Institute of Federalism 2000); Subir Bhaumik, "North-East India: Evolution of a Post-Colonial Region" in Partha Chatterjee (ed.), *Wages of Freedom: Fifty Years of the Indian Nation-State* (Oxford University Press 1998); Balmiri Prasad Singh, *North-East India: The Problem of Change* (Oxford University Press 1987).

With slightly less than 4 percent of India's population, but more than 25 percent of its tribal peoples, the region's persistent ethnic movements and political militancy, occasional ethnic genocides, and geographic isolation have made it a problem area of India. The large security forces deployed there are second only to those in Kashmir,[57] and the Armed Forces Special Powers Act (1958)(AFSPA) has regularly been in force in parts of the region. This has increased disaffection and increased support for insurgent movements, particularly in Manipur. The North-East's seven states (except Sikkim) of today are the result of many phases of territorial recasting since the early 1960s.

To begin with, Nagaland was the first state to be carved out of Assam in 1963 comprising the Naga Hills District of Assam. The British colonial authorities kept the hills as an "excluded area" but since independence different Tribal Councils governed the areas. The creation of Nagaland as a state in 1963 was something of an exception, as well as a trend-setter, in the history of territorial reorganization of the region for two reasons. First, the Nagas declared independence after the lapse of British suzerainty in India, but after protracted warfare with the Indian security forces and negotiations with the government, the famous Naga Peace Accord (known as the Naga-Akbar Hydari Accord June 26–28, 1947 at Kohima) was signed by the representative of ten Naga tribes and the Governor of Assam providing for the constitution of a Naga Council with a lot of autonomy in respect of land and other customary rights.[58] Second, this was followed by another accord called "the Sixteen Point Agreement," July 26–27, 1960, between the Naga People's Convention and the Government of India[59] providing for the creation of the State of Nagaland, essentially on an ethnic basis. Accordingly, the Indian Constitution was amended (Thirteenth Amendment 1962), which added a special provision, Article 371-A, providing for special autonomy for the state in relation to religious and social practices, Naga customary law (including civil and criminal justice), and ownership of land and its resources.

Tripura and Manipur had very limited political institutions of governance as the Chief Commissioner's provinces until they were granted Union Territory status in 1962, which was an improvement. The Union Territory status had been accorded to Mizoram and Arunachal Pradesh (NEFA renamed) in 1971. Meghalaya was made an autonomous sub-state in 1960 within the State of Assam (by the Assam Reorganization Act 1960) and made a state in 1971. Tripura and Manipur were also made states by the same North-Eastern States Reorganization Act 1971. Mizoram and Arunachal Pradesh became states in 1987. In the cases of Mizoram, Manipur, Tripura, and Arunachal Pradesh, the territorial trajectory was from a Union Territory to statehood with autonomous powers within the Indian Union. For the tribal dominated units such as Mizoram, Meghalaya, and Nagaland, the prior experiences in the Tribal District Councils (under the Sixth Schedule) seemed to have paved the way for demanding greater territorial status, such as Union Territory and finally statehood.

The Nagas set the trend in achieving statehood after insurgency and, in nearly all cases, militant political movements and ethnic peace accords have preceded the formation of the desired territorial status. Tripura and Manipur were cases apart as the former princely kingdoms, but both had political movements demanding statehood—in Tripura the movement was spearheaded by the Communist Party, which was the most powerful force locally. In the cases of the three Christian-dominated States (Mizoram, Meghalaya, and Nagaland), the local Baptist Mission in the late 1960s was quite active

[57] Bhaumik (n 56) 326.

[58] PS Datta, *Ethnic Peace accords in India* (Vikas Publishing House 1995) 156–60.

[59] ibid.

in pushing for statehood on the basis of religion, but soon switched to tribal ethnicity, realizing that a territorial entity based on religion would not be accepted.

The territorial reorganization in the North-East was quite distinct from that of mainland India in terms of the criteria and the constitutional evolution. But what was common was political mobilization; that is, there were political parties of different hues, mostly regionally based, which were at the forefront of movements for statehood. However, language was not a criterion here but tribal ethnicity was. With the exceptions of Tripura, Assam, and partly Manipur, other states were too linguistically diverse to use language as a criterion for territorial delimitation. Even though Manipuri is recognized as an official language, the persistent controversy about the right script has meant that official business is transacted in English and Hindi. In the case of Tripura,[60] the ancient identity with the princely region was the main plank of the CPI fighting for statehood status. None of the tribal-dominated states in the region has only one dominant tribe; for example, there are various groups of Nagas. In Arunachal Pradesh, the picture remains the same. In the latter, the protection of traditional cultural identity of the tribes was the main consideration.[61] While conceding tribal district councils (under the Sixth Schedule of the Constitution) was easier for tribal dominated areas, the statehood movements in Mizoram, Meghalaya, and Nagaland entailed long processes of ethnic violence and ethnic peace accords. Strategic considerations have played an important role in conceding statehood status to these small units in order to transform yesterday's ethnic rebels into tomorrow's stakeholders, who then take charge of upholding law and order and political stability. In most cases except Arunachal Pradesh, tribal leaders made use of the rhetoric of national self-determination, as is evident in the terms of the ethnic peace accords.[62]

The region today has a population of more than 30 million and eight states, most of which are very small, compared with other Indian states. It is not as violent as before although there are still ethnic militants, who often engage in extortion and mindless violence. However, a major and unresolved territorial issue remains; namely, the Bodoland question in Assam. A Bodo Territorial Council for the Bodos (plains tribes) was formed after two ethnic peace accords in 1993 and 2003 in an area where the Bodos are no longer a majority; even so, thirty of forty-six seats have been over reserved for the Bodos to the dismay and continuing discontent among the non-Bodo tribal and non-tribal communities which comprise about 70 percent of the population. With this outstanding exception, the successive states reorganization in the region has been responsible for enduring ethnic peace and political order.

India's reorganization of its territory has remained somewhat incomplete even today, although most of the potential roots of ethnic conflicts have been addressed. In many cases, the status of Union Territory, with very limited or no real autonomy and political institutions of governance, preceded the formation of states—as happened in Goa, Arunachal Pradesh, and Mizoram in 1987. Goa had its distinctive identity as a former Portuguese colony as well as the Konkani language, which was a factor. (Konkani was constitutionally recognized as an official language in 2004.) In the other two cases in India's North-East, strategic considerations, tribal ethnicity, and increased ethnic

[60] The SRC recommended its merger with Assam but the Government of India did not accept the proposal.

[61] Jhumpa Mukherjee, *Conflict Resolution in Multicultural Societies: The Case of India* (Sage Publications 2014) 90–2.

[62] In the rest of India, ethnic peace negations and accords were conspicuous by their absence because, unlike the rest of India, India's North-East were infested with militant and often underground ethnic militancy.

insurgency in the 1980s were factors—which led to the Ethnic Peace negotiations and Accords.[63] In 2000 the BJP-led coalition at the Center created three new states: Chhattisgarh out of Madhya Pradesh, Jharkhand out of Bihar, and Uttarakhand out of Uttar Pradesh.[64] In these cases, not language, but regional under- development, tribal ethnicity, and ecology were criteria, which represented a concession by the BJP-led National Democratic Alliance, which had believed in creating states only on administrative criteria. Finally, in the lead-up to the election of 2014, the Congress-led coalition at the Center addressed the long-standing question of Telangana, a new Telugu-speaking state carved out of Andhra Pradesh. Both the Congress and BJP-led party coalitions were committed to this for different reasons and for the first time the Union Parliament used its unilateral powers to create a state against the wishes of the state that was losing territory.

Outcome

State reorganization has happened in several phases: during the 1950s and 1960s; the early 1970s; the late 1980s; 2000s; and, finally in 2014. This political engineering has resulted in major changes in the federal political structure of India and been largely successful. Over time, the arrangements gave shape to Indian federalism. The late W.H. Morris-Jones observed:

> States Reorganisation is best regarded as clearing the ground for national integration. It seems at least likely that refusal to grant political recognition to the cultural areas would have focused and held all political attention on this one spot. The newly refashioned units, it is true, have a self-conscious coherence and pride but they are willing, thus equipped, to do business with the Centre, to work as part of a whole that is India.[65]

Linguistic states have not weakened the Center or paralyzed the federal structure—new states got themselves involved in cooperating with the Center for planning and economic development apart from maintaining the law and order, as an important competence of the states. Why India, the world's most socially and culturally diverse country, has been able to hold itself together despite many odds, is greatly due to the effective institutional engineering in the 1950s and 1960s, and subsequently too, which managed to recast and create subnational units with the purpose of making linguistically homogenous units as far as possible. As a result, the Telugus got their own state (Andhra Pradesh); Malayalis, their Kerala; Marathis, their Maharashtra; Tamils, their Tamil Nadu; Gujaratis, their Gujarat; the Sikhs, their Punjab, and so on. In the latter case, language could not be of the same use as in others, but the Sikhs were desperate and therefore finally even settled down with a truncated Punjab. As the late Khushwant Singh[66] commented, with a great dose of emotion:

[63] Datta (n 58) 142–52.

[64] Bhattacharyya, "India creates three new states" (n 28); Louise Tillin, *Remapping India: New States and their Political Origins* (Oxford University Press 2014).

[65] WH Morris-Jones, *The Government and Politics of India* (4th rev. edn., The Eothen Press 1987) 101.

[66] Khushwant Singh, *A History of the Sikhs, Volume 2: 1839–1964* (Princeton University Press 1966) 304–5.

The only chance of survival of the Sikhs as a separate community is to create a State in which they form a compact of groups, where the teaching of Gurumukhi[67] and the Sikh religion is compulsory.[68]

India's federation-building though is far from complete. There have been further demands for reorganization and more demands are being made even today. As of December 2017 there were demands for at least nine new states, all by way of bifurcating the existing ones, such as Harit Pradesh (from Western UP), Purbachal (from Eastern UP), Vidarbha from Maharashtra, and Bodoland from Assam. But language has since not figured prominently in calls for constitutional change. In the case of the North-East, with seven federal units where the process was largely completed in 1972, tribal affiliations rather than language played the most important role. In the three states created in 2000, a complex of regional identity, tribal identity, ecology, and underdevelopment were factors. The latest case of Telangana is a unique story[69] in the sense that with its creation in 2014 there are now two states in the south of India where inhabitants speak the same language, although the regional distinctiveness of Telangana has remained important.

Since the political parties have been the most important factor, or actors, in eking a new state out of an existing state, it is important to make some reference to the outcome of state creation on India's party system and the federation in general. That the provincial units of the Congress Party were themselves the main actors in successfully getting a state out of some existing ones helped resolve intra-party tensions and create a better base of party support in the new states. Up until the fourth general elections in 1967, state reorganization largely consolidated Congress's mass support in the regions and reinforced the one-party dominant "Congress system," as it was called. However, there were exceptions of strong ethnic- and regional-based parties, such as the Sikh-based SAD Party in Punjab, the Mizo National Front in Mizoram, and others in the North-East. After1967, Congress units in many states increasingly were not able to hold on to their bases as more parties with a sharp focus on ethnic or regional identity emerged to challenge Congress dominance. The GMK (1967) in Tamil Nadu is a strong case in point. Other such parties followed suit, adding fuel to the growing erosion of support for Congress in the states. Further regionalization of India's party system since the 1980s has meant the near end of the "Congress system," or the "one party dominance." As Congress's hold declined, it turned to regional parties as part of national level coalition governments and this has continued with BJP-led coalitions. Despite the very good majority obtained by the BJP in the 2014 Lok Sabha elections, it had to depend in a pre-poll alliance on various regional parties for its success. Since the late 1960s, Center-state relations have deteriorated with the states run by non-Congress parties asserting more autonomy, thereby creating considerable tensions in

[67] The script of the language (Punjabi).

[68] For details, see Khushwant Singh, *A History of the Sikhs, Volume 1: 1469–1839* (Princeton University Press 1960).

[69] The States Reorganization Commission of 1955 had not recommended for the creation of a separate state, but recognized the Telangana issue with due considerations: "After taking all factors into consideration, we have come to the conclusion that it will be in the interests of Andhra as well as Telangana if, for the moment, the Telugus area is constituted into a separate State which may be known as the Hyderabad State with provisions for its unification with Andhra after the general elections likely to be held in or about 1961 . . . ' See *State Reorganization Commission Reports, 1955, Vol. 2*, ch. 5, 107.

the dynamics of the federation.[70] The BJP (created in 1980) was hardly affected by the process, but the creation of three new states in 2000, when the coalition led by the party was in power, benefitted the BJP only temporarily because its political base in the new states dwindled. It has very often depended on state-based tribal parties or movements, such as the Jharkhand Mukti Morcha in the case of Jharkhand, for forming coalition governments in that state. In Chhattisgarh and Uttarakhand, the other two states it created when in office, it has seen its political fate alternate with that of Congress.

The creation of many subnational units through states reorganization has meant more democratic legitimacy to the whole federal system by bringing the government closer to the people in a large very populous country such as India. During the struggle for independence the Congress Party had created its Provincial Committees in accordance with ethno-regional considerations that brought the party closer to the people and linguistically more intelligible to them too. This had happened since the emergence of M.K. Gandhi in Indian politics in the early 1920s. This democratization accompanying states reorganization has not, however, produced equal political dividends for Congress because the latter upheld always, in public, pluralism, and hence could not fully identify itself with the subnational forces of ethno-regionalism; many strongly ethno-regionalist-oriented political forces emerged and took away the political mantle.

States reorganization has also produced another impact in the internal dynamics of state politics. Since some major caste and classes were the leading interests behind the demand for states reorganization, and the main beneficiaries, formation of new states has also resulted in the proliferation of region- and subregion-based political parties and groups demanding territories based on micro-ethnic identity. But given their size and concentration, they were not powerful enough to pose a serious challenge to the system as a whole. In some cases, substate-level territorial authority as per the Constitution has been conceded, which territorialized conflicts.

States reorganization has also created new, apparently insoluble, problems in some cases. Since the creation of Nagaland in 1963 as India's first tribal ethnic state, various Naga rebel groups kept demanding Nagalim, a greater Nagaland, which would incorporate the Naga inhabited areas in the neighboring states of Assam, Arunachal Pradesh, and Manipur. On August 3, 2015, Prime Minister Narendra Modi signed a "Framework Agreement" with the National Socialist Council of Nagaland (Issac-Muivah group) whose content is still not available publicly. On September 27, 2017, eight Naga groups were invited to New Delhi by the Union government for talks but so far nothing has come out as of spring 2018. There is, however, strong opposition from the affected states to part with their territory particularly because the affected states were not taken into confidence by Prime Minister Modi when he signed the "Framework Agreement." If the Nagas get their Nagalim, it would produce repercussions throughout India, and adversely affect the multicultural mosaic of the country and the states within it.

But such exercises, as above, have helped India recognize ethno-linguistic cleavages and identities, accommodated them by providing relative autonomy within the federation, and thus turned yesterday's ethnic rebels into today's and tomorrow's defenders of law and order, responsible also for the delivery of some public benefits. As I have

[70] Harihar Bhattacharyya, "Globalization and Indian Federalism: Reassertions of States' Rights" in Hans Lofgren and Prakash Sarangi (eds), *The Politics and Culture of Globalisation in India and Australia* (Social Science Press 2009) 99.

argued elsewhere,[71] this has satiated what I have termed "thick nations" and facilitated their willingness and role in the development of the "thin nation;" that is, the nation as a political community, which is in short supply still in India.

Lessons Learned

The fact that the states have relatively autonomous powers has meant that recognition of major territorial cleavages through state reorganization—whether linguistic, ethnic, tribal, or even quasi-religious (as in Punjab)—has been able to relieve tensions within the federation and provide major groups with a sense of self-government. In addition, the transfer of some territories between the states has promoted mutually congenial existence between some contiguous units, although inter-state border disputes remain in many cases, especially in the North-East. While statehood helped resolve conflicts and relieve tensions within the federation, it produced differential effects, notably those who spearheaded the movement for statehood—the political elites and groups (linguistic, caste, class, and tribal) that they represented—were the main beneficiaries.[72] Linguistic and other minorities within the new states were often disadvantaged or even discriminated against in civil service employment, political representation, and services, such as linguistic education. Thus the dominant castes of the Kammas and the Reddys in the Andhra movement, or the Lingayats and the Volkyaligas in the case of Karnataka, were the key players and the main beneficiaries in their states. In the case of Punjab, which became a Sikh-majority state, not all Sikhs benefitted equally: the Jat Sikhs, the dominant castes emerged in control, while the Harijan Sikhs (the poorer and laboring classes) had little influence in state politics. However, this very fact of dominance in certain states meant that the controlling groups were able to maintain political order and stability.

The criteria determining the creation of India's states have proven flexible, so that over time the federation has become composed of states that are very different in size and in their underlying character. The early state creations were essentially linguistic in character, though even then other criteria weighed and some major linguistic reorganizations, notably the creation out of Maharashtra and Gujarat out of Bombay, were put off in the first round. Over time other criteria became more central as the Center responded to insurgencies and political mobilization. Thus in the North-East, ethnic and tribal factors were key and they led to states that are much smaller than those in mainland India. In the case of Punjab, language was given as the primary official justification for creating the state, but the real pressure was more religious in character. In practice, certain informal criteria have developed and been widely accepted with regards state creation: demonstrable popular support; appropriate leadership; economic viability; and the non-secessionist nature of the movements. In all official pronouncements on the issue, language apart, the administrative convenience and economic viability have always been emphasized since the days of the Dar Commission (1948).[73]

[71] Harihar Bhattacharyya, "Federalism and Competing Nations in India" in Michael Burgess and John Pinder (eds), *Multinational Federations* (Routledge 2007) 50–68; Bhattacharyya, "Ethnic and Civic Nationhood in India."

[72] Roger King pointed out that why Jawaharlal Nehru was initially a little reluctant in conceding to linguistic statehood was because he saw in such "linguistic chauvinism" the lurking interests of the dominant castes and classes; see King (n 34).

[73] This was India's first linguistic commission formed in 1948 to advise the Constituent Assembly of India on linguistic statehood.

On process, India's unique arrangement whereby the Constitution assigns almost unilateral powers to the Union Parliament to redraw states has served the country well. In fact, it has almost always been done with the consent of the affected states (Telangana was an exception) and on occasion the Center has backed down on the inclusion of some territory in a new state in the face of resistance by the state of origin. But given the political map of India at the outset, and the progressive mobilization of territorial groups over time, the flexibility of the Indian Constitution has served the country very well. This procedure stands in stark contrast to that in most federations, where no state's boundaries can be altered without its consent. While at the end of the day the process is largely political, the use of official commissions, most notably the State Reorganization Commission in the 1950s, provided an effective way to come up with a coherent set of proposals, based on extensive study and consultations. There was never any question in India of referendums to validate such changes and it is hard to imagine that they would have been helpful. Each commission's recommendations were subject to political review and in some cases significant adjustment.

The staging of the process of new state creation served the country well. Most cases were conducted peacefully and through normal political debate and mobilization, though in some cases, notably in the North-East, reorganization came in response to violent ethnic mobilization followed by peace accords. It can be argued there were incoherencies in the staging of the process; for example, not dividing bilingual Bombay in the first round of linguistic state formation, but these were of minor long-term importance. What has been more significant has been the ability of the huge and complex Indian system to respond to developments and pressures affecting millions of people as they arise. There is no way that the current map of twenty-nine states could have been drawn in one step during the 1950s. And the process is not over. Even now, there are pressures for the creation of yet more states, such as breaking up Utter Pradesh, which has well over 100 million people. However, the unfulfilled cases of statehood demand are not the major issues in current Indian politics. That strongly suggests that the recurrent state reorganizations have worked in India in ensuring relative political order, unity, and peace despite complex diversity.

Another aspect of India's approach to progressive staging of state creation which holds lessons is that resizing did not always lead directly to full state powers for the new units, but in some cases was accompanied by a staging of the transfer of powers. This was especially the case in the North-East where the new units sometimes had different statuses—Union Territory, Sub-Statehood (Sikkim) or Tribal Autonomous District Councils with considerable autonomy, or Associate Statehood (Meghalaya and Sikkim)—before they became full states. India has various asymmetric arrangements, such as the Special Category States (financially very dependent on the Center) and the provisions for Autonomous Tribal District Councils (in the North-East) (as an example of asymmetric arrangement within asymmetry), which have added further flexibility to the process of accommodating diversity, while promoting better order and political stability.

The successes of achieving territorial ambition by the major ethnic groups have produced ill effects for the linguistic and ethnic minorities, who in turn have mobilized against "ethnic deprivation" and for the protection of their identity. Such minorities, often called "micro-minorities," are quite sizeable, in numbers and proportion. In other words, the political principle of majoritarian rule that is at work at all levels of the polity creates the fear among minorities of being dominated and deprived. This has not always resulted in demanding a separate statehood because of the lack of territorial compactness. The democratic protections of a non-territorial nature under Articles 345 and 347 of the Indian Constitution are supposed to help out. But these non-territorial safeguards are no match for the control over government and administration by an ethnic or linguistic majority. The 50th Report of the Commissioner for Linguistic Minorities (2013) found that most states have not ensured the use of local minority languages in official purposes.[74]

This calls attention to the effects of *majoritarian political principle* at work at all levels of the polity. India's social plurality has arguably not been reflected to the desired extent in the institutional arrangements. Too often, the institutional accommodation of identity has been essentially mono-ethnic, rather than multi-ethnic, within the territorial units. This reflects the majoritarian principle, but runs counter to the social and cultural plurality at the ground level. "The winners take it all" principle may not be as accommodative of plurality. In nearly all cases, right-sizing the states has produced linguistic and other ethnic minorities. Territorially dispersed as they are, their capacity to create effective political pressures are limited.

Finally, while state reorganization can answer some needs, it may not respond to others. The ongoing neo-liberal reforms in India since 1991, which have transformed India from a public sector dominated to a private sector, market-driven economy, may have rendered territorial demands for statehood less attractive than before. The states today have to compete for investment, foreign and indigenous, and promote trade and business in their realm; the days of assured central financial support and the Planning Commission (abolished in early 2015) grants to supplement the State Plans are gone. Not all the states have reaped the benefits of reforms since 1991, which are concentrated in a few so-called "Forward States." The states in the North-East, for instance, have not benefitted at all from investment because of a host of constraints (land-locked, remote location, security, and unproductive land). But then as India's "security region," they receive various kinds of grants for development from the Center. However, the latest reports on India's public policy performance strongly suggest that even the states in the North-East have performed well in a variety of welfare and empowerment activities, including better rule of law compared with India's advanced states.[75] This adds, arguably, to better social cohesion among the diverse population in these states too. One can safely conclude that India's recurrent territorial reorganizations have been the most powerful factor responsible for India's enduring political order and stability.

[74] 50th Report of the Commissioner for Linguistic Minorities in India (July 2012 to June 2013) (New Delhi: Ministry of Minority Affairs, Government of India).

[75] Rajeev Malhotra, *India's Public Policy Report 2014: Tackling Poverty, Hunger and Malnutrition* (Oxford University Press 2014).

6

Dealing with Territorial Cleavages in Constitutional Transitions in Iraq

*Zaid Al-Ali**

Overview

Iraq's territorial cleavage between Arabs and Kurds was prioritized throughout the entire transition process, but was so seriously mismanaged that it has caused detriment to the country's entire system of governance. The interim Constitution was the first attempt to resolve the issue, at least on a temporary basis. It provided for the establishment of Iraq's first federal arrangement and for provinces to merge together and form larger regions, which had the potential to seriously change Iraq's internal arrangements. The text was conceived through a US-led and undemocratic negotiation process that excluded a large number of Iraqi actors. After January 2005, the newly elected interim parliament composed a fifty-five- (later seventy-) member Constitution drafting committee. That committee adopted a majoritarian approach to decision-making, which pushed the draft in favor of a more traditional form of federalism, but which left minority views (generally those of the Kurdish negotiators) unrepresented. Rather than prolong the process and insist on a more consensual approach, the US embassy and a small number of Iraqi allies decided that the negotiations should continue on an invitation-only basis, which excluded a large number of actors. The draft Constitution that emerged from that new process was heavily inspired by the interim Constitution. Although that draft was approved in the October 2005 referendum, a large segment of Iraq's political class has refused to apply the federal system of government (the Constitution's cornerstone) and its provision on natural resources. The result is that Iraq's territorial cleavage has been left unresolved and has been festering since 2005.

Background

Iraq's population is highly diverse, and includes large numbers of religious and linguistic groups. Arabs form the country's largest group (at approximately 75 percent of the population) and speak Arabic as their mother tongue; by and large they do not speak any other languages.[1] They are not religiously homogenous, with Shia Muslims

* The author is grateful to Cale Salih, George Anderson, and Haider Hamoudi for their comments on an earlier draft of this chapter. I am solely responsible for the positions that are set out in this chapter and for any mistakes.

[1] The Baath Party and other nationalist movements argued for decades that Arabs constituted a unique ethnic group, but a survey of Iraq's own Arab population (which includes people of all colors) quickly dispels that notion.

Territory and Power in Constitutional Transitions. First Edition. Edited by Michael Anderson and Sujit Choudhry. Dealing with Territorial Cleavages in Constitutional Transitions in Iraq

constituting a majority and Sunni Muslims a minority.[2] Kurds form the second largest community.[3] They speak Kurdish as their mother tongue, although several dialects of the language exist.[4]

Many of Iraq's communities live in mixed areas, such as the capital Baghdad, Kirkuk, Mosul, Erbil, Basra, and others. Other parts of Iraq's territory are nearly homogenous. Arabs live and form a majority in almost all of the country's territory apart from the Kurdistan Region. Kurds are spread across Iraq, Turkey, Syria, Iran, and Lebanon and are often referred to as the world's largest stateless minority.[5] Iraq's Kurds are concentrated in the three northern provinces (Dohuk, Erbil, and Suleimaniya), which make up the autonomous Kurdistan Region. Many were traditionally villagers and farmers living in the distant mountain ranges along the borders with Turkey and Iran, where there was often poor access to basic services, including education and health care. Kurds also live in many other parts of the country, including in Kirkuk province and city, which has been a source of major controversy during the recent constitutional drafting process.

Iraqi history has become highly politicized. Some scholars maintain that Iraq had no historical precedent prior to the twentieth century and that its current territory had previously consisted of three Ottoman *vilayets* that had nothing to do with each other except all being controlled from distant Istanbul, so that Kurds and Arabs have little in common and should never have been made to live in the confines of the Iraqi state.[6] A number of historical studies have argued in response that while Iraq's current territory was part of the much larger Ottoman State, it was governed as its own administrative entity prior to the twentieth century, and that the three supposed Ottoman entities that housed what became Iraq's Arab and Kurdish populations themselves never existed, or at least never existed in the form that some assume.[7] Others have also maintained that regardless of the precise administrative arrangement, the territory known as Iraq and the Iraqi people have existed since antiquity.[8]

Regardless, as World War I came to an end, Iraq's territory fell under the United Kingdom's "protection" and it was under British auspices that the modern Iraqi state

[2] There is some argument as to how relevant that religious divide has been in history, but there is little point denying how important it has become since 2003, and in particular since 2014.

[3] A number of other communities exist in Iraq, including the Turkoman and Assyrian communities, but while some are concentrated in specific geographic areas and while appeals were made (and continue to be made) for this to be addressed in the Constitution, their situations provoked close to no interest amongst the constitutional negotiators at the time. This chapter will therefore limit itself to the controversies and discussions relating to the status of territories that were inhabited by Iraq's Kurdish population and to Kurdish language rights, as a reflection of the discussions that actually took place in the drafting chambers and not as a judgment on the validity of each community's position. There is some debate as to whether the controversies surrounding Sunnis and Shias are territorial in nature. I address this issue below.

[4] The main Kurdish dialect that is spoken in Iraq is known as Sorani, which is part of the Indo-European family of languages although it shares many words in common with Arabic. Several other Kurdish dialects are spoken in Iraq, including Badani and Fayli. Some Kurdish dialects are so far apart from each other in vocabulary and pronunciation that Kurds from different dialectical groups sometimes have to revert to a third language (usually Arabic, Turkish, or Farsi) to communicate with each other.

[5] Sonia Roy, "The Kurdish Issue" (2011) 13 Foreign Policy Journal, April 22, 2011.

[6] Anwar Anaid, "Learning From Iraq's Historical Lessons" (*Rudaw*, July 19, 2014) <http://rudaw.net/english/opinion/19072014>; Peter W Galbraith, *The End of Iraq: How American Incompetence Created a War Without End* (Simon & Schuster 2006).

[7] Reidar Visser, "Historical Myths of a Divided Iraq" (2008) 50 (2) Survival, 95.

[8] Abbas Kadhim, *Reclaiming Iraq: The 1920 Revolution and the Founding of the Modern State* (Kindle Edition, University of Texas Press 2012).

came into existence. The state quickly emerged as a monarchy. The country's population as a whole suffered from poverty, illiteracy, and disease. Faisal bin Hussein, a wartime British ally who was originally from the Hijaz area of modern-day Saudi Arabia, and who had very little connection to Iraq or to its population, was chosen to be the country's king. Shortly after he settled in the country, he described a majority of his subjects in the following terms: "This government rules over a Kurdish part, most of which consists of a majority of ignorant people [. . .] and an ignorant Shi'a majority that belongs to the same [ethnicity as] the government. But the oppression they had under the Turkish rule did not enable them to participate in the governance or give them the training to do so."[9] That contemptuous attitude toward Iraq's communities was reflected both in the legal rights that were afforded to them and to the treatment that they received.

By 1925, a new Constitution had been adopted.[10] It provided for a fully centralized state, which allowed for the country's new authorities in Baghdad to hoard all the powers that London had previously granted to itself. There was hardly any recognition of Iraq's rich history of multiculturalism. Arabic was the only recognized language (article 17) and the only provision dedicated to minority language rights left everything to law, thereby allowing the new authorities to give and take away community rights whenever they saw fit (article 16). In addition, the Constitution created administrative districts, but left their borders, powers, and administration entirely to law, practically guaranteeing that they would never have any authority whatsoever (articles 109–12). The absence of constitutional rights, combined with bigotry at the highest levels of government as well as geographic disadvantage of those who lived furthest from Baghdad, ensured that the state would continue to neglect the rights of the poorest and most destitute. The result was that Kurds who did not speak Arabic were often unable to read official documents, such as laws, regulations, court decisions and orders, none of which were translated on a regular basis; they were not afforded equal opportunities to employment; and the areas that they lived in were starved of public investment.

Although many other areas and communities in the country also suffered during that same period, discriminatory treatment against the Kurds was particularly acute firstly because human investment needs were so high, and secondly because their treatment was often coupled with military repression, including bombing campaigns first by the UK's Royal Air Force and secondly by the Iraqi military. A significant proportion of Iraq's Kurdish population was displaced from areas that were rich in natural resources (most notably from Kirkuk city) by virtue of government policy and as a result of the ongoing conflict, leading to serious charges of ethnic cleansing. In addition, successive governments redrew provincial boundaries to dilute Kurdish demographic weight in specific provinces.[11] A guerilla war that was concentrated in the northern mountains eventually broke out and lasted for decades.[12] An attempt was made in the 1970s by the then ruling Baath Party to bring the conflict to an end, which included

[9] ibid, 2782.

[10] All of Iraq's previous Constitutions, including the 1925 Constitution, are available here: Zaid Al-Ali's website, "Iraq's Constitution" (*zaidalali.com*) <www.zaidalali.com/resources/constitution-of-iraq/>.

[11] Mainly in Kirkuk province, which was officially named Tamim province.

[12] Although the guerilla war received significant support from regional powers that were seeking to exert pressure on the Iraqi authorities in Baghdad, foreign support alone would never have sustained operations against the Iraqi army for such a long period of time in the absence of strong support from the local population, which itself would not have been forthcoming without a strong sense of injustice. See Michael M Gunter, "Foreign Influences on the Kurdish Insurgency in Iraq" (1992) 12 (4) Conflict Quarterly 7.

the introduction in the 1970 interim Constitution of Kurdish national rights. Article 5 of the new Constitution specifically stated that Iraq was composed of both an Arab and a Kurdish nation, and also "acknowledge[d] the national rights of the Kurdish People and the legitimate rights of all minorities within Iraq's unity." The new Constitution was followed by the passage in 1975 of an autonomy law which provided for the existence of a Kurdistan autonomous region with an elected regional assembly for the first time. These reforms eventually failed to have any meaningful impact firstly because the autonomy that was offered actually left all real decision-making power firmly in Baghdad's hands and secondly because, modest as they were, the reforms were not properly implemented.

That failure was followed by a decade of conflict between Iraq and Iran during the 1980s. kurdish guerillas were involved in the fighting , ultimately culminating in a brutal military campaign by the Saddam Hussein's military against the bulk of the country's Kurdish citizens, including through the use of chemical weapons. More than a hundred thousand were killed, a million people were displaced, and thousands of villages were razed to the ground. That disaster was followed by the 1991 Gulf War, which ultimately led to the imposition by the USA of a "no-fly zone" which prevented the Iraqi military from reasserting control over the country's Kurdish north. The result was that Iraq's three northern provinces established themselves as a semi-independent region, with Erbil as its capital, which had virtually no contact with the rest of Iraq. It was not recognized as an independent country internationally, but to all intents and purposes that is what it was: it adopted a different currency from the rest of Iraq, it maintained its own foreign relations and trade with surrounding nations (although much of that consisted of cross-border smuggling), and it was separated from the rest of the country by a military front. The region was jointly governed by the two main Kurdish parties, namely the Kurdistan Democratic Party (KDP) and the Patriotic Union of Kurdistan (PUK). Each controlled separate territories (with the KDP mainly concentrated in Dohuk and Erbil, and the PUK in control of Suleimania province) and also maintained separate armed factions with rival military commands.

Although the region was supposed to be democratic (and indeed, elections were organized and resulted in the formation of a parliament and government), tribal land disputes eventually spiraled into a full-scale internal civil war. Eventually, in 1996, this led to the formation of an internal border that remained in existence until 2003. Despite these (and many other) problems, the region nevertheless managed to improve standards of living considerably, particularly in comparison with the rest of the country. The political atmosphere was far more open than in the rest of Iraq, and international organizations were given a much freer hand to operate. The rest of the country languished under the Baath Party and the most comprehensive sanctions regime ever devised.

By 2003, Kurdish national aspirations had evolved to the point where Kurds could conceive establishing their own state. The Kurdish parties had administered the territories under their control with some (albeit qualified) success. They entered the post-2003 era with the intention of securing (and possibly expanding) the autonomy that they had gained in 1991. They also hoped to expand their mandate over territories that they claimed historical rights to. Finally, control over natural resources was vitally important to Kurdish ambitions in large part because it would improve the chances of financial self-sufficiency for any future Kurdish state. It was therefore equally important to extend control over Kirkuk province (which included some of Iraq's largest deposits) and over the unexplored fields that existed within the Kurdistan Region proper.

In March 2003, Iraq was invaded by the militaries of the USA and the UK with some small support from Australia, ultimately causing the end of Baath Party rule in Baghdad a few weeks later. Many of Iraq's exiled opposition parties, including its main Kurdish parties, had long planned for the day after the Baath Party's fall, in particularly by preparing draft Constitutions of their own. Some had even participated in major conferences in which the country's political future was discussed. There is no question however that the main catalyst for the transition and the subsequent constitutional drafting process was the US-led military invasion. Were it not for the invasion, there would not have been a transition from Baath Party rule.[13]

Prior to 2003, many of the political parties that were based in exile, as well as the two main Kurdish parties, engaged in indirect and direct discussions on a number of occasions to debate how the Iraqi state should be structured if ever the Baath party's regime should fall. On occasion, one of the opposition parties would publish a draft Constitution that expressed that particular party's views on governance. For the most part, those documents were drafted without any significant debate, and were sometimes even the product of single individuals working without any significant oversight. Some of the draft Constitutions that were produced during that period provided for federalism, but included very little detail on how their proposed mechanisms would function. As the 2003 war approached, a small number of conferences and dialogue sessions were organized, mostly by the US and the UK governments, supposedly to allow for the opposition parties to debate their country's future constitutional framework in a more comprehensive manner. Although the sessions confirmed that the country's vertical distribution of power (and whether or not to adopt a federal model) was going to be crucial in any post-war environment, they were generally a failure in that the parties did not make any significant progress in reaching an agreement. The only principle that parties appeared to agree on was that Iraq should not be structured along ethno-sectarian lines, though this was with the notable exception of the two Kurdish parties.[14]

The Period of Constitutional Engagement

The dynamics of occupation dictated who participated in the Constitution drafting process. The USA and the UK created the Coalition Provisional Authority (CPA), the country's highest civilian authority from 2003 to 2004, which played a major role in determining how the transition process would be organized. The CPA itself created a separate body known as the Governing Council, which was populated by all of the USA's closest political allies in the country. The KDP and the PUK were perhaps the most important beneficiaries of that arrangement. They were considered by the USA to be the only parties that wholeheartedly welcomed the invasion and subsequent occupation of Iraq (other parties were at best enthusiastic about the fall of the Baath Party while being opposed to the US occupation that followed).[15] They were also among

[13] The question as to whether a transition from Baath Party rule might have taken place pursuant to the wave of uprisings that swept the region starting in 2011 is beyond the scope of this chapter.

[14] For more on the pre-2003 efforts by the USA and the UK to forge an agreement between Iraqi opposition groups, see Conference of the Iraqi Opposition, "Final Report on the Transition to Democracy in Iraq" (The Democratic Principles Workshop working document 2002) <http://www.wadinet.de/news/dokus/transition_to_democracy.pdf>.

[15] Henri J Barkey, "On-again, Off-again Alliance: The History of Washington and the Kurds" (*Foreign Affairs*, August 21, 2014) <www.foreignaffairs.com/articles/iraq/2014-08-21/again-again-alliance>.

the only sophisticated political actors in Iraq at the time, and benefited from the assistance of a number of foreign (including US) advisers who advocated on their behalf at the CPA and with the relevant authorities in Washington.[16] The two Kurdish parties utilized their privileged relationship with the USA to significant benefit during the subsequent constitutional negotiations.

The main (and in my view only) territorial issue that characterized the constitutional negotiation process was the relationship between the Kurdistan Region and the rest of Iraq, which related to who should have ultimate control over specific parts of territory. There were many controversies involving Sunni and Shia Arabs, but those were not territorial in nature. The main areas of contention between those two groups was first whether Iraqis should resist the US occupation,[17] and then revolved around who should be in control over the government in Baghdad. There was never any suggestion of exerting direct physical control over other communities' territories; nor were there ever any genuine political disputes between the two sides either. Sunni parties were strongly in favor of a strongly centralized form of government (a position that they inherited from the pre-2003 era) as were most Shia parties and movements (including the Sadrist movement as well as the Dawa Party, which would come to play a dominant role in Iraq from 2005 onwards).[18] Some years after the Constitution entered into force, in 2011, a number of Sunni politicians argued that Sunni-majority provinces should invoke Article 119 and transform into regions (which they hoped would grant them as much autonomy from Baghdad as the Kurdistan Region),[19] but even that evolution cannot be classified as a territorial dispute, given that an equal number of Shia politicians were also arguing in favor of the same outcome for Shia-majority provinces. The main motivation behind this changing political environment was uncontrolled and unchecked government corruption and brutality by Baghdad's security services that affected all Iraqi provinces, as opposed to a territorial dispute of any kind.[20]

The CPA and the Governing Council spent the end of 2003 and the start of 2004 drafting a document known as the Law of Administration for the State of Iraq (also

[16] This created a huge opportunity for foreign advisers to influence the process in ways that remain little understood today. Some of these individuals have in fact been remarkably forthcoming about the drafting process and about the influence that they had. Some advisers encouraged their Iraqi clients to adopt radical views that were very likely to increase tensions with other Iraqi actors over the long term, with little regard for the consequences. This applies to many issues including federalism, territorial rights, and natural resources. See, for example, Galbraith (n 6).

[17] Neither group was entirely decided on this point. Most mainstream Sunni (including the Muslim Brotherhood affiliated Iraqi Islamic Party) and Shia groups were totally invested in the US-led process, but many components of both communities (including the Sadrist movement, which was perhaps the most powerful Shia group at the time) rejected and actively resisted the US occupation through the force of arms.

[18] The only Shia party which held strongly federal positions was the Islamic Supreme Council of Iraq (ISCI). Although ISCI managed to dominate discourse within the Shia community at the time, it was only able to do so as a result of its superior organizational capacity and not because of the popularity of its views. In fact, based on subsequent electoral results, it emerged that ISCI enjoys between 5 percent and 7 percent popular support in the country (which is to say around 10 percent popular support within the Shia community). For more, see Zaid Al-Ali, "Constitutional Legitimacy in Iraq: What Role Local Context?" in Rainer Grote and Tilmann J Röder (eds), *Constitutionalism in Islamic Countries: Between Upheaval and Continuity* (Oxford University Press 2011).

[19] Article 119 of the Iraqi Constitution provides: "One or more provinces shall have the right to organize into a region based on a request to be voted on in a referendum submitted in one of the following two methods: (1) A request by one-third of the council members of each governorate intending to form a region. (2) A request by one-tenth of the voters in each of the provinces intending to form a region."

[20] Zaid Al-Ali "Iraqi Regionalism and its Discontents" (*Open Democracy*, December 3, 2011) <www.opendemocracy.net/zaid-al-ali/iraqi-regionalism-and-its-discontents>.

known as the "Transitional Administrative Law" or the "TAL"), which was designed as an interim Constitution.[21] It was similar in form to many other interim Constitutions that were enacted during periods of transition: it established a new system of government for the country, which was supposed to be applied throughout the interim period, and also included a road map for how Iraq would transition to a new and permanent constitutional arrangement. The key difference between the TAL and its counterparts from other countries is that it was not the product of a true negotiation between Iraq's main political actors: much of the drafting was carried out by a very small group of American and Iraqi-American officials, and the key political disputes were negotiated between the CPA (which took on that responsibility without any legitimate basis to do so) and the Kurdistan Alliance, without any involvement from other Iraqi actors. The result was that the TAL was widely viewed as wholly inadequate by a large segment of Iraq's political class, which agitated against the document as soon as it entered into force.[22]

Although the Kurdistan Region had already been in existence for twelve years at that point, the CPA did not immediately take it for granted that the Region would survive in its existing form. Senior level discussions took place during late 2003 and early 2004 between US and Kurdistan officials on how to resolve the issue—Iraqis from other parts of the country were not invited to participate. It was eventually decided that the Kurdistan Region would not surrender any of the autonomy that it had acquired since 1991.[23] That decision prompted some parties in the rest of Iraq to demand that they should also benefit from the same privileges that the Kurdistan Region was being granted.[24] Other issues of contention during the discussions included natural resources (namely which level of government should enter into contracts, should exploit resources, should market internationally, and should cash in revenues) and language rights.

Naturally, the question of how to correct what became known as the "disputed territories" was critical in the drafting of the TAL. This included a number of issues that needed to be resolved including: (a) individual property (mainly owned by Kurds) that had been seized by the Iraqi state, and redistributed to state institutions, to government officials or to other individuals, many of whom were encouraged to move to specific geographic areas by the state; (b) the displacement of individuals and communities from these same areas with a view to rebalancing demographics in favor of specific groups; and (c) the state's redrawing of internal provincial boundaries for the purpose of reducing the demographic weight of specific groups in a number of provinces (namely in Kirkuk province).

In 2004, the CPA established a Property Claims Commission, which had as its mandate to "resolve real property claims in a fair and judicious manner" for disputes arising from governmental actions that took place between July 17, 1968 and April 9, 2003. It allowed for immovable property that was "confiscated, seized, expropriated, forcibly

[21] For a history of how the TAL was negotiated, see Larry Diamond, *Squandered Victory: The American Occupation and the Bungled Effort to Bring Democracy to Iraq* (Holt Paperbacks 2006); see also L Paul Bremer III and Malcolm McConell, *My Year in Iraq: The Struggle to Build a Future of Hope* (Simon & Schuster 2006).

[22] Hamza Hendawi, "Shiites Won't Sign Interim Constitution" (*The Washington Post*, Baghdad, Iraq, March 5, 2004) <www.washingtonpost.com/wp-dyn/articles/A34345-2004Mar5.html>.

[23] See Bremer and McConell (n 21).

[24] Saad Sarhan and Ellen Knickmeyer, "Shiites Call for Own State in South" (*The Washington Post*, Najaf, Iraq, August 12, 2005) <www.washingtonpost.com/wp-dyn/content/article/2005/08/11/AR2005081101791.html>.

acquired for less than full value, or otherwise taken, by the former governments of Iraq for reasons other than land reform or lawfully used eminent domain. Any taking that was due to the owner's or possessor's opposition to the former governments of Iraq, or their ethnicity, religion, or sect, or for purpose of ethnic cleansing, shall meet this standard" (Article 9).[25] The Commission's establishment and the importance of its mandate were eventually incorporated into the TAL, which provided in relevant part that the "Iraqi Transitional Government, and especially the Iraqi Property Claims Commission and other relevant bodies, shall act expeditiously to take measures to remedy the injustice caused by the previous regime's practices in altering the demographic character of certain regions, including Kirkuk, by deporting and expelling individuals from their places of residence, forcing migration in and out of the region, settling individuals alien to the region, depriving the inhabitants of work, and correcting nationality" (Article 58(A)).

On the issue of territorial boundaries, the TAL provided that, prior to 2003, the Iraqi state "the Presidency Council of the Iraqi Transitional Government shall make recommendations to the National Assembly on remedying these unjust changes in the permanent constitution. In the event the Presidency Council is unable to agree unanimously on a set of recommendations, it shall unanimously appoint a neutral arbitrator to examine the issue and make recommendations. In the event the Presidency Council is unable to agree on an arbitrator, it shall request the Secretary General of the United Nations to appoint a distinguished international person to be the arbitrator" (Article 58(B)). Finally, the TAL defers final settlement of the disputed territories issue until "a fair and transparent census has been conducted and the permanent constitution has been ratified" (Article 58(C)).

Article 60 of the TAL provided that a Transitional National Assembly would be elected in January 2005, that the entire drafting process should take place in six months, and that it should be completed by August 15, 2005. A three-month public consultation process would follow, in which Iraqis would be given the opportunity to debate and discuss the draft, followed by a referendum that should take place on October 15, 2005. The TAL also provided that in the event an extension of time became necessary, a one-time-only six-month extension could be granted. Finally, the TAL stated that, assuming that the new Constitution would be approved in the referendum, new parliamentary elections should take place by December 2005.[26] Naturally, those parties and individuals which disapproved of the occupation and who considered its influence over the country's political future to be illegitimate played no role over the process and subsequent discussions.

Following the completion of the TAL, sovereignty was formally transferred to an Iraqi administration in June 2004, which had as its main responsibility to organize elections that were eventually held in January 2005. The electoral law provided that Iraq's entire territory would consist of a single electoral district and that the 275 members of the Transitional National Assembly (TNA) would be elected on a proportional basis. The elections were marked by significant violence but were generally considered to be free and fair. The United Iraqi Alliance, which purported to represent Iraq's Shia majority obtained close to majority of seats in the new assembly, while the Kurdistan Alliance was close to a quarter of seats. Representatives of Iraq's Sunni Arabs,

[25] The Property Claims Commission was established by virtue of CPA Regulation Number 8, which itself was later amended by Regulation Number 12, dated June 24, 2004.

[26] The details of the transition plan are set out in Article 60 of the Transitional Administrative Law, Law of Administration for the State of Iraq for the Transitional Period, March 8, 2004 (Iraq).

one of the country's main ethno-sectarian groups, boycotted the elections and as such were seriously underrepresented in the Assembly.[27]

Following the elections, a fifty-five-member Constitution-drafting committee (CDC) was appointed from amongst the TNA's members.[28] Although the CDC commenced work in May, fifteen additional members, who supposedly represented Iraq's Sunni Arabs, were allowed to join the committee in June. The first source of difficulty was the CDC's internal rules, which it drafted in May 2005, and which allowed for substantive issues to be decided on a majoritarian basis. That rule and the inclusion of the additional fifteen members created an unforeseen dynamic within the committee. The CDC, particularly after it was expanded from fifty-five to seventy members, included a large majority of members who were determined to establish a federal system of government but one in which the federal government in Baghdad would play a key role in maintaining national unity and in which regional autonomy (even in the Kurdistan Region) would be greatly reduced. Most Arab members of the CDC (Sunni and Shia alike) were also socially conservative and sought to reflect that perspective in their work. Kurdish members, who were generally in favor of maintaining the same federal system that was established by the TAL and who were also broadly more socially liberal than their Arab counterparts, found that they were systematically in a minority in the discussions.

The drafts that were produced by the CDC reflected the views of the majority of its members. Over time, the list of exclusive federal powers expanded from seven powers in the first iteration to more than twenty-one at the end of the CDC's tenure. The drafters had also included provisions that predetermined how any federal regions (including the Kurdistan Region) would have to be organized internally. During the CDC's tenure, the draft Constitution was evolving in a way that would have brought Iraq closer to some of the world's most well-established federations. Kurdish members of the CDC resisted this trend but were consistently outvoted, and found that they were unable to steer the discussions in a direction that was more to their liking. The CDC's drafts were also peppered with references to Islam and traditional family values. That was also particularly disconcerting to many US officials who were determined not to see Iraq establish itself as an Islamic republic under its watch.

By early August 2005, the CDC had made significant progress on a number of issues, but clearly required additional time to complete its work. The TAL included a provision that allowed for a single six-month extension and some members were calling for more time to be granted in order to allow for the negotiations to proceed. Instead, the CDC's work was discontinued and a new, informal body known as the "Leadership Council" was formed to continue drafting the text. The Council's first meeting took place at the US embassy in Baghdad, and then continued at the headquarters of the Kurdistan Alliance. Because the Council's meetings were informal, it is unclear to this day who participated, although there is general agreement that American and British diplomats were involved and that members of the Kurdistan Alliance played a key role in the discussion.[29] The Council continued making changes to the draft Constitution

[27] That level of underrepresentation was not reflected in the Constitutional Committee due to an ad hoc decision to include fifteen Sunni members of the Committee (see n 29).

[28] For a detailed account of Iraq's constitutional drafting process, see Zaid Al-Ali, *The Struggle for Iraq's Future: How Corruption, Incompetence and Sectarianism Have Undermined Democracy* (Yale University Press 2014); Haider Hamoudi, *Negotiating in Civil Conflict: Constitutional Construction and Imperfect Bargaining in Iraq* (University of Chicago Press 2013).

[29] See this discussion at Chatham House, in which the former UK ambassador to Iraq clearly states that he played a role in the negotiations; Chatham House, "Iraq's Political Systems" (*Youtube*, March 20, 2013) <www.youtube.com/watch?v=7AkLGqmPjU8>; the same former UK ambassador makes

until October 13, 2005, which is to say, two days before the referendum date. The Transitional National Assembly, which was elected to draft the Constitution, found that the drafting body that it appointed to carry out its work was dissolved and that it was not allowed to oversee, debate, or vote on the draft Constitution.

US and Iraqi officials who defended the Leadership Council did so on the basis that it was the only way in which the original referendum date (which was set for October 15, 2005 almost entirely for the benefit of US concerns about having a Constitution before the US elections the following year) could be met. Violence increased steadily in the capital and elsewhere throughout the summer of 2005, and some US and Iraqi officials considered that a new election would bring into existence a new political settlement that would allow for a gradual return to normalcy. Because a new election could only be organized after the drafting of the Constitution was completed, the implication was that the drafting process should be rushed, even if this meant doing so informally and without the formal mechanisms that had been agreed upon.

Not only did this justification turn out to be a terrible miscalculation (violence quadrupled following the December 2005 elections), it also obfuscates a key distinction between the CDC on the one hand and the Leadership Council on the other. As already noted, the Leadership Council's work was generally dominated by representatives from the Kurdistan Alliance and the US embassy, which was reflected in its work. As soon as the Council assumed control over the process, the drafts that it produced deleted all of the provisions on the federal system of government that the CDC had prepared and replaced them with the provisions from the TAL, which reflected the outcome of negotiations that had taken place between the US-dominated CPA on the one hand and the Kurdistan Alliance on the other. As a result, the final draft of the Iraqi Constitution, which was finalized by the Leadership Council, satisfied the interests of one party to Iraq's constitutional negotiations (albeit a major one) and a foreign occupying force. As we shall see, this posed a major issue for the implementation of the Constitution in the coming years.

The final Constitution established a federal system of government that placed Baghdad at a distinct disadvantage in comparison to the regions and the provinces.[30] It includes a short list of exclusive federal powers (Article 110), and an even shorter list of shared powers (Article 114). The key provision is Article 115, which firmly tilts the balance of powers in favor of regions and provinces, and provides that "[a]ll powers not stipulated in the exclusive powers of the federal government belong to the authorities of the regions and provinces that are not organized in a region. With regard to other powers shared between the federal government and the regional government, priority shall be given to the law of the regions and provinces not organized in a region in case of dispute." Taken together, these provisions leave the federal government significantly under-empowered. For example, Article 110 provides that the federal government is exclusively competent to "formulate and execute" national security policy while it is only responsible for "formulating" fiscal, monetary and customs policy. Given Article 115, which gives residual powers to the regions and provinces, this suggests that the federal government can formulate such policies but that it may not have the authority to execute its own policies. The federal government is therefore responsible for raising

the same admission in the following discussion, also at Chatham House, NCFAnalysis, "Ranj Alaaldin and Zaid Al-Ali Discuss Iraq at Chatham House" (*Youtube*, March 18, 2014) <www.youtube.com/watch?v=_mXX10rbDEE>.

30 An unofficial translation of Iraq's final Constitution is available at Zaid Al-Ali's website (n 10).

and maintaining a national army and police force but may not be allowed to directly raise any revenue to finance their operations.

The Constitution recognizes the existence of the Kurdistan Region but also keeps open the possibility, as did the TAL, that other regions might be formed (Article 117). Thus the informal arrangement that allowed for the Kurdistan Region to operate independently from Baghdad prior to 2003 was more or less adopted by the Constitution with some modifications (Baghdad would be responsible for a small number of exclusive federal powers, including determining fiscal policy and defense). In addition, Article 118 provides that the federal parliament "shall enact, in a period not to exceed six months from the date of its first session, a law that defines the executive procedures to form regions [for other provinces], by a simple majority of the members present." The constitutional drafters, clearly aware of the risk that a significant portion of the first post-Constitution federal parliament might not agree with the constitutional framework's spirit, established a normal threshold for passing such a law. In contrast, the parliamentary deputies and her two speakers can only be elected by "an absolute majority of the total number" of the parliament's members" (Article 55). Although a region-formation law was eventually passed pursuant to Article 118 in October 2006, a large number of political parties from various political groups and communities boycotted the vote and many also alleged that there was no quorum and that the vote should not have been allowed to take place.[31]

The ownership and management of oil and gas revenues were also particularly contentious during the constitutional negotiations. The final text is once again the result of the flawed bargains that were struck and last minute drafting behind closed doors by the Leadership Council and is perhaps the clearest illustration of the Kurdish Alliance's influence over that body. Article 112 in particular is worthy of attention here. It provides that "[t]he federal government, with the producing provinces and regional governments, shall undertake the management of oil and gas extracted from current fields." The reference to "current fields" is designed to create a distinction that had previously been unknown in Iraq and in other resource-rich countries between oil fields that are currently being exploited and those that have yet to have had any oil extracted from them. When read with Article 115, Article 112's drafters clearly intended for oil fields that were unexploited at the time when the Constitution was adopted to be under the sole control of "regions and provinces that are not organized in a region." It was not without coincidence that the bulk of Iraq's unexploited fields were located within the Kurdistan region or in Iraq's disputed territories. The combination between Article 112 and 115 were specifically designed to grant the KRG exclusive authority over the region's oil resources.

As such, not only does Article 112 create a distinction that has no technical or economic rationale in the management of national resources,[32] it also creates a hierarchy among Iraq's provinces and regions, given that the Kurdistan Region is the only part

[31] The region formation law has yet to be applied and Kurdistan remains the only federal region in the country. As indicated above, residents in several provinces (most notably Basra province) have repeatedly expressed an interest in making use of these provisions to vastly expand their autonomy. Several formal initiatives to transform some of Iraq's provinces into federal regions have been launched, but Iraq's federal institutions (including the Independent High Electoral Commission) have refused to cooperate. See Peter Schwartzstein, "Welcome to Basrastan" (*Foreign Policy*, Basra, Iraq, July 1, 2015) <http://foreignpolicy.com/2015/07/01/welcome-to-basrastan-iraq-basra-secession-oil-shiite-south/>.

[32] The only justification that was offered at the time was that other parts of Iraq could also benefit from this arrangement, and suggestions were made that significant unexplored deposits existed in what were considered to be resource poor provinces, such as Anbar province. There remains significant doubt as to whether such deposits exist, but in any event, no benefit has accrued to the inhabitants of these areas. See Gloria Lalumia, "Power Plays: Massive Iraqi Oil Reserves – Fact or

of the country that is known to have significant unexplored fields (reflecting the deliberate policy of Saddam Hussein's regime). Under the Kurdistan Region's interpretation of the provision, the Region shares with Baghdad the responsibility to "manage" oil and gas extracted from their own fields. Once again, under the Region's interpretation, this responsibility extends to allocating revenues that are generated from the sale of the relevant resources. The Region further argues that, given that Article 121(2) grants supremacy to regional law over national law in all areas apart from the powers that are exclusive to the federal government, the Region is entitled to disburse revenues generated from the sale of oil extracted from its own fields in accordance with its own, regional policies. Under its interpretation of these provisions, which were incorporated into the draft by Kurdish negotiators specifically to allow the Kurdistan Region to be able to make these arguments, the Region benefits from the distribution of national revenue that is raised through the sale of oil extracted from Iraq's vast southern oil fields, and it also keeps whatever revenue it raises from the exploitation of oil fields that were unexploited at the time the 2005 Constitution was drafted. Because no other part of Iraq has significant undeveloped oil fields, no other province can benefit from this arrangement, even if they transform into a region pursuant to Article 118.

Proponents of the Kurdish position have argued that the privileges that they obtained for themselves in the negotiations are necessary to redress decades of discrimination and oppression that Kurds were made to suffer under successive Iraqi governments. In response, Arab politicians and observers have convincingly argued that southern provinces were just as deserving of such preferential treatment, and that the Kurdistan Region's privileged status would inevitably contribute to resentment toward the Kurdistan region in the long term. That feeling could only be strengthened by the fact that the Kurdistan Region's privileged status is not stated openly in the constitutional text and that it only became apparent after detailed review and interpretation of several provisions coupled with detailed knowledge of the status of Iraq's various oil fields. That such an important constitutional principle can only be understood in this way suggests deliberate obfuscation by the drafters, which is always cause for suspicion and discomfort in any type of negotiation, particularly constitutional negotiations.

On the disputed territories of Kirkuk and elsewhere, the final Constitution does little more than to reiterate the provisions of the TAL on the same issue. It merely states that the "responsibility placed upon the executive branch of the Iraqi Transitional Government stipulated in Article 58 of the [TAL] shall extend and continue to the executive authority elected in accordance with this Constitution, provided that it accomplishes completely (normalization and census and concludes with a referendum in Kirkuk and other disputed territories to determine the will of their citizens), by a date not to exceed the 31st of December 2007" (Article 140). This therefore applies as much to individual property claims as well as to the effort to redraw administrative boundaries between Iraq's various provinces.

Outcome

The post-2005 phase of Iraq's transition was defined by the Leadership Council's coup against the constitutional process. The final Constitution's provisions on the most critical areas were not the result of a negotiated settlement by the country's dominant

Fiction?" (*Truth-Out.org World Energy Watch*, June 5, 2007) <www.truth-out.org/buzzflash/commentary/power-plays-massive-iraqi-oil-reserves--fact-or-fiction>.

political forces. It instead reflected the outcome of an undeclared coup against what was supposed to be a democratic process. Naturally therefore, when individuals who did not play a leading role in the Leadership Council's secret negotiations were elected to government, they found little in the Constitution that they agreed with and so simply refused to apply it. As a result, the Constitution's provisions on federalism, disputed territories and oil and gas, all of which were essential to resolving Iraq's territorial cleavage, were ignored.

Following the October 2005 constitutional referendum, parliamentary elections were organized in December 2005, bringing into power parties that for the most part did not participate in the drafting of the Constitution (particularly during the Leadership Council phase of the process). As soon as a new government was formed in May 2006, many parties and ministers immediately distanced themselves from the Constitution, and in particular from the federal system of government. Over the following ten years, in the vast majority of cases, these politicians' statements and positions were largely based on the biases that they inherited from the pre-2003 era, during which the entire system of government was heavily centralized. The Constitution's provisions on federalism were both alien and unclear to the bulk of Iraq's politicians outside the Kurdistan Region, who naturally refused to apply them.

As a result, the Arab parts of the country were administered on a strictly centralized basis. Even the Kurdistan Region, which managed to maintain significant levels of autonomy from Baghdad, was extremely centralized, causing officials in Suleimania and elsewhere to complain that every minor issue of policy would have to be approved by Erbil. Although provincial councils were directly elected by voters on several occasions, and governors were indirectly elected in every province, a provincial powers law that was passed in 2008 effectively stripped all of these offices of any authority. In addition, the federal government established ministries in a number of areas that it had no or limited constitutional authority over (including education and health care). Those ministries maintained offices in each of the country's provinces whose sole responsibility was to implement policy that was established at the federal level. The elected provincial authorities were powerless to influence the formulation of policy or its implementation.

In the meantime, corruption reached historic levels, while productivity in the country plummeted. Despite increased government revenue from oil exports, public services hardly improved for the general population. Over time, the general population grew increasingly frustrated with the federal government's failures to improve standards of living.[33] The justice sector was also in a lamentable state, with detainees constantly complaining of torture at the hands of security officials, and judges indifferent to their plight.[34] In response, groups of Iraqis in various provinces sought to make use of Article 118 to transform into regions and acquire the same status as the Kurdistan Region. This raised the possibility of the country fracturing along territorial lines. As a result, and despite the fact that it had no constitutional authority to do so, Baghdad blocked all these initiatives by refusing to allow the Independent Electoral Commission from

[33] Since 2005, Iraq has consistently ranked close to bottom of all international corruption-related rankings, including Transparency International. See, for example, Transparency International, *Corruption Perceptions Index 2016*, https://www.transparency.org/news/feature/corruption_perceptions_index_2016.

[34] See UNAMI Human Rights Office & Office of the High Commissioner for Human Rights, *Report on the judicial response to allegations of torture in Iraq* (United Nations in Iraq February 2015) <www.uniraq.org/index.php?option=com_k2&view=item&id=3429:report-on-the-judicial-response-to-allegations-of-torture-in-iraq-baghdad-february-2015&Itemid=650&lang=en>.

organizing referenda on the issue. Instead, as a sop to the disaffected oil-producing provinces, the federal authorities included a provision in the annual state budget to grant each of them US$1 for each barrel of oil produced. That innovation made close to no difference to the state of service delivery in these provinces (mainly because of corruption, mismanagement, and an absence of accountability mechanisms), which remains lamentable to this day.

The failure to apply the Constitution extended also to Article 140 on disputed territories. Although the Iraqi presidency did manage to produce reports on the matter as required by Article 58(C) of the TAL, the population census was never carried out. In December 2007, as the deadline imposed by Article 140 approached, the United Nations Assistance Mission to Iraq (UNAMI) was requested to make a series of proposals in the hope of resolving the matter. UNAMI's involvement lasted for three years and involved significant on the ground research to determine local context, dynamics, and preferences.[35] That effort was completed in 2009, and led to the formation of a high-level task force which was theoretically mandated to reach a solution, but never did. Instead, the following few years were characterized by stagnation and growing polarization. The 2009 provincial and 2010 parliamentary elections led to the emergence of Arab coalitions that were defined mainly by their opposition to Kurdish demands rather than any clear political vision of their own. In addition, federal security forces confronted the Kurdistan Region's own security forces on a number of occasions during this period, raising fears of a new conflict.[36] Tensions were so high that many observers feared that the relationship could break down altogether.[37] In a dramatic turn of events, as the Islamic State of Iraq and Syria (ISIS) invaded parts of northern Iraq in June 2015 from neighboring Syria, Kurdish security forces forcibly took possession of additional territory including Kirkuk city and some of the surrounding areas, arguing that the issue of disputed territories has now been finally resolved by virtue of facts on the ground.[38] Although Baghdad has refused to recognize Kurdish claims over these areas, the matter is unlikely to evolve until significant progress is made in the war against ISIS.

The relationship between the two sides also deteriorated on the issue of oil and gas. As early as 2004, the Kurdistan Regional Government (KRG) entered into direct contractual agreements with foreign oil companies, at first for exploratory contracts, but eventually also for extraction and export as well. After the 2005 Constitution entered into force, the KRG considered that these contracts were now retroactively brought into legal conformity, and also considered that it had full legal authorization to enter into new contracts with international oil companies to further its own industry.[39] Although the Constitution would be used to argue both sides of this argument, Iraq's federal

[35] For a summary of the efforts that were made by UNAMI, see Sean Kane, *Iraq's Disputed Territories: A View of the Political Horizon and Implications for U.S. Policy* (Peaceworks No. 69, United States Institute of Peace 2011).

[36] See Abdel Hamid Zebari, "Kurds Protest Iraqi Forces Sent to Syrian Border Region" (*al-Monitor*, Erbil, Iraq, March 8, 2013) <www.al-monitor.com/pulse/originals/2013/03/maliki-new-force-jazeera.html>.

[37] See International Crisis Group, "Iraq and the Kurds: Confronting Withdrawal Fears" (Middle East Report No. 103, International Crisis Group March 28, 2011).

[38] See Hunar Ahmed, "Official: Peshmerga Control 90 percent of 140 Previously 'Arabicized' Zones" (*Rudaw*, April 28, 2015) <www.rudaw.net/english/kurdistan/280420151>.

[39] In order to bolster its own position, the KRG obtained a legal opinion by James Crawford (Matrix Chambers, Gray's Inn, London) on January 29, 2008. The opinion is available online here: Kurdistan Regional Government Cabinet, "International Law Expert Confirms KRG's Authority to Manage Oil & Gas Resources" (*Kurdistan Regional Government*, February 5, 2008) <http://cabinet.gov.krd/a/d.aspx?s=010000&l=12&a=22631>.

authorities in Baghdad ignored any legal argument that it may have had to support its position favoring the use of power politics instead. Baghdad simply declared that all contracts with international oil companies should be signed by the federal ministry of oil and blacklisted all the companies that were operating in the Kurdistan Region from operating in the remainder of the country (a significant disincentive given that the bulk of Iraq's natural resources were located in the country's southern provinces). Meanwhile, Baghdad and the KRG worked to negotiate a federal oil and gas law; while a draft was published in 2007, it was never finalized, which has only contributed to the sense of uncertainty on this issue.[40]

Over Baghdad's objections, the KRG negotiated an agreement with Turkey to allow for the construction of a pipeline that ran from southwest of Erbil to the Mediterranean port of Ceyhan. After oil started flowing through the pipeline and some initial hesitations by the Turkish authorities, several tankers were loaded and departed in the expectation of locating international customers. Although the KRG ostensibly located a purchaser in Texas, its tanker was barred from entering US territorial waters after legal representatives of the Iraqi government laid claim to the cargo before a federal court.[41]

With time, the dispute surrounding the KRG's right to exploit and sell oil internationally caused the relationship between the two sides to suffer considerably.[42] Under former prime minister Nouri al-Maliki's administration, Baghdad sought to enforce its will by refusing to transfer the KRG's share of the national budget until the KRG accepted to work within the federal framework. The decision caused an unprecedented economic crisis in the Kurdistan Region. Construction contracts were frozen, and public servants were required to work for months without pay. Baghdad insisted that until the KRG allowed for all oil sales and international contracts to be managed by the federal authorities it would not resume any financial transfers to Erbil. Although the dispute was temporarily resolved through an agreement that was entered into in December 2014, it collapsed shortly thereafter.[43] Both parties accused the other of cheating, but more importantly, the sudden decline in world oil prices by

[40] An unofficial translation of the draw law is available here: Global Research, "The Official Draft of the Oil and Gas Law of the Iraq Republic, English Translation of the Leaked Document" (*Global Research*, February 20, 2007) <www.globalresearch.ca/the-official-draft-of-the-oil-and-gas-law-of-the-iraq-republic/4868>.

[41] The Iraqi government was eventually allowed to sue the KRG for possession of the oil. See Laurel Brubaker Calkins, "Iraq Allowed to Sue Kurds over Texas Oil Tanker in US" (*Bloomberg Business*, Iraq, January 8, 2015) <www.bloomberg.com/news/articles/2015-01-09/iraq-allowed-to-sue-kurds-over-texas-oil-tanker-in-u-s-1-> last updated January 8, 2015. The KRG eventually sold the oil to a buyer in Israel, which rendered the issue moot, according to the court. See Bruce Stanley and Laurel Brubaker Calkins, "Iraqi Kurds Dealt Setback by US Court Ruling on Oil Sale" (*Bloomberg Business*, Iraq, September 22, 2015) <www.bloomberg.com/news/articles/2015-09-22/kurds-lose-fight-to-sell-crude-oil-in-u-s-after-iraq-sues> last updated September 22, 2015.

[42] Importantly, the traditional rivalry between the KDP and the PUK meant that the relationship did not breakdown altogether. During the worst periods of tension between Baghdad and Erbil, the PUK's political leadership maintained strong ties with Baghdad, even saving Prime Minister al-Maliki from a no-confidence vote in 2012.

[43] The agreement provides that the KRG will provide 550,000 barrels of oil a day that will be sold through the federal government, with the proceeds divided between Baghdad and Erbil. This includes 300,000 barrels a day from Kirkuk, which has been under the KRG's physical control since June 2014. The agreement also provides that Baghdad will resume its budget transfers to the region, with special allocations for security personnel. The agreement already appears to be at the point of collapsing, with the KRG claiming that it has not received its full budget transfer, and Baghdad complaining that the KRG has halted oil exports through the federal authorities. See Rudaw, "Iraq PM Calls on Erbil to Honour Oil Agreement" (*Rudaw*, Erbil, Iraq, June 29, 2015) <www.rudaw.net/english/kurdistan/28062015>.

50 percent and the burdens brought by the war against ISIS have caused an economic crisis throughout Iraq. In particular, the KRG has found that it does not have sufficient funds to cover its administration's standard operating costs, causing many to doubt the KRG's claim to economic self-sufficiency.[44] The economic and security crisis was, in October 2015, compounded by a deep political rift between the KRG's main political forces which threatens to split the region apart, as during the 1990s.[45]

The KRG also suffered from an acute internal political crisis. Article 120 of the 2005 Constitution provides that regions were obliged to adopt regional Constitutions that should "define the structure of powers of the region." The Kurdistan Region's dominant parties tried to negotiate a text over a period of years, but were unable to reach an agreement mainly over disagreements on the regional president's term. Instead, the president's term and powers were governed by a regional law that was adopted in 2005.[46] Article 3 provides that the president could only serve two four-year terms. By 2013, the Region's dominant parties could not agree on how the president should be replaced or by whom, and instead agreed to extend his term by another two years. In 2015, the war against ISIS was used as a pretext by the regional president's party to delay any discussion of his term, which meant that he illegally remained in his post for two years. President Barzani dissolved the regional parliament after an opposition party grew too critical of his situation.[47]

By 2017, the KRG's economic and political crises continued to deteriorate. The regional president's party decided to organize an independence referendum on September 25, 2017. The regional president argued that independence was a constitutional right, based on a very particular interpretation of the constitutional preamble's final sentence.[48] In a thirty-page report that was published on the day of the report, the KRG argued that that sentence meant that Iraq was a "voluntary union" in which Kurdistan has "retained its sovereign status."[49] The report also listed a large number of constitutional violations by the Iraqi government, including the failure to resolve the status of disputed territories by the agreed deadline, which had expired ten years before. The report argues that the "voluntary union" is therefore no longer valid, entitling Kurdistan to organize an independence referendum in the territory that it controlled in September 2017, including the city of Kirkuk.

The report asserts this wording was deliberately chosen to allow Kurdistan to preserve its sovereignty, which it could exercise at any point by withdrawing from the union. But the wording itself—particularly the Arabic original—is so vague that it is essentially devoid of meaning. The idea that Iraq is made up of several sovereign states

[44] Mohammed Hussein, Patrick Osgood, and Rawaz Tahir, "Strikes Spreading over KRG Salary Delays" (*Iraq Oil Report*, October 6, 2015) <www.iraqoilreport.com/news/strikes-spreading-over-krg-salary-delays-16652/>.

[45] Kawa Hassan, "Kurdistan's Democracy on the Brink" (*Carnegie Middle East Center*, October 28, 2015) <carnegie-mec.org/2015/10/28/kurdistan-s-democracy-on-brink-pub-61810>; David Romano, "Is the KRG Failing the People" (*Rudaw*, October 23, 2015) <www.rudaw.net/english/opinion/23102015>.

[46] See KRG Law 1 (2005), <http://www.iraqld.iq/LoadLawBook.aspx?page=1&SC=&BookID=28025>.

[47] Luay al-Khateeb, "Kurdistan's Slow Rolling *coup d'état*" (*Brookings Institution*, October 15, 2015) <https://www.brookings.edu/opinions/kurdistans-slow-rolling-coup-detat/>.

[48] The preamble provides in relevant part that "[t]he adherence to this Constitution preserves for Iraq its free union of people, of land, and of sovereignty."

[49] See "The Constitutional Case for Kurdistan's Independence & A record of the violation of Iraq's constitution by successive Iraqi prime minister and ministers, the Council of Representatives, the Shura Council, the judiciary and the army" (Kurdistan Regional Government, September 24, 2017) <http://cabinet.gov.krd/a/d.aspx?s=040000&l=12&a=55856>.

is directly contradicted by a number of other provisions, including Article 1 that states Iraq is "a single federal, independent and fully sovereign state." Iraq's Federal Supreme Court issued a decision ordering the KRG to stay its referendum pending a final decision on a case on the same issue that was brought before the prime minister.[50] The KRG ignored the decision, preferring to challenge the Court's legitimacy.

The Iraqi government, regional powers such as Turkey and Iran, and international powers such as the USA, the UK, the EU, and the UN all encouraged the Kurdistan Region to abandon the independence referendum. The KRG pressed on however, based on an inflated appreciation of its own political importance, which was encouraged by a large number of international advisers who advised President Barzani that independence was assured.[51] The KRG's confidence was also based on its many successes during the 2005 constitutional negotiations. The referendum did take place, and the results confirmed that more than 90 percent of voters chose independence.

However, in the days and weeks that followed, Baghdad used its reconstructed army and affiliated armed groups to militarily reassert control over large parts of territory, including the divided city of Kirkuk. The Kurdistan Region was greatly reduced in size, and lost the majority of its oil resources in the process. Baghdad also forced the closure of the Kurdistan Region's airspace to all international travel, which all international airlines immediately complied with. Not a single regional or international power provided the KRG with any significant political support. The KRG was humiliated with the result and President Barzani resigned from his post and was not replaced.[52]

Lessons Learned

The Iraqi process is a powerful illustration of how negative negotiation tactics, and an unequal playing field, can impact the outcome of a constitutional drafting process. In an ideal situation, a Constitution should seek to achieve a number of objectives. First, it should reflect a sufficient degree of consensus between a country's political elites, particularly on the system of government. Majoritarianism, particularly in divided societies such as Iraq, can lead to disastrous outcomes, which is why whatever solution is reached should always be the product of a well-organized negotiation process.[53] Second, a Constitution should clearly define the relationship between the individual and the state in a way that imposes a burden on the latter to protect the rights of the former. Third, in countries that do not enjoy a strong judicial tradition, Constitutions should be sufficiently clear and detailed (wherever possible) to prevent major surprises

[50] Iraq Federal Supreme Court Decision 91 (2017) <https://iraqfsc.iq/krarat/1/2017/91_fed_2017.pdf>.

[51] See Ben Cohen, "Bernard-Henri Lévy Slams Turkish President Erdogan for Pushing 'Crudest, Worst' Antisemitic Campaign in Wake of Kurdish Independence Vote" (the Algemeiner, October 9, 2017). The article includes a by now infamous photograph of President Barzani surrounded by a dozen international advisers, including Peter Galbraith, Bernard Kouchner, and Bernard-Henri Lévy. President Barzani is sitting at a table and cutting an apple, with the advisers sitting beside him and standing beside him, almost all smiling.

[52] The decision not to replace President Barzani was only possible because of the constitutional vacuum in the Kurdistan Region. Because the regional Constitution was never adopted, the ruling parties decided to devise a new governance framework on their own without consulting the general public.

[53] Sujit Choudhry (ed.), *Constitutional Design for Divided Societies: Integration or Accommodation?* (Oxford University Press 2008).

that may arise from the implementation of the Constitution. In the event it is not possible to negotiate or draft detailed provisions on specific issues, the Constitution should either provide broad guidance or remain silent, leaving the matter to be resolved (hopefully) through subsequent legislation.

In Iraq, none of these principles were respected. The CDC was designed in a way that a majority of its members could easily control the drafting process regardless of what the minority thought. Its majoritarian approach pushed the drafting process toward an outcome that would have been unacceptable to the two Kurdish parties, and could have caused the entire process to fail altogether. Regrettably, the remedy that was imposed to resolve this problem was even worse than the disease. The Leadership Council's innovation was to abandon majoritarianism in favor of a perverse form of "minoritarianism;" only those individuals who agreed with a narrow version of federalism were allowed to participate in the discussions, creating a final Constitution that was far outside the popular mainstream.[54] The consequence was that, for the following ten years, the bulk of Iraq's political elites refused to apply many of its key provisions, and in the absence of rules to govern their behavior, they allowed for Iraq's key institutions (including its security apparatus) to completely fall apart.[55]

In addition, the constitutional drafters allowed for the negotiations to be dominated by their single-minded focus on constructing (or imposing) an elite pact. The only interests that mattered in that context were those of the political parties that were represented in the discussions, almost none of which are democratic in any sense of the word.[56] In that context, the interests of ordinary Iraqis were virtually ignored: almost no progress was made on a series of state-building issues (including improving the performance of the judiciary, and establishing mechanisms to improve the enforcement of rights), leaving ordinary Iraqis with very few tangible improvements to speak of.

Finally, the Iraqi Constitution is hopelessly vague (and on occasion completely contorted) on a large number of crucial issues, particularly those relating to the territorial dispute discussed above. Constitutional ambiguity is a useful tool in many circumstances. Some analysts have even argued that Iraq's constitutional negotiators were deliberately ambiguous on a number of issues.[57] There is no question that ambiguity can be useful to paper over disagreements on matters of general principle.[58] Fiscal

[54] Although the Constitution was approved by a large majority of the population in a referendum that took place in October 2005, the referendum results are not a good measure to assess the population's level of agreement with the actual text for a number of reasons, including but not limited to the following: (a) the final text of the Constitution was only shared with the general public two days before the referendum date; (b) the final text of the Constitution actually included a provision that specifically provided that the Constitution should be amended within four months, hardly reassuring for anyone that may have cast their vote on referendum day; (c) security deteriorated considerably during the constitutional drafting process, leading the general population to vote not on the basis of the draft's actual content (which, for the most part, no one had seen anyway) but on the basis of their own survival instincts; and (d) immediately after the new Constitution entered into force, many of the country's most senior leaders, including Moqtada Sadr and Nouri al-Maliki, who was prime minister from 2006 to 2014, insisted that the Constitution's federal system of government (the Constitution's cornerstone) should not be applied.

[55] Zaid Al-Ali, "Iraq's House of Cards" (*Foreign Policy*, Iraq, April 29, 2014) <http://foreignpolicy.com/2014/04/29/iraqs-house-of-cards/>.

[56] Almost all of Iraq's political parties are considered the personal property of families or specific individuals. To name but a few examples, the KDP has led by the Barzani family for decades. The same applies to the Islamic Supreme Council of Iraq, which has been led by the Al-Hakim family since 1982. Similarly, Al-Wifaq (a secular party) has been led by Ayad Allawi since 1991.

[57] Hamoudi (n 28).

[58] The negotiators successfully adopted that approach in relation to the status of Islam, which was granted the same status as the "principles of democracy" (see Article 2 of Iraq's final Constitution).

issues are very different in that if governments are to operate there needs to be clarity regarding revenue-raising authority. As soon as a Constitution enters into force, the following year's annual state budget will have to be drafted. In countries like Iraq, the same is true of natural resources given that, as a result of number of factors, monetary and fiscal prospects are entirely conflated with the state's capacity to generate income from the extraction and export of natural resources. On these issues, constitutional negotiators can adopt a number of approaches, including: (i) establishing clear constitutional rules that must be followed by future parliaments and government;[59] (ii) establishing broad principles that will have to be fleshed out in subsequent legislation in the immediate future; and (iii) remaining silent on the issue, therefore leaving the issue to be determined as soon as possible after the Constitution is completed.

Once again, however, the negotiators failed on this issue, and in spectacular fashion. They did not establish clear rules; nor did they set out broad principles; they did not even choose to remain silent. The final draft deliberately constructs a complex series of principles, which (only upon close inspection and through a feat of interpretation that would have been close to impossible during the drafting process) favored the Kurdistan Alliance in a unique way. Given the manner in which this arrangement was incorporated into the draft, it should not have come as a surprise that the bulk of Iraq's political class refused to respect it.

The long-term implications for this type of outcome are dire: the ruling elites' refusal to apply constitutional rules relating to federalism, natural resources and other crucial matters means that they are essentially running the country without any meaningful rules to govern their behavior. Iraq's ruling elites have learned not to trust the Constitution, the highest law of the land, and they have applied that same attitude to all subsequent legislation and agreements, few of which are respected. To make matters worse, the balance of forces in Iraq has changed since 2005: for a time in 2013 and 2014, the Kurdistan Region was being starved of funds by Baghdad, something that would have been unimaginable in 2005. The debacle following the failed 2017 independence referendum is another illustration of the changed and evolving balance of forces that Iraq has experienced since 2003.

The clock cannot be turned back to 2005. But if Iraq were somehow given a second chance to negotiate a new grand bargain, it would seem intuitive to recommend that no party should seek to enforce an agreement, whether through majoritarianism, a temporal advantage, or otherwise. All major decisions should be decided on the basis of consensus, which takes time. In Iraq, had more time been available and if the negotiation process had been constructed in a manner that encouraged consensus building, a more realistic and acceptable option for everyone might have been the construction of an asymmetric form of federalism, in which the Kurdistan Region enjoyed a greater level of autonomy than the rest of the country. Although analysts have been deliberating whether asymmetric federalism might have been appropriate for Iraq, we may never have the opportunity to apply that arrangement in practice.[60]

While that specific construction is yet to be understood, it allowed for what could potentially have become a major point of contention to be deferred until a later date.

[59] The German Basic Law is a good example of this type approach. See the Basic Law's Chapter 10 on financial issues. A translation of the German Basic Law is available here: <https://www.constituteproject.org/constitution/German_Federal_Republic_2014?lang=en>.

[60] Joost Hiltermann, Sean Kane, and Raad Alkadiri, "Iraq's Federalism Quandary" (2012) 118 The National Interest 20, 28.

Another obvious lesson is that, given how long consensus building can take, one has to make proper arrangements for what should happen in the interim period. And in that context, the effort of drafting an interim Constitution should be taken far more seriously, both procedurally and substantively, than it was in Iraq. An interim Constitution cannot and should not be considered merely as a 'stopgap' measure that will have no long term implications. By negotiating its terms, inexperienced political actors can build significant experience in negotiating and drafting, which can be crucial in the run up to the drafting of a permanent Constitution. In addition, the interim text's provisions, however conceived, will inevitably be reviewed and considered during the drafting of the permanent Constitution, and so therefore its tone and tenure are both very significant. If, however, the text is flawed and is the product of an undemocratic process, that will only encourage political actors to rush the drafting of the permanent Constitution, in order to be rid of the interim text.

Finally, one should also not hesitate to recommend that whatever arrangement is agreed upon should be recorded as clearly as possible so as to reduce opportunities for deliberate misconstruction or obstruction in the future. The experience of watching Iraqi politicians argue over poorly constructed constitutional provisions since 2005 has been a painful one and could so easily have been avoided had more emphasis been placed on organizing a deliberative constitutional process that had as its dual objective to build consensus on key issues and to construct a functioning state. Hopefully ours is an experience that other countries and peoples in similar situations will learn from.

7

Indonesia

"Special Autonomy" for Aceh and Papua

Jacques Bertrand

Overview

Indonesian politics have been characterized by a large number of territorial cleavages that have only been partially addressed since the beginning of democratization in 1998. It is a very diverse country with a history of several challenges to the state's external boundaries, as well as internal ethnic and religious conflict. A strong anti-colonial nationalist movement constructed a core set of symbols and ideas around which the nation and state of Indonesia were eventually created, including Bahasa Indonesia as the national language.[1] During three decades of authoritarian rule, the state primarily emphasized unity and national integrity over accommodating its diversity.[2] Repression was routinely used to quell rising grievances.

When the regime began to democratize in 1998, several groups mobilized and demanded more autonomous powers and resources. Most groups primarily grumbled over strong state centralization. Acehnese, Papuans, and East Timorese, however, developed sub-state nationalist movements, all of which demanded independence in response to deeply seated grievances. Decades of violent repression, human rights abuses at the hands of the armed forces, displacement, and marginalization fed strong resentment against the Indonesian state.

A "constitutional transition" began with the fall of President Suharto's authoritarian regime in May 1998 and ended with the adoption of the Law on Aceh in 2006. In the first instance, Indonesia's highest governing body, the People's Consultative Assembly (Majelis Permusyawaratan Rakyat, MPR) adopted several constitutional amendments between 1998 and 2002. While preserving the 1945 Constitution, which had formalized a strong centralist and authoritarian regime, the MPR nevertheless radically transformed its substance to support democratic change. Among its notable features, it enshrined principles of "wide-ranging autonomy" for Indonesia's diverse regions (Art. 18, sec. 2 and 5) and mandated the adoption of legislation that recognized the "particularities and diversity of each region" (Art. 18A, sec. 1). Legislation that addressed these issues includes two iterations of fiscal and administrative decentralization laws that applied to all regions of Indonesia, in 1999 and 2004.[3] The state adopted

[1] George McTurnan Kahin, *Nationalism and Revolution in Indonesia* (First published 1955, Cornell Southeast Asia Program Publications 2003); Benedict Anderson, *Imagined Communities: Reflections on the Origin and Spread of Nationalism* (Verso 1983) 113–14.

[2] Jacques Bertrand, *Nationalism and Ethnic Conflict in Indonesia* (Cambridge University Press 2004).

[3] Andrew Ellis, "Indonesia's Constitutional Change Reviewed" in Ross H McLeod and Andrew J MacIntyre (eds), *Indonesia: Democracy and the Promise of Good Governance* (Institute of Southeast Asian Studies 2007).

Territory and Power in Constitutional Transitions. First Edition. Edited by Michael Anderson and Sujit Choudhry. Indonesia: "Special Autonomy" for Aceh and Papua Published 2019 by Oxford University Press.

two special autonomy laws in 2001 to address grievances in Aceh and Papua. While the special autonomy law still governs Papua, it no longer applies to Aceh. Instead, new legislation ensures broad autonomy powers and highly favorable fiscal concessions under the 2006 Law on Aceh. East Timor obtained a referendum on independence in 1999, and seceded from Indonesia.[4]

In this chapter, I compare how Acehnese and Papuans negotiated this constitutional transition. While the Acehnese obtained very detailed and extensive powers under the Law on Aceh, Papuans have repeatedly rejected the Special Autonomy Law that they obtained in 2001. Conflict in Aceh has largely subsided, while it continues in Papua. I argue that Indonesia's incrementalist and responsive approach to constitutional change enabled a flexible and asymmetric accommodation of ethnic groups that has largely strengthened Indonesia's stability and democratic character. Nevertheless, it reached its limits in Papua, where the state's fear of secession fuels an overly defensive, and ultimately self-defeating approach. Furthermore, Papuans have been divided and much weaker than the Acehnese, whose sustained unity and insurgency placed strong pressure on the Indonesian government. As a result, low-level conflict continues to plague Papua and a more successful negotiated solution is still elusive.

Background

Indonesia was conceived as a unitary state, in spite of its vast diversity. The world's largest Muslim country, Indonesia's population of 242 million people is divided along a large number of ethnic groups, scattered across a vast archipelago. Major ethnic groups include the Javanese (42 percent), Sundanese (15.4 percent), Malay (3.5 percent), Madurese (3.4 percent), and Bataks (3 percent), all of the other fifty or so ethnic groups represent less than 3 percent of the population.[5] More than 300 languages are spoken. A large majority of the population is Muslim (87 percent), while 9.9 percent are Christian, 1.7 percent are Hindu, and others follow Buddhism and Confucianism.[6] Indonesia's diversity has been a perpetual challenge for crafters of the country's Constitution and democratic institutions.

Revolution and political instability marked Indonesia's early experience with ethnic minority accommodation, and set a path that supported strong, centralist tendencies. The Indonesian nation is a classic "imagined community" that was crafted out of a diverse population, whose main commonality was a shared experience of Dutch colonial rule. An anti-colonial nationalist movement emerged in the first decades of the twentieth century and coalesced around the promotion of a national language, Bahasa Indonesia, which was a dialect of Malay used as a lingua franca in large parts of the archipelago. Nationalist leaders Soekarno and Mohammad Hatta promoted unity among all peoples of the Dutch East Indies and shunned potentially divisive tools of mobilization, such as religion. Their views clashed with competing groups, such as the

[4] The case of East Timor is somewhat of an exception, and therefore not addressed in this chapter. Only a handful of countries had ever recognized Indonesia's integration of East Timor. There were therefore ongoing international negotiations with Portugal over its future status. International pressures at the time of the democratic opening, when Indonesia was also financially weakened, were decisive in the decision to allow a referendum.

[5] Republic of Indonesia, Badan Pusat Statistik, *Kewarganegaraan, Suku Bangsa, Agama dan Bahasa Sehari-hari Penduduk Indonesia – Hasil Sensus Penduduk 2010* (Badan Pusat Statistik 2011).

[6] Republic of Indonesia, Badan Pusat Statistik, "Penduduk Menurut Wilayah dan Agama yang Dianut" [Population by Region and Religion] in *Sensus Penduduk 2010* (Badan Pusat Statistik 2010).

political party Masjumi, which espoused Islam to create a unifying movement against the Dutch.

Nationalists under Soekarno and Hatta prevailed at the time of drafting a Constitution as the Japanese retreated in 1945 from occupying Indonesia for three years. In the brief window of opportunity before the Dutch returned, nationalist leaders, supported by Islamists and other political parties, declared independence. The 1945 Constitution enshrined a unitary state, and an institutional structure that created a strong and centralized presidential system. Its preamble recognized "Belief in One God," the first of five principles (Pancasila) that affirmed the basis of the state.[7] This principle constituted a rejection of an Islamic state, while recognizing the primary importance of religion in Indonesia. Furthermore, the original Constitution contained only one article devoted to regional governments, which were defined without reference to any ethnic group. An amended version of the 1945 Constitution remains in force today.[8]

Indonesia's leaders rejected federalism, which they considered divisive and destructive. When the Dutch returned in 1945, they slowly regained control over the archipelago. The Indonesian Revolution, as nationalists called it, fostered increasing unity among diverse populations that joined the fight against the returning Dutch. As they regained territorial control, the Dutch sought local support by creating several states that coincided with major concentrations of particular ethnic groups. From 1945 to 1949, the small army of the Indonesian Republic resisted Dutch advances but failed to gain the upper hand. Under international pressure from the United Nations, the Dutch finally agreed to grant independence to Indonesia but negotiated a constitution for the Republic of the United States of Indonesia (1949), which was based on a federation of the Dutch-created states with the Republic of Indonesia as one of its constituent parts. The constitution was short-lived as a unitarist movement swept the newly independent country and, within eight months, virtually all federal states voluntarily disbanded and joined the Republic.[9]

From this brief experience, federalism was subsequently shunned and virtually banished as a possible option to accommodate Indonesia's diversity. Instead, with a motto of "unity in diversity," Indonesia's political leaders strengthened the unitary state and the primacy of integrative policies over accommodating diversity.[10]

Indonesia's political leaders developed an almost obsessive emphasis on unity and centralization as the first decade of Indonesia's independence witnessed regional rebellions and deep divisions over the fundamental nature of the state. The first was an early secessionist attempt from South Makuku after the fall of the Dutch-sponsored federal state in 1950. The second blended regionalist rebellion with an Islamist agenda. The Darul Islam movement, which lasted until the early 1960s, rejected the Pancasila-based Indonesian state and sought to create an Islamic one. Yet, it found its roots in regions with very devout Islamic populations and strong regionalist resentment against

[7] The five principles, as stated in the Constitution are: belief in the One and Only God; just and civilized humanity; the unity of Indonesia; democratic life through deliberation among representatives of the people, and achieving social justice for all the people of Indonesia. See Kahin (n 1).

[8] The original one only came into force in the late 1950s, when Soekarno suspended the Constituent Assembly mandated to draft a new Constitution and declared a "return" to the 1945 Constitution.

[9] Arthur Schiller, *The Formation of Federal Indonesia, 1945–1949* (W Van Hoeve 1955).

[10] Kahin (n 1) 464; JD Legge, *Sukarno: A Political Biography* (first published 1972, 2nd edn, Allen & Unwin 1985) 223, 38–9; Hans Antlöv, "Federations-of-Intent in Indonesia, 1945–49" in R William Liddle (ed.), *Crafting Indonesian Democracy: International Conference toward Structural Reforms for Democratization in Indonesia* (Penerbat Mizan 2001).

the Indonesian state's centralizing tendencies. Its strongest supporters were based in South Sulawesi, West Java, and Aceh. Other regions also rebelled although not under the banner of the Darul Islam. The instability of the 1950s, and fears of secessionist activities, drove President Soekarno and part of Indonesia's political élite to favor strong state centralization and increasing repression to maintain unity.[11]

Under authoritarian rule, these tendencies were reinforced. Soekarno suspended in 1959 the Constituent Assembly that had been elected in 1955 to draft a new constitution. Although this measure came primarily from a deadlock between nationalist (pro-Pancasila) and Islamist visions for the future, regional rebellions loomed large and, in particular, those associated with the Darul Islam and the declaration of a Revolutionary Government of the Republic of Indonesia (PRRI) in 1958, which was the culmination of regional resentment at over-centralization—particularly in parts of Aceh, Sumatra, and Sulawesi—and an attempt to create an alternative Islamic state.[12] Its defeat strengthened the Indonesian armed forces' resolve to dissolve rebellions, and bolstered Soekarno's decision to establish authoritarian rule under his proclaimed Guided Democracy. As he decreed a "return" to the 1945 Constitution, Indonesia became firmly entrenched as a unitary state, with Pancasila as its foundation.[13]

The New Order regime of President Suharto, from 1965 to 1998, deepened state centralization. The new authoritarian regime resulted from a dramatic end to rising rivalry between the Communist Party and the armed forces under Guided Democracy. The armed forces won the upper hand and seized power directly under Suharto's leadership, while brutally eliminating its communist rival. Nevertheless, the 1945 Constitution was again upheld but used to strengthen even more the powers of the President and state institutions that supported authoritarian rule. The regime consequently repressed even more forcefully its perceived threats to the state's integrity and unity .

Against this backdrop, the regime banned mobilization along ethnic, religious, or regional lines. Expressions of political demands relating to SARA (Suku, Agama, Ras, Antar Golongan meaning ethnic, religious, race, or intergroup identity) were frowned upon, censored in the press, and generally prohibited. Political parties using Islam as a basis of organization were initially forced to amalgamate in 1973 into a party with no Islamic identifier (Unity Development Party, PPP). When the regime adopted regional law no. 5, 1974, it reaffirmed a division of the country into provinces and districts with no reference to ethnic groups. It recognized cultural diversity and celebrated different traditions but it reinvented cultural references to support the central Indonesian nation and Pancasila.[14]

Mobilization in Aceh and Papua arose against this strong centralizing regime. Yet, there were some important differences at the outset. Acehnese had fought with the Republic against the Dutch, and rejected Dutch attempts to create a federal state. Acehnese political leaders had supported Indonesian nationalism, and adhered to the idea of a united Indonesia. By contrast, Papuans were integrated into Indonesia only twenty years after the Revolution, because the Dutch retained West New Guinea at Indonesia's independence in 1949; therefore, they never shared the common struggle that united many ethnic groups against the Dutch.

[11] Cornelis van Dijk, *Rebellion under the Banner of Islam: The Darul Islam in Indonesia* (Martinus Nijhoff 1981).

[12] Barbara S Harvey, *Permesta: Half a Rebellion* (Cornell Modern Indonesia Project 1977).

[13] This implied a definite rejection of the Islamic state option, and the adoption of Pancasila's first principle, "Belief in One God."

[14] Law No. 5, 1974 on the Basic Principles of Administration in the Regions [*Undang-Undang No. 5, Tahun 1974 Tentang Pokok-Pokok Pemerintahan Di Daerah]* (Republic of Indonesia).

Late integration to Indonesia added a significant layer to grievances, since groups did not share the "myths" of revolutionary struggle against the Dutch. Papuans instead shared with East Timorese an experience of forced integration, repression, and assimilationist policies.[15] Soekarno made claims to West New Guinea throughout the first decade of independence. In response, the Dutch educated and prepared a small Papuan elite for independence. Yet, as tensions rose with Indonesia, the United Nations brokered an agreement in 1962 to cede the territory to Indonesia while a plebiscite was organized on its future. From 1963 to 1969, Papuans waited as part of Indonesia for the opportunity to choose whether to formally integrate it or become independent. East Timor was integrated even more forcibly. Soon after the Portuguese announced in 1975 plans for decolonization, Indonesia invaded the territory ostensibly at the invitation of one of the political parties struggling for power. Against the backdrop of a declaration of independence by one of the parties, Fretilin, the Indonesian armed forces intervened and brutally repressed subsequent resistance from Fretilin and its armed wing Falintil.[16]

Papuans were formally integrated through a United Nations sponsored process, the 1969 Act of Free Choice.[17] It constitutes Papuans' primary source of grievance. From 1963 to 1969, the New Order government repressed Papuans and implemented assimilationist policies. Then in 1969 it organized a process to meet the provision for a plebiscite that the UN had mandated. Instead of a referendum, however, it selected a little more than a hundred representatives that voted unanimously in favor of joining Indonesia. There is little doubt that the regime not only hand-picked these representatives but also intimidated them. Shortly after 1969, resistance began mostly with the creation of the Free Papua Movement (Organisasi Papua Merdeka).

Aside from this significant difference, Acehnese and Papuans shared a number of common grievances. First, they were both rich in natural resources, which began to be exploited under authoritarianism and whose benefits accrued primarily to the central government and large corporations. Second, against the backdrop of several decades of repressive and assimilationist policies, both regions were declared Military Operations Zones for the last decade of the New Order regime. Third and related to the previous point, human rights abuses were frequent.

Structurally, both groups are also similar but there are some important differences. Acehnese and Papuans are concentrated in defined territories, each at the western and eastern ends of the Indonesian archipelago respectively. Their populations are small, as they each constitute less than 2 percent of Indonesia's population. Yet, two characteristics differentiate them. The Acehnese are a much more cohesive and integrated group, as they share a single Acehnese language and view themselves as one ethnic group, while indigenous Papuans are divided between their overarching identity as Papuans and more localized identities. They speak a large number of local dialects, have strong tribal identities, and are politically divided among highlanders and coastal Papuans. Furthermore, they have become increasingly marginalized in their own land, after years of state-sponsored and spontaneous migration. Indigenous Papuans now constitute only a slight majority, whereas the Acehnese still constitute an overwhelming majority

[15] Bertrand, *Nationalism and Ethnic Conflict in Indonesia* (n 2).

[16] Fretilin (*Frente Revolucionária de Timor-Leste Independente*—the Revolutionary Front for the independence of East Timor) and Falintil (*Forças Armadas de Libertação Nacional Timor-Leste*—Armed forces for the National Liberation of East Timor).

[17] Pieter Drooglever, *An Act of Free Choice: Decolonization and the Right to Self-Determination in West Papua* (Oneworld Publications 2009).

in their region, which has seen very little migration from other areas of Indonesia. Finally, the Acehnese are generally more highly educated and their average incomes are much higher than Papuans, who rank among the poorest and least educated in Indonesia.

Before democratization in 1998, there were three significant phases to the conflict in Aceh. All of them arose partly out of the constitutional and institutional structures. As mentioned above, in the first phase Acehnese joined the Darul Islam rebellion against the Indonesian state. Aceh's leaders, mostly Islamic scholars, joined the rebellion and its broader objectives of an Islamic state for Indonesia. But they also resented the initial inclusion of Aceh within a much larger province of North Sumatra. The Darul Islam and the objective of an Islamic state were defeated, although Aceh regained its provincial status.

The next two phases were precursors to the more recent, violent conflict. The Free Aceh Movement (Gerakan Aceh Merdeka, GAM) first rose in 1976 when oil and gas were discovered offshore. The rebels resented that the central government and corporations extracted Aceh's resources with few local benefits.[18] The movement failed but rose again in 1989. At this point, its prime objective was clearly independence. Although it drew greater support, it was not entirely clear how broad its support actually might be. The armed forces brutally repressed the movement and attempted to weed out potential supporters by harshly repressing the Acehnese population over the following decade, during the period that it was declared a Military Operations Zone.

Papuans, for their part, remained divided and only mobilized sporadically. The Free Papua Organization (Organisasi Papua Merdeka, OPM) was mostly an umbrella organization of several more localized resistance groups, organized sometimes around local, tribal identities and loyalties, and other times around rival personalities. They were poorly armed and none of the groups ever mounted a significant armed rebellion. Their activities were limited to occasional attacks on soldiers, mines, or government offices. Even so, the armed forces strongly repressed Papuans, and conducted regular military operations to weed out suspected separatists. Only rarely did Papuans dare express their desire for independence, through the occasional flag raising. Periodic demonstrations in major cities often included demands for independence but were mostly focused on human rights abuses. Much of the violence was localized, particularly around Freeport-McMoran's large mining activities near Timika. With growing migration from other areas of Indonesia, indigenous Papuans became increasingly marginalized and displaced, while they remained poor, uneducated, and subjected to repressive state policies.[19]

The Period of Constitutional Engagement

The period of constitutional change began with the demise of authoritarian rule in 1998 and ended in 2006. After thirty-three years, the New Order regime of President Suharto collapsed, as a result of pressures to reform the regime, a leadership succession crisis, and the final catalyst of the Asian financial crisis of 1997. Under the leadership of

[18] Tim Kell, *The Roots of Acehnese Rebellion, 1989–1992* (Cornell Modern Indonesia Project 1995).

[19] Octovianus Mote and Danilyn Rutherford, "From Irian Jaya to Papua: The Limits of Primordialism in Indonesia's Troubled East" (2001) 72 Indonesia 115; Richard Chauvel, *Constructing Papuan Nationalism: History, Ethnicity, and Adaption* (East-West Center Washington 2005); Robin Osborne, *Indonesia's Secret War: The Guerilla Struggle in Irian Jaya* (Allen & Unwin 1985).

the transitional president, Habibie, Indonesia began to democratize. During the period from 1999 to 2002, the People's Consultative Assembly (Majelis Permusyawaratan Rakyat, MPR),[20] the country's highest legislative body, adopted four amendments to the 1945 Constitution. Through this evolutionary mechanism, the MPR transformed Indonesia's Constitution to support democratic change. Many of the major debates concerned direct presidential elections, the changing role of the MPR, and the changing role of the military.[21] Yet, in combination with several pieces of legislation culminating in the Law on Aceh (2006), these amendments altered Indonesia's relations between the center and regions. It transformed Indonesia from a centralized, unitary state to one still officially unitary but highly decentralized.

Prior to the 1999 elections, a consensus emerged within the MPR to preserve the Constitution instead of opening up negotiations for an entirely new one. The MPR represented the main political and military elite of the late New Order regime, as its members remained in place until the 1999 elections. This elite found a natural ally even among democratic reformers from political parties that had been opposed to the New Order regime, such as the Democratic Party of Indonesia for the Struggle (PDI-P) of Megawati Soekarnoputri, daughter of Indonesia's first president, Soekarno. They shared a strong commitment to preserving Pancasila and the principle of a unitary state. They resisted demands from street demonstrators demanding for deep reforms, including constitutional change. They feared that it might lead to deep divisions that could threaten Indonesia's unity and reopen the wounds of the past, particularly violence related to ideological challenges from the left and from Islamists. They passed the first amendment, the most important aspect of which was to impose a two-term limit on the presidency and strengthen the role of the legislature (Dewan Perwakilan Rakyat, DPR). By doing so, they sought to rebalance power toward the legislature, and curb the strong executive powers of the original Constitution of 1945 that enabled authoritarian rule. The MPR held the power to amend the Constitution by two-thirds of its representatives, with at least two-thirds of its members present. The formula was subsequently changed to allow amendments by 50 percent plus one with two-thirds of its members present.

After the 1999 elections and the formation of the new MPR, the crafting of constitutional amendments was delegated to a special ad hoc committee of the MPR (Panitia Ad Hoc I), composed of members of various political parties. Two parties dominated the committee and the new MPR; namely, the PDI-P of Megawati Soekarnoputri and Golkar, the old party of the New Order regime. The committee's work proceeded openly and with some public consultations, but was not a full-fledged, broadly advertised, consultative process. It proceeded through informal, interpersonal negotiations rather than truly open debate. Partly by design and partly by coincidence, the committee was able accomplish its work without broad awareness of the implications of the constitutional amendments, while public debate was more focused on the elections, the role of the military, a rising movement to oust President Wahid until 2000 and his replacement by Vice-President Megawati. It retained strong control over the process, and proceeded mostly by consensual agreement among all major political parties. As the President ruled with a multiparty cabinet and broad coalition within parliament, there were strong incentives to proceed by consensus. Despite the turmoil over President

[20] Under the New Order regime, the MPR was composed of members of the Indonesian parliament, representatives from the armed forces, and appointed members representing regions and a number of functional organizations.

[21] Ellis (n 3).

Wahid, its impact had little effect on this approach in the constitutional amendment process.[22]

The second and third amendments altered the structure of central-regional relations. Indonesia had several, hierarchically organized levels of administrative territorial organization: provinces, regencies/municipalities, districts, and villages.[23] Using a principle of "deconcentration," each level of government was responsible for implementing directives and policy from the central government. The Ministry of Interior appointed provincial and regency heads. Although provinces and regencies had their own parliaments, they essentially rubber-stamped central government policy.

The second amendment changed the basic principle of regional organization by providing wide-ranging autonomy to the 292 regencies (regions) and municipalities rather than to the twenty-six provinces.[24] They were given wide-ranging autonomy in all jurisdictions except those that, by law, were attributed to the central government. In combination with laws on administrative and fiscal decentralization, this constitutional change was designed to bypass the provinces and give more powers to regencies and municipalities. While the Jakarta elite supported the need for decentralization, it also feared that giving more powers to the provinces might revive regional tensions and demands for secession that haunted Indonesia's past and continued to challenge the central government in East Timor, Papua, and Aceh.

One clause also required that the "diversity of regions" be respected in adopting laws to regulate regional administration, while creating special units for "regional authorities that are special and distinct." This clause was a vague and hesitant attempt to introduce some asymmetry, and allow for different governance structures or a different set of powers to regions that have specific needs. The clause departed from the Indonesian government's previous insistence on homogenous structures and allocations of powers across regional units.[25] By accepting some asymmetry, it introduced more flexibility, and would make the Constitution consistent with the introduction of "special autonomy" laws to address specific conflicts in Aceh and Papua, while maintaining an across-the-board symmetrical, decentralized system at the regency level in the rest of Indonesia.

The second amendment did not create much controversy, in large part because legislation had already been adopted. In the late New Order, the central government had begun to think about decentralization as a possible solution for conflict in East Timor and Papua, but also as a necessary reform of the administrative system. When Habibie acceded to power, the "Team of Seven," mostly academics who were mandated to look into reforms of the political system convinced him to proceed with it. Most parliamentarians agreed with radical decentralization, as they saw it as necessary to

[22] Donald L Horowitz, *Constitutional Change and Democracy in Indonesia* (Cambridge University Press 2013) 74–6.

[23] For clarity, I use "regencies" to identify the territorial region below the province (*kabupaten*) and districts (*kecamatan*) for those below regencies. Other scholars use "districts" and "sub-districts" for *kabupaten* and *kecamatan* respectively.

[24] Krisztina Kis-Katos and Bambang Suharnoko Sjahrir, "The Impact of Fiscal and Political Decentralization on Local Public Investments in Indonesia" (Discussion Paper no. 7884, The Institute for the Study of Labor (IZA) 2014) 7. Because of the new resources available to this level of government, there was an explosion of requests to create new regencies and municipalities. As of November 2017, there were 514 regencies and municipalities. *Rekapitulasi Jumlah Ppid Provinsi, Kabupaten Dan Kota Update November 29, 2017* (http://www.kemendagri.go.id/media/filemanager/2017/12/04/f/i/file.pdf), accessed December 15, 2017).

[25] *Undang-Undang Dasar Republik Indonesia, 1945* (2006) (Constitution of the Republic of Indonesia 1945 (2006)).

reduce (or prevent) regional discontent. Furthermore, many bureaucrats, supported by foreign advisers, often hailed the advantages of decentralization to improve efficiency and accountability.

The Constitution itself did not specify the jurisdictions but the 1999 laws did. Law nos 22 and 25, 1999 on regional governance and fiscal decentralization respectively gave vast new powers to regencies. They obtained powers in all jurisdictions except foreign policy, defense, security, justice, and monetary and fiscal policy. In addition to these powers, new formulas redistributed much more fiscal resources to regencies, and provided them with new taxation powers.[26]

Some backlash occurred once the laws were introduced. Members of the armed forces, as well as PDI-P and Golkar, began to oppose the changes. As Smith notes, the armed forces realized that it would no longer dominate regional government once regency heads became elected. PDI-P and Golkar realized that they might lose control over their patronage networks and regional candidates. Nevertheless, the laws were upheld, as President Habibie and his cabinet emphasized the gains from "transparency" and "public participation," while downplaying the shift in power. In the end, Golkar members supported the laws and other parties accepted them reluctantly.[27]

Provincial governors were the strongest opponents of the 1999 laws, as they resented being by-passed while being expected to continue implementing central government directives. While the central government maintained a firm commitment to autonomy at the regency level, it made compromises by strengthening the position of provincial governors. In 2004, laws no. 32 and 33 replaced the 1999 laws.[28] Law no. 33 provided detailed modifications to the fiscal allocations previously specified in Law no. 25, 1999. The previous law was very ambiguous with respect to distributions between central, provincial, and regency governments of tax revenues, royalties, and other revenues from natural resources, which were to be determined by regulation. The law added many more details regarding the formulas for revenue allocation. Law no. 32, 2004 introduced direct elections for governors and regency heads. This change gave more independent voice to governors and regency heads who could claim direct popular support. The law replaced law no. 22, 1999, which was deemed to be confusing. Nevertheless, in terms of allocation of powers between the central government, provinces, and regencies, the net effect of the law was unclear and ambiguous. While it appeared to retain general principles of wide-ranging autonomy at the level of regencies, its wording also suggested more central and provincial government oversight to curtail some of those autonomous powers. Since much of the detail was relegated to regulations, and these were still being implemented several years thereafter, the final allocation of powers was unclear. More recently, there have been renewed debates to revisit once again these regional laws.

The third amendment created a Chamber of Regional Representatives (Dewan Perwakilan Daerah, DPD). As Horowitz has noted, it is an anomalous chamber as its members represent provinces, yet autonomous regions are at the municipal and district level: "A radical devolution is thus offset by a weak regional house that does not represent the principal units to which power is devolved."[29] As the military and the PDI-P

[26] Bertrand, *Nationalism and Ethnic Conflict in Indonesia* (n 2).

[27] Benjamin Smith, "The Origins of Regional Autonomy in Indonesia: Experts and the Marketing of Political Interests" (2008) 8 (2) Journal of East Asian Studies 211, 225–7.

[28] *Undang-Undang Republik Indonesia Nomor 32 Tahun 2004 Tentang Pemerintahan Daerah* (Law No. 32, 2004 of the Republic of Indonesia on Regional Government) (Republic of Indonesia).

[29] Horowitz (n 22) 127.

continued to strongly prefer a unitary and centralized state, they were most opposed to the DPD. Golkar and other parties with more support in regions outside of dominant Java sought a more genuine bicameral parliamentary system but they failed. The DPD was meant to represent regions equally, in spite of the fact that the island of Java, with only five provinces, holds about 60 percent of the total population. In the end, the DPD was formed out of a compromise. It is composed of three representatives from each province, but its total membership should not exceed a third of the total membership of the Indonesian parliament (DPR). More importantly, its powers were strongly diluted. It obtained no legislative powers; its role was to propose to the DPR bills that related to regions and their fiscal relationship to the center.

The process of adopting four amendments moved Indonesia decisively away from a unitary state. Its net effects, however, were uneven. It constitutionalized the principle of regional autonomy but at the same time decentralization laws undermined provincial power in favor of regencies.

For most of the regions of Indonesia, these changes responded to past grievances and were generally well received. Although the initial devolution in 1999 was designed in part to address deeper grievances in East Timor, Aceh, and Papua, the new laws had no effect on demands and mobilization in those regions. East Timor was offered early in 1999 a referendum on wide-ranging autonomy, which gave broad new powers at the provincial level. Although East Timorese rejected this option in the August referendum that led to independence, their experience created the strong precedent of allowing a referendum and, as well, of offering wide-ranging autonomy at the provincial level. These benchmarks became new bases for Acehnese and Papuans to claim similar options.

Aceh

The central government's limited attempts to address deep grievances in Aceh stimulated a new, unprecedented round of violent mobilization. In addition to decentralization toward regencies, many Acehnese resented the government's resistance to allowing a referendum, subsequent attempts to implement its own version of "special autonomy," as well as failure to address past human rights abuses.

In the initial phase, Acehnese were only marginally involved in changes affecting them. Their numbers were too small to be significant in the constitutional changes being discussed in Jakarta. Furthermore, after promises were made to East Timor, large masses demonstrated in the provincial capital, Banda Aceh, to ask for a referendum.[30] Instead, the government refused and supported an initiative from the governor of Aceh.[31] With a local team, governor Syamsuddin Mahmud drafted a special autonomy bill that was subsequently modified and passed in the Indonesian legislature. Although Acehnese local academics and government bureaucrats participated in this process, a much larger set of organizations and groups outside of the government wanted more extensive autonomy and a better consultative process.[32] Given Aceh's small population and number of representatives, Acehnese did not have opportunity to debate the bill

[30] Bertrand, *Nationalism and Ethnic Conflict in Indonesia*, 179.

[31] Governors under the New Order regime were all members of the government party Golkar, or members of the armed forces. They were appointed by the President, sometimes with consultation from the local provincial parliament. Governor Syamuddin Mahmud was appointed in 1993 and remained in place after the democratic transition, until 2000.

[32] Rodd McGibbon, *Secessionist challenges in Aceh and Papua: Is Special Autonomy the Solution?* (East-West Center 2004); Bertrand, *Nationalism and Ethnic Conflict in Indonesia* (n 2).

in the Indonesian parliament, but even at the local level they had few opportunities to articulate demands within the existing local institutions, which were still dominated by representatives tied to the interests of Indonesia-wide political parties.

Meanwhile, the Free Aceh Movement (GAM) responded to the government's unwillingness to hold a referendum by escalating its violent mobilization. After the brutal repression of 1989, the government had declared Aceh a "Special Operations Zone." Armed forces personnel frequently abused human rights in the search to weed out possible GAM supporters. Meanwhile, GAM quietly reorganized, both in Aceh and abroad, and reached a much greater degree of organizational strength than in the past. Beginning in early 2000, GAM increased its activities and the state responded with similarly stronger military force, so that the level of casualties, displacement, and disruption were high already by 2001.

Under these circumstances, moderate leaders in Aceh were powerless. The governor and his entourage could not credibly claim to represent the Acehnese as, by law, they represented and were appointed by the central government. As GAM escalated its violence, moderates outside of the government were crowded out. GAM enjoyed a fair amount of popular support but resentment grew from the destruction, displacement, and violence of the conflict.

The special autonomy law for Aceh of 2001 therefore was passed and came into force in 2002, just as the violent conflict was in full force.[33] It significantly increased autonomy and fiscal resources for Aceh as a province—in contrast to the weaker arrangements for provinces elsewhere—and it recognized autonomy on all matters under the province's jurisdiction, including provisions for the election of the governor and district heads, and created institutions that, at least in name, reflected local traditions. In fiscal matters, it provided more resources than the decentralization laws had for regencies: an 80 percent share of tax revenues from forestry, mining, and fisheries to accrue to the provincial government, and 55 percent of revenues from oil, and 40 percent from gas, for eight years.[34] Afterwards, these allocations were to be reduced to 35 percent on oil and 20 percent on gas. It also increased the provincial government's share of total tax revenues relative to what was retained by the central government. Overall, it gave new powers and resources that were well above what had been granted under the 1999 decentralization laws.

Yet, the law was insufficient to reduce the conflict because it was imposed rather than negotiated, and it was vague. GAM rejected the law and continued its insurgency, as it accused the government of failing to address grievances, hold a referendum, or negotiate the terms of more significant autonomy. The law was vague with respect to the autonomy that was promised. For instance, it was imprecise about the specific powers and jurisdictions that the provincial government obtained. Moreover, the governor and district heads were to be elected but the governor was also in charge of implementing central government policies, which created ambiguity over accountability. The central government also retained substantial powers of appointment and oversight in security matters and the judiciary, with no provincial oversight on military operations in the

[33] See *Undang-Undang Republik Indonesia Nomor 18 Tahun 2001 Tentang Otonomi Khusus Bagi Provinsi Daerah Istimewa Aceh Sebagai Provinsi Nanggroe Aceh Darussalam* (Law No. 18, 2001 of the Republic of Indonesia on Special Autonomy for the Province of Aceh) (Republic of Indonesia).

[34] As with all of the other laws on fiscal allocations, the wording in the law remained very ambiguous, with regulations meant to specify exact amounts and calculations. Revenue from royalties and other non-tax revenue were even less clearly allocated.

province, as well as primary control over the management of tax revenues. As a result of the sustained conflict, the law was never implemented.[35]

The failure was therefore a problem of substance but also of credible commitment. The Indonesian government showed little interest in negotiating and certainly refused to offer options to consult the population by referendum on the future status of Aceh. The state's reluctance to respond to demands for justice for the decade of human rights abuses contributed to raising suspicions as well. Overall, it left the impression that offers of autonomy were not genuine, and could easily be reversed.

Four factors finally combined to allow a peace agreement to succeed.[36] First, after four years of violent conflict, both sides began to experience combat fatigue, as casualties mounted but neither GAM nor the Indonesian armed forces gained the upper hand. Second, with presidential support, Vice-President Jusuf Kalla played an active role in finding a solution to the conflict. Third, the involvement of a neutral mediator, former President Martti Artisaari of Finland, contributed to building confidence and reaching a mutually acceptable agreement. Finally, the tsunami in December 2004 destroyed most of Aceh's capital, Banda Aceh, and devastated a large area along the coastline. It provided a catalyst for both parties to reach an agreement in order to focus on rebuilding the province.

The combination of strong commitment from the president and vice-president, as well as accepting third-party mediation, considerably augmented the chances of achieving a negotiated agreement. Mediation was not new in the Aceh conflict. Previously, the Henry Dunant Centre had brokered two cease-fires. Its role was unprecedented in a country with strong aversion to "foreign interference," but President Abdurrahman Wahid, who believed in accommodation to achieve peaceful solutions, opened the door for the Centre's crucial role. Negotiations in Helsinki, brokered by the Finnish former president, overcame problems with past externally mediated cease-fires, including the failure to narrow the gap in claims from both sides, the underestimation of the ability of "spoilers" to undermine the agreement, the lack of proper external monitoring of the cease-fire, and the fact that the cease-fire agreements were being implemented at the same time as the central government adopted a unilateral, top-down autonomy law.[37] With lessons learned from past mistakes, the "Helsinki process" better succeeded when it became clear that no side had gained any advantage from past resumptions of violence. As Aspinall notes, key points included the external mediator's insistence on having a full settlement before disarming, agreeing on a detailed template for Aceh's governance rather than only a framework toward reaching such an agreement, and obtaining GAM's abandonment of independence and acceptance of autonomy within Indonesia as a basis for peace.[38] The 2005 peace agreement led to the 2006 Law on Aceh, which was much more detailed and broad than the previous special autonomy law. It had 210 articles, which far surpassed either Aceh or Papua's special autonomy laws. This level of detail and breadth, obtained out of a negotiated process, had better chances of being broadly accepted. With strong monitoring mechanisms, it also increased the chances that the Law on Aceh would be implemented and that autonomy provisions would not be undermined by the regulatory process.

[35] Bertrand, *Nationalism and Ethnic Conflict in Indonesia* (n 2).

[36] This section is also based on interviews conducted in Banda Aceh, March–April 2008.

[37] Edward Aspinall, *Islam and Nation: Separatist Rebellion in Aceh, Indonesia* (Studies in Asian Security series, Stanford University Press 2009); Edward Aspinall, *The Helsinki Agreement: A More Promising Basis for Peace in Aceh?* (East-West Center 2005) 5–6.

[38] Aspinall, *The Helsinki Agreement* (n 37) 6.

The crafting of the law, based on the extensive peace agreement, showed the importance of detailed legislation. Laws in Indonesia, particularly those relating to autonomy and regional administration, are often vague. Such an approach delegates much of the law's substance to the executive, which then decides on the effective reach of the law through subsequent regulations. This process removes the issue from public debate and scrutiny, as it is relegated to the "mundane" task of implementation and administration. Yet, these regulations, more often than not, significantly strengthen or vastly dilute the intentions of the law. With a much more detailed law, GAM could hope that promises made in the peace agreement would be fulfilled.

The Aceh government obtained authority over all sectors except foreign relations, defense, national security, monetary and fiscal policy, and justice.[39] The law also allowed the Aceh government to implement and enforce Islamic law but the central government retained the power to appoint judges to the Islamic court. Even though security and defense remained under the jurisdiction of the central government, the Aceh government gained more oversight over security organizations. The governor and the Aceh legislature would be consulted on the appointment of the Aceh chief of police and before military troops were stationed in Aceh for defensive purposes. Restrictions were placed on the deployment of "special" forces, which were most involved in military operations in the past. Furthermore, the law spelled out specific requirements for the armed forces to respect human rights and local customs.[40]

The most controversial article was the right to organize local political parties, thereby creating an exception to national legislation requiring all political parties to have a national outlook. This article, which was one of the most sensitive points in the Helsinki peace negotiations, allowed the Free Aceh Movement to turn itself into a political party to run for gubernatorial and local legislative elections.

In fiscal matters, the Law on Aceh provided even greater resources than the previous Special Autonomy Law. It obtained 70 percent from oil and gas revenues and 80 percent from all other resources in the province, which is a much greater proportion than in the previous law. In addition, the Aceh government gained the authority to calculate these relative allocations and to administer natural resource exploitation in its territory. No such powers were ever granted to any other provincial or local government.

The Law on Aceh created many new precedents in Indonesia. It provided new autonomous powers and fiscal resources to the provincial government, whereas the 1999 autonomy laws targeted regencies. It allowed local political parties, where they are still banned elsewhere.

Papua

The gap between the Indonesian state and Papuans' aspirations is wide and almost unbridgeable. Despite some initial consultations after democratization, the Special Autonomy Law that the Indonesian parliament passed in 2001 left out important aspects that Papuans had raised. As a result, "Special Autonomy" (Otonomi Khusus) has been weak and many groups have rejected it.

Papuan groups seized on the democratic opening to make claims to revisit the 1969 Act of Free Choice, demand redress for past injustices, and a referendum on independence. As with the Acehnese, shortly after Suharto's downfall, demonstrators voiced

[39] *Undang-Undang Republik Indonesia Nomor 11 Tahun 2006 Tentang Pemerintahan Aceh* (Law No. 11, 2006 of the Republic of Indonesia on Aceh Government) (Republic of Indonesia), art. 6.

[40] On the police, see ibid art. 99; on military forces, see ibid art. 162.

these claims both in major cities of Papua, and in Jakarta. When President Habibie met with a delegation of 100 Papuan community leaders in 1999, he was shocked by their frank demand for independence in response to his query regarding their claims. From that moment, attempts for a dialogue were closed off.

Papuans used extra-institutional means and peaceful mobilization to advance their claims. In an unprecedented show of unity of purpose, representatives of all sectors of Papuan society gathered in two large congresses that adopted a set of demands on the Indonesian state and elected a Presidium of the People's Congress (Presidium Dewan Papua, PDP) to represent them formally. This process by-passed formal institutional channels, which included the provincial parliament and government, as well as representation in the Indonesian parliament. In the latter, Papuans had very few representatives, and their representation in the Indonesian cabinet was often non-existent or limited to one member. The provincial government was largely seen as serving the interests of the central government, being corrupt and ineffective. Papuans therefore embraced an alternative leadership to advance their claims.

In response, the Indonesian government repressed the PDP and instead adopted a special autonomy law to counter demands for independence. In 1999–2000, President Abdurrahman Wahid had shown openness and accommodation toward Papuans. He had allowed them on several occasions to raise the Morning Star flag, a symbol of independence that the armed forces had previously repressed. Wahid also supported the organization of the Congress. By October 2000, however, the MPR reprimanded him for his openness during his accountability report, and security forces began to crack down on flag raisings. Leaders of the PDP were also charged with secessionist activities, prosecuted, and some were imprisoned for a few months. After Wahid was forced to resign, his successor Megawati Soekarnoputri continued the repressive approach toward the PDP and any activity deemed to be separatist.

It was under these circumstances that the Special Autonomy Law of 2001 was adopted. Under the sponsorship of the central government, the appointed governor appointed a local team to draft the bill. After broad consultation, it was submitted to the national parliament (DPR) and passed as Law no. 21, 2001 on Special Autonomy (OTSUS) for Papua. While the law provided wide-ranging autonomy, it fell short of many of the clauses included in the original draft, such as provisions for a referendum on independence after five years and provisions to revisit the 1969 Act of Free Choice.

The Special Autonomy Law actually provided many new powers and resources to Papua. The Papuan provincial government obtained jurisdiction over all matters except foreign policy, defense, monetary and fiscal policy, religion, and justice, which is similar to what Acehnese obtained under their own special autonomy law and the subsequent Law on Aceh. The law also created a special assembly, the Papuan People's Assembly (*Majelis Rakyat Papua*, MRP), to represent *indigenous* Papuan groups. It included representatives from all sectors of Papuan society, such as religious groups, women, customary groups, and many others. While representatives came from different regions of Papua, the assembly was not organized along territorial lines. Its mandate was to promote and protect the rights and customs of *indigenous* Papuan people. Most of its powers, however, were consultative as the legislative powers resided with the Papua provincial legislature (DPRP), organized along a territorial basis. There were obligations to consult the MRP over candidates for the position of governor and over decisions and regulations relating to the basic rights of Papuans. In order to address past human rights abuses, the law provided for the creation of a Truth and Reconciliation Commission to investigate past abuses. Finally, Papua received vast new fiscal resources, including 80 percent of non-tax revenues from mining, forestry and fisheries, and 70 percent from oil and gas exploitation. In addition, a greater proportion of tax revenues were to accrue to the province and it obtained special autonomy funds for a limited number of years.[41]

Papuans therefore obtained a special autonomy law that the central government imposed. Although the drafting committee consulted several groups, the law was neither a product of negotiation nor of broad consultation, and it was not a faithful reflection of the original draft. Some of the most important issues for Papuans were left out. Papuans once again failed to be consulted, and their demands for a referendum on their future status within Indonesia was ignored. So were their demands for redress for past human rights abuses, more control over the armed forces in their territory, as well as better control over migration. Moreover, the PDP, and other representative groups were largely sidelined in the process of drafting special autonomy. From the outset therefore it had a very narrow basis of local support, restricted mainly to some officials within the Papuan government.

Outcome of the Process

The period of constitutional engagement produced significant change in Indonesia. While overall it contributed to a reduction of conflict around territorial cleavages, some important points of contention remain, particularly in Papua.

Decentralization has reconfigured the Indonesian state. It is no longer a strong unitary and centralized state. With autonomous powers in most jurisdictions, followed by significantly larger fiscal resources for districts, the Indonesian state has given important powers to districts to manage their own affairs. While there was some pressure at the outset for such significant decentralization, it was by no means a strong set of claims across the archipelago. In part a response to more significant conflicts in Aceh and Papua, decentralization laws ironically reconfigured all of Indonesia without resolving its deepest cleavages.

There are certainly some pressures to reverse some of the current decentralization. Before the 2014 elections, there were discussions inside and outside parliament to revise the 2004 decentralization laws which, in turn, had replaced the 1999 laws. The opposition leader, Prabawo Subianto, to undermine his rival and newly elected President Joko Widodo (Jokowi), used his 60 percent control over parliament to pass in October 2014 a law that canceled direct elections for provincial governors and regency heads (Law no. 22, 2014 on Regional Elections). It returned to the previous formula of provincial and regency parliaments electing governors and regents. By many accounts, he was attempting to prevent the rise of non-traditional politicians, such as President Jokowi, who benefitted from such elections as governor before rising to become an outsider in presidential elections, but it was also to recapture central party control over the process.[42] Yet, this tendency did not succeed. The new parliament once again reversed

[41] Jacques Bertrand, "Indonesia's Quasi-Federalist Approach: Accommodation Amid Strong Integrationist Tendencies" (2007) 5 (4) International Journal of Constitutional Law 576; Law no. 33/2004 gave similar percentages to regions for mining, fisheries, and forestry, but less for oil and gas (15.5 percent and 30.5 percent respectively). Law no. 33/2004 and subsequent regulations, however, were much more specific about fiscal categories, their definition, and precise methods of redistribution than the Special Autonomy Law for Papua.

[42] See Stefanus Hendrianto, "Indonesia's Constitutional Conundrum: The Weak Presidency, the Strong Opposition and the Regional Elections Law" (*International Journal of Constitutional Law Blog*, October 4, 2014) <www.iconnectblog.com/2014/10/indonesias-constitutional-conundrum-the-weak-presidency-the-strong-opposition-and-the-regional-elections-law/>.

the October law and passed legislation on January 20, 2015 to scrap law no. 22, 2014 and return to direct elections for governors and regency heads.[43]

The effect of decentralization has been mixed. The most significant consequence was a movement for the creation of new regencies. Decentralization laws were intended to prevent mobilization along ethnic lines. While bypassing provinces in favor of regencies, it could arguably have been successful in this respect. Yet, many of the new regencies were created precisely to make their boundaries correspond more closely with concentrations of particular ethnic groups. As a result, not only has the number of regencies and municipalities multiplied (from 292 in 1998 to 508 in 2013) but they now also coincide more strongly with territories defined along ethnic lines. This outcome creates a *de facto*, quasi-ethnically based territorial division of Indonesia. There have been no significant conflicts resulting from these re-divisions in recent years (except in Maluku, where other factors overlapped),[44] but there were few conflicts as well at the outset.

Most of the problems arising from decentralization involve its implementation. Local elections provided more legitimacy to district heads but became fierce contests for local resources. Larger fiscal pies became prime prizes for electoral winners. Since 2005, revenues for local governments (mainly regencies) have grown at a compound rate of 17 percent annually. Transfers to local governments accounted for 31 percent of the central government revenues in 2013 and they constituted about 80 percent of local revenues. In a system with poor judicial oversight and limited accountability arrangements, the new resources became sources of personal enrichment. While some local governments used the funds to stimulate new programs, infrastructure, and development, many others have taken advantage of this system of "decentralized corruption."

Against this backdrop, territorial cleavages in Aceh and Papua show contrasting outcomes. As the Law on Aceh was implemented, GAM disbanded, its members reintegrated into Acehnese society, and its leaders entered formal politics. In Papua, by contrast, OTSUS failed to be properly implemented, many Papuans remained disillusioned, and the conflict, while low in violence, remained deep.

The implementation of the Law on Aceh reduced conflict, even though some problems remained. Most importantly, GAM disbanded and elections allowed its former members to run for office. Two elections were held for the position of governor, first in 2006 and then in 2012. GAM turned itself into a political party (Partai Aceh), and was able to win a majority of seats in the local parliament in the legislative elections of 2009. GAM's ability to transform itself into a dominant local party and its leaders to become governor has been the greatest achievement of the Law on Aceh.

Yet, some significant problems have developed. Most significantly, the former movement split, largely because of rivalry between candidates for governor. Irwandi Jusuf, elected governor in 2006 as an independent, became a controversial figure as he took his distance from Partai Aceh and the former GAM. He even went so far as to create an alternative political party (Partai Nasional Aceh). This division, and tight competition for the position of governor in 2012, led to violent clashes, intimidation, and vote rigging. In the end, the Partai Aceh candidate Zaini Abdullah won as governor, but the

[43] Indri Maulidar, "Parliament passes new law on direct elections for regional government heads" (*DPR Sahkan Undang-Undang Pilkada Langsung) Tempo On-line* (January 20, 2015) <www.tempo.co/read/news/2015/01/20/078636244/DPR-Sahkan-Undang-Undang-Pilkada-Langsung> accessed March 20, 2015.

[44] See Gerry van Klinken, "The Maluku Wars: Bringing Society Back In" (2001) 71 *Indonesia* 1.

results were marred with accusations of unfair elections, including intimidation and vote-buying. The former movement has continued to divide, and popular support for the Partai Aceh has waned, as its showing in the 2014 legislative elections have shown; it lost a significant share of the Aceh provincial legislature to national parties, while the Partai Nasional Aceh failed to gain much support.

The regulatory framework for the implementation of the Law on Aceh has been partially put into place. Some important regulations relating to such issues as the establishment of local political parties, the appointment of the Regional Secretary, or consultations regarding policies affecting Aceh were passed. Other aspects of the LOGA were delayed, or postponed indefinitely. Provisions for a Human Rights Court and a Truth and Reconciliation Commission were not implemented. Regulations were still lacking on the management of land, forestry, and oil and gas management.[45]

Finally, on the socio-economic front the Aceh government delivered on some of the promises of the peace agreement. Hopes were high that former GAM members would be fully integrated. The Badan Rehabilitasi dan Rekonstruksi (BRR, Agency for Rehabilitation and Reconstruction) became the main institution charged with reconstructing Aceh after the destruction and devastation of the 2004 tsunami. It helped the local government rebuild Banda Aceh, and many of the villages and infrastructure that had been destroyed. The local government also put into place some compensation packages for former GAM members, better health and education services, as well as skills development. However, the large transfer of fiscal resources has yet to be used to stimulate new industries, strengthen existing ones, and generate new employment. As with decentralization more broadly, new fiscal resources have created new opportunities for personal enrichment. In an environment where former GAM leaders expected some dividends from peace, the potential for graft has been an easy route.

Overall, the constitutional settlement in Aceh has been positive. It has created peace, by allowing GAM to disarm and enter the political process. It has enjoyed strong popular support, as gains in elections have shown. In this respect, many grievances were addressed and, in particular, through more powers locally, better representation, autonomy, and fiscal resources. A lack of consistent implementation, slow motivation to seize opportunities provided, and divisions among former GAM members, however, remain shadows over the peace process.

In Papua, many local representatives and organizations have repeatedly denounced and "rejected" OTSUS. From the officially recognized Dewan Adat Papua (DAP, Papuan Customary Council) to various Papuan churches, a broad array of Papuans criticized OTSUS for failing to represent, empower, or improve Papuans' livelihoods. Even President Susilo Bambang Yudhoyono admitted in 2013 that significant changes were required to make special autonomy effective in the region.[46]

From the outset, the Indonesian government derailed OTSUS' implementation by dividing up the province. Only months after acceding to power, President Megawati issued decree no. 1, 2003 splitting the province into two: Papua and West Papua. Ostensibly done on the basis of creating more efficient governance over a very large territory, most Papuans rightly believed that the measure was also designed to divide Papuans in order to prevent secessionist tendencies. The division interfered directly with the implementation of OTSUS, as many groups as well as the governor of Papua

[45] Crisis Management Initiative, "Aceh Peace Process Follow-Up Project: Final Report" (Crisis Management Initiative 2012).

[46] Jacques Bertrand, "Autonomy and Stability: The Perils of Implementation and 'Divide-and-Rule' Tactics in Papua" (2014) 20 (2) Nationalism and Ethnic Politics 174.

strongly objected to the unilateral measure, while different levels of government and the courts debated whether and how special autonomy would be extended to both provinces under the existing law. Finally, the central government drew even more criticism when it divided the Papuan People's Assembly (MRP) into two, on the basis that there should be one for each of the provinces rather than a single body. By doing so, it weakened the voice of the single MRP to represent all Papuans, while gaining support from West Papuans to obtain their own assembly. This action contributed to further dividing Papuans.

OTSUS was also poorly implemented. It took four years before the MRP was created, only after criticism and pressures from local groups. Most of the regulations required to properly implement the law were not in place, more than a decade after the law came into effect. In fiscal matters, the central government retained control over the management and disbursement of fiscal resources despite the law's provisions for provincial management. Finally, while the law provided for a Truth and Reconciliation Commission, it was never implemented.

Against the backdrop of controversies surrounding the implementation of special autonomy, the central government's overall policies toward Papuans contributed to perpetuating their suspicion of the central government. Security forces regularly used repressive tactics, such as repressing flag raisings, and continued to arrest Papuans deemed to be involved in secessionist activities, such as the head of DAP after a Congress organized in 2012 that declared a new republic of West Papua. In November 2001, *Kopassus* (the armed forces special forces) assassinated the leader of the PDP. The armed forces and Mobile Brigades (Brimob), a special paramilitary force with the police, continued to conduct operations in remote areas and regularly overstepped their powers, as the Indonesian Human Rights Commission has noted on several occasions. Moreover, the central government managed to undermine the MRP when the latter gained visibility and credibility as three of its respected leaders regularly criticized the failings of OTSUS and the government's overall policy. At the end of the MRP's mandate in 2011, the central government interfered with the election of members so that its most vocal critics were sidelined and replaced by less competent members who were indebted to the central government.

There was very little indication, therefore, that the central government was strongly committed to finding a resolution to the territorial cleavage in Papua. Papuan groups, including the DAP, churches, and a number of non-governmental organizations, have been calling for "dialogue," by which they mean a reopening of OTSUS, a negotiated autonomy, a discussion of the Act of Free Choice, and a more legitimate process of continued relationship to Indonesia. The central government, by fear of secessionism, refuses to revisit the Act of Free Choice and appears reluctant to open discussions on autonomy and its final form.[47]

As a result, special autonomy continues to be implemented in Papua, but fails to produce expected outcomes. Instead, the large fiscal transfers since 2002 have not produced developmental outcomes. While some of the funds were invested into ad hoc programs and infrastructure, most have disappeared in wasteful spending and corruption. Poverty rates remain among the highest in Indonesia, at 36.8 percent in 2010, only marginally less than in 2003, at 38.7 percent, whereas the national average stood at 17.4 percent in 2010.[48] With little legitimacy to the framework, opportunists have

[47] ibid.

[48] By comparison, there was a reduction in Aceh from 29.6 percent in 2003 to 21 percent in 2010. See Dian RD Agustina, Wolfgang Fengler, and Günther G Schulze "The regional effects of Indonesia's oil and gas policy: options for reform" (2012) 48 (3) Bulletin of Indonesian Economic Studies 369.

seized positions in the local government and profited from revenues. The Papuan and West Papuan governments have been unwilling, or unable, to use the full extent of newly obtained powers under special autonomy to generate beneficial outcomes for Papuans.

Lessons Learned

Indonesia has been radically transformed since the beginning of democratization in 1998. Today it resembles more a highly asymmetrical form of federalism than the highly unitary and centralized state that characterized the previous decades. Decentralization and different forms of special autonomy have alleviated some of the more important sources of conflict but their implementation has created some significant problems as well.

A gradual and flexible process of constitutional change can produce deep transformation and greatly alleviate territorial cleavages. Had Indonesia gone the route of a formal constitutional negotiation, it would likely have created more conflict rather than reduce it, as shadows of the past, including deep ideological divisions and stalled constitutional negotiations, still hung over the transition. Indonesians avoided a constituent assembly to adopt a new Constitution and worked instead through several amendments. Within this discussion, they could constitutionalize the principle of autonomy for regions, but delegate to the legislature what form such autonomy should take. While not the central reason for this process of constitutional change in Indonesia, the gradual approach allowed different types of conflicts to be addressed through different institutional mechanisms.

Decentralization had mixed effects but was an effective tool to provide more powers and resources to ethnic groups, while not necessarily defining boundaries in ethnic terms. It was also useful, although largely coincidental, to have implemented a decentralization law while amendments were being introduced to the Constitution; it created a climate that was already favorable to principles of regional autonomy.

Decentralization allows for some flexible arrangements that do not congeal ethnic identities within administrative boundaries. Ironically, in Indonesia, groups have taken advantage of the opportunity to redraw regency boundaries precisely to coincide more greatly with the "homeland" of particular groups. They have gained more powers and fiscal resources without being given an explicit, ethnically defined territory.

Furthermore, bypassing provinces enabled the government to avoid a larger territory to obtain new powers and resources that could be used as a basis for secessionist demands. While tensions had been rising in various regions to loosen up the centralized state, they had not yet degenerated into open conflict and certainly not secessionism.

There have been opponents of decentralization but, so far, they have been unable to reverse the trend. Some members of large parties such as PDI-P and Golkar initially resented the potential loss of power from the parties, as well as looser control over their patronage networks. With the rise of new politicians, such as Jokowi, that are products of decentralization and direct elections for regency heads and governors, they attempted to reverse at least direct elections to regain some control. Yet, as discussed, such tendencies are in the minority and new parliament quickly reversed the law that had eliminated direct elections for these positions, even if it is controlled by the opposition coalition led by Jokowi's opponent, Prabowo Subianto. As a result, decentralization has been strengthened.

Decentralization was less successful at addressing deep cleavages, and it created new problems. One of its initial objectives was to defuse deep conflicts in Aceh, Papua, and East Timor but it had no impact. Instead, Acehnese, Papuans, and Timorese considered decentralization as a strategy to avoid addressing their claims. They continued to mobilize and demand for independence or much broader autonomy at the provincial level. At the same time, decentralization had the unintended consequence of stimulating demands for the creation of new regencies. While some of these new divisions coincided with ethnic groups, and might have preventively defused potential conflicts, many others were promoted by opportunists seeking access to resources, in a system of decentralized corruption that has led to very high leakage of government revenues. Despite attempts to claw back some of the powers devolved, the problems have remained.

The creation of a second chamber to represent regions, the DPD, did not respond to specific cleavages but recognized the need for regional representation in a diverse society. In theory, it was useful to preserve a strong common identity by not explicitly aligning regional representation with ethnic groups. At the same time, it responded to a desire to represent regions in the central government. Yet, the fear of giving more power to provinces ended up creating a chamber with few powers and with little use. By avoiding a true bicameral parliament that would have given more power to provincial representatives, the Indonesian government preserved its unitary character but created an institution that does not effectively represent regions.

Autonomy can be a useful institutional tool to manage territorial cleavages but is meaningless if not accompanied by a number of accompanying conditions, such as the symbolic recognition of ethno-territorial identities to address deep cleavages, a willingness to negotiate its content, clear and detailed legislation, and a credible commitment to implement it. There is no doubt that the Law on Aceh of 2006, and the very extensive autonomy that it gave the province, contributed most significantly to the elimination of violent conflict in Aceh and peace between GAM and the Indonesian state. The newly transferred powers to almost all jurisdictions in the province, vast new fiscal resources, and rights to establish political institutions that are different from other regions, including the right to create local political parties, were key to a settlement.

Yet, the granting of certain forms of autonomy failed to resolve conflict. In Aceh, the special autonomy law of 2001 barely had any effect on the escalating conflict between GAM and the Indonesian government. While in Papua, special autonomy has provided new resources and new powers at the provincial level, it has not resolved the conflict. Instead, it has contributed to dividing Papuans, and perpetuating their impoverishment and marginalization even though, ironically, the powers obtained, the degree of autonomy, as well as fiscal resources were very significant. While less than what Aceh obtained, they were still a radical departure from past centralization, and gave significant powers and resources at the provincial level, as in Aceh, in contrast to practices elsewhere in the country where autonomous powers and resources were largely granted to districts.

Three conditions were key in making Aceh a more successful case than Papua. First, the Law on Aceh of 2006 was a result of negotiations. Neither the special autonomy laws of 2001 in Aceh nor Papua were negotiated. There were some consultations locally, but the national parliament significantly altered the draft laws before passing them. As a result, representative groups in Aceh and Papua felt by-passed, whereas the Law on Aceh, negotiated between GAM and the Indonesian state, legitimized the new institutional arrangements and invested the local government with strong popular support.

Second, the Law on Aceh was much more precise and detailed than the previous special autonomy law, or the special autonomy law in Papua. Despite this, there have still been some areas where implementing regulations have diverged from the original intent of the negotiated peace. In the case of Papua, however, the central government has been able to significantly dilute aspects of local autonomy, particularly the powers and unity of the Papuan People's Assembly (MRP) and election of its members, and the management of fiscal resources. Implementation, while less in the public eye, is vital for making autonomy real, so having negotiations bring more precision and detail into the law can reduce the risk that implementation will dilute or erase the original intent.

Finally, external mediation was key to obtain a negotiated solution in Aceh. The involvement of the Dunant Centre and the former president of Finland helped to achieve a negotiated solution. Papuans have sought such external support but the Indonesian government considers it an internal affair, and does not welcome foreign intervention, whereas in the case of Aceh it was forced to accept such mediation to resolve violent conflict. Obviously, the unity of the Acehnese and the capacity to sustain an insurgency created intense pressure on the Indonesian government. With much less unity and no sustained insurgency, Papuans' mobilization has been much weaker and more disparate. They achieved their strongest moment of political pressure under the leadership of the PDP in the early 2000s, but state repression and internal division prevented them from sustained mobilization. The Indonesian government is much less willing to involve external parties, as several groups in Papua continue to view independence as the only solution and there is a risk for the Indonesian state that calls for a historical revision of the Act of Free Choice might find a sympathetic ear among some external actors.

After more than a decade of reforms, Indonesia has departed very significantly from its homogenous approach to diversity and adopted, instead, an asymmetric model that has proven to be stable. Asymmetry was shaped out of responsiveness to deep conflict in Aceh and Papua. Other regions have accepted the greater compromises made in these cases to reduce conflict. None have demanded similar powers and fiscal resources at the provincial level, as those obtained in Aceh and Papua. The Indonesian government has been willing to stand by decentralization at the regency level but they likely understand that making similar claims at the provincial level would be rejected and, possibly, lead to recentralization all together. There are still relatively strong advocates of a strong, unitary, and centralized state within all political parties and the armed forces. Should current arrangements be challenged, they would be given the political space to press for a reversal of decentralization.

Constitutional processes focusing on autonomy and decentralization can effectively manage territorial cleavages. Where they are negotiated, precise, and sometimes helped through mediation, they can help eliminate violent conflict. Nevertheless, there is a vast gap between autonomy in law and its implementation. The Indonesian case also shows how much implementation matters, and how it can very significantly alter and dilute autonomy. Conflict can become stalled under those circumstances, as the case of Papua shows.

8

Constitutional Transitions and Territorial Cleavages

The Kenyan Case

Yash Ghai and Jill Cottrell

> For heaven's sake, now that you have heard our cries, we, smaller communities, should be given a share of this national cake as a token (*Clapping from Honourable Delegates)* so that we become satisfied and happy and Kenya remains united, Mr. Chairman. I am glad to realize that many Kenyans have now realized that and we are happy nobody is seceding. All that we want is the power to be devolved politically, economically, socially, educationally and administratively to the district and location, Mr. Chairman.
>
> Maalim Abdi Mohamed, MP[1]

Overview

Kenya grew out of British annexation of territories of a number of communities, and immigrants from India and Britain. As independence drew near, Britain agreed to the demand of minority communities—against strong opposition from larger communities—for federal arrangements under which the regions would have power on matters of special concern to minorities. But soon after independence, regional governments were abolished, leading to a highly centralized system. Authoritarian rule, massive land grabbing, loss of rights, and marginalization of minorities followed.

For long, the government resisted demands for constitutional reform, but eventually conceded, under pressure from civil society—and from Western governments after the cold war. Agreement was reached on principles for reform and the Constitution of Kenya Review Commission (CKRC) was established, in 2000. This chapter focuses on the work of that commission and the National Constitutional Conference that followed, adopting a draft Constitution. It concentrates on issues surrounding devolution of power, on who demanded it and how the issues were resolved. By the time of the Conference in 2003–04, there was a new president. He reneged on promises of reform, and imposed changes, which weakened the draft Constitution, including its provisions on devolution. This revised draft was rejected in a referendum in 2005.

Serious violence, driven by ethnic incitement, followed allegedly rigged elections in 2007. International mediation led to a coalition government and the resumption of

[1] MP for Wajir East, speaking at the National Constitutional Conference. "Plenary Proceedings, Presentation of Draft Bill, Cont. of Chapter 10—Devolution of Power Held at The Bomas of Kenya on 23rd May 2003" (available on the Archives website of Katiba Institute) https://preview.tinyurl.com/NCCDBCh10

Territory and Power in Constitutional Transitions. First Edition. Edited by Michael Anderson and Sujit Choudhry. Constitutional Transitions and Territorial Cleavages: The Kenyan Case © Yash Ghai and Jill Cottrell 2019. Published 2019 by Oxford University Press.

constitutional reform. In August 2010, a new Constitution, based largely on the drafts of the commission and national conference, including on devolution, was adopted in a referendum.

Background

The historian Charles Hornsby writes, "None of the country's borders matched local languages, communities or physical geography; Kenya was an artificial creation, delineated by the British for their purposes, lumping together neighbours, enemies and some communities that had previously no contact whatsoever."[2] British colonial occupation went back to the 1880s mainly, with various agreements with other European countries, including the Treaty of Berlin of 1885, fixing those borders. The Coastal strip, about 10 miles wide, came under British control by agreement with the Sultan of Zanzibar. Part of what is now Kenya (roughly corresponding to the current Turkana and West Pokot counties) was transferred from (British) Uganda in 1926, while a large section of Somali territory (formerly "belonging" to the Sultan of Zanzibar) was transferred to Italy in 1924.

The census just before independence (1962) shows the following figures: Kikuyu 1,642,065, Meru and Tharaka 478,369, Embu and Mbere 133,819, Luo 1,148,335, Luhya 1,086,409, Kamba 933,219, Kisii 538,343, Kipsigis 341,771, Nandi 170,085, Maasai 154,079, Taita 83,613, Swahili 8,657; the total being 8,365,942, this left 1,647,178 others. The number of ethnic groups is variously reckoned to be between 40+ and 60+.

The British exercise of power affected the social and economic structures of the African communities, undermining their self-sufficiency. Although the colonial plan was to preserve a measure of traditional systems and to restrict movement of local people out of their traditional lands (except when these were seized for settlers), many forces drove society in new directions. There was greater contact among communities, as well as competition for access to the developing economy and benefits from the state. The basis of traditional egalitarianism was destroyed by the market and administrative practices, leading to differentiation among and within communities. The economy and livelihood of the people depended increasingly on policies and administrative measures of the state. These tendencies accelerated with the approach of independence, destroying trust within communities as well as between communities. Today the force driving ethnicity is electoral politics, building on colonial classification, nourished to considerable extent by patronage dependent on the plunder of the state.

The boundary drawing exercises resulted in several communities having kin in neighboring countries, such as the Luo (closely related to communities in Uganda, South Sudan and Tanzania), the Maasai (on both sides of the Tanzania/Kenya border) and the Somali.

A commission sent by the British to gauge the wishes of Somalis found overwhelming support for secession—but neither Britain, nor Kenya later, acted on it. There was also uncertainty in the run-up to independence about the Coast. In fact the British had no intention of not including the coastal strip in Kenya and the Sultan did not oppose them. But some on the coast hoped for something else. Especially coastal Arabs and Swahili and some Europeans favored autonomy for the Coast, or even resisted the idea of the 10-mile strip being confirmed as part of Kenya, wanting reunion with Zanzibar.

[2] Charles Hornsby, *Kenya: A History Since Independence* (IB Tauris 2013) 21.

Among the motivating factors was the beginning of major up-country migration to the coast. On the other hand, the coastal Mijikenda and the main political parties opposed both separation and ten-mile strip autonomy.[3]

At independence the Europeans numbered 55,759 or under 1 percent of the population, but they occupied nearly 16 percent of the arable land. That massive land grab displaced huge numbers of people, especially the Kikuyu, Maasai and Kalenjin, and coastal people. The consequences included that many people were not living in what they considered their ancestral lands—and were resented by the communities whose land they then occupied. The fate of the Europeans and the demand of African communities for the recovery of their ancestral land, especially from Europeans and the Kikuyu, dictated British (and to some extent Kikuyu) policy in the Constitution-making process.

Such a legacy tempts rulers toward centralization, while wisdom dictates distribution of state authority and functions. Kenya's constitutional history is full of tension between the two.

Political mobilization for devolution

The issue of the establishment of devolution arose in the lead-up to independence in 1963 and again in the 1990s when a new Constitution-making process commenced. In 1962–63, apart from some demands for secession by Somalis, Coastal Arabs, and the Maasai, not relevant for our present purpose, the territorial issue was *majimbo* (regionalism). In late 1961, as independence drew near, a consortium of mainly medium sized tribes became worried that the larger tribes would dominate the government, and that minority tribes would be discriminated against. Under the umbrella of a political party (Kenya African Democratic Union—KADU), they demanded the division of powers between the central government and seven regions (ensuring regional rule for some of their member tribes).

The key actors were the two major African political parties (only racial political parties were allowed) and the British government, plus a small but highly influential group of white settlers (capitalizing on their special relationship with the British government). The critical negotiations were conducted in London. The African political parties (KANU (Kenya African National Union) and KADU) became so antagonistic that they refused to be in the same room with each other.[4] This gave Britain the role of a mediator and vastly increased its negotiating powers, quite apart from its role as the ultimate authority which would decide the terms of independence.

Closely connected to the nature of the state—centralized or decentralized—was the issue of land and rights of property, notably including lands appropriated by the government, European settlers, and some local communities; KADU wanted the regions to control land. At one level the constitutional debate seemed a very intellectual exercise, assisted by constitutional experts from the USA, Switzerland, and Britain. But behind this intellectual facade, there was undoubtedly political "mobilization" engineered by the political parties and interests.

[3] Justin Willis and George Gona, "Pwani C Kenya? Memory, Documents and Secessionist Politics in Coastal Kenya" (2012) 112 (446) African Affairs 48; James R Brennan, "Lowering the Sultan's Flag: Sovereignty and Decolonization in Coastal Kenya" (2008) 50 (4) Comparative Studies in Society and History 831. Also see Hornsby (n 2) 62.

[4] For a detailed account of negotiations on the independence Constitution, see Robert Maxon, *Kenya's Independence Constitution: Constitution Making and End of Empire* (Fairleigh Dickinson University Press 2011).

A combination of factors—the initial British distrust of Kenyatta and his party KANU, collaboration between KADU and European settlers, and concern for minority protection—led the British to institute regionalism in the independence Constitution. However, regionalism did not last for long, as in general elections after the conference KANU won a majority and Kenyatta, to whom the British had warmed by then, maneuvered to abolish regionalism. But "majimbo" had entered the Kenyan lexicon.

Ironically, soon after the repeal of regionalism, its leading proponent, Daniel arap Moi, became Vice-President in Kenyatta's highly centralized government. When Kenyatta died in 1978, Moi succeeded to the presidency and his own presidency was just as centralized, violent, and corrupt as Kenyatta's—and geared toward the interests of a few people from his own tribe, regardless of the interests of other communities.

Between them Jomo Kenyatta and Daniel Moi managed to destroy democracy, used excessive violence against people opposed to them, looted the national treasury, and promoted the fortunes of a few from their respective ethnic groups, ethnicizing politics (though the great majority of their own communities scarcely enjoyed any benefits). Both of them, and their families, amassed huge fortunes by corruption—and are now among the world's richest people. Kenyatta managed to destroy all political parties except KANU, and Moi changed the Constitution to make Kenya a *de jure* one-party state. They were so obsessed about their greed and consolidating their ethnic support, that they cared little about promoting a Kenyan identity among the diverse ethnic, religious and culture communities.

Most people kept their heads down and went about their business, while increasing numbers fell into the poverty trap. But there was opposition, torture, detention without trial, victimization, and occasional murders of dissenters. Moi ruled for twenty-four years, and removing him became the main concern of the democratic movement, led by civil society, and including some religious groups and some politicians.[5] The first objective was the repeal of the constitutional provision declaring Kenya a one-party state.

The situation began to change with the end of the cold war, and the victory of Western capitalism, meaning that the West now saw little point in buttressing dictators. Multi-partyism in Kenya was restored in 1992. But the opposition proved incapable of putting forward one joint candidate, and Moi was returned to power in 1992 and 1997.

The move for more constitutional change, for a system that would make future Mois impossible, gathered momentum. A series of national conferences, bringing together a wide cross section of society, including religious groups, trade unions, professional associations, and political parties, were held to define the terms of reform. The agreement reached at these conferences (the last was attended even by Moi) became the terms of reference of the Constitution commission that was eventually established to draft the new Constitution. But slow progress led civil society (including religious and political groups) to set up a "People's Commission" to consult the people and draft the Constitution. Fearing that he might lose control over reform, Moi set up a state-sponsored commission, the Constitution of Kenya Review Commission (CKRC), in 2000.

When various civil society groups got together in the early 1990s to produce a draft Constitution, one of their demands was that "The executive power was to be shared with Parliament, local government, civil society organizations and the people themselves."[6] The draft they produced focused on local government, with considerably more

[5] An excellent study of the reform movement is Willy Mutunga, *Constitution-Making from the Middle: Civil Society and Transition Politics in Kenya, 1992–1997* (Mwengo 1999).

[6] ibid 53.

powers than the local authorities ever had.[7] Mutunga identifies as an important stage in the civil society discussions on a new Constitution, the publication in 1996 of a book by Peter Habenga Okondo[8] that included a detailed analysis of *majimbo*. Although not everyone accepted Okondo's espousal of ethnic federalism, there was now "an articulation of a *majimbo* constitution by one of the *majimbo* ideologues."[9] The word "devolution" was used first, it seems, in a civil society assembly in October 1997: "Executive power must be constitutionally trimmed and controlled and the principle of devolution of power upheld so that equality before the law, accountability, transparency and good government are a reality."[10] Calls for devolution became a key part of the calls for constitutional reform. Ten days after the 1997 civil society assembly the original Constitution of Kenya Review Act was assented to, without any mention of devolution. But an early amendment said the purpose of review included:

(d) promoting the peoples' participation in the governance of the country through democratic, free and fair elections and the devolution and exercise of power; . . .
(h) strengthening national integration and unity . . .

It also asked the CKRC to "examine the various structures and systems of government including the federal and unitary systems and recommend an appropriate system for Kenya."

Hornsby says, writing of 1998–99, that "KANU . . . went on a sales drive for federalism."[11] He goes on to say that the Kikuyu and Luo, and much of civil society, were opposed to this for fear of a breakup of the country. But it is not at all clear that people generally equated "devolution" with federalism, rather than simply bringing more decision-making closer to the people.

The existing administrative system comprised, in addition to national ministries, two elements: local governments and "Provincial Administration." Many local governments were very ineffective, and often corrupt. Provincial Administration was the arm of the national government in the local areas, indeed the arm of the ruling party. It had been strengthened in the wake of the end of the *majimbo* experiment, and was widely hated. It was supported by a separate police force, the Administration Police, originally the "Native Police." Provincial Administration was a hierarchical system, with Provincial and District Commissioners, down to District Officers, Chiefs and sub-chiefs. There were eight provinces, and had been forty-one districts at independence. From 1992 a presidential process of creating new districts—a vote-winning strategy—began. By 2002 there were seventy districts and by 2010 there were 265. But only forty-six, plus the Nairobi area, had been legally created.

Like the districts, the provinces had ethnic connotations: Central (Kikuyu), North-East (Somali), Coast (Swahili, Arab, Mijikenda), Eastern (Somali in the North, Meru, Embu and Kamba in the South), Western (Luhya), Nyanza (Luo and Kisii), and Rift Valley (Kalenjin), while Nairobi was very mixed.

[7] In Appendix D of Mutunga's book, ibid 348–50.

[8] PH Okondo, *A Commentary on the Constitution of Kenya* (Phoenix Publishers 1995). Mutunga writes that this book was "the genesis of the debate on *majimbo* (regionalism or federalism) in Kenya, and it gave a very concrete framework of operating regionalism in Kenya" in Mutunga (n 5) 135.

[9] Mutunga (n 5) in reference to Okondo's book.

[10] Mutunga (n 5) 475.

[11] KANU was by now Moi's party—he who had headed the pro-*majimbo* KADU in the early 1960s. Hornsby (n 2) 625.

The Period of Constitutional Engagement

The central focus of this chapter is on late 2000 to early 2004, part of a twenty-year process that ended only in August 2010 with the promulgation of the new Constitution.

We begin with the process, and then turn to the place in it of devolution debates.

Yash Ghai, chairing the official process, made it a condition of accepting the post that he be given a chance to bring together the official and the "People's" commissions because it seemed unlikely that either on its own would succeed in getting a new Constitution, particularly one commanding broad support—a precondition for successful implementation. The merger negotiations took months of shuttle diplomacy, and occasional threats to abandon the process. Ghai concentrated on Kenyans and their organizations, and avoided external involvement. He established a measure of public support and eventually of the religious communities who had promoted the "People's Commission." In the end, public support became quite critical, for neither side wanted to be seen as a "spoilsport."

The original CKRC consisted of fifteen members (supposedly with knowledge of the law or knowledge and experience in public affairs) nominated by the National Assembly and appointed by the President, plus the Attorney-General and the Secretary. Its final size, with some People's Commission members, was twenty-nine. It was required to conduct and facilitate civic education to, and collect the views of, the people, and on the basis of their views to prepare the draft Constitution. It established Constituency Constitutional Forums throughout the country, with small libraries and funds for public meetings to discuss recommendations for submission to the CKRC, all facilitated by a district coordinator, a CKRC employee. A Parliamentary Select Committee liaised with Parliament, especially on administrative and financial matters.

The CKRC's work began in earnest in May 2001, and its draft Constitution and report appeared in September 2002. The authors have described elsewhere its highly participatory process, as well as the efforts at politically, and personally, motivated sabotage.[12] The political motives were related to resistance to any change in system of government and curbing presidential powers rather than to devolution. When the CKRC was established without the participation of civil society or opposition people (they were boycotting the "official commission") Moi thought he would be able to dictate to it. But the merger of the two commissions greatly reduced his influence, though several commissioners—from each original body—took orders from him.

The various delays, before and during the process, led to a disproportionate emphasis, especially in the media, on when (or whether) there would be a new Constitution, rather than on its contents.

The CKRC draft Constitution went to the National Constitutional Conference (NCC) for discussion, amendment and adoption. The NCC was broad based: all members of the National Assembly (223); three representatives from each district (210); one representative of each political party (40); representatives of religious organizations (35), professional bodies (15), women's organizations (24), trade unions (16) and registered non-governmental organizations (24); members of CKRC, but without vote (29)—629 altogether. Thus, the political "class" comprised the bulk of the membership (573), even though few bothered to make submissions to the CKRC and their attendance at Bomas was poor. MPs tended to come from the largest ethnic group in

[12] Jill Cottrell and Yash Ghai, "Constitution Making and Democratisation in Kenya (2000–2005)" (2007) 14 (1) *Democratisation* 1.

their constituency, and, while the rules for electing district members insisted on at least one woman, there was no ethnic requirement for these or civil society members, though the religious body category ensured that all faiths were represented.

After a suitable period for people and organizations to study the CKR draft Constitution, the NCC was scheduled to convene on Monday October 28, 2002, after they had a week's introductory workshop on the draft (in which very few politicians participated) with experts. It was assumed that the NCC would conclude its work in about three months, with the delegates operating behind a "veil of ignorance" and adopting a Constitution before forthcoming elections. Then the draft would go for final decision by the National Assembly, so that the elections would be conducted under the new Constitution. Ghai tried to persuade Moi that he might (as the Constitution allowed) continue in office for some months, rather than dissolving Parliament prematurely. By this time, however, Moi was tired of the process as he had failed to implant his ideas through some commissioners beholden to him.

On the afternoon of Friday 25, as the introductory workshop wound up, Moi dissolved parliament, paving the way for elections in December. Work on the Constitution was suspended until a new government and parliament were in place, under the old Constitution. Moi could not stand again, and was shrewd enough to realize that it would be futile to try. But he nominated as surrogate Uhuru Kenyatta as KANU's candidate. The opposition groups (whose numbers increased even as the CKRC process progressed) formed a coalition, NARC (National Rainbow Alliance). The endorsement by Raila Odinga (himself a potential candidate) of Mwai Kibaki as the candidate of the opposition assured the opposition of victory, in both presidential and national assembly elections. Kibaki, who had long served under Moi before opportunistically switching to the opposition, promised that, if NARC won, it would adopt a new Constitution in 100 days. But soon NARC split into two factions due to Kabiki's refusal to honor a pre-election pact to appoint Odinga as prime minister. This also had an impact on the workings of the National Assembly where Kibaki was in the danger of losing his majority. The political maneuverings meant the NCC was not convened until late April 2003, well beyond the 100 days. But it is arguable that the sense of national euphoria that accompanied the election,[13] which brought the end of the Moi era and an optimism for the future, contributed to the ability of the NCC to work, within the walls of the Bomas of Kenya[14] and not on the streets.

Eventually the new government in turn decided that it was not so enthusiastic about the new Constitution that the NCC process was producing. Kibaki's Vice President and Minister of Justice staged a walkout when it appeared that the NCC was likely to vote in favor of a parliamentary system—which Kibaki himself had supported when in opposition, but now preferred an executive presidency. Consequently the closing stages of the NCC were conducted in their absence. This walkout, coupled with intelligence that a major court case was about to be heard directed at derailing the whole process,[15]

[13] Interestingly, Kenyan optimism seems to have been very high in the two months before the election. A Gallup poll held in November–December put Kenyans as the most optimistic in the world, cited in Kimani Njogu, *Youth and Peaceful Elections in Kenya* (Taweza Communications 2013) 112.

[14] The cultural center where the NCC met—and became known as "Bomas."

[15] The case was *Njoya v. Attorney-General* Miscellaneous Civil Application No. 82 of 2004 (OS) [2004] eKLR (2008) KLR (EP) 658. Available at <http://kenyalaw.org/caselaw/cases/view/16582>. Ghai was informed by a senior government official that Kibaki and ministers with ethnic affiliations to him intended to move to court to declare the process unconstitutional on the ground that it did not provide for a referendum. Ghai therefore speeded up the process and managed to complete it before the case was concluded. Among the unfortunate consequences of this haste was that interesting ideas about devolution could not be pursued.

led to something of a crisis atmosphere in those last days, and considerable pressure to agree on a draft as soon as possible, in contrast to the earlier lackadaisical approach.

There was provision for a referendum if the NCC was deadlocked over a particular issue but this was never resorted to. The final stage involved the submission of the draft as approved by the NCC to the National Assembly, whose only choice was to vote "Yes" or "No" on the Bill as a whole; it had no power to amend the Bill. In accordance with section 47 of the then Constitution, National Assembly approval required the vote of at least 65 percent of the members—within one week of submission to the Assembly.

Devolution debates

Homing in on devolution, we look first at the relationship between the political shenanigans and devolution. But we cannot understand this without understanding a little about Kenyan politics generally. Many politicians did not take the Commission process (or even perhaps the whole idea of a new Constitution) seriously because they assumed that they would have the last say through parliament (though politicians did play a more active role in the National Conference in its latter stages). Only two parties made major presentations to the CKRC. And this indifference to the process continued well into the NCC—until the Kibaki–Odinga coalition began to come apart, and Kibaki decided to keep the old presidency-friendly Constitution.

Then we saw politics at its rawest. Kenya politics is about capturing the state, for accumulating personal wealth. The key for politicians is to build support by stimulating ethnic conflicts in order to solidify their base in their own ethnic community, and then look for suitable partners from other communities to ensure a majority vote. Public policy is the least of their concerns or interests. These considerations began to pervade the CKRC as it reached the decision-making stage, and with it the gradual diminishing of the influence of civil society.

Although most political parties had made some sort of submission to the CKRC, when it came to the NCC it was very difficult to hold any sort of party line. If not concerned only with their personal advantage, MPs were largely motivated by ethnic considerations.[16] Of course, to the extent that the devolution issue was an ethnic one, this motivation might have been expected to produce ethnic/party positions on the topic. While MPs' engagement with the process was generally sporadic, a good number participated in devolution discussions.

Kibaki, a Kikuyu, and the key Luo leader, Odinga, differed on the form of government. Kibaki wanted the old type presidential system (although—when in opposition—he had told the CKRC that one of the problems with the old Constitution was the "imperial presidency"), and Odinga, the parliamentary. But there were also differences over devolution: Kibaki and his supporters from the Kikuyu and related ethnic groups wanted to keep the centralized system while Odinga wanted devolution with the provinces, and not the districts, as the principal site of power. When Kibaki's group embarked on their strategy of disbanding the NCC, there was fresh enthusiasm among Luo and some other ethnic groups for devolution and a parliamentary system, as more conducive to power-sharing.

[16] When Ghai asked Uhuru Kenyatta, leader in the NCC of KANU, why it did not have coherent positions, he said that it was impossible to impose party discipline in the face of ethnic factions.

The main party submissions to the CKRC came from Kibaki's Democratic Party and later from the National Alliance for Change of which his party was a part.[17] The latter's submission[18] spoke in terms of strong local government rather than using the language of devolution: "The new Constitution should create viable, well financed local authorities for its respective local government, the new constitution should also ensure equitable distribution of national resources, enhance participatory democracy and grass root development through local authorities."[19]

Mindful of the baggage that the word *majimbo* carried, the Commission was anxious to distinguish devolution from it.[20] Yet it was hard to articulate the distinction clearly. Debates in the country were already underway, and the predicted divisions were emerging. One speaker characterized both sides as motivated by fear: of ethnic economic marginalization on the one hand or ethnic cleansing on the other.[21] Some opposed *majimbo* because they feared would lead to people being evicted from their homes if they lived outside their ancestral home territory, and others feared the loss of their land.[22] In both the Coast and the Rift Valley land was a strong source of complaint, specifically that outsiders were taking land, and in the Rift Valley there was something of a history of being driven from their own land, especially by European and later by Kikuyu settlers. At the Coast and in the north, the religious factor was also a consideration.

Although opinion on specific aspects was divided, the vast majority wanted the main recipient of devolved powers to be the existing districts (but with possibility of change of boundaries)—the administrative unit they were most familiar with. They wanted local control of many functions which affected their everyday life.

CKRC Proposals

The Commission presented its recommendations as being neither federal nor unitary. It placed considerable emphasis on the objectives of devolution, which included the promotion of: democracy, accountability, national unity, self-governance, the interests and rights of minorities and marginalized communities, access to services, and, on a broader front, enhancement of checks and balances.

Districts were to be the principal level of devolution, with directly elected councils and administrators. Powers were distributed between councils and the center; certain powers were to be concurrent.

Provincial councils were to be indirectly elected from districts, with an executive comprising district administrators. They were to assist and support district governments, promote cooperation, and develop provincial infrastructure. The taxing powers of districts were to be determined by an Act of Parliament. In some respects the proposals on details were tentative in that many of these would be spelled out in a

[17] For this short-lived alliance, see Hornsby (n 2) 674–5.

[18] See CKRC, "Public Hearing—National Alliance for Change at Charter Hall Nairobi, on 07/03/02." Available on Katiba Institute Arches site <https://preview.tinyurl.com/NAKCharterHall>.

[19] Kiraitu Murungi presenting the submission.

[20] Clear from a seminar attended by local and foreign experts, including Professor Ron Watts, Christina Murray, and Richard Simeon in December 2001.

[21] Duncan Okello of the Society for International Development reporting on a meeting SID had held with two political parties.

[22] Maalim Mohammed, MP, CKRC, "Verbatim Report of North Eastern Provincial Round Up Held at Nomad Resort Hotel June 09, 2002" (on file with authors).

Devolution Act, including a mechanism to change boundaries. The CKRC proposal was for a system anchored on the seventy existing districts, which meant that the 1963 structure of eight regions (provinces) as the principal level of devolution was rejected, partly because some provinces were so large that their headquarters were as remote from most people as Nairobi itself, but also because of concerns around identity and potential conflict. As district boundaries were already contested, this was viewed as an interim proposal.

Devolution Discussion in the NCC

The NCC strongly and almost unanimously supported devolution, though there were considerable differences over the numbers of devolved units and the basis for them.[23] One speaker did say, "if we really want to devolve powers, we have to be very careful or else, instead of creating devolution, we shall create the devil himself."[24]

A number of delegates recommended that provinces cease to exist or be broken up. "That system has made us think in terms of tribes and we know tribalism is the biggest cancer in this country today," as an MP from Moyale (on the border with Ethiopia) said.[25] On the other hand, the former Vice-President of a Region in the majimbo period favored the provinces: "had we been allowed to continue, Chair, the story today in terms of development, would have been different. But because we allowed for the powers to be concentrated at the centre that was the genesis of corruption and the looting in this country."[26] Districts were the focus of identity for many, "I wanted it to go on record that we from the North don't want to be part of Rift Valley. With all due respect to Rift Valley, we've really suffered. You come to our headquarters in Samburu district, if there is a messenger to be employed at the D.C.'s office, the messenger is brought from Nakuru, the messenger is brought from Uasin Gishu. Why and yet we have very poor Samburus who could really work there?"[27] A factor in this was hostility to the Provincial Administration.

Some doubted the viability of districts as the main focus of devolution,[28] and some supported creating units in between existing provinces and districts, comprising a few existing districts merged.[29]

The CKRC set up a Task Force from its members to review the devolution recommendations. It considered the experience of many countries, drawing on the views of some CKRC members who had visited Germany and South Africa to study

[23] CKRC, Presentation of the Report of the Task Force on Devolution of Powers—Chapter 10, held at the Bomas of Kenya on August 21, 2003 (National Constitutional Conference) (available at https://preview.tinyurl.com/NCCDevTaskForce).

[24] Munene J. Othiniel, in debate at National Constitutional Conference, ibid.

[25] Galgallo Gurrach Boru MP NCC Plenary Proceedings, "Presentation of Draft Bill, Cont. of Chapter 10—Devolution of Power Held at the Bomas of Kenya, 22 May 2003" (available at https://preview.tinyurl.com/NCCDBChap10220503).

[26] Otieno Ogingo, Plenary Proceedings, "Presentation of Draft Bill, Cont. of Chapter 10—Devolution of Power Held at the Bomas of Kenya, 23 May 2003" (n 1).

[27] District Delegate Sophia Lepuchirit (n 25).

[28] E.g. Crispin Odhiambo Mbai—who became chair of the Devolution Technical Working Committee, and was murdered a few months later (probably not because of his work on this matter) (ibid).

[29] E.g. Charles Edward Ohare, a regional minister in the brief Majimbo days. CKRC National Constitutional Conference, "Verbatim Report of Plenary Proceedings, Presentation of Draft Bill, Cont. of Chapter 10—Devolution of Power Held at the Bomas of Kenya on 26th May 2003." Available at https://preview.tinyurl.com/NCCDBChap10-260503.

their devolution systems, as well as on the literature regarding various forms of decentralization and devolution.[30] One member, Mutakha Kangu, played a key role in guiding the committee toward the adoption of the South African model—particularly in terms of intergovernmental relations. But its conclusions still included the CKRC draft provision whereby, after adoption of the Constitution, laws would be made on many details of devolution as agreed in principle.[31]

The Task Force responded to concerns expressed at the NCC by proposing larger regional units as the principal locus of devolution: initially it suggested three options; namely ten, thirteen, or eighteen units (having also considered other possibilities even up to twenty-seven). One of the objectives was said to be "cultural homogeneity, harmony and integration, taking into consideration ethnicity and historical factors."[32] They reduced the number of levels of government to four (national, region/zone, county/district, and location).

By mid-September 2003 the conference had decided on one option: that of eighteen "zones."[33] Debate in the NCC on devolution focused to a considerable extent (by no means exclusively) on the zones. Specific objections tended to concern smaller communities and where they were to be located, with whom they were to be grouped, and how far the zone headquarters would be from them.[34] The main exception to this was the Somali community, which was initially proposed to be split into two zones, but was re-united in the final proposals.

The NCC Technical Committee on devolution, which completed the detailed work, was the most active and numerous committee, and given to passionate support of devolution.[35] The tensions are shown by two somewhat contrasting principles agreed at its meeting of September 22, 2003: "Ethnicity should not be used as criteria for devolution. It should be a way to assist the Marginalised," but "Historical and cultural background be considered when dealing with devolution of powers." At one point it proposed an additional, special, unit for the small Teso people "because of its peculiar historical and cultural background."[36] The Committee tried to take into account the requests of delegates from the areas concerned, such as "That Delegates from Samburu . . . proposed that Samburu be allowed to join Moyale, Marsabit and Isiolo because they have similar lifestyles and livestock economy is their mainstay," although

[30] Presented to the NCC on August 23, 2003—see CKRC, National Constitutional Conference, "Verbatim Report of Presentation of Report of The Task Force on Devolution of Powers Held at the Bomas of Kenya on 21st August, 2003" available at https://preview.tinyurl.com/PresTFonDevolution

[31] For a study of the similarities between devolution in South Africa and Kenya, see Nico Steytler and Yash Ghai (eds), *Kenyan-South African Dialogue on Devolution* (Juta Publishers 2016).

[32] The Constitution of Kenya Review Commission, "Special Working Document for the National Constitutional Conference: Report on Devolution of Powers" (Prepared by the Commission and Approved for Issue at a Steering Committee Meeting August 19, 2003) <http://katibainstitute.org/Archives/images/CKRC/CK/Special%20Working%20Documents/DEVOLUTION%20OF%20POWERS.pdf>.

[33] Constitution of Kenya Review Commission, "Verbatim Report of Plenary Proceedings, Presentation and Debate on The Draft Provision on Culture, Affirmative Action & Devolution, Held at Bomas of Kenya on 16th September 2003" (National Constitutional Conference September 16, 2003) available at https://preview.tinyurl.com/NCC160903.

[34] Particularly the Mount Elgon and Teso people.

[35] Constitution of Kenya Review Commission, "The Final Report of Technical Working Group 'G' on Devolution of Powers Approved for Issue at the 110th Plenary Meeting of The Constitution of Kenya Review Commission" (National Constitutional Conference November 30, 2005) <www.constitutionnet.org/vl/item/final-report-technical-working-group-g-devolution-powers>.

[36] The quotation is from the minutes of the Technical Committee on September 22, 2003, see n35.

at the same meeting[37] "Some delegates suggested that delegates have no mandate to take decisions on behalf of their districts."

The sensitivity of the issues is shown by the fact that the Committee chose, only on this one issue, to decide by secret ballot between options when discussing two zones in the North Rift area. The vote was very close and it took two or three Committee meetings before it was resolved in favor of the solution that was lost on the first vote. The proposers of the motions tended to be prominent Rift Valley politicians. Discussions and revisions of the grouping of districts into zones continued into late February 2004, again a sign of the difficulty of the issues.

At the end of January 2004, the Commission drew up a list of still "contentious issues" including: "Whether there should be three or four levels of devolution; Whether the constituency rather than the district should be a unit of devolution; The constitution of membership of legislative councils/assemblies below the national legislature; Mode of creation of units of devolution immediately below the national government; Distribution of powers between various levels of government."[38]

There were differences on three major issues: the system of government (parliamentary or presidential), devolution (the sites of power), and applicability of the *sharia* to Muslims in family matters. A variety of deadlock breaking strategies were employed. A political party initiative to resolve these issues outside the framework of the NCC failed, especially when "a number of government ministers began to project this initiative as a process alternative to the Conference [which] made rejection of its recommendations virtually certain."[39]

An intra-NCC consensus building group set up by the Steering Committee produced some recommendations on topics including the executive and devolution. The conference Rapporteur General, Professor Okoth-Ogendo, commented that most of the protagonists on these issues were members of the ruling party,[40] which was interesting in view of their low profile in the NCC itself. The Steering Committee of the NCC set up a committee to mediate between the two political groups, but failed. European diplomats requested Ghai to be given a chance to mediate—but also failed. The Conference itself set up a yet another body.[41] None of the last body's recommendations were accepted by the Conference, and this led to the walkout by the Kibaki MPs and supporters.

For reasons that are not really clear, the eighteen regions were reduced to fourteen in late February. This followed on a "retreat" of chairs of technical committees at which a new draft was hammered out.[42] The consequence was that five of the existing provinces remained intact. Committee members were given a weekend to consult with their fellow delegates about the division of the other provinces. A matter of days before the winding up of the NCC, Ghai produced a document: "A Compromise Proposal for Devolution" making it clear that there was still a good deal of confusion on the topic.[43] He suggested that the root of the problem lay with the question of what was the principal unit of devolution: "One group favours the district, the other the region. The compromise the committee struck (which reflects CKRC's proposal) is to

[37] Minutes for September 23, ibid.

[38] CKRC, "The Report of The Rapporteur—General to the National Constitutional Conference on its Deliberations Between January 12–March 23, 2004 at the Bomas of Kenya" (National Constitutional Conference 2004) http://katibainstitute.org/Archives/images/Rapporteur-%20Generals%20NCC%20Report%20on%20Bomas%20III.pdf Appendix A.

[39] ibid p. 11. [40] ibid p. 12. [41] ibid p. 13.

[42] "Final Report of Technical Working Group 'G' " (n 35).

[43] Dated March 7, 2004, on file with the authors.

vest significant devolved powers in the district but to find a not unimportant role for the region . . . This produces somewhat confused lines of authority as well as adding greatly to the cost of devolution." He suggested that one way to cut through this complex system was to reduce the levels of government to two, the national and the county/region, of which there would be about 20, with authority to set up a system of local government. Each county would have a real prospect of discharging its responsibilities. This proposal would achieve greater economies of scale than a system based on districts, while at the same time it would enable greater participation of people than would be possible in a system based on the existing provinces. The smaller regions would be less threatening to national unity and more protective of the interests of minorities. However, the NCC adopted, on March 11, 2004, fourteen regions, and seventy districts (the latter as the main recipient of powers).

The closing stages of the NCC were so rushed and politically charged that, even after the conference adopted a draft, the CKRC found it necessary to check it and made some revisions based on the official records, some of which affected the devolution chapter—but not the core issues.[44]

Process of adoption

The original scheme for adopting the new Constitution was that the Bill adopted by the NCC would go to parliament, which would apply Section 47 of the existing Constitution whereby the parliament had either to accept or to reject the document as a whole; it could not introduce an amendment.

It is now clear that in the closing stages of the NCC process, in late February 2004, most of the Commissioners of the CKRC were meeting with the Parliamentary Select Committee on the Constitution (PSC), without the full knowledge of the chair, but presumably at the initiative of the PSC, to discuss how the Constitution might be amended to give parliament a fuller role, so as to build consensus in parliament to ensure that it would be passed.[45] A PSC member said "I think what has been eluding us is how the elite itself arrives at a consensus so that that consensus joins with the consensus of Wanjiku[46] to give Kenya a Constitution."[47]

At the time, the Kibaki group members of the PSC were boycotting the NCC (the PSC Chair called it a strategic decision).[48] What they were proposing was a deviation from a process deliberately intended to limit the role of parliament, because all the MPs were members of the NCC. Yet what they were planning was to give themselves ("the elite," Kibwana called them) the power to defeat the will of the NCC. But they had decided to implicate the CKRC, and persuaded its members (seventeen of them) to come up with a proposal on how to do it—and to join them in presenting it to the media.[49]

[44] See the "verification" process <http://www.katibainstitute.org/Archives/index.php/ckrc-process/verification-proc-docs-verbatim>; the document on Chapter 14 is relevant to devolution.

[45] Constitution of Kenya Review Commission, *Verbatim Report of Meeting Between CKRC Commissioners and Members of The Parliamentary Select Committee (PSC) Held at County Hall, Nairobi on February 192004*(Nation Constitutional Commission February 19, 2004) <www.constitutionnet.org/vl/item/verbatim-report-meeting-between-ckrc-commissioners-and-members-parliamentary-select-4>.

[46] Wanjiku is a common Kikuyu name, used to represent the common person, especially since former President Moi asked what could Wanjiku know about a Constitution.

[47] Kivutha Kibwana.

[48] Minutes of the meeting of February 26, 2004.

[49] The irony was that some of the most ardent supporters of the Kibaki government position had previously followed Moi's instructions.

The decision of the court in the *Njoya* case[50] put a stop to the process that was supposed to lead smoothly from the NCC draft to enactment. It opened the way for the plans discussed between the parliamentarians and a section of the CKRC to amend the Review Act in favor of parliamentary discretion. (Ghai had tried repeatedly and unsuccessfully to persuade the Attorney-General to ensure that the Constitution was amended to entrench the process, to prevent precisely this sort of development.) This elicited a flurry of public activity, mostly directed at the idea that the initiative was being taken away from the people, though there was wide support for the referendum element in the scheme. There was a petition to parliament (only the second the Speaker had ever received), presented by William Ruto (who is now Deputy President), seeking deferment of discussion of a revised draft Constitution until the constitutionality of the Act to amend the process was established, as well as adoption of a constitutional amendment to guarantee a referendum.[51] A civil society-backed court action sought unsuccessfully to stop the National Assembly from debating revision of the NCC draft.[52] And the media reported that "Civil societies yesterday threatened to storm Parliament on July 19 unless MPs stop debate on the Draft Constitution."[53]

The new process was supposed to be one of consensus—and the parliamentarians, at a retreat, agreed on two levels of government: the national and the "county," the latter bigger than the districts but smaller than the NCC regions. The roles assigned to the regions, the districts and the locations in the NCC draft should be assigned to the counties. But, confusingly the current administrative districts would remain in place.[54]

In the event the Bill for a new Constitution that was prepared provided for the existing seventy districts to be the sole basis of devolution. The powers of districts were to be similar to those in the NCC draft, but could be changed by ordinary legislation. Although the hated Provincial Administration was to be abolished, there was no provision for a Senate. This would have been a much weaker form of devolution—small, presumably weak, units, with little guaranteed power and no supporting Senate. The draft also provided for a more presidential system of government. Parliament adopted the Bill, aided, at least in part, by an opposition boycott.

This draft, generally known as the Wako Draft after the Attorney General, who was widely believed to have taken over the process, was submitted to a referendum in 2005. It was rejected by 3.5 million to 2.5 million votes. Resentment at the take-over of the draft by parliament was no doubt one factor, but the geographical spread of the voting indicates that the main factor was a verdict on the presidency of Mwai Kibaki, in regional/ethnic terms. Only in the Kikuyu Central Province was the majority vote "Yes."[55]

Outcome

Opposition to the Bill had been led by former members of Kibaki's government (Raila Odinga and his LDP) and Uhuru Kenyatta, Moi and Ruto of KANU.[56] Hornsby says,

[50] See (n 16). [51] National Assembly Deb July 20, 2005, 2528–9.

[52] *Onyango v. Attorney General* [2005] KHC 677, [2005] Miscellaneous Civil Application 677.

[53] "Civil Society Opposed to Debate on Bomas Draft" *The Standard* (Nairobi, July 20, 2005).

[54] The Parliamentary Select Committee on Constitutional Review, Summary of Report of the Retreat, Sopa Lodge, Naivasha (National Assembly November 4–7, 2004) on file with the authors.

[55] For an account see Bård Anders Andreassen and Arne Tostensen, *Of Oranges and Bananas: The 2005 Kenya Referendum on the Constitution* (Chr. Michelsen Institute 2006) <https://www.cmi.no/publications/file/2368-of-oranges-and-bananas.pdf>.

[56] Hornsby (n 2) 739.

"The LDP was now effectively in opposition." The campaign changed Kenyan politics, and produced a new party and name: the Orange Democratic Movement (ODM), using as its symbol the orange, the symbol for the "No" vote in the referendum.

Although the government liked to say, for example, in reports to UN human rights monitoring bodies, that Kenya was working on a new, improved Constitution, little happened for the next two years. But in late 2007, there was considerable violence, death, and displacement on ethnic grounds following ODM accusations that the result of the presidential election was rigged. The ethnic tensions and violence in 2007 had not been exacerbated by the 2000–05 process, though it did reflect them. Indeed, it was felt that, had something like the Bomas Draft been in place, the disputes and violence of 2007–08 might not have happened.

A resolution of the crisis was found through an internationally brokered "National Accord," which not only brought Odinga into government, in the newly created position of prime minister,[57] but also included a commitment to produce a new Constitution, in recognition that this major issue was unresolved. A Committee of Experts on the Constitution was appointed in 2009, and it included three foreigners out of nine members,[58] like the other bodies appointed under the National Accord; namely, the commissions on the electoral systems, on the violence, and on truth and transitional justice. It took the NCC draft as its starting point, while consulting other drafts including the CKRC and Wako drafts. On devolution, its first draft envisaged districts as the main unit, with coordinating regions (the eight provinces). The regions were later dropped: comments suggested their roles were limited and unclear.

But the CoE opted, in their second draft, to base the structure on the last "legal" districts, before the presidents started on their district creation sprees. They reduced the districts (which they renamed "counties") from seventy-four in their first draft to forty-seven. The CoE was prompted in part by a court decision that only the forty-seven districts as of 1992 were legal.[59] The CoE introduced more features from South Africa, particularly in the area of conflict resolution and the financial system.

The CoE process was also taken over by parliamentarians who demanded various changes, in a consultation this time prescribed by law. Unlike parliament in 2005, this Parliamentary Select Commission did not abolish the proposed Senate, though they did describe it as "a Lower House with limited legislative role." The CoE disregarded some PSC innovations, but basically accepted the provision for the Senate to: "exercise oversight over funds devolved to the county governments"—the source of much current puzzlement—as it did the removal of the Senate's role in non-county-related legislation.

The Constitution was adopted—by a referendum—in August 2010, but the devolution provisions did not come into effect until the 2013 elections. Thus this major departure from previous governance has been in operation for only five years.[60] Only a tentative assessment can be made of the structures, policies, and performance of county governments and their relationships with the national government. However,

[57] This was done through an amendment to the Constitution. For a description of the whole process, see Office of the AU Panel of Eminent African Personalities, *Back from the Brink: the 2008 mediation process and reforms in Kenya* (African Union Commission 2014).

[58] These three were Christina Murray, Chaloka Beyani, and Frederick Ssempebwa.

[59] *Job Nyasimi Momanyi v. Attorney-General* [2009] HCK 68, (2009) eKLR 1. The 1992 Districts and Provinces Act was the relevant legislation.

[60] There is one major book on the system, but as a legal analysis not an evaluation, John Mutakha Kangu, *Constitutional Law of Kenya on Devolution* (Strathmore University Press 2015) 89. Kangu was the CKRC Commissioner who contributed a great deal to the devolution provisions.

in early 2014 the National Assembly established a Working Group, chaired by the Auditor General, to carry out an assessment of the Constitution, especially of its impact on the economy, public institutions, and society. It was widely believed that the MPs anticipated that the report would rubbish much of the Constitution, but the Auditor General and his team did not oblige. In this brief evaluation we draw on its report, published in 2016, [61] and other more anecdotal sources.

We have shown how central to debates were the number and size of devolved units. The Working Group observed that many of the counties are made up of people who "share a common history, undertake common economic activities, and speak the same language." They concluded that

> the county governments as presently constituted are favourable for ethnic and social inclusion. The individual units also comprise population that is not too large and not too small to promote local self-governance, democracy, and delivering quality basic services as envisaged under the Constitution.[62]

A central objective, and popular expectation, of devolution was improved service delivery.[63] The Working Group said that in all the counties, there is evidence of improvement in service delivery, with some counties experiencing services well beyond what they had received since independence.[64] But a Transparency International survey in 2016 reported that 48 percent of respondents could identify some service (including infrastructure) that had improved with county government, 21 percent said nothing had improved.[65]

The objective first mentioned in the Constitution is "democratic and accountable exercise of power."[66] The Working Group concluded that devolution had indeed "enhanced transparency and social accountability where citizens are more aware and hold leaders responsible on the use of their resources."[67] The Transparency International survey reported that 38 percent of people had had contact with their county assembly member about a problem, as opposed to 19 percent who had contact with their MP, which does suggest that government has been brought somewhat closer to the people by devolution.[68]

On the more negative side there is corruption. County assembly members are particularly criticized for selfishness and misappropriation or misuse of public funds, for example, it is said, sometimes coercing Governors with threats of impeachment. These impressions from the media are supported by the Working Group.[69]

Corruption has been a major cause of conflicts within counties. Corruption suspicions were involved in the first effort to impeach a Governor. He was removed by the Senate. The High Court reinstated him; he was removed again. The Court of Appeal reinstated him, reversing the High Court and holding that there was inadequate

[61] Office of the Auditor-General, "Report of the Working Group on Socio-Economic Audit of the Constitution of Kenya, 2010" (Office of the Auditor-General September 2016) <https://africacheck.org/wp-content/uploads/2017/01/SocialAudit2010.pdf>.

[62] ibid paras 4–24. [63] Constitution of Kenya, art. 174(f).

[64] Office of the Auditor-General (n 56), paras 4–10.

[65] Transparency International Kenya, "The Kenya County Government Status Report, 2016" (Transparency International Kenya 2016) p. 30 <https://tikenya.org/wp-content/uploads/2017/09/TI-Kenya_County-Governance-Status-Report_2016.pdf>.

[66] Constitution of Kenya, art. 174(a).

[67] Office of the Auditor-General (n 56), paras 6–83.

[68] Transparency International Kenya (n 60), p. 12.

[69] See also Michelle D'Arcy and Agnes Cornell, "Devolution and Corruption In Kenya: Everyone's Turn To Eat?" (2016) 115 (459) *African Affairs* 246.

public participation, that the factual basis for removal had not been established and that there was an appearance of bias on the part of the Senate Committee.[70]

In one county—Makueni—stalemate resulting from tensions between the county Governor and assembly, as well as from assembly members' siphoning off funds, got so bad that a Commission of Inquiry was appointed by the President.[71] It recommended that the President, and Senate, exercise their power to suspend the county government, but the President declined to act insisting that, despite the "most alarming and deplorable litany of failures" the evidence is not strong enough, and that other methods exist to deal with corruption,[72] as well as arguably for reasons of political calculation.

Intergovernmental relations have been somewhat problematic. The Auditor-General's Working Group identified lack of a solid assessment of costs of functions as a cause of disputes between levels of government. The insistence of the counties on a "big bang" transfer of functions instead of the phased approach envisaged by the Constitution, something that was also demanded by the expectations of citizens, has created its own problems. And counties have not always respected the limits of their powers, and, indeed, those limits are not always clear.[73] The Working Group observes that evidence suggests that what is supposed to be "cooperative" devolution is less than fully successful.[74] There has been some undermining of devolution by increased use of conditional grants by national to county government.[75]

Mediation of intergovernmental disputes is little used, and the mechanism poorly developed. As the Working Group commented, "In general, inter-governmental relations in Kenya devolution have been adversarial. Yet, cooperative devolved government requires that the society moves away from the adversarial approach to consultation, negotiation and consensus building approach."[76]

Senate has been as much a rival as a supporter of the counties. Senators have been taken aback by what they consider are their limited powers, and jockey for power and publicity with Governors and Members of the National Assembly. In the 2017 elections, several stood, some successfully, for Governor, a phenomenon not unconnected to the financial benefits available to the latter.

From a financial point of view some counties have shown weak capacity to raise their own revenue.[77] Second, there is no doubt it has been expensive. The burden of paying so many legislators is high: Kenyans are over-represented by expensive representatives.[78]

However, surveys show that Kenyans overwhelmingly support devolution, despite criticisms of corruption and often ineffectiveness.[79] This is borne out by the Working Group's own survey, which showed that devolution is "well embedded in people's lives."[80]

[70] *Martin Nyaga Wambora v. County Assembly of Embu* [2015] HCK 194 (2015) eKLR <http://kenyalaw.org/caselaw/cases/view/117084/>.

[71] The report of the Committee, chaired by Mohammed Nyaoga, has not been published, but has been widely reported on.

[72] Manoah Esipisu, "Statement by State House Spokesperson in the Matter of the Petition to Suspend Makueni County Government" (*Official Website of the President*, September 6, 2015) <www.president.go.ke/2015/09/06/statement-by-state-house-spokesperson-in-the-matter-of-the-petition-to-suspend-makueni-county-government/>.

[73] Transparency International Kenya (n 60), pp. 24–6.

[74] Office of the Auditor-General (n 56), paras 4–80 to 83. [75] ibid paras 4–113 to 14.

[76] ibid paras 4–83. [77] ibid paras 4–58 to 60. [78] ibid paras 6–95 to 96.

[79] "Ipsos" 1st Quarter SPEC (Social, Political, Economic and Cultural): Second Media Release: Devolution Support for the Principle, Critical of the Practice" <www.ipsos.co.ke/spr/downloads/polls/SPEC_Poll_Narrative_Report_22nd_April_2015.pdf>.

[80] Office of the Auditor-General (n 56), paras 4–9.

There is another set of issues: those related to ethnicity and to the reasons for having a new Constitution. The Working Group commented that county governments, like the national, had not been effective in ensuring that recruitment to public offices reflects regional and ethnic diversity.[81] Another author suggested that, "The new county governments and the political and economic largesse that comes with them are, if not managed equitably, likely to further exacerbate existing conflicts in the poor and conflict-prone counties of northern Kenya."[82]

Some have suggested that the 2013 elections were peaceful in part because devolution gave people an alternative focus for their interest and loyalties; the election for the presidency was not the only game in town. If so, whether this remains the case for future elections will presumably depend on how successful county government is perceived to be, something that will depend in part on how far the national government allows counties to govern and to do "their own thing."

Lessons Learned

The 2000–04 phase of the process showed that much can be done in Constitution making even in the absence of an immediate crisis. Indeed, after the elections of 2002 the heat had gone out of the question of Moi, but interest in the Constitution remained high. But one might reasonably take the view that the absence of a crisis made it easier for reactionary forces to strategize to defeat enactment of the Constitution. Almost certainly they were at least as happy in 2005 to remain with the existing Constitution as they would have been with the Wako draft. And in 2008–10 the sense of crisis, and the international community through Kofi Annan and some other eminent African leaders, played a critical role in pushing the process to conclusion, largely along the lines of the NCC draft. External pressure was lacking in 2002–03, when foreign countries were far more focused on having elections, and getting rid of Moi, than on a new Constitution.

On the face of it, the 2000–04 process made a lot of sense: broad consensus among key groups in a series of national conferences; consensus reflected in CKRC's mandate and process; emphasis on consultations with the people; a broad based constituent assembly (nearly one-third being civil society and one-third being MPs); and back to parliament for a "Yes/No" vote. Consultation with the people worked very positively, especially as the CKRC did very careful analyses of their views and recommendations, which were then widely circulated, and formed a basis of its own proposals. Realistic discussion could only begin once there were concrete proposals, which were made in the draft Constitution published by the CKRC in September 2002. But the earlier discussions with the public were an important factor in developing public support for the process, and almost certainly account in no small measure for the strong support, not always backed up by detailed knowledge, now expressed by ordinary Kenyans for the Constitution. At that stage, people were able to express their dominant concerns, not often in terms familiar to constitutional lawyers, and it was for the CKRC to reflect those concerns in its ultimate draft.

[81] ibid paras 12–18 to 24.

[82] Aden Abdi, "Clans, conflicts and devolution in Mandera, Kenya" (*Peace Insight*, October 14, 2014) <www.insightonconflict.org/2014/10/clans-conflicts-devolution-mandera-finding-durable-solution-conflict-degodia-garre/>.

The 2000–04 process was complex with perhaps too many institutions. There are some difficulties with a process that involves a draft, based on the wishes of the people, followed by an assembly largely of those with limited understanding of the constitutional matters. The design was that the NCC would refine and improve the CKRC draft, but, in the event, this did not happen as much as had been anticipated. However, the NCC process did improve the devolution proposals, as outlined above.

Would it have been better if politicians were given the dominant role at that later stage? Some might think so. But the nature of Kenyan politics must be taken into account. The dominance of personal interest, and the manipulation of ethnicity to achieve that, do not encourage one to have any faith in the national orientation of the politicians. Maybe if they had not been confident that they held the ultimate whip hand (as the post-NCC events showed) they might have taken the NCC more seriously and truly engaged in it. Certainly they could not have been kept out—and even if they were, they would still have manipulated by string-pulling. Having them fully in, without the last word being with the National Assembly, would perhaps have been better.

The right balance between politicians, experts, and civil society is hard to achieve. Arguably the Kenyan processes have suffered from a lack of expertise, and a dominance of politics. Neither the CKRC nor, later, the CoE, had a solid core of constitutional experts. But some members of both bodies made major contributions, and political interference was the major obstacle to the production of the highest quality of Constitution drafting. A stronger phalanx of legal and other experts might have enabled political interference to be mitigated—but that is not how Kenyan bodies are appointed.

The process was long drawn out. The first part—national conferences—was necessary, to build some kind of consensus after years of authoritarian and tribalist rule, requiring almost a catharsis. The principal approach to the process and substance of the new Constitution was agreed. This consensus, confirmed by what many people told the CKRC, facilitated the CKRC's role.

Deadlines and timing are always crucial. The irony is that the Kenyan processes have had in theory quite tight timelines. But an early act of the CKRC commissioners was to seek an extension for their work. On the other hand, the CoE had no deadline for submission of its first draft. It submitted it just before Christmas, but a timeline then kicked in giving little time for discussion.

If a process goes on for too long, it is not unlikely that parties might change their minds as they weigh the implications of change for themselves. This happened (as discussed above) with the Kikuyu group. Kibaki, who had from the beginning been a supporter of constitutional reform, became the very person (with two or three close advisers) who killed the draft Constitution, made after nearly four years of consultations, meetings, and negotiations. Senior officials in the Catholic and Anglican churches followed a line not dissimilar to that of Kibaki and his supporters.

What this underlines is the desirability of decisions being made behind Rawls' veil of ignorance.[83] If the initial process could have started moving sooner, this might have been possible. And if the CKRC had not been so successful in dragging its heels, to the financial advantage of the commissioners, again maybe the election would not have intervened. On the other hand, to have held the election within a matter of months after the new electoral law had come into force would have faced the Election

[83] John Rawls, *Theory of Justice* (Harvard University Press 1971).

Commission with an intolerable task. The CoE's process, by contrast, finished over two years before the next election.

Deadlock breaking is important and can be useful but in Kenya for various reasons did not work. Even mechanisms involving only politicians did not yield a final settlement. Again the possibility of trumping the process in parliament may have had something to do with this. But it does not explain the inability of opposition politicians to stick to an agreement. This suggests a lack of skill in negotiating, including not having a clear sense of what one's own position is, or perhaps not having made a clear decision in one's own party before embarking on negotiations.

Referendum

The notion of referendum played an important role, in politics as well as in the outcome. A referendum was not a requirement in the making of the old Constitution. A different scheme, of extensive consultations with the Somalis in the North-East, to find out if they wanted secession was applied (but their overwhelming support for secession was disregarded).

The CKRC Act provided for a referendum for each of the controversial issues at the NCC, seriatim. It was not used because it was considered complicated, expensive and time consuming. In turn, the adoption by the NCC of the draft Constitution was challenged because it was not put to a referendum; the Court upheld the challenge even though there was no such provision in the CKRC Act. The consequence was that the old, much maligned, Constitution was maintained. A referendum was prescribed for the process that resumed in 2008, after post-election violence, and 67 percent of voters supported the new proposal, though voting unfortunately split largely on ethnic lines (as in the 2005 referendum). The new Constitution requires a referendum for amendment of specified articles,[84] and also a referendum to initiate a separate process for constitutional amendments of the Constitution ("popular initiative").[85] The democratic and participatory nature of the new Constitution has increased support for referendums in changing the Constitution. But some remain skeptical about the values of referendums, especially if the process itself is highly consultative and participatory.

We have to be mindful of the nature of the overall Kenya political system, which is excessively driven by greed, corruption, ethnicity, and violence—in violation of constitutional values. In these respects devolution has replicated the national practice, particularly corruption and violence.

As noted, there is some controversy as to the consequences of devolution, there being greater support for it than criticism. It is almost universally agreed that devolved governments are much better than the national government as far as the administration of counties is concerned. Some of the benefits of devolution are the following: some easing of ethnic tensions as most communities have some autonomy (though national politics continue to be ethnic), freedom to make decisions about matters that are of daily concern, and visible signs of "development"—street lights, tarred roads, improved hospitals, and involvement of the people in the affairs of the county. An additional possible benefit, though not undisputed, may be some de-ethnicization of politics, since quite often a county has a huge majority of one community. This tends to lead to intra-group rivalries in that such counties operate a competitive political system. The

[84] See Article 255, Constitution of Kenya 2010. [85] Article 257.

salience of one ethnic group is also diminished somewhat due to the constitutional requirement of minority representation in both the assembly and the government.

Critics, on the other hand, tend to argue that the benefits to the people have been meager in relation to the sums of money transferred to counties, to the wastage of money through the large number of counties, the scale of corruption, and constant conflicts, often violent, among Governors and assembly members, and Governors and Senators.

Inevitably, these circumstances have propelled some discussion on the wisdom of some decisions on the design of devolution. Various issues as to the design are still debated. One is whether it was sensible to create so many counties, with their own governments, meaning that a great deal of money goes on institutions, salaries, and resources, leaving little for "development," or whether the ideas so much debated at Bomas about ten, twelve, eighteen, or twenty larger units should have been pursued. Indeed this issue features prominently in ongoing (late 2018) debates on constitutional reform. A second issue is whether it was wise to stick to county boundaries essentially drawn up in 1963 and based on ethnic homogeneity as the criterion, when Kenyans are trying to promote national unity and common identity. A third issue is whether sufficient attention was paid to the structure and role of the Senate, as its members do not have sufficient links with the county governments (as in South Africa), its powers are limited, and it is clearly subordinate to the National Assembly. There is also a sense, that comes out clearly from the Auditor-General's report, that the transition could have been better handled: inadequate understanding of the costs of functions to be transferred, transfers happening too fast, and too many existing staff foisted on the counties.

How these things happened has, we hope, been indicated earlier. The difficulties of ethnic accommodation, changing ideas in the Constitution-making bodies about the most appropriate main site of devolution, the weight of history, the hubris of MPs (behind the demotion of the Senate), and the dearth of people with knowledge and understanding of multilevel government systems are among the explanations.

Consequently, people ask if devolution was designed by people who understood its implications, and were aware of the structures suitable for their functions and for intergovernmental relations. Might the lesson be that for issues that are both political and technical, once the political basis for devolution is agreed upon, it might have been better to have had a constitutional requirement for a process first of expert drafting of the necessary legislation and then of gradual implementation as capacities developed, under the supervision of an truly independent and expert body? This, it must be said, was what was envisaged in the very first, 2002, draft Constitution.

9

"Godot Has Arrived!"

Federal Restructuring in Nepal

Mara Malagodi

Overview

This chapter analyzes the process and modalities that led to the federalization of Nepal's unitary state. It explores the historical circumstances in which demands for federalism emerged and the federal settlement enshrined in Nepal's new Constitution promulgated on September 20, 2015. The question of federalism gained prominence in Nepal's public discourse during the "People's War," the ten-year-long armed insurgency (1996–2006) launched by the Communist Party of Nepal (Maoist) to overthrow the government. In fact, the drafting of Nepal's seventh Constitution was part of the peace process that began in 2006. The new dispensation was expected to reflect the political commitment to "building a New Nepal"—an inclusive and democratic polity—through a radical program of state restructuring. The Maoists, together with various ethno-cultural and regional groups, argued that the 1990 Constitution, which was to re-democratize the country after thirty years of Panchayat monarchical autocracy (1960–1990), inadequately addressed—if not reinforced—patterns of exclusion of many groups on the basis of class and/or identity and they saw territorial autonomy for ethno-linguistic and regional groups as the key solution to the country's rampant discrimination.

In April 2008, the first Constituent Assembly (CA1) was elected. It featured a relative Maoist majority, but was politically fragmented. The CA1 was unable to finalize and promulgate the new document due to profound disagreements over key matters, with federal restructuring proving to be the most contentious issue. The CA1 process led to the polarization between "pro-ethnic federalism" political forces—the Maoists and various Madhesi parties—and "anti-ethnic federalism" forces—the Nepali Congress, the various National Democratic Parties (RPP), and to a certain extent the Communist Party of Nepal (United Marxist-Leninist) (UML). After four extensions, the CA1 was eventually dissolved in May 2012 and a second Constituent Assembly (CA2) was elected in November 2013. The elections brought a relative majority to centrist parties—the Nepali Congress and UML. Following the disastrous earthquakes that hit Nepal in April and May 2015, the drafting of the new Constitution was "fast-tracked" leading to its promulgation in September. The new document, however, was met with growing protests in the Terai plains near the Indian border and an unofficial trade blockade by neighboring "India." At the time of writing, the new dispensation has already been amended once, and negotiations over a second amendment have been ongoing for over a year with regard to the controversial demarcation of the federal units. It is important to note that at the time of writing in February 2018 the creation

Territory and Power in Constitutional Transitions. First Edition. Edited by Michael Anderson and Sujit Choudhry. "Godot Has Arrived!": Federal Restructuring in Nepal © Mara Malagodi 2019. Published 2019 by Oxford University Press.

of the federal units of government has just started to take place after the elections in 2017.

Background

The period between 1990 and 2006 was Nepal's second experiment with democracy. In 1990, an alliance of banned and underground political parties succeeded in putting an end to the autocratic monarchical Panchayat regime. Pro-democracy leaders sought to institutionalize a constitutional monarchy and parliamentary democracy through the promulgation of the 1990 Constitution;[1] however, for many Nepalis this was an unsatisfying settlement. Moreover, political instability marred the country's parliamentary politics from 1994,[2] and the beginning of the People's War in 1996 led to an escalation of political violence and a progressive militarization of the state. The royal massacre of 2001, combined with the growing military successes of the Maoists, who by 2002 controlled roughly half of Nepal's territory, led to a further erosion of democratic politics.[3] Two bouts of emergency rule were proclaimed in 2002–03 and 2005, paving the way for another spell of autocratic monarchical rule under newly crowned King Gyanendra, until an alliance between the mainstream political parties and the Maoists succeeded in restoring democratic politics in April 2006.

The main grievances with regard to the 1990 Constitution were the semi-constitutional position of the Shah monarchy, a strong executive dominance, the overly centralized nature of state institutions, and the ethnocentric institutionalization of the nation at the constitutional level. The triumvirate of Nepali nationalism—the Shah monarchy, Hinduism, and the Nepali language—was, in fact, given centrality in the constitutional text to enshrine *Parbatiya* dominance also on a symbolic level.[4] In substantive terms, this hegemony was reflected in the under-representation of Janajati, Madhesi, Dalit, religious minorities, lower castes, and women in all the branches of the Nepali state leading to clear exclusionary patterns on the basis of identity. Furthermore, the 1990 Constitution banned the formation of political parties on a communal basis,[5] and retained the thirty-year-old ban on proselytism.[6]

The extent of social exclusion in Nepal is even more significant when related to the degree of sociocultural diversity of the country's population. The 2011 Census illustrates the varied composition of Nepal's population with 125 caste and ethnic groups, of which only the largest six are above 5 percent of the total population and they are not territorially concentrated.[7] The two biggest groups are the Chetri (i.e. Kshatriyas of local Khas origins) (16.6 percent) and Bahun (i.e. Hill Brahmins) (12.2 percent);

[1] Michael Hutt, "Drafting the Nepal Constitution, 1990" (1991) 31 (11) Asian Survey 1020.

[2] Martin Hoftun, William Raeper, and John Whelpton, *People, Politics and Ideology: Democracy and Social Change in Nepal* (Mandala Book Point 1999).

[3] Genevieve Lakier, "After the Massacre: Secrecy, Disbelief, and the Public Sphere in Nepal" in Raminder Kaur and William Mazzarella (eds), *Censorship in South Asia: Cultural Regulation From Sedition to Seduction* (Indiana University Press 2009); Deepak Thapa and Bandita Sijapati (eds), *A Kingdom under Siege: Nepal's Maoist Insurgency 1996 to 2003* (The Printhouse 2004).

[4] Mara Malagodi, *Constitutional Nationalism and Legal Exclusion: Equality, Identity Politics, and Democracy in Nepal* (OUP India 2013), chs 3 and 4.

[5] Constitution of the Kingdom of Nepal, 1990, art. 112(3).

[6] Constitution of the Kingdom of Nepal, 1990, art. 19(1).

[7] Government of Nepal, Central Bureau of Statistics, "2011 Census Major Highlights" <http://cbs.gov.np/image/data/Population/Major%20Highlights/Major-Finding.pdf> accessed December 6, 2015.

together they constitute the Parbatiya group, to which Nepal's royal family and elites belong. In terms of historically marginalized groups, dalits (i.e. "former untouchables") form about 14 percent of Nepal's population. The sixty-three groups classified under the umbrella term Adivasi Janajati (i.e. "indigenous people"), who can be described as ethno-linguistic groups that do not use Nepali as their mother tongue, account for 36 percent of the total population. Madhesi groups (i.e. non-Pahari "Terai plain dwellers," often erroneously described as "of Indian origins") constitute slightly less than 20 percent of the population. While Nepali remains the *lingua franca* of the majority, only 44.6 percent named it as their mother tongue, alongside ninety-one other mother tongues.[8] After the re-democratization of 1990, the Nepali state became even more Kathmandu-centric with Parbatiya males even more over-represented in state bodies (parliament, government, judiciary, civil service, police, army, universities, etc.), especially in the higher echelons.[9] These patterns reveal a clear link between poverty, marginalization, and identity.[10]

The reason for the discrimination faced by many of Nepal's ethno-linguistic, regional, and religious groups dates back to the country's creation as a modern state entity in the late eighteenth century. The military conquests initiated by King Prithvi Narayan Shah of Gorkha, a small kingdom lying west of the Kathmandu Valley, led to the annexation of many small principalities and kingdoms under Gorkhali sovereignty.[11] Hinduism and its association to the Shah monarchy were used as an important legitimizing tool.[12] This discrimination continued under the later regime of the Rana family (1846–1951), which assumed the powers of the monarch without displacing him, especially in the design of the 1854 *Muluki Ain* (Country Code), which slotted all the various ethno-linguistic, religious, and caste groups of Nepal within a single "national" caste hierarchy reinforcing Parbatiya hegemony.[13] Regrettably, Nepal's first experiment with democracy lasted for less than a decade (1951–60) as in 1960 King Mahendra Shah, abruptly brought it to an end with the support of the Army. The royal coup inaugurated three decades of monarchical autocracy under the legitimizing umbrella of ethnonationalist propaganda, centered on the Shah monarchy, Hinduism, and the Nepali language, thus further reinforcing patterns of exclusion within the country's population.[14]

Nepal's current administrative structure dates back to the Panchayat arrangements introduced in 1961, so it continues the regime's lack of recognition of sociocultural diversity in a territorial form. The Panchayat administration was territorially organized along two levels: second-tier local government bodies (with 75 Districts, *jilla*, 3,995 Village Development Committees, *gaum*, and 36 Municipalities, *nagar*); and first-tier

[8] Nepal Central Bureau of Statistics, *Statistical Pocket Book – Nepal 2002* (Central Bureau of Statistics 2002).

[9] Dhruba Kumar, "Social Structure and Voting Behaviour" in Lok Raj Baral (ed.), *Elections and Governance in Nepal* (Sage 2005), 210–11.

[10] Krishna B Bhattachan, "Possible Ethnic Revolution or Insurgency in a Predatory Unitary Hindu State, Nepal" in Dhruba Kumar (ed.), *Domestic Conflict and Crisis of Governability in Nepal* (Centre for Nepal and Asian Studies, Tribhuvan University 2000).

[11] Kumar Pradhan, *The Gorkha Conquests: The Process and Consequences of the Unification of Nepal, with Particular Reference to Eastern Nepal* (Oxford University Press 1991).

[12] Richard Burghart, *The Conditions of Listening: Essays on Religion, History and Politics in South Asia* (Oxford University Press 1996).

[13] András Höfer, *The Caste Hierarchy and the State in Nepal: A Study of the Muluki Ain of 1854* (Universitatsverlag Wagner 1979).

[14] Richard Burghart, "The Political Culture of *Panchayat* Democracy" in Michael Hutt (ed.), *Nepal in the Nineties: Versions of the Past, Visions of the Future* (Oxford University Press 1994).

local government bodies (with 5 Development Regions, *kshetra* and 14 Zones, *anchal*). Significantly, the functions of the first-tier bodies remained unclear.[15] The Panchayat administrative structure corresponded also to the four tiers of the state's representative institutions. They were organized into a pyramidal structure where only the lowest level was directly elected, while the members of the other assemblies were indirectly elected by and among the representatives of the level immediately below.[16]

Following the re-democratization of 1990, the growing demands for social inclusion were channeled through moderate demands for institutional reform. In 1996, the government commissioned a report on decentralization and local self-governance, and created a task force to improve the situation of marginalized groups. As a result, the government committed to decentralization and devolution through the enactment of the Local Self-Governance Act in 1999.[17] Significantly, the Act also prescribed the mandatory allocation of 20 percent of seats at the Village level to women,[18] and provisions for the nomination of women and disadvantaged groups in the executive committees at Village[19] and District level.[20] However, the innovations introduced by the 1999 Act have remained to a great extent ineffective, as no local elections have been held for twenty years between 1997 and 2017. A modicum of recognition along identity lines was introduced by the National Foundation for the Development of Indigenous Nationalities (NFDIN) Act in 2002, which was intended to increase the participation of Janajati (i.e. ethno-linguistic groups similar to "tribes" in the Indian Constitution) in state institutions. However, the NFDIN Act only recognized fifty-nine groups as "indigenous nationalities,"[21] while the 2001 Census identified more than 100 caste/ethnic groups, which had previously organized in 1990 under the umbrella organization of the Janajati Mahasangh.

Nepali governments have been historically preoccupied with politics in the Terai, the long lowland area running along the open border with India, whose population is mostly Madhesi (i.e. "plain dwellers" as opposed to Pahari "hill dwellers"). They sought to keep a tight leash on the region. One of the most contentious issues in the Terai throughout the 1990s has been that of citizenship, with estimates that in 1994 about 3.5 million people did not have citizenship certificates. According to an ICG report, this was caused by the legal requirements of descent and knowledge of Nepali for naturalization, discriminatory linguistic policies by the state, under-representation in state institutions, and economic discrimination.[22] The 1990 Constitution featured clearly discriminatory and exclusionary citizenship clauses: Article 9(5) denied citizenship through matrilineal descent, a provision included to "protect" Nepali-ness given the heavy Indian influence in the Terai due to the open border, while Article 9(4)(a) made the ability to read and write in the Nepali language mandatory for the acquisition of citizenship.[23] The demand for equal citizenship has been at the core of the agenda of

[15] Susanne Hesselbarth, "Alignment Strategies in The Field of Decentralisation and Local Governance, Country Study of Practices And Experiences: NEPAL" (Development Partners Working Group on Local Governance and Decentralization International Development Partner Harmonisation for Enhanced Aid Effectiveness, October 2007) <https://vdocuments.mx/country-case-study-nepal-october-2007.html>.

[16] Leo E Rose and Margaret Welpley Fisher, *The Politics of Nepal. Persistence and Change in an Asian Monarchy* (Cornell University Press 1970) 53.

[17] Hesselbarth, "Alignment strategies" (n 15).

[18] Local Self-Governance Act 1999, s. 7.

[19] Ibid, s. 8.

[20] Ibid, s. 172(2)(e).

[21] National Foundation for the Development of Indigenous Nationalities (NFDIN) Act 2002, sch.

[22] International Crisis Group, "Nepal's Troubled Tarai Region" (Asia Report No. 136, International Crisis Group July 9, 2007), 4–5 <https://www.crisisgroup.org/asia/south-asia/nepal/nepal-s-troubled-tarai-region>.

[23] Malagodi, *Constitutional Nationalism and Legal Exclusion* (n 4) 164–8.

Madhesi rights activists since the 1950s. The movement found renewed strength in the 1980s and organized itself as an identity-based regional political party in the early 1990s. Identity politics had entered Nepal, and was there to stay.

Political opposition to the regime

Many grievances along identity and class lines marred Nepal's post-1990 political scene, and all of them presented an institutional dimension. In particular, it has been argued that the 1990 Constitution played "a significant role in the continued exclusion of the marginalized socio-cultural groups"[24] and their political opposition to it. In 1996, the Maoists—who had united the small far-left parties excluded from the 1990 Constitution-making process—submitted a list of forty demands to the central government.[25] These included: the end of Nepal's "feudal" monarchical political system; redistributory reforms of the economy; the declaration of Nepal as a secular state; equal rights for women, ethno-linguistic minorities, and Dalits (formerly known as "untouchables"); and the "promulgation of a new Constitution drafted by the People's elected representatives." With regard to territorial restructuring, they demanded that "in areas having a majority of one ethnic group, that group should have autonomy over that area." The Maoists' grievances focused on a multidimensional understanding of marginalization, encompassing both questions of class and identity.[26] Their notion of identity politics went beyond ethnicity to include other dimensions such as gender, caste, religion, and region in light of the country's profound sociocultural diversity. In short, Nepal's People's War was not an ethnic conflict per se, but it certainly featured an ethnic dimension. The Maoists and their ideas steadily gained ground, either by persuasion or coercion. Significantly, by 2002 they controlled by military means roughly half of Nepal's territory, especially in the countryside, while the presence of the state was limited to the strongholds of the District Headquarters. The CPN (Maoist) had become a formidable political force that the Nepali establishment had to reckon with.

Identity politics and demands for recognition, however, were not new in Nepal and their articulation in the public sphere dates back to at least 1951, although the democratic opening of 1990 marked an increase in political mobilization along identity lines. Many groups in addition to the Maoists have been historically well organized, including the Madhesi parties and the Nepal Federation of Indigenous Nationalities (NEFIN) formed in 1990. It was only in 1993 that NEFIN assumed the connotation of *adivasi* interpreted in Nepal as "indigenous" (as opposed to "tribe" in India). The claim to indigeneity, historically debatable in itself,[27] seems an instrumental political move to sustain claims for self-determination on a territorial basis, especially through international legal instruments such as the Indigenous and Tribal Peoples Convention (ILO 169) ratified in September 2007. But as Gellner illustrates, in Nepal there is a high degree of intermixture with people from many groups living together and in only fifteen of seventy-five districts does a single group make up more than 50 percent of the population.[28] The Terai itself, with roughly half of the country's population, has

[24] Mahendra Lawoti, *Toward a Democratic Nepal. Inclusive Political Institutions for a Multicultural Society* (Sage Publications 2005) 115–16.

[25] Michael Hutt (ed.), *Himalayan People's War: Nepal's Maoist Rebellion* (Hurst & Company 2004) 285–7.

[26] Thapa with Sijapati (n 3) 51–82.

[27] Rajendra Pradhan, "A Native by Any Other Name . . . " (1994) 7 (1) Himal 41.

[28] David N Gellner, "Caste, Ethnicity and Inequality in Nepal" (2007) 42 (20) Economic and Political Weekly 1823, 1827.

great sociocultural diversity, featuring Madhesi Janajati groups, Madhesi caste groups, Pahari migrants, and Indian migrants.[29]

There have also been demands for recognition from Dalits and various religious minorities' organizations, which are not territorially based. Overall, the majority of identity-based demands in Nepal have been of a civil nature (i.e. to compete for resources within the system).[30] There have been cultural demands for ethnic, linguistic, and religious equality, economic demands for a fair share of state resources and political demands for proportional representation and regional autonomy. However, the demands with a territorial element have not been so far of a secessionist nature and secessionist threats were only issued when all the demands for recognition and autonomy were thwarted at the center. However, the growing polarization between Pahari and Madhesi, together with the increasingly violent expression of political discontent and heavy-handed responses by the state, could easily escalate the political conflict and rapidly lead to a much more intractable situation.[31]

Mainstream political parties and political elites

During the 1990 constitutional experience, the main political forces were the Shah King (first Birendra, then Gyanendra) together with their royal clique and the highest echelons of the Army, the mainstream parliamentary parties (Nepali Congress, UML, RPP, Anandi Devi, etc.), and the Maoists. The constitutional ban on the formation of communal parties[32] made parliamentary politics almost the exclusive purview of ideology-based parties, with the notable exception of Anandi Devi, a Terai regional party advocating for Madhesi rights. Identity-based demands and concerns remained largely ignored by all the other mainstream political parties, which featured a staggering dominance of Bahun and Chetri males in the composition of their respective Central Committees.[33] Identity politics was mainly conducted outside parliament through the burgeoning Janajati organizations formed after 1990.

The Maoists were able to capitalize on this vacuum and successfully combined the politics of redistribution with the politics of identity in their political campaign. Moreover, they were successful in associating the Shah Hindu monarchy with traditional societal structures such as caste, and with Nepal's ethnonationalist discourse, which had historically oppressed many groups marginalized on the basis of identity. The Maoist demand for secularism weakened the legitimacy of the monarchy while offering a common rallying point for identity-based grievances. Moreover, the controversial accession to the throne of King Gyanendra in 2001 after the harrowing events of the royal massacre further destabilized the monarchy, leading to its eventual demise in 2008.[34]

[29] Pitamber Sharma, *Unraveling the Mosaic. Spatial Aspects of Ethnicity in Nepal* (Himal Books 2008) 82.

[30] Harka Gurung, "State and Society in Nepal" in David N. Gellner, Joanna Pfaff-Czarnecka, and John Whelpton (eds), *Nationalism and Ethnicity in a Himalayan Kingdom: the Politics of Culture in Contemporary Nepal* (Harwood Academics 1997) 530.

[31] International Crisis Group, "Watch List – July-December 2015" (EU Watchlist No. 5, International Crisis Group December 1, 2015) <https://d2071andvip0wj.cloudfront.net/watch-list-december-2015-compressed_0.pdf> accessed February 16, 2018.

[32] Constitution of the Kingdom of Nepal 1990, art.112(3).

[33] Kumar (n 9) 210–11.

[34] On June 1, 2001 King Birendra, Queen Aiswarya, and seven other members of the Royal Family were shot dead inside Kathmandu's Royal Palace of Narayanhiti allegedly by Crown Prince Dipendra who then attempted to commit suicide and died two days later. The country was ridden by shock, uncertainty and fear as the vast majority of Nepal's population did not accept the official explanation for the killings (see Manjushree Thapa, *Forget Kathmandu: An Elegy for Democracy* (Viking Books 2005),

The beginning of the peace process in April 2006 brought identity politics to the forefront of Nepal's political debates. The political achievements of the Maoists, combined with the rise of more radical Madhesi parties, significantly eroded the electoral base of both the Nepali Congress and the UML in the Terai, and forced the mainstream political parties to rethink their strategy concerning identity politics. As a result, all the biggest ideological parties created so-called "ethnic wings" to widen their support base, and counter the Maoists, the Madhesi parties, and the growing number of identity-based political organizations. However, the reins of the main political parties—including the Maoists—remained firmly in the hands of the old leadership, mostly formed by Pahari upper-caste Hindu males. The pressure brought by the *Madhesi Andolan* upon the Nepali political establishment led to a widespread commitment to federal restructuring—with the notable exceptions of the RPP and some smaller Communist parties—but that commitment ultimately proved to be tenuous, especially toward ethnic federalism.

The Period of Constitutional Engagement

Context and background of the CA1

The decision that there should be a new Constitution, which would meet the long standing Maoist demand for a Constitution drafted by the People's elected representatives, was taken in the last phase of Nepal's civil war. On November 25, 2005, the Twelve Point Agreement was reached in India between the Maoists and the mainstream political parties.[35] It included the commitment to elect a Constituent Assembly. The promise of a Constituent Assembly made by King Tribhuvan in 1951 was finally going to be met, even if half a century later. The success of the pro-democracy movement against King Gyanendra's authoritarian rule in April 2006 led to the restoration of the House of Representatives (Parliament's Lower House), which had been dissolved in 2002, in order to have a legislature while the CA elections were being organized. Nepal's return to parliamentary politics inaugurated a phase of exhilarating optimism for the advancement of democracy and social inclusion, and the beginning of what appeared to be a genuine "constitutional moment."[36]

In 2006, Nepal emerged from a ten-year-long armed insurgency in which more than 17,000 lives were lost and more than 3,000 Nepalis were "disappeared."[37] The peace process essentially entailed two steps: the integration of the Maoist combatants into the Nepal Army, which was eventually completed by April 2012, and the drafting of a new Constitution—Nepal's seventh—by a directly elected inclusive body. Radical constitutional change was widely viewed as the primary vehicle for state restructuring

7–47). Moreover, the succession to the throne of Gyanendra, late Birendra's second brother, was looked at with suspicion. Rumors spread about the involvement in the royal massacre of the new King and his son Paras. The accusation was made explicit by the Maoist ideologue Baburam Bhattarai's letter published on June 6, 2001 in the daily *Kantipur*. Gyanendra was accused of being India's pawn, while late Birendra was described as a "patriotic King."

[35] UN Peacemaker, "12-Point Understanding between the Seven Political Parties and Nepal Communist Party (Maoists)" (*UN Peacemaker*, November 22, 2005) <https://peacemaker.un.org/nepal-12pointunderstanding2005>.

[36] Bruce Ackerman, *We the People: Foundations* vol. 1 (Harvard University Press 1991).

[37] International Committee of the Red Cross, "Nepal: women from opposing sides of the conflict" (*ICRC*, March 6, 2012) <https://www.icrc.org/eng/resources/documents/news-footage/2012/nepal-tvnews-2012-03-06.htm>.

to address the peace process mantra of "building a new Nepal;" a new Constitution written by elected representatives would "deepen democracy" by securing the inclusion of marginalized groups in state institutions and breaking the hegemony of upper-caste Pahari (from the hills) Hindu elites (*Parbatiya*).

With regard to constitutional change, the Maoists were adamant to repeal the 1990 Constitution and successfully advocated for the drafting of an interim document to pave the way to the elections of the Constituent Assembly. A small commission of unelected delegates, selected by the various political forces, prepared the Interim Constitution. Shortly after its formation, the commission had to be expanded to accommodate women and Janajati delegates. On January 15, 2007, after months of negotiations, the 1990 Constitution was finally abrogated and the Interim Constitution promulgated. The most contentious issues included the position of the monarchy, the powers of the Interim Parliament and Government, the CA election process, the choice of the body to promulgate the Interim Constitution, and the issue of citizenship in the Terai.[38] The new document, while heavily based on the 1990 Constitution, remained silent on the issue of the monarchy devoid of most of the ethno-cultural references that characterized the previous document; it proclaimed Nepal to be a secular state, retained a parliamentary form of government with a unicameral Interim Legislature, and set out the institutional roadmap for the elections of the Constituent Assembly. However, if left a number issues open for later political negotiation, such as federal restructuring.[39]

Following the promulgation of the Interim Constitution, an agreed number of Maoist delegates joined the Interim Parliament in January 2007 and then the Cabinet in April 2007, opening the way to the final preparations for the CA1 elections. Given the lack of agreement on a replacement, the Interim Constitution remained in force until September 2015. The issue of federalism arose relatively late in this process. In January 2007, the *Madhesi Andolan*, a mass protest movement against governmental discrimination of the Madhesi population in the Terai, led to prolonged strikes and violence. To appease the protestors, the Interim Government eventually accepted their demand for the federalization of the country and amended the Interim Constitution accordingly. However, one legal expert aptly described the agreements between the Government and the agitating ethnic-regional activists, together with the amendments to the Interim Constitution that ensued, as "painkillers, not treatments."[40] Thus, federalism officially entered Nepal's institutional politics by way of a string of amendments to the Interim Constitution that expressly committed Nepal to federalization, but they fell short of a federal design and Nepal remained *de facto* a unitary state. Moreover, no local elections were held for two decades, making local government at village, municipal, and district levels entirely dysfunctional.

In April 2008, the elections for the CA1 were peacefully held.[41] The 601-member unicameral Assembly operated both as the country's legislature and Constitution-drafting

[38] Kiran Chapagain, "ICDC misses yet another deadline" *Kathmandu Post* (Kathmandu, August 10, 2006 OR 25 Shrawan 2063 BS) 1.

[39] Mara Malagodi, "Constitutional Change and the Quest for Legal Inclusion in Nepal" in Colin Harvey and Alexander Schwartz (eds), *Rights in Divided Societies* (Hart Publishing 2012) 169–93.

[40] International Crisis Group, "Nepal: Identity Politics and Federalism" (Asia Report No. 199, International Crisis Group January 13, 2011) 8, <https://www.crisisgroup.org/asia/south-asia/nepal/nepal-identity-politics-and-federalism>.

[41] The Carter Center, "Observing the 2008 Nepal Constituent Assembly Elections" (The Carter Centre April 2008) <http://www.cartercenter.org/resources/pdfs/news/peace_publications/election_reports/FinalReportNepal2008.pdf>.

body. To the surprise of many, the Maoist emerged as the largest party, with 35 percent of the seats in a body of over thirty parties. On May 28, 2008, at the CA1's first meeting, Nepal was proclaimed a federal republic and the commitment to federalization resulted in further amendments to the Interim Constitution. However, the CA1 remained deeply divided and even with four extensions to its term, it was unable to agree on a new Constitution, especially with regard to the modalities of federal restructuring. Hence, the CA1 was eventually dissolved in May 2012 leaving Nepal with neither a legislature nor a Constitution-drafting body in place for over a year. In November 2013, the CA2 elections signaled the electorate's change of mood—and possibly a new trajectory for the country's commitment to federal restructuring. The Madhesi uprising had succeeded in firmly putting the question of federal restructuring on the constitutional agenda through a series of amendments of the Interim Constitution, although they bore little substantive influence over the work and output of the CA1.

Actors and decision-making in the CA1 process

The election of the CA1, after some postponement, was eventually held on April 8, 2008. The process was conducted in a reasonably free and fair manner, with a turnout of above 60 percent of eligible voters.[42] The CA1 featured 601 seats of which 240 (42 percent) allocated by first-past-the-post in single-member territorial constituencies (essentially those of the general election of 1999) and 335 seats (58 percent) allocated by proportional representation in which the entire country functioned as a single constituency and the electorate voted for political parties, not individual candidates. The PR mechanism gave parties a free hand in the selection of candidates, subject only to the legal quotas relating to identity, 13 percent dalits, 37.8 percent marginalized groups, 4 percent backward regions, 31.2 percent Madhesi, and 30.2 percent Other Groups.[43] The remaining twenty-six seats were reserved for appointments made by the Cabinet after the election.

Twenty-five of the fifty-seven parties contesting the election found representation in the CA1, alongside two independent candidates. The results surprised many because the Maoists came on top with a relative majority of 35 percent of seats, capturing many constituencies that had long been held by Congress and UML, especially in the Terai. The Maoists won almost double the seats of each mainstream party: the Nepali Congress obtained 19 percent, while the UML 18 percent. The fourth biggest party, the Madhesi People's Rights Forum (MJAF), captured 9 percent, the fifth, the Terai Madhes Loktantrik Party, 3.49 percent. Only five other parties controlled more than 1 percent of the seats; sixteen parties fell below that threshold.[44] The uneven distribution of seats, the fragmentation of Nepal's political spectrum, and the polarization of diametrically opposed and competing visions of the Nepali polity within the CA1 set the stage for many rounds of political maneuvering.

[42] ibid.

[43] The sum of these percentages is more than 100 percent. "Explanation – As a number of candidates represent more than one group, the sum total of the percentage of the candidates of all groups appears to be more than one hundred." Election to Members of the CA Act 2007, Sch. 1. 33 percent of the total seats were also allocated to women.

[44] Also see Kåre Vollan, "System of Representation for the Constituent Assembly Elections in Nepal: An assessment and suggestions for future elections" (Paris–Oslo International Workshop on Democracy, Paris, October 18–20, 2010) <www.uio.no/english/research/interfaculty-research-areas/democracy/news-and-events/events/conferences/2010/papers/Vollan-SystemOfRepresentationNepal-2008.pdf>.

The life of the CA1 was marred by political instability from its inception. The relative majority of the Maoists resulted in them obtaining key posts, including that of the Prime Minister. Maoist supremo Pushpa Kamal Dahal (aka "Prachanda") took the reins of the Nepali Cabinet in August 2008, supported by the Madhesi parties, the UML, and a number of smaller parties, while the Nepali Congress remained firmly in opposition. However, Dahal was forced to resign in May 2009 after a row with the President over the sacking of the Chief of Army Staff, when he was succeeded by the UML leader Madhav Kumar Nepal, who was in office a little over a year. Another UML leader, Jhalanath Khanal, took the helm of the government in February 2011, after seventeen unsuccessful rounds of votes within the CA1. His tenure was particularly short-lived, and in August 2011 he was replaced by Maoist ideologue Baburam Bhattarai, who remained in office until the CA1's dissolution in May 2012. Throughout the life of the CA1, Nepali party leaders mostly concentrated their energies on political power play for governmental posts and on the Army integration process, which was only concluded in April 2012. They did not give the Constitution-making process their personal time or priority, which meant that the CA1 could not resolve key issues. Leaders turned to these only at the last minute, but by then they were unable to reach an agreement before the Assembly's dissolution.

Significantly, in 2008 the electorate had rejected a number of old party leaders, even though the electoral law allowed them to run in up to two first-past-the-post constituencies. However, former prime ministers Sushil Koirala and Madhav Kumar Nepal—to mention just two examples—still managed to secure seats in the CA1 as part of the twenty-six Cabinet-appointed posts. The appointment of leaders who had been rejected by the electorate was indicative of the attitude of the main political parties toward democratic decision-making and the CA itself. As illustrated in a Martin Chautari report, the party leaders were always confident that they would have the last word on any question of Constitution-making in the name of taking decisions by "consensus" (*sahamati*). As a result, decisions on key constitutional matters became the exclusive purview of the political leaders outside of the CA1 itself. This entirely delegitimized the drafting process in the CA, and the leaders remained unable to reach a consensus even outside of the CA.[45]

The commitment to "consensus" decisions was built into the Interim Constitution in all the clauses related to decision-making in the CA. For example, the *5th Amendment* added a subsection to Article 33 on the Responsibilities of the state "to develop a culture of resolving major political problems of the country with understanding, consensus, and cooperation amongst the major political parties." However, this section was non-justiciable so that decision-making through consensus under the Interim Constitution remained, legally speaking, purely aspirational. The Constitution provided for voting procedures for all the decisions to be taken by the CA, and most of them required a simple majority of members present in the House, with a quorum of one-fourth of the total CA members. Only constitutional amendments (Article 148) and the passing of the new Constitution (Article 70) required a two-thirds qualified majority. Legally, two-thirds of the CA members could, under the Interim Constitution, declare a new Constitution. Politically, however, it proved impossible to do so without the support of all the main political leaders (i.e. "by consensus"), which would secure the legitimacy

[45] Martin Chautari, "The Debilitating Dynamics of Nepal's Constituent Assembly (2008–2012)" (Briefing Paper No. 8, Martin Chautari March 2013) <www.martinchautari.org.np/files/BriefingPaper8_EngVer.pdf>.

of the new document. At the same time, this requirement made resolving several issues virtually impossible.

The institutional setup of the CA1

The CA1 held its first meeting on May 28, 2008, and in a historic proclamation declared Nepal a "Federal Democratic Republic," putting an end to the 265-year-old Shah monarchy. Having done so, its first task was to create its Rules of Procedure and in its second meeting a forty-four-member CA Rules Committee was established. By November, both the Rules and an eighty-two-week Timetable for the CA were approved. Then in December, the Constitution-drafting work was organized into committees: the Constitutional Committee, ten Thematic Committees, and four Procedural Committees. For proposals to pass within a Committee a simple majority vote was required. All the Thematic Committees concluded their work and submitted their reports and concept papers for discussion by the full Assembly between May 2009 and January 2010.[46]

Even if the CA1 Rules were silent on the issues of Caucuses and Party Whips, these institutions played a fundamental role in the work and demise of the CA1. CA Speaker Subhash Chandra Nemwang allowed for the spontaneous creation of cross-party Caucuses along identity and gender lines.[47] The formation of the Women, Janajati, Dalit, and Madhesi Caucuses demonstrated that other bonds of solidarity and political cooperation existed in the CA1 beyond party affiliation. In fact, on numerous occasions, CA members voted according to their conscience, ignoring party lines. The party leadership responded by unleashing their Whips on the defiant party members. However, the use of Party Whips in the CA1 not just on ordinary legislative matters, but also on votes on constitutional issues when rebellious members were subjected to a three-line-whip, effectively curbed many cross-party initiatives. This was especially significant for the rebellious CA members elected under proportional representation, as expulsion from their parties would result in the loss of their seat.[48] Thus, the main three political parties, including the Maoists, which were all dominated by upper caste Pahari Hindu males, succeeded in silencing voices of dissent and demands for inclusion within their own parties, and in the Assembly. Essentially, this situation severely limited the availability of "systemic" ways through which the demands of the marginalized groups could be accommodated within the institutional process.

The Committees' reports had all been discussed in plenary sessions by May 2010, but no agreement could be reached among the main political parties on the most contentious issues: federal restructuring, presidential versus parliamentary government, and the judiciary. As a result, the new Constitution could not be finalized. The CA1 then bought time by amending the Interim Constitution to extend its own term. At this point, the task of resolving these issues was removed from the open public debates

[46] See Alliance for Social Dialogue, "Chronology of Constituent Assembly – I" (*ASD.org.np*) <http://asd.org.np/nepal-in-transition/constitution/constitutionmaking/constitution-category/meeting-chronology-of-ca-i/>.

[47] Kamal Dev Bhattarai, "CA caucus debate rages; parties divided" *The Kathmandu Post* (Kathmandu, March 8, 2014) <www.ekantipur.com/2014/03/08/top-story/ca-caucus-debate-rages-parties-divided/386395.html>.

[48] Krishna Khanal, Frits Sollewijn Gelpke, and Uddhab Prasad Pyakurel, *Dalit Representation in National Politics of Nepal* (Nepal National Dalit Social Welfare Organisation 2012) <www.idsn.org/fileadmin/user_folder/pdf/New_files/Nepal/2013/Dalit_Representation_in_National_Politics_of_Nepal_-_2012.pdf>.

of the body directly representative of the Nepali people and put into the hands of the old guard of leaders of the main parties. These men negotiated crucial decisions about Nepal's new constitutional settlement, mostly through the High Level Political Committee (HLPC), which had been set up by G.P. Koirala in January 2010. As a result, no inclusive and transparent deliberations within the CA1 were allowed to iron out the differences between the various political forces. Ultimately, the modus operandi of backdoor secret negotiations and opaque deals devised by the High Level Political Committee outside of the Assembly undermined the legitimacy of the Constitution-making process itself. At the same time, the political leaders failed to forge a compromise solution, notwithstanding three further extensions of the CA1's term in May 2011, August 2011, and November 2011. "Postponing" or rather "delaying" the entire Constitution-making process was the strategy adopted by the main political parties, since no agreement could be found on key issues. Negotiations dragged on to the point that commentators started to use expressions such as "Nepal at a permanent crossroad," "the unending transition," and "counterrevolution by stealth." It is argued that this was a conscious negotiating strategy especially by the parties at the opposition within the CA1.

Federal debates: political actors and federalism

The question of federal restructuring has polarized Nepal's political spectrum since the beginning of the peace process. On the one hand, the Nepali Congress, UML, and other smaller conservative and left wing parties advocated for a weak form of federalism that essentially entailed territorial restructuring along the past lines of devolution, with no reference to ethnicity. Their resistance to ethnic federalism stems from traditionalist conceptions of the Nepali state and nationalism, a fear of losing their power bases, and an apprehension that a polarization of Nepal's highly diverse society along institutionalized ethnic lines may lead to a Balkanization of the country—and further conflict. While the specter of secession was mostly a rhetorical threat used by the Nepali Congress and the UML—as well as the parties advocating a unitary state (e.g. RPP)—many expressed genuine concerns that "ethnic" federal restructuring could lead to further marginalization and violence. On the other hand, the Maoists, alongside Madhesi and Janajati parties, demanded federal restructuring along ethnic lines to secure the inclusion of marginalized groups, and break the long-established Pahari upper-caste Hindu hegemony over the country. With time, it seems that the Nepali Congress and the UML accepted a degree of federal restructuring to appease their Janajati, Madhesi, and Dalit members and supporters, and to avoid exacerbating political conflict, but they remained opposed to an ethnically based approach. For their part, the Madhesi parties progressively moved away from their original demand for a unified Madhes in the Terai, because this one province would have had 51 percent of the total population, which would be destabilizing. But they remained supporters of federal restructuring on the basis of identity.

The debates on the nature of federal restructuring took place first in the Thematic Committee called the Committee on State Restructuring and Distribution of State Power. After thirteen months of deliberations, this forty-three-member committee completed its report and submitted it for plenary discussion on January 27, 2010. The majority in the Committee voted for a model featuring fourteen provinces based on the criteria of "identity" as well as "capability," which was to ensure the viability of the provinces; however, the names and boundaries of the provinces were mostly along ethnic lines.[49] The identity markers highlighted by the Committee were: ethnic/communal, linguistic, cultural, geographical/continuity of regional identities, and continuity with historical identities.[50]

Preferential political rights (*agradhikar*) were included in the Committee's report in the form of temporary reservations of a share of political offices for the majority group in each province. No other special entitlements were given to such majority ethnic groups, essentially because no province would have a clear ethnic majority, and all would still host many smaller ethno-linguistic groups. As a result, this model raised preoccupations about the position of smaller groups. Significantly, four UML members voted for the proposal in the Committee against the party line, allowing it to pass at the Committee stage. A number of Committee members did not support the proposal, leading to a Nepali Congress leader to put forward an alternative six-unit model defined solely on the basis of capability and not identity, where the federal units were strikingly similar to the existing Development Regions.

As reported by the ICG, "a plenary discussion of the proposals was attempted, but this led to shouting and disruption of Assembly proceedings by members who felt they were being ignored. The report was kicked to the Constitutional Committee, which simply added the federalism proposals to a growing list of contentious issues."[51] The question of federal restructuring was then moved out of the CA1 with the creation of a nine-member High Level State Restructuring Commission in November 2011. Significantly, the Commission members were not CA members, but political appointees deemed to have some specialized knowledge in matters of federalism. The elusive search for political consensus brought the deliberations on a key political issue outside the CA1, the only body representative of the Nepali people. However, the Commission as well proved incapable of resolving the deadlock and by February 2012 it submitted two separate reports to the Prime Minister.[52] The majority report put forward by six members[53] proposed eleven provinces (i.e. federal units) down from fourteen: namely, 1) Limbuwan, 2) Kirant, 3) Tamsaling, 4) Newa, 5) Narayani, 6) Tamuwan, 7) Magarat, 8) Dalits, 9) Karnali-Khaptad, 10) Madhes-Mithila-Bhojpura, and 11) Madhesi-Awadh-Tharuwan. These names reflected the mixed adoption of ethnic and geographical denominators (except in the extraordinary case of the dalits, which was to be a non-territorially based province).[54] The minority report put forward by three Commission members (NC and UML appointees) [55] proposed six federal units along the existing administrative structure, with the names to be decided

[49] The fourteen provinces identified by the CA1 Committee on State Restructuring and Distribution of State Authority were: 1) Limbuwan, 2) Mithila-Bhojpura-Koch-Madhes, 3) Kirant, 4) Sunkoshi, 5) Sherpa, 6) Tamsaling, 7) Newa, 8) Narayani, 9) Tamuwan, 10) Magarat, 11) Lumbini-Awadh-Tharuwan, 12) Karnali, 13) Jadan, and 14) Khaptad.

[50] CA1, Report of the Committee for Restructuring the State and Distribution of State Power 2010. See: http://constitutionnet.org/sites/default/files/concept_paper_restructuring_state_gtz_eng.pdf.

[51] International Crisis Group, "Nepal's Constitution: Evolution, Not Revolution" (Asia Report No. 233, International Crisis Group August 27, 2012) 6, <https://www.crisisgroup.org/asia/south-asia/nepal/nepal-s-constitution-i-evolution-not-revolution>.

[52] Alliance for Social Dialogue, "Two Separate Reports by the State Restructuring Commission (January 29-February 4)" (*Alliance for Social Dialogue*, February 5, 2012) <http://asd.org.np/political-updates/two-separate-reports-by-the-state-restructuring-commission-january-29-february-4/>.

[53] The SRC Coordinator Madan Pariyar, and members Stella Tamang, Malla K. Sundar, Bhogendra Jha, Krishna Hachhethu, and Surendra Mahato supported the majority report.

[54] Report of the Committee for Restructuring the State and Distribution of State Power 2012.

[55] SRC members Ramesh Dhungel, Sabitri Gurung, and Sarbaraj Khadka supported the minority report.

by parliament. The outcome of this process rather than moving forward the debate on federalism, revealed how polarized and intractable it had become.

With the May 28, 2012 deadline looming, the top party leaders, who had kept their distance from the CA, attempted a series of last minute agreements. On May 15 the leaders of the Nepali Congress, UML, and CPN (Maoist) agreed on an eleven-unit federal model with provisions for naming the territorial units through the first meeting of the respective provincial assemblies. The question of naming the provinces became deeply controversial and divisive because of its highly symbolic value. Thus, Janajati and Madhesi groups pressured the Maoist leadership to uphold its commitment to ethnic federalism in the new Constitution, so the Maoists backtracked from the deal on the eve of the impending deadline. As the ICG reported, "there were whispers about leaving federalism for later, with only an in-principle commitment in the new constitution." But Madhesi, Janajati, and Tharu groups opposed this, arguing there could be "no constitution without federalism and no federalism without identity." They also rejected the idea of Constitution-by-commission or anything less than the full Constituent Assembly.[56] With no agreement on the most contentious issue, the CA1 was eventually dissolved on May 27, 2012, four years after its first meeting, leaving Nepal without a new constitutional settlement in place.

Dissolution of the CA1

The failure and eventual demise of the CA1 resulted from a number of factors. First, the behavior of top political leaders marginalized the Assembly as the forum of deliberations relating to key constitutional issues. By undercutting the only truly representative body entrusted with the task of Constitution drafting, the entire constitutional process was delegitimized. Second, inter- and intra-party squabbles over offices and seats took precedence over meaningful and long-awaited institutional reforms. In this respect, Kanak Mani Dixit pointedly observed: "the fact that both the CA and Legislature-Parliament had the same members proved fatal, because government-formation always took precedence, adding both rancour and unprincipled compromise."[57] Third, both the Executive and the Supreme Court became progressively involved in matters relating to the proceedings of the CA1, leading to an unhealthy tension between the various branches of the Nepali state.

Public frustrations with the CA1 also resulted from the Assembly's inability to complete its task notwithstanding the total of four extensions of its term taking it from the originally established two years to four years. After the second such extension, the Supreme Court became involved into the growing controversy and eventually it adjudicated on the constitutional validity of such extensions in four instances—May, August, and November of 2011, and May 2012. In the landmark judgment of November 2011, the court stated that if the CA1 failed to promulgate the new Constitution by the extended deadline of May 2012, it would automatically expire. As a result, on May 22, 2012, when the Bhattarai government tabled a Bill supported by the four main political parties for yet another amendment to the Interim Constitution to secure a further three-month extension of the CA1, the Supreme Court responded by issuing a stay order, effectively disallowing any further CA1 extension. In an

[56] International Crisis Group (n 51) 8.

[57] Kanak Mani Dixit, "The Life and Death of the Constituent Assembly of Nepal" (2012) 47 (31) Economic & Political Weekly 35, 36.

unforeseen turn of events, Prime Minister Bhattarai dissolved the Assembly on May 27 and called for new elections.

Outcome of the Process

The dissolution of the CA1 in May 2012 left Nepal with neither a legislature nor a Constitution-drafting body in place for over year. At the same time, a Cabinet, composed by Ministers appointed by the political parties and headed by the Supreme Court Chief Justice (only on temporary leave from his judicial post and an adjudicator on two of the cases that led to the dissolution of the Assembly) and unburdened by any form of parliamentary accountability, was placed at the country's executive helm. Unsurprisingly, this interim period undermined the constitutionality of the political process by implicating the Supreme Court in executive politics and it further eroded public trust in state institutions and political actors, both perceived as caught up in partisan politics and incapable of delivering institutional reform. Officially, such constitutional manipulation was justified as an exceptional measure for exceptional circumstances. However, the manifest democratic deficit was coupled with the progressive deterioration of governance, and Nepal's "constitutional moment" seemed irremediably lost.

The elections to the CA2 took place on November 19, 2013, after having being postponed twice. First of all, the turnout was exceptionally high, approximately 77 percent, demonstrating that the vast majority of those entitled to vote actively participated in the exercise. Second, according to both national and international electoral observers, the polls were conducted in a free, fair, and efficient manner. Third, pre-election intimidation and violence were minimal and decreased as the poll date approached.[58] A number of political parties and candidates alleged electoral fraud, but these allegations have not been substantiated.

The CA2's composition mirrors the one of its predecessor: a 601-seat unicameral legislature functioning both as the country's parliament and its Constitution-drafting body. As before, it featured 240 members elected in first-past-the-post seats, 335 elected by PR, and twenty-six named by the Cabinet. The 2013 elections brought the main centrist parliamentary parties—the Nepali Congress and UML—back to the political forefront in that they emerged as the biggest two parties in the Assembly, while the Maoists were relegated to the third position. Of the 575 seats allocated through the elections, the Congress won 196 seats (34 percent), the UML 175 seats (30 percent), and the Maoists only eighty seats (14 percent). A further twenty-eight parties secured representation in the CA2, but they all won less than 5 percent of the total seats.[59] Commentators have interpreted the electoral setback of the Maoists as both the result of a successful campaign of the mainstream parties against the proposals for ethnic federalism and the electorate's frustration with the CA1's biggest party in not delivering a new Constitution in four years.

In March 2014, the CA2 finally succeeded in re-adopting the many agreements on the new Constitution previously reached by the CA1. However, the thorny issues that caused the CA1 to be dissolved without a new Constitution after four years proved divisive. The questions of federal restructuring and the form of government continued

[58] The Carter Center, "Carter Center Congratulates Nepal on Well-Conducted Election Process" (*The Carter Center*, November 20, 2013) <www.cartercenter.org/news/pr/nepal-112113.html>.

[59] 2013 electoral results.

to polarize Nepal's political spectrum. On the one hand, the Nepali Congress, UML, and other smaller conservative and leftwing parties advocated for a non-ethnic form of territorial restructuring and a weak form of federalism, while retaining a parliamentary form of government. On the other hand, the Maoists, alongside Madhesi and Janajati parties, promoted a federal restructuring along ethnic lines to secure the inclusion of the many marginalized groups, and a presidential system in which the President is elected by popular vote. The majority in the CA2 of the Nepali Congress and UML made the former institutional roadmap the one that was eventually adopted. However, the requirement for a two-thirds majority of CA members to pass the new Constitution made the two dominant parties short of a handful of votes and seemed that it could force a degree of compromise. Negotiations were protracted and until the earthquakes hit Nepal in the spring of 2015 little progress had been made with regard to drafting.

The CA2 did not succeed in promulgating the new Constitution within its original deadline of January 2015. Nepal's "constitutional moment" seemed irremediably lost and radical state restructuring became a very distant prospect. In this respect, the coalition government attempted to prohibit the formation of cross-party Caucuses in the CA2, while the use of Party Whips continued. Thus, as late as October 2014, the ruling coalition of the Nepali Congress and UML hinted at the possibility of passing the new Constitution "by process" (i.e. by a qualified two-third majority vote in the Assembly in accordance with the procedures of the Interim Constitution). In response, a Maoist-led alliance of twenty-two parties threatened to reject the document if not forged "by consensus," and to take to the streets and launch a program of protests.[60]

In the wake of the 2015 earthquakes, Nepal's political elites vowed to "fast track" the drafting of the new document and finally complete the peace process. On June 8, the main four parties (Nepali Congress, UML, Maoists, and Madhesi Forum-L) reached a political settlement known as the 16-Point Agreement, which was to form the basis of the new Constitution.[61] Significantly, the negotiations included only four of the thirty-one parties represented in the Assembly and made little effort to include representation from the marginalized groups. The Agreement featured a parliamentary form of government with a mixed electoral system and a separate Constitutional Court, but crucially sought to postpone the naming and demarcation of the federal units until the promulgation of the new Constitution and the elections of the central and provincial legislatures.

The postponement of the long-awaited process of federal restructuring immediately sparked protests across the country. As a result, petitions were filed in the Supreme Court to have the Agreement declared violative of the currently in force 2007 Interim Constitution. In an unprecedented move, on June 19, a single bench of the Supreme Court issued an Interim Order against the implementation of the Agreement's postponement of federal restructuring.[62] The apex Court arrived at its decision on the basis of Article 138(3) of the Interim Constitution, which mandates that "the final decision relating to the structure of the state and federal system shall be made by the Constituent Assembly." Politicians accused the Court of overreaching and the

[60] Bhagirath Basnet, "Illusive consensus: There must be pressure from all sides to come up with a constitution by the scheduled date, by consensus, and if not, by two-third majority" *myRepública* (Nepal, December 1, 2014) <myrepublica.nagariknetwork.com>.

[61] 16-point Agreement Nepali Congress—Communist Party of Nepal-Unified Marxist Leninist—Unified Communist Party of Nepal-Maoist—Madhesi Janadhikar Forum-Loktantrik) <http://www.satp.org/satporgtp/countries/nepal/document/papers/16-point_Agreement.htm> accessed January 11, 2016.

[62] Adv.Dipendra Jha, "English Version of the SC order" (*Twitter.com*, June 19, 2015) <https://twitter.com/dipjha/status/612139709553229824> accessed January 11, 2016.

Assembly's Constitution Drafting Committee (CDC) pressed on with the preparation of the draft on the basis of the 16-Point Agreement defying the Supreme Court's order.

Protests grew increasingly violent and the security forces' response heavy handed, especially in the Terai, where the demands for federalism and equal citizenship have been historically the strongest. In the meantime, the Assembly opted for a fast-track procedure to pass the new Constitution, allowing for a very brief period of public consultation over the draft.[63] Amid mounting tensions, on August 8, the political leaders relented and inked a six-province deal of federalism.[64] Tharu political leader Rukmini Chaudhary pointedly commented on the deal: "Accepting the six-state federal model is suicidal for the indigenous [. . .] we demanded two states in the Terai: Madesh and Tharuhat. There is an incomplete Madhesh, and no Tharuhat. We said we don't want a North-South federal model that puts the mountains and plains in the same state, but that's exactly what they have given us. Indigenous groups have been cheated. Rai and Limbu homelands have been lumped together as in one state. Magar and Gurung homelands are also lumped together, as have Tamang and Newar homelands. There is Pahadi Brahmin-Chhetri dominance in each state."[65]

As protests intensified, on August 21 the Nepali Congress, UML, and Maoists agreed on a new seven-province federal deal (essentially carving Province 7 out of Province 6 and maintaining the controversial longitudinal division of the country), while the Madhesi Forum-L did not support the scheme.[66] On August 23, the draft Constitution (with the seven-province model) was tabled in the CA2 for approval by the House as the MPs representing the marginalized groups walked out in protest.[67] Violent demonstrations and communal violence erupted across the Terai, leading to the death of security forces and protestors in Kailali, the imposition of a curfew, and the deployment of the Nepal Army.[68] While a Constitution was eventually framed, as expected it did not bring about radical institutional restructuring. In the end, while federalism was accepted, the framework adopted reflected the political balance between the federalist and anti-federalist forces. As such, the 2015 document provides for three tiers of government: Federal at the center (Parts VII–X, Articles 74–125), Provincial through seven Provinces identified by numbers in Schedule 4 (Parts XIII–XVI, Articles 162–213), and Local through Villages and Municipalities at the lower level and Districts at the higher level (Parts XVII–XIX, Articles 214–30). Part XX (Articles 231–7) of the Constitution defines the relationship between the three tiers of government and Schedules 4 to 9 provide for the apportionment of executive powers and legislative competence amongst the three tiers of government. Nepal's Local

[63] Nikhil Narayan and Sanhita Ambast, "Nepal's 'Fast-Tracked' Constitutional Process Trades Rights for Speed" (*The Wire*, August 1, 2015) <http://thewire.in/2015/08/01/nepals-fast-tracked-constitutional-process-trades-rights-for-speed-7673/> accessed January 11, 2016.

[64] The Nepali Times Blog, "Federalism deal signed" *The Nepali Times* (Kathmandu, August 8, 2015) <www.nepalitimes.com/blogs/thebrief/2015/08/08/federalism-deal-signed/> accessed January 13, 2016.

[65] Erisha Suwal, "Accepting six-state federal model is suicidal for the indigenous" (*The Record*, August 9, 2015) <https://www.recordnepal.com/perspective/accepting-six-state-federal-model-is-suicidal-for-the-indigenous/> accessed January 13, 2016.

[66] Karma99, "Timeline of proposed federal structures" (*Karma99*, April 2015) <http://www.karma99.com/2015/04/proposed-federal-structures-of-nepal.html> accessed January 13, 2016.

[67] Prakash Acharya, "CA on cusp of promulgating constitution" *The Himalayan Times* (Kathmandu, August 24, 2015) <http://thehimalayantimes.com/kathmandu/ca-on-cusp-of-promulgating-constitution/> accessed January 13, 2016.

[68] Human Rights Watch, ""Like We Are Not Nepali": Protest and Police Crackdown in the Terai Region of Nepal" (*Human Rights Watch*, 16 October 2015) <https://www.hrw.org/report/2015/10/16/we-are-not-nepali/protest-and-police-crackdown-terai-region-nepal> accessed 13/01/2016.

government structure has remained unchanged since its creation in 1961 and the 2015 Constitution simply recognizes the existing framework. It remains to be seen whether the results of the 2017 local elections will breathe life into the process of decentralization that the Local Self-Governance Act was expected to bring about when enacted in 1999, but which has remained dead letter until today.

The Constitution, however, remained silent on the name of the Provinces and adopted a hybrid solution to the various proposals for federal demarcation that were on the negotiating table. The Provinces were created by lumping together clusters of the existing seventy-five districts. Significantly, the demand for the creation of a single Madhesi Province in the Terai was refused and the controversial longitudinal division of the country adopted. Madhesi and Janajati activists contended that this demarcation entrenched *Pahari Bahun-Chetri* demographic dominance in each Province.[69] As a result, they continue to lobby for a constitutional amendment to redefine the boundaries of the Provinces. Moreover, the long-standing controversial demand for preferential rights (*agradhikar*) was dropped. The Constitution drastically moved away from the federal model based on ethnicity and language initially proposed. The new Constitution was promulgated on September 20, 2015, but amendment Bills were already being tabled in Parliament in December 2015 and January 2016, but these failed to quell protests in the Terai, which continued amid an unofficial Indian-enforced trade blockade and the increasingly vocal form of ethnonationalism embraced by the UML-led Nepali government. A new phase of political conflict has begun in Nepal and given the electoral success of the nationalist leftwing alliance (UML and Maoists) in the 2017 elections at federal, provincial, and local level, it seems that this political cleavage can only deepen in the near future.

Lessons Learned

The failure of Nepal's CA1 in relation to the question of federal restructuring inspires a number of reflections concerning the link between territorial restructuring, identity politics, and the range of institutional responses to demands for social inclusion.

First, the institutional choice of territorial reorganization along identity lines seems unsuitable in circumstances where groups are not territorially concentrated and, instead, dispersed down to the village level as in Nepal. Federal restructuring along identity lines also seems inappropriate where groups are not sizeable enough to be granted their own territorial unit. The 2011 Census identified over a hundred ethnolinguistic and caste groups inhabiting a relatively small country, with most of them constituting less than 5 percent of the total population. The combination of these two factors simply makes it impossible to design a federal structure that recognizes every single group and accords it a territorial dimension. Thus, the introduction of a federal regime prioritizing identity may entail the lack of recognition of a substantive number of groups, which could in turn lead to discontent and conflict due to feelings of further marginalization and newly institutionalized patterns of exclusion for certain groups. At the same time, groups' demands for recognition ought to be addressed through institutional reforms; otherwise their outright denial may eventually lead to secessionist attempts as the growing unrest and human violations in the Terai seem to indicate.

[69] Suwal (n 65).

Second, in Nepal, debates on federalism and legal entitlements on the basis of identity have hinged on the concept of preferential rights (*agradhikar*) as the priority entitlement of the majority ethno-linguistic group to political leadership positions in their respective future federal units. In Nepal, the debate has moved from ethnicity to indigeneity as Janajati leaders embraced the principles underpinning the UN Decade for Indigenous People, leading to the ratification of the ILO 169 Convention in 2007. The emphasis on indigeneity has been strongly connected to the demand for federal structures that embed preferential group rights. As illustrated above, the preferential treatment of "bigger" groups in the federal units bearing their name raised the problematic question of the position of "smaller" marginalized groups that did not succeeded in obtaining their own territorial unit. Thus, it is important to delink territorial from non-territorial forms of recognition, as one does not necessitate the other as argued by Shneiderman and Tillin.[70] Notably, the 2015 Constitution entirely moved away even from the symbolism of ethnic federalism and sidestepped the controversial process of naming the seven federal units it created by referring to the Provinces with numbers from 1 to 7.

Third, the Nepali state has historically been the almost exclusive political preserve of Parbatiya groups with a significant under-representation of marginalized groups in the legislature, cabinet, civil service, judiciary, higher army ranks, and educational sector—accompanied by lower levels of educational and economic performance.[71] As a result, the demands for social inclusion in Nepal have made the relationship between federal restructuring and the constitutional right to equality a particularly intimate and embattled one. The 1990 Constitution favored a negative view of equality based on the principle of non-discrimination. In fact, the document presented a formulation of the right to equality in which cultural, linguistic, ethnic and religious affiliation did not provide any basis to claim a positive legal right. Such features, instead, were treated as possible causes for negative discrimination. While the 1990 right to equality allowed for future special legislation for the advancement of the unprivileged segments of Nepali society, such future positive discrimination was not based ethno-linguistic or religious criteria. The conflict in 2015 and 2016 over the federal map is, in essence, a conflict between the numerous, but marginalized, Madhesis and Tharu groups of the Terai and the traditional Parbatiya Hindu elites, who are still trying to maintain their supremacy.

In a situation like that of Nepal, Kymlicka's polyethnic or representation rights may be more appropriate in providing protection to a group's culture through legislation or giving political voice in central institutions.[72] In fact, after 2006, steps were taken to redress the question of group marginalization in Nepal through the use of quotas. In relation to parliamentary representation, a mixed electoral system was adopted in the 2008 CA1 elections, with part of the Assembly's proportional seats allocated on the basis of identity. Moreover, the Interim Constitution took significant steps toward the recognition of group rights based on sociocultural criteria such as ethno-linguistic, caste, and regional identity. This served as the constitutional basis for ordinary legislation introducing quotas. Amendments were made between 2007

[70] Sara Shneiderman and Louise Tillin, "Restructuring States, Restructuring Ethnicity: Looking across Disciplinary Boundaries at Federal Futures in India and Nepal" (2015) 49 (1) *Modern Asian Studies* 1.

[71] World Bank Nepal, *Unequal Citizens: Gender, Caste and Ethnic Exclusion in Nepal* (The World Bank and Department for International Development 2006).

[72] Will Kymlicka, *Multicultural Citizenship: A Liberal Theory of Minority Right* (Oxford University Press 1996) 30–1.

and 2009 to a number of Acts regulating public sector employment (civil service, police, army, government-owned corporations) and educational institutions to introduce reservations for categories of Nepalis on the basis of their identity. These measures are similar to the Indian approach to positive discrimination with its focus on state institutions. Significantly, the 2015 Constitution introduced the new controversial category of "Khas-Arya" (namely, high-caste Pahari Hindus) to the list of protected categories entitled to benefit from affirmative action measures.[73] Historically dominant groups have now bought into the politics of recognition and its institutionalization. In this respect, it would be important to consider the benefits for Nepal of moving away from purely majoritarian decision-making at the center and designing institutions informed by the principles of power-sharing.

Fourth, participation in Constitution making and the openness of the debate over constitutional change seem to be of paramount importance to sustain an acceptable and durable institutional compromise.[74] In Nepal, however, the CA1 ended up being marginalized by the top political leaders, who focused on other concerns, such as immediate power-sharing, while disempowering the entire Constitution-drafting process. This was in the end also the outcome of the CA2, but in this case the top leaders did reach a conclusion, however strongly it may be contested by the Madhesi and Tharu. The First Amendment to the new Constitution was passed on January 23, 2016, but it has not resolved the discontent in the Terai and no agreement had been found by February 2018 on a second amendment and the redrawing of the federal units. Given the extensive mandate that ultra-nationalist political forces received in the 2017 elections, it seems unlikely that Nepal's federal demarcation will be revised any time soon. The question, however, remains whether the coalition supporting the new document will prove able to sustain it. Clearly a broader consensus would bring more stability to the constitutional settlement, but achieving such a consensus seems an ever more distant possibility in Nepal's increasingly polarized public discourse.

[73] Krishna Adhikari and David Gellner, "New Identity Politics and the 2012 Collapse of Nepal's Constituent Assembly: When the dominant becomes 'other'" (2016) 50 (6) *Modern Asian Studies* 2009–40.

[74] UNDP and Constitution Advisory Support Unit, "Constitution Making in Nepal: Report of a Conference organized by the Constitution Advisory Support Unit, UNDP" (United Nations Development Programme 2007).

10

Nigeria's Permanent Constitutional Transition

Military Rule, Civilian Instability, and the Unending Search for Democratic "True Federalism" in a Deeply Divided Society

Rotimi Suberu

Overview

As one of the world's most deeply divided countries, Nigeria perennially has sought to redesign constitutional institutions to contain inter-group conflict. The struggle to stabilize Nigeria's fragmented society has seen wide-ranging institutional experiments, including civilian and military rule, centrifugal and centralized federalisms, presidential and parliamentary systems, and various institutions for restraining the legendary political corruption at the heart of the country's disintegrative ethno-political conflicts.

This chapter analyzes the background, procedures, structures, and aftermath of Nigeria's constitutional transformation under military auspices from a relatively decentralized, parliamentary federation of four ethnic regions to a centrist, presidential, thirty-six-state federalism. There was a momentous constitutional transition over nearly thirty years of military rule from 1966 to 1999, with a brief civilian interregnum during the Second Nigerian Republic (1979–83), during which the military created a strong central government. The military dominated the constitutional transition process, despite the cooptation of civilian drafting committees and constituent assemblies. Despite the resilience and ingenuity of the military's constitutional legacy, significant challenges have developed since the return of civilian rule, reacting against the military's non-participatory procedures, centrist structures, and relatively weak investment in critical institutions of restraint. These challenges, which have often come under the rubric of "political restructuring" and a quest for democratic "true federalism," have spawned a relentless constitutional politics, underscoring the permanent or continuous nature of Nigeria's constitutional transition.

Background

Nigeria's constitutional evolution (see Table 10.1) can be demarcated into three broad phases as follows. First, over the period from 1914 until independence, the British "amalgamated" Nigeria into one single colonial entity, gradually transforming the new state into a parliamentary federation of three major ethnic regions. This British legacy unraveled shortly after Nigeria gained independence in 1960 with the collapse of the First Nigerian Republic in a bloody military coup in 1966 and the subsequent outbreak of the Nigerian civil war (1967–70).

Territory and Power in Constitutional Transitions. First Edition. Edited by Michael Anderson and Sujit Choudhry. Nigeria's Permanent Constitutional Transition: Military Rule, Civilian Instability, and the Unending Search for Democratic "True Federalism" in a Deeply Divided Society Published 2019 by Oxford University Press.

TABLE 10.1 Nigeria's Constitutional Development, 1914 to Date

Name/Year of Constitution	Constitution-Making Authority	Major Feature(s)
Constitution of the Colony and Protectorate of Nigeria, 1914	Colonial	Amalgamated the Colony and Protectorate of Southern Nigeria and the Protectorate of Northern Nigeria, into a single colony
The Hugh Clifford Constitution, 1922	Colonial	Consolidated unification with predominantly appointed Legislative Council for the whole country, but with jurisdiction largely in Southern Nigeria.
Arthur Richards Constitution, 1946	Colonial	Brought Northern Nigeria under the Legislative Council, members of which included nominees of Regional Councils of the Northern, Western, and Eastern groups of provinces into which Nigeria had been divided in 1939.
John Macpherson Constitution, 1951	Colonial	Quasi-Federal with three regions given defined independent legislative powers; introduced elected majorities in the Central and Regional Legislatures.
Oliver Lyttelton Constitution, 1954	Colonial	Thoroughgoing Federal System, with specified powers to the Central Government, and residual Powers to the three regions.
Constitution of the Federation of Nigeria, 1960.	Colonial	Independent Federal Parliamentary Country of the British Commonwealth.
Constitution of the Federal Republic of Nigeria, 1963	Civilian	Nigerian President as ceremonial Head of State replaced Queen; ended judicial appeals to UK; created fourth region in Mid-West.
Constitution of the Federal Republic of Nigeria, 1979	Military	American-style Presidential Federal Model with 19 states.
Constitution of the Federal Republic of Nigeria, 1989	Military	Modified Presidential Federal System, including mandatory two-party system, 21 states, and greater local government autonomy.
Constitution of the Federal Republic of Nigeria, 1995	Military	Additional modifications, including elaborate ethnic power sharing, greater decentralization, 30 states, 13 percent resource revenue minimum for producing states, return to multi-parties.
Constitution of the Federal Republic of Nigeria, 1999	Military	Basically restored 1979 Constitution, but with 36 states and the 13 percent derivation principle.
Constitution of the Federal Republic of Nigeria, 1999 (as amended)	Civilian	Modest amendments to 1999 Constitution, including electoral reforms and entrenchment of the National Industrial Court.

Source: Adapted from Ben O Nwabueze, *A Constitutional History of Nigeria* (C Hurst and Company 1982).

Second, during 1966–99, Nigeria's military rulers transformed the country's constitutional institutions in response to the failure of the First Republic and the outbreak of civil war. Three mega-constitutional changes defined this transition:

- a change from a federal territorial structure with a small number of large constituent regions to one with a large number of relatively small states;
- a huge expansion in the powers and resources of the central government and a corresponding reduction in the autonomy of subnational units; and,
- a shift from a parliamentary system of government to a presidential structure. Additionally, the military sought to create agencies for restraining the political malfeasance at the roots of the country's instability.

Finally, the period since 1999 is the longest phase of civilian rule in Nigeria's constitutional history. It has seen governmental, civic, and ethno-regional bodies immersing themselves in multifaceted and contentious constitutional politics in a bid to reform or restructure the military's centrist and allegedly undemocratic constitutional legacy. Nonetheless, the basic elements of this legacy (multiple states, centralized federalism, presidential governance, and the quest for credible agencies of restraint) have remained intact.

Nigeria's constitutional odyssey reflects a constant struggle to manage the country's extraordinary ethnic, regional, and religious diversity. With three major ethnic groups (the Hausa-Fulani, Igbo, and Yoruba), hundreds of smaller ethnic communities, and approximately equal numbers of Christian and Muslim adherents, British-created Nigeria is among the most ethnically diverse countries in the world. In order to hold Nigeria together during a colonial era of growing socio-economic modernization and ethnic mobilization, the British spearheaded various constitutional reform conferences that culminated in the grant of independence to Nigeria as a Westminster-style parliamentary federation of three major ethnic regions in 1960.

Nigeria's First Republic (1960–66), however, proved unviable. The extensive postmortems on the Republic have implicated at least four institutional factors; namely, the unbalanced federal territorial structure, the subversive power of large regional units vis-à-vis the central government, the fragmentation and weakness of the central political executive in the face of this regional divisiveness, and the fragility and paucity of institutions that could restrain manipulations of political power.

A flagrant defect of the First Republic's federalism was the size of the predominantly Muslim Northern Region, which was larger and more populous than the two Southern, predominantly Christian, regions (the Eastern and Western administrations) combined. This created a classic "dual power situation" (with the "core" Northern Region usurping and rivaling the central government), deepened ethnic insecurity and anxiety, and encouraged ethno-secessionism.[1] The fact that the North was poorer and less modernized than the South aggravated this structural defect, highlighting the tension between the political hegemony of the North and the socio-economic primacy of the South.

Another flaw of the federal system was that it denied a measure of self-government to Nigeria's minority ethnic communities, including the Kanuri, Nupe, Tiv, Igala, Jukun, and the Ilorin-Kabba Yoruba in the Northern region; the Edo, Urhobo, Ijaw,

[1] Henry E Hale, "Divided We Stand: Institutional Sources of Ethnofederal State Survival and Collapse" (2004) 56 (2) World Politics 165.

Itsekiri, and the Western Igbo in the West; and the Ibibio, Annang, Efik and Ijaw in the East. These groups, which constituted approximately one-third of the population of each region, alleged "political repression, socio-economic discrimination, and even cultural extinction by the majority groups."[2] Consequently, they spearheaded intense and sometimes violent statehood movements, including agitations for Middle Belt and Bornu states in the North, for Calabar-Ogoja-Rivers (COR) state in the East, and for Mid-West state in the West. Although Northern and Eastern politicians in control of the federal government successfully schemed to create the Mid-West in 1963 in a bid to dismember and weaken the opposition-controlled Western Region, they firmly resisted the excision of minority states from their own regions, thereby leaving the country's minority problems substantially unresolved.

Having so few regional units, which prevented the fluidity, flexibility, or crosscutting regional alliances that would have flowed from multiple regional actors, also undermined Nigeria's pre-military federalism. Instead, national politics polarized around a succession of bitter inter-regional conflicts over the control of central and regional governments. These fierce struggles culminated in the Western regional election fiasco of 1965, which directly precipitated the first military coup in January 1966.

The instability inherent in the federal territorial structure was compounded by the considerable constitutional powers of the regions, which reflected the strong inter-regional suspicion and contending ethnic nationalisms that led to the establishment of the federal system in 1954. The regions controlled all matters of internal policy and administration (including education, agriculture, health, public works, and secondary roads), and were assigned revenue sources (income tax, and the return to them on a derivation basis of major federally collected export, import, and mining taxes) designed to give them "maximum financial independence."[3] In addition, the regions were empowered by the fact that they became internally self-governing before the federation as a whole, by the concentration of talented indigenous personnel in the regional administrations (where career prospects were brighter due to early regional indigenization programs), by the regional character of the leading political parties, and by the absence of strong, united, or coherent political leadership at the federal level.

Indeed, one of the most widely criticized features of the First Republic was the perceived "lack of decisiveness and drive at the center" arising from the dual, collegiate, structure of the federal parliamentary executive.[4] In particular, the federal government was debilitated by a public clash of ethno-political interests between President Nnamdi Azikiwe and Prime Minster Tafawa Balewa over the composition of the federal government (with President Azikiwe unsuccessfully seeking to prevent the reappointment of Balewa as prime minister following controversial federal elections in 1964), over the control of the armed forces, and over the constitutional future of the federation.

The greatest source of instability in the First Republic was, however, the intense premium on the control of political power and the absence of strong countervailing institutions to prevent personal, factional, or sectional abuses of power. In an underdeveloped political economy like Nigeria, where access to political power is the primary avenue to affluence and influence for groups and individuals, political competition

[2] Larry Diamond, "Class, Ethnicity, and the Democratic State: Nigeria, 1950-66" (1983) 25 (3) Comparative Studies in Society and History 457, 474.

[3] John P Mackintosh, *Nigerian Government and Politics* (Northwestern University Press 1966) 31.

[4] ibid 64.

can become intensively destructive, and overwhelm and consume institutions like the judiciary and electoral administration that are designed to regulate the struggles for power. But the constitutional arrangements of the First Republic lacked effective mechanisms to strengthen or insulate such potential institutions of restraint. Instead, the First Republic was degraded and destabilized by the politicization, manipulation, or enfeeblement of major nonpartisan institutions like the judiciary, electoral administration, local police forces, and even the military, as ethno-political factions struggled violently for political power at national and subnational levels. Unrestrained by a rule of law or independent oversight institutions, political competition in the First Republic morphed into a succession of political shenanigans and electoral frauds "that heightened ethnic and regional polarization, intensified political violence and intolerance, and heavily eroded the popular legitimacy" of the Republic.[5]

The flaws in the constitutional institutions of the First Republic partly reflect pitfalls in the procedures by which those institutions were constituted. The institutions were fashioned in a succession of constitutional conferences between the British colonial authorities and a rising, but tiny and ethnically fragmented, nationalist elite. These processes generally privileged the preferences of "the British [colonial] Government . . . and the desires of Nigerian politicians," with hardly any influences from "such places as the United States or neighboring French colonial territories" or, more importantly, from the wider Nigerian population.[6] The catastrophic levels of electoral manipulation and political corruption and repression that were perpetrated by politicians of the First Republic reflected and compounded this lack of constitutional legitimacy. The overthrow of the Republic by the military in January 1966, therefore, enjoyed support from "a broad section of the population, which welcomed the coup in an effusive outpouring of joy and relief."[7]

Period of Constitutional Engagement: Military Rule and the Reconstruction of Nigeria's Constitutional Architecture

Plagued itself by chronic ethnic conflict and political corruption, and featuring eight different military heads of state (all but two of whom were Northerners), the Nigerian military responded to the collapse of the First Republic and the subsequent outbreak of civil war with milestone political reforms. Essentially, the military sought to reshape the Nigerian polity in accordance with its own centrist institutional structures and vision. Yet, confronted with the irrepressible diversity of Nigerian society, the military governed largely in a conciliatory rather than coercive fashion, incorporating into its governance many benign features that helped soften its inherent unitary authoritarianism. The military government, for instance, continued a civilian policy of recruiting the military organization on the basis of equitable inter-regional or inter-state quotas, which helped moderate domination of the military by the more populous Northerners, who had relatively limited competitiveness in non-military sectors, but played disproportionate roles in coups.

[5] Larry Diamond, "Nigeria: The Uncivic State and the Descent into Praetorianism" in Larry Diamond, Juan J Linz, and Seymour Martin Lipset (eds), *Politics in Developing Countries: Comparing Experiences with Democracy* (Lynne Rienner Publishers 1995) 424.

[6] Mackintosh (n 3) 17.

[7] Diamond, "Nigeria" (n 5) 427.

Successive military administrations also committed to maintaining the federal structure, following violent reactions to the 1966 unitary scheme of the first military administration under General Johnson Aguiyi-Ironsi. In addition, the soldiers legitimized their rule as a corrective intervention designed to lay the foundations for the transition back to democratic rule. Consequently, they permitted some multiparty politics, albeit often with restrictions and late into the military's tenures, as an important feature of the re-democratization process. What is more, they consistently coopted civilian bureaucrats and politicians as advisers, ministers, commissioners, members of committees or investigatory panels, and Constitution drafters.

The military's Constitution-making procedures were originally implemented during the making of the 1979 Constitution and were largely replicated subsequently in the eighties and nineties. They had five basic elements:

(1) ***Articulation of an unambiguous centrist constitutional vision***: The military set the broad parameters of Nigeria's post-civil war Constitutions. As enunciated with particular bluntness and clarity by heads of state like Generals Murtala Mohammed and Ibrahim Babangida, these included a closely regulated system of national (rather than ethnic) political parties, presidential government, a centralized and multi-unit federalism, an ethnically inclusive central government reflecting the "federal character" or ethnic diversity of the country, and a rejection of grand radical ideological philosophies like socialism.[8]

(2) ***Elaboration of the military's vision by civilian technocrats***: The military entrusted the elaboration of its centrist vision to groups of academics, lawyers, and other technocrats, who translated it into constitutional documents. During 1975–76, a forty-nine-member Constitution Drafting Committee (CDC) drafted the 1979 Constitution, which provided the template for subsequent military-initiated Constitutions in 1989, 1995, and 1999. The CDC, which included at least two members from each of the then twelve states, comprised both "learned members in disciplines [with] direct relevance to constitution-making [and] eminent Nigerians with some experience in constitution-making," all of whom "were committed to a strong federal authority."[9] Following the collapse of the Second Republic, successive military administrations constituted similar technocratic Constitution review bodies, including the seventeen-member Political Bureau of 1985, the forty-six-member Constitution Review Committee in 1987, and the twenty-two-member Constitution Debate Coordinating Committee (CDCC) of 1998. Despite occasional voices of dissent, these Committees mostly produced constitutional proposals in accordance with the military's specifications or centrist vision.

(3) ***Attempted legitimization of the military's vision through representative assemblies***: Reflecting its formal commitment to democratization, the military sought to give broad legitimacy to its constitutional blueprints through directly

[8] Keith Panter-Brick, "The Constitution Drafting Committee" in Keith Panter-Brick (ed.), *Soldiers and Oil: The Political Transformation of Nigeria* (Frank Cass and Company 1978); Rafiu Akindele, "The Constituent Assembly and the 1989 Constitution" in Larry Diamond, Anthony Kirk-Greene, and Oyeleye Oyediran (eds), *Transition Without End: Nigerian Politics and Civil Society Under Babangida* (Lynne Rienner Publishers 1997).

[9] Murtala Mohammed, "Address to the Opening Session of the Constitution Drafting Committee of 18 October 1975" reproduced in *Constitution of the Federal Republic of Nigeria 1979* (reprinted by New Nigerian Newspapers Limited, Kaduna 1981) 125; Brian Smith, "Federal-State Relations in Nigeria" (1981) 80 (320) African Affairs 355, 366.

or indirectly elected constituent assemblies. Comprising a total of 232 members in 1977–78, 567 delegates in 1988, and 369 members in 1994–95, these assemblies were tasked with debating and ratifying Constitutional blueprints produced by the military's constitutional technocrats. However, the limited powers of these assemblies were underscored by their more or less explicit designation as advisory or deliberative (rather than sovereign) bodies, by the injection of several military appointees into the assemblies, by the selection of the leadership of the assemblies by the military, and by the restrictions (so-called "no go areas") that the military often placed on the deliberative freedoms of the assemblies.

(4) ***Preservation of the military's constitutional sovereignty***: Most important, the military reserved to itself final authority to approve, reject, or amend any decisions made by constitutional drafting or debating bodies. In 1978, 1989, and 1995, for example, the military made significant amendments to Constitutions approved by constituent assemblies. In 1999, the military dispensed with a constituent assembly altogether and, acting on the CDCC's advice, simply amended and updated Nigeria's 1979 Constitution, promulgating it as the 1999 Constitution.

(5) ***Rigid constitutional entrenchment and irreversibility of the military's institutional legacy***: A relatively rigid constitutional amendment formula (involving ratification of any constitutional changes by concurrent legislative supermajorities at federal and regional levels) has been a broadly supported feature of Nigeria's constitutional settlement since the First Republic. But the military, while suspending constitutional niceties for much of its rule and restructuring the federation largely unilaterally, supported both the restoration of a rigid Constitution amendment formula as well as an expansion in the subjects included in Nigeria's post-military Constitutions. In 1978, for instance, the military decided to elevate two of its policies, the Land Use Decree and the National Youth Service Programs, from mere statutory decree-laws into provisions entrenched in the forthcoming 1979 Constitution.

It is therefore understandable that Nigeria's current constitutional framework has elicited the criticism that it was fashioned and imposed by the military, rather than by the people or their representatives.[10] This critique has resonated powerfully because of the often-comprehensive (and entrenched) nature of the changes that the military made to the country's territorial structure, federal distribution of powers, central executive and legislature, as well as institutions of horizontal democratic accountability or oversight.

Territorial reorganizations

The military implemented five rounds of territorial reorganizations during its reign, increasing the number of federal sub-units from only four regions at the end of the First Republic in 1966 to 12 states in 1967, 19 in 1976, 21 in 1987, 30 in 1991, and 36 states in 1996. In addition, the soldiers relocated the capital of the federation from

[10] Tunde Ogowewo, "Why the Judicial Annulment of the Constitution of 1999 is Imperative for the Survival of Nigeria's Democracy" (2002) 44 (2) Journal of African Law 135.

the Yoruba-dominated, southwestern Nigerian city of Lagos to Abuja, an ethnically more neutral area in the center of the country.

The 1967 reorganization was announced by the military administration on the eve of civil war without any public consultations. While it subdivided the dominant Northern Region into six different states, the reorganization was primarily designed to undercut the imminent secessionist bid of the Igbo-dominated Eastern Region, which was split into three new states. Of the three states, the Rivers and Southeastern states were established for oil-bearing minority non-Igbo communities, thereby leaving the Igbo-based East Central state landlocked and without significant oil deposits. Although it failed to prevent the Eastern Region's proclamation of itself as an independent Republic of Biafra and the outbreak of civil war, the 1967 reorganization decisively decapitated the secessionist Republic, ensuring federal victory in the war.

Unlike the 1967 restructuring, which responded specifically to ethnic minority demands and was mostly unpopular among major ethnicities, subsequent state reorganizations were undertaken in response to intense agitations by majority and minority ethnic communities in large part to take advantage of the enormous distributive advantages associated with forming a state. Indeed, since the 1967 reorganization, federal revenues and other economic and political benefits (federal educational institutions, ministerial appointments, bureaucratic positions) have been allocated largely on an equal basis among the states. Thus, a major ethnic group like the Igbo, which resisted balkanization into smaller states in the sixties, came vociferously to support new state creation in order to enhance its relative shares of federal resources. The Igbo bemoan the fact that the Igbo-based Southeast geopolitical zone has only five states as against six states in the Yoruba Southwest and seven states in the Hausa-Fulani Northwest. Such calls for new state creation led the military repeatedly to fragment, proliferate and, invariably, weaken constituent states.

The military explicitly repudiated the ethnic principle as a basis for reorganization. The principle was considered inconsistent with subdividing big ethnicities into smaller states (and reducing disparities in the population sizes of states), with the multiplicity and fluidity of Nigerian ethnic identities, and with the military's overriding emphasis on national unity. Indeed, in 1976 the military decreed that the names of the states were not to have any ethnic or regional connotations.[11]

The non-democratic processes of the military's state creations facilitated its exaggerated repudiation of ethnicity. The 1963 creation of the Mid-West in the First Republic was the only one that followed prescribed constitutional procedures, including ratification by national and subnational legislatures and by plebiscite in the area of the proposed state. All subsequent reorganizations were undertaken more or less unilaterally by military regimes, albeit often in response to very vigorous statehood agitations.

The military's first territorial reorganization in 1967 was imposed hurriedly in response to Biafra's imminent secession. On the other hand, the 1976 state creations followed the recommendations of a civilian panel, though the military significantly modified the panel's proposals regarding the regional distribution, ethnic composition and administrative capitals of new states. The 1987 and 1991 reorganizations were not preceded by special panels or hearings, but responded to political dissatisfaction with previous state creations. Finally, the military imposed the thirty-six-state structure in

[11] Rotimi T Suberu, *Federalism and Ethnic Conflict in Nigeria* (United States Institute of Peace 2001) 91.

1996 without reference to—or publication of—the recommendations of a recently established civilian Committee on State and Local Government Creation.

Overall, state reorganizations have enhanced access by subnational groups to federal economic and political patronage, while ending the flagrant structural imbalance inherent in the predominant size of the old Northern region, assuaging ethnic minority insecurities, and fragmenting each of the three major ethnic groups into multiple states. The reorganizations minimized the disparities in the populations of the states, reduced inter-group tensions by fragmenting some of the more culturally heterogeneous or politically conflicted states, and also enhanced the powers of the central government.

Centralization of constitutional functions and fiscal resources

The military's flagship decree empowered the "Federal Military Government to make laws for the peace, order and good government of Nigeria or any part thereof with respect to any matter whatsoever."[12] Essentially, successive military administrations, with the exception of the Ironsi government, maintained the formal constitutional status of the country as a federation, while shifting powers and resources massively to the center. This shift was greatly abetted by the unified command structure of the military, as well as by the emergency created by civil war, the enhanced credibility of the central government after its victory, and then the dramatic post-war expansion in centrally collected revenues.

Throughout its rule, the military enacted several decree-laws that encroached on previously subnational powers and resources, and it then entrenched these new competencies in the Constitutions it bequeathed to the civilian administrations. A comparison of the legislative lists of the pre-military 1963 Constitution and the 1979 Constitution shows the extent of this centralization. Sixteen subjects that were concurrent to both federal and regional governments in 1963 were made exclusively federal in 1979. The transferred subjects include: arms, bankruptcy, censuses, commercial and industrial monopolies, drugs and poisons, fingerprints and criminal records, labor, prisons, professional occupations, quarantine, business registration, regulation of tourism, traffic on trunk roads, public holidays, regulation of political parties and the execution of federal civil and criminal processes. New items, such as the enforcement of directive principles and fundamental objectives of public policy, were added to the exclusive federal list in 1979 for the first time; this list grew to sixty-seven items from forty-five under the 1963 Constitution.[13]

The 1979 Constitution and its successors further reinforced centralization by how they constructed concurrent powers over public safety, electoral laws, local governance, and revenue allocations. For example, although "public safety and public order remain a concurrent matter . . . the principal instrument for maintaining and securing them—the police and the armed forces—are centralized in the federal government, without the concession made to the regional governments by the 1960/63 Constitutions to establish local police forces on a provincial basis."[14]

Similarly, the federal government is given lead responsibility for electoral laws, while state legislatures are restricted to "making laws with respect to elections to a local

[12] ibid 31.

[13] Constitution of the Federal Republic of Nigeria 1963, Sch., pt. I, Exclusive Legislative List; Constitution of the Federal Republic of Nigeria 1979, Sch. 2, pt. I, Exclusive Legislative List.

[14] Ben O Nwabueze, *Military Rule and Constitutionalism in Nigeria* (Spectrum Books 1992).

government council in addition to but not inconsistent with any law by the National Assembly."[15] Moreover, states constitutionally cannot effect changes in the boundaries of their local governments without ratification by the National Assembly. In essence, although state governments continue to enjoy extensive powers over local elections, finances and administration, the Constitution now empowers the federal government to regulate local governance, which was a purely residual subject for regional governments under the pre-military regime.

Fiscally, Nigeria's current Constitution gives both federal and state governments the legislative powers to allocate public revenues, but it consolidates the most important revenues into a Federation Account, which is to be divided by the National Assembly vertically and horizontally among federal, state, and local governments. In addition, the federal government not only levies and redistributes the Value Added Tax (VAT), which replaced the subnational sales tax in 1993, but also legislates on the rates and bases of key taxes that are collected and retained by the states, including personal income tax. Overall, Nigeria's subnational governments depend for an average 90 percent of their revenues on unconditional, constitutionally mandated, transfers from the Federation Account and other federally redistributed revenues.

Vertically, the Federation Account is currently distributed in the proportions of 48.50 percent, 26.72 percent, 20.60 percent, and 4.18 percent to the federal government, states, local government, and federally controlled special funds, respectively. Horizontally, the Constitution requires that a minimum of 13 percent of natural resource revenues be paid upfront to the resource-bearing areas on a derivation basis. The general allocations to the subnational governments are then statutorily distributed among the states and among the localities on the basis of the following principles and accompanying weights: equality, 40 percent; population, 30 percent; social development needs, 10 percent; land mass and terrain, 10 percent; and internal revenue generation effort, 10 percent.

The 13 percent derivation principle emerged from a "consensus agreement" at the 1994/95 Constitutional Conference in response to persistent violent agitations for subnational resource control in the oil-rich Niger Delta. Yet, given the dependence of all governments on redistributed oil revenues, the application of the derivation rule has spawned profound distributional distortions and disparities, with nine southern oil-producing states typically receiving over half of total revenue transfers to the states, even though they account for less than one-fourth of the population.[16]

The preponderant weight for inter-unit equality and population in the general horizontal sharing formula, on the other hand, dates back to 1969, when the military imposed both principles as a straightforward formula for sharing revenues among newly created states "without resort to special commissions of inquiry or constitutional convention."[17] Overall, these horizontal distribution arrangements focused the attention of most subnational governments on revenue sharing, rather than on autonomous revenue generation, thereby reinforcing the centrist agenda of the military.

The political and fiscal over-centralization of Nigeria effectively meant that the residual powers retained by state governments would "be determined largely by what

[15] Constitution of the Federal Republic of Nigeria 1979, Sch. 2, pt. II, Concurrent Legislative List, Item E; Constitution of the Federal Republic of Nigeria 1999, Sch. 2, pt. II, Concurrent Legislative List, Item E.

[16] Wumi Iledare and Rotimi Suberu, "Nigeria" in George Anderson (ed.), *Oil and Gas in Federal Systems* (Oxford University Press 2012) 239.

[17] Lawrence Rupley, "Revenue Sharing in the Nigerian Federation" (1981) 19 (2) Journal of Modern African Studies 257, 264.

the Federal Government voluntarily chooses to leave to the states." [18] With such centralization, however, the military and its advisers also addressed the deep-seated fears of ethnic and regional domination at the center and in the states by introducing the celebrated constitutional principle of federal character, which requires the composition and conduct of the federal government and other public agencies to reflect the diversity or "federal character" of the country. Essentially, this "encouraged many Nigerians to view federalism not as a principle of non-centralized democratic government, but as simply a guarantee of ethnic and religious group representation in the institutions of government, no matter how centralized."[19] The federal character principle would apply to the composition of the federal cabinet, ministries, departments, agencies, commissions and armed forces, the state governments, the political parties and to the procedures for electing the federal and state chief political executives in Nigeria's new America-style presidential system.

Presidentialism

In an explicit rejection of Nigeria's parliamentary experiment in the First Republic, and consistent with a predilection for strong presidential political chief executives in other African countries, the military concluded in 1975 that the country required an "executive presidential system of government in which the president and vice-president are directly elected and brought into office in a manner that reflects the federal character of the country."[20] The election formula that was adopted after protracted constitutional debates required a successful presidential candidate to win a plurality of votes nationally plus a quarter of the votes in at least two-thirds of the states and in the Federal Capital Territory. Similarly, a successful gubernatorial candidate must win the highest number of votes plus at least one-quarter of votes in two-thirds of the local government areas in the state.

There was confusion regarding the procedure to be followed if these requirements were not met. The current formula for president provides for a run-off election between the candidate with the highest number of votes and the one among the remaining candidates with a majority of votes in the highest number of states. If neither candidate in the run-off meets the requirements for election, they will have a second run-off with the same requirements. If this still fails to produce a winner, the candidates will meet in a final run-off election, with the presidency or governorship going to the candidate with a majority of votes. In practice, with the exception of the inaugural presidential election of 1979 (when Shehu Shagari was controversially declared elected as president after obtaining the required one-quarter of votes in slightly less than two-thirds of the then nineteen states) no federal or state election has proved inconclusive because of the geographic distribution requirement, which has been remarkably successful in generating strong incentives for the construction of inclusive electoral coalitions.

The debates preceding the ratification of the presidential system in the 1979 Constitution were some of the most vigorous in Nigeria. The military and its supporters in the CDC and 1977 Constituent Assembly defended the choice of a presidential system on the grounds of its presumed compatibility with Nigerian and African

[18] Michael Joye and Kingsley Igweike, *Introduction to the 1979 Nigerian Constitution* (Macmillan 1982) 94.

[19] Ladipo Adamolekun and John Kincaid, "The Federal Solution: Assessment and Prognosis for Nigeria and Africa" (1991) 21 (4) Publius: The Journal of Federalism 173, 178.

[20] Mohammed (n 9) 125.

indigenous kingship or chieftaincy traditions. It was also argued that the system would provide strong executive leadership, avoiding confrontations like those that plagued the dual executive of the First Republic, and would give the country a pan-Nigerian symbol of unity, deriving from the direct national election and preeminent constitutional status of the presidency.

The presidential system was also defended as more consistent with Nigerian federalism in providing for effective inter-branch separation of powers (including independent judicial review) as well as a strong upper legislative chamber (the Senate) to represent regional interests. This contrasts with the parliamentary system, which typically subordinates the upper chamber to the sovereignty of the popular or lower parliamentary chamber. Finally, the presidential system was promoted for providing for the popular election of the executive, fixed presidential terms of office (a maximum of two four-year terms), and fixed non-discretionary electoral cycles, among other democratizing characteristics.

Skeptics, however, either preferred a return to the parliamentary system of the First Republic or the substantial modification of the presidential system, including a simpler procedure for presidential elections, the possibility of cabinet members coming from the legislature, and formal provisions for the ethno-regional rotation of the presidency.[21] A common concern was that a presidential system could promote a dictatorial presidency unless adequate restraining institutions were in place.

A corollary of the military's constitutional choice of an executive presidency with broad trans-ethnic electoral support was its ban on ethnic political parties and its insistence on the formation of truly national parties. Indeed, despite its longstanding commitment to political liberalization and democratization, the Nigerian military implemented ethnic party bans more "systematically" than any other African regime, often demonstrating a profound distrust for independent political organizing by Nigeria's ethnically based civilian elites and denying registration to tens of prospective parties for failing to establish a national presence.[22] This disapproval of ethnic political parties found its most extreme expressions in the military's suggestion in 1975 that the CDC should explore "means by which [democratic] Government can be formed without the involvement of political parties," and in the subsequent imposition under the 1989 Constitution of a system that limited political competition to only two, government-established, political parties.[23]

Under the 1979 and current 1999 Constitutions, and associated electoral laws, political associations, to be officially licensed as parties, are required to reflect the federal character in their names, ideology, leadership, membership, and geographical location and distribution of their national and branch offices. Implementation and verification of these often-contentious party registration requirements has been entrusted to a national electoral commission, one of Nigeria's longstanding, but beleaguered, agencies of restraint.

[21] Federal Ministry of Information, "Report of the Constitution Drafting Committee, Volumes 1–2" (Federal Ministry of Information 1976); Federal Ministry of Information, "Proceedings of the Constituent Assembly: Official Report, Volumes 1–3" (Federal Ministry of Information 1978).

[22] Matthijs Bogaards, "Ethnic Party Bans and Institutional Engineering in Nigeria" (2010) 17 (4) Democratization 730.

[23] Mohammed (n 9) 124.

Agencies of restraint

An important feature of Nigeria's constitutional transition has been the attempt to redress a perceived defect in the pre-military constitutional framework through the reform or expansion of oversight or "corrective institutions" charged with restraining the country's "cutthroat political competition." [24] The 1963 Constitution, for instance, had scrapped the Judicial Service Commission, leaving the Nigeria Police Council, Public Service Commission, Electoral Commission of the Federation, and the Advisory Council on the Prerogative of Mercy as the country's only constitutionally established commissions at the federal level. Furthermore, appointments to these commissions lacked adequate political insulation.

Thus the 1979 Constitution established ten federal councils and commissions, including the civil service, electoral, judicial service, population enumeration, and police service commissions as well as the code of conduct bureau and tribunal. Appointments to these commissions were to be more insulated politically in that they were often subject to consultation with the Council of State (comprising the president, governors, and former heads of state and chief justices, among others) and confirmation by the Senate.

By the time of the inauguration of the 1999 Constitution, these constitutionally entrenched federal bodies had increased to fourteen, including the federal character and revenue allocation commissions, and National Judicial Council (NJC). Indeed, the establishment of the NJC marked a milestone in innovating with the design of agencies of restraint in the Nigerian federation. Headed by the chief justice of the Supreme Court and comprising mainly senior judges, the NJC is largely appointed without the involvement of the presidency and has very broad powers. It recommends federal and state judges for appointment (by the respective executives and legislatures) on the basis of nominations received from federal and state judicial service commissions, and also disburses monies for the judiciary and exercises disciplinary control over judges.

This innovative model has inspired other constitutional and statutory initiatives to create or strengthen agencies that could constrain the use of presidential power, or political office more generally, for personal, factional, partisan, or ethnic advantage. There has been a strengthening of the operational and budgetary autonomy of the Independent National Electoral Commission (INEC), and the creation of new statutory oversight agencies like the Independent Corrupt Practices Commission, Economic and Financial Crimes Commission, and National Human Rights Commission. However, the failure of these investments in agencies of restraint to transform the corrupt and ethnically fraught nature of Nigerian politics has highlighted contradictions in the military's constitutional legacy.

Outcomes: The Centrifugal Backlash Against the Military's Centripetal Restructuring

To what extent has Nigerian governance under civilian rule conformed to what the military hoped for? Undoubtedly, the military's elaborate constitutional engineering has produced multiple integrative and stabilizing outcomes, helping to avert a recurrence of large-scale ethno-secessionist warfare. The multi-state federal structure, for instance, has "functioned reasonably (even remarkably) well to break up the hegemony

[24] ibid 125.

of Nigeria's largest ethnic groups, decentralize ethnic conflict, disperse development activity, foster crosscutting cleavages, expose intra-ethnic divisions, facilitate inter-ethnic alliances and in general contain the powerful centrifugal forces inherent in Nigeria's ethnic composition."[25] The fiscal and other advantages of state creation have produced strong movements for the creation of additional states, which have been frustrated to date because of the onerous constitutional hurdles in the way of state reorganizations and broad concerns about the costs of further states proliferation.

Similarly, the military's centralization has endowed the federal government with the political and fiscal resources required to contain various centrifugal challenges to national unity, including Islamic extremism in the Muslim North, resource nationalism in the Niger Delta, and the Igbo-based Biafran restoration movement. At the same time, the devolution of almost half of centrally collected revenues to subnational administrations has tempered centralization and means that these units have become important arenas of political competition, thereby helping to moderate the struggles for the control of the federal presidency.

Meanwhile, the idea of a broadly elected president has come to be adapted to Nigeria's multi-ethnic context, as evident in the development by major national political parties of various creative power-sharing formulas for balancing and rotating the presidency and vice-presidency among regional, religious, and ethnic constituencies. What is more, the geographic distribution rules for electing the president and the formal ban on ethnic parties have encouraged the development of inclusive coalitions and national political parties, including the National Party of Nigeria (NPN) in the Second Republic, the Social Democratic Party (SDP), and National Republican Convention (NRC) in the aborted Third Republic, and the Peoples Democratic Party (PDP) and All Progressives Congress (APC) in the Fourth Republic.

The investment in agencies of restraint is arguably the least successful element of the military's constitutional engineering given the persistently lawless and corrupt character of Nigerian politics. The performance of the NJC, in particular, has been underwhelming, failing to control massive judicial and other forms of corruption and to eliminate executive interference in the budgetary and appropriations processes of the courts, while provoking criticisms for concentrating so much power in the chief justice and for eroding subnational control over state-level judicial appointments. Nonetheless, the idea of building strong oversight agencies has become very influential, as evident in recent constitutional reforms that are designed to give the judiciary, electoral commission, and other agencies of restraint budgetary autonomy and considerable political insulation from the executive. Partly as a result of those reforms, the electoral commission in 2015 successfully umpired the first interparty alternation in government at the national level in the country's electoral history.

These accomplishments notwithstanding, Nigeria's current constitutional framework is beset by significant ethnic, regional and religious challenges to its stability. The multi-state structure, for instance, is closely associated with the intensification and proliferation of discriminatory practices against non-indigenes (Nigerians living or born in states outside of their historic, ancestral, or indigenous communities). Such discriminatory practices have escalated from the exclusion of non-indigenes from employment and educational opportunities at the state level, to so-called "internal deportations" of beggars and vagrants to their states of origin by state governments like Kano and Lagos. While indigenization practices predated the creation of states, successive state

[25] Larry Diamond, "Issues in the Constitutional Design of a Third Nigerian Republic" (1987) 86 (343) African Affairs 209, 210–11.

reorganizations have led to a progressive contraction of the territorial space in which a Nigerian could enjoy indigenous status and freedom from discrimination.

Lacking the capacities of the old regions, and funded almost entirely by unconditional federal transfers, Nigeria's current states have functioned more like conduits for the dissemination of corrupt patronage, than as true laboratories of decentralized, democratic governance. They have mostly failed to use their control of approximately half of federal revenues and direct government spending to complement national macroeconomic reforms, formulate and implement sound economic policies, provide critical infrastructures and services in support of local businesses, and effectively deliver education, health and poverty-alleviating social services.

The governance failures of the multi-state structure cannot be dissociated from multiple pathologies in Nigeria's oil-based revenue allocation system. Aside from its heavy dependence on the redistribution of volatile oil rents via unconditional and unmonitored transfers, the revenue allocation system is vexed by poor intergovernmental policy coordination, the absence of significant incentives for non-oil revenue mobilization, and by weak to non-existent mechanisms for ensuring transparency and accountability in the use of devolved revenues. Other weaknesses of the revenue allocation system include enormous per capita disparities in the inter-state allocations of transfers arising from the application of the derivation and inter-unit equality principles, the disconnection of the derivation funds from the ecological and developmental challenges of the oil-bearing communities, and the vulnerability of federal-local financial transfers to expropriation by state governments. A more generic problem is that the presidentially appointed national revenue commission entrusted with developing and monitoring the implementation of the revenue allocation formula remains a professionally weak, politically emasculated, and virtually redundant bureaucracy

The military's hopes for an ethnically unifying Nigerian presidency have hardly materialized. Rather, electoral contests for the Nigerian presidency have remained one of the major recurrent flashpoints of fierce ethno-political contention and polarization in the Nigerian federation. The first post-military presidential election in 1979, for instance, was tainted by the bitter legal struggle over the interpretation of the presidential election formula. The next presidential election in 1983 was disfigured by widespread electoral fraud that contributed directly to the overthrow of the Second Republic. This was followed by the Northern-dominated military's annulment of the result of the 1993 presidential election, won by a Southerner for the first time in the nation's history. Although general elections in 2015 produced a relatively peaceful inter-party alternation in the presidency, Nigerian presidential elections typically involve varying levels of ethno-political scheming and melee, including the 2011 elections in which almost a thousand Nigerians were killed in violent ethno-religious post-election protests.

Although their creative informal power-sharing strategies may have helped to moderate ethno-political contention for presidential power, Nigeria's major political parties remain fundamentally weak. Partly because of the military's tight restrictions on party formation processes, Nigerian parties have remained stunted, shallow, faction-ridden, personality-driven institutions lacking internal democracy, viable organizations, coherent policy platforms, robust social bases, or genuine cross-sectional appeal. Rather their main common enterprise remains the doling out of political patronage among fractious ethnically based elites.

The multiple shortcomings of the military's constitutional legacy have produced a groundswell of constitutional agitation for a political restructuring, which has focused specifically on the perceived procedural illegitimacy and centralizing structures of the military's constitutional engineering. Echoing broad public criticisms of the 1999

Constitution, for instance, Emeka Ihedioha, the Chairman of the Constitution Review Committee of the House of Representatives, argued in 2013 that the Constitution is "the product of a military decree and . . . suffer(s) a legitimacy crisis. Many Nigerians view it with contempt and its opening paragraph . . . 'We the People' . . . has been described as a lie as there was never a time that Nigerians participated in the making of the Constitution."[26] Three perspectives have emerged regarding how this procedural deficit may be rectified.

The first perspective, embraced by the federal executive and legislature, reflects a tension between a perceived lack of legitimacy to the 1999 Constitution because of its military authorship and a strong commitment to respect the legal framework that has been bestowed. Thus, this approach seeks procedural legitimacy for the Constitution through the implementation of the constitutional amendment formula written into the Constitution itself. This requires that a proposal to change the Constitution must be approved by not less than two-thirds of all the members of each house of the bicameral National Assembly or by a four-fifths majority of these members if the change concerns the constitutional amendment formula itself or the provisions of the Constitution on fundamental human rights, boundary adjustments, and the creation of new states and localities. In addition, all amendments must be supported by resolutions of at least two-thirds of state assemblies.

Despite these onerous requirements, three sets of constitutional alterations, focusing largely on electoral administration reform, were passed by the required majority of federal and state legislatures and ratified by the federal presidency in 2010–11. Subsequently, in 2014, the federal and state legislatures passed a Constitution (Fourth Alteration) Bill, which included modest reforms regarding indigene practices, intergovernmental legislative lists, social welfare rights, local government autonomy, the electoral process, autonomy of oversight agencies, and Constitution amendment rules. However, the presidency, citing procedural technicalities and more substantive concerns, declined to assent to the bill, thereby stymying this official path to constitutional change. Nonetheless, during 2016–17, the leadership of National Assembly committed the legislature to revisiting, and adding "fresh inputs" into, the Fourth Alteration Bill, while the federal executive inaugurated a Committee on Constitution and Electoral Reform with a mandate to "evaluate our democratic journey thus far with a view to fashioning out a more enduring system that will serve present and future generations."[27]

By early 2018, Nigerian state assemblies were deliberating on multiple constitutional amendments recently passed by the National Assembly. Incorporated in separate individual bills rather than consolidated into a single comprehensive bill, these amendments included proposals to curb executive prerogatives, extend or entrench the powers of national and subnational legislatures, guarantee local government autonomy, encourage the political participation of young persons and independent candidates in elections, and improve the independence, powers, credibility, and efficiency of key oversight institutions like the electoral administration, police and judiciary. During mid-2018, President Muhammadu Buhari ratified a set of constitutional amendments that enhanced the financial autonomy of subnational legislatures and

[26] Emeka Ihedioha, "Keynote Speech" in *The Review of Nigeria's 1999 Constitution: Report of a Consultation with UK Based Nigerians* (Chatham House 2013) 22.

[27] Fred Itua, "Constitution Review: National Assembly to Overrule Buhari on Alteration Bill" *The Sun* (Lagos, January 9, 2017); News Agency of Nigeria, "Ken Nnamani-led Constitution, Electoral Reform Committee Inaugurated" *Premium Times* (Abuja, October 4, 2016).

judiciaries, reduced age requirements for selected political offices (the presidency and membership of the federal house of representatives and state assemblies), and, in general, improved and clarified the country's electoral processes. But he also withheld assent from multiple constitutional alteration bills, including amendments seeking to extend legislative privileges and to curb executive veto and spending powers. Even as proposals like enhanced local government autonomy and curbs on executive powers have been consistently resisted by state governments and federal political executives, respectively, the National Assembly's amendments have been broadly critiqued for not addressing the more radical demands for restructuring, decentralization, or true federalism in the country. Nonetheless, the Assembly's initiatives underscore the continuing commitment of Nigeria's national political leadership to a path of incremental constitutional amendments.

A second perspective on constitutional change, supported by leaders of Southern Nigerian ethno-regional (Igbo, Niger Delta, and Yoruba) movements, proposes the convocation of a Sovereign National Conference (SNC) of diverse ethnic and social groups to make a decision on whether and how the various Nigerian groups would coexist in a restructured Nigerian federation. But the idea of the SNC is severely undermined by its unpopularity in the North (where it is seen as a recipe for the dismemberment of Nigeria); by the relatively poor record of SNCs in most of the Francophone African countries where they were adopted in the nineties; by the absence of any broadly accepted criteria for selecting ethnic and other representatives into the SNC; and by the difficulty of reconciling the sovereignty of the SNC with the authority of an incumbent elected national government.

Many of the aforementioned challenges of the SNC were evident in the travails of the 2014 National Conference, which was convened by the presidency in an attempt to assuage southern demands for the SNC. The National Conference was undermined by its unelected nature, its skewed and unbalanced composition (for instance, Muslims, who constitute approximately half of the Nigerian population, accounted for only 198 of the 492 delegates), its unwieldy, open-ended, mandate, and its establishment without any formal enabling legislation by the National Assembly, which saw the Conference as an attempt to usurp legislative authority. More important, the Conference was vexed by the fault-line between Southern decentralist and Northern centrist perspectives on federalism, leading to various conflicting and unsustainable proposals, which reinforced criticisms of the Conference as a mere talk shop or a jamboree.

A final perspective, supported most consistently by the Citizens Forum on Constitutional Reform (CFCR-an alliance of Nigerian civil society groups), seeks the ratification of a redrafted or amended Nigerian Constitution by a popular referendum. Influenced greatly by the global rise of a paradigm of participatory constitutionalism, proponents of this third path to constitutional reform have disparaged Nigeria's existing Constitution-making methods as shallow, elitist, and restrictive, while advocating for a fully democratic, bottom-up, process-led, people-driven, and participatory approach. While there has been some official receptivity to the call for broader popular participation, the idea of a referendum has not obtained much official traction, presumably because it would further complicate Nigeria's already rigid Constitution-amending formula.

The post-military era has witnessed considerable contention not only about the appropriate procedures for reforming the military's constitutional legacy, but also the substantive reforms required to nurture a more viable democratic federalism. One common proposal seeks a more competitive and decentralized federalism through the consolidation of the states into between six and eighteen autonomous, ethnically based regions. Other proponents of "true" federalism advocate the deletion from the current list of exclusive federal legislative powers of items like prisons, police, evidence, labor, wages, mines and minerals, public holidays, land use, and fundamental socio-economic, political, educational, and environmental objectives. They also demand an end to federal interventions in local government, which they contend should be entirely a residual matter for the states.

There are constitutional reform proposals to make the contest for the presidency less ethnically polarizing by constitutionalizing the informal, but widely embraced, rotation and matching of presidential tickets on a regional and/or religious basis; by limiting the president's tenure to a single 4–7-year term; by splitting the federal executive between an executive president and a prime minister responsible to the legislature; or by restoring the parliamentary system of the First Republic.

The most compelling constitutional reform proposals for de-polarizing the struggle for the presidency, however, revolve around the establishment of strong institutional restraints on presidential power. For instance, a presidentially appointed Electoral Reform Committee (ERC) in 2008 called for the nomination and appointment of the board of national electoral commission by the NJC and the Council of State, respectively, rather than by the presidency.[28] Similarly, the aborted Constitution (Fourth Alteration) Bill, 2014 included various proposals to enhance the operational and budgetary autonomy of oversight institutions like the revenue allocation commission, security agencies, and offices of auditor-general, attorney-general, and accountant-general of the federation. However, these proposals have met with resistance from the political executive.

In essence, with the exception of the minor constitutional alterations implemented in 2010–11 and in 2018, Nigeria has not achieved any formal change to the military's constitutional legacy. This is not unlike the experiences of other federations with relatively rigid constitutional amendment formulas, including the USA and Canada. Nonetheless, comparative experience suggests that "deliberate constitutional reform is not the only or the most frequent source of change" in federal systems.[29] Thus, although countries like Germany, Switzerland, and the UK have recently accomplished formal constitutional change, federations like Canada, Spain, and Australia have witnessed more informal or non-constitutional evolution, adaptation, or renewal.

Indeed, in the absence of significant formal democratic constitutional change, Nigeria has experienced important non-constitutional development through judicial arbitration, legislative supplementation, and even "constitutional infidelity" or circumventions.[30] The states, for instance, have launched judicial challenges against the center's administration of the natural resource revenue allocation system, interventions in local governance, use of national policing powers, and manipulation of subnational electoral processes. While mostly upholding the prerogatives of the center in federal-state constitutional disputes over natural resource control and public security, major rulings of the Supreme Court on local governance and electoral disputes have

[28] Federal Republic of Nigeria, "Report of the Electoral Reform Committee" (Federal Republic of Nigeria 2008).

[29] Arthur Benz and Cesar Colino, "Constitutional Change in Federations: A Framework for Analysis" (2011) 21 (4–5) Regional and Federal Studies 381, 382.

[30] John Kincaid, "Constitutional Change in Federal Countries: Comparative Considerations" in Arthur Benz and Felix Knüpling (eds), *Changing Federal Constitutions: Lessons from International Comparison* (Barbara Budrich Publishers 2012) 31–50.

buttressed states' rights.[31] Indeed, owing partly to stronger judicial enforcement of revenue allocation laws as well as a reassertion of states rights by newly elected subnational governments, the end of military rule in 1999 witnessed "greater transparency and clarity in important aspects of intergovernmental fiscal relations . . . and . . . stricter observance of constitutional provisions on fiscal federalism" leading to "increased revenue flows to subnational governments."[32]

Furthermore, in a remarkable use of federal legislative power to enhance subnational resource rights, the National Assembly passed the "Allocation of Revenue (Abolition of Dichotomy in the Application of the Principle of Derivation) Act 2004," which abrogated the distinction between onshore and offshore oil in the calculation of the 13 percent of natural resource revenues constitutionally due to oil-bearing states on a "derivation" or region-of-origin basis. This legislation responded to fierce opposition by the oil-rich states to an April 2002 ruling of the Supreme Court, in *AG Federation v. AG Abia & Ors*, that natural resources in Nigeria's continental shelf belong to the federation as a whole and, therefore, cannot be said to be derivable from the adjoining littoral states for revenue allocation purposes.[33]

In addition to benefiting from judicial arbitration and legislative supplementation, the states have resorted to creative circumvention of centrist constitutional rules. In the most controversial assertion of states' rights since 1999, for example, twelve Northern Muslim states exploited a loophole in the Nigerian Constitution to extend the jurisdiction of Sharia courts from personal to penal matters. Similarly, several states have created so-called Local Council Development Areas (LCDAs) as a way of tinkering with their local government boundaries, thereby sidetracking the Constitution's entrenchment of the country's 774 local government areas. Other examples of constitutional infidelity include the proliferation of various subnationally funded or maintained law-enforcement or quasi-police units, the growing formalization of six geopolitical zones (three each in the North and South) as a tier of federalist coordination, administration, and representation outside the states and localities, and the informal rotation of the powerful office of the presidency on a North–South and/or Muslim–Christian basis.

Lessons Learned

The Nigerian experience with constitutional transformations under military rule holds multiple lessons for the management of ethno-territorial conflict in deeply divided societies. One key lesson is the potential role that a system of soft authoritarianism, like Nigeria's comparatively liberalized military regimes, can play in designing the constitutional institutions required to sustain relative stability in an ethnically fractured state. Confronted with the imminent secession of the Eastern Region, the military transformed the unwieldy ethno-regional federalism inherited from Britain into a more stable multi-unit system. For all the criticisms of the military's constitutional legacy, the overall impact of the military's political reforms has been to endow the country with a political system approximating many of the features generally associated with a robust federal design, including a relatively large number of constituent states, incentives for national multi-ethnic parties, provisions for inter-segmental

[31] Rotimi Suberu, "The Supreme Court and Federalism in Nigeria" (2008) 46 (3) Journal of Modern African Studies 451.

[32] World Bank, *Nigeria State Finances Study* (World Bank 2003) 43.

[33] Suberu, "The Supreme Court and Federalism in Nigeria" (n 31) 451–8.

representation in the national government, and a strong central administration with capacity to confront threats to national unity.[34]

A more sobering lesson of the Nigerian constitutional experience relates to the damage that inadequate participatory procedures can inflict on the legitimacy of otherwise sound constitutional designs. For all its efforts to involve civilian elites in the reconstruction of Nigerian political institutions, the military maintained firm control over the country's constitutional future and never once subjected its constitutional engineering to a truly sovereign constituent assembly or to popular ratification in a referendum. This lack of popular participation has engendered significant constitutional agitations in Nigeria in a period where the global ethos of participatory constitutionalism has been widely embraced by many African countries, including Nigeria's direct neighbors like Benin and Niger.

In more substantive terms, the Nigerian experience clearly demonstrates the advantages for stability of having a large number of small constituent states, rather than a small number of large units. Although violent ethnic, regional, and religious conflicts continue to plague Nigeria, the multi-state structure has functioned to disperse and defuse these antagonisms, making them less likely to morph into the kind of large-scale ethno-regional confrontation that produced the Nigerian civil war. Nonetheless, the very fluid, fragmentary, multilayered, and instrumental nature of ethnic identities in the African context greatly facilitated the military's reconfigurations of Nigeria's internal federal boundaries. In situations where ethnic identities are more crystallized and historically and symbolically embedded, such facility with internal territorial configurations may be more difficult to achieve.

The Nigerian experience also illustrates the imperative of balancing shared rule and self-rule in deeply divided societies. In their bid to create a strong central government, the military and its civilian advisers implemented policies that moved Nigeria too far in an over-centralizing direction, thereby producing a centrifugal backlash. The elimination of local level police forces and the imposition of a uniform system of local government, for instance, particularly detract from the country's federalist traditions and aspirations. Perhaps the use of more participatory constitutional ratification procedures would have prevented some of the centrist excesses of the military. Much of the current agitation for "true" federalism may be interpreted as less of a wholesale rejection of the military's integrative strategies than of an attempt to rein in the military's centralization and restore some balance to Nigeria's intergovernmental relations.

Yet another lesson of the Nigerian experience involves the potentially polarizing effects of a strong executive presidency in a deeply divided state. As correctly predicted by scholars like Arend Lijphart, such a powerful position, rather than serving to integrate Nigeria's divided society has fuelled a fierce ethnic, regional, and religious competition for political advantage.[35] The implication is not to abandon a presidential system, which remains a very attractive choice for developing countries for reasons that have been well enunciated in the Nigerian context. Rather, strong institutions of horizontal accountability are required to restrain presidential powers, to constrain the general propensity to manipulate and corrupt public power for personal and sectional ends in neo-patrimonial contexts like Nigeria, and to promote inter-group security and equity. However, the dysfunction and corruption that have degraded a key

[34] Rotimi Suberu, "Federalism in Africa: The Nigerian Experience in Comparative Perspective" (2009) 8 (1) Ethnopolitics 67.

[35] Arend Lijphart, "Constitutional Design for Divided Societies" (2004) 15 (2) Journal of Democracy 96.

independent agency like the NJC suggest that designing and constituting effective oversight institutions will remain an overwhelming challenge in the Nigerian polity.

Finally, the Nigerian experience underscores the continuity and complexity of constitutional transitions in deeply divided, developing states just emerging from extended periods of authoritarian rule and/or disintegrative internal conflicts. While the basic features of the military's constitutional transformation (multi-state federalism, a strong center, and presidential government) seem inviolable, agitations to adapt this institutional legacy to the imperatives of a post-military, deeply divided society will persist. This persistence was underlined by President Buhari in his nationwide new year address in January 2018. On one hand, he controversially critiqued "the ongoing debate about restructuring" Nigeria into a less politically centralized entity, including "shrill cries for a return to the parliamentary system," contending that "our problems are more to do with process than structure." On the other hand, Buhari assured Nigerians that "government is ever receptive to ideas which will improve governance and contribute to the country's peace and stability," conceding that the country's political structures "must periodically be perfected according to changing circumstances and the country's socio-economic developments."[36] In essence, Buhari's address represents an endorsement of the modest, incremental path to constitutional change that is promoted by the National Assembly (discussed earlier in this chapter), as distinct from the more radical agitations for restructuring (or "true federalism") and participatory constitutionalism that are popular with Southern Nigerians and with civic organizations, respectively.

Nonetheless, constitutional agitations will continue to focus on reorganizing subnational (especially local-level) territorial boundaries, rebalancing the relative powers and fiscal resources of central and constituent governments, restraining and managing presidential power struggles, extending the frontiers of horizontal accountability as a key ingredient of inter-ethnic security, and promoting popular participation in constitutional reforms. And constitutional politics in Nigeria will continue to invoke and evoke diverse strategies of constitutional change, including demands for wholesale constitutional replacement, the implementation of incremental constitutional amendments, legislative supplementation, judicial arbitrations, and even acts of constitutional infidelity. For the foreseeable future, Nigeria's constitutional transition will remain a work in progress.

[36] "Full Text of Muhammadu Buhari's 2018 New Year Address," *Punch* (Lagos, January 1, 2018).

11

The Philippines

Peace Talks and Autonomy in Mindanao

Bryony Lau

Overview

The Philippines has been wracked by an insurgency in its Muslim south since the early 1970s. A negotiated settlement at last seemed within reach by 2015. Moros, an umbrella term for thirteen ethno-linguistic groups that practice Islam, make up roughly 5 percent of the population in the predominantly Roman Catholic Philippines.[1] They are concentrated in two non-contiguous areas: the central portion of Mindanao, the large island in the country's far south; and in the Sulu archipelago, which stretches from the western tip of Mindanao to Sabah in eastern Malaysia. Moros began mobilizing against the Philippine state in the late 1960s and launched an armed rebellion in 1972. The first of several peace agreements to grant Moros autonomy was signed in 1976 under martial law.

The 1987 Constitution envisioned a Moro autonomous region within the unitary republic. The government created this region by fiat in 1989 but it had few powers and remained under Manila's control. The insurgents did not believe it was truly autonomous. As peace talks dragged out, the armed movement splintered and divisions among Moros deepened. The original organization, the Moro National Liberation Front (MNLF), fractured along ethnic lines in the 1980s, signed a final peace agreement in 1996, and then fragmented further in the early 2000s. The main breakaway group, the Moro Islamic Liberation Front (MILF), has posed the most serious threat to the Philippine state since then. A settlement looked less likely with the MILF, as negotiations were constrained by autonomy provisions in the Constitution. When a breakthrough agreement was reached in 2008, spoilers in Mindanao and Manila fiercely opposed it and the Supreme Court ruled it was unconstitutional. Despite these setbacks, the government and the MILF signed new peace agreements in 2012 and 2014.

This chapter explains why it has taken so long to resolve the territorial cleavage in the southern Philippines even though both sides recognize autonomy as the solution. Political interests in Mindanao and in Manila have repeatedly stood in the way, even while the 1987 Constitution made autonomy possible. A major constraint has been procedural: to create a Moro autonomous region, the Constitution requires legislation in Congress and a plebiscite in affected areas. This two-step process has

[1] In the Philippine context, Moro is not considered a derogatory term. The thirteen ethnic groups are Badjao, Iranun, Jama Mapun, Kalagan, Kalibugan, Maguindanao, Maranao, Molbog, Palawani, Sama, Sangil, Tausug, and Yakan.

Territory and Power in Constitutional Transitions. First Edition. Edited by Michael Anderson and Sujit Choudhry. The Philippines: Peace Talks and Autonomy in Mindanao © Bryony Lau 2019. Published 2019 by Oxford University Press.

allowed opponents of autonomy to block its implementation or to limit the territory and powers of such a region.

Background

For decades, peace eluded the southern Philippines for two reasons: the central government tried to impose autonomy unilaterally, and it frequently backpedalled on its promises. Over time, positions on both sides hardened, and the Constitution became a sticking point in the negotiations. Four key moments elucidate the difficulties: the 1976 Tripoli agreement signed under martial law; the drafting of the 1987 Constitution and the creation of the Autonomous Region of Muslim Mindanao in 1989; the 1996 final peace agreement with the MNLF and its partial implementation by Congress in 2001; and the 2008 memorandum of agreement on ancestral domain with the MILF.

History and more recent political grievances fuelled the insurgency. The MNLF and the MILF trace the Moro right to self-determination back to the existence, centuries ago, of distinct Muslim political structures. When the Spanish colonized the rest of the archipelago in the 1500s, they never gained control over these Islamized areas. It was only during the American period (1898–1946) that Moros were incorporated into what later became the Philippine state. Colonial administrators governed via Moro elites, which established enduring ties between local strongmen and Manila.[2] From the 1930s onwards, migration of Christian settlers from the Visayas islands and Luzon, and discriminatory land policies pushed the Moros into an ever-shrinking portion of central Mindanao and the Sulu archipelago.[3] During this period and after independence in 1946, Moro nationalism and identity emerged, initially among educated Muslims.[4]

The 1968 Jabidah massacre sparked Moro anger. Moro recruits to the Philippine military were killed by their commanding officers when they mutinied rather than foment rebellion in Sabah, in eastern Malaysia.[5] The incident radicalized Nur Misuari, a university lecturer from Sulu teaching in Manila. He and other younger, educated Moros as well as some elites mobilized in support of secession.[6] By late 1969, Misuari and eighty-nine others underwent military training in Malaysia; they formed the nucleus of the MNLF when it was set up in 1971. Meanwhile, violence between Moros and Christian settlers in central Mindanao escalated. When President Ferdinand Marcos used this unrest to justify martial law in 1972, the insurgency began. The MNLF, with the support of Malaysia and Libya, became the standard bearer for the

[2] Thomas McKenna, *Muslim Rulers and Rebels: Everyday Politics and Armed Separatism in the Southern Philippines* (University of California Press 1998) ch. 5.

[3] Patricio Abinales, *Making Mindanao: Cotabato and Davao in the Formation of the Philippine Nation-State* (Ateneo de Manila University Press 2000).

[4] Muslims in Mindanao were not becoming more religiously observant but rather more conscious of their unifying ethnic identity as Moros. McKenna (n 2) chs 5–7.

[5] The basic facts of the Jabidah massacre, and indeed whether it even occurred at all, are disputed. Marites Danguilan Vitug and Glenda M Gloria, *Under the Crescent Moon: Rebellion in Mindanao* (Institute for Popular Democracy 2000). The Philippine government still claims Sabah. See Gerald Sussman, "Macapagal, the Sabah claim and Maphilindo: the politics of penetration" (1983) 13 (2) Journal of Contemporary Asia 210.

[6] McKenna refers to this as a "counter-elite," McKenna (n 2) ch. 7.

armed separatist movement. The fighting took a huge human and economic toll.[7] Misuari and other senior leaders left to rally support in the Muslim world.[8]

The first agreement, signed in Tripoli, Libya, in 1976, yielded a ceasefire and proposed a Moro territory with distinct powers within the Philippine state. It included thirteen provinces in the "areas of autonomy," even though most no longer had a Muslim majority.[9] A provisional government would rule while the new political structures were set up. All subsequent negotiations have adhered to this formula: territory, powers and transition arrangements. The Tripoli agreement also set a precedent for third party involvement in peace negotiations; the pact was co-signed by Libya and the Organization of Islamic Conference (OIC).

A final clause made the Philippine government responsible for "all necessary constitutional processes" for implementation. Under the 1973 Constitution, which consolidated executive and legislative power in Marcos' hands, this simply meant he would decide.[10] In 1977, Marcos unilaterally created two separate autonomous zones, one in central Mindanao and one in western Mindanao and the Sulu archipelago, which were run by co-opted Moro elites. Fighting resumed, but not at the same level. The MNLF fractured along ethnic and geographic lines by 1984. Hashim Salamat, who served as the MNLF's head of foreign affairs, broke away to set up the MILF, taking the central Mindanao-based forces with him. This rivalry has complicated negotiations ever since.

The 1986 democratic transition ended the Marcos era but not the conflict in Mindanao. President Corazon "Cory" Aquino commissioned a draft Constitution, which contained autonomy provisions for Muslim Mindanao. In January 1987, weeks before the new Constitution was to be ratified, government negotiators and Nur Misuari signed an accord in Jeddah, Saudi Arabia, which asked the president to suspend the autonomy provisions so the MNLF could conduct consultations with Moros.[11] Yet the 1987 Constitution came into force with these provisions intact.[12] The first read:

> There shall be created autonomous regions . . . consisting of provinces, cities, municipalities, and geographical areas sharing common and distinctive historical and cultural heritage, economic and social structures, and other relevant characteristics within the framework of this Constitution and the national sovereignty as well as the territorial integrity of the Republic of the Philippines.[13]

[7] The most widely cited figure is 120,000 killed since the 1970s. A World Bank study estimated the economic cost of the conflict from 1970 to 2001 to be as high as $2–3 billion. Salvatore Schiavo-Campo and Mary Judd, "The Mindanao Conflict in the Philippines: Roots, Costs and Potential Peace Dividend" (The World Bank Social Development Papers, Conflict Prevention and Reconstruction February 2005) <http://siteresources.worldbank.org/INTCPR/214578-1111996036679/20482477/WP24_Web.pdf>.

[8] International Crisis Group, "Southern Philippines Backgrounder: Terrorism and the Peace Process" (Asia Report No. 80, International Crisis Group July 13, 2004) <www.crisisgroup.org/asia/south-east-asia/philippines/southern-philippines-backgrounder-terrorism-and-peace-process>.

[9] Tripoli Agreement (Government of the Republic of the Philippines-Moro National Liberation Front) (December 23, 1976) <www.hdcentre.org/wp-content/uploads/2016/06/The-Tripoli-Agreement-1976.pdf>. The thirteen provinces were Basilan, Sulu, Tawi-Tawi, Zamboanga del Sur, Zamboanga del Norte, North Cotabato, Maguindanao, Sultan Kudarat, Lanao del Norte, Lanao del Sur, Davao del Sur, South Cotabato, and Palawan.

[10] 1973 Philippine Constitution <www.gov.ph/constitutions/1973-constitution-of-the-republic-of-the-philippines-2/>.

[11] Jeddah Accord (Government of the Republic of the Philippines-Moro National Liberation Front) (January 3–4, 1987) <www.ucd.ie/ibis/filestore/Jeddah%201987.pdf>.

[12] Jacques Bertrand, "Autonomy and nationalist demands in Southeast Asia" in Alain-G Gagnon and Michael Keating (eds), *Political Autonomy in Divided Societies: Imagining Democratic Alternatives in Complex Settings* (Palgrave MacMillan 2012) 206.

[13] 1987 Philippine Constitution, art. X (Local Government), s. 15.

The new Constitution specified neither the structure of government nor the exact powers of the autonomous region in Muslim Mindanao. Congress would determine them in legislation to be ratified by a popular vote in the areas included.[14] This vested power in the legislature, although peace negotiations had always been handled by the president. The second step, the plebiscite, meant it would be difficult to include Christian-majority areas in an autonomous region as the MNLF wanted.

The Philippine government set up the region although the MNLF objected. In 1989, Congress passed legislation to create the Autonomous Region in Muslim Mindanao (ARMM).[15] In the plebiscite, only Sulu and Tawi-Tawi from the Sulu archipelago and Maguindanao and Lanao del Sur in central Mindanao voted to join. The two major cities in central Mindanao, Cotabato City and Marawi City, both stayed out. ARMM failed to satisfy Moro nationalist aspirations and the insurgent organizations continued to enjoy popular support.

Decentralization in 1991 transferred fiscal and other powers to provinces, cities, municipalities, and *barangay* (villages) across the country.[16] This strengthened local politicians, meaning the patriarchs and scions of sprawling families who wield political power in the Philippines.[17] For Moro-elected officials, these changes were welcome as their primary interest is running their communities and controlling the resources of local government.[18] Decentralization increased their access to central government funds and their fealty to Manila. This put Moro politicians increasingly at odds with the insurgents.

The Constitution also allowed for an autonomous region in the Cordillera, in northern Luzon. It was never set up. Indigenous highlander communities launched an armed rebellion against the government in the late 1970s during martial law.[19] Unlike in Mindanao, the main insurgent organization, the Cordillera Peoples Liberation Army (CPLA), and other highlander groups backed the autonomy provisions in the 1987 Constitution. A plebiscite in 1990 failed due to disagreements between those who drafted legislation on autonomy and groups like the CPLA. Internal rifts deepened and a second plebiscite in 1998 did not rally enough votes to create the region.[20] Meanwhile, decentralization and the 1997 Indigenous Peoples Rights Act allowed

[14] ibid art. X (Local Government), ss 20–1. Section 20 provided nine powers to be specified in this legislation, known as an organic act: administrative organization; creation of sources of revenues; ancestral domain and natural resources; personal, family and property relations; regional urban and rural planning development; economic, social, and tourism development; educational policies; preservation and development of cultural heritage; and "such other matters as may be authorized by law for the promotion of the general welfare of the people of the region."

[15] Republic Act No. 6734 "An act providing for an organic act for the autonomous region in Muslim Mindanao" August 1, 1989 (Philippines) accessed at <www.lawphil.net/statutes/repacts/ra1989/ra_6734_1989.html>.

[16] Republic Act No. 7160, "An act providing for a local government code of 1991," October 10, 1991, (Philippines) accessed at <www.lawphil.net/statutes/repacts/ra1991/ra_7160_1991.html>. Cities and municipalities are distinct administrative units in the Philippines. The act did not give local government comparable powers to those in a federal system, however.

[17] Their power remained undiminished even during martial law. Paul D Hutchcroft and Joel Rocamora, "Strong Demands and Weak Institutions: The Origins and Evolution of the Democratic Deficit in the Philippines" (2003) 3 (2) Journal of East Asian Studies 259.

[18] Alfred McCoy (ed.), *An Anarchy of Families: State and Family in the Philippines* (University of Wisconsin Press 2009).

[19] They opposed the Cellophil logging and pulp project in Abra province, and a proposed dam on the Chico River. The Communist Party of the Philippines and its armed wing, the New People's Army, were largely responsible for mobilizing highlanders.

[20] Gerard A Finin, "'Igorotism', rebellion and regional autonomy in the Cordillera" in Rosanne Rutten (ed.), *Brokering a Revolution: Cadres in a Philippine Insurgency* (Ateneo de Manila University Press 2008) 114–19; and David Hyndman, "Organic act rejected in the Cordillera: Dialectics of a continuing fourth world autonomy movement in the Philippines" (1991) 16 (2) Dialectical

highlanders to manage their own affairs.[21] These other laws proved more effective at addressing their grievances.[22] In Mindanao the same laws made it even harder to get autonomy to work.

The next president, Fidel V. Ramos, signed a final peace agreement with the MNLF in 1996 that would enhance the powers of ARMM and expand its territory.[23] The peace agreement, brokered by Indonesia under OIC auspices, envisioned two phases. In Phase I, lasting until 1998, the government would create a Special Zone of Peace and Development spanning all the provinces the MNLF had claimed in the 1976 Tripoli agreement, and provide development assistance throughout. In Phase II, the law passed to create ARMM in 1989 would be amended or repealed with new legislation that would reflect "the pertinent provisions of the final peace agreement;" another plebiscite would then be held with the MNLF's blessing throughout the special zone. The peace agreement explicitly stated that interim arrangements in Phase I and the new regional autonomous government to be set up in Phase II would have powers consistent with national laws and the 1987 Constitution.

In 2001, Congress acted unilaterally and produced a bill that omitted elements of the 1996 agreement.[24] The MNLF was unhappy with this process, as it did not have a clearly defined role in drafting the legislation under the terms of the peace pact. It was also dissatisfied with the substance of the law. A subsequent OIC-led review of the implementation of the 1996 agreement generated a list of forty-two consensus points between the MNLF and the Philippine government on necessary amendments to the 2001 law.[25]

The 1996 agreement was a partial success. In a plebiscite held in 2001, Marawi City in Lanao del Sur and Basilan (but not its capital Isabela City) voted in favor. All five Muslim-majority provinces were now within the autonomous region, but further expansion would only be possible if Christian-majority provinces (or portions of them) joined. The 2001 law strengthened ARMM but it was still not genuinely autonomous. The regional legislative assembly did not exercise the full powers accorded to it by Congress; for example, by failing to pass enabling laws. Line agencies and offices of the central government did not devolve their powers and budgets to ARMM; they were required to do so under the 1989 law and again in the 2001 law, yet regional agencies

Anthropology 169. In both plebiscites, only one province out of the six that comprise the Cordillera voted in favor.

[21] Republic Act No. 8371, "An act to recognize, protect and promote the rights of indigenous cultural communities/indigenous peoples, creating a national commission on indigenous peoples, establishing implementing mechanisms, appropriating funds therefor, and for other purposes" October 29, 1997 (Philippines), accessed at <www.gov.ph/1997/10/29/republic-act-no-8371/>. The act created new forms of land titles for indigenous peoples, known as certificates of ancestral domain.

[22] One scholar argues that the pan-Cordillera identity was simply never fully embraced and that autonomy has greater meaning at village level, Steven Rood, "Closure for the CPLA, Autonomy for Cordillera Villages" *Newsbreak* (Manila July 9, 2011) <http://archives.newsbreak-knowledge.ph/2011/07/09/closure-for-the-cpla-autonomy-for-cordillera-villages/>.

[23] Final Peace Agreement with the Moro National Liberation Front (Government of the Republic of the Philippines-Moro National Liberation Front) (September 2, 1996) <http://www.incore.ulst.ac.uk/services/cds/agreements/pdf/phil16.pdf>.

[24] Republic Act No. 9054, "An act to strengthen and expand the organic act for the autonomous region in Muslim Mindanao, amending for the purpose Republic Act No 6734" March 31, 2001 (Philippines) <www.lawphil.net/statutes/repacts/ra2001/ra_9054_2001.html>.

[25] "Updated Q&A on the status of the peace process between the GPH and MNLF" (*Slidedocument.org*, November 18, 2013) <https://slidedocument.org/updated-q-a-on-the-gph-mnlf-peace-process>.

still did not function autonomously. Provinces and the lower levels of local government remained more financially autonomous than ARMM.[26]

The MNLF temporarily gained power through the 1996 peace agreement but failed to transform into a peaceful political actor. Misuari became regional governor but proved hapless. In 2001, President Gloria Macapagal Arroyo and her advisers ousted him as chairman of the MNLF and the organization fragmented. Although thousands of MNLF members were integrated into the military and police,[27] others remained armed. Misuari loyalists in his home province of Sulu lashed out violently in late 2001; Misuari himself fled to Malaysia only to be deported and placed under house arrest in Manila until 2008.

Meanwhile, the MILF quietly built itself up and established camps, such that it controlled strategic portions of central Mindanao by the mid-1990s. Negotiations led to a ceasefire in 1997. Nonetheless, in 2000 the military launched an offensive against the main MILF camp. In 2001, the Philippine government invited Malaysia to facilitate peace talks. In 2003, the military launched another offensive. MILF founder Salamat Hashim died of natural causes the same year and was replaced by Al Haj Murad Ebrahim. By 2005, peace talks were finally moving. International attention had increased because of the presence of foreign jihadists in Mindanao and their ties to individuals within the MILF and the Abu Sayyaf Group, an extremist breakaway of the MNLF.[28] The Philippine government had a stronger incentive than ever to end the conflict. But five factors made the quest for a peace agreement increasingly complex.[29]

First, the MILF needed to broker a better deal than the MNLF, with a form of autonomy significantly different from ARMM, to justify its own armed struggle. Second, the MILF simply refused to recognize the 1987 Constitution because it was biased against Moros. By extension the MILF resisted the constitutional process for creating an autonomous region through legislation and a plebiscite. Third, the Philippine government lacked credibility. Fourth, divisions among Moros had deepened, not only between the MNLF and the MILF, but also between local politicians and the insurgent organizations. Fifth, the Philippine public was increasingly skeptical of peace talks and the MILF, partly due to its terrorist links.

Starting in 2005, negotiations with the MILF tackled territorial demands first, and left governance on the back burner. Talks stalled whenever the government insisted that new areas could only join the autonomous area via a plebiscite as required by

[26] The International Bank for Reconstruction and Development/The World Bank, "Joint needs assessment for reconstruction and development of conflict-affected areas of Mindanao: local governance and institutions report, vol 5" (The World Bank 2005) <www-wds.worldbank.org/external/default/WDSContentServer/WDSP/IB/2011/07/04/000386194_20110704071222/Rendered/PDF/630270WP0Local00Box0361499B0PUBLIC0.pdf>.

[27] 5,750 into the Armed Forces of the Philippines and 1,500 into the police.

[28] Jihadist groups in Southeast Asia have used Mindanao as a training ground from the 1990s onwards. Some MILF were willing to host the foreigners, notably Indonesians responsible for the 2002 Bali bombings. The MILF leadership expelled foreign jihadists from central Mindanao in November 2005 for the sake of the peace talks; they and their Abu Sayyaf Group allies went to the Sulu archipelago, where they were targeted by the Philippine military, with extensive U.S. support. See Patricio Abinales and Nathan Gilbert Quimpo (eds), *The U.S. and the War on Terror in the Philippines* (Anvil 2008); and International Crisis Group, "The Philippines: Counter-insurgency vs. Counter-terrorism in Mindanao" (Asia Report No. 152, International Crisis Group May 14, 2008) <www.crisisgroup.org/~/media/Files/asia/south-east-asia/philippines/152_counterinsurgency_vs_counter_terrorism_in_mindanao.pdf>.

[29] On the challenges facing the peace process see also, Malcolm Cook and Kit Collier, "Mindanao: A Gamble Worth Taking" (Lowy Institute Paper 17, Lowy Institute November 20, 2006) <www.lowyinstitute.org/files/pubfiles/Cook_Collier%2C_Mindanao.pdf>.

the Constitution.[30] Yet in mid-2008, the two sides reached the breakthrough memorandum of agreement on ancestral domain, which proposed a "Bangsamoro Juridical Entity" to replace ARMM.[31] The memorandum was a triumph for the MILF. The Philippine government made significant concessions on territory and agreed to sweepingly vague language on governance. At no point did the memorandum mention the Constitution, which would prove to be its downfall.

The memorandum proposed a modest "core territory" for the Bangsamoro Juridical Entity, comprising the five provinces in ARMM, plus six municipalities in neighboring Lanao del Norte that had voted yes in the 2001 plebiscite, but there was scope for significant future expansion in two steps. Areas listed in category A would vote in a plebiscite held in twelve months' time; areas in category B would vote in twenty-five years' time, after receiving socio-economic assistance. Together, this was a huge expanse of Mindanao, although much less than the MNLF's original thirteen provinces. It was unlikely all areas in categories A and B would vote yes; for example, the projected territory included portions of Christian-majority Zamboanga City (the economic hub of western Mindanao) and the lands belonging to non-Islamized indigenous peoples who do not self-identify as Moro.

Unlike the MNLF, which based its territorial demands on history, the MILF tried to expand the appeal of Moro nationalism to justify a larger autonomous region. This was the rationale for changing the name to the Bangsamoro Juridical Entity. The 2008 memorandum defined the "Bangsamoro" as Moros, indigenous peoples, and spouses and descendants of both, thus including some Christians as well. This definition of Bangsamoro identity was contested, both by Moros who identified more strongly with their smaller ethno-linguistic group, and especially by indigenous peoples who perceived the memorandum as a land grab by the MILF.[32] Christians in areas earmarked for future expansion similarly mistrusted the MILF.

The memorandum had scant information on governance, but the most detailed provision said the relationship between the central government and the Bangsamoro Juridical Entity would be "associative characterized by shared authority and responsibility . . . based on executive, legislative, judicial and administrative institutions with defined powers and functions in the comprehensive compact."[33] The MILF and the Philippine government were to negotiate the comprehensive compact next, but the language on governance was loose enough to alarm Philippine nationalists.

The memorandum quickly proved unworkable. Christian politicians from Mindanao petitioned the Supreme Court to intervene. Clashes broke out between MILF forces,

[30] See the book written by MILF chief negotiator Mohagher Iqbal, published under the pen name Salah Jubair, *The Long Road to Peace: Inside the GRP-MILF Peace Process* (Institute of Bangsamoro Studies 2007).

[31] Memorandum of Agreement on the Ancestral Domain Aspect of the GRP-MILF Tripoli Agreement on Peace of 2001, unsigned agreement negotiated in Kuala Lumpur, Malaysia, 2008 (2008 Memorandum of Agreement) <https://peacebuilderscommunity.org/moa-ad-between-grp-and-milf/>.

[32] Non-Moro indigenous peoples would like titles to what they also call their "ancestral domains" under the 1997 Indigenous Peoples Rights Act. None of these groups that live within ARMM has ever received a title for ancestral domain, and their land rights are not secure. For the most part unarmed, indigenous peoples have been caught between Christian settlers and Moro insurgents in violent disputes over land and have often been displaced from their traditional areas. International Crisis Group, "The Philippines: Indigenous Rights and the MILF Peace Process" (Asia Report No. 213, International Crisis Group November 22, 2011) <www.crisisgroup.org/~/media/Files/asia/south-east-asia/philippines/213%20The%20Philippines%20-%20Indigenous%20Rights%20and%20the%20MILF%20Peace%20Process.pdf>.

[33] 2008 Memorandum of Agreement (n 31) Governance, para. 4.

Christian militias, and the military. In Manila, Arroyo's opponents believed she was trying to use the peace process as a Trojan horse to change the Constitution, which limits the president to a single six-year term.[34] The memorandum seemingly hinted at constitutional change where it guaranteed automatic "amendments to the existing legal framework."[35] By early September, the Arroyo government announced it would not sign the memorandum in any form.[36]

Most damaging of all was the Supreme Court ruling in October.[37] It concluded that the Bangsamoro Juridical Entity would create "a state in all but name." The ruling objected strongly to the idea of an "associative relationship" with Manila because this would be fundamentally different from that of ARMM. The justices also concluded that President Arroyo exceeded her authority in guaranteeing the MILF changes to the "legal framework," which the court interpreted to mean the Constitution. The power to amend the 1987 Constitution resides in Congress, a constitutional convention or the Filipino people through a referendum.[38] The president could only recommend but not promise changes to the Constitution. In short, the memorandum of agreement on ancestral domain was unconstitutional.

2008 was a major setback for the peace process. The MILF concluded that constitutional change was imperative; the government could not meet its demands otherwise. Yet future presidents were likely to be even more hesitant to broach the issue after the Supreme Court had clarified the limits of executive authority. The chance of a deal with the MILF looked increasingly remote.

The Period of Constitutional Engagement

The "constitutional moment" for resolving the Mindanao question began in mid-2010 when Benigno Aquino III, the son of Corazon Aquino, became president. The Philippine government and the MILF signed the framework agreement in October 2012 and the comprehensive agreement in March 2014.[39] These agreements laid out a vision of a larger, more powerful autonomous region called "the Bangsamoro." Remarkably, both substantively and procedurally, they appeared compatible with the Constitution. The MILF made significant concessions to secure the deal, believing that President Aquino would be able and willing to implement the agreements in full, unlike his predecessors.

The peace agreements were a clear improvement over the existing autonomous region in terms of territory and powers. The core territory of the Bangsamoro would be all five provinces currently in ARMM; the six municipalities in Lanao del Norte

[34] 1987 Constitution, art. VII (Executive Department), s. 4.

[35] 2008 Memorandum of Agreement (n 31) Governance, para. 7.

[36] International Crisis Group, "The Philippines: The Collapse of Peace in Mindanao" (Asia Briefing No. 83, International Crisis Group October 23, 2008) <www.crisisgroup.org/~/media/Files/asia/south-east-asia/philippines/b83_the_philippines___the_collapse_of_peace_in_mindanao.pdf>.

[37] *The Province of North Cotabato v. The Government of the Republic of the Philippines Peace Panel on Ancestral Domain*, En Banc, GR No. 183591, October 14, 2008 <http://sc.judiciary.gov.ph/jurisprudence/2008/october2008/183591.htm>.

[38] 1987 Constitution, art. XVII (Amendments or Revisions).

[39] Framework Agreement on the Bangsamoro (The Philippine Government–Moro Islamic Liberation Front) (October 15, 2012) <http://peacemaker.un.org/sites/peacemaker.un.org/files/PH_121015_FrameworkAgreementBangsamoro.pdf>; Comprehensive Agreement on the Bangsamoro (The Philippine Government–Moro Islamic Liberation Front) (March 27, 2014) <http://peacemaker.un.org/sites/peacemaker.un.org/files/PH_140327_ComprehensiveAgreementBangsamoro.pdf>.

and thirty-nine *barangay* in another neighboring province in central Mindanao, North Cotabato, that had voted yes in the 2001 plebiscite; and Cotabato City (in Maguindanao) and Isabela City (on Basilan). This was in fact larger than the core territory proposed in 2008. But unlike the failed memorandum, the new agreements avoided naming specific areas beyond the core territory that might join the Bangsamoro; instead, they allowed for "additional contiguous areas" to join the core territory if there was sufficient popular support.[40]

The sections on governance described an asymmetrical relationship with the central government, with a long list of exclusive (to the Bangsamoro), concurrent, and reserved (for Manila) powers. In contrast to ARMM, the Bangsamoro would have a parliamentary system headed by a chief minister, elected by and accountable to members of parliament. Seats in parliament would be allocated by district, by proportional representation and by sector.[41] In ARMM, voters have separately and directly elected the executive and legislative branches, just as they do for national elections. The MILF argued that a parliamentary system would build consensus among Moros and encourage the formation of political parties, which are weak throughout the Philippines. Regional policing powers were another major triumph for the MILF. Its negotiators consistently argued for a regional police force because local police frequently have ties to the perpetrators of violence, whether they be politicians, criminals, or extremists like the Abu Sayyaf Group.[42] Like the MNLF, the MILF would get to run the region in an interim capacity as the new governance structures in the Bangsamoro were set up. The first elections under the new system would take place in 2016, timed to coincide with general elections and the end of Aquino's term.

The MILF was also determined that the Bangsamoro enjoy fiscal autonomy so that it could govern independently of the central government. While recognizing that the Bangsamoro would be unable to raise enough revenue on its own for many years, the MILF negotiated provisions on taxation and natural resources with this objective in mind. For example, income from exploitation of fossil fuels would be shared equally, but the Bangsamoro would keep 75 percent of income from metallic minerals.[43] The MILF also negotiated for the Bangsamoro's budget to be released automatically by Manila, akin to how the provinces, municipalities, and *barangay* receive their internal revenue allotment, which is a percentage share of national taxes as specified in the 1991 decentralization law.[44] This would help correct for ARMM's dependence on Manila and the comparative freedom enjoyed by local governments. However, the peace agreements also made it clear that a stronger regional government would not weaken the provincial governors and mayors, who would continue to have the same

[40] Framework Agreement on the Bangsamoro (n 39), s. V (Territory).

[41] The parliament will have a minimum of sixty seats, with 50 percent drawn from a party-list system open only to regional political parties, 40 percent elected by district, and the remaining 10 percent for under-represented sectors. Assuming the Sulu archipelago joins, the islands will have thirteen district seats in the parliament, while central Mindanao would have nineteen district seats. The election of the chief minister is by majority vote, including through a runoff if necessary. Removal of the chief minister requires a higher threshold: a two-thirds vote of no confidence. Draft Bangsamoro Basic Law, art. VII (The Bangsamoro Government).

[42] ibid art. XI (Public Order and Safety), s. 2 (Bangsamoro Police).

[43] 2013 Annex on Revenue Generation and Wealth Sharing, s. VII (Natural Resources).

[44] 1991 Local Government Code, Title III (Shares of Local Government Units in the Proceeds of National Taxes), ch. I (Allotment of Internal Revenue), ss 284–8. By law, 20 percent of the internal revenue allotment should be spent on development projects.

powers and budgetary allocations, unless changes were necessary to promote "good governance."[45]

Unlike the failed 2008 memorandum, the framework and comprehensive agreements on the Bangsamoro were not immediately denounced by opponents in Mindanao and Manila. Christian politicians and indigenous peoples who had been up in arms only a few years ago were less fearful. The provisions on identity and territorial expansion of the Bangsamoro were carefully worded to respect the freedom of choice of non-Moros. Government and MILF negotiators had also reached out to likely opponents before the agreements were finalized.[46] Moro politicians with poor relations with the MILF were unlikely to be happy with any peace deal that strengthened their rivals, but they did not feel the agreements threatened their interests and their budgets, at least not immediately, and stayed quiet. Nur Misuari of the MNLF was angry, predictably, as he felt the new agreements were diminishing what his organization had achieved for the Moros, but he had little capacity to derail their implementation. Pundits and members of Congress in Manila objected to certain aspects of the peace agreements, but these were criticisms of technicalities rather than of the principle of stronger autonomy.

Whether the peace agreements were compatible with the Constitution was a matter of opinion. The government, namely the Office of the Presidential Adviser on the Peace Process which led the negotiations, was confident none of the substantive powers of the Bangsamoro necessitated constitutional change. The chief negotiator was in fact a constitutional law expert who had had to persuade skeptical members of the cabinet to agree to risky concessions. For example, the Constitution does not specify the form of government for autonomous regions; however, the legality of the parliamentary structure could be challenged.[47] The peace agreements would also create in the Bangsamoro a number of regional equivalents to national institutions, some of which have mandates defined by the Constitution.[48] For example, under Article X on local government, the Constitution refers to local police agencies in autonomous regions, which would appear to sanction the creation of a Bangsamoro police,[49] but Article XVI on general provisions mentions only one police force.[50] President Aquino's advisers felt that provided regional bodies were responsible and answerable to their national counterparts in Manila, the peace agreements were constitutional.

[45] "The privileges already enjoyed by the local government units under existing laws shall not be diminished unless otherwise altered, modified or reformed for good governance pursuant to the provisions of the Bangsamoro local government code." Framework Agreement on the Bangsamoro (n 39), s. I, pt 3.

[46] The MILF even appointed a representative from the Teduray tribe in Maguindanao as an alternate member of its negotiating team for the peace talks.

[47] Interview with a senior official, Office of the Presidential Adviser on the Peace Process (OPAPP) (Manila, the Philippines, January 26, 2012).

[48] The Commission on Elections, Commission on Audit and Civil Service Commission are called the "constitutional commissions" and are the subject of art. IX in the 1987 Constitution. The Commission on Human Rights is discussed under art XIII (Social Justice and Human Rights), ss 17–19. The Office of the Ombudsman is described under art. XI (Accountability of Public Officers), ss 5–14.

[49] "The preservation of peace and order within the regions shall be the responsibility of the local police agencies which shall be organized, maintained, supervised and utilized in accordance with applicable laws. The defence and security of the regions shall be the responsibility of the National Government." 1987 Philippine Constitution, art. X (Local Government), s. 21.

[50] "The State shall establish and maintain one police force, which shall be national in scope and civilian in character, to be administered and controlled by a national police commission. The authority of local executives over the police units in their jurisdiction shall be provided by law." 1987 Philippine Constitution, art. XVI (General Provisions), s. 6.

The MILF took the opposite view and believed it had eked out powers that surpassed those permitted under the Constitution. To understand how the two sides had managed to sign the peace agreements nonetheless, it is necessary to look in more detail at the three reasons why the MILF wanted to change the Constitution—to maximize Moro autonomy, to avoid constitutional procedures for setting up an autonomous region, and to ensure irreversibility of new autonomy arrangements—and how the government addressed these concerns in the negotiations.

First, the MILF wanted to maximize Moro autonomy within the Philippine state and believed that the unitary character of the Philippine republic, as protected by the 1987 Constitution, was an unfair constraint in peace negotiations. In the initial phases of the talks under President Aquino, the MILF pushed to discuss constitutional change up front, which the government resisted. Instead, Aquino's negotiators proposed focusing first on political demands, and then assessing whether these could be accommodated under the current Constitution. Rather than refuse to consider constitutional change, the government side conveyed to the MILF that the president was open to it, but only if necessary. A meeting between MILF Chairman Murad and President Aquino in Tokyo, Japan, in August 2011 began to build trust between the two sides. The MILF subsequently agreed to park the issue of constitutional change rather than allow it to bog down the negotiations, perceiving that the president sincerely wanted peace in Mindanao and could be trusted to act in good faith.

Second, the MILF wanted to avoid the constitutional procedure for creating an autonomous region. Unless the peace agreements were implemented through legislation in Congress and a plebiscite, it would be necessary to change the constitutional provisions on autonomous regions. The 2008 Supreme Court ruling had clarified that the president lacked authority to implement the peace agreements otherwise. For the MILF, the problem with the constitutional procedure was twofold: it was justifiably concerned about legislators interfering in a peace process many knew very little about, and doubted that future plebiscites would favor territorial expansion. Given the MNLF's experience, the MILF feared legislators would mangle the agreements as they were enshrined in domestic law, by omitting or changing important provisions, and that the results of a plebiscite would be disappointing.

The MILF, however, agreed to implement the peace agreements according to the Constitution. The 2012 framework agreement contained a section on transition and implementation which specified that a new piece of legislation, called the Bangsamoro Basic Law, would be passed and a fresh plebiscite held.[51] The MILF backed down because it perceived that President Aquino had sufficient sway over Congress and the ability to push through priority legislation such that the Bangsamoro Basic Law would faithfully reflect the peace agreements.[52] The two sides also came up with a way for the MILF to participate in drafting the legislation. The peace agreements created a Bangsamoro Transition Commission, whose fifteen members would be nominated by the government and the MILF, and would reflect the diverse communities within the Bangsamoro. Chaired by the MILF chief negotiator, the commission's main responsibility would be to write the Bangsamoro Basic Law. In addition, it would propose constitutional amendments necessary to accommodate the powers of the Bangsamoro.[53]

[51] 2012 Framework Agreement, s. VII (Transition and Implementation).

[52] President Aquino's ruling Liberal Party and its allies in Congress had successfully pushed through the controversial reproductive health bill.

[53] 2012 Framework Agreement, s. VII (Transition and Implementation).

The real revelation was where the plebiscite would be held. The core territory of the Bangsamoro and the provisions on the plebiscite were among the last issues negotiated for the framework agreement. The government's stance was that a fresh plebiscite would have to be held in all areas comprising the core territory of the new region, not just those areas that lay outside ARMM, as had been the case in the 2001 plebiscite.[54] This reflected the 2008 Supreme Court ruling, which had clarified that results from previous plebiscites could not apply if the proposed autonomy arrangements diverged substantially from current ones.[55] This troubled the MILF, and ran the risk of the Bangsamoro ending up smaller than the existing autonomous region because of opposition within the Moro community.

The MILF has claimed to be acting in the best interests of all Moros, but this is contested by Moro elites from the three provinces in the Sulu archipelago. Competing ethnic identities have always circumscribed the appeal of Moro nationalism. These divisions have been more problematic for the MILF than the MNLF, because the former is only really present in central Mindanao. MILF Chairman Murad and other senior leaders are Maguindanao, with a sprinkling of Maranao, the ethnicity from Lanao; almost all of its 12,000 fighters are from the same areas.[56] The MILF has few followers among the Tausug, which is the largest ethnic group in the Sulu archipelago. The Tausug, however, have historically played a leadership role among Moros, yet would likely be sidelined for the foreseeable future with the MILF or its Maguindanao allies poised to run the Bangsamoro on an interim basis and possibly afterwards. The MILF was concerned that Sulu elites might use a new plebiscite as an opportunity to persuade their constituents to vote no, and to reject the new autonomy arrangements as negotiated by the MILF. In other words, rather than expanding the autonomous area, the plebiscite could become a means for provinces to opt out of the Bangsamoro. Not only would this damage the MILF's credibility, and reverse the territorial gains made by the MNLF, it would also deprive the Bangsamoro of a potential source of revenue: taxes from offshore oil and gas believed to lie beneath the Sulu Sea.

The MILF acquiesced because it had little choice. When the government tabled its position on the plebiscite, the parties were very close to finalizing the framework agreement. The MILF was otherwise happy with governance arrangements and the economic and fiscal powers it had negotiated, and was reluctant to let these slip away by taking a hard line on territory and the plebiscite. Third parties directly involved in the negotiations also played a constructive role in back-channeling to secure the MILF's agreement. The members of the International Contact Group, an advisory body comprising foreign governments and international non-governmental organizations that have sat in on the talks since 2009, and the Malaysian facilitator held quiet meetings with MILF central committee members in Mindanao.[57] Aquino's advisers also assured the MILF that the president would lean on Moro politicians in the Sulu archipelago to rally votes in support of joining the Bangsamoro. In agreeing to the plebiscite and to implementing the peace agreements through legislation in Congress, the MILF had moved very far from its stance in 2008, when it had rejected

[54] Interviews with MILF and government negotiators and members of the International Contact Group (Manila, the Philippines, September 2012).

[55] 2008 Supreme Court ruling.

[56] The MILF has a base command in the southeast corner of Basilan but is hardly present in Sulu or Tawi-Tawi.

[57] The International Contact Group was comprised of the United Kingdom, Japan, Turkey, Saudi Arabia, Muhammadiyah, the Asia Foundation, the Centre for Humanitarian Dialogue and Conciliation Resources.

constitutional processes entirely. The MILF was reluctant to admit it had backed down, and the mandate of the Bangsamoro Transition Commission to propose constitutional amendments later helped save face.

The third reason why the MILF wanted to change the Constitution was to ensure irreversibility. By implementing the peace agreements through ordinary legislation, the MILF was running the risk of a future Congress rolling back the powers of the Bangsamoro. By enshrining core provisions of the peace agreements in the Constitution, it would be much more difficult to reverse these gains. Here too, however, the MILF eventually backed down. Instead of constitutional change, the MILF opted to use international involvement in the peace process as a way of keeping the government honest. In 2009, the MILF supported the creation of the International Contact Group because it believed the presence of internationals around the peace table would make it harder for the government to backpedal future agreements, like the Arroyo government had with the 2008 memorandum. This was formalized in the 2012 framework agreement, which proposed creating a third party monitoring team to provide regular reports on implementation and eventually to sign off on an exit agreement.

Resolving the territorial cleavage in Mindanao within the parameters of the 1987 Constitution had seemed next to impossible after the collapse of the peace process in 2008. Yet the Philippine government and the MILF managed to negotiate a new deal only four years later. The breakthrough was due largely to the MILF's willingness to be flexible once it became clear that President Aquino was personally committed to the success of the peace process. On the government side, it is unclear if the president was ever really open to changing the Constitution, or whether his negotiators perceived that the only way of developing momentum in the early phases of the talks was to convince the MILF that the option was on the table.

Once the framework agreement and the comprehensive agreement were signed, both parties shifted their attention to the urgent matter of implementation. President Aquino was adamant that Congress pass the Bangsamoro Basic Law and that the plebiscite be conducted before his term ended in 2016. The MILF was of the same view and ultimately did not propose any constitutional amendments through the Bangsamoro Transition Commission, despite its mandate. Steering clear of constitutional change made it more likely that the peace agreements would be implemented quickly, while President Aquino still retained sufficient political capital to control Congress as it reviewed the Bangsamoro Basic Law.

Up until January 2015, implementation was delayed but on track. After prolonged back-and-forth over the final wording with the MILF, the president's office submitted the Bangsamoro Basic Law to Congress in September 2014.[58] A specially convened ad hoc committee, chaired by Congressman Rufus Rodriguez from Cagayan de Oro in northern Mindanao, led deliberations on the bill in the House of Representatives and held public hearings around the Philippines in late 2014. A committee in the Senate, chaired by Ferdinand "Bongbong" Marcos, Jr, the son of the former president, deliberated and held its own public hearings in parallel, but was expected to follow the lead of the lower house on the bill. It seemed likely Congress would pass the draft law, with some revisions but none too drastic. Most legislators were not under any pressure from their constituents on the matter; the Philippine public was largely ambivalent

[58] The final negotiations were a closed-door session between three MILF representatives and three government representatives, one of whom was the president's chief legal adviser. Interview with a member of the International Contact Group (Manila, the Philippines, March 2015).

and had confidence in Aquino's leadership.[59] While some legislators queried the constitutionality of certain aspects, such as policing powers, and Moro elites in the Sulu archipelago grumbled during the public hearings, there was little to be gained from vociferously opposing a bill that the president was intent on passing. It seemed the MILF had been right to pin its hopes on President Aquino and let its desire for constitutional change fall by the wayside.

Outcome of the Process

In January 2015, President Aquino's political capital evaporated in the wake of a botched counter-terrorism operation in central Mindanao. The final stages of the peace process hinged entirely on the president's ability to sway Congress and Moro elites in the Sulu archipelago to implement the peace agreements to the MILF's satisfaction. With the president's approval ratings in freefall, skeptics in Manila and Mindanao no longer felt compelled to stay quiet. The strategy for implementation suddenly looked short-sighted. The peace process went nowhere as attention turned to campaigning for the May 2016 elections. The victory of Rodrigo Duterte, the former mayor of Davao City, the country's first Mindanawon president, and a committed federalist, dramatically shifted the politics of the peace process yet again.

On January 25, 2015, elite police commandos entered Mamasapano, Maguindanao, a village under MILF control, to kill Malaysian extremist Zulkifly bin Hir alias Marwan and his local ally Basit Usman. They were hiding with members of an MILF splinter group that rejects the peace process, called the Bangsamoro Islamic Freedom Fighters.[60] The police did not inform the MILF of this risky operation despite coordination mechanisms on counter-terrorism.[61] A deadly firefight broke out between the police and MILF members; forty-four police, seventeen MILF, and five civilians were killed. Marwan was dead too, but the political and human cost was extremely high. The Philippine public was outraged and angry at the MILF.

The Mamasapano incident was the first major clash between the MILF and government forces in central Mindanao since 2008–09. Information emerged that the president had been closely involved in planning and overseeing the police operation.[62] With

[59] Public hearings by the two congressional committees were largely attended by Muslims, as the Bangsamoro Basic Law was perceived as a Moro issue. Interviews with government officials, OPAPP (Manila, the Philippines, March 2015).

[60] For more details on Marwan, see Institute for Policy Analysis of Conflict, "Killing Marwan in Mindanao" (Report No. 17, Institute for Policy Analysis of Conflict March 5, 2015) <http://file.understandingconflict.org/file/2015/03/IPAC_17_Killing_Marwan_in_Mindanao.pdf>. For details on the BIFF's split from the MILF, see International Crisis Group, "The Philippines: Back to the Table, Warily, in Mindanao" (Asia Briefing No. 119, International Crisis Group March 24, 2011) <www.crisisgroup.org/~/media/Files/asia/south-east-asia/philippines/B119%20The%20Philippines%20%20Back%20to%20the%20Table%20Warily%20in%20Mindanau>.

[61] The police could have informed the MILF through the Ad Hoc Joint Action Group, through which intelligence related to criminal and terrorist activity is shared.

[62] The police were the first to release a report on the Mamasapano incident in March; full text of the Board of Inquiry's report can be downloaded from the Philippines Star website "DOCUMENT: PNP Board of Inquiry's Mamasapano Report" *Philippine Star* (Manila, March 13, 2015) <www.philstar.com/headlines/2015/03/13/1433196/full-text-pnp-board-inquirys-mamasapano-report>. Next was the Senate; for a comparison of its findings and those of the Board of Inquiry, see Camille Diola, "Juxtaposed: BOI and Senate panel Mamasapano probe findings" *Philippine Star* (Manila, March 19, 2015) <http://www.philstar.com/news-feature/2015/03/19/1435317/juxtaposed-boi-and-senate-panel-mamasapano-probe-findings>. Later in March, the MILF released its own investigation, MILF Special Investigative Commission, "Report on the Mamasapano Incident" (Moro Islamic

the 2016 national elections less than eighteen months away, senators seized an opportunity to grandstand and to question the president's judgment, the MILF's sincerity, and the peace process as a whole in televised inquiries. The president's approval ratings fell below 50 percent for the first time.[63] The Aquino government was on the back foot and there were no real champions of the MILF and the Bangsamoro Basic Law beyond the executive branch. The chair of the ad hoc committee, Congressman Rodriguez, ratcheted up his rhetoric against the MILF even while he assured anxious members of the International Contact Group that Congress would still pass the Bangsamoro Basic Law.[64] Legislators criticizing the bill and the president had little grasp of how difficult it had been to broker a deal, and how many concessions the MILF had made in the negotiations. The firestorm in Congress proved the MILF had been right to be wary of exposing the peace agreements to the politicking of legislators.

The Mamasapano incident changed perceptions of the Bangsamoro Basic Law and refocused attention on the trustworthiness of the MILF. Arguments about defending the Constitution and the Philippine state were now more potent. Skeptical legislators and political opponents of the MILF in Mindanao had an opening to water down the bill. In June, a group of former politicians and Catholic church officials filed a petition with the Supreme Court challenging the constitutionality of the peace agreements and requesting the justices issue a temporary restraining order to prevent their implementation. Some within the MILF perceived the delay as an opportunity to reopen negotiations and push yet again for constitutional change, if it proved impossible to implement the framework and comprehensive agreements.[65] Hopes for passing legislation on President Aquino's watch dimmed and then were finally snuffed out as the May 2016 elections approached.

During his campaign for the presidency, Duterte pledged to bring lasting peace to Mindanao and to shift the Philippines to a federal system. After his inauguration in June 2016, the new president's vision for what this would mean practically began to take shape. First, his administration reconstituted the Bangsamoro Transition Commission and expanded its membership such that it represents groups who felt excluded previously—notably the MNLF. The new commission crafted a revised version of the Bangsamoro Basic Law, which reflected the framework and comprehensive agreements signed with the MILF, as well as the 1996 final peace agreement with the MNLF, and any other relevant legislation. In mid-2017, the draft law was submitted to Congress. Progress toward passage of the bill remained slow but it was finally passed in mid-2018. The constitutionality of key provisions, notably on a regional police force, remained in question; language in the bill was modified to reflect these concerns. Meanwhile, a parallel process to introduce federalism—which would require sweeping changes to the Constitution—is underway.[66] How peace agreements struck with

Liberation Front March 2015) <http://www.gmanetwork.com/news/story/458026/news/nation/full-text-report-of-the-milf-on-the-mamasapano-clash>.

[63] His approval rating declined from 59 percent to 28 percent from November 2014 to March 2015; his trust rating declined from 56 percent to 36 percent during the same period. See Kristine Angeli Sabillo, "Pulse Asia: Aquino trust, approval ratings at their lowest after Mamasapano incident" *Philippine Daily Inquirer* (Manila March 17, 2015) <http://newsinfo.inquirer.net/679329/aquino-trust-approval-ratings-plunge-to-lowest-levels-after-mamasapano-clash>.

[64] Interview with a member of the International Contact Group (Manila, the Philippines, March 2015).

[65] Interview with a technical advisor, the MILF (Cotabato City, the Philippines, March 2015).

[66] As per the 1987 Philippine Constitution, art. XVII (Amendments or Revisions), ss 1–4.

insurgents in Mindanao will be reconciled with Duterte's federalist ambitions before the end of his term in 2022 is unclear.

The election of a federalist to the presidency is an unforeseen twist in the peace process. The MILF had never sought to make common cause with the federalist movement to advance its campaign for constitutional change, even though it ought to be easier to grant more extensive powers to Moros under a federal system. Rather, the MILF stuck to demanding an asymmetrical arrangement within a unitary system. Its leaders did so for good reason: Philippine nationalists who defend the 1987 Constitution have always criticized the peace agreements because they believe granting Moros more autonomy encourages other regions or provinces to demand the same. Now that the campaign for federalism is being led openly by the president himself, the political calculations look very different. For the MILF, they have little choice but to back President Duterte's iconoclastic vision for peace in Mindanao, and hope that he finally succeeds where his predecessors have failed.

Lessons Learned

For four decades, the Philippine government negotiated, intermittently, with Moro insurgents. The contours of the 1976 Tripoli agreement were broadly the same as the 2012 and 2014 agreements. Even when autonomy was clearly the solution and constitutionally viable, it was the politics of implementation that mattered. Several lessons can be drawn from the Philippine experience.

First, it may be possible to resolve a territorial cleavage without changing the Constitution. The democratic transition in 1986 was a missed opportunity to end the conflict and draft the 1987 Constitution such that it addressed insurgent grievances. While recognizing the limits of the unitary Philippine republic by allowing for decentralization and two autonomous regions, the Constitution has constrained the negotiating position of the central government in peace talks with Moros and, more problematically, it has given a prominent role to Congress in implementing autonomy. Nonetheless, when the political will was there on both sides of the negotiating table, it was possible to reach a deal compatible with the Constitution.

Second, majority opinion is unlikely to favor granting more power to a marginalized minority. The Philippines has an armed rebellion in Mindanao precisely because Moros feel the rest of the country is not sympathetic to their plight, yet the Constitution has an inherent tension: it gave Congress, whose members reflect the views of the majority, the ability to decide what powers this minority could have. There is a strong vein of anti-Moro sentiment in the Philippines that politicians are all too willing to tap for their own purposes, as demonstrated in 2015. In democratic societies like the Philippines, the legislative branch can play an important role in endorsing the devolution of power. In situations where there is a territorial cleavage, however, political solutions like asymmetric autonomy may be unpalatable to a majority that fears for the unity and integrity of the country.

Third, plebiscites may be necessary to democratize an elite-brokered settlement but come with risks. The Aquino government framed the plebiscite not just as a constitutional necessity but also as a means for making the peace process more inclusive. The prospect of the plebiscite encouraged the MILF to reach beyond its natural constituency in central Mindanao. Yet political mobilization in Mindanao has weakened since the conflict first began in the 1960s and 1970s. Divisions within the Moro community are deep. The political interests of Moro elites and their capacity to manipulate voters cannot be ignored. The plebiscite will require a well-organized public information campaign and must be conducted cleanly if it is to imbue the peace process with democratic values, as the Aquino government intended. If these conditions are difficult to obtain in a country with regular elections and reasonably good state capacity, they will be even more elusive elsewhere.

Fourth, sequencing of negotiations and constructive ambiguity are crucial to the success of constitutional transitions. By reaching agreement on easier issues first, and postponing the hard questions, the MILF and the government were able to build momentum in the talks. This made it easier to overcome the sticking points on territory and the plebiscite later. The government was also sensitive to the MILF's need to save face even when making major concessions, as it did on constitutional change and territory. Giving the MILF-led Bangsamoro Transition Commission a mandate to look into constitutional amendments was crucial. Territorial provisions for contiguous areas to join the Bangsamoro in the future allowed the MILF to claim that it had not really given up any territory, even if Christian areas that were once inhabited by Moros will never join. However, ambiguity in governance provisions in the 2008 memorandum angered Philippine nationalists and contributed to the collapse of the peace talks. A keen understanding of political context and dynamics between negotiating parties is essential to sequencing and using ambiguity effectively.

Fifth, third parties can provide important support. The International Contact Group was a particularly innovative aspect of the talks under the Aquino government. They championed the peace process when it stalled and provided technical expertise, particularly to the MILF, to bridge the gap in knowledge on constitutional and other legal issues. The blend of foreign states and non-governmental organizations in the International Contact Group meant the MILF and the Philippine government had access to different perspectives. Third-party leverage was limited, however, once Congress was making the decisions on implementation. There were also instances in which third parties could have done more, especially the OIC which only intermittently engaged, despite its leverage over the MNLF and its capacity to convene the Moro insurgent leadership. The peace talks have had a high degree of international involvement, yet it has remained a Philippine-owned process throughout, and the credit for reaching the 2012 and 2014 agreements is owed to the MILF and the Aquino government.

The Philippines shows how autonomy can address territorial cleavages within a unitary state. However, autonomy could only end violent political mobilization if negotiated with Moro insurgents. The 1987 Constitution made autonomy possible, but also forced the government to implement any peace agreement through legislation and a plebiscite. This exposed the peace process to political forces that proved difficult to control, even for a president as popular and as committed to ending conflict in Mindanao as Benigno Aquino III.

12

The Withering Away of Politically Salient Territorial Cleavages in South Africa and the Emergence of Watermark Ethnic Federalism

Nico Steytler

Overview

The policy of apartheid was an attempt to territorialize the white/black racial cleavage through the creation of bantustans, confining black political aspirations to 13 percent of the country, while the remainder of the country continued under white minority dominance. This was to be done by fracturing blacks into ethnic-based territories. The failure of, and resistance to, apartheid resulted in the "constitutional moment" from 1990 to 1996 where the two major protagonists, the white minority, represented by the National Party (NP) and the African National Congress (ANC) sought to unmake the political salience of these manufactured territorial cleavages; they created a new narrative of a non-racial, non-ethnicity society and thereby undercut the salience of territory. This project was violently resisted by polities whose very political base lay in territory—the Afrikaner right wing and Zulu nationalists. However, the non-racial, non-ethnic narrative was dominant, although allowances were made for very limited accommodation of ethnic-based territories.

After twenty-five years the unmaking of the salience of territorial cleavages has largely been successful; territorial politics based on race and ethnicity have largely withered away. Right-wing Afrikaners and Zulu nationalists' demands for an ethnic homeland have evaporated. Although ethnicity amongst the Africans has not disappeared, it is currently well catered for through a weak federal system. The non-territorial black/white divide, manifested by the continued inequality in wealth between the two racial groups, is still the dominant cleavage, which has led to the increasing questioning of the non-territorial comprise between the ANC and the NP over the protection of property rights.

The important lessons from the successful unmaking of territorial politics include: a common commitment to peace; the framing of the transition to democracy in non-racial terms; the willingness to make asymmetrical deals with obdurate ethnic entrepreneurs; the strategic use of ambiguity in agreements and temporizing final outcomes; the very limited use of foreigners in the negotiations; and the holding of elections both to structure the process as well as providing legitimacy to the end product—the constitutional settlement.

Territory and Power in Constitutional Transitions. First Edition. Edited by Michael Anderson and Sujit Choudhry. The Withering Away of Politically Salient Territorial Cleavages in South Africa and the Emergence of Watermark Ethnic Federalism Published 2019 by Oxford University Press.

Background

The major political, economic, and social cleavages in the South African society have been racial—black and white—with no clear territorial boundaries between the two groups. Of less political salience are ethno/linguistic cleavages within the two race groups. The cultural and linguistic division among whites—Afrikaners and English-speakers—was politically significant for most of the twentieth century, but is now limited to a few fringe parties representing the far-right Afrikaners. Among the black group, an apartheid distinction was made, on the basis of race, between Africans, colored and persons of Indian origin, a distinction still used by the new democratic government for the purposes of affirmative action policies. The colored community predominated in the south and western parts of the country, while here is a high concentration of Indians in the urban area of Durban on the east coast. Among the Africans the nine linguistic groups—isiZulus, isiXhosa, Sepedi, Setswana, Sesotho, Xitsonga, SiSwati, TshiVenda, and IsiNdebele—all have strong territorial concentrations.

After 300 years of racial dominance and segregation by whites, the NP came to power in 1948, representing Afrikaners, and sought to find a territorial solution to consolidate and justify white dominance. Commencing in the 1960s, the constitutional transition of grand apartheid sought to locate and constrict black political demands to territorial enclaves amounting to no more than 13 percent of the land mass, while dreaming of having white numerical dominance in the remaining 87 percent.

The central tenant of grand apartheid was that South Africa was a country of ethnic minorities, an ideology that did not apply to whites. To secure white dominance, the black majority was to have only a right to self-determination through ethnically based bantustans. In rejection of the NP's racial and ethnic vision of South Africa, the black majority, mainly led by the ANC, embarked in 1961 on an armed struggle to realize a unified South Africa, which "belongs to all who live in it, black and white," in the words of the Freedom Charter, a 1955 policy statement, advanced by the ANC that presented an alternative vision for the future.[1]

Grand apartheid was not federal but envisaged instead that each black ethnic group would transition into an independent country, while black workers would sell their labor to the white-owned mining and industrial complexes as temporary sojourners in the South African republic. A constitutional process commenced with the establishment of ten self-governing territories for each African ethnic group—the bantustans. As the end goal was territorial disaggregation, the federal element of shared rule never featured; it was all about self-rule. But, because the territories allocated for self-governance were far removed from the economic productive areas, the bantustans were entirely dependent on revenue transfers from the apartheid government. The first "independent" homeland was the Transkei (1976), followed by Bophuthatswana (1979), Venda (1979), and the Ciskei (1981). None of these bantustans ever achieved international recognition of their "independence." The remaining six bantustans, so-called "self-governing territories", did not progress to "independence." Chief Mangosothu Buthelezi, while accepting the self-governing status of KwaZulu, refused the end goal of independence, insisting to remain part of South Africa. The geographic distribution of the ten bantustans is depicted in Figure 12.1.

[1] See David Everatt, "The Freedom Charter in historical perspective" in Nico Steytler (ed) *The Freedom Charter and Beyond: Founding Principles for a Democratic South African Legal Order* (Wyvern 1991) 21–43.

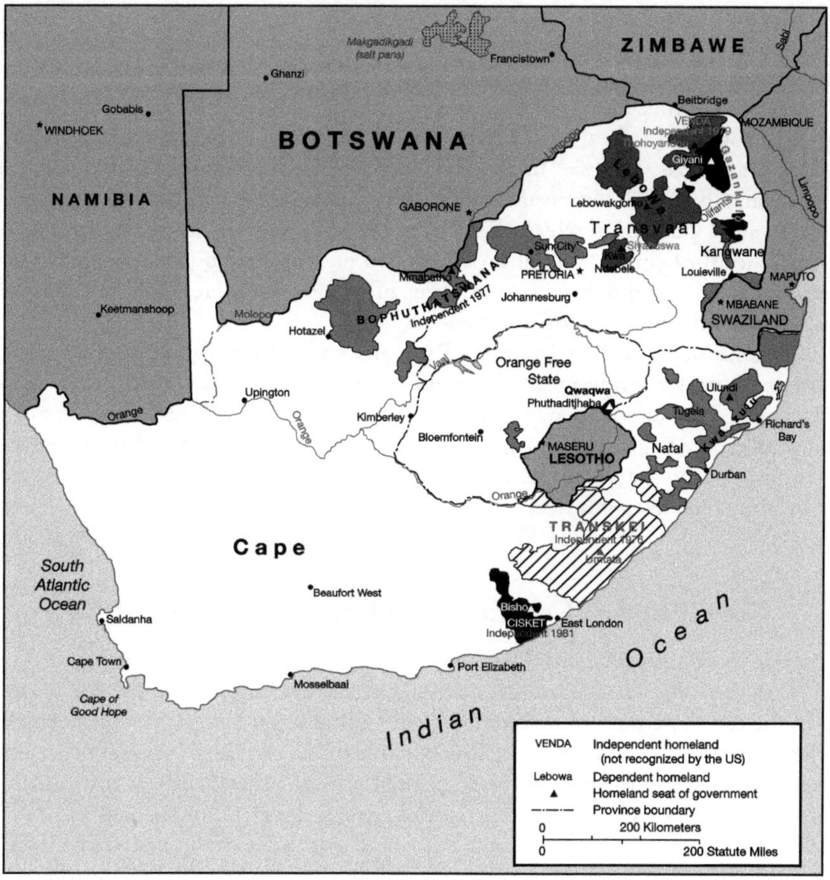

Figure 12.1 South Africa's "homeland" areas under the apartheid system
Source: http://www.worldstatesmen.org/South_African_homelands.html

The bantustans had a formidable bureaucracy, if nothing else, providing the main form of employment in these areas. By 1990, 700,000 of all the 1.2 million civil servants in the whole of South Africa were employed in the ten banstustans, comprising 16 percent of the workforce in those areas.[2]

In terms of apartheid ideology, two race groups proved to be problematic—the colored and Indian communities. The coloreds were a mixed race grouping sharing the main social characteristic with Afrikaners—language and religion—but politically white racism was paramount in determining their treatment so in the 1960s the ideology of apartheid produced the notion that the coloreds were "a nation in the making," who, although having no exclusive territorial concentration, ought to have their own political destiny. A separate legislative body the Colored Representative Council, was established and some, as yet undefined, form of weak federalism was foreseen. The Indians comprised a small minority, and attempts in the 1950s at repatriation floundered, so a small measure of local self-government was allowed for them.

[2] Louis A Picard, *The State of the State: Institutional Transformation, Capacity and Political Change in South Africa* (Wits University Press 2005) 300.

As these non-territorial arrangements for coloreds and Indians were manifestly unviable, the next step was to draw whites, coloreds, and Indians together into a consociational model of governance, but which excluded Africans. The Constitution of 1983 established three houses of Parliament, one for each race group, implementing a form of personalized federalism. Social services (education, health, social welfare) were provided on the basis of race. In all other matters, the three houses had to agree, all sitting separately, but if consensus could not be reached, the conflict was resolved by the Presidential Council in which the whites had an in-built majority. It was thus not the usual model of consociationalism where two or more groups have an equal say in decision-making, but a skewed one in terms of which white interests could, and did, trump those of the two "junior" partners.

The establishment of the tri-cameral Parliament added fuel to black resistance and led to the outbreak of widespread civil unrest, which was a low-intensity civil war that two declared states of emergency could not quell. By the late 1980s in the face of internal conflict, economic sanctions, and international isolation, the edifice of apartheid was crumbling, and the government began talks with Nelson Mandela and the ANC in a bid to bridge the deep political chasm.

The Period of Constitutional Engagement: 1990–96

The fall of the Berlin Wall in November 1989 (graphically signaling the end of the Cold War), the collapse of communist regimes in Eastern Europe, and the end of proxy wars of the two superpowers were dramatically seized upon by the NP.[3] President FW de Klerk announced on February 2, 1990 the unbanning of the ANC and other liberation movements and the beginning of negotiations for a new South Africa. Although secret talks had been initiated before 1990 between the government and the ANC,[4] the close link between the ANC and the South African Communist Party (SACP) was a stumbling block; the government could talk to the "nationalists" in the ANC (Mandela and others), but balked at the specter of its own making—the ungodly red peril manipulated from Moscow. With the Moscow-venom pulled from the SACP's sting, the government could unban it alongside the ANC.

The negotiations process was framed in an important way by a shared commitment to peace and a fear of a descent in a vortex of destruction,[5] which animated all principal players at crucial moments. A second framing principle that quickly emerged was that race could no longer be an organizing principle. Due to the apartheid past, a consociational solution where race or ethnic groups would qua groups find consensus, was simply not an option. Adopting the ANC's vision of non-racialism, all parties in the negotiations eventually abandoned race-based solutions. However, the historic racial cleavages were effectively still present in that some groups couched demands around language, culture, and ethnicity, often with a territorial base. In this context, two separate visions of the state framed the negotiations: the one depicting an undivided unitary state, while the other sought to give territorial expression to linguistic, cultural, and ethnic polities.

[3] See Dennis Cruywagen, *Brothers in War and Peace: Constand and Abraham Viljoen and the Birth of the New South Africa* (Zebra Press 2014) 118.

[4] See Willie Esterhuyze, *Endgame: Secret Talks and the End of Apartheid* (Tafelberg 2012).

[5] Kader Asmal and Adrian Hadland, with Moira Levy, *Kader Asmal: Politics in My Blood – A Memoir* (Jacana Media 2011) 132.

The players

The NP, in power for forty-two years, was no longer a purely Afrikaner party. In the 1989 general election for the tri-cameral Parliament, it won 60 percent of the vote, while the Conservative Party, which had broken away from the NP in 1981 because of the latter's deviation from a petty apartheid, attracted nearly half of the Afrikaner voters (46 percent). The NP's constituency was mostly the urban, propertied classes of both linguistic groups.

The NP's vision of the future evolved during the negotiations. A race-based consociational model was mooted but soon found it to be unviable.[6] Similarly, an attempt to focus on group rights, with the focus on culture and language, but this did not have much traction in urban settings. A cantonal system, suited to an urban environment, was also mooted, but it too failed because it was about preserving race-based privileges in the suburbs. In the final push, the NP abandoned the idea of protecting ethnic minorities, but sought to entrench the role of minority parties through power sharing arrangements. Although the NP proposed federalism, this would provide few direct advantages to it because its support base was geographically dispersed across the country. At best it could claim regional majorities only in the Western Cape and the Northern Cape—and even then only on the back of colored votes. Thus federalism, at best, could provide only a limited check on a center, which inevitably would be controlled by the ANC. The NP's more fundamental objective was the protection of key privileges of white constituency through safeguarding accumulated property, civil service jobs, and pensions.

The ANC, as the foremost liberation movement in South Africa, came to the negotiating table with a clear vision: a non-racial centrist state on its way to socialism. Although it did not win the armed struggle, it was armed with the moral imperative of non-racialism. Further, the principle of non-ethnicity was a counter to the apartheid strategy of divide-and-rule through the bantustans. Ethnicity was equated to "the demon of tribalism," with many traditional leaders discredited for collaborating with the apartheid government.[7] The ANC's vision of the state was thus one of a unified, centrist state which controlled the levers of state power to undo the ravages of apartheid. Consequently, it viewed federalism as a device to perpetuate grand apartheid and weaken a transformative central government. Legitimate concerns about language, culture and ethnicity would be addressed on an individualized basis by a bill of rights, with an equality clause as its center piece.[8]

The very fact that the ANC and the NP framed the negotiations on non-ethnic lines (because neither was ethnically based[9]) galvanized two sets of groups—right-wing Afrikaners and bantustan leaders—who found common ground in their opposition to the ANC and the NP and saw their future in territorial terms.

The right-wing Afrikaners, represented by the Conservative Party, were implacably opposed to the ANC whom they branded as communists, a view widely shared among the leadership of the South African Defense Force (SADF) and the South Africa Police

[6] See Anthony Butler, *Cyril Ramaphosa* (Jacana Media 2007) 280, quoting Roelf Meyer, the chief negotiator of the NP.

[7] David Welsh, *The Rise and Fall of Apartheid* (Jonathan Ball Publishers 2009) 488.

[8] See Heinz Klug, "How the Centre Holds: Managing Claims for Regional and Ethnic Autonomy in a Democratic South Africa" in Yash Ghai (ed.) *Autonomy and Ethnicity: Negotiating Competing Claims in Multi-ethnic States* (Cambridge University Press 2000) 102.

[9] Allister Sparks, *Tomorrow is Another Country: The Inside Story of South Africa's Negotiated Settlement* (Jonathan Ball Publishers 1995) 179.

(SAP), whose very *raison d'être* over the previous three decades was combatting the ANC and the SACP. On the far right there were also para-militia formations, most notably the *Afrikaner Weerstandsbeweging* (Afrikaner Resistance Movement). However, even they abandoned race by replacing it by the politically more acceptable notions of language and culture; the Afrikaners' language (Afrikaans), identity and culture had to be protected and preserved. The goal became that of self-determination of minority groups, and the demand for a *volkstaat* (people's state) in an own territory. What made this grouping powerful was its support in the military and the police, as well as its willingness to resort to violent means.

Making common cause with the right-wing racists were the former beneficiaries of grand apartheid—some of the bantustan governing elites. While the leaders of "independent" Transkei and Venda sided with the ANC, the rest feared the end of their power-base and thus coalesced around strong federal demands. The governments of Bophuthatswana and Ciskei had military forces, while KwaZulu had a police force. The governing party of the latter, the Inkatha Freedom Party (IFP) led by Chief Mangosuthu Buthelezi, was of particular importance because, unlike the other bantustan leaders, the IFP could claim broad support among traditional Zulu society. The IFP's demands were for a highly federalized country, hinting at a threat of secession. The KwaZulu legislature adopted in 1993 a draft Constitution for KwaZulu which provided for a confederal system of government, with KwaZulu having an own military force and a high-level of self-governance.[10]

Trajectory of the constitutional process

The transition from apartheid to democracy commenced in the late 1980s with secret meetings between the apartheid government and the ANC, followed by a number of peace-making agreements in 1990 and 1991. When negotiations about the future commenced, at the first formal meeting on 13 November 1991, called the Convention of a Democratic South Africa (CODESA I), participation was broadened to include all major political parties and the governments of South Africa, Ciskei, and Venda.[11] However much the inclusiveness of the process was projected, decisions merely required "sufficient consensus," a vague term which indicated that the two main protagonists—the ANC and the NP[12]—had to agree.[13] The IFP did not sign the first step setting out the beginnings of a road map for negotiations (the Declaration of Intent) because Buthelezi felt affronted that he was not regarded as an equal negotiating partner with the NP and the ANC.

When Codesa was reconvened (CODESA II) in 1992, the NP was emboldened by an all-white 1992 referendum which gave 68.7 percent support for the NP to continue with negotiations for a new Constitution, but without specifying any content. The negotiations deadlocked, however, on, among other matters, the process of adopting a Constitution. The ANC insisted that it had to be done by an elected constitutional assembly, while the NP, at first, wanted that it be negotiated because it would then be

[10] Stephan Ellman, "Federalism Gone Awry: The Structure of Government in the KwaZulu/Natal Constitution" (1993) 9 (2) South African Journal on Human Rights 165.

[11] See Sifiso Mxoli Ndlovu, "The ANC, CODESA, Substantive Negotiations and the Road to the First Democratic Elections" in South African Democracy Education Trust (eds), *The Road to Democracy in South Africa, Vol. 6 [1990–1996] Part 2* (Unisa Press 2013).

[12] For the purpose of this paper, the NP and the apartheid government are treated as synonymous, and referred to as the NP.

[13] Butler (n 6) 292.

in stronger bargaining position. Eventually it accepted an elected body, but demanded high majorities of 70 and 75 percent, depending on the matter. During this period, violence had continued unabated in Natal and on the Reef. When a group of Zulus migrant workers attacked a hostel on the Reef at Boipathong, leaving forty-two dead, the ANC broke off formal negotiations on the ground that the government was complicit in the violence or did not do enough to control it, which was done with the intent to destabilize the negotiations.[14]

Back channel negotiations continued between the ANC and the NP and in September 1992 the ANC and the NP signed a Record of Understanding. The NP, in the light of Codesa II's failure, rethought and abandoned their position on group rights. The ANC, in turn, accepted a two-stage process of Constitution-making: a negotiated interim Constitution, which also contained a set of constitutional principles which would bind an elected constitutional assembly.[15] Further, agreement was reached on power-sharing at the center for a limited interim period.

This agreement was seen by Buthelezi as a betrayal by his old ally, the NP.[16] He then turned to the racist Afrikaner right-wing and other bantustan leaders, forming the Concerned South Africans Group (COSAG). The language of territorial politics increased; the right to self-determination was claimed by the Afrikaners, and the IFP talked of unilateral secession and the creation of a Zulu state.[17]

Based on the "Record of Understanding," signed by the ANC and the NP, constitutional negotiations resumed in April 1993 in the form of the Multi-Party Negotiating Process (MPNP) with twenty-six parties present, including the Afrikaner right-wing (grouped as the *Afrikaner Volksfront* (Afrikaner People's Front) and the IFP. The setting in July 1993 of the election date on April 27, 1994 gave urgency to the negotiations between the NP and the ANC, but also led to the walk-out by the *Afrikaner Volksfront* and the IFP. In a desperate attempt to get the IFP on board, the ANC agreed to the IFP's demand for international meditation on "outstanding constitutional matters."[18]

The ANC/NP deal: the interim Constitution of December 1993

The ANC and the NP negotiated an interim Constitution, which was eventually adopted on December 20, 1993, ironically, by apartheid's tri-cameral Parliament as the NP insisted on legal continuity. The primary objective of the interim Constitution was to address the black/white cleavage; it had to provide for black majority rule, yet safeguard white interests. This was done by focusing on co-government, a weak form of federalism, constitutionally protected individual rights (including language and cultural rights), an independent judiciary, and the protection of accrued wealth (property, pensions, civil service jobs), and a process of reconciliation. The latter element later found expression in the Truth and Reconciliation Commission which could give individual pardons for past atrocities on the basis of full disclosure.

First, for the first five years a government of national unity would operate; any party with 20 percent of the votes could nominate a deputy president and with five percent support was entitled to a cabinet position.

[14] ibid. [15] ibid 302.

[16] Jabulani Sithole, "The Inkatha Freedom Party and the Multiparty Negotiations" in South African Democracy Education Trust (eds) *The Road to Democracy in South Africa Vol. 6 [1990–1996] Part 2* (Unisa Press 2013) 870; Sparks, *Tomorrow is Another Country* (n 9) 143.

[17] Butler (n 6) 302; Sithole (n 16) 871. [18] Welsh (n 7) 511.

Second, provinces were to be established, each with an elected legislature and executive to which the co-governance mechanism also applied. The legislatures were given a substantial list of legislative competences, but they were all concurrent with the national Parliament and thus subject to potential national laws. The functional areas included: agriculture, education (excluding tertiary education), environment, health services, welfare services, housing, language, public transport, limited policing, roads, trade and industrial promotion, and urban and rural development. In cases of conflict with a national law a low threshold "override" clause applied in favor of the center; national legislation would prevail, for example "on any matter that cannot be regulated effectively by provincial legislation."[19] The powers were little more than what the four provinces exercised before the advent of the 1983 tricameral Constitution.

A guiding principle for demarcating the new provinces was that they could not reflect the ethnic-based bantustans. A small committee of experts was mandated to determine the number of provinces and their boundaries in accordance with a set of criteria, which included economic feasibility, functionality, geography, and community accommodation. Within the allotted six weeks nine provinces and their boundaries were recommended, following largely the Development Bank of South Africa's "economic" or "developmental" regions. Linking boundaries to "economic/development" thus avoided any reference to an ethnic base. Also, although in seven of the nine provinces there were linguistic majorities, the names stayed clear of any ethnic reference. The new provinces were a combination of history and geography: the Cape Province was split into the Eastern Cape, Western Cape, and Northern Cape; the Transvaal province was dismembered into North-West, Northern Transvaal, Eastern Transvaal, and Pretoria-Witwatersrand-Vereniging; and the two "old" provinces, untouched by demarcation, retained their old colonial names of the Orange Free State and Natal. All the boundaries were not cast in stone; in the case of given local expressions of support in a referendum, the boundaries with regard to specified areas could be amended. Moreover, the Northern Cape could be disestablished and the Eastern Cape split into two.[20]

Third, in the absence of group rights and group protection, a supreme Constitution would provide individual security through an enforceable bill of rights, which included rights against discrimination on the basis of race, language and ethnicity. Such rights would be protected by an independent judiciary, with a powerful Constitutional Court at the apex. Fourth, accrued wealth would be protected through an entrenched property clause (providing for just compensation in cases of a state taking), security of pensions, and the continuation of civil service jobs after the transition to a majority government.[21] Fifth, through a process of truth and reconciliation indemnity for the apartheid security forces was secured.

Self-determination and a volkstaat: bringing the right-wing Afrikaners on board

While the ANC and the NP were negotiating their compromises, the ANC was fearful of the Afrikaner right-wing's ability to unleash violence that could wreck the transition to democracy. The *Afrikaner Volksfront* (AVF), formed in May 1993 and comprising forty Afrikaner organizations, was led by General Constand Viljoen, the retired chief

[19] Interim Constitution of South Africa (Interim Constitution), s. 126(3).

[20] Interim Constitution, s. 124(2) read with sch. 1(2).

[21] Welsh (n 7) 526; Asmal and Hadland, with Levy (n 5) 126.

of the Defense Force. The AVF claimed that it could muster a volunteer army of over 50,000 trained former SADF members, and could rely on disaffected sections of the SADF.[22] In contrast, the ANC was less concerned about the IFP, which they thought they could crush militarily.[23] Starting in August 1993, the ANC, led by Mandela, engaged in secret negotiations with Viljoen.[24] Foreign players in the persons of the US Ambassador to South Africa, Princeton Lyman,[25] and the British Ambassador, Robin Renwick,[26] played a limited but valuable facilitation role in this process.

During January and February 1994, the ANC brokered a deal with a group within the *Afrikaner Volksfront*, led by Viljoen, which entailed two crucial concessions: the recognition of the right to self-determination, and the possibility of expressing this right in an own territory, a *volkstaat*, should there be sufficient support for it. This agreement was reduced to the first amendment to the interim Constitution which was signed into law on March 3, 1994.[27]

A twenty-member *Volkstaatraad* (People's State Council) would be established from among those elected members of Parliament who supported the idea of a *volkstaat*. The aim of the *Volkstaatraad* was to provide a "constitutional mechanism to enable proponents of the idea of a Volkstaat to constitutionally pursue the establishment of such a Volkstaat."[28] The Council's mandate was to investigate the feasibility of a *volkstaat*, including boundaries, powers, and functions, and its relationship to the national and provincial governments, and make recommendations to the Constitutional Assembly for the possible establishment of the *volkstaat*. In this regard, the established provincial boundaries were not to be a bar to the creation of a *volkstaat*. A further concession was that there would be two ballots papers—one for the national legislature and the other for the provincial legislatures. The results of the provincial ballot could then be used to test right-wing support for a *volkstaat*.

These concessions were also cemented in the Constitutional Principles. If a *volkstaat* was established before the adoption of the final Constitution, its continuation had to be entrenched in the latter.[29] Given the uncertainty of the establishing a *volkstaat*, a very watered down right of self-determination was enshrined in the Constitutional Principles:

> (1) This Schedule [the Constitutional Principles] and the recognition of the right of the South African people as a whole to self-determination, shall not be construed as precluding, within a framework of the said right, constitutional provision for a notion of the right to self-determination by any community sharing a common cultural and language heritage, whether in a territorial entity within the Republic or in any other recognized way.
>
> (2) The Constitution may give expression to any particular form of self-determination provided there is substantial proven support within the community concerned for such a form of self-determination.[30]

This Constitutional Principle set the parameters of the right to self-determination very narrowly. First, it did not entail the right to secession; it was to be exercised within the ambit of the South African people's right to self-determination. Second, it was a *notion*

22 Cruywagen (n 3) 138. 23 ibid 140. 24 ibid 167. 25 ibid 206.
26 Robin Renwick, *Mission to South Africa: Diary of a Revolution* (Jonathan Ball 2015).
27 Constitution of the Republic of South Africa Amendment Act 2 of 1994 (Act 2 of 1994).
28 Interim Constitution, s. 184(B), added by Act 2 of 1994, s. 9.
29 Constitutional Principle XXXIV(3), added by Act 2 of 1994, s. 13.
30 Constitutional Principle XXXIV(1) and (2), added by Act 2 of 1994, s. 13.

of right, not the right itself. Third, any recognition need not be territorially based. Fourth, there had to be substantial support from the community sharing a common cultural and language heritage.

These constitutional provisions were sufficient for Viljoen to break away from the *Afrikaner Volksfront*, to establish his own party, the *Vryheidsfront* (Freedom Front), and registered it for the election moments before the registration deadline of March 10, 1994.[31] Despite the constitutional text, implementing the deal, the Freedom Front still insisted that a tri-party agreement between it, the ANC, and the government/NP, reflecting the constitutional amendment, be signed by their respective leaders to cement a personal commitment to the deal. The agreement was eventually signed by Mbeki, De Klerk, and Viljoen on April 23, 1994, four days before the election.[32]

Recognizing Zulu nationalism: bringing the Inkatha Freedom Party on board

Both the ANC and the NP sought to bring Buthelezi and his party to participate in the election. Natal was by then a veritable killing field as the IFP (clandestinely assisted by the SADF and the SAP) fought ANC supporters across the province as well as on the Reef.[33] Buthelezi would not budge and insisted on international mediation on outstanding constitutional issue between the IFP and the main protagonists. Mandela eventually agreed in exchange for the IFP undertaking to register provisionally as a party contesting the election, which it did an hour or so before the Freedom Front.[34]

At the same time as accommodating the right-wing demands in the first amendment to the Constitution, a sop was thrown by the ANC and NP to the IFP by strengthening the federal elements in the Constitution. These federal provisions did not form part of a comprehensive agreement with the IFP, aimed at securing the latter's electoral participation. They were a concession by the ANC and the NP in the hope that the IFP may come to the party. Some foreign influence may have contributed to this "peace offer;" US Ambassador Lyman may have played a role in ANC's rapprochement, having repeatedly sought to persuade the ANC to address Buthelezi's demands for federalism.[35]

The strengthened federal provisions entailed the following: First, the only exclusive provincial power, that of the drafting of a provincial Constitution, was initially very narrow in scope; the provincial Constitution had to be consistent with the interim Constitution. The amendment allowed provinces, however, to devise "legislative and executive structures and procedures different from those provided in the Constitution."[36] Second, a number of functional areas were added to the concurrent list: airports, consumer protection, provincial sport, soil conservation, and "indigenous law and customary law."[37] The inclusion of "indigenous law and customary law" was significant because for the first time the link between ethnicity and provinces was made. Third, original, albeit limited, fiscal powers were introduced. In the original text, any provincial tax had to be authorized by national legislation, reflecting a financing model in terms of which provinces would be dependent on transfers from revenue

[31] Cruywagen (n 3) 187.
[32] ibid 210; the agreement is reproduced in Cruywagen (n 3) appendix II 233–5.
[33] See Mary de Haas, "Violence in Natal and Zululand: The 1990s" in South African Democracy Education Trust (eds) *The Road to Democracy in South Africa, Vol. 6 [1990–1996] Part 2* (Unisa Press 2013).
[34] Welsh (n 7) 511; Cruywagen (n 3) 187.
[35] Welsh (n 7) 491.
[36] Act 2 of 1994, s. 7.
[37] ibid s. 14.

raised nationally. The amendment gave provinces exclusive taxing powers on "casinos, gambling, wagering and lotteries, and betting,"[38] an important source of the "independent" bantustans' meager own revenue. Fourth, a further Constitutional Principle was added: in the final Constitution, provincial powers and functions "shall not be substantially less than or inferior to those provided in [the interim] Constitution,"[39] thus affirming the permanent nature of the concessions. Finally, in an amendment aimed specifically at the IFP, there was a name change: Natal became "KwaZulu/Natal,"[40] the forward slash signifying that the name could go either way in the future.[41] This symbolic move placed for the first time an ethnic label to a province, breaching the non-ethnic principle for subnational governments.

These amendments did not enticed Buthelezi to participate in the election and he obdurately insisted on international mediation of constitutional matters.[42] In April the NP and ANC relented. Henry Kissinger, the former US Secretary of State, and Lord Carrington, the British diplomat who oversaw the negotiations for a democratic Zimbabwe, were engaged but their mandate had not yet been agreed upon when they stepped off the plane in South Africa. The IFP was insisting that the election date by placed on the agenda, a demand the ANC and the NP refused to agreed to; both were anxious to bring the transition period to finality. This stalemate sent the two eminent diplomats packing within two days of their arrival. As Cyril Ramaphosa, the chief ANC negotiator, said, "if we fall in the trap of mediating the election date, the entire process could have been scuttled."[43] Another foreigner, the Kenyan theologian and old friend of Buthelezi, Washington Okumu, apparently convinced him that staying out of the elections would simply lead the IFP into the political wilderness and more bloodshed would follow.[44] A week before the election day Buthelezi stepped back from the brink, accepted Mandela's proposal for the constitutional recognition of the Zulu monarch,[45] and agreed to participate in the election, gaining an ostensibly insignificant amendment to the Constitution. A provincial Constitution could provide for "the institution, role authority and status of a traditional monarch in the province," and in the case of KwaZulu/Natal, there must be a provision for the "Zulu monarch."[46] The recognition of a traditional monarch, lying at the apex of an ethnicity culture and identity, would give those provinces with a majority ethnic group, a distinct ethnic color. In the case of KwaZulu/Natal the reference to the Zulu monarch made that province unmistakenly Zulu. Moreover, this was not a transitional arrangement; the provision in a provincial Constitution relating to "the institution, role authority and status of a traditional monarch" was cemented in the Constitutional Principles.[47] The agreement with Buthelezi further included that the IFP issues with the 1993 Constitution were to be addressed by international mediation.[48]

[38] Act 2 of 1994, s. 4. [39] Constitutional Principle XVIII(2), Act 2 of 1994, s. 13.

[40] Act 2 of 1994, s. 1.

[41] In the final Constitution the name became hyphenated: "KwaZulu-Natal," indicating a joining together of two parts.

[42] Welsh (n 7) 510. [43] Quoted in Sparks, *Tomorrow is Another Country* (n 9) 174.

[44] Welsh (n 7) 516. [45] Sparks, *Tomorrow is Another Country* (n 9) 173.

[46] Constitution of the Republic of South Africa Second Amendment Act 3 of 1994 (Act 3 of 1994), s. 1.

[47] Act 3 of 1994, s. 2, amending Constitutional Principle XIII. [48] Welsh (n 7) 516.

The Constitution of 1996

The miraculously peaceful election on April 27–9, 1994 swept the ANC into power with 62.6 percent of the vote. The National Party garnered 20.4 percent, the IFP 10.5, and the Freedom Front (FF) 2.2. The NP was thus entitled to a deputy presidency and the IFP to two ministerial posts in the Government of National Unity. The IFP's support was primarily located in the most populous province of KwaZulu/Natal, where it got 50.3 percent of the vote. Evidence suggests, however, that the ANC chose not to contest the fairness of the balloting process in KwaZulu/Natal, despite strong evidence of irregularities such as ballot box stuffing, which favored the IFP, in order to have the IFP part of the new governance regime.[49] The FF's overall support of 424,555 votes on the national ballot and over 640,000 on the provincial ballots was spread across the provinces, with no more than 6 percent in any province. While the IFP won the governance of a province, the seven elected FF MPs could not find any territory where there was "substantial proven support within the community" for a *volkstaat*. While white support for the NP was diluted across the country, it could only capture the Western Cape with the support of colored voters.

In KwaZulu/Natal the IFP, in a show of hubris, immediately commenced a process of drafting a provincial Constitution, aiming to establish a truly federal dispensation, including its own police force and Constitutional Court. On the face of it, the adopted provincial Constitution, cynically supported by the ANC to achieve two-thirds support in the provincial legislature, conflicted sharply with the interim Constitution. As the Constitutional Court had to certify that the provincial Constitution was consistent with the interim Constitution, the KwaZulu/Natal Constitution floundered spectacularly before the new apex court.[50]

With the distribution of political power crystalized, the Constitutional Assembly proceeded with negotiating the final Constitution. The ANC was shy of the required two-thirds majority to go it alone, so compromises with the NP or the IFP were required. The NP was, however, under the cosh; if they failed to reach agreement, the Constitution, approved by a simple majority, would be submitted to a referendum where only 60 percent support was required for final approval. The IFP, although taking up cabinet posts, withdrew from the CA on the grounds that that the ANC reneged on a promise to submit constitutional disputes to international mediation. However, before exiting the CA, the IFP submitted a detailed proposal for a fully fledged American-styled federation, drafted by Buthelezi's close confidant and adviser, the American-born Mario Ambrosini.

Negotiating from a position of strength the ANC sought to reclaim some ground that it lost in the negotiations. The powers of the provinces were overall reduced, despite the fact that, in compliance with the Constitutional Principles an "anorexic" list of exclusive powers were added to the concurrent ones.[51] One of the areas of loss was their control of local government. In the interim Constitution local government was

[49] See Peter Harris, *Birth – The Conspiracy to Stop the '94 Election* (Umuzi 2010); Welsh (n 7) 556.

[50] *In re: Certification of the Constitution of the Province of KwaZulu-Natal, 1996* [1996] (11) BCLR 1419 (CC). The Constitutional Court also failed to certify on the first round a Western Cape provincial Constitution, through a narrow reading of the new Constitution, which was similar to the interim Constitution on this point (*In re: Certification of the Constitution of the Western Cape* [1997] (9) BCLR 1167 (CC)).

[51] The Constitutional Court, having to certify that the Constitution was in accordance with the Constitutional Principles, found that provincial powers were substantially less than in the interim Constitution, *In re: Certification of the Constitutional Text 1996* [1996] (10) BCLR 1253 (CC). With a few minor amendments, which did not significantly increased provincial powers, the final text was

a competence of provinces. In the final Constitution local government was elevated to a "sphere of government" alongside the national and provincial governments, and its original constitutional powers effectively hollowed out some provincial powers.[52] The result has been referred to as South Africa's "hour-glass federation:" the provinces are squeezed thin between a powerful local government (led by the metropolitan municipalities) from the bottom and a dominant national government from the top.[53]

The asymmetrical provisions to placate the Afrikaner right wing and the Zulu nationalists disappeared. The interim Constitution's requirement of the mandatory recognition of the Zulu monarch was absorbed in a generalized provision that a province may give recognition to a traditional monarch in a provincial Constitution.[54] The *Volkstaatraad*'s quest for a *volkstaat* proved quixotic; there was no identifiable area where right-wing Afrikaners could muster substantial support. The ANC's calculated risk was vindicated. The FF's next glimmer of hope was the establishment of the Commission for the Promotion and Protection of the Rights of Cultural, Religious and Linguistic Communities. However, the mere fact that this Commission also included religious communities, constrained the Commission from performing any protective role for territorially based ethnic communities.[55] All that remained of the original deal was the inclusion of the very circumscribed "notion" of the right to self-determination.[56]

The peace-making Constitution-building process that ensued after the unbanning of the ANC in 1990 proved to be very effective; after a period of six years a stable, legitimate, and highly regarded constitutional dispensation was established which dealt decisively with the political salience of territorial cleavages of the time.

The Outcome

In celebrating two decades of democracy in 2014, a remarkable feature has been the withering away of the politics of territory. All major parties are national parties. Right-wing Afrikaner territorial claims have evaporated, KwaZulu-Natal is now firmly supportive of the ANC and its centrist ideology. The provincial system has not spawned territorially based political parties, yet it provides a safety net for residual ethnic interests. However, the black/white cleavage remains endemic so that the economic compromise remains open to question.

The search for a territorial *volkstaat* evaporated soon after its articulation. Already by 1996 the dream of an Afrikaner homeland was shown to be a mirage. By 2003 Allister Sparks, a veteran political commentator, could declare that the separatist movement was dead.[57] It did not, however, mean the end of fringe groups clinging to the idea, some resorting to violence. After a ten-year trial, nineteen *Boeremag* members (Boer Force) were sentenced in October 2013 to between ten and forty-eight years' imprisonment for conspiring to overthrow the ANC government in the early 2000s. The

approved, *In re: Certification of the Amended Test of the Constitution of the Republic of South Africa, 1996*, [1997] (1) BLCR 1 (CC).

[52] Nico Steytler and Jaap de Visser, *Local Government Law of South Africa* (LexisNexis 2007) ch. 1.

[53] Nico Steytler, "National, Provincial, and Local Relations: An Uncomfortable *Menage a trois*" in Harvey Lazar and Christian Leuprecht (eds), *Sphere of Government: Comparative Studies of Cities in Multilevel Governance Systems* (McGill-Queen's University Press 2007) 229–56.

[54] Nico Steytler and Johann Mettler, "Federal Arrangements as a Peacemaking Device during South Africa's Transition to Democracy" (2001) 31 (4) Publius: Journal for Federalism 93, 99.

[55] ibid 100–1. [56] Constitution of 1996, s. 235.

[57] Allister Sparks, *Beyond the Miracle: Inside the New South Africa* (Jonathan Ball Publishers 2003) 4.

Afrikaner settlement of Orania, established on the banks of the Orange River in 1990, has attracted over the next twenty-five years no more than a thousand adherents. The *volkstaat* dream has become more modest and local; in the capital city of Tshwane (Pretoria) a small group of Afrikaners at Kleinfontein, around a thousand souls, seeks some level of local self-government within the larger municipality. The Freedom Front (now styled Freedom Front Plus after incorporated other fringe Afrikaner parties) attracted less than 0.9 percent of the national vote in 2014, obtaining only four seats in Parliament.

The failure to install the Zulu monarch in KwaZulu-Natal, foreshadowed the demise of Zulu nationalism under the tutelage of the IFP. From the start, there was no unified Zulu political grouping. The Zulu community was divided between ANC-supports in the urban areas and rural, traditionalists IFP-supporters. From the outset the ANC drove a wedge between King Zwelentini and Buthelezi. The 1994 election results further indicated that the IFP "managed" only half of the vote in the province. Ever since then the party has been in decline. In 1999 the IFP lost its majority (41.9 percent), but was still the largest party, followed by the ANC (39.4 percent), and the two parties formed a coalition provincial government. By the 2004, the ANC was the dominant party (46.9 percent) and it formed the government without the participation of the IFP. By 2009 the ANC, now under the leadership of Jacob Zuma, who, with his four wives, is more of a Zulu traditionalist than Buthelezi, was victorious with 63 percent of the vote against the IFP's 22. The 2014 election was almost the death knell of the IFP; while the ANC maintain its support level at 64.5 percent, the main national opposition party, the Democratic Alliance, superseded the IFP as the official opposition with 12.9 percent to the IFP's 10.9 percent of the vote.[58]

The ascendency of Zuma in the ANC has provoked fears of the "Zulufication" of the national executive. More than a quarter of all ANC members now hail from KwaZulu-Natal.[59] Former President Thabo Mbeki has also warned against the rising phenomenon of tribalism, referring to appointment of "homeboys" by ministers (the largest proportion coming from KZN),[60] although Mbeki's administrations were accused of favoring Xhosa-speakers—the so-called "Xhosa Nostra." The ANC has, however, over its long history managed to rise above ethnic politics in its ranks by being inclusive in both its appeal and practice. Nevertheless, this brings the question of the role of provinces and ethnic mobilization or accommodation to the fore.

The nine provinces were established immediately after the 1994 election, each with its own administration. In six provinces this entailed the absorption of the ten existing Bantustan administrations, including their incapacity, inefficiency and corruption. The result has been that the majority of provinces have not added much value to governance over the past twenty years, and some have shown signs of state failure. The ANC, which only reluctant embraced the idea of devolution, soon questioned whether provinces were any longer necessary because they have served their role in the transition to democracy. At its 2007 national conference, three options were presented: abolish the provinces, keep the status quo, or reduce their number and refine their functions. At the next ANC national conference in 2012, the answer was that "provinces [should] be

[58] The IFP's traditional support base was also eroded by the splintering off of the National Freedom Party which attracted 7.3 percent of the provincial vote.

[59] Susan Booysen, "KZN ANC – King-making and Zulufication in the Time of Zuma" (*SABC News*, November 6, 2012) <http://www.sabcnews.com/sabcnews/kzn-anc-king-making-and-zulufication-in-the-time-of-zuma/> accessed November 2018..

[60] City Press, "Thabo Mbeki tackles tribalism" (*News 24*, January 14, 2014) <www.news24.com/Archives/City-Press/Thabo-Mbeki-tackles-tribalism-20150429> accessed January 28, 2015.

reformed, reduced and strengthened."[61] Significantly, the option of abolition has fallen by the wayside. I have argued that the support for province no longer comes from its earlier adherents—the NP and the IFP—but from the ANC itself; local political elites have captured the lucrative provincial expenditure responsibilities (disposing of 43.5 percent of national budget, compared to the 47.5 percent of the national government[62]), and have in effect provincialized the once centrist ANC.[63] The urge within the ANC to reduce the number of provinces is primarily aimed at eliminating the Western Cape, which has entrenched opposition rule through the support of the coloreds, the majority population group in that province.[64] It was further contended by Yonatan Fessha that the provincial system serves an ethnic equilibrium as it placates "the demon of tribalism;"[65] with language majorities in seven of the nine provinces, it provides the major ethnic groups access to government largesse. As ethnicity was never overtly the rationale for the provinces, they nevertheless reflect below the surface a diluted "watermark" of ethnic federalism.

Lessons Learned

The South African constitutional settlement—the miracle of a negotiated revolution that brought three centuries of colonial and white political dominance to an end—has its obvious lessons: a common commitment to peace; the development of trust between the main protagonists; the use of back channels of communications when negotiations deadlocked or broke off; and the willingness to negotiate in the face of violence. For Kader Asmal, a member of the ANC Constitutional Committee and later cabinet member, the commitment to peace was the most important, as he observed: "Where there is a commitment to peace, there is *always* a way."[66]

The lessons emanating from resolving territorial politics are no less instructive. When the interim Constitution was agreed upon principally between the ANC and the NP, they avoided framing the provinces in linguistic/ethnic terms; the weak form of federalism eschewed any reference to ethnicity. However, this framework did not foreclose their willingness to accommodate the two spoilers with explicit ethnic-territorial agendas—the right-wing Afrikaners and Buthelezi's IFP—in an asymmetrical system. Effecting a divide among the right-wing Afrikaners, and enticing a significant group, the Freedom Front, to join the election were the result of the Mandela magic, shrewd negotiations, facilitation by foreign individuals at key moments, and calculated risk. The ANC agreed to the unthinkable—an ethnic Afrikaner territory in the form of a *volkstaat*. But it was a calculated risk, in which the ANC was confident of the outcome because it bound the Freedom Front into a democratic process to seeking a mandate and location for the *volkstaat*. The strategy was an open-ended process which allowed the quest for a *volkstaat* to play itself out. As everyone else but the Freedom Front could see, it was quixotic from the start.

[61] ANC, "53rd National Conference Resolutions: Legislatures and Governance" (December 2012) Resolution 4(2)(1).

[62] National Treasury, *Budget Review 2014* (National Treasury 2014) 94.

[63] Nico Steytler, "The Politics of Provinces and the Provincialisation of Politics" in Tiyanjana Maluwa (ed.), *Law, Politics and Rights: Essays in Memory of Kader Asmal* (Brill/Nijhoff 2014) 191–214.

[64] ibid.

[65] See Yonatan Fessha, *Ethnic Diversity and Federalism: Constitution Making in South Africa and Ethiopia* (Ashgate 2010).

[66] Asmal and Hadland, with Levy (n 5) 132 (emphasis in the original).

Dealing with the Zulu nationalism of the IFP and an obdurate Buthelezi, a not entirely dissimilar strategy was followed which resulted in the partially asymmetrical constitutional accommodation of March 1994. The weak federal arrangements were symmetrically strengthened for all provinces, while limited asymmetrical accommodation of ethnicity was countenanced. Going against the grain of the ANC ideology of non-ethnicity, the bantustan name KwaZulu was added to the colonial Natal. Moreover, the provinces were given the concurrent competence over customary law, which was most developed in KwaZulu/Natal. It is important to note that the negotiating process preceding the March 1994 amendments was made in the absence of the IFP as a direct negotiating party. The result was that the enlargement of the provincial powers did not bind the IFP into the election, but it had the important effect of undercutting some of the IFP's federal demands. When direct negotiations with the IFP did commenced on the eve of the April election, it was largely a symbolic, asymmetrical gesture of recognizing the Zulu monarch for KwaZulu/Natal. Although the very notion of recognizing a monarch in a republican form of government is a contradiction in terms, this political system was applied supplely enough to accommodate a localized political solution.

What drove the innovative strategies for, and solutions to, territorial politics was a common desire for peace. The deal the ANC struck with the Freedom Front was driven by both the ANC's fear of the potential destructive force the right wing could command to scupper the democratic transition, and Viljoen's aversion to unleash a civil war. Peace also was also a key factor in Buthelezi's joining the elections. But peace on the ground was conditional on progress toward full democracy; negotiations continued against the backdrop of violence. Although the overall approach was that the process toward democratization could not be upheld by the side issues of lesser players, the potential for violence by the spoilers gave urgency in the negotiations and the willingness to negotiate quite fundamentally. It was the rigidity of the election date that allowed the impossible to happen. Seven days before the election date Buthelezi joined in, the interim Constitution was amended two days later, and the IFP logo was glued to 80 million printed ballot papers.

When De Klerk announced the unbanning of the ANC on February 2, 1990, it was not conceivable that the first democratic election would be held four years later, followed by a final Constitution two years hence. The election date of April 27, 1994 was only fixed nine months before the event. However, the process culminating in that event had in the main evolved in a planned manner. Hard at work were the main protagonists devising a road map, starting with the cessation of hostilities in the first accords in 1990, to the election date. Given that the main areas of contention between the ANC and the NP dominated negotiations, there was no road map for the territorial issues. Only as an add-on, raised by the spoilers' capacity to unleash violence, were these major issues dealt with in the six months before the election.

The participation of the FF and the IFP illustrates best the limited role of international actors played in managing the process. Indirectly, the end of the Cold War prompted the process toward democratization, but there was no direct involvement in the process itself or for any one of the main protagonists. There were international funds and advisers for some parties, including experts on minority rights advising the right wing and the IFP. The ambassadors of the USA and Britain played a useful facilitative role at key moments at an interpersonal level. The only attempt at direct intervention was when Buthelezi demanded international mediation, but Henry Kissinger and Lord Carrington returned empty handed. On the whole, the process was managed and completed without the help of outsiders,[67] which has the important benefit of

[67] Sparks, *Tomorrow is Another Country* (n 9) 151.

South Africans owning the process and the products, seeing themselves as the makers of "the small miracle." However, South African negotiators drew much on foreign experience and experts on particular aspects of the Constitutions. The German model of federalism based on the principle of *Bundestreue* was important for the ANC agreeing to the provincial system in the interim Constitution and the Bundestag was the basic model for the National Council of Provinces in the 1996 Constitution.

In the search for compromises (all of which were per definition reluctantly made) the legal text of agreements was often couched in ambiguity in key areas. Textual ambiguity worked in two ways. First, the ambiguous or open text provided both the principal protagonists with sufficient language to convince their followers that "we got what we wanted," an important face-saving exercise. Second, ambiguity also allowed the parties to calculate that the open text may swing their way by anticipated future dynamics. A further important negotiating device was temporizing, allowing the temporary compliance with the requirements of the occasion, but avoiding a final commitment.

On the agreement by the ANC and the NP of the interim Constitution in November 1993, Joe Slovo, a key ANC negotiator, is quoted saying that the agreement would not be "*remotely* a federation . . . We've managed to give them devolution without losing control."[68] Earlier Roelf Meyer, the chief NP negotiator, claimed that "we have a regional dispensation with all the hallmarks of federalism."[69] Both could subjectively be correct if each understood federalism in their own particular way, but this is not likely. David Welsh, the eminent historian, commented that "underpinning the 'sufficient consensus' was the illusion of agreement between the ANC and the NP concerning provincial powers whose actual extent was shrouded in vagueness."[70] He further conjectures that Meyer probably believed that the text established a "proto-federal Constitution" and that once the provinces were established, they would use their limited space to press for more powers in the Constitutional Assembly.[71] As Welsh astutely notes, "federal systems create political subsystems at the regional level, and then, in time tends to federalise national parties," a fact that the NP may then have thought could benefit it, the NP, and not the ANC.[72] In temporizing on the extent of provincial powers by leaving it to the Constitutional Assembly, the opposite occurred; the ANC managed to reduce the powers of provinces to become little more than administrations. We have argued elsewhere that the use of ambiguity in "federal solutions" is a dominant pattern followed in most "federal" dispensations in Africa, giving rise to the notion of "fragile federalism"—ambiguous provisions that are in practice decidedly skewed in favor of the center resulting in weak subnational governments.[73]

Temporizing and ambiguity was the name of the game that the ANC played with Viljoen. No final decision was made on a *volkstaat* but left it to the future depending on actual support for the idea and following an agreed constitutional process. The only concrete measure Viljoen could extract from the ANC was entrenching the principle of self-determination for cultural/linguistic groups. As quoted above, the text expressing the principle is so ambiguously worded and circumscribed, that it has no constitutional purchase and remains an empty promise. The seasoned journalist, Dennis Cruywagen, more cynically concludes that the ANC never had any intention of granting Viljoen

[68] Quoted in Welsh (n 7) 508 (emphasis in the original). [69] ibid. [70] ibid.
[71] ibid. [72] ibid 495.
[73] Nico Steytler and Jaap de Visser, "'Fragile Federalism' and the Dynamics of Devolution" in Francesco Palermo and Elisabeth Alber (eds), *Federalism as Decision-Making: Changes in Structures, Procedures and Policies* (Brill/Nijhoff 2015) 79–101.

his *volkstaat*; this goal was from the beginning to trap the general into participating in the election and turning his back on armed resistance.[74]

Referendums and elections played a definitive role in achieving democratization. The referendum among white voters emboldened De Klerk to continue with the process of negotiations toward majority rule. However, the NP's negotiating positions was constrained by the agreement in the interim Constitution that should the Constitutional Assembly fail to pass the text by a two-thirds majority, the text approved by a simple majority would be submitted to a referendum requiring only 60 percent support. And the 1994 election results indicated that the ANC could go it alone.

The 1994 election was key to the success of the process of democratization. First, setting the date in July 1993, and cementing it in the political process and popular expectations, meant that the negotiating process for the interim Constitution had a finite time frame. Second, it gave urgency to get the spoilers on board and also for them to make hard decisions. Viljoen had to decide whether to embark on a bloody civil war or register the Freedom Front for the election, which was done moments before the final registration date for political parties expired. While the date for joining the election was flexible, the election date was not. With a week to go before the April 27 election, Buthelezi buckled and joined the election process. The election not only ushered in majority rule, but also provided a popular mandate for the Constitutional Assembly. As Kader Asmal strongly asserted, without such a mandate the Constitution would have no legitimacy.[75]

Elections also run risks of upsetting political compromises. In the violence-steeped KwaZulu/Natal, the ANC must have strategized that keeping Buthelezi and the IFP in the governance fold was key to peace in that province. Squeaking in with barely 10 percent of the vote nationally ensured Buthelezi a cabinet position in the Government of National Unity. Losing the highly contested KwaZulu/Natal legislature to the ANC, would have rendered the IFP a bystander in the Zulu Kingdom. When the IFP garnered a bare 50 percent of the vote, the ANC did not allow its party's provincial leaders to contest the fairness of the elections despite clear evidence of irregular voting practices and ballot box stuffing. For the sake of peace, the ANC leadership allowed the IFP to elect the premier of the province.

In conclusion, looking back with the hindsight of twenty-seven years, it is clear that the Constitution-making process and products did solve the problem of territorial politics. The political salience of territorial cleavages, in the form of the Afrikaner right-wing and Zulu nationalist, has withered away. However, as Sparks remarked already in 1995, "[t]hough ethno-nationalism may not again become the driving force in South African politics, it is a devil to be watched."[76] The ever-present danger of "the demon of tribalism" or ethnic mobilization has to same extent been undercut by the provincial system that provides oblique accommodation to linguistic/ethnic communities, although chauvinistic politics at the center may undo this function. The black/white cleavage, however, remains the dominant one. With wealth distribution still highly unequal in favor of whites, black political demands are that the political transition must now be followed by an economic revolution, in which the ANC/NP compromise on property rights may not have a place.

[74] Cruywagen (n 3) 208. [75] Asmal and Hadland, with Levy (n 5) 129.
[76] Sparks, *Tomorrow is Another Country* (n 9) 180.

13

Spain

Constitutional Transition through the Gradual Accommodation of Territories

Luis Moreno, César Colino, and Angustias Hombrado

Overview

Spain's peaceful transition to democracy (1975–79) offers an example of how a political agreement could overcome internal confrontations. In contemporary times, Spain experienced a cruel Civil War (1936–39) and a long period of dictatorship under General Franco's rule (1939–75). At the death of the dictator, the opposition mobilized around left-right cleavages as well as around several territorially based nationalist movements that had been repressed by Francoism. The moment of constitutional transition, which would last from 1977 to 1979, arose from an alliance between moderate reform factions in the elites of the old dictatorship, supported by the new King, with opposition elites. Together, they agreed to call for elections and establish a full-fledged democratic regime amid a great economic crisis, intense public mobilization, and some instances of political violence. This constitutional moment would culminate in the passing of the 1978 Constitution, although the implementation of new territorial institutions would extend for several more years. But in less than a year-and-a-half, from 1976, the country experienced the self-dissolution of the Francoist Parliament, the legalization of the Communist, and many other, parties; the call for democratic elections; the signing by all political and social forces of pacts to resolve the economic crisis; the restoration of the Generalitat of Catalonia and other pre-autonomy regional regimes; and, finally, the approval of a democratic Constitution in December 1978.

This constitutional pact "refounded" the Spanish state as a democracy and reinstituted the rule of law. It laid down the preconditions for the creation of a welfare state and the overcoming of the economic crisis. By recognizing nationalities and regions throughout the Spanish territory, it responded to old aspirations of autonomy not just in the territories with nationalist movements but also in all regions, which shared the aspiration for economic development and democratization of the state. Thus, based on a wide consensus of both the national parties of the left and right as well as of the regional parties, the 1978 Constitution enabled the creation and institutional accommodation of seventeen regions and nationalities or "autonomous communities" (*Comunidades Autónomas*, ACs). This was given effect subsequently by the constitutional recognition of regional home-rule and cultural diversity and the extensive decentralization of powers and finance.

This recognized the existence of different languages, political traditions, and distinct civil-law traditions. It also endorsed some constitutional asymmetries notably concerning the funding of some ACs. Decentralization would enable nationalist parties both to form governments in Catalonia and the Basque Country during the first thirty

Territory and Power in Constitutional Transitions. First Edition. Edited by Michael Anderson and Sujit Choudhry. Spain: Constitutional Transition through the Gradual Accommodation of Territories Published 2019 by Oxford University Press.

years of democracy and to participate in governance at the center. This promoted the integration and legitimacy of the new Spanish system for many years, though challenges remain. The Spanish case also shows the importance of a conscious willingness of reconciliation among the elites and its determination to avoid the mistakes considered to have led to the demise of democracy and to civil war in the 1930s. Moreover, the introduction of a moderately proportional electoral formula, countrywide elections early in the process, and the design of a very inclusive and deliberative process of Constitution-making to produce new institutions created a positive dynamic. This operated together with the moderation and demobilization of the mass movements and the support of new and "reborn" parties from both the left and ethnic-regionalist, in favor of a successful negotiation and accommodation between elites of a new Constitution. Despite profound continuing disagreements among the parties, a large majority of the political actors and the electorate approved the final results of the negotiations without producing clear losers of the process. Only persisting ethnonationalist violence in the Basque Country for three decades, now finally ended, can be regarded as an exception to this overall positive assessment. The current secessionist bid of a radicalized Catalan nationalist movement and the government of Catalonia also raise questions about the sustainability of the model.

Background

The lack of accommodation and integration of the territorial dimension of Spanish political life had been an unresolved problem for most of the twentieth century. The Second Republic, established in 1931, had tried to contribute to resolve the country's ethno-territorial conflicts, but it ultimately failed to do so, if only because of its short duration. Its most notable improvement was the regional model of the Constitution, situated somewhere between a unitary and a federal state. This led to the approval of Statutes of Autonomy for Catalonia, the Basque Country and Galicia. In addition, Aragon, Andalusia, Asturias, the Balearic Islands, the Canary Islands, both Castilles, Leon, and Valencia had expressed autonomist claims by the time of the military uprising on July 18, 1936; though many had not yet taken the legal steps required by the 1931 Republican Constitution, a significant number had begun some part of the process. Thus the regional autonomist process, though incipient, was spreading throughout Spain by the time the Civil War broke out.[1]

The issue of regional autonomy versus centralism was fundamental to the political polarization prior the outbreak of the Civil War (1936–39) and it also created innumerable controversies within the Republican forces themselves. The victory of General Franco's forces in 1939 ultimately destroyed the republican democracy and all chances of setting up a territorially structured state. A long period of dictatorship and political centralization ensued, aiming at imposing a uniform Spain.

The Francoist conception of national unity degenerated into an obsessive and reactionary ideology that denied Spain's plurality and dominated the country uninterruptedly from 1939 to 1975. However, Francoism not only failed to eliminate Spain's internal ethno-territorial diversities, it achieved exactly the opposite[2]. The governing

[1] Luis Moreno, *The Federalization of Spain* (Routledge Taylor & Francis Group 2001).

[2] As Conversi stated: ". . . behind its centralist façade, Francoist Spain had at the very end brought about substantial political disunity. Indeed, the result of years of Francoist repression was further disintegration;" Daniele Conversi, "The Smooth Transition: Spain's 1978 Constitution and the Nationalities Question" (2002) 4 (3) National Identities 223.

classes, together with the military and the Catholic hierarchy, had advocated a peculiar and artificial idea of Spain that made unitary centralism and dictatorship concomitant concepts. The result was that by the beginning of the democratic transition in the 1970s, the very concept of anything Spanish was regarded by the democratic forces as synonymous with repression and cultural hegemony.[3] During the phase between 1967 and 1975, internal conflicts within the regime resulted in weak institutional measures to deal with the post-Franco transition. The Organic Law of the State and the personal decision of Franco that his succession fell on the figure of Juan Carlos de Borbón effectively discarded the idea that some Francoist political staff had of a closed political project to continue in power after the death of the "Caudillo." Their internal conflicts greatly determined the form and substance of how the transition was carried out.[4] The same happened with opposition elements that proved unable to impose their objective of a clean rupture and so, had to reduce their pretensions and settle on a framework of democratic coexistence, including some political forces of the past.

Although the Spanish transition has been fundamentally explained as an actor-driven process, the role of civil society should not be underestimated, as the works by both Threlfall for the case of Spain as a whole and Balfour, looking specifically at Catalonia demonstrate.[5] Arguably, political mobilization in the early stages of the Spanish transition was crucially driven by parties of the left and trade unions. And they were, at least at that time, more the expression and voice of civil society than were most state institutions holding state power. As Threlfall puts it, "civil society organizations (the Workers' Commissions, the whole spectrum of Left parties, organized students and women, and opposition media) were the chief drivers of the waves of protests that undermined the first government of the monarchy and closed off all options other than democratization."[6] The mobilization in factories, faculties, neighborhoods, farmers, professional associations, and associations of women found echo in the media and contributed to the opening cracks and divisions among the regime's supporters—the church, army, judicature, and big money. For the most part, civil society organizations have been praised for their role in moderating their rank and file, which certainly facilitated the success of the democratization process. But they also played an equally important, more active, and somehow counterbalancing role leading public demonstrations and strikes that paralyzed large industries as well as public services in big cities, including Madrid, Seville, Cordoba, Barcelona, Zaragoza, Bilbao, and Pamplona, as well as smaller ones.[7] The regime dealt with these protests in the street with harsh repression and a significant number of injured or dead. At the same time, the transition was throughout accompanied by terrorist attacks by the terrorist group ETA as well as by recurrent violence from both the extreme right and the extreme left, not to mention police violence. According to the French historian Sophie Baby, between 1975 and 1982 there were 3,200 violent actions and 700 deaths in Spain, 530 of them caused by terrorism, with 361 murdered by ETA, and the rest by GRAPO, the extreme right, the police, the dirty war, and repression.[8]

[3] Salvador Giner, "Ethnic Nationalism, Centre and Periphery in Spain" in Christopher Abel and Nissa Torrents (eds), *Spain: Conditional Democracy* (Croom Helm 1984).

[4] Álvaro Soto, *¿Atado y bien atado? Institucionalización y crisis del franquismo* (Ed. Biblioteca Nueva 2005).

[5] Monica Threlfall, "Reassessing the Role of Civil Society Organizations in the Transition to Democracy in Spain" (2008) 15 (5) Democratization 930; Sebastian Balfour, *Dictatorship, Workers, and the City: Labour in Greater Barcelona Since 1939* (Oxford University Press 1989).

[6] Threlfall (n 5) 940.

[7] ibid 938–42.

[8] Sophie Baby "Estado y violencia en la transición española: las violencias policiales" in Baby, Sophie, Olivier Compagnon, and Eduardo González Calleja (eds), *Violencia y transiciones políticas a*

Several opposition groups joined forces in cross-party platforms toward the end of the Franco period. In July of 1974, as a result of previous initiatives by the Spanish Communist Party (PCE), the *Junta Democrática* (JD) was established, incorporating other left-wing parties, trade unions, and some independent opposition activists. Of the twelve claims put forward by the Junta, there was an explicit demand to recognize the territories of Catalonia, the Basque Country, and Galicia as political subjects, and to extend this to any other region that so decided. A few months before the death of General Franco on November 20, 1975, the *Plataforma de Convergencia Democrática* (PCD) was established under the auspices of the Spanish Socialist Party (PSOE) and the Christian-Democrats of *Izquierda Democrática*. No regional forces or nationalists from Catalonia and the Basque Country joined the PCD or the *Junta*, but in October 1976 regional representatives did integrate into the much broader *Plataforma de Organizaciones Democráticas* (POD). This included the *Platajunta*, which had merged the previous JD and PCD, but it also brought in the Basque Nationalist Party (PNV), the *Assemblea de Catalunya*, and other regional platforms.

There is some historical continuity from the party system during the Second Republic and that which emerged after 1977. This was especially true of parties of the left, which had not dissolved but remained active underground or in exile. In the so-called "historical nationalities" of Catalonia, the Basque Country, and Galicia, the forces opposed to Francoism had developed a political discourse that combined denouncing both the absence of democracy and the continuous official attacks on their national identities and cultures. So for these nationalities democratic and ethno-territorial vindication became fused. Every time that Basque and Catalan opposition groups negotiated secretly in exile with other democratic forces, the demand for one thing was invariably tied to the assertion of the other. In this way the ideology of political decentralization made its way into contemporary Spanish democratic consciousness.[9]

In Catalonia, the clandestine *Assemblea de Catalunya*, founded in 1971, was capable of organizing an illegal, persecuted, and heterogeneous political opposition. Its activities were based on a simple four-point program: political amnesty, freedom, a statute of autonomy, and democracy. It gathered together in a clandestine movement opposed to the Franco regime representatives of various political groups (Liberals, Christian-Democrats, Socialists, or Communists), trade union leaders, representatives of local movements from Barcelona, groups of university students and teachers, as well as intellectuals and citizens in general. It was highly representative of Catalan society in the 1970s. Its ability to create a democratically legitimate alternative to the Franco regime in Catalonia constituted a unique precedent for the peaceful transition to liberal democracy the whole country was later to enjoy.[10] On the other hand, Greer argues that the strength of Catalonia's web of regional social organizations facilitated the organization and weight of Catalan demands for autonomy during the Spanish democratic transition.[11] Although Catalan society had been largely demobilized under Franco's authoritarian regime, clandestine collective action did not disappeared entirely, and

finales del siglo XX. Europa del Sur America Latina (Casa de Velazquez 2009). See also Xavier Casals, *La Transición española. El voto ignorado de las armas* (Pasado & Presente 2016).

[9] Even regions that had previously shown only weak aspirations for autonomy or home-rule discovered regional identities and found reasons to claim these rights later in the 1970s.

[10] Josep M Colomer, "Transitions by Agreement: Modeling the Spanish Way" (1991) 85 (4) American Political Science Review 1120. Carme Molinero and Pere Ysàs, *La cuestión catalana: Cataluña en la transición española* (Planeta 2014).

[11] Scott L Greer, *Nationalism and Self-Government: The Politics of Autonomy in Scotland and Catalonia* (State University of New York Press 2007).

even more relevant, regional business and professional organizations throve during that time, creating a "distinct, sizeable and interconnected organizational infrastructure of Catalonia." In Greer's view, the survival of an organizational web in Catalonia under the dictatorship fostered the creation of a party system that structurally favored autonomy, leading to what he refers to as the "Catalan autonomist consensus." In his words, "the existence of a shared Catalan agenda in the pacted transition was possible because two political forces—the Catalan communist party (Partit Socialista Unificat de Catalunya, Unified Socialist Party of Catalonia, PSUC) and the activist Jordi Pujol—were able to mobilize most of the available activists, dominate sources of social protest, and thereby prevent any other leadership espousing anything else from finding activists." [12] These two parties were Catalanist parties, and their commitment to Catalanist goals made it possible for Catalonia to represent itself in the transition as a comparatively united nation.[13]

In the Basque Country, the separatist guerrilla group ETA[14] found considerable popular support, and given the oppressive political circumstances, it developed some links with the democratic movement. In 1973, ETA assassinated Admiral Carrero Blanco, Franco's Prime Minister, appointed by the dictator to become his political heir. At the time, those who advocated political violence against the Franco dictatorship were not regarded without sympathy by some sectors of the population, even beyond the Basque country. With the advent of liberal democracy, however, many who had felt such sympathy repudiated the ETA, which had paradoxically intensified its terrorist actions.[15] Several factors explain the violent nature and the historical origins of terrorism in the Basque Country. These include according to Fernández[16] broader contextual factors, such as the Franco dictatorship, the decline of the Basque language, the arrival of immigrants, the ambiguity or passivity of the Basque Nationalist Party (PNV), and the model of anti-colonial movements, as well as factors internal to the movement,, the influence of the ultranationalist groups in exile, an intergenerational clash, ETA's war imagery and ideological evolution, and more personal factors such as the emotional state of its leaders and the internal dynamics of the group.

Conversi maintains that the contrasting paths taken by Catalan and Basque nationalism, and their contrasting strategies played into the successful transformation of Spain.[17] While Basque radicalism and violence was largely directed toward destroying the old order, Catalan peaceful mobilization largely worked toward the building of a new state framework. For Payne, the differences between Basque and Catalan mobilization is rooted in their contrasting origins and ethos.[18] Catalan nationalism has from

[12] Scott L Greer, "Who Negotiates for a Nation? Catalan Mobilization and Nationhood before the Spanish Democratic Transition, 1970–1975" (2015) 23 (4) Democratization 615.

[13] ibid.

[14] Founded in 1959 in opposition to Franco's regime, ETA (*Euskadi Ta Askatasuna*, "Basque Homeland and Freedom") has advocated secession for *Euskalherria* with the annexation of Navarre and the French Basque Country by means of armed violence. ETA has been responsible for killing nearly 900 people. On October 20, 2011, ETA announced a "definitive cessation of its armed activity."

[15] See Diego Muro, "The Basque Experience of the Transition to Democracy" in Alonso, Gregorio and Muro, Diego (eds), *The Politics and Memory of Democratic Transition: The Spanish Model* (Routledge/Canada Blanch Studies on Contemporary Spain 2011). Disregarding the transitional process to democracy, the military nucleus of ETA decided to maintain a strategy of increasing political violence insisting that the supporters of the Basque national liberation movement continued to be the victims of centralist oppression.

[16] Gaizka Fernández, *La voluntad del gudari. Génesis y metástasis de la violencia de ETA* (Tecnos 2016).

[17] Conversi (n 2) 224.

[18] Stanley G Payne, "Nationalism, Regionalism, and Micronationalism in Spain" (1991) 26 Journal of Contemporary History 479.

its origins, and largely since, pursued the restructuring of the Spanish state and has sought to play an active role in the process. Conversely, Basque nationalism has always been more oriented toward separation. These differences showed in the different position they adopted toward rupture or an agreed solution. Following the approval of the 1976 Law of Political Reform, popular support for gradual change rose in most of Spain, including among Catalan political forces, thus leading the opposition to discard the idea of rupture. However, in Euskadi, where all nationalist parties kept to an intransigent line, the rupture strategy remained dominant. The ETA was a more radical and leftist movement that emerged in late 1950s as an informal student group with no direct connection with the first Basque nationalism of PNV and Sabino Arana. In the underground conditions in which it had to operate, it became progressively more radical and "the choice of violence became irrevocable by the mid-1960s at a time when dictatorial measures, coupled with economic boom, produced new strains in Basque society."[19] This was a deliberate, conscious choice to assume a paramilitary form, following the classic insurrectional model of "cycle of action-repression-action," in which the more the state increased repression, the more the radical separatists gained support. Payne also suggests that some additional factors may have influenced the extreme radicalization of Basque nationalism compared with that in Catalonia. The Basque provinces were "the region which suffered the most intense repression during the final decade of Franco regime, creating a persecution complex which only redoubled fanaticism and for the first time gave credence to the nationalist position in the minds of tens of thousands of formerly skeptical." Taxes paid by the Basque economy did not reverted in equivalent public services in the Basque provinces. There was even some resentment after Franco's death that negotiations for Catalan autonomy proceeded more rapidly and smoothly.

Spain's possible integration into Europe had an important effect in facilitating compromise among economic, political, and social actors in the transitional period. Decades of international isolation and ideological and economic autarchy since 1939 led many Spaniards to believe that complete modernity was unattainable. Thus, becoming a fully fledged European country was viewed as a necessary condition for political and institutional modernization. The dictatorship of General Franco fought liberal democracy and human rights, the very pillars on which the European Union was built. After 1975, recycled Francoists and opposition politicians shared the view that the transition toward democracy in Spain would be legitimized by the popular desire to return to mother Europe and to repudiate the anti-European sentiment of "Spain's exceptionalism."

The Period of Constitutional Engagement (1978–83)

Key elites played a crucial role in the successful establishment and consolidation of democracy. They showed skillful leadership, but they did not act in a social or political vacuum, since larger mobilization within the population provided a positive context for the success of the elites negotiations that defined and consolidated the new regime.[20] On June 15, 1977, general democratic elections were held for the first time since the Second Republic. Appointed by the King Juan Carlos, Prime Minister Adolfo

[19] Conversi (n 2) 225.

[20] Ignacio Sánchez-Cuenca, *Atado y mal atado. El suicidio institucional del franquismo y el surgimiento de la democracia* (Alianza Editorial 2014).

Suarez and Parliament Speaker Torcuato Fernández-Miranda had strategically led the legislature of the Franco regime to pass the Law on Political Reform[21] and granted an extensive political amnesty to all political prisoners.[22] The new law initiated a process of legalization of all political parties and a wide inter-party consensus set the basis for Suarez's call for fully democratic elections.

The distribution of seats in the new Parliament contributed to reaching compromise. The two largest parties, the conservative-liberal UCD and socialist PSOE, won similar shares of votes. The UCD got 166 out of the 350 seats, ten seats short of a parliamentary majority. Support for nationalist parties was similar to that of the Second Republic in the 1930s, and while they emerged as strong political forces, they were still not the main ones in their territories—in Catalonia the Socialists and Communists won almost half the vote. However, the claims of these parties were further strengthened by protests and large demonstrations. The election result produced a minority government that would be preoccupied with the issue of the demands of the historic nationalities. This configuration also increased the opportunities for the Basque and Catalan nationalist formations (PNV and CiU) to influence the constitutional negotiations. With both the two main statewide parties, and in particular the governing UCD, falling short of absolute majorities in both the 1977 and 1979 general elections, the Basque and Catalan nationalists were able to exact a price for supporting minority governments and their demands provided a decisive input in the process of decentralization. This regional leverage continued after the Constitution was approved because no party won a parliamentary majority in the elections of 1989, 1993, and 2004 (in all of which the PSOE led), and 1996 (in which the PP, successor to the UCD, led).

An immediate issue for the new Prime Minister Suarez was dealing with the urgent regional demands of the Catalan and Basque nationalists and he took very astute preliminary steps to start winning their trust. First, he reached back to the previous democratic legality of the Second Republic and brought back President Tarradellas of the Catalan government, which had gone into exile. Secondly, he implemented "pre-autonomy" regimes by decree-laws, first in favor of Catalonia and then of the Basque Country at the end of 1977. These rather symbolic initiatives were aimed at securing the support of Catalan and Basque nationalists, and it was hoped they would appease the climate of political violence in the Basque Country promoted by ETA. Such "pre-autonomy" decrees were regarded as "promissory notes" that regional autonomy would be recognized by the coming democratic Constitution.[23] Moreover, the provisional regimes of autonomy devised to accommodate Catalan and Basque demands for self-government, were also offered to other territories if requested.[24]

The country was in economic crisis and its political situation remained fragile. So representatives of the main political parties, the new unions and employers negotiated the Pactos de la Moncloa, which were signed in October 1977. These Pacts showed moderation between government, employers and trade unions and were explicitly

[21] Georgina Blakeley, "'Keeping up Appearances': Torcuato Fernández-Miranda, 'Heresthetics' and the Spanish Law for Political Reform," Revista Española de Investigaciones Sociológicas (2016), 154, 3–20. Sánchez-Cuenca (n 20).

[22] The Government of Adolfo Suarez, a key figure in the transitional period who forged his political career within Franco's regime, issued a partial political amnesty in July 1976, freeing 400 prisoners, which was eventually extended to a blanket amnesty in May 1977.

[23] Paul Heywood, *The Government and Politics of Spain* (St. Martin's Press 1995).

[24] In fact, by the time the Constitution was passed, up to thirteen regions had been granted a provisional regime of autonomy.

designed to support harsh reforms necessary to combat the economic crisis and thereby "consolidate democracy." All social agents accepted increases in taxes and unemployment insurance payments, cost-containment in public spending, together with the avoidance of strikes and lock-outs and wage restraints in order to allay the fears of a military uprising.[25] Other Pactos also included an agreement not to use past history, with its traumatic memories of civil war, repression, and exile, as a political weapon. The focus would be on the future.[26] The negotiation of the pacts set the pace and the tone for the subsequent negotiations for a new constitutional order.[27]

The UCD government wanted a commission of experts to write the initial constitutional draft, but the other parties refused and insisted that the Parliament itself should do it. Political parties, including some that were short-lived, were thus the key stakeholders in negotiating the constitutional draft. They channeled views on the right-center-left political spectrum as well as on centralism versus decentralism. Parties agreed to appoint a drafting commission of seven deputies, most of them constitutional experts or professors (*ponencia*), representing different parties, tasked with drafting a first constitutional proposal. These seven politicians were to be known as the "fathers of the Constitution;" they represented the AP conservative party (1 member), the UCD center-right party (3 members), the PSOE socialist party (1 member), the PCE–PSUC communist party (1 member, also a Catalan), and the CDC Catalan nationalist coalition and the Basque Nationalist Group (1 member from the Catalan nationalists).

The constitutional process followed a complex procedure. The drafting commission was regarded as a subcommittee of the Parliament's Constitutional Committee composed of a larger number of deputies representing several parties. The Parliament (*Cortes Generales*) thus turned into a constituent assembly. The drafting group of seven began its deliberations in an atmosphere of compromise and cooperation. Despite the fact that conservatives, liberals, centrists, socialists, communists, and substate nationalists disagreed over a wide range of issues concerning the state organization, education, industrial relations, divorce, and abortion—just to name a few—they were finally able to broker a broad political agreement whose fundamental aim was to achieve a comprehensive democratic transition.[28]

This commission, met from late August until mid-December of 1977, when a first draft of the proposed Constitution was leaked to the press. Several conflicts aroused and coalitions formed within the commission that almost led to the point of breakup. All parties then had a period to propose amendments for consideration by the *ponencia*. After a second deliberative round, the commission submitted its final proposed draft in late March 1978. The text was then reviewed by the Constitutional Committee of the Congress of Deputies, which over two months engaged in much sophisticated discussion of the draft, for instance about the nature of Spain.[29]

[25] Robert M Fishman, "The Labor Movement in Spain: From Authoritarianism to Democracy" (1982) 14 (3) Comparative Politics 281.

[26] Carsten Humlebæk, "The 'Pacto de Olvido'" in Gregorio Alonso and Diego Muro (eds), *The Politics and Memory of Democratic Transition: The Spanish Model* (Routledge/Cañada Blanch Studies on Contemporary Spain 2011).

[27] Xosé M Núñez Seixas, Lina Gálvez Muñoz, and Javier Muñoz Soro, *España en democracia, 1975–2011* (Critica/Marcial Pons 2017).

[28] Soledad Gallego-Diaz and Bonifacio de la Cuadra, *Crónica secreta de la Constitución* (Tecnos 1989).

[29] Andrea Bonime-Blanc, *Spain's Transition to Democracy. The Politics of Constitution-Making* (Westview Press 1987).

After successive readings within the Constitutional Committee a revised text was submitted to plenary sessions of the lower house of the Parliament, where it was further revised, and then sent to committee and plenary deliberations in the Senate. A joint subcommittee of the two houses was required to solve differences between the texts passed by each, but party leaders had limited the extent to which the Senate had modified the text. The document got final parliamentary approval on October 31. It was then submitted to a popular referendum on December 6, 1978, and was ratified by a vote of 88 percent,[30] with all provinces voting in favor. This completed the process of establishing a legitimate new democratic order.

The consensual approach among parties that had facilitated the economic pacts and the pre-autonomy regimes was also employed in the ensuing constitutional negotiations in the Parliament. As a consequence, and for the first time in the Spanish history, the new Constitution was not to be the product of the winning side or the majority party, but represented a broad inter-party compromise. The very process of negotiation confirms this point. Elite negotiation and accommodation of diverse interests continued to be the practice even after the transitional period. There were various methods adopted for the constitutional negotiations as ways to help reach agreement. Meetings of the negotiators were often carried out informally so as to avoid the "interference" of the public eye when compromising about sensitive issues. Among the latter, the territorial organization of the state and the institutional design of the general administration of the country were considered the most difficult set of constitutional provisions to agree upon.[31]

Several negotiating strategies facilitated deliberation and reaching an agreement. First, at the request of the opposition parties, the UCD governing party did not provide a constitutional blueprint, but the *ponencia* undertook the drafting of the whole text from scratch. Second, as strong conflicts between the parties became more evident once the public parliamentary debates started, representatives from UCD and PSOE improvised dinner meetings at the Restaurant José Luis, which has become famously recognized as the place where the decisive "game of nocturnal consensus" took place. There, both political forces were able to resolve their deep-rooted differences behind the scenes. Although Communists and Catalan nationalists did not participate directly in these private bipartite negotiations, they were previously consulted on the issues.[32] Third, in order to avoid undisciplined behavior of party members, when the draft Constitution text entered the Second Chamber, party leaders imposed greater party discipline upon their Senate delegations, forcing them, in some cases, to withdraw amendments.[33]

Regarding the territorial issues in the constitutional negotiations, the center-periphery conflict aligned the intensely Spanish-nationalist AP against the Basque

[30] In the popular referendum held on December 6, 1978, the Spanish *Carta Magna* received 87.9 percent "yes" votes, 7.8 percent "no" votes, and 4.3 percent null or blank votes. Abstention reached 32.9 percent of the registered electorate.

[31] Josep M Colomer, *Game Theory and the Transition to Democracy: The Spanish Model* (Edward Elgar 1995); Andrea Bonime-Blanc, *Spain's Transition to Democracy. The Politics of Constitution-Making* (Westview Press 1987); Soledad Gallego Diaz and Bonifacio De la Cuadra, *Crónica secreta de la Constitución* (Tecnos 1989).

[32] Richard Gunther, "The Spanish Model Revisited" in Gregorio Alonso, and Diego Muro (eds), *The Politics and Memory of Democratic Transition: The Spanish Model* (Routledge/Canada Blanch Studies on Contemporary Spain 2011).

[33] Richard Gunther, "The very model of the modern elite settlement" in John Highley and Richard Gunther (eds), *Elites and Democratic Consolidation in Latin America and Southern Europe* (Cambridge University Press 1992).

and Catalan nationalists, with proposals ranging from a unitary and highly centralized system, to a symmetrical federal structure and even to some form of confederal arrangement, as was implicit in the Basque parliamentary group's proposal to re-establish the pact between the historic charter (foral) institutions and the Spanish Crown. The Catalan nationalists sought autonomy within a Spanish state that acknowledged Catalonia's distinctiveness. The territorial question was strongly divisive within the ruling party itself with some key members of UCD fiercely favoring a general decentralization throughout all Spain against others supporting some kind of institutional differentiation and special treatment for the historic nationalities.

Most of the constitutional draft proposed by the drafting commission was not substantially modified in the Constitutional Committee of the Parliament. However, the very controversial nature of the territorial question made it the exception and it led to substantial changes late in the parliamentary debates.[34] The positions of the main parties on the territorial question were very divergent. On the right, the inheritors of late Francoism were willing to accept changes for democratization, but they were also aware that the *poderes fácticos* (or "powers in the shadow," especially the Armed Forces) would not be prepared to witness impassively reforms that could jeopardize the "indissoluble" unity of Spain. On the other hand, parties at the left—the PSOE and PCE—mostly identified with the principles of pluri-nationality and even the right of self-determination. However, and above all, they were the most convinced supporters of federalism (in its conventional symmetrical expression after the German model). At this difficult constitutional juncture, they managed to overcome an ideological approach and adopt an essentially pragmatic strategy in the constitutional bargaining. In this sense, they gave up their federal goal, in exchange for being part of the constitutional consensus.[35] They opted instead for an open-ended model that tried to build a bridge between the unitarist aspirations of certain groups of the right and the confederalist stance of some regional nationalist parties.

The identity of Spain, of the nationalities, and the nature and location of sovereignty in the new regime were fraught with symbolism, which is often the most emotional and difficult element in finding constitutional consensus. The constitutional authors sought to assert the identity of Spain as a nation while simultaneously restructuring its territorial organization. They spent several days on provisions such as Articles 1 and 2, which ascribed sovereignty to the whole Spanish people and had introduced the term "nationalities" in the Constitution. This required a great effort in consensus-building, since such language sought to accommodate the ideas both of those who postulated the existence of a Spanish nation, as the social basis for the Spanish state, and of those from the so-called "peripheral" nationalities who sought recognition of differentiated sub-state national identities, especially in Catalonia and the Basque Country.

These highly divided positions on the territorial structure of the state and the nature of the political community prevented an agreement on a definitive and closed territorial model and led to a hybrid and open-ended one. Article 2 of the 1978 Constitution acknowledged the existence of sub-state "nationalities and regions" with a right to autonomy and home-rule within the "indissoluble unity of the Spanish nation," but the Constitution did not derive clear institutional consequences from this distinction in the territorial organization of Spain. Some asymmetries were constitutionally

[34] Jordi Jaria, "La Forma del Estado en los Debates Constituyentes" in Miguel Angel Aparicio (ed.), *La Descentralización y el Federalismo: Nuevos Modelos de Autonomía Política (España, Bélgica, Canadá, Italia y Reino Unido)* (Cedecs 1999).

[35] Jaria (n 34).

preserved, but the recognition of co-official languages[36] and the maintenance of traditional civil-law systems in some ACs did not give them greater legislative or administrative powers. The preservation of the Basque Country and Navarre's special system of *de facto* fiscal independence and the special provisions on the VAT for the Canary Islands were the only exceptions in relation to powers. These latter asymmetries have subsequently fueled demands for the recognition of a "differential status," particularly in the Basque Country, Catalonia, and, to a lesser extent, Galicia.[37]

The main Basque nationalist party deployed a rather ambivalent strategy during the parliamentary negotiations. Unlike the Catalan nationalists, no Basque representative was a "father of the Constitution" so Basque nationalists were not directly involved in the constitutional negotiation, though one of the members of the *ponencia* from the center-right UCD was rather sympathetic to their positions and expectations. In fact, a notable provision was added to the constitutional text before its approval that "protects and safeguards the historical rights of the so-called charter (*fuero*) regions (Basque Country and Navarre)," and that establishes that any "general revision" of its financing system (a special arrangement of fiscal independence) is to be carried out "in accordance with the Constitution and the Statutes of Autonomy of the Basque Country and Navarre." The parliamentary group of the PNV Basque nationalists, however, abstained in the final voting of the constitutional draft and advocated an "active abstention" in the referendum campaign for the approval of the 1978 Constitution. In two of the three Basque "historical territories" (Gipuzkoa and Biscay), abstention reached 56 percent of the registered electorate, although a majority of 67 percent of the total turnout in the Basque Country voted for the 1978 Constitution so that "Yes" votes amounted to 31.3 percent of the registered electorate.[38] These figures have subsequently been subjected to no little speculation. The abstention percentage in Gipuzkoa and Biscay was interpreted as a manifestation of the limited extent of the Spanish state's legitimacy in Euskadi. Following the inception of the 1978 Constitution, the Statute of Autonomy of the Basque Country was also submitted to a referendum in 1979, in which nearly 90 percent of those voting, or 59 percent of the registered electorate, supported the Basque constitutional law. Once again, such figures made secessionists and sympathizers of ETA point out the lack of legitimacy because the Statute received little more than a simple majority of eligible votes (53 percent according to data provided by the Basque Government).[39]

[36] *Castellano* (Castilian), most commonly known elsewhere as Spanish or *Español*, is Spain's official language. Nonetheless, regional languages are co-official in the territories where they are spoken: namely, Aranese (*Aranés*, a variant of Occitan) in Catalonia; Basque (*Euskera*) in the Basque Country and Navarre; Catalan (*Català*) in Catalonia, the Balearic Islands, and the Valencian Community (officially as *Valenciano*); and Galician (*Galego*) in Galicia. Asturian (*Asturianu*), though not official, is a "protected" language in Asturias. There are also some surviving minority Romance languages or dialects such as Astur-Leonese, Leonese, Extremaduran, Cantabrian, and Aragonese. Unlike Aranese, Basque, Catalan/Valencian, and Galician, these minority languages have no official status because of their very small number of speakers.

[37] César Colino, "The Spanish model of devolution and regional governance: evolution, motivations and effects on policy making" (2008) 36 (4) Policy & Politics 573; Luis Moreno, "Federal democracy in plural Spain" in Michael Burgess and Alain-G. Gagnon (eds), *Federal Democracies* (Routledge 2010), 160–77.

[38] Juan J Linz, Manuel Gómez-Reino, Francisco Andrés Orizo, and Darío Vila Carro, *Conflicto en Euskadi* (Espasa-Calpe 1986).

[39] Juan Díez Medrano, *Divided Nations. Class, Politics and Nationalism in the Basque Country and Catalonia* (Cornell University Press 1995); André Lecours, *Basque Nationalism and the Spanish State* (University of Nevada Press 2007).

It is important to underline that not only historic nationalist parties, notably the Basques and Catalans, had been decisive in lobbying for the decentralization of power, but statewide parties, notably the PSOE and even the UCD, also embraced the demands for increased autonomy of the regions and, thus, greatly contributed to Spain's federalization and the articulation of territorial interests, either "top-down" or "bottom up." The new elites of all parties shared a consensus on the need for the transition to solve the "territorial question," especially in those regions with traditional nationalist movements. In this regard, the support given by the PSOE and other statewide, left-wing parties to the political agendas of the peripheral nationalist parties led to significant constitutional concessions, which recognized the historic nationalities as special. This was an acknowledgment of their autonomous status in the Second Republic. Therefore, they were automatically recognized as ACs under the new regime and could acquire autonomy more quickly, while for the other ACs this possibility was left open over the next five years. Furthermore, the Constitution recognized historical economic and fiscal rights for the Basque Country and Navarre.

Spain had fifty provinces, which was considered to be too many jurisdictions for the extent of devolution envisaged. The Constitution required most of them to merge in a manner satisfactory to the Cortes if they were to qualify to receive the powers that could be devolved in an autonomy agreement. With mergers, seventeen autonomous communities appeared, only a few of which had been single provinces before. The mergers were decided, in most cases, by votes of the provincial and municipal counselors, though in a few cases the issue was put to local referendum. The proposed mergers then had to be ratified by the Cortes.

As the new ACs were established, each could chose its own sphere of powers within the framework of two constitutional lists of shared and exclusive competences, which effectively provided a menu for decentralization à la carte. Regional *Estatutos de Autonomía* were approved by democratically elected regional assemblies. In the cases of the "nationalities," which opted for the fast-track established in Article 151 of the 1978 Constitution (Basque Country, Catalonia, and Galicia, and later Andalusia), the statutes were also approved in popular referenda during 1979 and 1980 preceding final assent by the Spanish Parliament.

Outcomes

The Constitution finally approved provides for an open-ended model of decentralization. It had not really resolved the ultimate territorial structure of the state: it did not specify the constituent units but it set forth various alternative paths for the creation of Autonomous Communities. The Statutes of Autonomy are organic laws, which must be approved by the national Parliament, represent a sort of regional constitutional laws so that Spain's effective "constitutional moment" carried on through the preparation of these statutes. To that aim, and in accordance with a "principle of voluntariness" (the so-called *principio dispositivo*), the Constitution left the decision to opt for autonomy to the very territorial entities that were to benefit from it.

The Constitution did not create the State of Autonomies; it did not constitute the ACs, delimit their territory, establish their organization, or determine their powers. It created principles, conditions, and procedures for these in which the protagonists were: (a) the regional representatives who must manifest their desire for autonomy; (b) the central institutions, and, in particular, the lower Chamber of the Spanish Parliament (*Congreso de los Diputados*); and (c) the Constitutional Court, in its role of supreme interpreter of the constitutional text.[40] In fact, Title VIII of the 1978 Constitution (section "On the Territorial Organization of the State") reflected many of the tensions and political stumbling blocks that existed at the time of the inter-party discussions on the territorial organization of the state. This issue was highly contentious even in the general consensual climate during the transitional period. A constitutional "open model" for political decentralization unleashed later on a process of federalization geared at providing internal territorial accommodation by combining both federal principles of self-rule and, to a lesser degree, shared rule. As was graphically expressed by the Minister of Economy during the period 1979–82:

> Title VIII [of the Constitution] allows Spain to have one regional autonomy, or three, or a few, or all, or none, according to the will expressed by the people or the representatives of a given territory, and allows that autonomy to be wide or restricted, and that different communities should have the same or different degrees of autonomy, and that they organize themselves homogeneously or heterogeneously, and for the mistakes made in the process to be rectified.[41] [Original in Spanish, translated by the authors]

The period after the passing of the Constitution (1978–83) brought about deep institutional changes and the setting up of a new constitutional order in Spain. Key changes materialized in the promulgation of the Statutes of Autonomy—of the seventeen *Comunidades Autónomas*. The latter were fully implemented according to the following chronological sequence: Basque Country, 1979; Catalonia, 1979; Galicia, 1981; Asturias, 1981; Cantabria, 1981; Andalusia, 1982; Aragon, 1982; Castille-La Mancha, 1982; La Rioja, 1982; Murcia, 1982; Navarre, 1982; Valencia, 1982; Canary Islands, 1982; Balearic Islands, 1983; Castille and Leon, 1983; Extremadura, 1983; and Madrid, 1983.

Given their strong identity as "historical nationalities," the Basque Country, Catalonia and Galicia aimed at replicating the powers and symbols of the Spanish central state by having their own police forces, official visits to foreign places, specific public policies in the field of education and health, police, external and ornamental signs such as the flag, the anthem, and so forth—all of which was permitted by the new Constitution. A second group of *Comunidades Autónomas* with "earlier" aspirations for home rule (Andalusia, Canary Islands, Navarre, Valencia) then attempted in the 1980s to "imitate" the institutional outlook of the "historical nationalities" as they developed their autonomy statutes. Finally, a third group of "late-comer" regions in the home-rule process of decentralization (Aragon, Asturias, the Balearic Islands, both Castilles, Extremadura, Murcia) struggled not to feel discriminated against by the achievements of those "early rising" regions referred to in the second stage of the mimetic sequence. In the end, they sought to copy the powers assigned to the other, even though they had less well-defined ethno-territorial identities.[42] Thus what was thought, at the time when the Constitution was passed, might be a very asymmetric system, with the historic nationalities having greater devolved powers than the other ACs, turned out to be remarkably symmetric because of the imitation effect reflected in the Autonomy Pacts of 1981 and 1992. So in practice, the extension of home-rule to all Spanish ACs

[40] Enric Fossas, "Assymmetry and plurinationality in Spain" (Working Paper 167, Institut de Ciències Polítiques i Socials-UAB 1999). Victor Ferreres, *The Constitution of Spain: A Contextual Analysis* (Hart Publishing 2013).

[41] Jaime García Añoveros, "Autonomías, un proceso abierto," El País, May 29–31, 1984.

[42] Certain areas lacking in self-governing experience suddenly professed aspirations to autonomy. Cantabria, La Rioja, and the province of Madrid became uni-provincial autonomies although they had never had a tradition of self-government. Moreno, *The Federalization of Spain* (n 1).

implied the genesis of a *de facto* federal state in all but name.[43] The evolution of the Constitutional Court rulings on the issue have consolidated the notion that the ACs have formal, constitutional equality and the right to the same elements of autonomy (with the important exception of the special fiscal privileges of the Basque Country and Navarre).

The Basque Country and Navarre achieved a special regime with its own tax arrangements (the *concierto económico*). This allows them to levy their own taxes and negotiate a transfer to Madrid to pay for common services. This system has subsequently created some resentment in other ACs, because the Basque Country and Navarre are able not only to have a higher level of regional public expenditures per capita but also to remain outside the structured system of statewide fiscal equalization, despite being among the wealthiest ACs in Spain.[44] According to the constitutional provisions, the economic agreement of the charter (*fuero*) regions (Basque Country and Navarre) builds on a political agreement or pact between the central and Basque governments, which is to be ratified by the two parliaments (regional and central) without possibility of amendment (legally it has the same procedure as international treaties). According to this procedure, the only role of the Spanish Parliament is to ratify an agreement previously reached between the Basque institutions and the Spanish state government. Thus, Spain's Cortes is not entitled to modify such rules unilaterally. This ensures an advantageous bilateralism between the *fuero* regions and the State and strengthens the position of both Basque Country and Navarre, since the approval of measures is dependent upon the existence of special agreements. The genesis for the enactment of "shared sovereignty" was highly conditioned by the political circumstances under which negotiations were taken place, and was regarded as a means to appease Basque nationalism and to prevent violence by ETA.

After twenty-five years of constitutional decentralization, some *Comunidades Autónomas* decided to renegotiate their Statutes of Autonomy to gain more autonomy and resources.[45] The practice of bilateralism or "executive federalism," which is characterized by meetings in Ministers councils and negotiations between the central and regional governments, has been reinforced to a great extent by the atrophy of the Senate as the upper chamber for territorial representation and decision-making. Centralists encroached in sections of the public administration, and the main Spanish parliamentary parties have favored bilateral and *ad hoc* center-periphery relationships to the detriment of advancing a common shared rule as in most federal regimes. All this has given impetus to a certain centrifugal political dynamic, which is particularly felt in Catalonia and the Basque Country. Secessionists in these ACs have found new "windows of opportunity" to advance their agendas for secession.

The most dramatic events have been in Catalonia. In 2006, this AC negotiated a new statute of autonomy, which was then passed by the legislature in Catalonia, by the Parliament nationally and then in a referendum by Catalan voters. However, the Popular Party challenged this before the Constitutional Court and the Court finally ruled in 2010, striking down some provisions and curtailing others. It ruled against giving the Catalan language a status above that of Spanish and said that "The

[43] Ronald L Watts, "Spain: A Multinational Federation in Disguise?" (Paper prepared for the conference on "The Federalization of Spain-Deficits of Horizontal Cooperation," Saragossa, Spain March, 27–8 2009).

[44] Luis Moreno and César Colino "Kingdom of Spain" in Luis Moreno and César Colino (eds), *Diversity and Unity in Federal Countries* (McGill-Queen's University Press 2010), 288–319.

[45] These were: Aragon (2006); Catalonia (2006/2010); Valencia (2006/2011); Andalusia (2007); Balearic Islands (2007); Castille and Leon (2007); and Extremadura (2011).

interpretation of the references to 'Catalonia as a nation' and to 'the national reality of Catalonia' in the preamble of the Statute of Autonomy of Catalonia have no legal effect."

Several drivers or sociopolitical preconditions—such as the successful creation of a collective grievance discourse, a postulated democratic right to decide, considerable and sustained popular support through mobilization of the civil society, as well as the interests and behaviors of some leaders immersed in an outbidding electoral competition for the nationalist vote—lie behind the current secessionist bid.[46] Both the Court's ruling and the central government's refusal to accept a new fiscal pact was used by the Catalan prime minister's Mas to justify a sudden and far-reaching tactical and strategic change, which took advantage of the soaring secessionist sentiment among the Catalan population, in part due to the economic crisis. In 2012, in a large demonstration held on September 11 in Barcelona, proliferating civil society secessionist organizations, with the support of the Catalan official public media and the Catalan government itself, were able to mobilize the general discontent of thousands of Catalans due to the crisis and other grievances around the banner of sovereignty. A very effective populist rhetoric against "Spain" and focused on the "plundering" or "pillaging" of Catalonia by Spain and the alleged disregard for Catalonia within Spain was utilized. The secessionist program, after snap regional elections by the end of 2012, was built on the 2013 Parliament declaration, the coalition agreements, and the so-called roadmap of January 2015. It has sought to reach independence either by legal means or through unilateral action.

After an illegal pseudo-referendum at the end of 2014, with scarce turnout, in October 2017 the Catalan government under Premier Puigdemont and his short majority proceeded to pass two unconstitutional laws in the regional Parliament providing for a binding self-determination referendum and the transition to a new independent republic. These two laws were suspended by the Court but the vote was held anyways, without any of the usual guarantees, and where allegedly a 92 percent voted in favor of independence, but again with a very low turnout. The Spanish government had ordered police to try to stop the illegal referendum vote forcibly, which led to highly publicized confrontations. The events became critical, with the Spanish and Catalan governments testing one another. The Spanish government threatened direct rule, but said it would back off it the AC would hold elections. But on October 27, the Parliament of Catalonia declared independence from Spain unilaterally. This led the Spanish government to invoke its constitutional power to assume direct control over some of the AC's government's powers; it proceeded to dismiss Puigdemont and his cabinet, and to dissolve the Parliament and to call regional elections in December 21. The elections were narrowly won by the secessionist parties, but many of their elected candidates have been arrested or fled the country because of charges of rebellion against them and this has left them without a majority and unable to form a government as of April 2018. This crisis has led to significant polarization of opinion within Catalonia, while in Spain it has produced a hardening of attitudes toward the demands of Catalonia. It has also demonstrated the lack of international support for a unilateral declaration of independence by a region within a democratic country. Its longer-term impacts on Spanish politics and government are highly uncertain.

[46] See César Colino and Angus Hombrado, "Besieged and paralyzed? The Spanish State facing the secessionist Challenge in Catalonia and coping with the Reform imperative" in EZFF (ed.), *Jahrbuch des Föderalismus 2015* (Nomos 2015), 293–317. Andrew Dowling, *The Rise of Catalan Independence: Spain's Territorial Crisis* (Routledge 2018).

Lessons Learned

While our account above ends with the Catalan crisis of 2017–18, it should not obscure Spain's relatively successful transition to democracy in the late 1970s and its consolidation in the early 1980s. It gives confidence that Spain will deal with its challenges peacefully and democratically. The transition in the late 1970s shows the importance of a combined action by old and new elites for developing a broad consensus on a new constitutional order. The old elites of the former regime still had important powers over key institutions, while the new elites, who had been politically excluded, now had the support of new or rejuvenated political parties and much of civil society that had been mobilized during the socioeconomic and cultural modernization in the latter years of Franco. The nature of the former regime, a skillful leadership by the King during the transition, the moderation of the elites and a very encouraging international environment in Europe were all factors that shaped the approaches of the main political actors and promoted the constitutional transition to a stable and legitimate regime in Spain. The central objective of the key economic, political and social actors during the period of constitutional engagement (1975–79) was to overcome constraints so as to make democratization and decentralization possible. To this end, all stakeholders involved in the political negotiations were prepared to limit their sectional interests for the sake of achieving a common agreement.

Elite negotiation and accommodation of diverse interests continued to be the normal practice after the transitional period, whether through intergovernmental relations or informal practices, such as the presence of important regional leaders from different ACs in the central cabinet. The Spanish case also shows the importance of the willingness of reconciliation among the elites and its determination to avoid the mistakes of the past. Moreover, early elections at the central level soon in the process and the design of a very inclusive and deliberative constituent process to produce new institutions, operated together with the moderation and demobilization of the mass movements to guarantee a successful negotiation between elites of a new Constitution. Despite the profound existing disagreements among the parties most political actors and the electorate accepted the final results of the negotiations without producing clear losers of the process.

There may have been a breakdown in this pattern of elite reconciliation over the future of Catalonia—as currently seen in the standoff and the lack of communication between Catalan separatists and the national government—that has been precipitated by several domestic Catalan factors and in part by the ruling of the Constitutional Court, which was construed as overriding a major political compromise on Catalonia's revised Statute of Autonomy in 2006, and the subsequent inaction of the Central government, as well as by the extraordinary nature of the issue in question: the right or not of a region to secede. Spain is by no means unusual amongst democratic states in maintaining there is no such right, but declaring any issue out-of-bounds for political discourse creates challenges in a democracy.

We can then summarize several characteristics and preconditions of success of the Spanish case that may be useful elsewhere, especially in similar processes of transitions from similar authoritarian regimes with mobilised territorial cleavages:

- A particular sequence of elections and decentralization, with national elections having place prior to regional and local elections which gives the central government and leaders initiating the transition legitimacy to deal with regional demands for more autonomy and establishes clearly the subject of the "stateness" and of the constitutional process.
- A general perception and consensus among the new transition elites from all the parties of the need to solve the "territorial question," especially in those regions with traditional nationalist movements. The supporting role of statewide left-wing parties to the programs and agendas of the peripheral nationalist parties during the transition is a case in point. It led to the decision to establish two paths toward full autonomy and the constitutional decision to distinguish two tracks according to the autonomy granted in the Second Republic. It also led to the recognition of historical rights for the Basque Country and Navarra that were respected and constitutionalized.
- Pervasive memories of the previous conflicts or civil wars and wish for reconciliation to avoid repetition of the past. These memories of past civil conflicts and repression are transmitted alongside political cultures in an intergenerational fashion. The Spanish transition shows the positive persistence or resurgence of nationalist parties that were the same or the heirs of parties in the Second Republic. This accounted for their rapid organization and capacity and their integrative force as substate nationalist parties that moderated their stances and demands. The Spanish case also featured the return of several political leaders, active during the Second Republic, from exile into political activity again. Opposition forces have also to renounce some of their past symbols for the sake of compromise.
- The strength and predominance of support for statewide parties (or their regional branches) in national elections in all regions. This profoundly affected the political dynamic because there were no regions, including Catalonia and the Basque Country, in which nationalist parties were stronger than statewide parties. This reflects the presence of dual Spanish and regional identities among citizens.
- The decision for a reinforcement of the party system to favor larger parties. The proportional electoral system had majoritarian effects due to the type of electoral district chosen (the old provinces) and to the public financing of parties, which produced a rationalized and functional Parliament.
- The decision to create "pre-autonomy regimes" that set the stage for a possible generalized devolution.
- The design of the scheme of devolution. The favoring of shared competences over exclusive competences, but with national paramountcy; give each AC a role in designing its statute of autonomy and its own public policies; but a meaningful framework legislative role for the central Parliament.
- The conscious use of constitutional ambiguities and silences as a device for accommodating diverse interests and aspirations and different definitions of the national community. The Spanish Constitution is a paradigmatic example of ambiguity of the constitutional pact in territorial issues. The type of open-ended territorial arrangements agreed as a compromise among unitarist, federalist, and confederalist visions were the only possible consensual solution. Issues where

complete agreement could not be reached were left to be resolved when democracy was fully consolidated.

- Finally, the bilateral way in which devolution would be subsequently negotiated step by step in bilateral committees with representatives of the central government and new regional authorities.

14

Sri Lanka's Failed Peace Process and the Continuing Challenge of Ethno-Territorial Cleavages

Asanga Welikala

Overview

Despite an auspicious start to independent statehood following British decolonization in 1948, Sri Lanka soon dissipated its early promise in a quagmire of ethnonationalism, institutional decay, authoritarianism, and civil war.[1] Compared with the complexity of many other Asian and African post-colonial states contending with ethno-territorial pluralism, including notably India, the Sri Lankan situation seems at first straightforward. Its ethno-territorial conflict stems from the Sinhala-Buddhist majority's dominance over the island's politics and government, and in response, the minority Tamils' desire for self-government in the northeast. The ethnic division between Sinhalese and Tamils is thus replicated in a territorial cleavage between the "south" and the "northeast", so that fairly conventional constitutional strategies of nation-building and power-sharing would seem adequate to accommodate these competing claims.[2] Yet the conundrum is that the Sri Lankan state has consistently failed to devise a constitutional order in congruence with its societal pluralism, and, despite over half a century of reform attempts, this seemingly easy problem has so far defied resolution.

This chapter focuses on one of the most concerted attempts made to find a constitutional resolution of the conflict: the Norwegian-facilitated peace process between the government of Sri Lanka and the Liberation Tigers of Tamil Eelam (LTTE), roughly from 2001 to 2005. This process was marked in significant ways by methods associated with the liberal peace-building model, while simultaneously reflecting the closed and elitist character of Sri Lankan constitutional politics.[3] Its failure led to a final phase of military conflict in which the government comprehensively defeated the LTTE in May 2009 and then, as victor, was hostile to any concessions to Tamil aspirations to regional autonomy—something which has changed only recently with a change of government. The chapter highlights various weaknesses of this model of conflict transformation and

[1] Harshan Kumarasingham, *A Political Legacy of the British Empire: Power and the Parliamentary System in Post-Colonial India and Sri Lanka* (IB Tauris 2013) ch. 7.

[2] John McGarry, Brendan O'Leary and Richard Simeon, "Integration or Accommodation? The Enduring Debate in Conflict Regulation" in Sujit Choudhry (ed.), *Constitutional Design in Divided Societies: Integration or Accommodation?* (Oxford University Press 2008) ch. 2, 85–7.

[3] Christine Bell, *On the Law of Peace: Peace Agreements and the Lex Pacificatoria* (Oxford University Press 2008) ch. 2, ch. 5; Jonathan Goodhand, Jonathan Spencer, and Benedikt Korf (eds), *Conflict and Peacebuilding in Sri Lanka: Caught in the Peace Trap?* (Routledge Contemporary South Asia Series Book 38, Routledge 2011); Kristian Stokke and Jayadeva Uyangoda (eds), *Liberal Peace in Question: Politics of State and Market Reform in Sri Lanka* (Anthem Press 2011).

Territory and Power in Constitutional Transitions. First Edition. Edited by Michael Anderson and Sujit Choudhry. Sri Lanka's Failed Peace Process and the Continuing Challenge of Ethno-Territorial Cleavages Published 2019 by Oxford University Press.

constitutional transition, in a context of limited constitutional imagination on both sides, hyper-competitive southern electoral politics, the breakdown of cohabitation at the center, the failure to mitigate the effects of ethnonationalist antagonisms, and the critical absence of public participation. The failure to inform and engage skeptical constituencies in particular led to a significant democratic deficit in the process.

Constantly harried by day-to-day challenges of political crisis management, the peace process never matured sufficiently for constitutional negotiations of any depth to take place, although the parties did manage on one occasion to articulate the fundamental principles of a constitutional settlement, embodied in the Oslo Communiqué of December 2002, that may well be of relevance for the future.

The election of a more moderate government in January 2015, the successful enactment of several democratic and governance reforms in May, the election of a new Parliament in August in which moderate parties across the ethnic divide emerged victorious, and the commencement in March 2016 of a constitutional reform process through Parliament sitting as a Constitutional Assembly, gave rise to cautious optimism that devolution reforms would follow. But that process too has stalled with a breakdown in the cohabitation relationship between the President and Prime Minister in late 2017, and a major constitutional crisis in late 2018 that rules out any further reforms in the current Parliament.[4] It therefore remains a story of failure, from which, nonetheless, lessons can hopefully be drawn as and when Sri Lanka returns to constitutional reform in the future.

Background

The Sri Lankan polity is characterized by rich ethnic and religious pluralism, albeit with an overwhelming Sinhala-Buddhist majority of almost 75 percent of the population, which sees itself as the historic national community of the island.[5] In the Sinhala-Buddhist nationalist worldview, the island is the only homeland of the Sinhalese people, who are, moreover, the inheritors of a sacred duty to preserve and protect Theravada Buddhism. This is the heritage of race and religion that the Sinhala-Buddhists have defended with much sacrifice and resilience against South Indian Tamil-Hindu and European-Christian invaders from time immemorial. These central elements of Sinhala-Buddhist nationalism are elaborated and reproduced in a powerful tradition of historiography, which continues to inform contemporary political and cultural discourse, in particular in relation to a specific view of the form and foundations of the Sri Lankan state.[6] In this view, there is no distinction between the collective identity of the ethnic majority and the Sri Lankan nation-state.[7]

It follows from this that ethnic and religious (and indeed, ideological) minorities are expected to acknowledge the primacy of the majority's political and cultural dominance over the historical and territorial space of the state. Sinhala-Buddhist nationalism

[4] Asanga Welikala, "Sri Lanka's Long Constitutional Moment" (2015) 104 (5) The Round Table 551; for frequently updated research on the ongoing constitutional reform process, see: "Constitutional Reforms in Sri Lanka: Books & other material related to constitutional reform in Sri Lanka" (*Centre for Policy Alternatives*) <http://constitutionalreforms.org>.

[5] According to the latest (and first post-war) 2012 census, the total population of Sri Lanka is 20,359,439, of which Sinhalese are 15,250,081 (74.9 percent), the Sri Lankan Tamils 2,269,266 (11.15 percent), Sri Lankan Moors (Muslims) 1,892,638 (9.3 percent), and the Indian Tamils 839,504 (4.12 percent): Department of Census and Statistics, *Census of Population and Housing of Sri Lanka 2012* (Government of Sri Lanka 2012) Table A3, <www.statistics.gov.lk/PopHouSat/CPH2011/Pages/Activities/Reports/FinalReport/Population/FinalPopulation.pdf> accessed April 4, 2017.

[6] Stanley Jeyaraja Tambiah, *Sri Lanka: Ethnic Fratricide and the Dismantling of Democracy* (University of Chicago Press 1991) 93–102.

[7] Michael Roberts, "Ethnic Conflict in Sri Lanka and Sinhalese Perspectives: Barriers to Accommodation" (1978) 12 (3) Modern Asian Studies 353.

is therefore unequivocally hegemonic, but it is not assimilationist; minorities enjoy tolerance of their distinctiveness to the extent commensurate with the dominant nation's view of its primacy, meaning that constitutionally the Sri Lankan state must be unitary in form, foster Buddhism, and privilege the Sinhala language and culture. The commitment to the unitary state is important both symbolically and substantively. Symbolically, it is the modern continuation of the ancient Sinhala-Buddhist state tradition, in which an encompassing monarchy was the synecdoche of a hierarchical social order and state[8] (this justification is also strongly implied in modern arguments in favor of centralizing presidentialism[9]). Most importantly, it registers a clear constitutional rejection of Tamil territorial claims to federal autonomy. Thus substantively, the centralization of power and authority in the unitary state ensures that executive and legislative institutions are permanently under majoritarian control.[10]

This forceful nationalism has been politically ascendant ever since independence, shaping and defining the character of the Sri Lankan nation-state at every significant constitutional moment, and permeating the discourse and practice of ordinary electoral politics. Thus, soon after independence, legislation was enacted to deprive citizenship rights from large sections of the Indian Tamil population.[11] In 1956, the "Sinhala Only Act" sought to make Sinhala the sole official language.[12] During the late 1950s and mid-1960s, attempts at introducing a bilingual official language policy and devolution to Tamil-majority areas were derailed by processes of ethnic outbidding among the major political parties within the south. The non-discrimination and minority protections of the independence Constitution had proved ineffective in the hands of a deferential judiciary, and when the country became a republic in 1972, the unitary state, a "foremost place" for Buddhism, and the primacy of Sinhalese, were all constitutionally enshrined.[13] The Constituent Assembly, which drafted and enacted the first republican Constitution, completely rejected Tamil demands for equal treatment, secularism, and especially federal autonomy.[14]

The Sri Lankan Tamils, distinct from the Indian Tamils and the largely Tamil-speaking Muslims, see themselves as the other historic national community within

[8] Roshan de Silva Wijeyeratne, *Nation, Constitutionalism and Buddhism in Sri Lanka* (Routledge Contemporary South Asia Series, Routledge 2014) ch. 4.

[9] Asanga Welikala, "Nation, State, Sovereignty and Kingship: The Pre-Modern Antecedents of the Presidential State" in Asanga Welikala (ed.), *Reforming Sri Lankan Presidentialism: Provenance, Problems and Prospects* (Centre for Policy Alternatives 2015) ch. 13, <http://srilankanpresidentialism.org/wp-content/uploads/2015/01/21-Welikala.pdf> accessed April 4, 2017.

[10] Asanga Welikala, "The Sri Lankan Conception of the Unitary State: Theory, Practice and History" in Amaranth Amarasingham and Daniel Bass (eds), *Sri Lanka: The Struggle for Peace in the Aftermath of War* (Hurst & Co 2016).

[11] The Indian Tamils, also sometimes known as Upcountry Tamils or Estate Tamils, are Tamils brought down from Southern India as indentured labor for tea, rubber and coffee plantations during the British colonial era. While a large number were repatriated to India in stages after independence, they are still the dominant ethnicity in plantation labor in the central hill country. They are distinct from the indigenous Sri Lankan Tamils who originate in the northern and eastern regions of the island, and they make no territorial claims.

[12] Neil DeVotta, *Blowback: Linguistic Nationalism, Institutional Decay, and Ethnic Conflict in Sri Lanka* (Stanford University Press 2004) ch. 4.

[13] Rohan Edrisinha, "Sri Lanka: Constitutions without Constitutionalism: A Tale of Three and a Half Constitutions" in Rohan Edrisinha and Asanga Welikala (eds), *Essays on Federalism in Sri Lanka* (Centre for Policy Alternatives 2008).

[14] Nihal Jayawickrama, "Reflections on the Making and Content of the 1972 Constitution: An Insider's Perspective" in Asanga Welikala (ed.), *The Sri Lankan Republic at 40: Reflections on Constitutional History, Theory and Practice* (Centre for Policy Alternatives 2012) ch. 1, available at <http://republicat40.org/wp-content/uploads/2013/01/Reflections-on-the-Making-and-Content-of-the-1972-Constitution1.pdf> accessed April 4, 2017.

the island.[15] There is little doubt about their historic presence in the island and the legitimacy of their constitutional claims on this basis. But this is not to say that Tamil nationalist ideology always presents convincing arguments about its claims, illustrated, for example, by Tamil nationalism's attempts to encompass the Muslims of the north and east within the Tamil nation under the rubric of "Tamil-speaking people." Muslims, however, have resisted this attempt at assimilation and insisted on their separate religion-based identity.[16]

Sri Lankan Tamil claims to constitutional accommodation are based on three principles: that they are a distinct nation, with a traditional homeland in the northeast of the island, and entitled on these grounds to the right to self-determination.[17] On this basis, they have asserted an entitlement to self-government, whether in the form of autonomy within a federal Sri Lankan state, or, if not, as a separate state. Under the British, the Tamils had been content to regard themselves as a minority (albeit historically coeval with the Sinhala majority), and to seek representation in the colonial state on that basis.[18] Industrious and educated, the Tamils, or at least a prominent Tamil elite, gained disproportionate social advancement under British colonialism compared to the Sinhalese, although the land-owning Sinhalese colonial elite was always the dominant faction. Nevertheless, Sinhala-Buddhist nationalists fed upon, and contributed to, the perception that Tamils were colonial lackeys whose social and economic successes were at the cost of poor Sinhalese in their own land.

As the prospect and potential of Sinhala-Buddhist domination became more apparent after independence, the Tamils rearticulated their collective identity as a distinct nationality, with a demand for federal autonomy. The Federal Party, the main vehicle of parliamentary Tamil nationalism even today, was established in 1949 for this purpose.[19] Deteriorating ethnic relations and the Tamils' sense of beleaguerment, especially after the Sinhala Only Act, have ensured that parties committed to the Tamil national, territorial, and self-determination claims have won majorities in every election in the north and east since 1956. The Tamils' consistent commitment to these principles was even affirmed in the several rounds of post-war elections after 2009, notwithstanding the devastating military defeat of the LTTE.

In the first two decades after independence, the Federal Party's various attempts to negotiate official bilingualism, devolution (short of federalism), and equitable solutions to discriminatory measures (such as affirmative action favoring rural Sinhala youth for university entry) had been unsuccessful. Recourse to courts and constitutional safeguards also proved largely unfruitful. Particularly notable, in anticipating the pattern of failure of future agreements, was the government's unilateral abrogation—under pressure from its Sinhala-Buddhist constituency—of the Bandaranaike-Chelvanayakam Pact of 1958, signed between the prime minister and the leader of the Federal Party,[20] which would have provided for bilingualism and some territorial

[15] Tambiah (n 6) 102–13.

[16] Farzana Haniffa, "Conflicted Solidarities? Muslims and the Constitution-making Process of 1970-72" in Asanga Welikala (ed.), *The Sri Lankan Republic at 40: Reflections on Constitutional History, Theory and Practice* (Centre for Policy Alternatives 2012) 228–38; Zarin Ahmad, "Contours of Muslim Nationalism in Sri Lanka" (2012) 3 (2) South Asian History and Culture 269, 269.

[17] Rohan Edrisinha, Mario Gomez, VT Thamilmaran, and Asanga Welikala (eds), *Power-Sharing in Sri Lanka: Constitutional and Political Documents, 1926–2008* (Centre for Policy Alternatives 2008) ch. 15.

[18] A Jeyaratnam Wilson, *Sri Lankan Tamil Nationalism: Its Origins and Development in the 19th and 20th Centuries* (Penguin 2000) ch. 4.

[19] ibid ch. 6.

[20] Edrisinha and others, *Power-Sharing in Sri Lanka* (n 17) ch. 9.

autonomy for the northeast. When the Constituent Assembly of 1970–72 peremptorily rejected the Federal Party's rather conservative scheme for a federal Constitution, militant groups overtook the parliamentary Tamil nationalists. The militants were Tamil youth radicalized by discrimination as well as revolutionary doctrines of the era. They demanded a separate state and advocated armed struggle to achieve it.[21] The humiliation inflicted by the first republican Constitution in 1972 united the parliamentary and militant nationalists in a 1976 convention, which passed the "Vaddukoddai Resolution" calling for a separate, independent state of "Tamil Eelam" for the first time.[22]

A low-intensity insurgency commenced during this period with a proliferation of armed youth groups fighting Sri Lankan armed forces, and, indeed, each other in vying for dominance of Tamil nationalist politics. This transformed into a full-scale civil war between these groups and the Sri Lankan government after the anti-Tamil pogrom of July 1983.[23] Following the killing of an army patrol in the Jaffna peninsula by Tamil terrorists, the Sri Lankan government aided and abetted a riot against Tamil civilians in the south, especially Colombo, with massive loss of life, destruction of property, and displacement.[24] The Indian government was now drawn into the conflict because of widespread support among Tamils in the Indian state of Tamil Nadu for their co-ethnics in Sri Lanka. Indian mediation led to the Indo-Lanka Accord of 1987, by which the Sri Lankan government undertook to establish provincial councils for all nine provinces—though the main objective was the devolution of power to the new North-Eastern Provincial Council (NEPC). These changes were introduced by the Thirteenth Amendment to the 1978 Constitution and other consequential legislation. The settlement included the "merger" of the existing Northern and Eastern Provinces into one administrative unit, so as to encapsulate the region of historical Tamil habitation.[25]

India undertook to disarm the rebels and ensure their compliance with the settlement. It succeeded except for the LTTE, which rejected the Accord and began a military campaign against the Indian Peace Keeping Force (IPKF) of approximately 100,000 troops at peak. The militant groups who had accepted the Accord and assumed control of the NEPC soon encountered an uncooperative central government that obstructed meaningful implementation of devolution. Frustrated, the NEPC attempted a unilateral declaration of independence in 1991. The central government responded by dissolving the NEPC and suspending devolution in the province. After the departure of the IPKF, hostilities between the LTTE and the government continued, interspersed with brief ceasefires and half-hearted attempts at negotiation.[26]

This period also saw the LTTE's consolidation of its hold on Tamil politics, which would end only with its battlefield defeat in 2009. The LTTE proved ruthless in its use of terror against opponents. Its leader Velupillai Prabhakaran's single-minded pursuit of an independent Tamil Eelam became invested with a sense of nationalist purity and authenticity; other militant groups and political parties were seen as

[21] Wilson (n 18) ch. 7.

[22] Edrisinha and others, *Power-Sharing in Sri Lanka* (n 17) ch. 12.

[23] Ketheshwaran Loganathan, *Sri Lanka: Lost Opportunities: Past Attempts at Resolving Ethnic Conflict* (Centre for Policy Research and Analysis 1996) ch. 4.

[24] While no wholly reliable figures exist, a widely cited estimate is that some 150,000 Tamils were displaced as a result of the pogrom, and well over 1,000 and up to 3,000 killed. See Nancy Murray, "The State against the Tamils" (1984) 26 (1) Race & Class 97, 106.

[25] Loganathan (n 23) ch. 5; Edrisinha and others, *Power-Sharing in Sri Lanka* (n 17) chs 16–17.

[26] Loganathan (n 23) ch. 5.

too willing to cut deals, or in hock with Indian interests if not with the Sri Lankan state. Prabhakaran's campaign of unrestrained violence against more moderate Tamil politicians, intellectuals, and other militant groups bore fruit in 2001, when just ahead of the parliamentary elections of that year, nearly all the remaining mainstream politicians and ex-militants, including the venerable Federal Party, formed the Tamil National Alliance (TNA). While ostensibly an attempt to ensure a single Tamil voice in future negotiations, it was in reality the subordinate electoral arm of the LTTE, founded on the principle that the LTTE was the "sole and authentic" representative of the Tamil people. It is testament to how far the Sri Lankan state had radically alienated the Tamil people that such a violently anti-pluralistic and autocratic force as the LTTE was able to capture, barring a few courageous individuals, the imagination of an entire community as the only plausible agent of its liberation from oppression.[27] Yet it is also true that the LTTE's dominance was as much due to its unparalleled capacity to crush dissenting voices within the Tamil community.

In 1994, the People's Alliance (PA) government assumed power with a commitment to a negotiated settlement and a broadly liberal attitude to devolution and power-sharing. Its preliminary talks with the LTTE however soon collapsed, whereupon the PA adopted its "War for Peace" policy. This involved waging war on the LTTE while inviting all other parties to deliberate on constitutional reforms within a parliamentary select committee, which included the Federal Party and other Tamil parliamentary parties. The government published a series of proposals in 1995, 1996, 1997, and, in 2000, it presented a draft Constitution Bill to Parliament.[28] None of the PA proposals won sufficient support in Parliament to be enacted. Sinhala-Buddhist nationalists were in uproar about the government's conciliatory approach, and the war with the LTTE showed no signs of a rapid conclusion. Following a series of military setbacks for the government, including debilitating terrorist attacks in the south, the parliamentary election in December 2001 was won by the opposition United National Front (UNF) on a clear promise to call a ceasefire and enter into negotiations with the LTTE. In the northeast, the newly formed TNA swept all the seats, reflecting its role in bringing all major Tamil groups and parties together as well as the LTTE's control of large parts of the area.

The election resulted in control of Parliament and the presidency being divided between the two main parties, which was the first occurrence of "cohabitation" within the semi-presidential Constitution adopted in 1978. The independently elected executive president from the PA, Chandrika Kumaratunga, was compelled to appoint a prime minister, Ranil Wickremesinghe, and a cabinet from the new UNF parliamentary majority. The "dual-mandate" of cohabitation seemed promising at first. While there was little disagreement between Kumaratunga and Wickremesinghe on the fundamentals of a political solution—both were committed to some form of federal-type devolution—the question was whether they could transcend the highly competitive nature of Sri Lankan party politics, build a southern consensus in negotiating with the LTTE, and share credit in achievements. It was in this context of cohabitation in the south, as well as the LTTE's strong military position and substantial control of territory in the north and east, that the Norwegian government was invited to facilitate a ceasefire with a

[27] See also Joanne Richards, "An Institutional History of the Liberation Tigers of Tamil Eelam (LTTE)" (2014) The Centre on Conflict, Development and Peacebuilding Working Paper No10 <http://repository.graduateinstitute.ch/record/292651/files/CCDP-Working-Paper-10-LTTE-1.pdf >.

[28] Edrisinha and others, *Power-Sharing in Sri Lanka* (n 17) chs 21–6; Sunil Bastian (ed.), *Sri Lanka: The Devolution Debate* (5th edn, International Centre for Ethnic Studies 2006).

view to commencing negotiations. Prior to discussing this peace process, is necessary to examine the territorial dimension of the Sri Lankan conflict more closely.

Among all the claims associated with the Tamil challenge, none has caused greater controversy or resistance than the claim to a "Tamil traditional homeland" in the north-east of the island. Opponents dispute both the historical rationale and the purported physical boundaries, and they include not only Sinhala-Buddhist nationalists but also those who fear such an ethnic enclave would pose an anti-modern threat to building a civic culture for the Sri Lankan nation-state.[29]

Intertwined with the territorial claim is a disputatious debate about the demography of the north and especially the east. The Federal Party's original political program opposed Sinhalese "colonization" of the east through state-aided programs of agricultural resettlement because it altered the area's demographic balance. Tamil nationalists have seen colonization as insidious demographic engineering designed to consolidate Sinhala-Buddhist hegemony over the whole island and render Tamils a minority even in Tamil areas. Considerable credence can be attached to this especially once colonization became a Sinhala-Buddhist nationalist ideological issue after the watershed election of 1956. However, earlier colonization policy by the British colonial administration, and later by Ceylonese politicians and civil servants under the Donoughmore dispensation,[30] were technocratic, not ideological, attempts to develop sparsely populated agricultural lands by resettling Sinhala peasants in them, thus easing pressure on agricultural land in the island's southwest and center.[31]

Thus, those who stress the economic imperatives of resettlement as the basis of the colonization policy, see the homeland argument as historically spurious Tamil nationalist myth-making.[32] There are two facets to how the Tamil nationalist territorial claim was articulated (and contested) in the post-independence period that require consideration: namely, what Tamil nationalists have meant by the concept of a "Tamil traditional homeland," and what they have seen as its physical boundaries.

Hellmann-Rajayanagam, who notes that the term "homeland" is "used loosely and is nowhere defined in the literature,"[33] dates its occurrence in English language discourse in Ceylon to legislative debates and memoranda of the 1930s. She suggests that it is an English "translation of a term widely used in the Tamil writings" which literally means "Regions where Tamil-speaking people have traditionally (or from generation to generation) lived."[34] From the evidence she and others have offered, it seems that the idea of a traditional homeland, even though its exact boundaries were amorphous, was a politically resonant and commonly accepted notion among Tamils. Critically, it preceded the Federal Party's presentation of Tamil politico-constitutional claims in terms of a distinct nation from 1949 onward.[35]

[29] HL de Silva, *Sri Lanka: A Nation in Conflict: Threats to Sovereignty, Territorial Integrity, Democratic Governance and Peace* (Visidunu Prakashakayo 2008); Dayan Jayatilleka, *Long War, Cold Peace: Sri Lanka's North-South Crisis* (rev. edn, Vijitha Yapa 2014).

[30] Michael Roberts, "Narrating Tamil Nationalism: Subjectivities and Issues" (2004) 17 (1) South Asia: Journal of South Asian Studies 87, 106–8; Dagmar Hellmann-Rajanayagam, "The Concept of a 'Tamil Homeland' in Sri Lanka – Its Meaning and Development" (1990) 13 (2) South Asia 79, 95.

[31] Hellmann-Rajanayagam (n 30) 93–5, 103–6.

[32] KM de Silva *The "Traditional Homelands" of the Tamils: Separatist Ideology in Sri Lanka: A Historical Appraisal* (3rd rev. edn, International Centre for Ethnic Studies 2013); Gerald H Peiris, "An Appraisal of the Concept of a Traditional Homeland in Sri Lanka" (1991) 9 (1) Ethnic Studies Report 13.

[33] Hellmann-Rajanayagam (n 30) 81. [34] ibid 82.

[35] Arular R Arudpragasam, *The Traditional Homeland of the Tamils* (Kanal Publications 1996).

Moreover, Sinhalese opposition to a Tamil traditional homeland appears to have intensified only once it was asserted as part of a Tamil *national* claim. As Hellmann-Rajanayagam has argued, in the debates over territorial and communal representation in the early twentieth century, the notion that the north and east were not merely Tamil-speaking majority areas, but were "Tamil *homelands*," seems to have been assumed by Tamils and Sinhalese alike. Indeed, as she further argues, in the run-up to independence, Sinhalese leaders met Tamil demands for special constitutional protections against Sinhalese dominance with the argument that Tamils would obtain sufficient territorial representation under democracy because of their preponderance in the northeast.[36] During the period between the late 1930s and independence in 1948, the dominant Tamil demand was for a proto-consociational scheme of representation at the center known as "50-50", which envisaged, not federalism as after the Federal Party's emergence in 1949, but legislative representation on the basis of 50 percent of seats for the Sinhalese and 50 percent for the minorities. The scheme's rationale was to offset the dominance of the Sinhalese and guarantee minority representation, but it was rejected by the Soulbury Commission which recommended the independence Constitution.[37]

The absence of precisely demarcated boundaries to the homeland has created difficulties for the Tamil territorial claim as a legal and constitutional proposition. This is evidenced in the shifting nature of the territorial claim. The Federal Party's founding manifesto in 1949 merely stated, "The Eelam Tamils are a nation of their own, they have a homeland of their own."[38] Resolution No. 1 at its First National Convention in 1951 asserted Tamils' "territorial habitation of definite areas which constitute over one-third of this Island," but nevertheless called for "a plebiscite to determine the boundaries of the linguistic states" of the future federation.[39] It was more specific in the Memorandum and Model Constitution submitted to the Constituent Assembly in 1971, which set out a federal scheme for the future republican Constitution. This proposed that, "The Northern Province and the Trincomalee and Batticaloa Districts of the Eastern Province will form one Unit. This will be a Tamil majority State. The Amparai District [in the southwest end of the Eastern Province] will form a Muslim majority State."[40] In the Vaddukoddai Resolution of 1976, which registered Tamil nationalism's paradigm shift from federalism to secessionism, the Tamil United Liberation Front (TULF) identified the Northern and Eastern Provinces as the territory of the future state of Tamil Eelam. Since then, Tamil nationalists have generally put forward the Northern and Eastern Provinces as the territorial extent of the Tamil homeland, although more maximalist claims have been made.[41]

While it is generally conceded by all except the most recalcitrant Sinhala-Buddhist nationalists that the Jaffna Peninsula and most of the Northern Province are areas of historic Tamil habitation, the Tamil claim to historic habitation in the rest of the area comprising the Northern and Eastern Provinces has been constantly challenged.[42] These territorial disputes have concentrated on the areas to the interior of the Eastern littoral and the interior areas between the North-Central Province and the southern end of the Northern Province. This vast area, the whole of which was once known as

[36] Hellmann-Rajanayagam (n 30) 83; see also Sir Ivor Jennings, *The Constitution of Ceylon* (3rd edn, Oxford University Press 1953) 6–8.

[37] Edrisinha and others, *Power-Sharing in Sri Lanka* (n 17) ch. 6.

[38] Hellmann-Rajanayagam (n 30) 82.

[39] Edrisinha and others, *Power-Sharing in Sri Lanka* (n 17) 212.

[40] ibid 140.

[41] Peiris (n 32) 14; Edrisinha and others, *Power-Sharing in Sri Lanka* (n 17) chs 16–17, ch. 27.

[42] Hellmann-Rajanayagam (n 30) 82.

the Vanni, was until the 1930s universally regarded as a "wild country . . . covered in jungle, full of wild animals . . . and malaria-infested swamps."[43] Notwithstanding this, it was the transition from communal to territorial representation in the late colonial period that made the Tamils realize that, rather than being one of the two founding nations in the island as they had hitherto regarded themselves, they too were now a minority in a Sinhala-majority polity. From the Colebrooke-Cameron reforms of 1829–33 to the Donoughmore Constitution of 1931, the model of (limited) native representation in the colonial state was on a communal basis. The various reforms in-between adjusted the number of representatives allocated to the Sinhalese, Tamils, Moors, and Burghers in legislative and executive councils. However, in 1931 the Donoughmore Constitution introduced universal franchise, bringing with it the radical innovation of territorial democracy. This new model of territorial democracy—idealistically but perhaps naively—sought to encourage Ceylon's people to shed their communal identities and build a civic "Ceylonese" identity in moving toward fully responsible government.[44]

The expectation that universal franchise would promote modern political parties and reframe political competition along ideological or policy programmatic lines turned out to be misplaced. Instead, political mobilization not only continued along communal lines but also gave Sinhalese politicians the awareness that they were now transformed into a governing class with a perpetual majority. This strengthened the Tamils' resolve to protect their identity and preserve its homeland. Thus, even before peasant colonization in the northeast became invested with a Sinhala-Buddhist ideological mission to negate Tamil claims to the territory, Tamils strongly resisted it. This is why the spatial possession of a homeland assumed such fundamental significance to the Tamil identity and sense of dignity, even if large parts of the area claimed as a homeland were sparsely populated and undeveloped.[45]

The Period of Constitutional Engagement

By the time we come to the specific period of constitutional engagement on the ethno-territorial question that is the focus of this chapter, Sri Lanka's conflict had reached a "mutually hurting stalemate"[46] with neither side in the armed conflict able to deliver a knockout blow (although in retrospect, not so mutually hurting as to convince either side that war was no more an option).[47] The exploration of a third-party facilitator had begun much earlier than the election of the UNF-led cohabitation government in December 2001, when President Kumaratunga's government approached the Norwegian government in 1997.[48] Norway was chosen as a small power with no strategic interests in the region, its long record of peace diplomacy, and because it was

[43] ibid 93, 95; Roberts "Narrating Tamil Nationalism" (n 30) 102–8.

[44] Edrisinha and others, *Power-Sharing in Sri Lanka* (n 17) ch. 2.

[45] Hellmann-Rajanayagam (n 30) 97.

[46] I William Zartman, "Ripeness: The Hurting Stalemate and Beyond" in Paul C Stern and Daniel Druckman (eds), *International Conflict Resolution after the Cold War* (The National Academies Press 2000) ch. 6.

[47] Gunnar Sørbø and others, *Pawns of Peace: Evaluation of Norwegian Peace Efforts in Sri Lanka, 1997–2009* (Evaluation Department Norad 2011).

[48] Jayadeva Uyangoda, "Government-LTTE Negotiation Attempt of 2000 through Norwegian Facilitation: Context, Complexities and Lessons" in Kumar Rupesinghe (ed.), *Negotiating Peace in Sri Lanka: Efforts, Failures and Lessons*, vol. 1 (2nd edn, Foundation for Co-Existence 2006) ch. 12.

acceptable to both the government and the LTTE as well as India.[49] The main objective in the early stages appears to have been ceasing hostilities and beginning a process of talks, with no clear commitment on either side to a "constitutional" engagement.

The Norwegian-facilitated peace process between the UNF government and the LTTE began with the Ceasefire Agreement (CFA), signed between the two parties on February 22, 2002. It formally ended on January 16, 2008, but it had effectively been dead months if not years before that.[50] In fact, there had been no meaningful engagement between the two parties after 2005, when the attempt to jointly deal with the aftermath of the Asian tsunami proved unsuccessful. Fighting had progressively escalated from early 2006 onward, so much so that from May 2007 onward the Sri Lanka Monitoring Mission (SLMM), set up under the CFA, ceased making determinations over the increasingly widespread violations of the CFA by both parties.

Two key factors are generally adduced to explain why the two parties agreed to a ceasefire.[51] For the government, it had become clear that President Kumaratunga's "War for Peace" strategy had failed to make the expected military gains let alone defeat the LTTE. The LTTE had a series of battleground gains, which secured control over substantial territory and cut off the Sri Lankan forces' supply lines to the north, and its terrorist attacks in the south, notably on the country's only international airport in July 2001, proved devastating. In 2001, the economy went into contraction (1.4 percent negative growth) for the first time since independence and the Central Bank warned that "the country cannot continue to bear the cost of prolonged war, and hence, a speedy resolution of the conflict is essential."[52] Morale of the armed forces was low, and the country at large was war weary. These factors led to Wickremesinghe's victory in the December 2001 election on the promise to enter into a ceasefire with the LTTE, to commence negotiations on a political settlement, and to rebuild the economy.

The LTTE for its part was pushed toward a ceasefire by domestic and international factors. By December 2001, it had made sufficient territorial and military gains to feel that it had strategic parity with the government, and could enter a process of negotiations from a position of strength. But it was also coming under considerable international pressure in the post-9/11 environment against terrorism, with several proscriptions against it in major countries and other international measures aimed at curtailing its funding and arms procurement networks. There was now little tolerance and no legitimacy accorded to those who practiced terrorism.[53]

When the CFA was signed, President Kumaratunga protested vehemently that she had been not been consulted. While it was perhaps understandable that the UNF government, desirous of rapid progress in the aftermath of the election, had excluded her, this was an ominous portent of how the government's two power centers would be unable to work together on the peace process in the future. The first round of talks took place in September 2002 in Thailand, with five further rounds at regular intervals until the last in March 2003 in Japan. The third round, in December 2002 in Oslo, is especially significant for the present discussion.

[49] Kumar Rupesinghe, "Interview with Erik Solheim: Minister of International Development" in Kumar Rupesinghe (ed.), *Negotiating Peace in Sri Lanka: Efforts, Failures and Lessons*, vol. 2 (Foundation for Co-Existence 2006) ch. 13; see also Mark Salter, *To End a Civil War: Norway's Peace Engagement with Sri Lanka* (Hurst & Co 2015).

[50] International Crisis Group, "Sri Lanka: The Failure of the Peace Process" (Asia Report No. 124, International Crisis Group November 28, 2006).

[51] Charan Rainford and Ambika Satkunanathan, *Mistaking Politics for Governance: The Politics of Interim Arrangements in Sri Lanka 2002–2005* (International Centre for Ethnic Studies 2009) 18–20.

[52] As cited in ibid 18.

[53] ibid 20.

As direct engagement got underway, the LTTE was keen to address urgent issues directly impacting on the daily lives of people of the northeast initially, for which it demanded a formalized interim administration, and only then deal with matters concerning constitutional change. The government and the international community, while initially sympathetic to this, would perhaps have preferred to work on substantive matters much earlier. But in hoping to keep the LTTE on-board, the issue of an interim administrative structure for the northeast under LTTE control came to dominate the agenda. While a Joint Task Force was mooted in the first round, it was clear this would possibly be open to legal challenges as well as opposition from a hostile president; consequently, in the second round in October 2002, more informal joint committees were established. These were: the Subcommittee on Immediate Humanitarian and Rehabilitation Needs (SIHRN), the Subcommittee on De-escalation and Normalisation, and the Subcommittee on Political Matters, which was chaired by the heads of the two delegations, Professor G.L. Peiris MP for the government, and Anton Balasingham, the LTTE's senior theoretician.[54]

As noted, the talks were between the government of Sri Lanka (or more precisely, its UNF component) and the LTTE, which claimed to be the sole authentic representative of the Tamil people. While the Muslims would ideally have liked separate representation, the LTTE would not agree. The leader of the Sri Lanka Muslim Congress (SLMC), which was part of the UNF, served in the government delegation.

The most significant development in these talks for the purposes of the present discussion was the agreement reached on December 5, 2002 in Oslo with regard to the outlines of a constitutional settlement. This was to form the basis for further discussions within the Subcommittee on Political Matters. The official communiqué issued by the Norwegian government recorded the agreement as follows:

> The parties agreed on a working outline defining the objective as well as a number of substantive political issues for negotiation . . . Responding to a proposal by the leadership of the LTTE, the parties agreed to explore a solution founded on the principle of internal self-determination in areas of historical habitation of the Tamil-speaking peoples, based on a federal structure within a united Sri Lanka. The parties acknowledged that the solution has to be acceptable to all communities . . . Guided by this objective, the parties agreed to initiate discussions on substantive political issues such as, but not limited to: Power-sharing between the centre and the region, as well as within the centre; Geographical region; Human Rights protection; Political and administrative mechanisms; Public finance; Law and order.[55]

While lacking in detail and precision, this brief statement was, at this stage, both appropriate and realistic in outlining only broad principles. But it did reflect symbolically some significant concessions from both sides. In ethnonational conflicts, symbols are often as salient as policies and institutions; seemingly positive constitutional concepts like "federalism" or "unitary state" or "self-determination" may be highly charged ethnonational symbols for both sides. Thus, the use of such terms often denotes a kinesic significance outside any more rationalist frame of analysis. Nevertheless, certain specific issues in the final sentence, especially "geographical region," related to long-standing and central issues in the conflict, but because the discussions on these issues never progressed into any detailed constitutional negotiations, it is impossible to determine what the Oslo principles, subject to further, difficult negotiation, might have produced as a concrete institutional design.

[54] ibid 23–5.

[55] Edrisinha and others, *Power-Sharing in Sri Lanka* (n 17) ch. 27.

That said, a joint statement of intent seemed to portend a promising start to future constitutional negotiations. The two striking concessions were: first, the LTTE's agreeing to explore a solution based on a united Sri Lankan state, breaking from their commitment to a separate state; and secondly, the Sri Lankan government agreeing to contemplate federalism despite being constitutionally wedded to a unitary state. The federal but single Sri Lankan state would also be asymmetric, in recognizing the right to "internal self-determination" of Tamil-speaking peoples in their areas of historical habitation—a right not recognized for any other province—even though secession was implicitly ruled out by limiting this right to its internal aspect. Recognition that the territorial unit in the northeast was based on a Tamil right to internal self-determination may well have translated into greater powers for it than the other provinces, resulting in an asymmetrical federation. But as noted, no further discussion on these matters took place.

While avoiding inflammatory rhetoric, the communiqué nonetheless addressed the spirit of Tamil claims to autonomy, recognition, and representation. On the other hand, the avoidance of terms like "Tamil nation" and "traditional homeland," the principle that any solution must be acceptable to all communities, and the putative safeguard against secession and the disintegration of the state were all meant to assuage Sinhala and Muslim fears. This was therefore a distillation of the essence of a constitutional settlement that could meet the competing ethnic demands within an institutional balance that took account of the requirements of both unity and diversity.[56]

The strength of the Oslo statement arguably was that it provided a good basis, however skeletal, for the Subcommittee on Political Matters to build upon by fleshing out the principles and exploring institutional options for a new Constitution. Optimism was also stimulated by the position of the two co-chairs, Peiris and Balasingham, as moderates within their respective parties who seemed to have a reasonable working relationship. In the event, however, this subcommittee was never properly constituted and never met, so the hopes generated by Oslo were soon scattered.[57] In the single meeting Peiris and Balasingham held after Oslo, they decided that the subcommittee would commence discussion on fiscal and financial issues first. It is unclear how this decision was reached, and it would have been difficult to discuss such issues without knowing the overall federal scheme, including the allocation of competences. It seems likely that they regarded fiscal matters as technical and less politically charged than, for example, the territorial re-demarcation of the northeast, human rights, or police powers.

The government was attacked by Sinhala nationalists in the south for agreeing to federalism and self-determination, which they saw as synonymous with separatist demands. The LTTE too began to backtrack on the Oslo principles almost immediately, emphasizing that the intention was merely to "explore" the matters mentioned in the statement, and that the parties had not reached a final agreement. It stated that if the government did not or could not deliver the promised autonomy in an acceptable manner, then Tamils would reserve their right to external self-determination. It has sometimes been speculated that Balasingham exceeded his brief in agreeing to federalism, to which Prabhakaran would never agree, which would explain the LTTE's backsliding on Oslo immediately after they agreed to it. While certainly a likely

[56] Rohan Edrisinha and Asanga Welikala, "The Interim Self Governing Authority Proposals: A Federalist Critique" in Rohan Edrisinha and Asanga Welikala (eds), *Essays on Federalism in Sri Lanka* (Centre for Policy Alternatives 2008) ch. 12.

[57] ibid 78.

scenario, there is no evidence with which to prove this. What is clearer, however, is that by this time the LTTE was becoming concerned that it was being led into a "peace trap" by the Sri Lankan government and international community, whereby it would be locked into a constitutional process which, while offering some amorphous prospect of autonomy, would progressively limit its political options, especially with regard to secession. Moreover, given the precarious power balance of cohabitation within the Sri Lankan government, it was also (quite justifiably) skeptical about the UNF government's capacity to deliver the radical constitutional changes promised. Rather than building upon the positive gains of Oslo, therefore, both parties increasingly put constitutional issues aside, while the lack of progress on normalization and reconstruction took center-stage.

By mid-2003, the LTTE withdrew from the talks claiming that the internationalization of the peace process favored only the Sri Lankan government, with no concomitant benefits of international legitimacy for itself. It insisted again that a suitable interim administration for the northeast under its sole control be set up, so that it could deliver reconstruction and have an institutional basis as the representative of the Tamil people. The government agreed in principle and during mid-2003 made three different proposals for an interim administration, all of which the LTTE rejected. The government's proposals reflected both legal constraints of the Constitution and the severe opposition in the south to an interim administration for the LTTE, but they went to the utmost limit in trying to accommodate the latter's demands.[58] After the last of these was rejected, the government invited the LTTE to propose its own framework, and the LTTE made its proposals for an Interim Self-Governing Authority (ISGA) in November 2003. The ISGA, which was to be in sole control of the LTTE, was to be vested with "plenary powers" to administer the northeast as if it were a constitutionally established government.[59]

While ostensibly a proposal for an interim administration, it was clear that the ISGA was much more. It was an attempt not only to institutionalize the political and military power in LTTE-controlled areas, but also to reinforce the LTTE's dominance over both government and civil society in those areas. In centralizing authority in the unelected LTTE, the proposal paradoxically imitated the centralizing pathology of the Sri Lankan state, and worse, given the LTTE's record of violent intolerance of dissent and political pluralism within the Tamil community, the ISGA proposal caused serious concern from the perspective of democracy and human rights. It effectively sought to reframe negotiations on a final constitutional settlement from the federalization contemplated at Oslo to more of a confederal model.[60] In short, it was clear to its many critics that the LTTE had not abandoned its goal of a separate state and that anything less would merely be treated as a stepping-stone to that goal at some future point. This serious doubt regarding the LTTE's commitment to the federalist Oslo principles fatally undermined advocates of federalism and power-sharing in the south. Both, legitimate concerns and political opportunism, therefore ensured a storm of protest in the south when the LTTE's proposal was published, and President Kumaratunga used the occasion to take over three key ministries including defense by dismissing their UNF ministers without consulting Prime Minister Wickremesinghe.

Attempts to resolve or mitigate the crisis within the government proved unsuccessful. The president dissolved Parliament in January for fresh elections in April 2004,

[58] Rainford and Satkunanathan (n 51) 87–90. [59] ibid 91–117.

[60] A "coming together" as opposed to a "holding together" dynamic, A Stepan, *Arguing Comparative Politics* (Oxford University Press 2001) ch. 15.

at which the UNF was defeated. For this election, President Kumaratunga created an electoral alliance, the United Peoples Freedom Front (UPFA), made up of southern parties opposed to the peace process and federal-type power-sharing, even though her views about both were more in line with her vanquished rival Wickremesinghe. Ironically, she tried to resurrect the peace process after the election, but her insistence that any interim administration must be part of a final constitutional settlement found no favor with the LTTE, for whom an interim administration was a condition precedent to negotiations on a final settlement. In this way, opposition from both the LTTE and the president's new parliamentary allies prevented any resumption of the peace process.

During this period of fruitless engagement between the new government and the LTTE, the Asian tsunami struck Sri Lanka on Boxing Day 2004, with some of the worst devastation occurring along the northeastern coastline. This created an opportunity for the government and LTTE to jointly respond to the disaster, and perhaps build on that cooperation to restart some form of constitutional negotiations. Given the mutual recognition of the need for joint action, as well as international pressure for some shared institutional basis for the disbursement of relief funds, the two parties fairly expeditiously agreed an institutional structure called the Post-Tsunami Operational Management Structure (P-TOMS).[61] However, the Janatha Vimukthi Peramuna (JVP), the hard-line party of Sinhala nationalists with whom President Kumaratunga had gone into coalition before the 2004 general election, challenged the constitutionality of this. In a highly controversial judgment in July 2005, the Supreme Court found that some aspects of the P-TOMS arrangement violated the Constitution, in particular that its spending powers would infringe Parliament's exclusive control over public finance.[62] That signaled the end of the P-TOMS, as well as any prospect of further cooperation between the two parties. Moreover, the LTTE was widely suspected in August 2005 of assassinating Kumaratunga's widely respected Foreign Minister Lakshman Kadirgamar, an ethnic Tamil, and the government reintroduced the proscription on the LTTE.[63]

President Kumaratunga's two terms in office came to an end in 2005, and in the ensuing presidential election, her prime minister and successor Mahinda Rajapaksa narrowly defeated Ranil Wickremesinghe by 50.29 percent to 48.43 percent of the vote.[64] While Rajapaksa initially adopted a conciliatory stance with regard to the LTTE and the peace process, his ideological orientation was clearly Sinhala-Buddhist nationalist and committed to the unitary state.[65] Especially after the Kadirgamar assassination, he also tapped into hardening attitudes in the south toward the LTTE, with the Wickremesinghe government now widely seen as having appeased a terrorist organization that was irredeemably separatist. Controversially, the LTTE had enforced a boycott of the presidential election in the areas under its control and this decisively benefitted

[61] ibid 48–54.

[62] Edrisinha and others, *Power-Sharing in Sri Lanka* (n 17) 724; *Wimal Weerawansa and Others v. The Attorney General and the Minister for Relief and Rehabilitation* (2005) SCFR App Nos 228/05, 229/05 & 230/05, SCM 15.07.2005.

[63] Sinha Ratnatunga, "Lakshman Kadirgamar: The Lawyer Turned Politician" in Adam Roberts (ed.), *Democracy, Sovereignty and Terror: Lakshman Kadirgamar on the Foundations of International Order* (IB Tauris 2012) ch. 3, 57.

[64] Department of Elections, Government of Sri Lanka, "Results of the Presidential Election 2005" <www.slelections.gov.lk/web/images/pdf/past-presidential-election-results/result-of-presidential-election-2005(summary).pdf> accessed April 4, 2017.

[65] International Crisis Group (n 50).

Rajapaksa in the presidential election, given that this Tamil vote would have gone to the more conciliatory Wickremesinghe otherwise. Had Wickremesinghe won, the subsequent course of history could have been dramatically different. Unsubstantiated allegations suggest there may have been some secret understanding on the boycott between Rajapaksa and the LTTE, but it seems clear that the LTTE had by 2005 concluded that a resumed peace process with Wickremesinghe in full control of the government and enjoying considerable international standing, especially in the west, would not be in its interests. It had consolidated its military strength and territorial presence during the previous few years of the ceasefire, and seems to have calculated that it could hold its own against a hostile government led by Rajapaksa.

The parties did meet for talks in 2006, but neither was interested in negotiations and the CFA was effectively dead with daily violations and significant military clashes between the two sides. The Supreme Court made its own unhelpful contribution by declaring unlawful the merger of the Northern and Eastern Provinces effected under the terms of the Indo-Lanka Accord, on an application made by members of the JVP.[66] Although the NEPC had not been operational since 1991, it was highly significant that the new Rajapaksa regime was increasingly willing to undo past commitments with regard to the Tamil territorial claim. From mid-2006 onward, the military conflict escalated, and by 2007, it was unambiguously a situation of war, with the government clearing the Eastern Province of the LTTE. The government formally abrogated the CFA in January 2008 and the final phase of the Sri Lankan war commenced in the north, to conclude in May 2009 with the total defeat of the LTTE amid allegations of serious violations of international human rights and humanitarian law from both sides.

The Outcomes of the Process

The Norwegian-facilitated peace process failed in its central purpose: to find a constitutional settlement for Sri Lanka's ethno-territorial cleavage. This legitimized critics of the peace process and a negotiated settlement, and enthroned a government hostile to the accommodation of Tamil grievances. President Rajapaksa's war victory against the LTTE won him political capital—beyond what any other post-independence Sri Lankan leader had had—with which he could have pursued reconciliation and reforms. But any expectation of Rajapaksa's capacity for magnanimity and statesmanship was soon extinguished. Instead, a crude form of unadulterated Sinhala-Buddhist triumphalism became the leitmotif of the post-war state. Rather than offering devolution and democracy, in September 2010, the regime enacted the Eighteenth Amendment to the Constitution,[67] which abolished the presidential two-term limit, and significantly weakened other constitutional restraints on presidential power. This form of "abusive constitutionalism"[68] was further extended with the impeachment of the Chief Justice in 2013 when the Supreme Court tried to ensure the procedural validity of government legislation.[69]

[66] Edrisinha and others, *Power-Sharing in Sri Lanka* (n 17) ch. 35.

[67] Rohan Edrisinha and Aruni Jayakody (eds), *The Eighteenth Amendment to the Constitution: Substance and Process* (Centre for Policy Alternatives 2011).

[68] David Landau, "Abusive Constitutionalism" (2013) 47 University of California Davis Law Review 189.

[69] Niran Anketell and Asanga Welikala, "A Systemic Crisis in Context: The Impeachment of the Chief Justice, the Independence of the Judiciary, and the Rule of Law in Sri Lanka" (Centre for Policy Alternatives 2013) <www.cpalanka.org/the-impeachment-of-the-chief-justice-the-independence-of-the-judiciary-and-the-rule-of-law-in-sri-lanka/> accessed April 4, 2017.

The country's constitutional framework was thus altered to reflect the political dominance of the Rajapaksa regime: propounding a highly chauvinist reinterpretation of Sinhala-Buddhist nationalism; rampantly using patronage, populism, and corruption as means of mobilizing its political majority; and deploying legal authoritarianism and extra-legal violence to ensure control. The military victory against the LTTE was repetitively portrayed as the triumph of the Sinhala-Buddhist owners of the state against the impertinent Tamil minority. The use of ancient Sinhala-Buddhist chronicles, the inflammatory invocation of their myths and symbols, and their hegemonic tropes of state, territory, race and religion, became the dominant political and cultural discourse of the south, propagated not merely by the state but also by a triumphalist media and intelligentsia. Like the heroic warrior-kings of folklore, Rajapaksa had reunified the island and restored the primacy of the Sinhala-Buddhist nation, overcoming the depredations of a powerful Tamil rebellion.[70]

Such regimes find validation and electoral sustenance by invoking a permanent enemy, so in the absence of the LTTE, not only Tamils but also the Muslim minority became demonized "others" within, while the UN and international community more broadly were demonized for insisting on accountability for alleged atrocity crimes of the Rajapaksa regime. Useful and moderate policy recommendations made by bodies appointed by Rajapaksa himself, such as the All Party Representative Committee (APRC)[71] on devolution reforms, and the Lessons Learnt and Reconciliation Commission (LLRC) on reconciliation policies, were ignored. At the height of the Rajapaksa administration's popularity, the new control regime seemed capable of permanently destroying Sri Lanka's—brittle but long-held—democratic traditions, and altering forever the nature of the Sri Lankan state itself. The pervasive undermining of the rule of law endangered the state's institutional capacity to check the regime's excesses, including the unprecedented nepotism and kleptocratic corruption. However, these excesses and especially the extravagant corruption in turn ensured a major decline in its popularity within its own core constituency among the Sinhalese, so that Rajapaksa was defeated in the presidential election of January 2015 by the common opposition promising major constitutional and governance reforms.

While the new government of President Maithripala Sirisena is markedly more moderate and conciliatory, the parties behind his victory were careful to avoid any reference to Tamil and other minority demands in building its coalition of political and civic forces against Rajapaksa, focussing initially instead on presidential and governance reforms. The new government's first reform act, the Nineteenth Amendment to the Constitution passed in May 2015, focussed entirely on reducing and restructuring presidential powers.[72] While the TNA and other minority parties supported Sirisena's candidacy unconditionally, given that he could not have prevailed without the support of the minorities, there is an implicit but strong expectation that devolution and power-sharing reforms building upon the existing framework of the Thirteenth Amendment will be addressed in the new Constitution currently being discussed in the Constitutional Assembly process. The manifesto of Prime Minister Wickremesinghe's winning coalition, the United National Front for Good Governance, in the August

[70] Nira Wickramasinghe, "Producing the Present: History as Heritage in Post-War Patriotic Sri Lanka" (Research Paper No. 2, International Centre for Ethnic Studies 2012).

[71] Edrisinha and others, *Power-Sharing in Sri Lanka* (n 17) ch. 37.

[72] Asanga Welikala (ed.), *The Nineteenth Amendment to the Constitution: Content and Context* (Centre for Policy Alternatives 2016) <http://constitutionalreforms.org/the-nineteenth-amendment-to-the-constitution-content-and-context/> last accessed April 4, 2017.

2015 parliamentary election promised "maximum devolution within the unitary state." The shape and form of this, however, is yet to be seen.

Lessons Learned

The Sri Lankan peace process from 2002 to about 2005 is disappointing overall, adding to the countless failed attempts since independence, as well as several post-war attempts after 2009, at constitutionally accommodating the country's ethno-territorial cleavage. However, its unintended outcomes changed the nature and circumstances of the conflict radically. What lessons can be drawn from the peace process that could have relevance in future attempts at constitutional reforms to address the territorial issue?

With the defeat of the LTTE and its ideological commitment to secession, the Tamil political claim to territory has reverted to the more traditional demand for federal-type autonomy, though some Tamil groups still insist that their nationality claim be recognized within a federal framework.[73] But it is now uncontested that any settlement will be within a united Sri Lankan state. This therefore revives the salience of the principles enunciated in Oslo in 2003, and even if provocative terms like "nation," "self-determination," and "federalism" are avoided for practical political reasons, it is clear their conceptual substance will need to inform future constitutional reforms.

The Sinhala-Buddhist chauvinism that opposed the peace process and its federalist direction, and which saw a massive upsurge in the aftermath of the war, may have receded somewhat, but it would be a cardinal error to discount the continuing political force of Sinhala-Buddhist nationalism in the south. Even in the great reformist moment of early 2015, more expansively liberal plans to abolish the executive presidency were thwarted by parties and individuals who wished to retain a strong presidency, which comports with deeper Sinhala-Buddhist nationalist perspectives on the nature and form of the Sri Lankan state.[74]

Two features of Sri Lanka's political culture were highlighted in the failure of the peace process: the hyper-competitive nature of party politics, and a non-transparent, uncommunicative, and unresponsive style of elitist constitutional politics. These both constrict the space for public participation and deliberation in constitutional choices, with fatal consequences for building public consensus around a negotiated constitutional settlement. The good governance reforms mandated in the elections of 2015 enjoyed a very broad public consensus. In bringing the two main parties (and many others) together in a government of national unity, President Sirisena and Prime Minister Wickremesinghe, seemed initially to be addressing the first of these problems. But with dispiriting inevitability, that crucial underpinning of a national consensus on constitutional reform broke down within two years, again almost entirely on the personal dynamics of the relationship between Sirisena and Wickremesinghe, as it was the case between Kumaratunga and Wickremesinghe during the peace process. The Constitutional Assembly process, after a period of engagement with civil society and the public, soon retreated into the traditionally secretive habits of Sri Lankan political

[73] Tamil People's Council, "Report of the Sub-Committee on Finding a Political Solution to the National Question" (Tamil People's Council January 31, 2016) <http://www.tamilguardian.com/files/File/TPC/Highlevelframework.pdf > accessed April 4, 2017.

[74] Asanga Welikala, "Sri Lanka's Long Constitutional Moment" (2015) 104 (5) The Round Table 551.

culture, and its lack of engagement with the public ensured not only public apathy when its interim proposals were published in late 2017, but also that the opponents of reform were left free once again to distort and misrepresent the proposals.

Although Sri Lankan politics reflects a proliferation of both ideology and ethnicity-based parties, governments are always formed with either the United National Party (UNP) or the Sri Lanka Freedom Party (SLFP) as their core and main element. This was the case with Wickremesinghe's UNF and with Kumaratunga's PA and UPFA during the peace process. Despite the substantial underlying consensus between Kumaratunga and Wickremesinghe with regard to the process and the substance of a constitutional settlement, neither was able to resist the pressures and temptations of partisan advantage. In this, they were demonstrating not only the traditionally poor quality of political leadership shown by their predecessors but also their inability to transcend the established trajectory of Sri Lankan party politics, characterized by ethnic outbidding between the two major parties and their allies, and the zero-sum nature of electoral competition. Normal politics might be conducted on such a basis, which may even be seen as healthy democratic competitiveness offering greater choice to the citizen. But in addressing the constitutional challenge of uniting an ethnically and territorially divided polity and providing a stable basis for the conduct of pluralistic constitutional politics, such a political culture has proved disastrous. The failed peace process in this sense is only one instance in a longer history of a systemic failing in the structure of politics.

Once the exclusive preserve of a wealthy and anglicized elite, Sri Lankan politics has hugely democratized since the 1950s in opening the vocation of politics to all classes. This, however, has not meant the democratization and modernization of the culture of politics. The otherwise politically literate population only really plays a part in the democratic process during elections, whereas in-between the institutions of government function without much transparency and public involvement. This culture was replicated in the peace process, and was exacerbated by the LTTE's primitive hostility to political pluralism within its own community. As the ICG piquantly noted, "For the most part, the [. . .] peace process consisted of discussions in hotels abroad between small groups of men from only two of the parties to the conflict."[75]

As noted, this lesson goes unheeded today. Opinion polls over the period of the constitutional reform process since 2015 consistently demonstrate very low levels of public awareness and engagement.[76] As a recent statement of civil society groups observed, the government's failures of political communication, generate "public apathy and allow anti-reform forces to control the political narrative." Noting the regrouping of Rajapaksa-led anti-reform forces, which "would hold back the social, political, economic, and constitutional progress of our country for decades," the statement urged the government to "act fast to regain the initiative . . . and ensure conducive conditions for the constitutional referendum to come."[77]

Even though both the government and the LTTE established official Peace Secretariats, there was no credible program by either party to engage the public, share information, encourage debate and discussion, promote inter-communal dialogue,

[75] International Crisis Group (n 50).

[76] See Centre for Policy Alternatives (CPA) polling data from February and October 2016 and March 2017, CPA, "Constitutional Reforms in Sri Lanka" (*Centre for Policy Alternatives*) <http://constitutionalreforms.org> accessed April 4, 2017.

[77] See Centre for Policy Alternatives, "Rebooting the Constitutional Reform Process: A Civil Society Statement" (*Centre for Policy Alternatives* March 20, 2017) <www.cpalanka.org/rebooting-the-constitutional-reform-process-a-civil-society-statement/> last accessed April 4, 2017.

and in these ways build public support for the process. While civil society organizations attempted such outreach, they were a poor substitute for political parties or government. In this context, gratuitous opportunities were provided for spoilers in southern politics to exploit Sinhala fears through misinformation and distortion, such as the way in which the federal idea was transmogrified into a synonym for appeasement and separatism without any meaningful counter-response from the government. In the north and east, the LTTE merely used the opportunity to eliminate dissent, promote the personality cult of its leader, and orchestrate political events aimed at whipping up an infantile form of nationalist hysteria among Tamils. These approaches to public involvement had the predictable consequences of eroding southern support and hardening northern attitudes, and thereby undercut the crucial element of public support for the process.

A brief word on the international role in the process is also necessary, an aspect that has been extensively discussed elsewhere.[78] The Norwegian government was invited by both parties to serve as facilitators and not mediators, which determined a relatively non-interventionary role from the outset. This meant that beyond facilitation of other international expertise, for example through the Forum of Federations advising the parties on federalism at Oslo, the Norwegians had little substantive input. While this was appropriate for political and constitutional matters due to issues of ownership and credit, some commentators have pointed out that the facilitator's minimalist role especially in the form and content of the CFA weakened the process. In particular, the CFA included neither human rights guarantees nor enforcement mechanisms. This allowed the parties to act with impunity, especially the LTTE, which as reported by the SLMM was responsible for the vast majority of violations of both the CFA and human rights. This validated the spoilers and critics of the peace process, and seriously if not fatally undermined the legitimacy and public confidence in it.[79]

An issue related to the last point was the extreme desire of the drivers of the constitutional reform process since 2015 to be seen to be conducting a nationally owned process, a sensitivity directly derived from the experience of the peace process. However, in this pursuit of national ownership and authenticity, it also meant that the political elite saw a need not merely to do without international expertise but also to exclude local civil society groups from the process. The adverse consequences were not merely for the quality of the technical deliberations and the design choices, but more importantly, in the alienation of the process from the public, and ultimately the erosion of public support and investment in it.

A deeper question in any retrospective review of the peace process is whether it was doomed to failure from the start. The absence of a southern consensus, the uncompromising attitude of Sinhala-Buddhist chauvinism, and not least, the recalcitrant nature of the LTTE and in particular the obdurate commitment of Prabhakaran to both separatism and violence, have all fostered the view in some quarters that, notwithstanding the considerable social and economic costs of military conflict, the adversaries had not yet reached the stage where negotiations were the only political option open to them. There is considerable credence that can be attached to such a view. However, the circumstances of late 2001 in which the peace process began, outlined above, reminds us that there were many incentives for both the state and the LTTE to enter into a facilitated ceasefire and negotiations. Motives might be questioned, but without both the state and LTTE agreeing, the peace process would not even have begun. Once underway, however, its

[78] Goodhand, Spencer, and Korf (n 3); Stokke and Uyangoda (n 3); Sørbø and others (n 47).

[79] On all these issues, see esp. Mark Salter, *To End a Civil War: Norway's Peace Engagement in Sri Lanka* (Hurst & Company 2015).

many weaknesses were unable to withstand the major pressures put on it, and these might be summarized in the following terms.

Elite-led processes of constitutional transition are untenable without public acceptance, which in turn necessitates sustained efforts to inform and involve the polity at large, and engage and contain antagonistic constituencies within it. The design of the peace process reflected the elitist nature of Sri Lankan politics, but without transcending its extreme partisan dynamics. The negotiations and their content were barely understood by people at large, and the lack of public awareness and information about efforts to resolve the conflict reinforced suspicion and mistrust among ethnic communities. The process never matured enough for the difficult negotiations on concrete details of a constitutional settlement to begin. But the process did not even begin to create the pre-constitutional political consensus involving the key stakeholders (including potential spoilers) about the need for peace and justice, and the rationale for a negotiated settlement.

To ensure the legitimacy of the process and to allay mutual suspicions among the antagonistic communities, there has to be some sort of shared normative framework that determines the bounds of acceptable behavior. A joint commitment to shared and expressly articulated human rights norms may have been one such basis in the Sri Lankan context, but such an agreement proved impossible due to the reluctance of the parties, and especially the LTTE, and the inability of the facilitators to compel the parties.

A minimum consensus on the overarching importance of peace through a constitutional transition assumes crucial significance among parties who are otherwise in electoral competition with each other. As Paikiasothy Saravanamuttu noted, "Political competition can continue to be possible on the basis of differing approaches, emphases and tactics, rather than on the strategic objective of a peace settlement through talks."[80] Without this crucial requirement, the constitutional transition itself falls victim to the vagaries of electoral competition and ethnic outbidding.

Sri Lanka has been an uninterrupted procedural democracy since 1931, but the substantive content of its democracy has been unable to transcend the problem of ethnicized majoritarianism to accommodate minority claims in a plural polity, rendering it a deeply divided society. The dominance of ethnicity and sectional nationalisms in democratic politics, and their competing historical, cultural, and political claims, often make even routine policy decisions the subject of fundamental disagreement. This has entailed the constitutional evolution of the Sri Lankan state in ways that have hardened the majority's tendency to control the state, and the principal minority's resolve to resist that hegemony. Overcoming this deep ethnonational and territorial division through normative and institutional alternatives constitutes the central challenge if Sri Lanka is to build a stable and just constitutional order. The peace process commencing with the ceasefire of 2002 was aimed at addressing this challenge, but was itself unable to surmount the structural and systemic problems of the Sri Lankan polity.

[80] Paikiasothy Saravanamuttu, "Democratization of the Peace Process: Sri Lanka" in Judith Large and Timothy D Sisk (eds), *Democracy, Conflict and Human Security: Further Readings* vol. 2 (International IDEA 2006) 218.

15

After the Scottish Independence Referendum

Toward a Federal Moment for the United Kingdom?

Stephen Tierney

Overview

This chapter addresses the independence referendum in Scotland which took place on September 18, 2014 and its aftermath, which together have created an extended and ongoing constitutional moment, the implications of which for the future of the United Kingdom (UK) remain uncertain. In the referendum 55 percent of Scots said "No" to the question: "Should Scotland be an Independent Country?". It was a very dramatic event but it should also be seen as part of a long process in the gradual devolution of power in the UK, not only to Scotland but also to Wales and Northern Ireland, a process which continues to move ahead at speed. Although the referendum did not result in a vote for independence, it has sparked a further process of decentralization. The Smith Commission, established in the days after the referendum,[1] was a body given the task of drawing up further radical powers for the Scottish Parliament. This resulted in the Scotland Act 2016, which sets out a series of powers that could make Scotland one of the most autonomous substate territories in the world. In this chapter I discuss the institutional arrangements and political conditions that formed the background to the referendum, the referendum itself, and the aftermath in which we saw such a quick move toward further, radical constitutional change. Insofar as the referendum marks a constitutional moment it is a fluid one, with the question now being asked: is the UK edging in a federal direction?[2]

The independence referendum stemmed from the electoral success of the Scottish National Party (SNP) which, having ruled as a minority government since 2007, won an overall majority in elections to the Scottish Parliament in May 2011. The aspiration for independence has been the key project of the SNP since the 1970s and for over three decades the party has also accepted that a referendum would be required to legitimize this claim. The SNP has taken the view that were it to put to the UK government a clearly expressed democratic demand for independence, endorsed by the people of Scotland in a direct way, the political legitimacy of this claim would be irrefutable. Similarly, it has long been established at the level of the UK state that, as a political principle, if a majority of Scots wish to leave the UK the territory should be allowed to do so.

[1] The Smith Commission, "The Smith Commission: About" (*UK Government National Archives*, December 2, 2015) <http://webarchive.nationalarchives.gov.uk/20151202171047/http://www.smith-commission.scot/about/> accessed February 25, 2015.

[2] Stephen Tierney, "Is a Federal Britain Now Inevitable?" (*UK Constitutional Law Association*, November 27, 2014) <https://ukconstitutionallaw.org/2014/11/27/stephen-tierney-is-a-federal-britain-now-inevitable/> accessed February 25, 2015.

Territory and Power in Constitutional Transitions. First Edition. Edited by Michael Anderson and Sujit Choudhry. After the Scottish Independence Referendum: Toward a Federal Moment for the United Kingdom? © Stephen Tierney 2019. Published 2019 by Oxford University Press.

In the end the referendum ended in a victory for the "No" side, and a result of 55 percent to 45 percent seems on the face of it to be a clear victory for the unionist side. However, I explore in this chapter how the referendum was certainly not the start of the debate about the territorial organization of the UK, and by the same measure it has not served not to end this debate. Rather, the referendum has led constitutional deliberations in a new direction, inspired by the political commitments made toward the end of the campaign by the main unionist parties which promised further powers for the Scottish Parliament in an effort to persuade wavering Scots to vote "No." And it was certainly not the end of the story. Reform of the UK's territorial Constitution is now also over-shadowed by the decision taken by the British people to leave the European Union (EU) in the "Brexit" referendum held on June 23, 2016. It is unclear what this will mean for devolution, and even for Scotland's place in the UK itself, with the current SNP government "seriously considering" a second independence referendum in order to keep Scotland inside the EU.[3]

Another important outcome of the September vote was the success of the referendum itself as an exercise in popular decision-making. The poll was widely hailed as a success in engaging the electorate, resulting in a turnout of nearly 85 percent, and producing a national conversation which energized citizens. This experience will strengthen the arguments of those who seek to make the referendum itself a stronger feature of future processes of significant constitutional change in Britain and elsewhere; the Brexit referendum being a sign of the continued prominence of direct democracy.

Background

The lead up to the Scottish independence referendum was one of regular constitutional politics: electoral victory in the Scottish parliamentary elections of 2011 by the SNP led to the organization of a referendum as promised in its manifesto. One of the reasons why the referendum emerged from, and was organized within, the normal contours of constitutional democracy is that Anglo-Scottish relations within the UK are not burdened by ethnic strife. The territory of Northern Ireland is in the eyes of many a divided society, but Scotland is not and in the same way its relationship with England and the rest of the UK is, when compared with troubled regions of the world, an amicable and democratic one; any sense of historical injustice is now rhetorical and of little contemporary political salience.

It is for this reason that many observers looking at the situation from outside the UK no doubt wonder why the mood for independence became so strong within Scotland, falling just 5 percent short of majority support in the referendum. To explain the strength of nationalism in an otherwise harmonious constitutional environment it is necessary to analyze the referendum as the culmination (or more accurately, the latest stage) in a long-term mobilization of national sentiment in Scotland which has built upon a strong residual national identity that never fully dissipated after the Anglo-Scottish parliamentary union of 1707. It is also important to see the referendum as an event which, although dramatic and of great significance, was run on the basis of fairly prosaic arguments, with nationalists presenting a largely pragmatic case that Scotland would be economically better off determining its own affairs. For many voters the

[3] Jon Sharman, "Scottish SNP government 'seriously considering second independence referendum next year'" (*The Independent*, February 24, 2017) <http://www.independent.co.uk/news/uk/politics/scottish-snp-government-second-indepedence-referendum-union-uk-britain-a7596881.html>.

calculation to be made was indeed a practical one: whether independence would deliver a more or less prosperous country in which to live and not, as in other countries, a principally emotional decision to quit an oppressive state.

The UK is also unusual compared with most of the other situations addressed in this book in that the independence referendum process took place without any period of major political upheaval or of significant extra-parliamentary activity. The referendum was the direct result of the SNP's electoral victory, but it was also a consequence of the UK state's acceptance of the legitimacy of the demand for a referendum, and the state's acquiescence in not only permitting, but also facilitating, the staging of this referendum. In order to discover how Scotland and the wider UK got to the situation where, on the one hand a party promoting independent statehood became so popular that it won a general election to the Scottish Parliament, and on the other, the UK state was willing to cooperate with the manifesto commitment of that party to hold a referendum on independence, it is necessary to explain the constitutional history of the UK and the key part Scotland has played in the formation of the "union state." Central to the story are long-term as well as short-term factors in the development of Scotland as a polity within the UK, both of which combined to create the path to the 2014 referendum.

The institutions through which nationalists in Scotland were able to organize a referendum were created by the Scotland Act 1998. The passage of this piece of legislation by the UK Parliament created the Scottish Parliament and Scottish Executive (now called the Scottish government[4]), at the same time as devolution was also extended to Wales and Northern Ireland in other pieces of legislation.[5] The Scottish National Party came to govern under these institutions and it was, ironically, the very institutions created by UK legislation in 1998 which offered the SNP the institutional infrastructure with which to organize the referendum itself. In addition, fifteen years of self-rule (the Scottish Parliament was inaugurated in 1999), gave the Scottish people a taste of autonomy, with their domestic Parliament enjoying an extensive range of powers over matters such as education, health, transport, the environment, law and order, and local government. However, notably this regime of autonomy did not include taxation or other economic levers as a UK government publication has observed.[6] This disjuncture has allowed nationalists to point to the limitations as well as the advantages of the devolved arrangements.

The starting point for any meaningful study of Scottish devolution and of the path toward the independence referendum is not, however, 1998. Instead we need to return to the origins of the UK state itself and the key role Scotland played in "forging"[7] that state. We also need to account for the fact that since 1707 Scotland has retained its own national identity within a plurinational UK. Another important background factor which lay behind the relatively amicable circumstances within which the independence referendum was agreed to by the UK state and subsequently organized by the Scottish Parliament is the unique nature of the UK's constitutional arrangements. The UK has an unwritten Constitution which has provided the flexibility with which to change the Constitution fundamentally simply by way of legislation of the UK Parliament. This allowed very different models of devolution to be created for Scotland, Wales,

[4] Scotland Act 2012, s. 12.

[5] Government of Wales Act 1998; Northern Ireland Act 1998.

[6] Scotland Office, *Scotland in the United Kingdom: An Enduring Settlement* (Cm 8990, 2015) para. 2.3.6.

[7] Linda Colley, *Britons: Forging the Nation 1707–1837* (Yale University Press 1992).

and Northern Ireland through simple acts of Parliament, resulting in a heavily asymmetrical system. It has also allowed ad hoc changes to the system to be made very easily; for example, through the Scotland Act 2012, which is again an ordinary act of Parliament but one which cedes further and not insignificant competences (discussed further below) to the Scottish Parliament.[8]

In historical terms, the "union" persona of the state is central to an understanding of the UK Constitution. Although not federal, the UK was founded in full recognition of the national differences of which it was composed and, at least in the case of Scotland, there was a constitutional commitment to continue to recognize these differences in the functioning of the state. The territories of the UK came together, at least formally, in processes of legal union. England's union with Wales was clearly the result of conquest, but even here this was given legal recognition by an Act of the English Parliament.[9] Of greater constitutional significance, the modern British state was shaped by the later and more sophisticated legal unions between England and Scotland to form the UK in 1707,[10] and that between the UK and Ireland in 1800, the legacy of which is Northern Ireland's ongoing membership of the UK.[11]

Although these different unions brought with them distinctive points of constitutional identity, the one with the most enduring constitutional differences is the Anglo-Scottish union. It is the retained sense of difference within Scotland, made manifest in its political and administrative heritage, which kept alive that sense of discrete national identity which, when the political circumstances were conducive to the nationalist movement, led to the referendum of 2014. It is also important to note that the UK state has long accepted the reality of its multinational composition, and it is this recognition of national pluralism which lay behind the acceptance by the UK state of the legitimacy of Scots to elect a party committed to a referendum on independence.

The feature of Scotland's institutional distinctiveness that is particularly significant after 1707 is the retention of an independent legal system. This in turn helped keep alive a particular understanding of the constitutional status of the union within the Scottish legal system which in some respects has differed from the clear acceptance of the doctrine of parliamentary supremacy within the English legal system. From time to time it has been suggested that the very authority of the UK Parliament derives from the Acts of Union of 1707.[12] This argument is now of only historical interest, given both that it was always extremely unlikely that a Scottish court would seek to strike down an Act of the UK Parliament by invoking these Acts, and the subordination of the Acts of Union within the Scotland Act 1998,[13] a statute which (in its amended form) is now treated almost universally as the modern restatement of the Anglo-Scottish union. However, the survival of the idea that Scots and the Scottish legal system looked to a different rule of recognition in the post-1707 period, left open the argument (in constitutional and not just political terms) that Scotland as a society

[8] For example, this statute extends further tax powers to Scotland. Other constitutional changes have been brought about by the Government of Wales Act 2006 and the Wales Act 2014.

[9] This is traditionally titled in England, the Laws in Wales Act 1535 (27 Hen VIII, c 26), and in Wales, the Act of Union 1536.

[10] Union with Scotland Act 1706 (6 Anne c 11); and the Union with England Act 1707 (asp 7), 406.

[11] Union with Ireland Act 1800.

[12] *MacCormick v. Lord Advocate* [1953] UKSC 396, at 411 and see Faculty of Advocates, Response to the consultation paper by the Secretary of State for Constitutional Affairs and Lord Chancellor: Constitutional Reform: a Supreme Court for the United Kingdom (November 2003).

[13] Scotland Act 1998, s. 37.

retained its own constituent popular power as a rival source of sovereignty to that of the UK state embedded in Parliament. In other words, the origins of the UK as a mutually agreed union created a historical and constitutional legacy that in turn helped to shape how the constitutional significance of the devolution settlement for Scotland in 1998 was widely perceived in Scotland. Even after devolution Scots retained the claim that having entered the UK voluntarily, and having retained a strong sense of nationhood including the institutional infrastructure of nationhood within the state, secession would always be a legitimate constitutional option if sought by a majority of Scots. By contrast it is also worth noting that in many ways the Anglo-Scottish union was a far more harmonious one than that with Ireland, which is better characterized as one of conquest. Scotland and England were united by a common Protestantism, which was a particular resource in fostering nation-building, particularly at the time of the Napoleonic wars.[14] This led to a constitutional arrangement which allowed Scotland to keep a number of its own cultural institutions and which operated in greater harmony with the UK state than did those in Ireland which throughout the late eighteenth century, and more markedly at the end of the nineteenth century, helped foster a strong impetus toward independent statehood.

Scotland maintained some degree of governmental autonomy which was consolidated by the creation of the office of Secretary of State in 1885 and of the Scotland Office in 1928.[15] This period of "administrative devolution" not only allowed for discrete civil and administrative patterns to continue to develop, but also it created a civil service infrastructure within the Scottish Office that was easily adapted to run the new system introduced by the Scotland Act 1998 which created the Scottish Parliament.

Another notable phenomenon during the period of "administrative devolution," was the rise of Scottish nationalism, particularly since the 1960s. The SNP was founded in 1934 but did not win a seat in Parliament until 1967. Its breakthrough came in 1974 when in the October General Election it won eleven seats in the UK Parliament with 30 percent of the Scottish vote. Ironically its representation within the UK Parliament was never so high again until May 2015 when it won fifty-six of the fifty-nine Scottish seats with 50 percent of the Scottish vote. It now seems set to play a pivotal role in debates about the UK's constitutional future, particularly by offering an oppositional voice on the Brexit negotiations with Brussels.

The SNP has, at least until 2015, enjoyed its greatest success in the Scottish Parliament rather than at Westminster. Although in opposition following the first two elections to that Parliament in 1999 and 2003, it formed a minority Scottish government in 2007. It built upon this success to win an overall majority of seats in the Parliament in 2011, the first party to do so, which allowed it to pass legislation to hold the referendum.

The rise of the SNP over the past half-century does raise the question why, in such a closely integrated country and one that does not have any notable ethnic cleavage between Scotland and England, the SNP emerged and grew as such a political force. Michael Keating identifies a number of the key features which in the past two centuries had established the bonds of loyalty between Scotland and the rest of the UK.[16] In addition to the historical-cultural factors such as Protestantism,[17] in the nineteenth century

[14] See Colley (n 7).

[15] Rodney Brazier, *Ministers of the Crown* (Oxford University Press 1997) 9.

[16] Michael Keating, *The Independence of Scotland: Self-Government and the Shifting Politics of Union* (Oxford University Press 2009).

[17] See Colin Kidd, *Union and Unionism: Political Thought in Scotland 1500–2000* (Cambridge University Press 2008).

Scotland benefitted from, and many Scots played a very prominent role in, the British Empire. In the twentieth century, with the rise of the Labour Party across the UK, many Scots came to share in a sense of social solidarity, and consequently in a shared commitment to the welfare state and the National Health Service, as well as to cultural institutions such as the BBC. Keating discusses how the commitment to each of these has dissipated in time and that as a consequence the union has come to seem less relevant to many Scots. The period of Conservative government in the UK from 1979 to 1997 placed a particular strain on the union, since in this period the Conservatives were markedly less popular in Scotland, with their vote in Scotland dropping progressively from 31 percent in 1979 to 17.5 percent in 1997. Opposition became merged with national identity, and into this vacuum came the Scottish National Party which was able to build support by combining a nationalist approach with a social democratic agenda for social and economic reform.[18] The creation of the Scottish Parliament provided the SNP with the catalyst to turn this support into real governmental power, and it has used this opportunity to the full.

The Scotland Act 1998 is itself a remarkable development since it was passed by ordinary legislation, a product of the flexibility of the UK Constitution. The backstory was the campaign by the political opposition from 1979 to 1997 to bring about devolved government. 1979 was a pivotal year not only because it began an eighteen-year period of Conservative Party rule but also because the first attempts to implement devolution for Scotland and Wales failed in referendums held that year. The legislation provided that if fewer than 40 percent of the total electorate voted "Yes" in the referendum, the measure would not pass.[19] The result in the Scottish devolution process was 51.6 percent support for the proposal, but with a turnout of 64 percent this represented only 32.9 percent of those registered to vote.[20] The measure therefore failed and became a source of political grievance among nationalists during the 1980s and 1990s. The first concerted reaction came with the Campaign for a Scottish Assembly (CSA) which was launched in 1985 and issued the document, *A Claim of Right for Scotland*, in 1988 declaring the inherent right of the Scots to self-government.[21] This asserted that "sovereignty" in Scotland rested with the Scottish people and as such they had the right to initiate changes to Scotland's constitutional position. This led to a cross-party Scottish Constitutional Convention (SCC) which was inaugurated in 1989. Over the next seven years it embraced much of Scotland's political elite, involving *inter alia* the Labour and Liberal Democratic parties (although not the SNP who objected to the fact that independence was not on the agenda for discussion or the Conservatives who were at that time opposed to devolution), local authorities, churches, and the Scottish Trades Union Congress.[22] Although not established by any official route, it was composed of fifty-nine of Scotland's seventy-two Westminster MPs and all six of its Members of the European Parliament. This resulted in a series of publications, the most important of which, *Scotland's Claim, Scotland's Right*,[23] that set out a detailed blueprint for devolution, which proved to be very influential, the

[18] Keating, *The Independence of Scotland* (n 16).

[19] Scotland Act 1978, s. 85(2); Wales Act 1978, s. 80(2).

[20] Richard Dewdney, "Results of Devolution Referendums (1979 & 1997)" (1997) 97 (113) House of Commons Library Research Paper <http://researchbriefings.parliament.uk/ResearchBriefing/Summary/RP97-113#fullreport>.

[21] A Claim of Right for Scotland (1988), 19. Its title was, of course, intended to echo the radical spirit of the pre-Union Scottish Parliament's revolutionary Claim of Right of 1689.

[22] Jean McFadden, "The Scottish Constitutional Convention" [1995] Public Law 215.

[23] ibid.

eventual model of devolution enacted through the Scotland Act 1998 being remarkably similar to it.

This allowed the Labour Party when in government to hold a referendum in 1997 which endorsed the plan for devolution and then to legislate for this by 1998. In many respects the devolution model of 1998 was the direct creation of the Scottish Labour Party which had been the dominant voice on the SCC. This demonstrated how constitutional change can be effected in the UK very easily, as happened again with subsequent changes to the devolution model through the Scotland Act 2012. This latter Act implemented many of the key recommendations of the Calman Commission, which had been established in 2007 by the main unionist parties in the Scottish Parliament—Labour, Conservative, and Liberal Democrats—to "review the provisions of the Scotland Act 1998 in the light of experience and to recommend any changes to the present constitutional arrangements that would enable the Scottish Parliament to serve the people of Scotland better, improve the financial accountability of the Scottish Parliament and continue to secure the position of Scotland within the United Kingdom." This was in political terms an attempt to see off the SNP proposal for independence by establishing more powers for the Scottish Parliament, including more tax-varying powers. In the end its proposals were quite modest in their reach. They were passed by the UK Parliament with the consent of the Scottish Parliament, as it is now a constitutional convention that the Scottish Parliament should consent to changes to the devolution settlement. This consent was also needed for the Scotland Act 2016 which provides radical new powers for the Scottish Parliament.

To conclude, 1998 for Scotland was clearly not year zero. The devolved arrangements which emerged have their roots in a historical story in which Scotland's relationship with the central state began in the reality of retained cultural institutions after 1707 which in turn were supplemented by gradually strengthening political institutions. This kept alive a strong sense of Scottish national identity which was fully accommodated within a British union, which also shared strong cultural totems—the English language, Protestantism, solidarity forged in European wars, and a developing social state. But ironically it was this retained national identity which would, by the end of the twentieth century, make independence seem a feasible and reasonable constitutional option as the reasons for union, in the eyes of many Scots, began to dissipate. The SNP was to become the vehicle for this option as it set out to hold a referendum from the moment it was elected as a minority government in 2007.

The Period of Constitutional Engagement

A feature of the 2014 referendum, which surprises many external observers, is the fact that the UK government acquiesced in the process and even cooperated in framing the rules for the vote. The process of the 1980s and 90s emphasizes the lingering sense of nationhood within Scotland, but it also demonstrates how attuned the UK state was to this, and the lengths it was prepared to go to in order to accommodate it. When the SNP won its Scottish Parliament majority in 2011 the UK government did not oppose the principle that the Scottish government could pursue its manifesto commitment to hold a referendum on independence. However, this is not the whole story and as we will see, the UK government's decision to cooperate in the process was in large measure tactical. The UK was certainly not going to let Scotland go without seeking to influence the process, and to this end it questioned the legal basis upon which the Scottish government proposed to act. It was one thing to concede the principle that Scots could have a referendum, it was another to accept that the Scottish Parliament had the lawful authority under the Scotland Act 1998 to organize one. By the start of 2012 it was clear that a legal dispute could well emerge as to whether or not the Scottish Parliament had such a power, with the UK government adamant that only the UK Parliament could authorize such a process, and the Scottish government determined to press ahead with its independence plans.

In January 2012 the Scottish government announced its intention to hold a referendum on independence, announcing that this would take place in the autumn of 2014. A draft Referendum Bill to this effect was published, which asserted the authority of the Scottish Parliament to hold such a referendum, while a public consultation exercise was set in motion.[24] The UK government, a coalition of Conservatives and Liberal Democrats, immediately challenged the legislative competence of the Scottish Parliament to pass this Bill and in doing so launched its own consultation process.[25] It appeared for a time that the matter would end in the courts as there was considerable disagreement between the two governments as to whether s. 29 of the Scotland Act 1998, from which the Scottish Parliament derives its competence, entitled the Scottish Parliament to hold a referendum of a consultative nature only.[26]

To the surprise of many, on October 15, 2012 an agreement ("The Edinburgh Agreement"[27]) was reached between the two governments which led to the UK Parliament devolving to the Scottish Parliament the competence to legislate for a referendum, providing that it had to be held before the end of 2014 and only on the issue of whether Scotland should become independent of the rest of the UK.[28] This condition is the key to understanding why, in a very short space of time, the UK government moved from a potentially confrontational stance to one of agreement. Constitutional principle and the sociological reality of a multinational state helped inform this decision, but it is also the case that political calculation was at work. Given that there was disagreement as to whether the Scottish Parliament could hold a consultative referendum, the Scottish government had declared that it would do so, and that it would include a third question on the ballot concerning more powers for the Scottish Parliament—"devo-max" as it came to be known. The UK government strongly opposed such a move and also wished to avoid a court case which, even if successful from their point of view, would almost certainly help stoke nationalist support. On the other hand, by agreeing to a referendum the UK was able to gain a say in the process rules, in particular making sure the referendum was on the issue of independence and nothing else. Thus, the main benefit of the Edinburgh Agreement from the UK government's point of view was that the referendum was a straight contest between independence on the one hand and the status quo on the other. Opinion polls in 2012 (as they had for

[24] Scottish Government, *Your Scotland – Your Referendum – A Consultation Document* (Scottish Government 2012) <www.scotland.gov.uk/Publications/2012/01/1006>.

[25] Scotland Office, *Scotland's Constitutional Future* (Cm 8203, 2012).

[26] For commentary on this dispute, see Adam Tomkins, "The Scottish Parliament and the Independence Referendum" (*UK Constitutional Law Association blog*, January 12, 2012) <http://ukconstitutionallaw.org/2012/01/12/adam-tomkins-the-scottish-parliament-and-the-independence-referendum/>; and Gavin Anderson and others, "The Independence Referendum, Legality and the Contested Constitution: Widening the Debate" (*UK Constitutional Law Association Blog*, January 31, 2012) <http://ukconstitutionallaw.org/2012/01/31/gavin-anderson-et-al-the-independence-referendum-legality-and-the-contested-constitution-widening-the-debate/>.

[27] Scottish Government, *Agreement between the United Kingdom Government and the Scottish Government on a referendum on independence for Scotland* (*Government of Scotland Website*, October 15, 2012) <www.scotland.gov.uk/About/Government/concordats/Referendum-on-independence>.

[28] Scotland Act 1998 (Modification of Schedule 5), Order 2013.

most of the preceding four decades) rarely showed popular support for independence in Scotland above 30 to 35 percent, and so the government was confident of victory on this issue. Another condition contained in the Edinburgh Agreement was that the referendum be conducted so as to command the confidence of both parliaments, both governments and the people. The stated aim of the Agreement was that the referendum "deliver a fair test and a decisive expression of the views of people in Scotland and a result that everyone will respect."

Regardless of the degree of political calculation behind the deal that was eventually reached, this agreement paved the way for the referendum to be organized through legislation of the Scottish Parliament in a lawful way with the full consent of the UK state. It is of considerable significance that the UK government accepted the fundamental principle that the Scottish people have the right, by way of referendum, to achieve independence, bearing in mind the protracted and difficult way in which the issue of secession has played out in many parts of the world, including liberal democratic states such as Canada and Spain.[29] This in turn encouraged the Scottish government to act in a consensual way on process issues. The Scottish government was willing to adapt the general regime of referendum process law used for UK referendums and to accept the oversight of the independent UK regulator—the Electoral Commission—so much so that both governments accepted the Electoral Commission's review of the referendum question.

The Scottish government sent its proposed question to the Electoral Commission. The initial formulation was: "Do you agree that Scotland should be an independent country? Yes/No." The Electoral Commission took the view that "based on our research and taking into account what we heard from people and organizations who submitted their views on the question, we consider that the proposed question is not neutral because the phrase 'Do you agree . . .?' could lead people towards voting 'yes'." It therefore recommended the following alternative question: "Should Scotland be an independent country? Yes/No."[30] This was accepted by the Scottish government and this was the question included in the Scottish Independence Referendum Act,[31] and ultimately put to the voters.

There was also no debate within the UK as to the franchise for the referendum. It was accepted that this would be based upon residence, using the same franchise rules as Scottish Parliament elections.[32] One difference from the existing franchise, however, was the provision in the Scottish Franchise Act extending the vote to those aged 16 and 17.[33] This was a notable departure; never before had people under the age of 18 been entitled to vote in a major British election or referendum.[34] On the one hand this could be seen as a cynical ploy to empower younger voters who would be more likely to vote "Yes." On the other, it has long been SNP policy that younger people should be allowed to vote and this was the first electoral event where this could be put into practice. In the end it did not arouse particular controversy within the Scottish Parliament's

[29] Stephen Tierney, *Constitutional Law and National Pluralism* (Oxford University Press 2004).

[30] The Electoral Commission, "Referendum on independence for Scotland: Advice of the Electoral Commission on the proposed referendum question" (The Electoral Commission 2013) <www.electoralcommission.org.uk/__data/assets/pdf_file/0007/153691/Referendum-on-independence-for-Scotland-our-advice-on-referendum-question.pdf>.

[31] Scottish Independence Referendum Act 2013, s. 1(2). See also Andrew Black, "Scottish independence: SNP accepts call to change referendum question" *BBC News* (Scotland, January 30, 2013) <www.bbc.co.uk/news/uk-scotland-scotland-politics-21245701>.

[32] Scottish Independence Referendum (Franchise) Act 2013.

[33] ibid s. 2(1)(a).

[34] Representation of the People Act 1983, s. 1(d).

Referendum (Scotland) Bill Committee. Now that the Scottish Parliament has the power to set the franchise for the Scottish Parliament elections in May 2016,[35] it has used this to extend the vote to those over 16 years of age for this election.[36] It is also worth noting also that there was no suggestion that the referendum should be decided on the basis of any rule other than 50 percent plus 1. In fact this is not particularly unusual. Of course supermajority requirements do exist in certain states such as Australia (where successful amendment requires a referendum in which a majority nationally and majorities in a majority of states vote for the proposition), and in other systems referendums can be a part of a wider amendment process in which various levels of support require to be achieved. But most referendums around the world are settled on a 50 percent plus 1 basis, some with a participation threshold,[37] and the provision of a supermajority requirement is very much the exception rather than the norm.[38]

It is interesting how the polling data changed in the course of the campaign. As has been noted, historically support for independence has rarely moved above 35 percent over the past decade, and it was still at this level when the Scottish government announced the referendum in 2012 and did not change significantly until very late in the campaign. What then led to support for independence reaching 45 percent in the actual vote? A number of factors may have been at work, including the success of the "Yes" campaign in allaying the fears of voters about the economic future, and the fact that it was able to improve the share of female support for independence during the campaign. The latter factor is notable since women often gave economic uncertainty as a key reason for their intention to vote no. It is also widely thought that the "No" (Better Together) campaign was not very effective, and that some of the negative campaigning may have been counter-productive. Another feature was the very high turnout of over 84 percent which mobilized many people who do not normally vote, particularly in the lower socioeconomic groups, and polling data shows that they voted heavily for independence.[39]

Outcome of the Process

The outcome of the referendum was a victory for the "No" campaign, but the move to radical constitutional change which followed hot on the heels of the referendum was not what many expected even one month before the vote. Rather than a period of calm reflection after the referendum, the UK immediately embarked upon a process of potentially radical constitutional change, with the prospect of many more powers being devolved to the Scottish Parliament.

In the aftermath of the referendum the UK government developed a speedy timetable for this extensive decentralization, a process which by January 2015 had resulted

[35] Scotland Act 1998 (Modifications of Schedules 4 and 5 and Transfer of Functions to the Scottish Ministers etc.) Order 2015.

[36] Scottish Elections (Reduction of Voting Age) Act 2015.

[37] Stephen Tierney, *Constitutional Referendums: The Theory and Practice of Republican Deliberation* (Oxford University Press 2012) 272.

[38] ibid 274.

[39] Alberto Nardelli, "Were Scottish independence opinion polls misleading?" *The Guardian* (September 19, 2014) <www.theguardian.com/politics/2014/sep/19/scottish-independence-opinion-polls-referendum-vote>; see also John Curtice, "Scotland's Decision: So How Well Did The Polls Do?" (*Centre on Constitutional Change blog*, September 22, 2014) <www.centreonconstitutionalchange.ac.uk/blog/scotlands-decision-so-how-well-did-polls-do>.

in the publication of draft clauses for a new Scotland Bill which the three main UK parties—Conservative, Labour, and Liberal Democrats—committed to legislate upon following the UK general election in May 2015.[40] With a Conservative victory in that election the process moved on quickly and the Scotland Act 2016 was passed in the spring of the following year.

The background to this development is one of political panic. In the two weeks immediately preceding the independence referendum the opinion polls seemed to suggest that the "No" side's lead, which had been pretty solid throughout the campaign, was narrowing dramatically, with the occasional poll now predicting that the "Yes" side may even be poised to win. On September 16, two days before the vote, the UK leaders of the Conservative, Labour, and Liberal Democrat parties issued "the Vow,"[41] undertaking that in the event of a majority "No" vote they would produce agreed proposals on additional powers for the Scottish Parliament, and setting out a short time frame within which these powers would be agreed.

The result was that the day after the referendum, the Prime Minister announced that Lord Smith of Kelvin, a non-political figure, had agreed to oversee the process to take forward this commitment to grant further devolution to the Scottish Parliament.[42] The Terms of Reference of the Smith Commission were:

> To convene cross-party talks and facilitate an inclusive engagement process across Scotland to produce, by 30 November 2014, Heads of Agreement with recommendations for further devolution of powers to the Scottish Parliament. This . . . will result in the publication of draft clauses by 25 January. The recommendations will deliver more financial, welfare and taxation powers, strengthening the Scottish Parliament within the United Kingdom.[43]

On November 27 the Smith Commission published its report proposing radical new powers for the Scottish Parliament, in particular tax powers including control over income tax in Scotland and responsibility for certain important welfare powers. The Heads of Agreement in the Smith Report are divided into three pillars:

- Pillar 1 Providing for a durable but responsive constitutional settlement for the governance of Scotland;
- Pillar 2 Delivering prosperity, a healthy economy, jobs, and social justice;
- Pillar 3 Strengthening the financial responsibility of the Scottish Parliament.

This process is open to considerable criticism. The Smith Commission arrived at Heads of Agreement very rapidly.[44] This left little time for full consultation with the UK Parliament, with the Scottish Parliament, and other devolved legislatures, or with the citizens of Scotland or the wider UK. This is not to criticize the work of Lord Smith, the ways in which the Smith Commission members approached their task, or

[40] *Scotland in the United Kingdom* (n 6).

[41] David Clegg, "David Cameron, Ed Miliband and Nick Clegg sign joint historic promise which guarantees more devolved powers for Scotland and protection of NHS if we vote No" *Daily Record* (September 15, 2014) <www.dailyrecord.co.uk/news/politics/david-cameron-ed-miliband-nick-4265992>.

[42] Government of the United Kingdom, "Press release Scottish Independence Referendum: statement by the Prime Minister" (*Gov.UK*, September 19, 2014) <www.gov.uk/government/news/scottish-independence-referendum-statement-by-the-prime-minister>.

[43] "The Smith Commission Report," The Smith Commission (Edinburgh, November 27, 2014).

[44] Stephen Tierney, "Solomon Grundy Does Constitutional Change: The Smith Commission Timetable to Transform the Scottish Parliament" (*UK Constitutional Law Association,* October 31, 2014) <https://ukconstitutionallaw.org/2014/10/31/stephen-tierney-solomon-grundy-does-constitutional-change-the-smith-commission-timetable-to-transform-the-scottish-parliament/>.

deliberated together, or the conclusions they came to in their report. It is rather a reflection of the remit which the Commission was set and the speed with which it was required to conduct its work.[45]

The proposals, which have now largely been replicated in the Scotland Act 2016, promised the most extensive reorganization of territorial government in the UK since 1998. In light of the significance of the changes that have resulted, the brevity, exclusiveness, and lack of transparency in the process runs counter to good practice in relation to constitutional reform. Regardless of how sensible or popular constitutional changes prove to be or how well they work in practice, the health of a democratic system depends upon the propriety and legitimacy of the process by which constitutional changes within it are effected. As the House of Lords Select Committee on the Constitution stated in its report on the Fixed-term Parliaments Bill:

> Process is critical in terms of upholding, and being seen to uphold, constitutional values: particularly those of democratic involvement and transparency in the policymaking process. Moreover, we believe that a proper process is the foundation upon which successful policy is built: the lack of a proper process makes an ineffective outcome more likely.[46]

In many ways the UK method of constitutional change through parliamentary legislation has been advantageous. It allowed devolution to be created quickly in 1998 and for this to be done in incremental and heavily asymmetrical ways for each of the three devolved territories, without the need for an overarching constitutional settlement for which there was little political appetite. In other words, devolution was achievable, meeting the specific needs and desires of each of the territories without abandoning Britain's unwritten Constitution and without juridifying a political Constitution that has worked well for centuries. Furthermore, the flexibility in the system has allowed for further constitutional change from time to time, responding to further demands or correcting what seem to be anomalies or outdated features of devolution.

But a disadvantage in the system is that there are ultimately no procedural checks. Parliament can effect any constitutional change it wishes and it can do so by way of ordinary legislation. In this respect the lack of citizen involvement in the process toward such significant constitutional change, change which in the end was passed in the Scotland Act 2016 by the UK Parliament without a referendum, is very different from the long period of citizen engagement we saw in the referendum. This reminds us of the extent to which the UK remains an outlier among modern democracies for the degree of flexibility in its constitutional arrangements.

In terms of the substance of the proposals, the Scotland Act 2016 has realigned significantly the balance of competences currently set out in the Scotland Acts of 1998 and 2012 ("the 1998 Act" and "the 2012 Act"). The Scottish Parliament is assuming a range of new powers in policy areas such as taxation, welfare, employability, transport, energy efficiency, fuel poverty, and onshore oil and gas extraction. These proposals have required significant amendments in particular to Schedules 4 and 5 of the 1998 Act. It is the provisions on taxation that have attracted the most attention. In light of the Scotland Act 2016 Scotland will acquire far more fiscal responsibility.[47] In particular

[45] House of Lords Constitution Committee, "Proposals for the devolution of further powers to Scotland" (Constitution Committee March 18, 2015) <www.publications.parliament.uk/pa/ld201415/ldselect/ldconst/145/14502.htm>.

[46] Constitution Committee, "8th Report (2010–2011): Fixed-term Parliaments Bill" (UKHL Paper 69), para. 160.

[47] Constitution Committee, "Proposals for the devolution of further powers to Scotland" (March 18, 2015) para. 95, <www.publications.parliament.uk/pa/ld201415/ldselect/ldconst/145/14502.htm>.

it has been given extensive powers in relation to income tax raised in Scotland, which is important in symbolic as well as practical terms. This builds upon the more modest tax powers which were included in the 2012 Act, a number of which are still to be implemented.

In introducing this measure, the UK government noted that: "Under the Scotland Act 1998 (the 1998 Act), the Scottish Parliament is responsible for almost 60% of public spending in Scotland (e.g. health, education, housing, policing, justice, etc.) but is responsible for only around 10% of Scottish tax (council tax and non-domestic (business) rates). While the Scottish Government is also able to vary the basic rate of income tax in Scotland (by up to 3p) it has never used this power."[48] But: "As a result of the Smith Commission Agreement, the Scottish Parliament will control around 60% of spending in Scotland and retain around 40% of Scottish tax. This will therefore make the Scottish Government one of the most powerful subcentral governments in the OECD, just behind the Canadian provinces and Swiss cantons. Importantly, it will therefore give the Scottish Government substantial choices in relation to levels of tax and spending in Scotland."[49] There is, of course, disagreement about what this will mean in practice with some skepticism as to the extent to which these powers can be used to produce variation across the state.[50]

The 2016 Act also changes the constitutional status of the Scottish Parliament, providing: "A Scottish Parliament is recognised as a permanent part of the United Kingdom's constitutional arrangements."[51] It is difficult to see what constitutional effect this might have, given the UK's doctrine of parliamentary sovereignty,[52] but the very statement could be a steer to the courts to consider Scottish devolution now to be an entrenched arrangement at the level of constitutional principle.[53]

The future for the UK is now very unclear. The Conservative government claims a mandate to pursue further reductions in public spending, the possible repeal of the Human Rights Act 1998 and an agenda of constitutional reform designed to enhance the legislative power of English MPs. This is the so-called English votes for English laws (EVEL) issue, designed to correct the anomaly whereby MPs from the devolved territories can vote, and in some circumstances could even hold the casting votes, in Westminster on bills which will in practice only affect England (the West Lothian question). Although, with a Conservative majority in the Commons, such a casting vote is unlikely to be an issue in practice, the current government moved ahead with a model whereby English MPs in the House of Commons are guaranteed a decisive say on such legislation.[54]

[48] *Scotland in the United Kingdom* (n 6) para. 2.3.6.

[49] ibid para. 2.2.10. See also House of Lords Select Committee on the Constitution, "10th Report of Session 2014–15: Proposals for the devolution of further powers to Scotland" (UKHL Paper 145, March 24, 2015).

[50] Michael Keating, "Not Devo-Max Yet" (*Centre on Constitutional Change blog*, November 27, 2014). https://www.centreonconstitutionalchange.ac.uk/blog/not-devo-max-yet

[51] Scotland Act 2016, s. 1.

[52] Mark Elliott, "The Draft Scotland Bill and the sovereignty of the UK Parliament" (*Public Law for Everyone blog*, January 22, 2015) <http://publiclawforeveryone.com/2015/01/22/the-draft-scotland-bill-and-the-sovereignty-of-the-uk-parliament/>.

[53] Kenneth Campbell, "The draft Scotland Bill and limits in constitutional statutes" (*UK Constitutional Law Blog*, January 30, 2015) <http://ukconstitutionallaw.org>.

[54] England's position itself is arguably untenable, and the UK government proposes a change to parliamentary procedure to ensure "English votes for English laws." The plan is that when a Bill is designated as "England only" by the Speaker of the House of Commons, it will be considered only by English MPs at the Committee stage. The Bill would still need the support of a majority in the House to pass, but in effect English MPs will have a veto power. UK Cabinet Office, "English Votes for English Laws: An Explanatory Guide to Proposals" (*Gov.UK*, July 2015) <https://www.gov.uk/

The government is at the same time challenged by an equally assertive block of Scottish nationalists. The SNP claims the political legitimacy to fight austerity and demands implementation of its own constitutional priorities which include powers which go further even than the Smith Commission recommendations. The most explosive development was the Brexit referendum in June 2016. Given that a majority of Scots (62 percent to 38 percent) voted to remain in the EU, the Scottish government sees this result as entitling it to reopen the issue of independence. Depending upon how Brexit negotiations develop, such a poll is a very distinct possibility. In this context the Brexit referendum now poses a very real threat to the future of the Anglo-Scottish union.

Leaving the impact of Brexit to one side, the UK seems to be at a crossroads offering two possible constitutional directions: toward a UK where Scotland is treated as a separate entity in some kind of quasi-independent, confederal arrangement where its influence on the rest of the country is further marginalized, or toward a UK where devolution is reconfigured to include not only the dynamics of autonomy but also the imperative of integration. Notably the issue of federalism has rarely been discussed as a constitutional option for Britain. There are, of course, very significant objections to both the feasibility and desirability of federalism for the UK. In terms of feasibility it is a standard trope that federalism is a bad fit for the UK, first because England is too big. There are also other more normative objections: a federal system would bring with it a fundamental restructuring of the Constitution by way of a written Constitution for which there has traditionally been little appetite. This would also mean the end of parliamentary supremacy, the keystone of the British system of government. Third, it would deliver new layers of government, a step which does not enjoy significant support in England. And finally, the lessons of other countries where federalism has been grafted onto a parliamentary system is that the role for the courts expands significantly, portending the juridification of Britain's traditionally "political" Constitution.

If we consider federalism to be in effect a balance between autonomy for substate territories and representation of these territories in the central organs of the state: "self-rule" and "shared rule," the UK devolution system has emphasized the former and almost entirely ignored the latter.[55] The trajectory of the post-referendum proposals leading quickly to a new Scotland Act 2016 are being followed by proposals for further powers for the Welsh Assembly[56] and may also lead to further changes to the powers of the Northern Ireland Assembly. The UK is therefore heading toward more and more self-rule without any real efforts to build institutions of shared rule.

The prospects for federalism look far less propitious today than they would have in the case of a hung parliament with different parties holding the balance of power along a range of possible governmental configurations; the prospect of Brexit has also done little to promote comity in Scotland and Northern Ireland where majorities voted to remain in the EU. In any case the lack of a formalized approach to shared rule is at present the biggest gap in any federal vision for Britain, although the high level of

government/publications/english-votes-for-english-laws-proposed-changes/english-votes-for-english-laws-an-explanatory-guide-to-proposals>. See also Mark Elliott and Stephen Tierney, "House of Lords Constitution Committee Reports on 'English Votes for English Laws'" (*UK Constitutional Law Blog*, November 2, 2016) <https://ukconstitutionallaw.org/2016/11/02/mark-elliott-and-stephen-tierney-house-of-lords-constitution-committee-reports-on-english-votes-for-english-laws/>.

[55] Stephen Tierney, "Giving with one hand: Scottish devolution within a unitary state" (2007) 5 (4) International Journal of Constitutional Law 730; "Federalism in a Unitary State: A Paradox too Far?" (2009) 19 (2) Regional and Federal Studies 237.

[56] Wales Bill, October 20, 2015.

asymmetry in the system is also extreme by federal standards. In institutional terms, however, it can be argued these are not insurmountable challenges, but the political question is, who wants it? In other words, is it already too late to forge the political will across the Union for a "holding together" model of "shared powers" federalism? Scottish nationalists remain focussed upon independence. At the same time there is Northern Ireland where a federal solution would surely be viewed with deep suspicion for its integrative dynamics by Irish nationalists. Furthermore, can federalism be achieved at a price deemed to be worth paying in England; that is, without massively diminishing English influence in the state, without imposing a fully codified Constitution, without creating new layers of regional government, and without abandoning parliamentary supremacy? It would seem that these challenges are in practical terms manageable; the recent, incremental moves toward English votes for English laws shows one way forward. Both the UK Constitution and federalism as an idea for government are sufficiently flexible and adaptable to arrive at a new territorial accommodation for the UK. The real obstacle is that such a solution does not appear to be in the political interests of either the Conservative Party or the SNP. Federalism could work for Britain, indeed it may be the only constitutional system which can now hold the country together, but the irony is that two rival political forces are now in place at Westminster neither of which is likely to prefer it to the prospect of a more detached Scotland.

Lessons Learned

The 2014 referendum offers a number of lessons: the first relates to the democratic potential of the referendum as an instrument of constitutional change; a second is some guidance on how to reach an amicable and consensual settlement of the secession issue; and a third is that territorial issues may in the end never be settled within a complex plurinational state where territorial societies might always seek to reposition themselves in relation to the central state. The constitutional future of the UK will turn on political will more than constitutional capacity. I will discuss each in turn.

A remarkable feature of the Scottish referendum was the level of popular participation. The turnout of 84.65 percent was the highest for any UK electoral event since the introduction of universal suffrage, significantly trumping the 65.1 percent who voted in the 2010 UK general election and the 50.6 percent who bothered to turn out for the 2011 Scottish parliamentary elections. But turnout is only part of the picture. Evidence suggests that citizens felt greatly empowered by the referendum and the role they had in making such a huge decision, seeking out information about the issues at stake and engaging vociferously with one another at home and in public spaces to an unprecedented degree in British politics, on social media, etc.[57]

The fact that the process was agreed by both governments was a great benefit here. Voters had plenty of time to discuss and reflect upon the issue (the plan to hold a referendum was announced in January 2012) and the question ("Should Scotland be an Independent Country?") was very clear, having been reviewed by the independent Electoral Commission. One of the most empowering elements of the entire process

[57] Ailsa Henderson, Liam Delaney, and Robert Liñeira, "Risk and Attitudes to Constitutional Change" (ESRC Scottish Centre on Constitutional Change Risk and Constitutional Attitudes Survey August 16, 2014) <www.futureukandscotland.ac.uk/sites/default/files/news/Risk%20and%20Constitutional%20Attitudes%20Full%20Survey%2014%20Aug.pdf>; "AQMen Data Science for Social Researchers" (*AQMen Research*, 2017) <http://www.aqmen.ac.uk/>.

was the way in which, as September 18 approached and opinion polls narrowed, political elites on both sides had to sit on the side-lines, aware that the power to change or not to change the UK state lay entirely in the hands of the Scottish people.

A related consequence is that arguments of principle against the use of the referendum to make major constitutional decisions have been further undermined by the success of the Scottish process. It does often appear that the opposition we find to referendums in political theory and among political scientists owes more to a broader skepticism with popular politics altogether. Referendums are stereotyped as democratically problematic, not because citizens are in fact ill-informed voting fodder (if this were the case how could we legitimize representative democracy?) but because they get in the way of politics as an almost exclusively elite process interspersed by the occasional inconvenient election. The referendum is not a perfect device, and if not properly regulated it can indeed be manipulated by elites. But if the process is properly designed we now know it can work well.

The success of the referendum as an electoral event comes at a time of great proliferation for the referendum.[58] The success of the Scottish process may well encourage other states to use the referendum for major constitutional decisions and may also encourage other substate nationalists to lobby for a referendum.[59] The referendum is indeed on the rise in many other states, and this is itself part of a wider process of grassroots political engagement by citizens through non-conventional avenues. The politics of protest has been much talked about in recent years, but at a more prosaic level the internet has opened up a far more diverse range of sources of information for citizens, and at the same time has presented platforms for horizontal engagement among citizens through social media in ways which even ten years ago were barely feasible. Many citizens who are engaging in political argument to an unprecedented extent with many more interlocutors than ever before will not be satisfied unless they also have the power to make political decisions.

A second outcome of the referendum is that it arguably serves as a case study in how the issue of secession can be resolved in a consensual way. The fact that the UK accepted the democratic legitimacy of the SNP government to hold a referendum on the basis that it had won an election with this as a manifesto commitment, and the cooperation of the UK state in making the process free, fair, and democratic, is one that other countries might draw lessons from. That a majority of Scots voted "No" in the referendum may be testimony to the fact that a state which behaves in this way toward a national minority may well encourage members of this minority not to vote for secession. In this way the UK process may be seen as something of a gentle civilizer[60] of the secession question. Of course, other countries will argue that secession is simply not permissible under their Constitution, at least not without a constitutional amendment which requires broad consensus across the state,[61] and I am certainly not making the case for a general right of constitutional secession. But the UK/Scottish model does

[58] Tierney, *Constitutional Referendums* (n 37).

[59] Stephen Tierney, "'And the Winner is . . . the Referendum': Scottish Independence and the Deliberative Participation of Citizens" (*International Journal of Constitutional Law Blog*, September 26, 2014) <www.iconnectblog.com/2014/09/and-the-winner-is-the-referendum-scottish-independence-and-the-deliberative-participation-of-citizens/>.

[60] Martti Koskenniemi, *The Gentle Civilizer of Nations: The Rise and Fall of International Law 1870–1960* (Cambridge University Press 2001).

[61] This is the position taken by both the Spanish government and the Constitutional Court in Spain.

offer a template for how a good process can be arrived at, which does offer hope for good relations after the referendum, whatever the outcome.

A final lesson from the process comes with the way in which the referendum has been followed by moves to further constitutional change. The UK immediately embarked upon such change. Although the flaws in the process are deeply frustrating, particularly for people elsewhere in the UK who feel disenfranchised by a process that seems to have been all about Scotland, the reality of the contemporary plurinational state is that there may never be a "settlement" as such. This may in the longer term prove to be pathological for the UK unless some kind of federal solution can be found which has the buy-in of the UK's four main territories. In the end, all that can be done is to appeal to the consent of these peoples to commit to the UK. In light of the UK's history as a union of nations, built upon consent, simply to proscribe secession and refuse to accept the democratic will of substate peoples is both undemocratic and potentially counter-productive.

Demands for further constitutional change will likely be a permanent feature of constitutional politics in the UK as they have been in other states such as Canada, Spain, and Belgium. The best that can be done is to try to manage these demands within an evolving state. Frustrating though this may be for those who seek constitutional closure, many situations discussed in this book show that endless constitutional disagreement is far from the worst affliction for multicultural and multinational polities.

16

Dealing with Territorial Cleavages

The Rise and Fall of Ukraine's Faustian Bargain

Lucan Ahmad Way

Overview

This chapter explores efforts in Ukraine to create a constitutional system that accommodates the country's stark regional differences. The Ukrainian case highlights the fact that, even in a context of deep cross-regional differences, regional demands for autonomy are not necessarily enduring but may fluctuate quite dramatically over short periods of time depending on the political situation in the center. Demands by territorially concentrated groups for constitutional accommodation varied significantly from the breakup of the USSR in 1991 until 2015. With the partial exception of Crimea, central actors alleviated demands for decentralization and federalism by giving key regional interests and identities a stake in central power. By the mid 1990s, a powerful coalition for centralization—sometimes referred to as the "pact with the devil"—emerged between national democrats seeking state support for Ukrainian language and national symbols on the one side; and eastern economic interests on the other seeking access to rents and administrative mechanisms for maintaining power. The collapse of this arrangement from 2010 to 2014 contributed to the onset of violent conflict.

Background

While divisions in Ukraine have sometimes been described in ethnic terms, they primarily reflect broader, historically grounded and regionally concentrated disagreements over Ukraine's place in the world. This divide can best be described as one between "Ukrainophile" and "Russophile" visions of Ukraine. Ukrainophiles have core preferences for Ukrainian language, culture, history, and symbols and support alliances with Europe rather than Russia. Russophiles generally support Ukrainian independence but view Ukraine as part of Russia's "civilizational space," speak Russian, and support geopolitical alliances with Russia rather than the United States or Europe.[1]

Ukraine: West, East, and Center

The relative strength of Russophile and Ukrainophile views has varied enormously in different regions. A patchwork of areas with quite distinct histories, Ukraine can

[1] Oleh Protsyk, "Majority-Minority Relations in the Ukraine" (2008) 1 Journal on Ethnopolitics and Minority Issues in Europe 1, 6.

Territory and Power in Constitutional Transitions. First Edition. Edited by Michael Anderson and Sujit Choudhry. Dealing with Territorial Cleavages: The Rise and Fall of Ukraine's Faustian Bargain

roughly be divided into three regions—west, center, and east—that reflect historical and ethnolinguistic differences.[2]

First, western Ukraine, populated by Ukrainian speaking ethnic Ukrainians, is mostly dominated by provinces that only became part of Russia or the USSR after World War II. In particular, Galicia was under Austro-Hungarian rule prior to WWI, within Poland in the interwar period and was only incorporated into the Soviet Union in 1939. Galicia is the center of modern Ukrainian nationalism.[3] Austro-Hungarian authorities in the nineteenth century actively promoted Ukraine as a separate nationality as part of an effort to divide the local population from the neighboring Poles on one side and Russians on the other. Most critically, the Austrian government actively promoted the expansion of mass schooling in the Ukrainian language, which as a result became "the working language of many and diverse social, cultural, economic, and political associations."[4] Following its incorporation into the USSR after WWII, anti-Soviet insurgents operated in western Ukraine through the early 1950s. This region was a particularly potent source of anti-Soviet dissidents during the Soviet period.

By contrast, eastern/southern Ukraine, which became part of the Russian empire before the nineteenth century, has been the region most integrated into Russia. It is dominated by Russophones, and exhibited a relatively underdeveloped sense of Ukrainian identity. Within eastern Ukraine, the Donbas region (Luhansk and Donetsk) has possessed a strong regional identity. An important coal-producing region, Donbas became a major industrial center in the late nineteenth and early twentieth centuries and attracted immigrants from throughout the Russian empire and later Soviet Union. During the Soviet era, leaders from eastern Ukraine (including Leonid Brezhnev (Dnipropetrovsk) and Nikita Khrushchev (Donbas)) were over-represented in top-level Soviet leadership positions.

At the end of the Soviet era, the region witnessed major strike activity by miners that threatened Soviet power. After the collapse of the Soviet Union, Donbas was host to a highly profitable metals industry and was beset by violent conflicts among competing mafia groups. In addition to major steel and coal production in Donbas, Dnipropetrovsk in the east was the site of the USSR's largest missile factory—*Yuzhmash*—whose director, Leonid Kuchma, became President in 1994.

Next, Crimea in the south stood out as the only region with a Russian ethnic majority and the region most recently incorporated into Ukraine. In 1954, Khrushchev incorporated Crimea into the Ukrainian republic as part of an effort by the recently selected General Secretary of the Party to solidify his support in the Central Committee.[5] Within Crimea, the Crimean Tatars, constituting about 10 percent of the population, represented a vocal and relatively well organized minority. Native to the region, the Tatars suffered deportation by Stalin for alleged collaboration with the Nazis during WWII. In the late 1980s and 1990s, several hundred thousand Tatars returned to Crimea. Tatars, represented by a council (*Mejlis*), have been strong supporters of the Ukrainian government, which has been seen as an ally against Russian aggression.

[2] Dominique Arel and Andrew Wilson, "The Ukrainian Parliamentary Elections" (1994) 3 (26) Radio Free Europe/Radio Liberty Research Report 1, 6; Valeriy Khmelko and Andrew Wilson, "Regionalism and Ethnic and Linguistic Cleavages in Ukraine" in Taras Kuzio (ed.), *Contemporary Ukraine: Dynamics of Post-Soviet Transformation* (ME Sharpe 1998).

[3] Roman Szporluk, *Ukraine, a Brief History* (Ukrainian Festival Committee 1979) 78, 88; Keith Darden, *Resisting Occupation in Eurasia* (Cambridge University Press forthcoming).

[4] Szporluk (n 3) 78, 88; Darden (n 3) 101–2.

[5] Mark Kramer, "Why Did Russia Give Away Crimea Sixty Years Ago?" (*Wilson Center*, March 19, 2014) <www.wilsoncenter.org/publication/why-did-russia-give-away-crimea-sixty-years-ago2014>.

Finally, central Ukraine lacked the history of intense nationalism found in much of western Ukraine but consisted of a greater number of Ukrainophones than in eastern and southern Ukraine. Effectively, it functioned as a "swing" region in the 1990s and 2000s. In 1991 and 1994, it voted overwhelmingly for the more Russophile candidate. However, by the early 2000s, support in central Ukraine had shifted away from Russia. In 2004 and 2010, over 60 percent of central Ukrainians voted for Ukrainophile candidates.

Divisions between east and west Ukraine have reflected distinct attitudinal communities. While surveys have suggested relatively equal levels of support for democracy, there are striking differences in foreign policy attitudes—including support for NATO, the EU, and Russia.[6] Polarization between Russophile and Ukrainophile attitudes was "an enduring fact of Ukrainian political life" in the post-Soviet era.[7]

Overall, the central regional tensions in Ukraine have not reflected typical conflicts between minorities on the one side and a dominant majority on the other. Certainly, traditionally defined territorially concentrated minorities existed in Ukraine—Tatars in Crimea, Hungarians in Zakarpatiia, Romanians in Bukovyna, and Bulgarians and Gagauzians in Odesa. However, with the partial exception of the Tatars in Crimea, these groups were weakly mobilized and never presented a serious challenge to Ukrainian statehood.

At the same time, the Russian "minority" shared many characteristics of a dominant group in post-Soviet Ukraine. While ethnic Russians represented fewer than 20 percent of the population,[8] Russophile identity has been quite powerful. After 70 years of mostly pro-Russian Soviet rule, Ukrainian language and culture in the 1990s and 2000s were on the defensive. Just over a third of the population spoke Ukrainian at home; a third spoke Russian and just under a third spoke both about equally.[9] Culturally, Russian has been dominant. Outside of western Ukraine, Russian was spoken in large cities—including the capital Kyiv. Almost no movies were dubbed into Ukrainian and Ukrainian language publications were dwarfed by Russian language ones.[10] Indeed, the Ukrainian language was widely perceived as requiring positive discrimination as a way of countering its perceived marginalization under Soviet rule.[11]

Russophile strength also emerged from Russian government support, industrial production, and the fact that a plurality of the country– just under 50 percent—resided in the east. By contrast, just over 50 percent lived in central (30 percent) and western (20 percent) Ukraine. Critically, the relative distribution of power in the country meant that both Russophiles and Ukrainophiles (with the support of populations in central Ukraine) had a plausible chance at national power.

In turn, support for regional autonomy in Ukraine has fluctuated significantly depending on whether or not regional groups could expect to gain national power. In the nineteenth century, nationalist Ukrainian intellectuals supported federalism as a means of promoting Ukrainian culture within the Russian empire, which Ukrainians could never expect to dominate.[12] In the late Soviet period, politicians in Galicia

[6] Pippa Norris (2014). "Ukrainians Are Not That Divided in Their Views of Democracy." Washingtonpost.com. March 3.See also Ivan Katchanovski, *Cleft Countries: Regional Political Divisions and Cultures in Post-Soviet Ukraine and Moldova* (Ibidem-Verlag 2006) 113, 114.

[7] Dominique Arel and Valeriy Khmelko, "The Russian Factor and Territorial Polarization in Ukraine" (1996) 9 (1–2) The Harriman Review 81, 90.

[8] All figures here refer to the pre-2014 borders of Ukraine. [9] Protsyk (n 1) 24.

[10] ibid 2–3. [11] ibid 21–2.

[12] Kataryna Wolczuk, *The Moulding of Ukraine: The Constitutional Politics of State Formation* (Central European University Press 2001) 68.

advocated Galician autonomy in order to protect the region from a pro Communist majority that dominated the rest of Ukraine—but quickly abandoned autonomy as "anti-state" once Ukraine became independent.[13]

In the post-Soviet period, Ukrainophiles have had the greatest stake in Ukrainian unity—and therefore have consistently supported unitary structures. By contrast, the east has often been on the defensive. As we see below, the evolution of support for federalism in the post-Soviet era was a direct reflection of the east's perceived stake in national power in Ukraine. In the early 1990s, insecurity, fostered by the sudden break with Russia and the first President's anti-Russian policies, created the basis for strong support for federalism and a brief experiment with decentralization. However, the rise to power of Leonid Kuchma, a former head of Yuzhmash missile factory in eastern Ukraine, created the basis for a powerful coalition for centralization rooted in a Faustian bargain between western Ukrainophiles and eastern economic interests—a bargain that lasted in various forms until 2010.

The Period of Constitutional Engagement: 1991–96

It can be said that the entire post-Soviet period has been one large constitutional moment. Outside a couple of years after the passage of the 1996 Constitution, major political forces have contested and renegotiated core elements of the constitutional structure. In the early 1990s (1991–96), Ukraine operated under the old Soviet Ukrainian Constitution that was amended over 220 times.[14] In June 1996, politicians finally negotiated a new Constitution that mostly remains in force today. However, since then, major efforts were undertaken to strengthen (2000–02; 2004–10) or weaken (2002–04; 2014) Presidential power. In particular, a reduction of Presidential power was introduced in 2005, reversed in 2010, and re-introduced in 2014. At the same time, center-periphery relations have only been the subject of contestation for part of that time—1991–96 and after the 2014 crisis. This chapter focuses on these two periods.

From the beginning, the process of Ukraine's independence was a product of compromise between east and west. On the one hand, western Ukraine was a major site of anti-Soviet mobilization—and therefore an attractive Western ally at the start of the 1990s when Soviet rule had been heavily discredited by economic breakdown and political crisis. Western Ukraine became a "a hotbed of nationalist dissent" and "by far the most politicized region of Ukraine."[15] At the same time, the east hosted most of the population and the industrial wealth—without which an independent Ukraine was unimaginable.

Out of this distribution of forces, there emerged what might be thought of as the first Faustian bargain between Leonid Kravchuk, Ukraine's first President, on one side and western Ukrainian nationalists on the other. The Party Ideology Secretary in the late 1980s, Kravchuk was selected to take charge of the Ukrainian legislature in 1990. The Communist establishment, which had previously shown no interest in Ukrainian independence, selected Kravchuk because he was one of the few members of the political elite who dared debating leaders of the pro-Ukrainian Rukh movement

[13] ibid 72. [14] ibid 128.

[15] Mark R Beissinger, *Nationalist Mobilization and the Collapse of the Soviet State* (Cambridge University Press 2002) 192; David R Marples, "Elections in Ukraine: An Analysis" *Ukrainian Weekly* (Kiev, March 4, 1990) 15.

that had emerged in 1989.[16] But instead of combating demands for independence, Kravchuk quickly co-opted the cause of Ukrainian independence. He challenged efforts by Gorbachev to negotiate a new union treaty in 1990 and early 1991. In a referendum on December 8, 1991, Ukrainians voted overwhelmingly for independence. In a Presidential election held on the same day, Kravchuk won in the first round—capturing a majority in eastern Ukraine and a plurality of most western oblasts.

Yet, Kravchuk was unable to hold onto the support of eastern industrial interests for long. Economic collapse, Ukraine's dysfunctional state, and fears of Ukrainianization fostered increasing demands for decentralization in the east and south in the early 1990s. First, rather than facilitating economic growth as many had hoped, the sudden breakup of the Soviet Union contributed to a severe economic downturn and hyperinflation in Ukraine. This crisis severely tested support for independence among forces in the east that had backed sovereignty as a means of promoting economic growth.[17]

Simultaneously, the sudden dissolution of Soviet power in mid-1991 deprived Ukraine of a functional center—a fact that encouraged many in the east to seek greater autonomy. Many important state institutions—including the army, security services, and key economic ministries—had been controlled directly by Moscow prior to the Soviet collapse. Further, the Communist Party, the main means of central control in the Soviet period, disappeared without a trace in 1991. New central mechanisms of control had yet to be institutionalized. In the early 1990s, "the juxtaposition of the elements of the system of Soviets with Presidentialism meant that regional leaders could decide on their own allegiance: either to the President, the Prime Minister, or the chairman of parliament."[18] Regional presidential prefects, established in March 1992 to increase central executive power,[19] simply added to the confusion at the local level about who was in charge.[20]

In this context, many—including Volodymyr Hryniov, the deputy head of parliament—thought the best solution was to strengthen local control as a way of avoiding the dysfunction in Kyiv.[21] Hryniov argued that federalism would stimulate bottom-up reforms and innovation and that unitarism would only hasten centrifugal tendencies in Ukraine.

Simultaneously, President Kravchuk's embrace of Ukrainian nationalism fostered fears of Ukrainianization in the east. The President encouraged the use of the Ukrainian language in the media, education, and government and limited cooperation with Russia.[22] Partly as a result, trade with Russia significantly declined.[23] Kravchuk's efforts to ensure that central state television broadcast in Ukrainian had the unintended consequence of alienating many in the east.

In response, heads of heavy industries with previously strong ties to Russia—coal mining and steel—became vocal proponents of decentralization and federalism. They supported groups such as the Interregional Block for Reforms (IBR), headed by Hryniov, which claimed to represent eastern and southern Ukraine. The most

[16] *Foreign Broadcast Information Service Daily Report, USSR* December 6, 1991, p. 74.

[17] Andrew Wilson, *Ukrainian Nationalism in the 1990s: A Minority Faith* (Cambridge University Press 1997).

[18] Wolczuk, *The Moulding of Ukraine* (n 12) 139.

[19] The prefects, appointed by the President, were given the right to annul decisions of local radas, see Wolczuk (n 14) 122.

[20] *Nezavisimost'* (newspaper) June 22, 1994: 5.

[21] Wolczuk, *The Moulding of Ukraine* (n 12) 73.

[22] Paul D'Anieri, *Economic Interdependence in Ukrainian–Russian Relations* (SUNY Press 1999) 139.

[23] ibid 112.

important proponent of decentralization became Leonid Kuchma, the former head of the *Yuzhmash* missile factory in Dnipropetrovsk. Supported by the IBR and a wide range of enterprise directors, Kuchma became Prime Minister of Ukraine in mid-1992.

Demands for decentralization abounded during this period—particularly in Donbas and Crimea, which both had strong ties to Russia.[24] First, Donbas became the most vocal region outside Crimea in support of decentralization. While there was little support in the east for separation from Ukraine, many supported greater autonomy.[25] Donetsk and Luhansk councils voted in favor of regional autonomy in June 1993; while Luhansk voted that Russian should be the official state language alongside Ukrainian. During the March 1994 parliamentary elections, Luhansk and Donetsk held local referendums calling for full membership in the CIS, a federal structure for Ukraine, and the immediate introduction of Russian as an official language alongside Ukrainian in the Donbas region.[26] Most critically, in early 1993, coal miners, backed by regional leaders and enterprise heads, struck throughout the region demanding regional autonomy, higher wages, and a referendum on early parliamentary and presidential elections. Partly in response, Efim Zvyahilsky, the mayor of Donetsk and the head of one of the largest mines in Donbas, was brought in as acting Prime Minister.

The early 1990s also witnessed powerful movements against the center in Crimea, the only region in Ukraine with a Russian ethnic majority. In early 1991 before the Soviet collapse, a referendum passed overwhelmingly in Crimea to make the region an autonomous republic directly subordinate to Moscow rather than Kyiv. After the collapse of the USSR in late 1991, however, the referendum was essentially ignored and Crimea became an autonomous republic within Ukraine. In May 1992, Crimean leaders passed the Constitution of the Republic of Crimea that proclaimed the territory to be a sovereign state that "enters the state of Ukraine and defines its relations with Ukraine on the basis of contract and agreements."[27] The Ukrainian parliament immediately rejected this Constitution and a compromise Constitution was agreed upon in September 1992 that made Crimea a constituent part of Ukraine. Separatism reached its peak in 1994 with the election of a pro-Russian president Yurii Meshkov. Meshkov called for the boycott of Ukrainian parliamentary elections that year[28] and his "Russia Blok" won fifty-four of ninety-eight seats in the regional assembly.[29] Meshkov changed Crimea to Moscow time.

These powerful forces for devolution ushered in a period of significant *de facto* regional decentralization. In 1993, the Ukrainian legislature abolished central control of regional executives instituted by Kravchuk and transferred control over these administrations to the local assemblies. In 1994, regional heads became directly elected. The leaders of regions combined responsibilities of local self-government and representatives of the central state. They could not be dismissed by the central government.[30] In June 1994, newly elected heads of oblast administrations gained "extensive"

[24] Wolczuk, *The Moulding of Ukraine* (n 12) 70; Valentyna Romanova, "Regionalist Origins of Centralisation in Ukraine" (2012) 20 (1) Sfera Politicii 54, 57.

[25] Jaroslaw Martyniuk, "Ukrainian Independence and Territorial Integrity" Radio Free Europe/Radio Liberty Research Report (March 27, 1992). According to surveys in September and October 1991, 6 percent of easterners and fewer than 10 percent of Donetsk residents supported seceding to Russia.

[26] Wolczuk, *The Moulding of Ukraine* (n 12) 71.

[27] ibid.

[28] Due to turnout requirements, this boycott resulted in twelve of twenty-three national parliamentary seats remaining vacant through 1998, see Gwendolyn Sasse, "The 'New' Ukraine: A State of Regions" (2001) 11 (3) Regional and Federal Studies 69, 88.

[29] ibid.

[30] Romanova (n 24) 55–6.

powers over their territories.[31] 1994–95 would end up being the period of greatest regional decentralization.

Then in 1994, Kuchma was elected as President on a platform supporting federalism and closer ties to Russia. Kuchma's close advisor was Hryniov, a vocal proponent of federalism. Yet, the new President made a stunning shift in policy once in power—establishing a powerful coalition for centralization between eastern oligarchs and Ukrainophiles in western Ukraine. First, Kuchma preserved Ukraine's western orientation—downgrading Ukraine's membership in the CIS and seeking NATO membership.[32] Kuchma's rise to power in 1994 also represented a fundamental reorientation of eastern economic interests away from Russia and toward Ukraine. The rise of large financial-industrialists in Russia in the mid-1990s generated fear among many in Ukraine's economic elite that Russians would use their greater access to wealth to grab valuable properties and out-compete Ukrainians in such vulnerable sectors as banking and finance.[33] As Andrew Wilson notes, the eastern industrial elite began "to realize the new Ukrainian state could make them very rich indeed."[34]

Simultaneously, Kuchma rapidly abandoned support for federalism. Several factors seem to have encouraged this conversion. First, national democrats feared that decentralization would only heighten regional differences and "provide centrifugal forces with symbolic legitimacy and material resources."[35] Decentralization was thought to be especially dangerous in a country "haunted by the spectre of centrifugal forces."[36]

At the same time, Kuchma's control over central institutions made it very easy for him to convince his supporters to abandon support for decentralization. Many oligarchs sought central state subsidies and access to the central state provided ample opportunities for enrichment.[37] With a clear stake in the central government, eastern interests had little reason to continue to press for decentralization. Simultaneously, centralization was considered essential for Kuchma to maintain national power.[38] By the late 1990s, Kuchma used regional appointments in order to promote a system of electoral corruption. The ability to bring in votes for the President and his allies would become an important criterion for advancement under Kuchma.

After his election, Kuchma took immediate steps to centralize state power: he issued decrees to restore Presidential control over regional administrations that had been handed over to regional councils, and subordinated elected heads of regional councils to the President. To allay concerns of regional leaders, he created an advisory (but largely powerless) Council of Regions consisting of heads of oblasts and the mayors of Kyiv and Sebastopol.

Kuchma also centralized control over Crimea. In response to separatist tendencies in Crimea, Kuchma pushed through a "law on the Autonomous Republic of Crimea" in March 1995 that abolished its presidency and placed executive authority directly under Kuchma's control.[39] The Crimean President Meshkov, facing divisions within his own ranks, was unable to fight back. From 1995 until June 1996, the government

[31] Wolczuk, *The Moulding of Ukraine* (n 12) 70.

[32] Dominique Arel, "Ukraine: The Muddle Way" (1998) 97 (621) Current History 342, 344.

[33] Rosaria Puglisi, "Clashing Agendas? Economic Interests, Elite Coalitions and Prospects for Cooperation between Russia and Ukraine" (2003) 55 (6) Europe-Asia Studies 827, 836.

[34] Andrew Wilson, *The Ukrainians: Unexpected Nation* (Yale University Press 2000) 195.

[35] Wolczuk, *The Moulding of Ukraine* (n 12) 74. [36] ibid 65. [37] ibid.

[38] Kimitaka Matsuzato, "All Kuchma's Men: The Reshuffling of Ukrainian Governors and the Presidential Election of 1999" (2001) 42 (6) Post-Soviet Geography and Economics 416,

[39] Kataryna Wolczuk, "Catching Up with 'Europe'? Constitutional Debates on the Territorial-Administrative Model in Independent Ukraine" (2002) 12 (2) Regional & Federal Studies 65, 71.

chipped away at Crimea's effective sovereignty but agreed to allow Crimea to retain the title "Autonomous republic," a Constitution, and a regional assembly.[40] The Ukrainian President was given the power to appoint a powerful presidential representative and key ministers. The ministry of internal affairs and security forces were staffed entirely by Kyiv. The responsibilities of the Crimean legislature remained limited. However, Gwendolyn Sasse argues that the protracted negotiations themselves were a "vital mechanism in defusing conflict potential."[41] "The process itself, rather than the constitutional status, was the key to conflict prevention."[42] The government responded to tensions by repeatedly delaying decisions on controversial issues such as dual citizenship. While probably not part of a conscious strategy, these delays meant that the final negotiations took place "when the emotional dust had settled and the potential for conflict had by and large been resolved."[43]

After gaining power, Kuchma also set about passing a new Constitution.[44] Until then, negotiations over the new Constitution had taken place entirely within the confines of the legislature and had gone nowhere. In October 1994, Kuchma created a relatively inclusive new Constitutional Commission as a "state commission" combining representatives of both the executive and legislative branches. However, the Commission got bogged down in the highly contentious issue of how to describe the sovereign people and could not agree on procedures for passing the Constitution.

Realizing that this commission was unlikely to achieve any results, Kuchma decided to push for a "stop gap" Constitution that could be passed as a regular law with fewer votes in the legislature.[45] Initially Kuchma met with little success. To resolve the deadlock, Kuchma pushed through the creation of a special ad hoc commission in which each parliamentary faction was given one representative—a system that favored national democratic parties that were much smaller than the left-wing factions. He succeeded in doing this by threatening to hold a referendum on the confidence in the President and parliament. Given the unpopularity of the legislature, the head of parliament, Oleksandr Moroz, agreed.

Finally, a temporary "Constitutional Agreement" to replace the old Soviet Constitution was passed with the support of six center-right parties and Moroz. After significant negotiation (and likely a fair amount of bribery), the agreement was voted on and signed by a majority of 240 deputies. The accord strengthened Presidential powers and subordinated provincial and rayon executive administrations directly under Presidential control. To allay the concerns of provincial heads, Kuchma promised to retain existing officials in their positions.[46] The agreement was set to expire after one year.

However, progress on passing a Constitution remained slow. Kuchma at this point abandoned the Commission and instead relied on ad hoc expert commissions over which he had much greater control. In March 1996, he supported a "March draft" Constitution that gave the President significant power and created a directly elected bicameral legislature consisting of an upper house in which Ukraine's provinces would be given equal representation. Bicameralism was widely opposed—even by many pro-Presidential groups—because it gave disproportionate representation to more lightly populated western provinces and because it was thought to undermine collective action and influence of the legislative branch. National democrats feared that an upper house would create a back door route to federalism. In this draft, local self-government

40 Sasse, "The 'New' Ukraine" (n 28) 92–3. 41 ibid 91. 42 ibid 94.
43 ibid 93.
44 Unless otherwise noted, this description draws from Wolczuk, *The Moulding of Ukraine* (n 12).
45 A simple majority rather than two-thirds majority. 46 Matsuzato (n 38) 424.

was guaranteed in cities and villages. However, rayon and provincial administrations were made directly subordinate to President and Cabinet of Ministers. The March draft, which was widely opposed by parties across the political spectrum, went nowhere in the legislature.

Then, on June 26, Kuchma threatened that, if a Constitution was not passed, he would hold a popular referendum on the much-hated March draft. While such a referendum had no legal status (and indeed a similar constitutional referendum held in 2001 went nowhere), the prospect that the March draft might become law concentrated the minds of deputies. In a 23-hour session on the night of June 27–8, Moroz led a non-stop debate in which article after article were voted on by the legislature. With help from the Presidential administration (and bribery[47]), a Constitution was passed on the morning of June 28 with 315 of 450 votes.

The Constitution was a formal articulation of the Faustian bargain that defined Ukrainian politics in its first decades. On the one hand, Ukrainophiles obtained ratification of Ukrainian national symbols and Ukrainian language as the sole official language of the country. On the other hand, eastern elites obtained effective control over the state apparatus to maintain power and secure rents. Seeking to use state power to promote Ukrainian language and culture, the national democrats strongly supported a unitary state structure. They viewed both parliament and decentralization as threats to Ukrainian statehood—parliament because it was dominated by the Russophile left in the 1990s and decentralization because it was seen to promote centrifugal forces.

Kuchma, on the other hand, did not care much about the national issue but cared deeply about creating a strong vertical of state power that would give him the administrative resources necessary to maintain power. Kuchma opposed the Communists who sought to undermine Presidential power. Thus to appease the right, Kuchma quickly adopted the rhetoric of statehood—firmly supporting Ukrainian national symbols, and anthem.

Within two short years then, Kuchma helped to kill elite support for federalism in Ukraine. In 1995–96, he built a powerful coalition for centralization that brought national democrats interested in supporting Ukrainian statehood together with oligarchs interested in protection from powerful Russian economic interests, central state subsidies and the use of central administrative resources to maintain power. By the late 1990s, federalism had almost completely disappeared from political discourse.[48]

Outcome

After the passage of the Constitution, the Faustian pact evolved into different forms: a single pyramid compromise 1996–2004 characterized by strong Presidential power; and a double pyramid compromise 2004–09 characterized by stronger parliamentary authority.[49] During the first period, increased Presidential power embedded in the 1996 Constitution gave Kuchma enlarged capacity to promote electoral fraud. The centrally controlled tax administration, and other government agencies, were systematically used to coerce businesspeople, politicians, and local officials into backing the

[47] Yuri Lukanov, *Tretyi Prezident: Polytichnii portret Leonida Kuchmi*. Kyiv: Tak Spravi, 1996, i155–6*)*.

[48] Sasse "The "New" Ukraine" (n 28) 82; Protsyk (n 1).

[49] These terms come from Henry Hale, *Patronal Politics: Eurasian Regime Dynamics in Comparative Perspective* (Cambridge University Press 2015).

regime during elections.[50] Simultaneously, regional officials were now held accountable for success in bringing in votes for the President and his allies. Officials who did not bring sufficient votes in Kuchma's 1999 reelection were let go.[51] Indeed, the rise of Viktor Yanukovych, who was governor of Donetsk in the late 1990s, can be directly traced to his ability to mobilize support in Donetsk, which had previously been dominated by the Communists. After bringing disproportionate support for pro-Kuchma forces in the 2002 parliamentary election, Yanukovych was selected as Prime Minister and became Kuchma's chosen successor in 2004.

Simultaneously, Kuchma built a system of wealthy "oligarchs" who relied on Kuchma for access to rents. In exchange for support for Kuchma, oligarchs gained "privileged access to privatisation, budget subsidies, quotas and licences for the import and export of oil, gas, wheat, vodka and tobacco."[52] For these figures, centralization offered greater access to resources—including massive subsidies from the state budget.[53]

For a very long time, Ukrainophile forces were happy to support Kuchma because Kuchma consistently resisted Russian interference into Ukrainian domestic affairs. The President refused to join the Russian-dominated Eurasian Customs Union and fought back efforts by Russians to take ownership over Ukrainian gas pipelines. Domestically, Kuchma supported the existing language law that made Ukrainian the sole official language of the country.

This arrangement, however, began to unravel in 2000 with the release of secretly recorded tapes of Kuchma that exposed massive corruption and seemed to suggest that Kuchma ordered the murder of the Internet journalist, Georgi Gongadze. After the release of the tapes turned Kuchma into a Western pariah, Russia became Kuchma's virtually major ally. Then in 2002 Kuchma selected Viktor Yanukovych, the governor of Donetsk, to be Prime Minister and to run as the government's candidate in the 2004 Presidential election.[54] Yanukovych marked a striking break from Kuchma. He was closely associated with the Donetsk "clan" and stridently pro-Russian.

In the run-up to the election, the opposition coalesced around the candidacy of Viktor Yushchenko, Prime Minister from 1999 to 2001, who was highly regarded in the West. Yushchenko, whose popularity was bolstered by a surge in the Ukrainian economy during his tenure, was strongly supported in Western Ukraine. In the months before the election, polls consistently showed Yushchenko with a slight lead over Yanukovych. However, on election day on November 21, blatant fraud in Donetsk and several other provinces[55] resulted in a narrow official victory of Yanukovych.

In response to this fraud, protest—primarily by western and central Ukrainians exploded. Hundreds of thousands of protesters took to the streets for three weeks in the center of Kyiv.[56] Galicia, which made up about 10 percent of Ukraine's

[50] Keith Darden, "Blackmail as a Tool of State Domination: Ukraine Under Kuchma" (2001) 10 East European Constitutional Review 67.

[51] Matsuzato (n 38).

[52] Puglisi "Clashing Agendas?" (n 33) 837.

[53] Romanova (n 24) 58.

[54] While Kuchma faced a two-term limit in 2004, he engineered a court ruling allowing him to run for a third time. In the run-up to the 2004 election he kept open the possibility that he would run—but ultimately chose not to because he was so unpopular that a victory would have come at enormous cost.

[55] For discussions of fraud, see Karatnycky (2005); Lucan Way, "Kuchma's Failed Authoritarianism" (2005) 16 (2) Journal of Democracy 131.

[56] Lucan Way, *Pluralism by Default: Weak Autocrats and the Rise of Political Competition* (Johns Hopkins University Press 2015); also Mark R. Beissinger "The Semblance of Democratic Revolution: Coalitions in Ukraine's Orange Revolution" (2013) 107 (3) American Political Science Review 574, 581–2.

population, accounted for about 36 percent of all pro-Yushchenko protesters—more than double the share of protesters (14 percent) from the capital, Kyiv, where the main demonstrations took place.

Despite their powerful capacity to bring people to the streets, Ukrainophile forces demonstrated an acute awareness of the need to avoid alienating pro-Russian forces in 2004. While Yushchenko's "Our Ukraine" coalition included several radical nationalists in its ranks, the movement strenuously avoided using nationalist symbols during the Orange Revolution.[57] Most critically (and in contrast to EuroMaidan) Yushchenko refrained from seizing power unilaterally in late 2004. While Yushchenko initially had himself sworn in as President a day after protests began in November 2004, pro-Orange forces backed off for fear of sparking regional tensions. According to Taras Stetskiv, "fear of splitting Ukraine" dissuaded activists from seizing power and encouraged them to negotiate a settlement with Kuchma forces.[58] Indeed, in late December Yanukovych attended a short-lived "All-Ukrainian Congress of Deputies" held in the Donetsk city of Severodonetsk. The congress, whose keynote speaker was Iuri Luzhkov, the Mayor of Moscow who supported Russian annexation of Crimea, called for a "federal South-Eastern republic based in Kharkiv."[59] Yanukovych threatened to organize a referendum on this question if Yushchenko became President.

However, talks between Yushchenko and Kuchma in Kyiv cut short these demands. Yushchenko negotiated a constitutional settlement with Kuchma forces to weaken the Presidency in exchange for a rerun of the election.[60] As a result of a two-thirds constitutional agreement in mid-December 2004, the legislature became responsible for selecting the prime minister and approving most cabinet members nominated by the prime minister. Such reforms would help spur significant competition in the Yushchenko era.

Split pyramid bargain 2005–09

The victory of Yushchenko marked an important milestone for Ukrainophile forces. Yushchenko was a much more ardent supporter of Ukrainian nationalism than was Kuchma. In 2006, Yushchenko helped push through a highly controversial law that officially declared the 1932–33 man-made famine in the Soviet Union as a "genocide" against the Ukrainian people—a move that was strongly opposed by Russophile forces.[61] Yushchenko also honored highly controversial figures in the Ukrainian nationalist resistance in WWII.[62]

[57] Anton Shekhovtsov, "The Creeping Resurgence of the Ukrainian Radical Right? The Case of the Freedom Party" (2011) 63 (2) Europe-Asia Studies 203, 211.

[58] Tatiana Silina, Serhii Rakhmanin, and Olga Dmitricheva, "Anatomiia dushi maidana" *Zerkalo Nedeli* (Kiev December 11–17, 2004).

[59] Taras Kuzio, "Nationalism, Identity and Civil Society in Ukraine: Understanding the Orange Revolution" *Communist and Post-Communist Studies* 43, No. 3 (September 2010): 285

[60] Silina, Rakhmanin, and Dmitricheva (n 58).

[61] Jan Maksymiuk, "Ukraine: Parliament Recognizes Soviet-Era Famine As Genocide" (*Radio Free Europe/Radio Liberty* Research Report, November 29, 2006) <www.rferl.org/a/1073094.html>. While the famine resulted in the deaths of millions of Ukrainians, there is no scholarly agreement about whether this policy was specifically aimed at Ukrainian nationals or was instead part of a much broader murderous policy under Stalin.

[62] RFE/RL, "Yushchenko Defends Making Bandera, Shukhevych 'Heroes Of Ukraine'" (*Radio Free Europe/Radio Liberty*, March 23, 2010) <www.rferl.org/a/Yushchenko_Defends_Making_Bandera_Shukhevich_Heroes_Of_Ukraine/1991175.html>.

At the same time, the Orange Revolution unified political forces in the east—giving them a powerful means to contest for central power. Under Kuchma, the east had divided among a loose collection of parties and non-party politicians. The Orange Revolution united this electorate into the Party of Regions headed by Viktor Yanukovych. While the party had reaped just 17 percent in the east in coalition with other parties in earlier elections, the party by itself won close to 60 percent in the east in 2006 and 2007. Yanukovych himself garnered 77 percent of the vote in the east and a respectable 44 percent nationally in the final, relatively free round of the Presidential election in 2004. Founded in Donetsk in the late 1990s, the party initially demanded greater decentralization of power in Ukraine. However, with the rise of Yanukovych, it dropped such demands and continued to support Ukraine's top-down administrative structure. With a well-organized party, massive industrial wealth, and solid control over almost half of the country, the party dominated parliament for much of the late 2000s.

For five years, this situation resulted in a de facto balance of power between the strongly Ukrainophile President Yushchenko and the Russophile Party of Regions. However, this balance of forces would be shattered by Yanukovych's election in early 2010—an election that ushered in the breakdown of the Faustian bargain and war in 2014.

The breakdown of the Faustian bargain and conflict 2010–14

Two dominant and competing narratives have shaped our understanding of Ukraine's stunning and totally unexpected descent into violent conflict in March 2014. The least-grounded interpretation comes from the Russian government, which has portrayed the war as emerging from domestic resistance to an anti-Russian right-wing fascist government that seized power in a coup in late February 2014. From the Russian perspective, the fall of Yanukovych was not a homegrown revolution but the product of Western intervention and a US government effort to undermine Russia. This interpretation is fatally flawed. While the Ukrainian opposition did indeed adapt highly divisive Ukrainian national imagery during protests, the government that came to power did *not* in fact undertake *any* effective measures prior to the war that were genuinely threatening to Russophones in the eastern Ukraine or elsewhere. Next, while it is true that the opposition ended up seizing power from Yanukovych, such a seizure was made unavoidable by Yanukovych's sudden decision to flee the country on February 21, 2014. It was thus not a coup. Finally, there is extremely little evidence that Western support was critical to the success of Euromaidan.

A second, much more empirically grounded interpretation focuses on Russia's highly aggressive behavior toward Ukraine. Indeed, it is clear that the crisis after Yanukovych's exit would never have turned violent absent Putin's invasion first of Crimea and then the Donbas. There is also abundant indication that plans for the invasion of Crimea were years in the making. Putin indicated in the late 2000s that he saw Crimea's 1954 incorporation into Ukraine as legally dubious. To put it simply, there is a villain in this story and his name is Putin.

That said, an exclusive focus on Putin provides an inaccurate understanding of the roots of war in Ukraine. First, history is littered with examples of irredentist claims that were never successfully acted upon.[63] The simple existence of irredentist claims does

[63] Austria and South Tyrol; Hungary and Transylvania; Bulgaria and FYROM; Sweden and the Åland Islands. I thank Keith Darden for pointing these out.

not mean that invasion is inevitable. Very few predicted Putin's annexation of Crimea and virtually no observers argued that the Russian government would intervene in Donbas. Indeed, many accounts of decision-making suggest that it was haphazard, ad hoc, and on the fly.[64]

In a nutshell, the war in Ukraine would almost certainly not occurred were it not for the domestic crisis in Ukraine. To understand the sources of this crisis, we need to understand how Ukraine's Faustian bargain broke down in early 2014. The bargain that resulted in the relative equal inclusion of Ukrainophile and Russophile forces in Ukraine began to erode with the election of Viktor Yanukovych as President in early 2010.

After taking office, Yanukovych rapidly monopolized power and pushed Ukraine in a starkly pro-Russian direction. In April 2010, the legislature, dominated by a tightly cohesive Party of Regions, approved a highly controversial agreement with Russia extending Russia's lease over the Black Sea Fleet.[65] Subsequently, the party was able to use its dominance of the legislature to cow the courts. This subordination of the judiciary greatly enhanced Yanukovych's capacity to impose authoritarian rule. Perhaps most importantly, subordination of the courts helped Yanukovych to quickly reverse the constitutional reform of 2004. Such a reversion was hampered by the fact that—according to the law—the court could invalidate the reforms, but did not have the authority put into effect other changes—such as a re-imposition of the pre-reform presidential and legislative terms—that would be necessary to fully revert to the Kuchma-era system. Further, according to most experts, such changes would only take affect after new parliamentary and presidential elections.[66] Yet, Yanukovych's dominance of the court was sufficient that the courts simply cut through the legal morass and declared by a vote of 17 to 1 both that the changes of 2004 were unconstitutional *and* that the old 1996 Constitution immediately valid.[67] In turn, Yanukovych's government and "loyal" parliament "promptly" sponsored and passed legislation to make these changes effective.[68]

Euromaidan and the collapse of Yanukovych

In late 2013, Yanukovych was securely in power. His party dominated the legislature while the opposition was fragmented and almost completely sidelined. Yet, a string of events was to lead to his sudden downfall three months later. It all began in late November, when, under pressure from Russia, Yanukovych suddenly withdrew from negotiations on an Association Agreement with the European Union. Within days, tens of thousands took to the streets to demand membership in the Association. Following a half-hearted attempt to crack down on protesters on November 30, the "Euromaidan" protests swelled to hundreds of thousands.

[64] See Steven Lee Myers, "Russia's Move Into Ukraine Said to Be Born in Shadows" *The New York Times* (Moscow, March 7, 2014) <www.nytimes.com/2014/03/08/world/europe/russias-move-into-ukraine-said-to-be-born-in-shadows.html?search-input-2=Russia%27s+move+into+ukraine+shadows>.

[65] Neil Buckley and Roman Olearchyk, "Ukraine: A nation on guard" *Financial Times* (EU Energy, October 21, 2010) <www.ft.com/content/43cdd390-dc8b-11df-a0b9-00144feabdc0>.

[66] See "Ne zamakhnut'sia li . . ." Biznes (September 25, 2010); "Mnogostradal'naia Konstitutsiia" *Chaspik*, (No. 38 [491], September 26, 2010); "Konstitutsionnyi otkat. Ianukovich stanet Kuchmoi?" *ForUm* (October 1, 2010).

[67] Buckley and Olearchyk (n 65).

[68] Alexei Trochev, "Editor's Introduction: The Constitutional Court of Ukraine: Back to the 1996 Constitution" (2011) 46 (3) Statutes and Decisions 4, 5.

In stark contrast to the protests in late 2004, which were tightly organized by pro-Yushchenko supporters, the demonstrations in late 2013 and early 2014 were highly spontaneous and lacked clear leadership. The protesters—the vast majority of whom came to the demonstrations on their own rather than with any organized group[69]—initially lacked obvious political demands. The rallies, dominated by handwritten signs, had the homegrown feel of the American Occupy protests in 2011. The protests could have gone in a number of directions—including one that emphasized opposition to corruption, which would have unified east and west, rather than union with Europe, which divided the country. Ultimately, however, the protests took on a starkly anti-Russian and pro-European tenor. This direction was detrimental to the opposition movement as multiple surveys showed a lack of majority support for joining the European Union.[70]

There is no evidence that protests were driven by right-wing Ukrainian nationalist ideology. Most surveys instead showed that opposition to Yanukovych united people who showed up at the demonstrations.[71] Subsequently, far right parties obtained tiny support in parliamentary and presidential elections. Nonetheless, the far right *did* play a quite visible role in the protests. One of the three opposition parties that gave support to the protests was the Svoboda Party, which was clearly on the far right. Svoboda, which until 2004 had called itself the Social Nationalist Party of Ukraine and employed neo-Nazi and SS symbols, did not hide its glorification of the nationalist Organization of Ukrainian Nationalists. In December they held a torchlight rally on the Maidan to honor the WWII-era nationalist leader, Stepan Bandera, and they regularly flew the red and black flag of the OUN, which was banned as a racist symbol at soccer matches by the International Football Federation (FIFA).

The explicit harkening back to the songs, slogans, and symbols of the nationalist movement of the 1930s and 1940s—with its aspiration to achieve an ethnically pure Ukrainian nation-state free of Russians, Jews, and Poles—was one of the main differences between these protests and the Orange Revolution of 2004. Svoboda's deputies controlled the opposition-occupied Kiev city administration building, its flag was widely visible and a portrait of Bandera hung in the central hall.

Although these symbols alienated Russophile Ukrainians, they likely inspired numerous Ukrainophile activists. Indeed, while initially about half of the protesters in Kyiv were from the capital, western Ukrainians (representing 20 percent of the population) accounted for about half of the protesters in Kyiv by late January.[72] Across the country, a disproportionate share of protests was concentrated in western Ukraine.[73] According to one survey, 53 percent of western Ukrainians participated in the protests

[69] Fond Demokratichni Initsiatyvy, "Від Майдану-табору до Майдану-січі: що змінилося?" (*Fond Demokratichni Initsiatyvy*, February 6, 2014) <http://dif.org.ua/article/vid-maydanu-taboru-do-maydanu-sichi-shcho-zminilosya>.

[70] Most surveys showed around 40 to 45 percent support for European integration as compared with about 30 to 40 percent support for the Customs Union—a plurality for Europe but hardly a clear mandate. See, for example, "Дані загальноукраїнського соціологічного дослідження моніторингу «Україна і українці»" <www.slideshare.net/Luxarxl/2014-31960903>.

[71] Fond Demokratichni Initsiatyvy "Від Майдану-табору до Майдану-січі: що змінилося?" (n 69).

[72] ibid. According to the series of surveys conducted by Democratic Initiatives, Kyivites represented about half of the protesters in December and about 20 percent by late January.

[73] "Статистика протестних подій Майдану: учасники, географія, насильство" (https://issuu.com/irf_ua/docs/dp-2014-7).

as compared with 17 percent of central Ukrainians and 2 to 4 percent of southern and eastern Ukrainians.[74]

At the same time, Yanukovych remained largely intransigent—refusing to negotiate a reduction in Presidential power or early elections. And then, quite suddenly, Yanukovych's regime collapsed. On February 20, government snipers fired on protesters killing about seventy people. This sparked a rebellion within the ruling party, which effectively lost its majority in the legislature. After that point, the Party of Regions more or less ceased to function as a coherent political unit. Yanukovych, sensing his own vulnerability, agreed to significant concessions during negotiations overnight.

However, government security forces began to fragment. The authoritarian state ceased to function in significant parts of the country. In particular, forces around Yanukovych dissolved—leaving the President vulnerable to attack. That night, he fled the capital and then the country. The next day, parliament voted to dismiss Yanukovych and elected Oleksandr Turchynov, Tymoshenko's close ally, as acting President. For the first time since independence, Ukraine experienced a leadership turnover that occurred completely outside the electoral process. The Party of Regions, which had essentially monopolized power in the east for nine years, suddenly ceased to exist as a viable political force. For the first time since independence, the east was deprived of effective representation in the halls of central power.

In turn, large sections of the Ukrainian state collapsed. Police and special forces "disappeared from the streets." The new authorities in Kyiv lacked any effective means of imposing order—outsourcing security functions to local oligarchs and opposition paramilitaries.[75] At the same time, the new government faced severe distrust in the southeast of the country. While those in western and central Ukraine saw the events as a democratic revolution, half of the population in the southeast—and 70 percent of Donetsk and Luhansk—viewed the new government as illegal.[76] Opposition to the new government in the east was far higher than it had been following Yushchenko's accession to power in 2005.

The combination of a total loss of popular support in the east and (more importantly) the breakdown of the state created an important opening for Putin to sow disorder. Thus, when insurgents began to seize local governments in March and April in cities in Donetsk and Luhansk, local authorities did nothing to stop them and may have given them assistance. "Once protests started seizing government buildings across the region, police either fled or defected to the protesters' side."[77] Top leadership within the Party of Regions did not support the war, comparing Donetsk's secession to tossing the oblast "from a tenth-floor window."[78] Yet by March, the party ceased to function and could do nothing to shape events.

[74] Fond Demokratichni Initsiatyvy, "Річниця Майдану – опитування громадської та експертної думки" (http://dif.org.ua/article/richnitsya-maydanu-opituvannya-gromadskoi-ta-ekspertnoi-dumki).

[75] Rosaria Puglisi, "A Regional Perspective on Post-Maidan Domestic Security" (University of Ottawa 10th Annual Danyliw Seminar on Ukraine, Ottawa, October 31, 2014).

[76] See KIIS, "Думки Та Погляди Жителів Південно-Східних Областей України: Квітень 2014" (*Kiev International Institute of Sociology*, April 20, 2014) <www.kiis.com.ua/?lang=ukr&cat=news&id=258> accessed June 2014.

[77] Sergiy Kudelia, "Domestic Sources of the Donbas Insurgency" PONARS Eurasia (Eurasia Policy Memo No. 351, PONARS Eurasia September 2014).

[78] Lucan Way, "Putin's Move" (*The Walrus* June 16, 2014) < https://thewalrus.ca/putins-move/>.

Developments after the fall of Yanukovych and future directions for Ukraine

Euromaidan and the war that followed have fundamentally destroyed the fundamental set of compromises that contributed both to massive corruption and peaceful relations between east and west. First, the conflict resulted in the disenfranchisement of Russophiles within what was left of Ukraine. In large part due to polarization from the war, pro-Russian political forces were in retreat. In the presidential election held at the end of May, pro-Russian candidates together gained less than 15 percent of the vote. In the parliamentary elections of October 2014, the only Russophile party to gain seats was the Opposition bloc, consisting of former Party of Regions leaders, that garnered 9 percent of the vote. As a whole, pro-Russian forces (including the Communist Party and another party that failed to gain seats) garnered a stunningly low 16 percent of the national vote. These poor results appear to have resulted both from the loss of highly Russophile voters in Crimea, Donetsk, and Luhansk, as well as from dramatically reduced turnout in those parts of the east that remained under Ukrainian control.

Once again, issues of federalism and decentralization became salient in Ukraine. The insurgents in Donetsk and Luhansk called for federalism. In mid-March, Prime Minister Yatseniuk reached out to Russophones in the east announcing plans for increased decentralization.[79] Yet, federalism was intensely unpopular among Ukrainophiles and was widely seen as a backdoor means for Russia to control Ukraine. Thus, Putin's proposals would have essentially made it impossible for Ukraine to join European institutions without the support of representatives in the east. For many in the Ukrainian elite, federalism was seen as a means for Putin to revive the Soviet Union.[80]

At the same time, Ukraine faced considerable pressure from Russia and the West to carry out a plan of decentralization. The Minsk agreements to end the conflict—conducted in September 2014 and February 2015—included commitments by the Ukrainian government to decentralize power. The agreements incorporated a provision calling for constitutional reform by the end of 2015 creating "special status" for Donetsk and Luhansk.

As part of a Ukrainian effort to fulfill this agreement, a law was passed in September 2014 that would amnesty "participants of the events in Donetsk and Luhansk regions" and that included a provision for local militias created by local councils. Further, an initial draft of constitutional reforms, passed in its first reading in September 2015, included mention of a "special status" for Donetsk and Luhansk—stating that "The specifics of executing local governance in certain counties of the Donetsk and Luhansk regions are defined by a separate law." While highly controversial, these mentions of special status seem to have been included to abide by the letter (rather than spirit) of the Minsk agreements. Indeed, an amendment to the September 2014 law, passed in March 2015 dictated that the law would only take force after local elections conducted under Ukrainian law and monitored by international observers. Furthermore, the Minsk agreement stated that reform would only come into effect after a return of

[79] Gwendolyn Sasse and James Hughes, "Building a federal Ukraine?" *The Washington Post* (March 19, 2014) <www.washingtonpost.com/news/monkey-cage/wp/2014/03/19/building-a-federal-ukraine/?utm_term=.49d378937b3f>.

[80] See Zerkalo nedeli, "Путин выступает за федерализацию Украины" *Zerkalo nedeli* (November 17, 2014) <https://zn.ua/POLITICS/putin-vystupaet-za-federalizaciyu-ukrainy-159013_.html>.

border control to Ukraine.[81] Indeed, rebel leaders in Donetsk referred to constitutional reform as a "farce."[82]

At the same time, more genuine moves toward decentralization were also made. Subnational governments receive about 40 percent of public revenues—a share that has increased slightly since 2014. On August 31, 2015, a decentralization reform package passed its first reading in the Ukrainian Rada but stalled in the parliament due mostly to nationalist opposition

The reforms, if passed, would significantly bolster decentralization. Most importantly, the proposed reform gives elected representatives the power to select local executives, which since 1996 have mostly been appointed centrally. At the bottom (*Hromada*) level, Ukrainians would separately elect executives and legislators. At the district (*rayon*) and regional (*oblast*) levels, Ukrainians would elect legislators who would then choose an executive.

Yet, the constitutional drafts of late 2015 retained key elements of centralization. In particular, the draft created a centrally appointed prefect within each region to coordinate and supervise the legality of local actions. Specifically, they were given the power to countermand provisions passed by the local government. Such supervision was seen by President Poroshenko as an important "vaccination" against separatism and rogue local councils.[83]

Such provisions reflect a long standing but mistaken view that formal centralization of power is key to preventing secession. Observers of Ukraine forget that Crimea separated even though power at that point was highly centralized.[84] There is little reason to think that secession could have been prevented if power had been even more centralized in Kyiv. Furthermore, past experience with prefects—under Kravchuk in the early 1990s discussed above—was not particularly encouraging. Such figures did more to generate confusion about who was in charge than to provide any kind of serious break on secession. Overall, the conflict had and has little to do with the degree of centralization in Ukraine.

Indeed, it is worthwhile to separate the issue of secession and fears of Russian interference from questions of decentralization. Decentralization needs to be carried out for its own sake—because it provides an institutional basis for policy innovation, and economic development.[85] At the same time, no amount of decentralization is likely to convince rebels in Donetsk and Luhansk to give up territories under their control. As argued above, the war was not the product of a lack of local autonomy per se but Russian aggression, extreme distrust of new authorities in Kyiv, and a breakdown of state institutions in the spring of 2015. Putin chose to interfere in the spring of 2014 not because he was particularly concerned by the lack of local autonomy (or by any

[81] See Kirill Mikhailov, "Ukraine's decentralization and Donbas 'special status': what you need to know" (*Euromaidan Press* September 1, 2015) <http://euromaidanpress.com/2015/09/01/ukraines-decentralization-and-donbas-special-status-what-you-need-to-know/>.

[82] Sounak Mukhopadhyay, "Ukraine's constitutional reform 'a farce': Donetsk People's Republic leader" *International Business Times* (Australia, September 3, 2015) <www.ibtimes.com.au/ukraines-constitutional-reform-farce-donetsk-peoples-republic-leader-1464254>.

[83] William Partlett, "Agendas of Constitutional Decentralization in Ukraine" (*Constitution Net* July 23, 2015) <www.constitutionnet.org/news/agendas-constitutional-decentralization-ukraine>.

[84] Of course, the separation of Crimea was instigated by Russian military intervention. Nonetheless, broad (if not necessarily majority) support for integration with Russia meant that there was more or less no resistance within Crimea to this move.

[85] Decentralization is also likely as well because decentralization is likely to create a reservoir of new and good politicians, a training ground for national leaders, see Oleh Zahntiko, "Decentralization vs Anti-Centralization" (*Vox Ukraine*, August 19, 2015) <http://voxukraine.org/2015/08/19/decentralization-v-anti-centralization/>.

supposed discrimination against Russophones) but because the breakdown of state authority in Ukraine made it *possible* to intervene. It is hard to see how any of these factors could have been affected by a different constitutional design—either more or less centralized.

As argued in this chapter, the experience of the last twenty-five years in Ukraine suggests that a better way to reduce tensions and limit Russian opportunities for intervention is to ensure that Russophile parts of the population feel that they have a stake in central power. Giving Russophiles such a stake need not involve increased formal decentralization of power (although that is likely a good idea for other reasons). Ukraine's regions have always been able to use Russian as often or as little as they wish. Instead, this means not enforcing centralized Ukrainization policies aimed at imposing Ukrainian language or anti-Soviet cultural policies on the populations of eastern Ukraine.

Such inclusion has been made substantially harder by the war. First, the war motivated a series of so-called anti-communist laws enacted in the spring of 2015 that restricted the use of Communist-era symbols and dictated positive assessments of certain, highly controversial figures in Ukrainian history.[86] The OSCE has criticized these laws for their negative impact on free speech in Ukraine.[87] While other countries such as Poland and the Czech Republic have passed laws citing the "criminal" nature of the Communist regime, the Ukrainian laws go much further by imposing penalties for expressing contrarian points of view.[88] In July 2015, the Ministry of Justice stripped the Communist Party and two of its satellites[89] of the right to participate in elections.[90] These laws potentially antagonize populations in the southeast that have so far resisted Russian efforts to foster tensions. Thus, a poll in early 2015 showed that half of the populations of Kharkiv, Dnipropetrovsk, and Zaporizhia in the southeast and 70 percent of those in Donbas regret the collapse of the Soviet Union.[91]

At the same time, the Russian invasion has deprived Russophile forces of effective representation in Kyiv. The only Russophile party to win seats in the Rada in 2014—the Opposition Bloc—is almost completely excluded from the political process in Kyiv. As noted above, electoral turnout in the east seems to have declined dramatically since the Euromaidan revolution. Official turnout in eastern Ukraine in the Presidential election went down from 66 percent in 2010 to about 50 percent 2014. In the October 2014 parliamentary elections, less than half showed up in the east and south. It is likely that some of this decline is due to disenchantment with the political process and the dearth of parties representing their interests.[92] War with Russia made

[86] At the same time, Russian language continues to be widely used in regional governance in southeast Ukraine. There has been very little evidence of forcible linguistic Ukrainianization.

[87] Organization for Security and Co-operation in Europe, "New laws in Ukraine potential threat to free expression and free media, OSCE Representative says" (Press Release, OSCE May 18, 2015) <www.osce.org/fom/158581>.

[88] This point was made to the author by Oxana Shevel, Tufts University.

[89] The Communist Party of Ukraine (renewed) and the Communist Party of Workers and Peasants.

[90] Mariana Antonovych, "Ukraine's Justice Ministry outlaws Communists from elections" *The Kyiv Post* (Kiev, July 24, 2015) <www.kyivpost.com/content/ukraine/ukraines-justice-ministry-outlaws-communists-from-elections-394217.html>.

[91] Only about 30 percent in Kharkiv, Dnipropetrovsk, and Zaporizhia and 10 percent of those in the Donbas expressed positive views of the Soviet collapse. See Fond Demokratichni Initsiatyvy, "Що об'єднує та роз'єднує українців – опитування громадської думки України" (*Fond Demokratichni Initsiatyvy* 2015) <www.old.dif.org.ua/en/polls/2015a/sho-obednue-ta-rozednue-.htm>.

[92] Tadeusz A Olszański, "A strong vote for reform: Ukraine after the parliamentary elections" (*The Centre for Eastern Studies*, October 29, 2014) <www.osw.waw.pl/en/publikacje/analyses/2014-10-29/a-strong-vote-reform-ukraine-after-parliamentary-elections>.

it substantially harder for politicians to mobilize Russophile support. The pro-Russian population in 2014 was demoralized, and weakly organized, and substantially smaller.

It is possible to argue that such marginalization is a good thing. After all, this population would seem to be less supportive of reform and the Opposition Bloc includes some of the most corrupt politicians in Ukraine. Yet, such exclusion is both normatively and pragmatically problematic. First, Ukrainian democracy will remain flawed and unrepresentative so long as major parts of the population are not included and do not feel welcome in the political process. Second, such exclusion is likely to render eastern Ukraine more vulnerable to Russian interference. Indeed, a critical priority would seem to be the promotion of loyally Ukrainian and less corrupt Russophile parties. In the short term, inclusion of such groups may promote territorial integrity but threaten reform. Yet, reform grounded in wider political participation and consensus is likely to be more enduring.

Lessons Learned

This chapter has explored the changing ways in which territorially concentrated populations and interests in Ukraine engaged with the constitutional process after the collapse of the Soviet Union in 1991. In a nutshell, eastern interests supported centralization when they have had a stake in central power and fought for federalism when they have felt threatened. In the early 1990s, a deeply flawed Faustian bargain between national democrats and eastern economic interests created the basis for a unitary system. In 2010, this bargain began to break down with the election of Viktor Yanukovych. Then in early 2014, the sudden departure of Yanukovych and the collapse of the Party of Regions, which had monopolized control over the east for nine years, created an opening for Putin to sow unrest in Ukraine.

The Ukrainian case highlights the fact that the existence or absence of politically salient demands for local autonomy often hinges on the nature of politics at the center. Demands for autonomy may diminish when groups are given a direct stake in central power. By contrast, exclusion of important groups may foster such demands. An important lesson of this study is that the best way to reduce tensions and opportunities for Russian intervention is to strengthen representation of loyal Russophile forces in the center.

What can be done to ensure that Russophile Ukrainians feel included in the Ukrainian state? One relatively simple step is to avoid central measures such as the anti-communist laws that impose symbolic changes (such as eliminating Soviet-era names) that are alien to a large share of the population in the east. A much harder problem is what to do about the marginalization of pro-Russian parties in the center. Polarization caused by the war makes it much harder include such parties in the government. Such inclusion is made much harder by the fact that the Opposition bloc is led by formerly pro-Yanukovych officials whose attachment to Ukrainian independence is deeply suspect. Some form of consociationalism might be an answer. Yet, such measures seem unlikely to attract support in the context of war.

A longer-term (but perhaps no easier) solution would be to break from the confines of the Faustian bargain. This could be done through grassroots efforts to create powerful Russophile parties that support Ukrainian statehood and but that are not—in contrast to the Opposition bloc—tied to Yanukovych and the corrupt Donbas elite. The rise of Russophile forces not tied to Yanukovych's disastrous regime may facilitate the inclusion of such parties in coalitional politics. Given the fact that only small minorities of the southeast oppose Ukrainian independence, there would seem to be political space for such parties.[93] None of this will be easy—especially given the government's strong ties to oligarchs. Nonetheless, those who want Ukraine to be a viable and united state need to think seriously about ways to create political space for the majority Russophiles in the country who want to remain in an independent Ukraine.

[93] For example, a Democratic Initiatives poll in early 2015 showed that just 15 percent of residents in Dnipropetrovsk and Zaporizhia, Mykolaiv, Odesa, and Kherson in the south and a third of residents in Kharkiv and Donbas oppose independence. See Fond Demokratichni Initsiatyvy, "Що об'єднує та роз'єднує українців – опитування громадської думки України" (n 91).

17

Yemen's Failed Constitutional Transition

George Anderson[*]

Overview

Yemen's constitutional moment started with the exhilaration of the country's Arab Spring and ended with the outbreak of civil war. In 2011 a popular uprising resulted in the resignation of the autocratic president, Ali Abdullah Saleh. Neighboring Arab countries quickly became engaged in steering the process, which included an election to legitimate the succession of the vice-president to the presidency, a government of national unity composed of old line parties, and, at the urging of the United Nations, a National Dialogue process on national goals and the design of a new Constitution. The dialogue process was intended to be highly inclusive and non-partisan, but suffered from its inability to resolve tough questions, the absence of key political players, and the role of spoilers, including Saleh. It recommended a new federal regime, but its design was only partially developed and failed to resolve the critical issue of the number and boundaries of states. The president created a committee that endorsed his preferred scheme, which was deeply resented in the South, where there was strong mobilization around secession, and by the Houthis in the north. A Constitutional Drafting Committee was commissioned to prepare a draft. Throughout this process, the government was very dysfunctional, while the economy and security situations were deteriorating. By the summer of 2014, Houthi insurgents had progressed to the edges of the capital Sanaa, when a government decision to end fuel subsidies led to massive demonstrations and the entry of the Houthi into Sanaa, causing a crisis for the government. The Constitutional Drafting Committee finally delivered its document to the president in January 2015 and this became the trigger for civil war. The country has become even more fractured with the humanitarian disaster of the conflict and there is little sign of consensus on its constitutional future.

Background

For thirty-three years, Ali Abdullah Saleh as President of the Republic of Yemen had played off factions in a regime that had the trappings of democracy, but might better be classified as "competitive authoritarian."[1] He had succeeded in uniting the two Yemens in 1990, when the southern People's Democratic Republic of Yemen was badly weakened by the collapse of the Soviet Union. The Southerners felt badly exploited

[*] The author thanks Zaid al-Ali, Christine Bell, and Robert Foster for comments and assistance in an earlier version of this chapter.

[1] Steven Levitsky and Lucan A Way, *Competitive Authoritarianism: Hybrid Regimes After the Cold War* (Cambridge University Press 2010).

Territory and Power in Constitutional Transitions. First Edition. Edited by Michael Anderson and Sujit Choudhry. Yemen's Failed Constitutional Transition © George Anderson 2019. Published 2019 by Oxford University Press.

after unification and had revolted in a bloody civil war in 1994, which Saleh ruthlessly crushed. Yemen was already politically stressed when the Arab Spring erupted and quickly brought the fall of the presidents of Tunisia and Egypt. Saleh's rule faced increasing opposition because of economic problems, youth unemployment, falling oil revenues, water and food scarcity, and serious regional alienation in the South as well as in Sa'ada, the Houthi area of the north. Outside regional capitals, the security situation was poor. In the south, state dominance was challenged by Al-Qaeda and the secessionist Southern movement, known as Hirak. In the north, the governorate of Sa'ada was primarily under the control the Zaydi revivalist militias known as the Houthi. While Yemen was the poorest Arab country, its political regime appeared more liberal than most in the region, with a largely free press, significant civil society and competing political parties, but real control was strongly centralized in Saleh through an extensive system of patronage and corruption.[2] Just before the Arab Spring erupted, the political class was divided by the possibility that Saleh might change the constitution to permit his indefinite tenure—and, potentially, pave the way for his son to succeed.

The initial reaction to the Tunisian uprisings was muted, with small student rallies calling for Saleh to step down, while the group of opposition parties in parliament—the Joint Meeting Parties (JMP)—also held rallies, but with demands for political reform, not Saleh's resignation. With Mubarak's demise demonstrations became much larger, notably in Sana'a, Aden and, especially Taiz. Students and civil society leaders made Saleh's resignation a basic demand prior to dialogue and in March the JMP developed a five-point roadmap for transition, which included Saleh's resignation by the end of the year. Later that month, Saleh's troops killed fifty-two student demonstrators in Sana'a, which led to the defection of several important supporters of the Saleh regime. By May, fighting had erupted between government troops and fighters loyal to the head of the Hashid confederation, Sheikh Sadiq al-Ahmar, as well as a faction of the First Armored Division, under the command of Ali Mohsen al-Ahmar. This conflict reflected the deep animosity between the families of Sheikh Al-Ahmar and President Saleh and risked dragging the country into civil war. The politics of transition became dominated by the reconfigured elite groups and armed actors.

The JMP roadmap for transition called for Saleh to be replaced by his Vice-President, Abd Rabbuh Mansur al-Hadi; a transitional government would be formed and elections held. There would be an immediate restructuring of the security forces and an investigation of state-led violence against demonstrators. This plan left open the possibility of Saleh's future prosecution and was firmly rejected by him.

Given its poverty, Yemen had long experienced interventions in its internal politics by outside powers—whether the Egyptians and Saudis in the northern civil war in the 1950s, the Soviets in South Yemen, or the Americans after the attack on the USS Cole in 2000 and the underwear bomber in 2009. The Saudis aided Saleh in his wars with the Houthis and had deep links with many tribal chiefs. Thus it was not surprising that in April 2011, the Gulf Cooperation Council should step in as mediator in Yemen's crisis. While the UAE, Kuwait, Oman,[3] and Bahrain have tended to fall in with the Saudis on Yemeni matters, Qatar has been something of an outlier, both in being quite independently active (e.g. in trying to mediate a truce with the Houthis in 2007–08) and in its close relations with the Muslim Brotherhood element within the Islah Party. The Arab states provided $1 billion in aid to Yemen from 1990 to 2004, compared with $250 million from the EU, and in 2006 they pledged $2.5 billion in aid, more

[2] Sarah Phillips, *Yemen and the Politics of Permanent Crisis* (Routledge 2011)

[3] Though Oman kept its distance from the recent Saudi-led war against the Houthi–Saleh alliance.

than half of the total of $4.7 billion pledged by all donors—though much of this was never delivered.[4]

The GCC proposed an alternative to the JMP plan, which importantly included immunity for Saleh. This was agreed by Saleh's Party, the General People's Congress (GPC), and the JMP and indeed by Saleh himself. However, Saleh unexpectedly refused to sign at the absolute last second, according to insiders, because Saleh's son, in particular, flatly rejected the entire deal. This public rejection of the GCC deal heightened the divisions within Yemen, including within the military—and was widely seen as an insult to the Saudis assembled for the signing. The crisis deepened on June 3 when in an assassination attempt Saleh was badly burned and then flown to a military hospital in Saudi Arabia. Vice President Hadi became acting President the next day, but was always in the shadow of Saleh's possible recovery and return. When Saleh did recover, the Saudis apparently kept him under virtual house arrest.

Around the middle of 2011, the Special Representative of the UN Secretary General, Jamal Benomar, became an important actor. He pushed successfully for a national dialogue, which had not been part of the original package. His small team worked to supplement the GCC Initiative with what became the Implementation Mechanism, with significantly more detail on how the transition process would be managed. Remarkably, Benomar's initial involvement was not specifically mandated by the Security Council. In September, protesters marched en masse toward central Sana'a. Allowing them into the city would have cut off regime loyalists from all the key government areas and so the military opened fire on the unarmed protestors, killing scores and wounded hundreds. A week of gunfire and shelling followed, which added to the sense that the crisis was desperate. It seems that this precipitated a sudden and secret decision by Saleh to return to Yemen, despite the Saudis making it clear to him that he was expected to stand down and not return to Yemen. But on September 22, they allowed Saleh to bid farewell to some family at the airport and he somehow eluded his guardians and boarded a private flight to Aden, whence he was driven to Sana'a. On September 23 it was announced that he was back, and taking full control again, completely surprising Hadi.

These events precipitated greater international focus and concern. In October 2011, the United Nations Security Council-passed resolution 2014, which marked the start of a more aggressive international policy on Yemen. It endorsed the GCC Initiative, signaling the Security Council's desire for Saleh to be removed from office, something that it had not done in any other country in the region. It called for both a Yemeni-led process of political transition and political settlement. The UN's action was sensitive given the GCC's view that it should be the dominant voice in the region.

Saleh again became involved in the discussions being held by Benomar and finally agreed to the GCC initiative plus the supplementary "Implementing Mechanism." This spelled out the process for a transitional government, a national dialogue, and a new Constitution that would be the basis for countrywide elections. Saleh signed both documents in Riyadh in November 2011. This was seen as his acceptance of the leadership of the Saudis, who guaranteed his immunity. Importantly, there was to be no legal or other restriction on Saleh's participating in future political processes and he remained head of the GPC (which was also Hadi's party). Most thought he would stay out of the country, but there was no plan for this and he soon returned from medical treatment in the USA, angry and seeking revenge. Equally important, there was no restriction on

[4] Edward Burke, "*One blood and one destiny*"? *Yemen's relations with the Gulf Cooperation Council*, June 2012, www.lse.ac.uk/LSEKP/

his son and others in the former leadership; on the contrary, they were expected to be active players. And so Saleh was placed to pull levers as a major spoiler.

The GCC deal and Implementation Mechanism documents dealt with three key issues:

- First, were the terms of Saleh's resignation. The formal transfer came after Hadi's election in an early national vote and parliament had granted immunity to Saleh. He was also explicitly granted immunity by the text of the GCC Initiative.
- Second, were the interim provisions for governance. The presidential election would follow within ninety days. Prior to that, a government of national unity was formed, made up equally of ministers from the GPC and from the Joint Meeting Parties. (The initial GCC proposal for some ministers from civil society groups did not happen.) The Prime Minister was to come from the JMP (in practice, Islah). The government was to operate on the basis of consensus, though Hadi could decide in the absence of consensus and was charged with all functions relating to military and foreign affairs. The government was to deal with day-to-day governance and had no role in the emerging constitutional debate or National Dialogue Conference (NDC).
- Third, was the process for the NDC. It was to be very inclusive and had a broad mandate on national goals and the content of a Constitution. It was to be followed by a constitutional drafting commission that would implement the results of the conference. The NDC was to conclude within five months and the constitutional drafting four months after that. The draft would be submitted to a referendum on the Constitution and then elections would be based on the new order. In the event, these timetables proved highly unrealistic.

The Friends of Yemen, a body of thirty-nine countries established in 2010, met in Riyadh in September 2012, eight months after Saleh's resignation. A document prepared by the Yemeni government with the World Bank painted a picture of unprecedented deterioration in the economic and humanitarian situations, serious food insecurity, critical fiscal shortfalls, and unemployment over 50 percent for youth and even over 40 percent for those of prime working age.[5] Donors responded with pledges of \$6.4 billion in aid for the period up to April 2014, which led the Yemeni government to draft its largest budget in 2012. However, when the Friends met in April 2014, only 36 percent of the pledged funds (which had grown to \$7.9 billion) had been disbursed, \$1 billion of which was a deposit by Saudi Arabia into Yemen's central bank (though 97 percent of the pledged funds had been allocated to projects). The original plan had focused heavily on major infrastructure projects, which proved impossible to deliver quickly; the Gulf States, which were to be the key funders, resisted switching to projects that could move more quickly. It emerged that the Yemeni government did not have the capacity to absorb much of the planned aid quickly and efforts by the World Bank and others to build capacity came too late. Thus the economic stimulus that was to have been a central contribution of the international community during the critical first two years of transition largely failed to materialize.

The GCC Initiative was essentially a deal between the GPC and the JMP—the old parties. It excluded the civil society groups that had occupied the public squares, as well as Hirak, the Southern movement, which was agitating for major autonomy or

[5] Ministry of Yemen, *Transitional Program for Stabilization and Development, Yemen Donor Conference, Riyadh*, September 4–5, 2012

secession, and the Houthis, who had fought six brief wars against the regime and effectively controlled a significant part of the north. Thus the leaders of the excluded factions were never full parties to the GCC Initiative or the ensuing steps, which undercut the standing of whatever agreements were reached later on. Both Hirak and the Houthis were excluded from the Government of National Unity. It was not easy to engage with Hirak or the Houthis. Hirak was a loose coalition of at least seven large factions and several smaller ones, whose demands ranged from secession to devolution to the redress of past wrongs. The Houthis were in armed defiance of the government and told they would have to disarm to participate in government. The government never functioned collegially and Hadi had the cooperation of only a few ministers because some of the GPC ministers were Saleh loyalists while still others were on the fence, fearful of his influence. Hadi did not play a forceful role in day-to-day governance, where many issues were allowed to fester and corruption was rampant.

The political configuration was deeply problematic. The elephant, Saleh, was not in the room, but in his private compound in the center of the capital. The international community shunned contact with him, while he called upon the loyalty or fear of most of the prominent members of the GPC. He had significant influence over parts of the army and the security apparatus and had what was effectively a private militia. He was suspected to be behind targeted assassinations and acts of sabotage on power lines and pipelines, which led to blackouts and lost government revenues. Hadi was no match for Saleh. He had no real political base, weak political skills, and little understanding of government. The last parliamentary elections had been in 2003, when the GPC, a ministerialist party of no fixed ideology, won two-thirds of the seats. Islah, a broadly based Islamic party, was the largest opposition group, while the Socialists and Nasserites harkened back to earlier periods and had very limited support. Thus the "government of national unity" was based on a fairly decadent old order. Similarly, those outside government lacked coherence and leadership: Hirak was highly fragmented, as were the street protesters and youth. The Houthis had a strong—even authoritarian—leader in Adbul-Malik al-Houthi, but he stayed in the north and was disengaged from both the government and the NDC. Despite their unity, the Houthis had no clear political agenda, so they were peripheral to political developments in the capital during the early phases of the transition. They continued to fight and gain ground as the transition progressed. While there was a hurried and effectively uncontested national election to ratify Hadi's succession to the presidency, the view of election experts and political advisors was that it would be impossible to hold effective parliamentary elections in the near term given the security problems and lack of a reliable voter registry. Thus it was impossible to say what real support different political factions had within the population.

The National Dialogue Conference (NDC) started with high public expectations as the great set-piece of Yemeni politics, but it moved much more slowly than planned and failed to produce clear decisions on central questions, so the public became progressively disenchanted with it. The dysfunctionality of the government and deterioration of public services and security were equally or more important in causing public disenchantment. The government was caught up with internal politics, patronage, and graft while the basic security and economic situations worsened severely. Because the Houthis had remained outside government, they were able to sell themselves as the enemies of corruption to a deeply disillusioned public.

Framing the Constitutional Process

The National Dialogue was to bring "all forces and politics actors" together for a comprehensive discussion of:

- The process of drafting the Constitution.
- The reform of the Constitution, to be submitted as amendments to the people in a referendum.
- The issues of the South and in Sa'ada.
- Steps to build a democratic system, including the civil service, judiciary and local government.
- National reconciliation and transitional justice and measures to protect human rights.
- Legal and other means to protect vulnerable groups, including children, and to advance women.
- Measure for economic reconstruction and development.

President Hadi, elected in February 2012, took until May before naming a liaison committee to engage potential actors on the NDC and until July before naming the Technical Preparatory Committee. This committee, which included all political factions and constituencies, developed an elaborate agreement on the structure, procedures, and management of the NDC, its secretariat, a Presidium, and nine working groups. It reported only in December 2012 and the NDC itself commenced in March 2013, over a year after the election of the president.

The Technical Committee took an unexpected but important initiative by entering into the substance of two major challenges when, in August 2012, it formulated twenty "demands" for the president. Most addressed the southern situation, including the return of property and funds illegally taken, the release of detainees, an official apology for the 1994 civil war, the compensation for those who lost their positions after 1994, and the replacement of senior administrators in the south. Others addressed the Houthis and the north, including an end to punishment, cessation of hostilities, an official apology, compensation for past damage, and the release of persons being held relative to the Sa'ada wars. The major successful follow-up to these demands was $350 million in compensation payments for victims of unfair dismissals in the south (thanks to Qatar's contribution). However, the commission to address land and property issues in the south faced a more complicated task and never benefitted from an endowment, so land grievances continued to fester. While Hadi endorsed the twenty demands, his lack of vigorous response missed a key opportunity to improve the political climate.

The NDC had 565 delegates. Parties and other groups, including the Houthis, named their own delegates, subject to the requirement that there be 30 percent women. There were to be 145 youth delegates, of whom 105 were affiliated with parties and forty were independent. The President could make additional appointments and final decisions on all appointments. Half of the representatives were nominally southerners, though many represented old-line parties and had been long-resident in the north. Hard-liners from Hirak refused to participate, so Hadi resorted to representatives from Hirak's less extreme supporters. The overrepresentation of southerners, who form about 20 percent of Yemen's population, caused some resentment, but the more fundamental problem was the lack of truly representative southerners prepared to engage in negotiations.

The NDC Presidium was nominally chaired by President Hadi with broad representation of parties and groups. After the conference had been operating for several weeks, the President also established the Consensus committee, which was to reach consensus on controversial issues and coordinate outcomes of the working groups, also broadly representative but including the chairs of the nine working groups and with 50/50 membership. Benomar of the United Nations attended as well. It met periodically but proved weak and unable to resolve controversial issues. The secretariat was headed by Ahmed Awad bin Mubarak, originally from Aden and a member of the Revolutionary Youth's Coordination Council. It had over 120 personnel and almost eighty volunteers, and it worked closely with the office of the special UN advisor, notably regarding the provision of expertise.

The primary work was done in nine working groups. Each had a balanced membership of about sixty members. The topics were all embracing:

- Southern issue
- Sa'ada issue
- National reconciliation and transitional justice, including previous political conflicts and violations of rights in 2011, displaced persons, combatting terrorism
- State-building: identity and form of state, electoral system, legislative, judicial and administrative arrangements
- Good governance: rule of law, accountability and transparency, corruption, popular participation, public administration, parties, foundations of foreign policy
- Army and Security Agencies: national and professional foundations, role of the army in political life, security organization as a civil entity
- Independent bodies and special social and environmental issues: civil service, media, religious endowments, human rights, Grand Mufti, supervisory agencies, political parties, civil society groups, revenge, weapons, armed outlaw groups, qat, diversity and tolerance, water and the environment
- Rights and freedoms: general (political, economic, etc.) and special (women, children, marginalized, marriage of minors, persons with special needs, expatriates, minorities, displaced persons)
- Development: economic, cultural, educational, human, health, social, political, role of state and private sector, use of resources, external support

The Progression of the Constitutional Process

The conference was committed to public outreach and received over 1,500 submissions from groups all over the country, with working group field trips to eighteen governorates. The media provided more than 7,700 hours of television time and hundreds of printed articles, all of which built up public expectations. There were three public plenary sessions, which received blanket coverage. The most difficult issues related to the South, Sa'ada, the structure of the state, and transitional justice.

The southern committee was initially chaired by a Hirak supporter, who struggled to maintain his legitimacy with militants. He insisted that a federal Yemen have only two regions—north and south—with essentially equal power-sharing at the center, and that after three or five years there should be a referendum in the south on independence. This found no traction with northerners, so he and his allies started boycotting meetings and Hadi eventually replaced them by a more amenable group. The southern issues proved so difficult in the full NDC that eventually a special committee, called the 8+8 (half northerners, half southerners) was struck under the chairmanship of Benomar. The committee met thirty-two times before concluding in December with a meeting with the President to sign the "Just Solution" document. This addressed southern grievances, proposed a federal regime based on certain principles, and a constituting period for capacity building before implementing federalism. It called for a more inclusive national government. While it was signed by representatives of seventeen parties and civil society groups, it was rejected by most of the Hirak movement, a faction within the GPC loyal to Saleh, and by the Socialist and Nasserite parties.

The issues relating to representation in central institutions, the regional structure, and oil and gas were among the most difficult.

- Representation in Central Institutions: While some advocated different representation in the constituting period than permanently, the GPC advocated one permanent arrangement from the outset based on land and population. This would mean 40/60 South/North membership, but with the south having a veto on matters of vital interest. However, Hirak, the Houthis and the Socialists called for 50/50. The committee concluded that the south should have virtually equal weight in the central parliament for several years of transition, with a promise of longer-term overrepresentation.
- Regional Structure: Yemen has twenty-one governorates, but it was decided that the federal system would have a smaller number of regional unit (while retaining the governorates). The number and boundaries of regions was deeply divisive. Hirak strongly favored one southern region (and perhaps one northern region), but this was opposed by the GPC, which feared a united south. Unable to resolve how many regions there should be, two major options were referred to the president to deal with through an additional process.
- Oil and Gas: There was agreement that ownership would be with the people of Yemen and that federal legislation would deal with the distribution of revenues, subject to their being a special benefit for the producing region. Management arrangements were more contentious: the GPC favored strong central authority, with some participation of regions and governorates, while Hirak and the Houthis favored regional and governorate responsibility in cooperation with the federal government. The ultimate decision on control of oil and gas was ambiguous with considerable overlap regarding the powers for the federal, regional, governorate and even communal governments.

The northern working group had an easier time because the Houthis, perhaps surprisingly, were less radical in their demands. Historically they identified with a strong Yemeni government and they came round to federalism largely in solidarity with the south, with little idea as to what it might mean. Their priority was a more representative and perhaps a more technocratic central government, with an extended transitional period. They astutely declared their support for a secular state, not a return to the imamate. The structure of the state working group eventually pronounced in favor of federalism, but this was a paper-thin consensus with fundamental tensions on the nature of federalism, the religious or secular identity of the state, and the choice between a presidential or parliamentary regime. With a weak chair, the group failed to resolve any of the fundamental federalism design issues around the allocation of powers and central institutions and the consensus committee was unable to resolve these matters as well. The other working groups were less contentious (with the notable exception of that on reconciliation and transitional justice, where the issue of Saleh's immunity was hotly discussed), but they faced a daunting range of complex issues given the limited time and their often limited expertise. The NDC ended up taking ten months, rather than the six originally planned. Its final day, January 21, 2014, was clouded by the assassination of a senior Houthi member of the NDC and the bombing of the car of the secretary general of the Islah Party, wounding his son.

The 8+8 Committee had been unable to reach agreement on the number and boundaries of the regions of the new Yemeni federation, so shortly after the NDC concluded Hadi created the Regions Committee to choose between the six region and two region options. It was chaired by Hadi and had twenty-two members chosen by him and generally sympathetic to his views. It met four times, hearing experts and having special presentations on Sana'a and Aden. By February 10, it reported there was a "consensus of most members" in favor of six regions, four in the north and two in the south, with Sana'a being a federal city autonomous from all regions while the city of Aden would have special status, with independent and executive powers, within the Aden region. This was very much Hadi's preferred option, which many considered he had forced through. The report indicated which governorates would constitute each region, subject to a possible review of borders after one or more electoral terms. It included provisions regarding the representation of all governorates within each region's legislature and executive and called for criteria on equitable distribution of revenues from natural and non-natural resources, with special consideration for producing governorates and regions.

All of the committee's members signed the report, apart from the Socialists (who objected to the division of the south). The decision infuriated Hirak, which insisted on a united southern region. Its most serious political consequence however was its total rejection by the Houthis: their area was to be within a new region of Azal, with no access to the sea, little water, and few resources; the Houthis would be a minority in their own region. They wanted to be united with the resource-rich neighboring Jawf governorate and the Hajjah governorate, which has access to the sea—this would have produced a region on an east-west axis, not a north-south, axis. They viewed the map as designed to disempower and impoverish them, while leaving the GPC and JMP positioned to control the Azal region. This decision on the federal map was a critical breaking-point in the political process.

The NDC was to be followed by a Constitutional Commission, which "shall prepare a new draft Constitution within three months" and propose the necessary steps for the submission of the draft for referendum "in order to ensure broad popular support and transparency." Within three months of the adoption of the new Constitution by referendum, parliament was to enact a law convening national parliamentary (and, if provided for in the Constitution) presidential elections. In March 2014, two months after the NDC, Hadi created the Constitution Drafting Commission (CDC). It had seventeen members, with 50 percent from the South and 30 percent women; the members selected their own chair and two deputies. At least half of those deemed to be from the South had not lived there for years. None was associated with Hirak. One was associated with, but was not a formal member of, the Houthis. Most had backgrounds in the law, government, or universities. The CDC was to report in four months. It was to seek to achieve consensus, but when not possible, decisions would be made by a 75 percent majority.

If a decision on this basis proved not possible, it was to be referred to the National Body for Monitoring the Implementation of the Outcomes of the NDC. This was an entirely unforeseen body, which Hadi created in April 2014. He chaired it and it had balanced membership of eighty-two. The National Body would determine the conformity of the CDC's draft with the decisions of the NDC. It could be referred back and revised until the National Body was satisfied. Should the National Body fail to reach agreement, the President would make the final, binding decision. In fact, the National Body met only once and had no role in approving the final draft.

The CDC met from March until June, but worked casually and made little progress so it was decided it would spend three weeks in Berlin in June, with a dedicated team of experts to assist. The focus was on the structure of a federal system, including the division of powers and fiscal arrangements. A final push to conclude came in October in Abu Dhabi. The United Nations (aided by other organizations such as International IDEA) provided substantive advice. Progress on the draft proceeded faster in Abu Dhabi than previously, but the CDC was still confronted by gaps and contradictions in the NDC outcomes and by its own internal structural tensions. For example, the NDC included two different appointment mechanisms to the Constitutional Court: the Good Governance Working Group decided its members should be "elected by a general assembly of judges,"[6] while the State Building Working Group decided that 70 percent should be elected by the "general assembly of judges," 15 percent by the Bar Association, and 15 percent by the Council of Faculties of Sharia and Law in state universities.[7] Many CDC members were aware that the judiciary was replete with regressive and corrupt judges, and so either option would result in a new Constitutional Court dominated by those same elements. They therefore decided that "[t]he President of the Republic shall nominate half of the [fourteen] members and the Supreme Judicial Council, universities and the Bar Association shall nominate the remaining half" (Article 329). All nominees would have to be confirmed by a three-fifths majority in the upper chamber of parliament. Thus, in a clear illustration of the NDC's weaknesses, its decisions on this issue had close to no impact on the final outcome.

Close to a quarter of the CDC's final draft relates to details of the federal system of government on which the NDC never reached conclusions. Chapter 5 sets out extensive lists of powers for each level of government. Article 335 provides that the federal authorities should be exclusively responsible for "air navigation, civil aviation, meteorology and regulation of marine navigation," "intellectual property," and "national environment protection and climate change policy," among many others; Article 337 provides that the regional governments should be exclusively compete over "lands and real estate in the region," "agriculture," "tourism," and "telecom services," etc.; finally, Article 338 provides that "wilayas (governorates) and localities" are exclusively responsible for "civil defense," "regulation of markets," and "medium and small enterprises," etc. The NDC had never determined how these responsibilities should be allocated in a federal system of government. This was doubly problematic, because the CDC enjoyed less legitimacy than the NDC, but also because the proposed arrangements

[6] See Final Report for the Second Semester of the Working Groups, Working Group on Good Governance, September 2013, para. 30.

[7] See Final Report for the Second Semester of the Working Groups, Working Group on State Building and Constitution Principles and Foundations, August 2013, 24.

were probably not workable.[8] The result was that some actors who were not involved at the CDC stage took to alternative means to scuttle the process.

The international community was deeply engaged throughout the period of the NDC and the CDC. The World Bank communique following the donors meeting in April 2014 called on the Yemeni government to deal with "ghost workers" and, particularly, fuel subsidies, whose cost grew to a staggering $3 billion in the first half of 2014, at a time when oil revenues were plummeting. While the IMF had been negotiating a loan program for a progressive end to subsidies, on July 29, 2014 the government eliminated the subsidies in one fell swoop without any mitigating measures; observers commented that the "rollout was an unmitigated disaster—a perfect case study of how not to introduce subsidy reform."[9] People poured into the streets and the Houthis took advantage of this to rally support,[10] moving their militias into Sana'a and causing a full-scale crisis. On September 21 the Prime Minister resigned and Benomar brokered the formation of a new "unity" government, which had Houthi acquiescence but not their direct participation. In many ways, the collapse of the transition process really began with the public outrage around the end of fuel subsidies, which paved the way for the Houthi take-over of Sana'a.

The UN Security Council had regular sessions on Yemen throughout the transition period. A central preoccupation was what to do about "destabilizing actors," the first of whom was Saleh, who was clearly using his leadership of the GPC to block progress in the NDC but was thought to be engaged in more concrete acts of sabotage. As the Houthis descended from the north, they too became a major concern. Finally, in November 2014 Saleh, Abd-al-Khaliq al-Houthi and Abd-al-Khaliq Badr-al-Din al-Houthi were, by UNSC resolution 2140, put under sanctions, meaning a freeze on their assets and travel ban measures. The Houthis were charged with violence against the army and plotting a coup, while Saleh was charged with undermining the authority of the government, creating discontent within the army, plotting a coup, and using AQAP operatives to conduct assassinations and attacks on the military.

It was in this fraught context that the CDC was working and urged by the international community to report quickly. Ten months after its creation, the CDC submitted a draft to Hadi on January 3, 2015. By this time, the political, economic, and security situations in the country had deteriorated dramatically. There was turmoil throughout the autumn, with the government in disarray. The Houthis had agreed to a new prime minster, but they and the GPC refused to participate in the new government. The Houthis opposed the appointment of the new army chief and blocked his entry into his office. There were competing demonstrations in the capital. The delivery of the draft Constitution has been described as the "trigger for the Houthi final takeover of Sana'a and then the start of full civil war (so) the importance of the constitutional drafting process" cannot be overestimated.[11] Within two weeks the President's chief

[8] Among other things, the CDC did not include any official representatives of the powerful Houthi movement. One CDC member was ideologically in agreement with the Houthi movement but had not formally adhered to the movement and did not present himself in the CDC's discussions as a Houthi. Similarly, the southern representatives on the CDC were not representative of the majority of the Southern movement.

[9] Danya Greenfield and Svetlana Milbert, "Protests in Yemen Expose Weak Governance and Poor Economic Planning," September 2, 2014, at Atlantic Council.org

[10] Though by July 2015 the Houthis, by then in control of Sanaa, were forced to backtrack and remove the subsidies once again because their ally Saleh was no longer able to pay for them.

[11] Helen Lackner, *Yemen's "Peaceful" Transition from Autocracy: Could it have Succeeded?* International IDEA, p. 58

of staff, Ahmad Awad bin Mubarak, was abducted by the Houthis and on January 22 both the President[12] and the Prime Minister resigned. The GCC and UN-sponsored political transition had come to an end.

Outcomes

A harsh assessment would be that the transitional process in Yemen produced a deeply flawed draft Constitution and contributed to the outbreak of civil war. The transition failed for many reasons. The process itself was incredibly complicated and unable to meet any of its deadlines. The original GCC agreement had serious design weaknesses, notably the ill-considered interim governance arrangements and the terms of Saleh's resignation, which permitted him to become a major spoiler. The NDC was ill-equipped to take on the huge responsibilities assigned to it. The necessary measures to stimulate the economy and reform the military were not achieved. However, all of the weaknesses in the original agreement and those which followed were less important than the deep cleavages amongst leading political actors who had little disposition to make the necessary compromises. There was a dire lack of leadership, which Hadi proved incapable of providing. The virtual collapse of effective governance along with deteriorating security, military insubordination, sabotage of electricity and the petroleum sector, and economic and fiscal distress completed the constellation of factors that led to Yemen's breakdown.

The outcomes of the NDC, as confused as they often were, also reflected the fundamental problems with the representativeness of the NDC. The Houthis and Hirak as well as the youth and other civil society groups were not part of the GCC agreement and never endorsed the process. Despite this, most youth and civil society groups in the north were prepared to participate in the NDC, as were the Houthis (though their true engagement was limited). However, representation from the south was always a problem in that the more hardline elements from Hirak and civil society stayed away. The Houthis, for their part, played a rather passive role in the NDC, partly because the federal issues were of marginal interest to them. (They showed their hand more clearly in September 2014 when they negotiated the Peace and Partnership Document, but even here they remained outside the new government and therefore in some degree marginal.) One other major actor, Al-Qaeda in the Arab Peninsula, was never considered for inclusion because of its terrorist activities. Even the GPC was divided between loyalists to Saleh, to Hadi, and fence-sitters, while the Joint Meeting Parties were a heterogeneous lot, some of which had lost any real claim to a popular constituency.

The government started to come apart in the summer of 2014 largely because of the economic situation and the end of fuel subsidies. This opened the way for the Houthis to enter the capital. The delivery of the draft Constitution was the *coup de grace*, and within days the president was in exile and Sana'a was in the hands of Saleh, the great spoiler of the transition, and his new allies the Houthis. It was a marriage that could not last and it found its end with Saleh's murder by Houthis militants. The country in 2018 is effectively a collapsed state, more deeply fractured than ever.

[12] Though Hadi subsequently withdrew his resignation.

Lessons Learned

There are many lessons, but perhaps the first may be the limits of the possible in deeply divided societies undergoing major political transitions. Could a different process or constellation of actors have reached a happier outcome? Was the part played by outside actors positive? There are three broad kinds of lessons we might draw.

The role and design of sub-national governance arrangements

A central issue relates to how conflicts within the country were addressed—or could have been—by sub-national governance arrangements. Yemen had been highly centralized since unification in 1990, but the state had a limited presence in many regions and Saleh's style of patronage politics progressively lost its ability to "dance on the heads of snakes" and maintain balance between competing forces. The deeply alienated south, crushed in the 1994 civil war, sought regional empowerment, but its favored option was secession, not federalism; paradoxically then, it was the separatist challenge from the south that led to the NDC consensus on the need for federalism. Hirak never bought into Hadi's six-region federal model, though some in Hirak might have agreed to a two-region model, or at least a model in which the south was a single unit. Hadi feared a single-unit south, which would replicate the boundaries of the old People's Democratic Republic, as a way-station to secession. The Houthis, for their part, while in principle not opposed to federalism, also rejected the proposed federal map because of their hostility to the region in which they would be located. The two leading established parties in the north, the GPC and Islah, were both centralist in orientation and resistant to dramatic devolution within a federal structure that might have won some support in the south. Thus, sub-national governance arrangements were certainly at the center of the political agenda, but the NDC consensus in favor of federalism was very fragile and far from providing the basis for a real and lasting political agreement. The draft Constitution—with all its problems—was unable to resolve the divisions and Hadi's imposition of his map of the regions was guaranteed rejection by the Houthis and the South.

Designing federations in deeply divided societies, especially those with significant territorial cleavages, presents major challenges, especially in post-conflict or potentially violent contexts. Most successful federations have emerged in peaceful contexts, either through democratic coming together of formerly separate units, or through a constitutional transition toward devolved arrangements in a functioning democracy. To function well, a federation needs citizens who have a sense of belonging both to the national and their regional communities. Some federations, such as the USA and Nigeria, have survived bitter civil wars once secessionist forces have been defeated militarily, but it took decades to transition to normal, democratic politics and the traces of the conflicts can still be seen in both countries. The victors in Ethiopia's civil war designed a federal regime, but it is effectively a highly centralized one-party system, which has suppressed dissident voices and failed to deliver truly autonomous self-government to the more dissident regions.

Did the international actors mistakenly steer the Yemenis toward federalism when some better approach might have proven more viable and appropriate? An argument has been made that a strong and effective, centralized state should be established as a first step, before moving to serious devolution through federalism.[13] As desirable as this

[13] Peter Salisbury, *Stemming the Rise of a Chaos State*, Chatham House, 2016, https://www.chathamhouse.org/publication/yemen-stemming-rise-chaos-state

might seem, it is hard to imagine it being acceptable in a political context of southern secessionism. Thus any viable political arrangement in Yemen seemed bound to provide for some significant devolution, at least for the south. The central choice was between an asymmetric arrangement, with the south having devolution while the rest of the country remained under the central government (e.g. as in the UK) or a federation. Given that there was no appetite for asymmetry among northerners, the default option became federalism, which raised myriad questions about the allocation of powers, the definition of the regional units, and key central institutions including the parliament, the executive, and the associated electoral laws. In a society with such high mistrust, it was inevitable there would be some power-sharing or "consociationalism" at the center—at least during an extended transition.

As much as the political geometry seemed to require federalism with some kind of north-south power-sharing at the center, the Constitution-making process was inadequate to the challenge of designing such complex arrangements. Moreover, given how weak Yemen's state capacity was, any successful transition to such arrangements would have required a staged process of implementation during which there might have been enhanced power-sharing at the center and perhaps international guarantees and support regarding the staged implementation.[14] The Constitution that was drafted had some of these elements, but it would still have proven inadequate should it have been ratified. While there are lessons about the substantive design of a Constitution for Yemen, the major problems in terms of the international role were not in relation to its advisory support regarding specific design features, but in relation to the process—the timetable, sequencing, and actors—that was supposed to produce a new Constitution.

The NDC, with all its faults, provided a rare opportunity for an inclusive dialogue among Yemenis, though some stayed away and others worked to undermine it. It did produce a weak consensus on the need for federalism, but almost none on the precise model: the number and boundaries of regions; power-sharing at the center; the allocation of powers. The decision to keep the governorates as a separate tier of government while creating the regions could only add to the complexity of the new regime, while taxing the country's capacity beyond the possible. There appeared to be recognition that any move to federalism would have to take place over a period of years, during which capacity would be developed in the regions and the design of the system would be refined. Any such prolonged transition period (which presumably would be as necessary as ever given the devastation of the civil war) will put the issue of the transition arrangements and form of a transitional government front-and-center. This would suggest a much stronger focus on power-sharing arrangements at the center, notably within the new government (the executive), not just the legislature. A related question will be whether there should be a new legislature of some kind during the transition and if so, how it might be chosen and constituted. Somali experience in operating for an extended period without elections may prove relevant (if rather sobering).

Hadi's model of six regions—four in the north and two in the south—was probably the most offensive element of the federal design to both Hirak and the Houthis. Moreover, the continuing attachment of Yemenis to the governorates meant that the NDC opted for a three-tier federation—center, regions, and governorates—whose

[14] Ethiopia, in a totally different political context, provides an example of the progressive development of regional administrations and governments in a new federation in a country that had extremely low governmental capacity. There was a sophisticated capacity building strategy, led by a senior minister for capacity development.

design was confusing and whose implementation was probably beyond the human and financial capacity of the country. While in principle there may be some advantages to a federation with a small number of regions, the model that emerged was unacceptable and probably unworkable. This suggests that a model of federalism based on the twenty-one governorates would prove more acceptable and manageable. It would build on existing governmental infrastructure. While twenty-one units is fairly large for a federation of 28 million people, it is within the bounds of comparative experience (e.g. Kenya's model of devolution). Almost all the governorates have a population of more than half a million. And there could be arrangements to permit or encourage governorates to amalgamate through some kind of bottom-up process.

Political legitimacy and process in a constitutional transition

A striking feature of the transition in Yemen was the very low political legitimacy of most of the political actors engaged in the process. Those who represented the GPC and JMP could, at best, claim electoral mandates that were won ten-years before in an entirely different context. The GPC itself was divided between supporters of Saleh and of Hadi and fence-sitters. There was little structure to civil society and Hirak was deeply fractured—with its representatives at the NDC coming from the most accommodationist and least representative groups. The Houthis were united and disciplined, but their leader paid little attention to the issues confronting the NDC. So politics had very little structure and anchorage and this greatly impeded the ability to develop consensus within groups and agreements across groups. President Hadi won a mandate of sorts from his election, but his term was meant to be for only two years and this became an issue as the transition progressed and his popularity declined.

The classic method to bring greater clarity to such a situation is to hold elections. The GCC Agreement and Implementing Mechanism outlined a series of activities that were to prepare for parliamentary (and possibly presidential) elections within two years. In the event, only the initial presidential election was held. A large international team worked on preparing for further elections, but it was frustrated by the partisan character of the commission for elections, as well as the huge challenges of developing a new voter registry. The GCC Agreement stipulated that new elections were to be held only under a new voter registry, but it was never realistic that this could be done in two years. And as the security situation deteriorated, the option of holding elections became ever more remote.

Might legislative elections have been held at the outset, like the presidential election? And would this have been helpful? Technically, it would have been difficult.[15] Also, elections carried the risks of Hirak winning most seats in the south and perhaps of the GPC, with its infrastructure largely in place, winning most seats in the north (and even having an overall majority, with the attendant dangers). Failing new elections, there might have been an attempt to create a more inclusive government of national unity or a government of technocrats (as many called for by 2014). The government that was created was unrepresentative of key groups seeking major change, highly partisan, of very low competence, and very corrupt.

In addition, the Yemeni case demonstrates the problems of leaving the former strong man in a position to play a major role. He was excluded from any direct role—the

[15] International Foundation for Electoral Systems, *The Role of Elections in a Post-Conflict Yemen* (Arlington, VA: 2016) retrieved at http://www.ifes.org/publications/role-elections-post-conflict-yemen

international community would not meet with him—but remained head of the largest political party and controlled much of the activity of its representatives. So by definition he became a spoiler. When the UN Security Council finally imposed sanctions on him,[16] they proved ineffective. By extension, in a country where the military have traditionally played a central role in politics, a transitional process must give high priority to military reform because otherwise nostalgia in the military for the old regime may lead it to subvert the transition—as they eventually did in Yemen, as they did in Egypt, and as they tried to do in Spain. It became clear in 2014 that Saleh had continued to have high-level military support in significant parts of the army, including elite units.

What lessons does this suggest? First, interim governmental arrangements dominated by the old political elite and excluding strong constituencies for change are seriously problematic: there is always a likelihood interim arrangements may last for several years; even if they do not, such arrangements can discredit the larger process of transition and poison the political environment. The structure in Yemen—where the old parties ran the government, while the NDC was meant to be a broader forum—relegated those most ardent for change to the talk shop dealing with the longer term. A true government of national unity would have been difficult to construct given the Houthis continued belligerency and Hirak's strongly secessionist orientation, but trying to develop a more inclusive government would have been a better than what emerged. For example, some had suggested the alternative of a government of technocrats. When Khaled Bahah was named Prime Minister in 2014 he was seen as a technocrat and there were periodic calls for a transitional government of technocrats. If a more inclusive government of national unity, perhaps with a strong injection of technocrats, could have been achieved, it could not have been worse than the weak and corrupt government made up of the old parties.

Moreover, a heavily bottom-up process such as the NDC needs to be complemented by some top-down arrangements: in some countries, such as Kenya, an arm's length and relatively apolitical group or commission has been charged with developing a draft Constitution, which is then referred to the legislature or some popular body; in other countries, such as South Africa, the main negotiations were between a small number of political leaders, with their draft then being subjected to a process of review and revision by a larger body. It is extremely difficult to reach an agreement on a Constitution without buy-in from senior political leaders—so identifying and engaging them in the process must be a major objective. The NDC was given an impossibly wide mandate combined with the most difficult decision-rule of all—consensus—and the real political leaders were not there to bargain. The decision-rule within the CDC was more realistic (two-thirds majority). In practice, there must be a balance between a fairly flexible decision-rule and a political recognition that even a supermajority cannot ram through certain changes over an important and deeply alienated minority.

Arguably, the architecture of the transitional process was too ambitious and all-inclusive. In such a highly divided and conflictual environment, it was optimistic to think that a sequence all the way to a new Constitution and elections could be set out with a tight timetable. While it is understandable that donors, often for their own ideological, geopolitical, or budgetary reasons, look for a complete plan with deadlines, this is often unrealistic. Experience in such cases is that mediators and advisors must pay attention to the importance of sequencing when incremental political agreements

[16] *Final report of the Panel of Experts on Yemen established pursuant to Security Council resolution 2140 (2014)*, United Nations, January 26, 2016, S/2016/73.

and trust-building are required. This implies a clear sense of staging and the need for iteration, with mediation as necessary in brokering agreement at different steps. It necessarily involves elite bargaining as well as securing broader social buy-in. The GCC process made limited progress in achieving some agreements among the old parties and some of the civil society participants, but it never truly engaged the Houthis and many of the key leaders in Hirak (which was admittedly very fractured), and it dealt with Saleh, the major spoiler, through proxies, but even here without a clear leading representative. Finally, there was no attempt to engage AQAP, which was reasonable given its terrorist activities, but longer term the issue of how to deal with AQAP will need to be considered.

The priority in ending Yemen's civil war will be to develop initial arrangements for governing the country. It is most unlikely that a peace agreement itself will embed a new Constitution (the Bosnian model) because any such Constitution would be highly contested. At most, the peace agreement might include certain principles and benchmarks that should inform the process and substance of future Constitution-making. Hammering these out would be a major challenge, but the process should avoid the mistake of having completely separate tracks for governance and Constitution-making and it should recognize the importance of engaging key leaders in both and having bridges between them. The 8+8 Committee was the only forum associated with the NDC in which there was serious bargaining among the parties.[17] Its format was totally different: only sixteen around the table with Benomar as chair. This brought a focus that was not achieved in the NDC, though even this failed to resolve some of the major questions before it, notably the federal map and petroleum. The President's decision to impose his version of a federal map was disastrous and stands as a lesson on the danger of settlements imposed on powerful, territorially based groups. A new process will need a clear sense of the main bargaining table or tables (the South African model, where the central negotiations were between the ANC and the National Party but there was a second-tier table of other key parties which might provide some inspiration) as well as a view regarding the broader involvement of the public.

A more integrated approach to transitions

The political process in Yemen—notably the NDC and CDC—was complex and time consuming. Even if these processes had been better designed they would have taken a long time to develop a consensus around a Constitution. But while the NDC and CDC were working, the economy and security situation deteriorated drastically and this undermined public confidence in both the government and the dialogue process. Arguments have been made that the provision of basic services, security sector, and the rule of law should have been prioritized, and that this was the result of a failure of political will, so that any future peace process "must be coupled with genuine attempts to address needs and grievances at the local level or it will be doomed to fail."[18] The story is perhaps more complex, but such transitions do need the international community to make every effort to have a "whole of government" approach, which means conscious linkage and coordination. In Yemen, the different actors operated in quite a siloed fashion, though there were steps in the latter stages to improve coordination, notably in having a World Bank officer assigned to Benomar's team. The security issues—reform

[17] Early on, the Presidium was in some ways a tight negotiating group, which did produce the twenty demands, but it never had to resolve major substantive conflicts.

[18] Lackner, N12 64–8.

within the military, the Houthi advances—might also have been brought more directly into the general approach of the international community. Security reform was only partial, despite attempts, so Saleh retained sway over key units of the army. There was a failure to improve security in many governorates.

In addition to focusing on the larger issues of economic management, security, and service delivery, a strong focus on government can deliver immediate, tangible contributions to a transition process. For example, an opportunity was missed with the relatively weak follow-up to the twenty demands that the Presidency of the NDC put forward regarding the South and Sa'ada. The lesson here is that there should be focused attention on "quick wins"—tangible measures that address key grievances—early in a transition process. This can help build political capital in favor of the transition and give it momentum.

In other words, the international community needs to recognize that a political process of transition cannot succeed in a climate of economic and security collapse. Those leading the political and economic efforts need to work together. For major donors an important lesson may be the need to give priority early on to shoring up the economy so as to help the political process. This may mean funding projects that may not be the most strategic, long-term economic investments but are designed to provide aid that can be delivered quickly. The donor package of large infrastructure projects largely failed to materialize and donor spending fell well short of pledges. A good example of very targeted aid that was politically helpful was Qatar's contribution for payments to southerners who were dismissed in 1994. This addressed a key grievance and put money quickly into the economy. Unfortunately, no similar funding was available for addressing the land and property grievances, which could have contributed significantly to the political environment in the south. Other short-term priorities to shore up an economy during a political transition can include make-work projects and support for key government services.

Of course, a strong focus on early economic improvement requires an appropriate plan to build delivery capacity as quickly as possible, with the appropriate checks and controls. A major reason why funds did not flow was because donors considered that the delivery capacity was not present, but arguably the focus on big infrastructure projects, which are very complicated to deliver, was an even greater impediment. Finally, when federalism is on the agenda, this should include a plan to start building capacity early on, even if just through pushing administrative decentralization. Yemen did nothing to build up the governorates during the transition and was unable to start building capacity for the new regions because they were not defined yet. This adds to the logic of building transitional devolution on existing structures if possible.

Finally, the Yemeni experience demonstrates how limited the influence of outside powers and advisors may be. Even had they had a better strategy and delivery, it is not clear that there could have been a successful process in Yemen, with its deep divisions, weak leadership, and inadequate capacity.

18

Processes of Constitutional Transitions in the Face of Territorial Cleavages

Cheryl Saunders

Introduction

Process is a significant factor in successful constitutional transitions.[1] Success for this purpose encompasses not only workable substantive outcomes but a perception of the legitimacy of the process by which they were produced that can assist to sustain the new arrangements over the longer term.[2] In relation to the Constitution itself, around which transition centers, the legitimacy derived from process reinforces its status as the fundamental law that provides the framework for the exercise of public power.[3] The ideal is a Constitution that provides a viable framework for government to which all can subscribe, conveying a sense of the shared ownership of the state.[4]

Much of the attention in relation to the process of transition has focused on the relative significance of public participation and elite buy-in.[5] While the jury is still out on this debate, the common sense answer surely must be that both are important, but in degrees that are likely to vary with the conditions of particular transitions.[6] In any event, however, this is by no means the only aspect of the process for constitutional transition that may affect outcomes, deserving consideration for this reason. Questions of process are raised from the time of the first tentative moves toward transition until well after new constitutional arrangements are in place. They may include, for example, bases for the initial selection of negotiating partners, the manner in which the agenda for transition is set, the potential of an interim Constitution or other instrument to buy time for consideration of more lasting arrangements, the choice of institution for

[1] Vivien Hart, "Democratic Constitution Making" (Special Report 107, United States Institute of Peace July 2003); United Nations, "Guidance Note of the Secretary-General: United Nations Assistance to Constitution-making" (UN April 2009); United Nations Development Programme, "Constitution-Making Support" (UNDP Guidance Note 2014) 23–4.

[2] Alvaro Vasconcelos, "Introduction: Prioritising the Legitimacy of the Process" in Alvaro Vasconcelos and Geral Stang (eds), *Constitutional Reform in Times of Transition* (Arab Reform Initiative 2014) 8, 9. On other possible elements of "success" see Jennifer Widner, "Constitution Writing in Post-Conflict Settings" (2008) 49 William and Mary Law Review 1513.

[3] On the need for caution in assessing legitimacy without reference to context, see William Partlett, "The Dangers of Popular Constitution-Making" (2012) 38 (1) Brooklyn Journal of International Law 193; David Landau, "Constitution-Making Gone Wrong" (2013) 64 (5) Alabama Law Review 923.

[4] Nicholas R L Haysom, "Constitution Making and Nation Building" in Raoul Blindenbacher and Arnold Koller (eds), *Federalism in a Changing World* (International Conference on Federalism 2002) 225–6.

[5] Fernando Mendez and Jonathan Wheatley, "The Constitution-Making Process: An Analytical Framework" in Jonathan Wheatley and Fernando Mendez (eds), *Patterns of Constitutional Design* (Ashgate Publishing 2013) 13.

[6] Abrak Saati, *The Participation Myth* (Umea University 2015) 269–78.

Territory and Power in Constitutional Transitions. First Edition. Edited by Michael Anderson and Sujit Choudhry. Processes of Constitutional Transitions in the Face of Territorial Cleavages Published 2019 by Oxford University Press.

deliberation on a new Constitution, the rules for decision-making at key points in the process, the timing of elections, the utility of a referendum, the plan for constitutional implementation.[7] Process obviously comprises legal instruments, institutions, and formalized procedures. In most cases, however, it will involve the exercise of judgment on less tangible matters as well, of which the way in which incentives might affect behavior and the most effective means of building trust are examples. In many transitions, the influence of international actors or the manner of their involvement may be questions of process as well.[8]

Conflicting interests, insecurities, and the significance of the stakes make decisions about process difficult enough in any constitutional transition. The degree of difficulty is exacerbated when, as usually is the case, there are significant divisions within the community along political, cultural, or socioeconomic lines.[9] But the challenges of constitutional transition have an additional dimension still when such cleavages are territorially defined, weakening the central state, reinforcing sub-state identity, and offering alternative sites of loyalty in reality or perception. Conditions of this kind imply the need to consider a range of measures specifically designed to reinforce shared ownership of the state and confidence in its operations.[10] Those relevant to the substantive constitutional framework include federalism and related forms of constitutionally protected devolution, balancing self-rule and shared rule; consociational or other power-sharing techniques at the center; and carefully calibrated protection of sensitive individual and group rights. These may be complemented by extra-constitutional strategies of various kinds to support reconciliation and build solidarity.[11] In addition, however, significant cleavages that are territorially defined have implications for the process of constitutional transition, to maximize acceptance of workable outcomes without freezing lines of identity in time. These are the subject of this chapter.

Territorial cleavages are a feature of many of the constitutional transitions that have taken place over the decades that followed the end of the cold war. In analyzing the implications of territorial cleavages for the process of transition, this chapter draws on the wide variety of cases included in this volume: Bolivia, Bosnia-Herzegovina, Cyprus, Ethiopia, India, Indonesia, Iraq, Kenya, Nepal, Nigeria, the Philippines, Scotland, South Africa, Spain, Sri Lanka, and the Ukraine. These by no means exhaust recent world experience of such transitions, however. Additional cases that offer insights that can be useful for this purpose include Belgium, Canada, the South Tyrol, and Northern Ireland. Others, in which the implications of territorial cleavages for the process of constitutional transition are or may in time be an ongoing concern, include Bougainville, Libya, Myanmar, Somalia, the Solomon Islands, Tanzania, and Yemen.

Questions about process arise at any point along the spectrum of constitutional transition, from the first intimations of the possibility of change to the bedding down

[7] For a detailed compendium of these and other processes see Michele Brandt, Jill Cottrell, Yash Ghai, and Anthony Regan, *Constitution-making and Reform: Options for the Process* (Interpeace 2011).

[8] Andrew Ladley, *Constitution Building After Conflict: External Support to a Sovereign Process* (Policy Paper, International IDEA May 2011).

[9] See Sujit Choudhry (ed.), *Constitutional Design for Divided Societies* (Oxford University Press 2008).

[10] The distinction between nation building and state building is usefully elaborated in Armin von Bogdandy, Stefan Häußler, Felix Hanschmann, and Raphael Utz, "State-Building, Nation-Building, and Constitutional Politics in Post-Conflict Situations: Conceptual Clarifications and an Appraisal of Different Approaches" (2005) 9 Max Planck Yearbook of United Nations Law 579.

[11] Keith G Banting and Will Kymlicka, *The Political Sources of Solidarity in Diverse Societies* (Research Paper No. RSCAS 2015/73, The Robert Schuman Centre for Advanced Studies 2015).

of the new dispensation over time.[12] Transitions in which the management of territorial cleavages is a significant issue are no exception. The section on "Dimensions of Process" explores the ways in which territorial cleavages may affect the processes of transition at the most obviously salient points: when the agenda is set; as constitutional changes are designed; when final decisions are made; and during the period of implementation. "Postponements" deals with an additional, related phenomenon, commonly associated with constitutional transitions of this kind: the postponement of final decisions on key matters through deliberate ambiguity, incomplete prescription, or reliance on the future operation of Constitution amendment rules. This technique again draws attention to the reality that constitutional transition may extend well beyond the point at which constitutional implementation might normally be understood to end, in order to encompass the eventual resolution (or non-resolution) of sensitive questions.

One purpose of this volume is to draw insights from world experience for constitutional transitions that are presently in train or for others that are not yet underway. Insofar as these affect process, they are identified by way of conclusion at the end of the present chapter. As I observe in the conclusion, however, it is necessary also to appreciate that each instance of constitutional transition is shaped in myriad ways by its own circumstances, including the nature of the transition; the characteristics of the territorial cleavages; the challenges confronting statehood, in practice or theoretical conception; and the geopolitical context in which the transition occurs. This consideration does not prevent valuable insights being drawn from comparative experiences with constitutional transition. It requires understanding of relevant differences, however, so that allowance can be made for them and insights drawn at the level of generality at which they can be a reliable guide. The following section explores the potential relevance of contextual difference more closely and indicates how and why it matters.

Context

The process for constitutional transition within a state in which there are significant cleavages along territorial lines is always affected by context. It is not feasible to exhaustively identify and categorize all elements of context for this purpose. Nor should individual features of a particular process for transition be considered in isolation from the others, which collectively contribute to a constitutional dynamic. The purpose of this section, therefore, is merely to draw attention to four, broad variables that are likely to affect the process of any constitutional transition, in order to illustrate the point.

The nature of the transition

One is the nature of the transition itself. This may vary in a range of ways, any of which may affect the process adopted. At least three features of transition deserve consideration for this purpose.

First, in some cases constitutional transition is a response to violent conflict, as in Bosnia-Herzegovina, Nepal, or the Philippines.[13] This circumstance may call for measures that differ from those available to a transition taking place in more peaceful

[12] Cheryl Saunders, "Constitution-Making in the 21st Century" (2012) 4 International Review of Law 1.

[13] See generally Alexander Rasmbotham and Achim Wennmann (eds), *Legitimacy and Peace Processes: From Coercion to Consent* (Accord 25, Conciliation Resources 2014) 6.

conditions, of which Scotland is an example at the opposite end of the spectrum. Conflict may inject an additional element of urgency into a process of transition, although this will be less where the conflict is "frozen," as in the unusual situation in Cyprus. Conflict may cause the transition itself to begin with a peace agreement in which constitutional pre-commitments are made, as in Nepal.[14] It makes it more likely that the international community will be involved in the transition, in one form or another.[15] The more serious the conflict, the greater is the possibility that international involvement will be prescriptive, in relation to process as well as substance. A history of conflict also may create pressure for additional procedures to secure transitional justice and pursue reconciliation, demanding consideration of what these involve and how they can be achieved without jeopardizing the prospects for peace.[16]

Significantly, conflict adds yet another dimension to the identification of partners in a constitutional transition, by requiring decision about whether to deal with former combatants or not.[17] Refusal to deal with combatants by definition precludes negotiation and may prolong and deepen the conflict; Sri Lanka is a case in point. The inclusion of combatants facilitates a negotiated peace as, for example, in the Philippines and Nepal. In the longer term, nevertheless, it may add another layer of complexity to transition to a form of government in which disputes are resolved through constitutionalized politics and law, unless counter-measures are taken.[18] Conflict also may preclude or complicate recourse to some of the familiar tools for constitutional transition, including elections for a legislature or a constituent assembly, a referendum, or even widespread public education and participation, as the example of Iraq shows. The impact of conflict is most serious when it is current or recent. Even where violent conflict is long past, however, as, for example, in Spain, the memory may create apprehension and contribute to a dynamic that can range from mistrust to an urge for reconciliation.[19]

Second, considerations of process differ between transitions characterized by constitutional continuity and those characterized by rupture. These categories are not necessarily mutually exclusive as the examples of India, South Africa, and Bolivia show.[20] In some transitions, also, of which Indonesia and Sri Lanka are examples, there is a genuine choice to be made between creating a new Constitution and amending an old one, which itself constitutes an element of process. In most cases, nevertheless, the distinction is significant and may determine the process to be followed. Most obviously, in conditions of continuity, the process for adopting new constitutional arrangements

[14] Christine Bell, "Peace Agreements: Their Nature and Legal Status" (2006) 100 (2) The American Journal of International Law 373.

[15] Ladley (n 8).

[16] The significance of context in this regard is emphasized by Jeremy Sarkin and Erin Daly, "Too Many Questions, Too Few Answers: Reconciliation in Transitional Societies" (2004) 35 (3) Columbia Human Rights Law Review 101.

[17] Alexander Ramsbotham and Achim Wennmann, "Introduction" in Alexander Rasmbotham and Achim Wennmann (eds), *Legitimacy and Peace Processes: From Coercion to Consent* (Accord 25, Conciliation Resources 2014).

[18] Veronique Dudouet, "Transformation of Coercive Actors" in Alexander Rasmbotham and Achim Wennmann (eds), *Legitimacy and Peace Processes: From Coercion to Consent* (Accord 25, Conciliation Resources 2014).

[19] In one view, the cautious "pact" that characterized transition in Spain in 1978 has left unfinished business. Ashifa Kassam, "Spaniards aim for a new democracy and end to Franco's long shadow", *The Guardian* (Madrid, November 20, 2015) <www.theguardian.com/world/2015/nov/20/spaniards-aim-for-a-new-democracy-and-end-to-francos-long-shadow?CMP=share_btn_link>.

[20] Arato explores other ways in which the boundaries of "amendment" and "replacement" have been blurred, from the perspective of the continental European constitutional tradition, in Andrew Arato, *Post Sovereign Constitution Making: Learning and Legitimacy* (Oxford University Press 2016).

will be constrained by the requirements for constitutional change laid down by the existing Constitution; Sri Lanka is a case in point. In a related scenario, where an existing Constitution is deemed to impose substantive constraints on the measures that can be put in place in response to a territorial cleavage, as in the Philippines, these must be managed by the process that is followed as well.[21] Continuity also makes it likely that an existing regime will stay in place, at least for a limited period, giving it considerable influence over the terms of the transition as occurred, for example, in Kenya. It may be feasible, in these circumstances, for government as usual to be carried on while the transition occurs.

By contrast, in conditions of constitutional rupture as in Nepal or Iraq, the mode of Constitution-making must be determined on the basis of first principles, whatever they may be conceived to be. The choice may have a bearing on the perceived legitimacy of the new regime. Under these conditions, also, it always will be necessary to make arrangements for the ordinary business of government to be carried out, until a new Constitution comes into effect as the framework for government. An interim Constitution offers one option for this purpose, which also can provide a roadmap for the remainder of the process.[22] On the other hand, an interim Constitution also must be made through a process that attracts a degree of support that is sufficient in the circumstances, even if it falls short of the procedural expectations for a final Constitution.[23] Iraq offers an object lesson in the consequences of failing to meet such minimum requirements. Where the process of transition involves the same institutions in both governing and Constitution-making questions may arise about how the two can be distinguished so as to ensure that each function is effectively performed. Constitution-making arguably calls for a more far-sighted, consensus-oriented approach to decision-making, which can be harder to achieve when questions of immediate political moment intrude. South Africa balanced the two functions well, but in Nepal ordinary politics often seemed to overwhelm the Constitution-making process.

Third, the character of the regime from which transition occurs may have an impact on the nature of the transition itself, in ways that affect the process adopted. An authoritarian regime that is still in control may be prescriptive about options for both process and substance in ways that reflect its own preferences and concerns. Of the cases in this volume, Nigeria and Ethiopia offer examples, which also show that, ironically, an authoritarian regime may insist on substantive constitutional solutions, including federalism, that would not be possible if broader consensus were sought. A democratic regime that remains in control may be prescriptive too, as was the government of the United Kingdom in relation to the Scottish referendum, but its demands will be tempered by considerations of what can be defended to its constituency.[24] Even the

[21] A similar problem has arisen in connection with the peace process in Colombia, see Carlos Bernal-Pulido, "Transitional Justice within the Framework of a Permanent Constitution: The Case Study of the Legal Framework for Peace in Colombia" (2014) 3 (4) Cambridge Journal of International and Comparative Law 1136.

[22] For a range of uses of interim Constitutions including, for example, as a mechanism to facilitate continuity, as in South Africa, see Kimana Zulueta-Fülscher, *Interim Constitutions: Peacekeeping and Democracy-Building Tools* (Policy Paper, International IDEA November 2015).

[23] Vicki Jackson notes that in some circumstances the shortfall may be due to international involvement: Vicki C Jackson, "What's in a Name? Reflections on Timing, Naming and Constitution-Making" (2008) 49 (4) William and Mary Law Review 1249.

[24] The terms of the Edinburgh Agreement 2012 make the point: Scottish Government, "Agreement between the United Kingdom Government and the Scottish Government on a referendum on independence for Scotland" (October 15, 2012) <www.gov.scot/About/Government/concordats/Referendum-on-independence>.

character of an earlier regime that has lost control may affect the dynamic of a transition in one way or another. Examples include the continuing, indirect influence of the former colonial regime on transition in India; the effect of the minority apartheid regime on the processes for transition in South Africa; and the relevance of the former, elitist, monarchical regime on the course of the transition in Nepal.

The nature of the territorial cleavage

A second variable in the context in which a transition occurs that is likely to affect the process adopted is the nature of the territorial cleavage. Again, this variable can manifest itself in different ways, two of which are canvassed here.

One might loosely be described as the depth of the cleavage, understood to be identifiable from a range of possible characteristics: the period of time over which a distinct regional identity has endured; the factors on which it is based; the existence of discrete regional, institutional arrangements; the relative significance of the cleavage as a contributing cause of the transition. Evaluating depth is no easy task. Historical identity can often be argued to be present in some degree in any transition in which territorial cleavage plays a part. Ethnic difference can be exploited for political purposes, masking other forms of discontent. Grievances stemming from perceptions of discriminatory or unfair treatment, including undue centralization of power and resources, usually play a role in feeding a conflict that precedes transition, even when distinct regional identity is clear.[25] Where borders are porous, populations are likely to be intermixed across regional lines. In some cases, nevertheless, the depth of the territorial cleavage can readily be accepted. Historical identity in a reasonably well-defined territory in which a distinctive population is concentrated is well established in, for example, Catalonia, Scotland, the Bangsamoro, Kurdistan Iraq, and Turkish Cyprus, even though the grievances associated with the cleavage are exacerbated by other factors. In each of these cases, also, the people of the region in question either have formal institutions of their own or, in significant numbers, regard political representation at the regional, rather than the national, level as a more authentic reflection of their aspirations.

Collectively, these features of a transition tend not only to strengthen demands for territorial autonomy but also to affect the process of transition as well by, for example, requiring recognition of territorial representatives as parties to the negotiations on transition and making their identification relatively straightforward. The outcomes are not invariable, however, even where these features are present. In South Africa, for example, despite the relatively distinctive identity of KwaZulu-Natal, territorial cleavage was a less significant factor during the process of transition and the outcome was weak in terms of regional autonomy. In this case, other considerations were predominant in constitutional negotiations and the African National Congress was widely accepted as adequately representing the interests of the vast majority of the people, irrespective of regional divisions.

The process of transition may also be affected by spatial dimensions of a territorial cleavage. This feature also may take different forms. One is the distinction between a territorial cleavage affecting only parts of the state, as in the Philippines, Indonesia, or

[25] Thomas Fleiner, Walter Kalin, Wolf Linder, and Cheryl Saunders, "SCIENTIFIC BACKGROUND: THEME PAPER Federalism, Decentralisation and Conflict Management in Multicultural Societies" in Raoul Blindenbacher and Arnold Koller (eds), *Federalism in a Changing World* (International Conference on Federalism 2002) 202.

Sri Lanka, and cleavages that arguably apply across the state as a whole, as in Nigeria, Nepal, India, and Kenya. This distinction has obvious implications for outcomes potentially leading, in the former case, to asymmetrical forms of devolution.[26] It may also affect process, however. A territorial cleavage that applies in only part of the county pits a minority against a majority that may not see its own interests in supporting a territorially based response at all, adding to the difficulties of negotiation and creating an incentive to seek a solution within the bounds of an existing Constitution. The prospect of asymmetry also may lead to consideration of equal treatment for other parts of the state, as in Spain or generate resentment, as in Sri Lanka.

The spatial dimensions of a cleavage may affect process also where, as frequently is the case, territorial boundaries are unclear or contested. This situation adds a new factor to the negotiations, of which either side may take advantage. It also necessitates a process to finally determine territorial boundaries, at the point where new constitutional arrangements come into effect, over time, or both. The examples of Nepal, India, Nigeria, and Iraq illustrate the complexities and significance of this issue.[27]

Finally, whatever the state of the territorial boundaries, where the identity of the population within a particular territory is mixed as, again, usually is the case, the process for transition should, in principle, give minorities a voice, both for the purpose of inclusion and to ensure that substantive outcomes take their interests into account. This adds yet another layer of complexity to constitutional transition, if territorial autonomy is envisaged. In a variation on this problem, where internal leadership within a territory is divided, as in the Philippines, the process of transition will involve a choice of negotiating partners, with potential for further dissention down the road.

The challenges confronting statehood

The concept of statehood may have implications for a process of constitutional transition, in both theory and practice, which are heightened in conditions of territorial cleavage. Almost by definition, constitutional transition involves the organization of power within an existing or proto-state and, in that sense, involves state building. Territorial cleavages within a state that call for territorial solutions may be regarded as a threat to the integrity of the state even where, as should be the case, steps also are taken to strengthen shared rule.

In practical terms, the process of transition will be affected by whether or not the state already is in existence. A transition that involves the aggregation of previously distinct territorial entities, to constitute a new or renewed state, is likely to require a process in which each of the entities has representation of its own. Territorial representatives may have significant bargaining power in these circumstances. Procedural questions about proportional representation and decision-making rules may arise in an acute form. Of the cases in this volume, the most obvious example of a transition of this kind is Cyprus, at least if attention is confined to the recent past. There are elements of aggregation in other cases too, however. India is an example, which also

[26] John McGarry, Brendan O'Leary, and Richard Simeon, "Integration or Accommodation? The Enduring Debate in Conflict Regulation" in *Constitutional Design for Divided Societies* (Oxford University Press 2008) 41, 63–6.

[27] See generally, George Anderson, "Creation of Constituent Units in Federal Systems" (2014) Centre for Constitutional Transitions at NYU Law Working Paper <www.constitutionaltransitions.org/wp-content/uploads/2017/05/Creation-of-New-Units-June-18.pdf>.

shows how the effects of aggregation can be cushioned by a degree of pre-existing unity in addition to, in the case of India, the context of decolonization.

Nevertheless, in the circumstances of the twenty-first century, territorial cleavages more commonly are a feature of transitions within pre-existing states, creating pressure for the devolution of authority from the center. Among the large group of states in this category, further variations can be identified, with implications for process. In some cases, there is an immediate or perceived threat to the physical integrity of the state itself as in Spain, the UK, or, perhaps, Ukraine. In others, of which Nepal is an example, transition is prompted more immediately by a threat to peaceful coexistence. In some, as in the UK, the Philippines and Spain, the apparatus of the central state functions normally during the transition. In others, the institutions of the central state also need to be substantially rebuilt in the course of the transition. South Africa, Ethiopia, Nepal, and Iraq are examples, which also demonstrate the widely varying circumstances in which state building may occur.[28] None of these groupings is mutually exclusive. Each of these situations, however, has implications for the process of transition, potentially affecting incentives, bargaining power and negotiating strategies as well as the more structural dimensions of the transition and the challenges to be met.

Conceptual differences in the understanding of the state can affect the process of transition as well. In some deep-rooted territorial cleavages, differing visions of the form of the state may result from different interpretations of the past or preferences for the future, which need to be accommodated in the process of transition. The UK is an example of the former, where competing views about the implications of the Acts of Union of 1707 in Scotland and England respectively fed into debate on the secession referendum, as Stephen Tierney explains. Cyprus illustrates the latter, in which the two communities have diametrically opposing views on whether transition involves devolution within an existing unitary state, as Greek Cypriots would have it, or the union of two founding states, on the Turkish Cypriot account. In a further variation on this problem, some such differences go to the very concept of the nature of a state or, at least, of the state in contention. Thus, in Spain, an understanding of the state as constituted by a united nation with indivisible sovereignty places limits on the depth of autonomy exercisable by territorial components of it, fuelling tensions and limiting outcomes in ways that also complicate process.[29] In somewhat similar vein, in the Philippines, the concept of the state as enshrined in the Constitution is argued to preclude some forms of autonomy without constitutional change, adding yet another complex factor to the problems requiring resolution before constitutional transition can occur.

International involvement

Most constitutional transitions in the twenty-first century involve international actors of some kind, at some stage. These may be international institutions, individual or groupings of states, intergovernmental or non-governmental organizations or advisers acting under a variety of auspices.[30] In at least some such cases, international actors will have a significant influence on the process of transition. How international

[28] Von Bogdandy and others (n 10).

[29] This theoretical perspective is well explained in Eoin Daly, "The Indivisibility of the French Republic as Political Theory and Constitutional Doctrine" (2015) 11 (3) European Constitutional Law Review 458.

[30] Ladley (n 8).

involvement occurs, and with what effect, varies dramatically, however. Three examples illustrate the range. In some cases, international influence is effectively irresistible. Thus, in the admittedly unusual example of Iraq, the invasion and occupation of the state by the USA and its allies determined key stages of the constitutional process that followed, despite the limitations of international humanitarian law.[31] Similarly in Bosnia-Herzegovina, the Dayton peace process that brought the conflict to an end also settled the Constitution for the new state. These are still extreme cases; there are also other examples, including Cyprus and Kenya in which representatives of the international community are active participants but play a less determinative role. In a second category of cases, now much less usual than it once was, a retreating imperial power sets the scene from which transition occurs in a way that theoretically can be changed but in practice affects the course of events, as the examples of India and Nigeria show.[32] In a third and much more common category of case, of which Nepal is an example, international influence is exerted through the presence of international advisers, working under the auspices of international or foreign national organizations. While this form of influence depends on voluntary acceptance by the state in transition, pressures for compliance with what sometimes are portrayed as global standards give such advice more authority than may at first appear. To the extent that this form of international involvement diminishes local ownership and understanding of new constitutional arrangements, affecting their implementation in practice it hinders, rather than helps, constitutional transition. In any event, none of these and other forms of international influence should be overlooked in examining the dynamics of particular transition experiences.

Two other forms of international involvement merit more specific consideration because they recur frequently and are significant in their effect.

One derives from the geopolitical context in which a transition occurs. The international players in this case will often be neighboring or regional states but may also be powerful states or groupings of states that for one reason or another take an interest in the case. The role of formalized regional groupings, of which the European Union and the Council for Europe are amongst the most developed examples, deserve particular attention in this context, as illustrated by the case studies of Bosnia-Herzegovina and Cyprus. In any event, geopolitical considerations will often be triggered by conflict, for which sometimes they are also a catalyst. They may have particular salience in transitions characterized by territorial cleavage, where ethnic identity is shared across borders or strategic advantage is perceived to be at stake. It is not feasible to determine an effective process for constitutional transition without taking these influences into account and, in some cases, involving international stakeholders directly at particular stages of it. Many of the case studies in this volume illustrate the point. The Ukraine is an obvious example, where territorial cleavages, such as they are, have been exacerbated by the competing attentions of Russia and Western states, to the point of encouraging separatist tendencies. Similarly, determination of the process for transition in Nepal

[31] Tristan Ferraro (ed.), "Occupation and other forms of administration of foreign territory" (Report, International Committee of the Red Cross 2012) <www.icrc.org/eng/assets/files/publications/icrc-002-4094.pdf>.

[32] Differences in the context for transition left by the respective colonial powers is usefully described in Roger D Congleton and Dongwoo Yoo, "A Test of the Unravelling Hypothesis: Constitutional Bargaining and the Quality of African Institutions" (Public Choice Society Meetings, Charleston 2014) <http://ssrn.com/abstract=2444759>.

requires understanding of the roles of neighboring India and China. In Spain and the UK it requires an appreciation of the incentives and disincentives to territorial autonomy and secession that membership of the EU brings to the table.[33]

A second, increasingly significant form of international involvement concerns the role of the United Nations, when it is actively involved in a constitutional transition. In recent decades the UN has contributed to transition in a variety of ways ranging from authorizing the initial use of force or withholding permission for it, as in Libya and Iraq respectively, to offering assistance with aspects of the process through country-specific missions or the UNDP.[34] In some transitions, in addition, the United Nations is directly involved on the ground, as an interim administration, as in Timor Leste[35] or as facilitator of negotiations, as in Cyprus. In circumstances of this kind, international actors are themselves part of the process from whom lessons can be learnt and to whom lessons may apply.

Dimensions of Process

Phases of a transition process

Territorial cleavage may affect any or all phases of a process of constitutional transition. For the purposes of identifying how this might take place, it is useful to distinguish four of these. Each occurs in every constitutional transition, although not necessarily in neat sequence. The first phase is the period at the outset of a process during which its principal features are determined, deliberately or inadvertently. The main stakeholders or negotiating partners are identified; the general contours of substantive change begin to emerge; the process of transition itself is decided; an interim constitution may be made; a "round table" or other negotiating forum may occur.[36] The second phase involves deliberation on substantive change, often in an assembly of some kind, although several institutions may be involved, one or more of which is constituted so as to be representative of the people, however determined.[37] During a third phase, which may overlap with the second, the constitutional changes that frame the transition are ratified or brought into law, by a vote in the assembly, a referendum, or some other means that is deemed to confer legitimacy.[38] The fourth and final phase encompasses the implementation of the new constitutional arrangements, in terms not only of logistics but attitudinal and cultural change. Public participation is likely at some phase of the process and potentially may occur in some form throughout.[39] The ordinary business of government also must be carried out by one means or another during the transition process. The dynamics of government as usual are not necessarily conducive

[33] Any regional organization of which a state is part may influence constitutional transition, in ways and degrees that vary between regions: Raul Cordenillo and Kristen Sample (eds), *Rule of Law and Constitution Building: The Role of Regional Organisations* (International IDEA 2014).

[34] UNDP (n 1).

[35] Simon Chesterman, "East Timor in Transition: Self-Determination, State-Building and the United Nations" (2002) 9 (1) International Peacekeeping 45.

[36] On the phenomenon (and merits) of a round table format see Andrew Arato, "Conventions, Constituent Assemblies and Round Tables: Models, Principles and Elements of Democratic Constitution-Making" (2012) 1 (1) Global Constitutionalism 173.

[37] A table of processes that have been used, drawn from nineteen different case studies, is found in Laurel E Miller, "Designing Constitution-Making Processes: Lessons from the Past, Questions for the Future" in Laurel E Miller (ed.), *Framing the State in Times of Transition* (US Institute of Peace Press 2010) 601, 607–10.

[38] ibid. [39] Brandt and others (n 7) 80–148.

to the more consensus-building style required by constitutional transition unless this tension is anticipated and managed, as in South Africa.

While the detail of the impact of territorial cleavage on process depends on the context in which it occurs, some generalizations can be made on the basis of collective experience, using the phases of transition as an organizing principle.

Agenda setting

In any transition, the initial phase of the process is the time to identify the substantive issues to be resolved, to establish a workable and legitimate process for doing so, to determine the key stakeholders, to build trust and to begin to work toward securing sufficient consensus on a new constitutional dispensation.[40]

These are tasks for a process of transition characterized by territorial cleavage as well. In conditions of territorial cleavage, however, some take a distinctive form.

In the first place, territorial cleavage is likely to give rise to a particular set of issues that need to be dealt with in the course of the transition. Where the territorial cleavage is the principal driving force for the transition, this will be obvious from the outset. Among the cases in this study, Cyprus, the Philippines, and the UK are examples. Even where the transition has multiple causes, the relevance of territorial cleavage may be assumed, as in Ethiopia, India, and Nigeria. This is not always the case, however. In some transitions, of which Nepal is an example, there is initial resistance to the implications of territorial cleavage, for reasons of historical practice or apprehension of the consequences. In most if not all cases, nevertheless, there is much to be gained from perceiving the potential of territorial cleavage early, in order to ensure that the need to manage it is clearly on the agenda.[41] There is a range of possible constitutional responses to the problems that underlie territorial cleavage, of which a measure of self-rule is only one.[42] A holistic solution can be assisted by identifying the constitutional and other issues associated with the cleavage and managing the responses to them. A solution developed in this way also can take into account the position of minorities in territorially defined areas, if a degree of territorial autonomy is part of the transition package. Measures for self-rule can be balanced with those for shared rule. Devolution of some kind, arguably desirable in any event for reasons of good government explored in the chapter on Kenya, can be adapted as an element of the response to territorial cleavage, although not necessarily along the same geographical lines.[43]

At the risk of anticipating the next part, this approach to designing constitutional solutions in the face of territorial cleavage, once seeded from the beginning of the process, should be carried forward into the deliberation phase. Where federalism or some variant of it is sought, it is tempting and, indeed, may be appropriate to identify this as one of the constitutional themes for detailed examination by a committee of the Constitution deliberation body. Arrangements for self-rule should never be considered

[40] On the importance of building the climate for constitutional transition, see Nicholas Haysom, “Negotiating a Sustainable Political Settlement—Part 2 Legitimation: Lessons from the South African Transition” (Toward Inclusive and Participatory Constitution Making conference, Kathmandu, August 3–5, 2004) <www.idea.int/news/upload/Nepal%20-%20Haysom.pdf>.

[41] Donald Horowitz, “Conciliatory Institutions and Constitutional Processes in Post-Conflict States” (2008) 49 William and Mary Law Review 1213, 1230.

[42] Haysom, “Constitution Making and Nation Building” (n 4).

[43] This decision, and others, may be guided by the choice between approaches that emphasize consociation between groups with different interests and “centripetal” approaches that offer incentives for cross-ethnic coalitions: Horowitz (n 41).

a discrete part of a constitutional package, however. They are always interdependent with other aspects of a system of government: shared institutions at the center; protection for minority rights; constitutional adjudication; the formula for constitutional change. Where a thematic committee is used in this way, cross-fertilization with the ideas emerging from other committees is desirable and coordination of the final recommendations of all committees is essential.

Second, in conditions of territorial cleavage there is likely to be an additional range of potential stakeholders to be taken into account, representing territorially defined communities. These stakeholders may have a critical role to play, in negotiating agreed outcomes that prove durable and as a voice for the views of people in these areas. In some cases the choice of stakeholders is more straightforward than others. Some areas defined by territorial cleavage have their own institutions and leaders authorized to speak for them are likely to be known. Scotland is an obvious example but Kurdistan in Iraq and Catalonia in Spain are in this category as well. Even in these cases, the scope of the authority of regional spokespersons may be contested, by opposing views within the region or by regional representatives in central institutions, as the example of Catalonia shows. Nor can official representatives always be relied on to deliver majority support from their communities; the response of Cypriot communities to the Annan plan is a case in point. These cases nevertheless offer a contrast to others in which there are no formal indicia of those with authority to speak on behalf of their communities. Thus, in the Philippines, several groups claimed to represent the Bangsamoro. Negotiations proceeded with the group considered to hold out the best prospects of success, but there is potential for conflict with others, further down the track, which also needs to be managed. More difficult still are cases in which territorial cleavage is politically salient but territorial solutions are contested by the central state and there are no obvious or acceptable representatives of those pressing for them. Nepal and Ukraine illustrate the point; and the former, at least, also demonstrates the costs of failure.

In all these circumstances, it is desirable to identify effective local leaders with a strong claim to legitimacy on a basis that is as inclusive as possible. In the real world this may be a difficult task, however, particularly for international actors without considerable inside knowledge, who cannot judge the adequacy of the authority of local partners. In some cases, in reality, there may be no such leaders, requiring a transition process that takes account of territorial cleavage in other ways. Elections may offer one solution. Fair elections may be impossible, however, in a post-conflict context. Premature elections can also have other untoward effects, polarizing positions on the configuration of new constitutional arrangements at a time when consensus building is needed.[44]

Third, territorial cleavage throws up issues for the transition on which the negotiating parties may have starkly different views, placing a premium on the effectiveness of negotiation. The preferred outcome from the perspective of the central state tends to involve limited concessions to territorial claims, particularly where these involve a measure of territorial autonomy. Proponents of the territorial cause, on the other hand, are likely to seek maximum constitutional protection for their concerns, including through a degree of territorial autonomy. International actors may have views as well, rightly or wrongly, which almost always will be opposed to secession but will often encourage a substantial degree of devolution. The range of mutually acceptable outcomes is finite, making compromise essential, on both sides. The range may be considerable,

[44] Christine Bell and Kimana Zulueta-Fulscher, *Sequencing Peace Agreements and Constitutions in the Political Settlement Process* (Policy Paper No. 13, International IDEA 2016).

nevertheless. Strategic choice of particular procedures at particular times may advance the priorities of either the central state or territorially based interests. Thus, for example, in relation to South Africa, Nico Steytler describes how strategic choices by the African National Congress, at the time of the negotiation of the Interim Constitution, ultimately contributed to the "withering away" of the salience of territorial cleavages.

Deliberation and ratification

The phases during which deliberation takes place on proposed new constitutional arrangements, and they are reduced to draft form and brought into law, present further challenges to any process that purports to be representative and inclusive, in conditions of territorial cleavage. Most obviously, they raise questions about whether and, if so, how, the people of the territorially defined areas are represented as such for the purposes of deliberation and determination. Resolution of this problem generally involves striking an acceptable and accepted balance between the democratic standard of one vote one value and the organization of interests on a territorial basis in which population numbers are not decisive. In many cases, including Sri Lanka, the Philippines, and South Africa, this problem pitted majority against minority. It may also map onto divisions between the central state and segments of its territory, as these examples also show. The problem may present itself in a variety of guises during deliberation and ratification of new constitutional arrangements: in the composition of a deliberative body and its constituent parts; in voting rules on key issues; in the framework for any elections that are part of the process; in the decision rules for a referendum; in the Constitution of any transitional government. While the issue is most commonly associated with these intermediate phases of a constitutional transition it may also be encountered earlier. This might occur, for example, in determining the composition of a "national dialogue" that is designed to scope the ambit of constitutional change or in laying out a road map for the process of transition in an interim Constitution.[45]

This problem of reconciling territorial representation with majoritarian voting tends to be resolved in favor of the former in "coming together" federations of which the USA and Australia are examples.[46] In these, now historical, constitutional transitions, polities considering federation were represented in deliberative assemblies in equal numbers, despite substantial differences in population size, and they retained a veto over their own participation at the point of ratification, at least as a matter of law. Constitutional transitions involving the aggregation of distinct polities now are rare, however, and claims based on the principle of the equality of representation of territories, as territories, have correspondingly been diminished, at least for this purpose. The principle has by no means disappeared, however. Thus in the somewhat more recent example of India, the Constituent Assembly was constituted indirectly by election by state legislatures and appointments by princely rulers, although the territories were not equally represented. Successful transition in Cyprus will require majority support from both communities.

[45] Katia Papagianni, "National Dialogue Processes in Political Transitions" (Civil Society Dialogue Network Discussion Paper No. 3, Civil Society Dialogue Network 2014).

[46] On the various ways of categorizing federations by reference to their origins see Michael Burgess, *In Search of the Federal Spirit: New Theoretical and Empirical Perspectives in Comparative Federalism* (Oxford University Press 2012) 139–40.

These days, a deliberative constitutional assembly or other body is more likely to be constituted by direct election, which in turn is more likely to adhere to the principle of one vote one value, generally on the basis of proportional representation. All else being equal, elections are a powerful legitimating tool for a new Constitution, particularly in conditions of constitutional rupture. On the other hand, elections based solely on population numbers may fail to produce an assembly in which representatives of particular groups, territorially based or otherwise, have a sufficient voice in the Constitution-making process, jeopardizing the longer-term prospects for peace.[47] Iraq is an extreme example but this is, or was, an issue in Libya too.[48] Similar tensions arise where final ratification of a Constitution requires a statewide referendum. In principle, again, a referendum is one obvious way of legitimizing a new Constitution, by demonstrating the support of the constituent power. In conditions of territorial cleavage, however, a referendum risks giving inadequate voice to territorially based views, undermining its legitimacy in the eyes of these communities.

Two types of solutions are suggested by past practice, which are not necessarily mutually exclusive.

One involves qualifying the majority principle, at the point of selecting a deliberative body or in determining decision-making rules. Whether this is appropriate and, if so, how it is best done varies with the circumstances of each case. Decisions on these issues should take account of the potential impact of the chosen process on broad public acceptance of the Constitution. In addition, as in any Constitution-making exercise, process design should be informed by an understanding of the way in which what Elster has described as "upstream" and "downstream" effects might influence a successful conclusion.[49] Where, as is usually the case, final decisions by a larger body are effectively negotiated by a smaller group, whether formalized or not, the territorial dimensions of the conflict are relevant to the composition of the smaller group as well.

At one extreme, the process for constituting a deliberative body might provide for election or selection of representatives of the people territorially organized, thus giving full weight to the implications of territorial cleavage. There are lesser options as well, however, that seek a balance with the majority principle. The number of representatives of the people territorially organized might be determined partly or wholly by reference to population share, in a system of weighted representation; additional seats, whether elected or appointed, might be reserved for territorial interests in a deliberative body otherwise elected on the basis of equal national citizenship; if a deliberative body is bicameral, the second chamber might represent the people, territorially organized; supermajorities might be required to make key decisions in the deliberative body; less formally, the deliberative body might generally agree to operate on the basis of "sufficient consensus," the meaning of which should be understood by reference to the conditions of the particular transition;[50] and a supermajority requirement might be applied to the turnout quorum or decision rules in a referendum as

[47] The importance of inclusion in maintaining peace in ethnically divided communities is emphasized in Andreas Wimmer, *Waves of War: Nationalism, State Formation, and Ethnic Exclusion in the Modern World* (Cambridge University Press 2012) ch. 6.

[48] Jason Gluck, "Constitution-building in a political vacuum: Libya and Yemen in 2014" in Melanie Allen and others (eds), *Annual Review of Constitution-Building Processes* (International IDEA 2014) 43, 45–6.

[49] Jon Elster, "Forces and Mechanisms in the Constitution-Making Process" (1995) 45 Duke Law Journal 364, 373–5.

[50] Haysom, "Negotiating a Sustainable Political Settlement" (n 40).

well.[51] How these procedures work can be illustrated by examples. In South Africa, the voting rules for adoption of the final text of the Constitution required a two-thirds majority of all the members of a bicameral legislature, sitting as a Constitutional Assembly. For alterations to the boundaries of the provinces, there was a super-added requirement of a two-thirds vote in the second chamber, in which the provinces were equally represented. Supermajority voting rules were used for other purposes as well, including appointment of a committee of experts, to act as a circuit breaker in some conditions of disagreement. In an example of another kind, Iraq used unusual supermajority requirements in prescribing the decision-making requirements for a referendum to ratify the Constitution. Under the Transitional Administration Law, the Constitution would be ratified if, at referendum "a majority of the voters in Iraq approve and . . . two-thirds of the voters in three or more governorates do not reject it."[52]

A second type of solution to the problem of providing some protection for territorial interests in the course of a constitutional transition is to devise some other form of safeguard instead of, or in addition to, qualification of the majority principle. Any such arrangement is likely to depend both on trust and on institutional integrity. South Africa again provides an example. In South Africa, the process for constitutional transition involved pre-commitments on a general framework for multilevel government in the principles appended to the Interim Constitution, famously secured by a requirement for certification by the Constitutional Court that the final draft complied with the principles. Importantly also, this part of the Interim Constitution was expressed to be unamendable during the Constitution-making process.[53]

There is a need for care in any event in the use and timing of elections and referendums in the course of constitutional transition. Despite their democratic credentials, both also have downsides that may be exacerbated in conditions of territorial cleavage if, indeed, a fair and inclusive vote is feasible in post-conflict conditions at all. Elections can deepen social and political divisions, making it more difficult to create the broad consensus that, ideally, Constitution-making requires. While elections are inevitable at some point in a democratic transition, in some cases postponement may be possible and desirable and they should always be managed with the particular challenges of transition in mind. Referendums are not necessarily essential to constitutional transition. They offer an important tool for the purpose, however, and in some cases there may be compelling reasons for their use.[54] On the other hand, referendums may be divisive too, in a constitutional transition in which there are strongly held competing views. A referendum in any event can be a blunt instrument for decision-making, providing only for acceptance or rejection, risking failure from objection to particular provisions, relying for its rationale on a level of understanding among voters that they may not possess. These considerations suggest that a decision to include a referendum in a process for constitutional transition should be taken with full understanding of its suitability for the purpose and should be coupled with techniques to minimize potential disadvantages. These might include, for example, efforts to ensure agreement between opinion leaders before the referendum occurs and preparation of the voters,

[51] For a critique, arguing in favor of other devices to build prior agreement, see Stephen Tierney, *Constitutional Referendums: The Theory and Practice of Republican Deliberation* (Oxford University Press 2012) 275–82.

[52] *Law of Administration for the State of Iraq for the Transitional Period*, art. 61(c).

[53] *Constitution of the Republic of South Africa 1993*, s. 74(1).

[54] On the proliferation of referendums see Stephen Tierney, "Whose Political Constitution? Citizens and Referendums" (2013) 14 (12) German Law Journal 2185.

in their respective constituencies, to accept the constitutional compromises that inevitably will have been made.[55]

In some circumstances, in conditions of territorial cleavage, a referendum is held in a territorially defined area, rather than across the state as a whole. Parallel, territorially based referendums are an obvious mechanism for securing public support and bolstering legitimacy where autonomous polities are considering union, on some basis, in a single state. Cyprus offers a relatively rare contemporary example of their use in this way; in this case, as a mechanism for reuniting two parts of a deeply divided polity. The rejection of the referendum in Cyprus also demonstrates the risk, however, where the incentives for a positive vote are wrong and leadership is weak or uncommitted. Other cases in this study show how a territorially confined referendum may be used for other purposes, in the course of a constitutional transition. In Scotland and Catalonia the referendum has been seen as a mechanism to secure an expression of popular will to secede from the larger state. In the Philippines, it is proposed ultimately to be used to ratify the Bangsamoro Basic Law, if and when this is approved by the Congress of the Philippines. In South Africa, the National Party used a referendum directed only to its own supporters to strengthen its authority to proceed with negotiations over constitutional transition. While this was not a case of a cleavage along territorial lines, it offers an example that could also be used for such purposes. In each of these cases, the referendum played a useful role. In all of them, also, however, it offers the same risks: of deepening division, undervaluing minority views, and courting rejection.

Implementation and other matters

Territorial cleavage has implications also for the final phase of constitutional transition, during which new constitutional arrangements are put into effect. Precisely what this involves depends on the detail of the constitutional arrangements themselves, but attention to implementation is likely to have at least three dimensions.

First, action is required by the institutions of the central state to put in place and secure the effective operation of all aspects of the new constitutional dispensation; in particular, for present purposes, those designed to reflect the settlement of the issues raised by territorial cleavage. These may include, for example, devolution of legislative or executive power; power-sharing arrangements within national institutions; and procedures to facilitate the use of language rights or new electoral laws.[56] Where difficult constitutional questions have been postponed, using a technique that is considered in the next part, implementation requires progress with these as well.

Second, where, as is the usual case, the Constitution is interpreted and enforced through courts, it is important to ensure that courts understand and give effect to the spirit of the new arrangements. This may be particularly challenging where the state is moving from a unitary to a more decentralized form of government, as Sri Lanka found, following the passage of the Thirteenth Amendment.[57] Of course, this

[55] Haysom makes a similar point in relation to "confidence-building measures" for constitutional negotiations more broadly: Nicholas Haysom, "Negotiating the Political Settlement in South Africa: Are there Lessons for Other Countries?" (2002) 11 (3) Track Two s 4.

[56] In a development that still is unusual, the Constitution of Kenya provided for the establishment of a Commission for Implementation of the Constitution for a period of five years: Constitution of Kenya, sch. 6(5). The tasks of the Commission included oversight of the legislation and administrative procedures necessary for the implementation of the constitutional provisions relating to devolution.

[57] Asanga Welikala, "Devolution within the Unitary State: A Constitutional Assessment of the Thirteenth Amendment with reference to the experience in the Eastern Province" in Centre for Policy

dimension of implementation must be pursued in a way that preserves respect for judicial independence. Much can be done in this regard, however, without raising concern about separation of powers, even where the former judges remain in place and retain constitutional jurisdiction. Among other things, the state should adopt a position in litigation before the court that furthers effective implementation of the Constitution.

Third, a constitutional transition that involves substantial autonomy at the sub-national level requires sub-national implementation as well. Sub-national constitutive documents may be required which, once in place, also will require implementation. In any event, the effective operation of the sub-national level of government will be critical to the success of the constitutional transition as a whole, in the exercise of the powers and functions for which it is responsible and merits explicit attention to capacity building. The relative novelty of sub-national government also can open the door to corruption, as the cases of Indonesia and Kenya show, unless preventative action is taken.

Two final, general, observations should be made about the process of constitutional transition before examining the techniques associated with postponement in the next part.

The first concerns public participation. Public participation in some form is a likely feature of almost any constitutional transition in the twenty-first century. It is regarded as important for purposes that range from deepening the legitimacy of the new Constitution to enhancing its effectiveness to attempting to ensure its approval at referendum. Conditions of territorial cleavage may affect the planning for public participation in several ways. Most obviously, territorial division adds to the number, complexity and potential sensitivity of the issues that are raised for popular consideration in the course of public participation. These realities should be borne in mind in designing both the procedures for public participation and the information material on which they are based. In some circumstances, moreover, the emphasis placed on particular issues in the course of public participation may differ in parts of the country in ways that call, properly, for different approaches. Cyprus offers an example, where the information needs and interests of people in the Greek and Turkish areas are likely to differ in significant respects.

The second observation concerns the role of international advisers. International advisers may be involved at various stages of a process of constitutional transition. At their best, they bring to a process a body of useful knowledge about both procedural and substantive solutions that is suggested by experience elsewhere and that is capable of being adapted to local needs. They may also bring insights, informed by experience, about what is likely to work and what is not. In some transitions, they offer a neutral force that can assist effectively with negotiation or mediation.

There is a danger, however, that international advisers bring predilections of their own about what should be done in relation to both process and substance, on the basis of knowledge that is confined to a relatively narrow range of their own experience, which they assume to have more universal application. The issues presented by territorial cleavage for resolution through constitutional transition are likely to be deeply rooted in local history and politics, however. Outsiders may have limited capacity to identify local leaders with real authority. They may be unaware of aspects of past history that make some solutions less palatable than others. Transplanted institutions, principles and practices, if appropriate at all, are likely to require careful selection and

Alternatives (eds), *Devolution in the Eastern Province: Implementation of the Thirteenth Amendment and Public Perceptions 2008–2010* (Centre for Policy Alternatives 2010) 15–19.

adaptation that is informed by local conditions. The challenges of implementation will be ongoing, long after the international advisers have left. It is critical that solutions adopted are workable in the local context and are owned and understood by those to whom they will apply. With these imperatives in mind, international advisers should conceive their role primarily as offering knowledge and insights from experience elsewhere in a form that facilitates local choice. They should be selective in the constitutional models that they bring to the table, in a way that is informed by comparative understanding.

Postponements

A Constitution enshrines the framework for government that has emerged from the transition in a form that is difficult to change. The potential rigidity of a new constitutional settlement may be daunting in a state undergoing transition, particularly when some aspects of it are novel. This consideration alone may inhibit agreement on new constitutional arrangements. In any event, issues may arise in the course of negotiations over a new constitutional settlement that are, at least for the moment intractable and on which no agreement seems possible. Unless resolved in some way, such issues have the potential to derail a transition altogether.[58] These problems apply in any transition, but may be pronounced in conditions of territorial cleavage. The stakeholders may be divided over desirable outcomes. Some of the solutions on the table may be unfamiliar, including those that require substantial devolution. Devolution within a previously highly centralized state may need to be phased in, to build local capacity, as in Kenya. There may be particular apprehension about the number of devolved units and the location of boundaries, unless these were relatively well established beforehand.

These problems can be ameliorated in a range of ways. Strategic flexibility is one. A constitutional amendment formula that is less rigid, generally or in relation to parts of the Constitution, can reduce the stakes of constitutional entrenchment, although at some cost to the security of the constitutional bargain.[59] A Constitution can provide internally for a measure of flexibility by, for example, formally prescribing a transitional period during which new constitutional arrangements come into effect or old arrangements stay in effect, or enabling functions to be transferred by agreement between levels of government.[60] Alternatively, in an example of a different kind, the costs of constitutional transition can be reduced by retaining some arrangements from the past and confining innovation to matters on which change is demonstrably needed.[61]

A degree of flexibility in the operation or alteration of new constitutional arrangements can indirectly postpone difficult decisions by ensuring that they are not necessarily final in effect. In addition, however, there are other, more direct techniques for postponing decisions, where that might contribute to the success of the transition

[58] Widner (n 2) 1534.

[59] Context may affect the way in which an apparently flexible amendment procedure operates in practice: Tom Ginsburg and James Melton, "Does the Constitution Amendment Rule Matter at All? Amendment Cultures and the Challenges of Measuring Amendment Difficulty" (2015) 13 (3) International Journal of Constitutional Law 686.

[60] The Australian Constitution offers an example of all three: one state was empowered to continue to impose customs duties for a transitional period (s. 95); the introduction of free trade and some revenue arrangements was postponed during a transitional period (s. 92, s. 94); the Commonwealth Parliament may make laws on matters referred by State Parliaments (s. 51(xxxvii)).

[61] Ozan Varol, "Constitutional Stickiness" (2016) 49 UC Davis Law Review 899, 928.

overall. At one extreme, negotiation of a new Constitution might be avoided entirely in the short term by relying on an existing Constitution, with amendments if necessary, until conditions stabilize sufficiently for Constitution-making to occur.[62] Two other postponement techniques are explored further below. The first involves deliberate ambiguity in drafting potentially disputed provisions; the second, a considered decision not to resolve particular controversial issues leaving, at best, a place-holder in the text of the Constitution.[63]

Many parts of most Constitutions prove to be ambiguous until their meaning is settled through interpretation or practice. Ambiguity that equates with postponement, however, involves agreement on a contentious issue in a form that is understood differently by different parties and is acceptable on this basis. Examples from the cases in this volume include South Africa, Cyprus, and Iraq. In each case the ambiguity enabled constitutional transition to progress to the next stage. At least in the short term, it could be portrayed as a win for both sides, and it preserved the possibility of ultimate victory for either, once the constitutional settlement was in place. In South Africa, Steytler notes that the strategy was effective; the deliberate ambiguity over the extent of the federal character of the state created a position that all parties could accept.[64] In Iraq, Al-Ali argues that the strategy was effective in managing differences over the constitutional status of Islam but destructive in other respects. In Cyprus, ambiguity in relation to the federal character of the state became a cause célèbre during the referendum campaign, contributing to the rejection of the agreement.

Failure to resolve a contested question is a related technique of a different kind. Any Constitution leaves some matters to implementation by legislation or other means; what is included and what is not are matters for fine judgment. The technique of postponement, however, involves the deliberate omission from the Constitution of a matter that otherwise would be likely to have been included but on which agreement could not be reached, at least in the time available. India is one of many examples. Controversy over a uniform civil code at the time of constitutional transition was overcome by postponement of any definitive decision, apart from conferring an enabling power on the parliament and encouraging progress through a directive principle;[65] in India also, a more radical restructuring of existing territorial boundaries was postponed until a later date. Iraq is another example of postponement, where the Constitution of the second chamber of a bicameral legislature was left to subsequent legislation.[66] Spain offers a further, pertinent example, where the 1978 Constitution acknowledged the "nationalities and regions" that constituted the state but merely put in place procedures for regionalization once the Constitution was in place.[67] In Indonesia, also, while the Constitution recognized the principle of autonomy, its realization in Aceh and West Papua was left to subsequent legislation.[68]

[62] The "small Constitution" in Poland offers an example: Lech Garlicki and Zofia A Garlicka, "Constitution Making, Peace Building, and National Reconciliation" in Miller (ed.) (n 37) 391, 393–6.

[63] All three contribute to what Hanna Lerner has characterized as the "incrementalist approach to constitution making": Hanna Lerner, *Making Constitutions in Deeply Divided Societies* (Cambridge University Press 2011) ch. 2.

[64] The ambiguity on this point in South Africa stemmed from the terms of the constitutional principles, the use of which reflected the technique of postponement more generally: Heinz Klug, "Constitution-Making, Democracy and the 'Civilizing' of Irreconcilable Conflict: What Might We Learn from the South African Miracle?" (2007) 25 (2) Wisconsin International Law Journal 269, 286.

[65] Lerner (n 63) ch. 4.

[66] Constitution of Iraq, art. 65.

[67] Constitution of Spain, s. 2(8)(3).

[68] Constitution of the Republic of Indonesia, ch. VI.

These techniques are important and useful in appropriate circumstances. They can be employed to secure agreement on constitutional transition in the face of an apparent impasse in deliberations. They can be coupled with measures to provide some assurance that the postponed items will remain on the agenda, for subsequent solution by, for example, providing for the establishment of a commission for inquiry and report. They should be used with discrimination, however, and with an eye to any potential for unexpected judicial interpretations. They may not be suitable for matters that go to the heart of the causes of constitutional transition. They should be used with caution for matters that are closely integrated with other features of the new constitutional dispensation as, for example, in relation to the second chamber in Iraq. And they should be used in the understanding that their effect may be to leave some matters permanently unresolved. Spain had been something of a success story in this regard, although the continuing conflict between the state and the region of Catalonia, which in part stems from the playing out of matters not resolved at the time of transition, suggests the need for caution.[69] In India and Iraq, however, the contentious issues postponed at the time of transition have never been finally been resolved.[70] In Indonesia, postponement led to further conflict, requiring a further process to be put in place to resolve it.

The techniques associated with postponement may have a particular application in constitutional transitions involving the delimitation of boundaries for the purposes of federalization.

In some cases, both the number and boundaries of federated units are relatively settled and are assumed for the purposes of constitutional transition. In other cases, boundaries are less clearly established as transition gets underway. In most such cases, they are settled in the course of transition. The delimitation of boundaries may be a highly controversial exercise, however, requiring principles to guide boundary drawing and a decision-making process in which the principles are applied. The Ethiopian Boundary Commission, representing the political parties equally and established during the period of the transitional government is an example.

All Constitutions that provide for a form of federalism or entrenched regionalism are likely to include Constitution alteration rules that allow for the alteration of boundaries and the creation of new units. In some cases the rules are relatively rigid, involving the consent of the units concerned, in some form.[71] In others, however, where greater flexibility is judged to be required over time, the Constitution may enable unit boundaries to be altered more readily, sometimes by a unilateral decision of central institutions in which regions are represented. As the example of India shows, in context, this amounts to a form of postponement.

Some cases of constitutional transition more deliberately adopt the techniques of postponement in relation to the boundaries of federated units. In Iraq, by way of example, the new Constitution recognized the status of Kurdistan as a federal unit but merely empowered other governorates to establish themselves as part of the federal order, individually or by amalgamation, through a referendum vote.[72] In Nepal, an

[69] Josep Valles, "Catalonia and Spain: Conflicting Majorities" (*Centre on Constitutional Change*, August 14, 2015) <www.centreonconstitutionalchange.ac.uk/blog/catalonia-and-spain-conflicting-majorities>.

[70] In relation to India, see Lerner (n 63). The position in Iraq is described by Zaid Al-Ali, in this volume.

[71] Germany is an example: *German Basic Law* art. 29; Rudilf Hrbek, "New delimitation of the German Lander: A continuously discussed but still unresolved political project (1948–2012)" in Stelio Mangiameli (ed.), *Federalism, Regionalism and Territory* (Guiffre Editore 2013) 78.

[72] Constitution of Iraq, arts 117–19.

early draft of the final Constitution would have established a commission to draw the boundaries of the federated units after the Constitution came into effect.[73] The storm of criticism that greeted this decision caused a succession of hasty changes to the draft to settle the provincial boundaries.[74] These remain contested, however, even under the Constitution as finally promulgated, presenting decision-makers with a dilemma over how the boundaries might be changed.[75] Time will tell what lessons can be drawn from this aspect of the constitutional transition in Nepal. As matters stand, it is tempting to suggest that the question of boundaries should have been more effectively tackled at an earlier stage in the process, however difficult that may have been.

Postponement offers one technique for dealing with the sensitive question of the boundaries of federated units. It also offers flexibility to respond to needs that may arise over time. India is a positive example in this respect. Flexibility in the delimitation of federal units has other consequences as well, however, which should be borne in mind. Unless the boundaries eventually settle down as, for the most part, is the case in India, flexibility can detract from the potential of self-rule. Federated units in these circumstances are unlikely to have their own constitutive instruments. More significantly still, they may have less capacity to establish themselves as functioning polities in a federated order. It may be tempting also for central institutions to use their power to determine the number and boundaries of units to weaken the sub-national order by causing the proliferation of states. This appears to have been the case in Nigeria, where the large number of federated units is a contributing factor to centralization and represents one of the issues that another round of Constitution-making may need to resolve.

Conclusions

The wide range of case studies examined in this volume confirm that significant territorial cleavages are likely always to have implications for a process of constitutional transition, normatively and in practice. What is appropriate or desirable from a normative point of view, however, may vary with the different perspectives of stakeholders. A process that seems optimal from the perspective of the central state may well be unacceptable to some or all territorial interests, and vice versa. Resolving these differences, in the interests of a workable outcome that is acceptable to all parties, is a core matter for negotiation, in which strategic calculations will play a part. Where agreement cannot be reached it may be necessary to take steps to ensure that the disappointed party or parties can live with the outcome. A process that has been broadly accepted as fair may assist in this regard.

No two transitions are the same. The process that is followed at each of the phases of transition depends on context. This chapter has canvassed some of the more likely variables, in terms of the nature of the transition, the characteristics of the cleavage, conceptions of the state, and the dynamics of international involvement. This list is by no means exhaustive, however. There are many other factors that in practice can influence the course that a particular transition can and should take.

[73] Draft Constitution of Nepal, July 2015, s. 60.

[74] Constitution of Nepal 2015, art. 56, sch. 4.

[75] "Supreme Court clears decks for constitutional amendment" *The Himalayan Times* (Kathmandu, January 2, 2017) <http://thehimalayantimes.com/kathmandu/supreme-court-clears-decks-for-constitution-amendment/>.

Nevertheless, the now-extensive world experience with constitutional transitions in conditions of territorial cleavage offers some insights that can usefully be applied at an appropriate level of generality, with all the necessary caveats. It is likely always to be useful to identify and acknowledge the territorial cleavage from the outset of negotiations, when a variety of measures may be available to resolve the issues that arise. In principle, all substantial stakeholders should be included in all phases of the transition, although it is acknowledged that, in some circumstances, this is a counsel of perfection. Deliberate attempts should be made to strike a fair and acceptable balance between majoritarian and territorial interests in determining the process to be followed and in deliberating on the terms of the final settlement. Care should be taken in timing and structuring events such as elections and referendums that are inherently majoritarian in character. Implementation is a key phase, on which the success of a transition may depend, particularly where new constitutional arrangements involve significant devolution of governmental authority. The techniques of postponement should be used strategically, with a clear eye to their pros and cons. International involvement should be focused and constructive, in recognition of the need for local ownership of both the process of transition and its outcomes.

19

Constitutional Design and Territorial Cleavages

Tom Ginsburg

Introduction

This chapter surveys constitutional options for resolving and managing enduring territorial cleavages, drawing on the case studies in this volume. It divides constitutional tools into three sets, based on a reading of the literature: those that involve allocation of decision-making to different levels of government, including federalism, autonomy and various forms of devolution; those that concern central government institutions, including representation of territorial interests at the center, budget redistribution, and rights; and those that allow the territorial units to exit. We also discuss the role of institutional guarantors and international actors in constitutional enforcement. It goes without saying that these approaches can be used in various combinations, and that some constitutional mechanisms work at more than one level. Federalism, for example, usually combines local autonomy over certain policy areas with explicit representation in the formation of central policy. It also bears emphasizing that the best normative approach in any particular situation will depend on contextual factors. Nevertheless, it is possible to generalize about the costs and benefits of the particular constitutional options, and the case studies provide a rich set of material from which to draw conclusions.

The perspective I take here is one that is explicitly political. I draw on the image of a Constitution as a political bargain concluded by a small set of decision-makers.[1] These decision-makers may represent political parties, different regions of the country, a center, and periphery, or different ethnic and social groups. To adopt a new Constitution, a sufficient plurality of powerful parties must believe they are likely to be better off within the prospective arrangement than outside it. Furthermore, the arrangement they produce must be "self-enforcing," meaning that significant deviations are punished by actors within the system. This does not mean that constitutional arrangements are always happy affairs: stability and endurance may require mechanisms of mutual threat and discipline to keep the arrangement in place. But successful Constitutions channel conflict through their institutional arrangements. This last point provides us with a normative lens through which to evaluate the various design options considered here.

We note that the focus of most of the case studies is on the maintenance of existing state structures rather than the integration of new ones; that is, the emphasis is on what Stepan calls holding-together federalism rather than coming-together federalism.[2] This

[1] See Barry Weingast, "The Political Foundations of Democracy and the Rule of Law" (1997) 91 (2) American Political Science Review 245; Zachary Elkins, Tom Ginsburg, and James Melton, *The Endurance of National Constitutions* (Cambridge University Press 2009).

[2] Alfred Stepan, "Federalism and Democracy: Beyond the U.S. Model" (1999) 10 (4) Journal of Democracy 19.

Territory and Power in Constitutional Transitions. First Edition. Edited by Michael Anderson and Sujit Choudhry. Constitutional Design and Territorial Cleavages Published 2019 by Oxford University Press.

is not completely true, in that the Turkish side would characterize the Cyprus case as one of coming-together federalism, as might the Russians in their characterization of the Crimean peninsula. But for our analytic framework, we focus on the more common problem of holding diverse countries together.

In the context of enduring territorial cleavages in existing states, the key issue over which bargaining will occur is the degree of autonomy, including the definition and powers of the subsidiary units. At one extreme, forces in a territorial unit ultimately may threaten secession or violence or both. At the other extreme there is the possibility of total integration in a unitary state without any local autonomy. In between these two extremes lie many possible configurations, over which the parties may bargain. A simple heuristic to capture the dynamic is to think about Albert Hirschmann's framework of Exit, Voice and Loyalty.[3] The bargaining is typically over *how much voice to give the territorial unit to avoid exit and achieve a degree of loyalty.*

Because of the close association of territory and sovereignty, as well as the perceived zero-sum nature of each, territorial cleavages are very high stakes issues, going to the heart of the definition the political community, national identity, and statehood. Constitutional bargaining over territory, one might say, is like that which occurs over other kinds of issues, only more so. That is, bargaining is likely to be emotional, difficult, and not always amenable to permanent resolution. We have, in the case studies here, some examples of bargains that never materialize, such as that recounted by Welikala in his discussion of Sri Lanka. Of course, a successful bargain will incentivize parties to invest in mutually beneficial arrangements, and so is worthwhile to pursue.

However, to foreshadow a point made below, the fact that agreement is reached does not mean that it is a good or optimal one. One of the themes that emerges from the set of cases in this volume is that some of the bargains, which may have been the best possible under the circumstances, are institutionally dysfunctional.

Constitutional bargains require enforcement and monitoring. Once the parties agree to undertake certain actions, they must be able to determine when the other party is violating the agreement. This implies the ability to monitor the performance of the other side. It also implies the utility of some third party who can help the parties to coordinate their understandings of what their agreement requires. These might be institutions that are endogenous to the agreement, such as constitutional courts or federalism commissions, or they might be third parties outside the borders of the territory. So institutional arrangements are not only the direct topic of constitutional bargains, but often necessary to help them persevere. For this reason we conclude our discussion with some thoughts on guarantors.

Allocating Decision-Making across Space: Federalism and Devolution

Constitutional federalism

Constitutional federalism is, of course, the standard mechanism for dealing with territorial difference, and it is here that we shall start.[4] Federalism is the classical approach

[3] Albert Hirschmann, *Exit Voice and Loyalty: Responses to Decline in Firms, Organizations and States* (Harvard University Press 1970).

[4] Ugo M. Amoretti and Nancy Gina Bermeo (eds), *Federalism and Territorial Cleavages* (John Hopkins University Press 2004).

to thinking about regulatory variation across space within a single state. In a federal system, there is a constitutional division of authority between a central government and one or more subunits, the distinguishing feature of which is that there are some topics on which the subunit rules will stand in the face of central opposition.[5] Roughly 11 percent of all countries are nominally federal in the sense that the Constitution uses the term explicitly; roughly 18 percent are actually so in the sense that one or more regions has designated policy areas in which it has a veto or final authority.[6] Figure 19.1 shows these trends over time. The solid line shows nominally federal countries, and the dashed line adds other countries that are in fact federal as defined above.

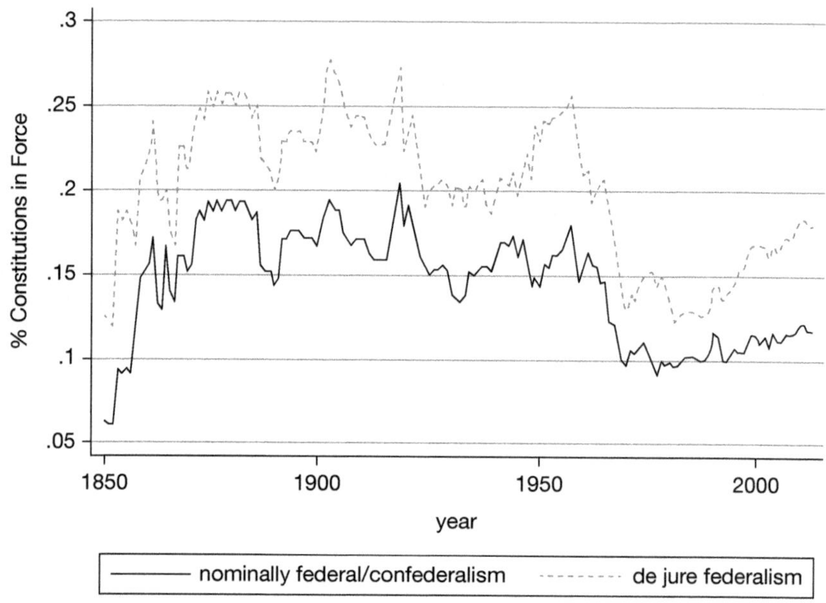

Figure 19.1 Federalism over time

While some of the benefits of federalism might be obtained through other means, proponents argue that constitutionalization allows the polity to *commit* to the policy of decentralization. Constitutions, by virtue of their entrenched nature, allow for greater reliance by citizens and foreigners on their promises than does ordinary law or policy.[7] Amendment formulas for modifying federal schemes are frequently more onerous than is the case in unitary regimes, in that they may require special approval of the subunits in some form and combination.[8] Having some realm of authority that cannot be

[5] This is my working definition from the Comparative Constitutions Project. Note the slight distinction from Will Kymlicka's definition of federalism as a system "which includes a constitutionally entrenched division of powers between a central government and *two* or more subunits, defined on a territorial basis, such that each level of government has sovereign authority over some issues" (emphasis added). Will Kymlicka, "Is Federalism a Viable Option for Secession?" in Percy Lehning (ed.), *Theories of Secession* (Routledge Press 1998) 119.

[6] Data on file with author, from the Comparative Constitutions Project.

[7] Stephen Holmes, *Passions and Constraint* (University of Chicago Press 1995).

[8] George Anderson, *Federalism: An Introduction* (Oxford University Press 2008).

unilaterally retracted by the central government allows units in a federal system to be more credible. In the context of enduring territorial cleavages, some effective commitment device is likely to be necessary.

Importantly, constitutional federalism need not treat all the subunits equally. In India, Kashmir and several other regions get special constitutional treatment by virtue of the terms of their accession to the Union or other historical legacies. As described in the chapter in this volume by Moreno, Colino, and Hombrado, Spanish regions under the 1978 Constitution were granted "autonomy" over crucial cultural policies as a reaction to the excessive centralism of the Franco regime, and this was expected to be asymmetric, though the degree of asymmetry has declined over time. And the United Kingdom has evolved into a system of asymmetric arrangements among its component parts, with Scotland having pushed the boundaries of autonomy quite far.[9]

The literature on federalism is vast, and its advantages extend well beyond resolving territorial cleavages. The founding fathers of the United States of America argued that multiple governments can reduce the risk of tyranny, as having power divided into two different levels of government would serve to limit domination by either one.[10] Madison saw the danger of tyranny arising not just from the government, but from the society as well. Federalism would ensure that no single region would be permanently dominated, but also that minority interests within any particular territory would be better respected, as they could leave to another jurisdiction (or obtain help from the center as eventually occurred later with African American constituents). This benefit of federalism implies the need for subnational autonomy within a broader national framework, as distinguished from having a large number of independent countries.

Beyond the promotion of liberty and the protection of rights, several other crucial rationales are often given for federalism. First, federalism allows public goods to be produced on a smaller scale than that of an entire country, presumably allowing for better overall alignment between preferences and policies for certain types of goods.[11] Only if there are externalities that impose costs across regions should an issue area be allocated to a higher level government. This is basically the principle of subsidiarity as it has been articulated in European Union law, and is a powerful motive for the global shift toward devolution even in unitary states. Of course, the theory does not mean that actual allocations of powers match the ideal, since they are subject to the political negotiation highlighted above.

A second, related point is that jurisdictions that compete with each other for citizens will be encouraged to produce optimal sets of policies for a diverse society. The basic idea is that citizens will "vote with their feet" and move to different jurisdictions that better reflect their particular preferences.[12] This will lead to more responsive government.

Third, federalism allows for experimentation in policies. In the USA, it is often said that the states are policy laboratories for democracy.[13] If policies work in one state, it

[9] W Elliott Bulmer, *Constituting Scotland* (Oxford University Press 2016).

[10] James Madison, Federalist No. 51, available at the Avalon Project, http://avalon.law.yale.edu/18th_century/fed51.asp last accessed December 21, 2017.

[11] Dennis C Mueller, *Public Choice III* (Cambridge University Press 2003) 287; Mikhail Filippov, Peter C Ordeshook, and Olga Shvestova, *Designing Federalism: A Theory of Self-Sustainable Federal Institutions* (Cambridge University Press 2004) 2.

[12] Charles M Tiebout, "A Pure Theory of Local Expenditures" (1956) 64 (5) The Journal of Political Economy 416.

[13] The phrase comes from Justice Louis Brandeis in *New State Ice Co v. Liebmann* 285 US 262 (1932) [311] (Brandeis L) ("It is one of the happy incidents of the federal system that a single

might provide the basis for the adoption of the policy elsewhere, either at the center or through horizontal, peer-to-peer processes, such as imitation or learning.

Fourth, it is sometimes argued that federalism has systemic advantages in providing "minor league" environments for the training of political leadership. This refers to the idea that politicians can gain executive experience at a lower level of government, which might make them more attractive as national leaders. Prime Minister Modi of India shares something in common with four of the last seven US presidents: they all had experience as chief executives of states.

All of these rationales are general, and may have little purchase on the problems of territorial cleavages, in which issues of identity are at the fore. As Sujit Choudhry and Nathan Hume note, federalism in post-conflict settings is qualitatively different from "old" or traditional federalism.[14] They argue that the principal goals in such contexts "are not to combat majority tyranny or to provide incentives for states to adopt policies that match their citizens' preferences, but rather to avoid civil war or secession."[15] In the context of territorial cleavages, the need to hold the country together, and to defuse or resolve conflict is primary. There may be a localized anti-tyranny concern, in which a unit fears domination at the center. One way to think of territorial cleavages is that they arise because of sharply different preferences—over policy, distribution of resources or identity—that correspond with internal geographic divisions. Aligning preferences with power can prevent minority domination by a majority, if that minority predominates in a subunit. But the other general advantages of federalism—jurisdictional competition, policy laboratory, and minor league for political leadership—may not be found at all in the context of enduring territorial cleavages, and indeed may be undermined by the particular arrangements adopted.

To develop this point we need to recall that Constitutions are often political bargains concluded by a small set of decision-makers. Political bargains are subject to the threat of renegotiation. This is consistent with one theme in the literature on federalism; namely, that it is less a one-time allocation of duties and powers than an ongoing and dynamic set of negotiations.[16] When working well, this iterated quality of constitutional federalism allows multiple levels of government to adjust their responsibilities over time to better serve citizens. But ongoing or repeated iterations of renegotiation can also be a source of tension, and in some cases may even allow the development of secessionist movements.

Dividing authority over crucial issues can help reduce the stakes of the overall constitutional bargain and thus facilitate agreement. For example, if a territorial cleavage overlaps with a distinct religious or ethnic identity, allowing language and religion to be determined locally might make an overall constitutional bargain possible. Language, in particular, does not allow for neutrality, as official business must be conducted in some language. Federalism reduces the zero-sum nature of having an official language, reducing alienation and increasing efficacy. This parallels the public goods argument for federalism. However, the particular bargain that is concluded will not necessarily

courageous State may, if its citizens choose, serve as a laboratory; and try novel social and economic experiments without risk to the rest of the country"); James A Gardner, "The 'States-as-Laboratories' Metaphor in State Constitutional Law" (1996) 30 (2) Valparaiso University Law Review 475.

[14] Sujit Choudhry and Nathan Hume, "Federalism, Devolution and Secession: From Classical to Post-Conflict Federalism" in Tom Ginsburg and Rosalind Dixon (eds), *Comparative Constitutional Law* (Edward Elgar 2013).

[15] ibid.

[16] Carl J Friedrich, *Trends of Federalism in Theory and in Practice* (Pall Mall 1968).

overlap with the overall optimal scheme for producing public goods. It may be the case that, for example, granting special fiscal benefits to a particular sub-unit leads to high overall rates of taxation, as both the center and sub-unit impose duplicative taxes. Likewise, such a policy may lead to relatively higher taxes in the rest of the country. Consider Nigeria's 13 percent formula for allocation of the revenues from resources to the producing states, as described by Suberu in his chapter. Allowing the relatively rich southern states more revenues has led to tensions similar to those in the well-off Basque region of Spain.[17] It has also led to successful further lobbying efforts by the oil-rich states for expanding the tax base by including the continental shelf. This is a different form of jurisdictional competition—not a positive sum competition to attract citizens through the adoption of good policies, but a negative-sum exercise in what is called rent-seeking, reducing the pie for other states.

The federal solution also risks institutionalizing interests and creating the capacity for re-negotiating the bargain later on, perhaps even leading to pressures for secession. Indeed, one study shows that mechanisms for integrating minorities may succeed in resolving some problems, but ultimately reduce attachment to the national state.[18] Philip Roeder has argued that a key element in the probability of successful secessionist movements is what he calls the segment state. Sub-states with administrative infrastructure and other indicia of statehood, such as regional institutions of government, had a much easier time seceding than those that do not.[19] Having a sub-unit in place that is already capable of producing some public goods, and allowing for the formation of collective voice, might lead local elites to promote secession, and give them some credibility in re-opening negotiations down the road.[20] This dynamic was particularly apparent in the breakups of the socialist federalisms of Yugoslavia and the Soviet Union, in which each sub-unit had a dominant ethnicity for whom it was named.

The track record of federalism on political mobilization has been decidedly mixed.[21] Dawn Brancati notes that a corollary to decentralization is that regional parties can thrive, creating pressure for secessionist movements. She argues that certain variables will be more likely to exacerbate regional tensions: the presence of regional legislatures, for example, can lead to a locally dominant party with an interest in pushing the regional identity. This has been the case in Catalonia, for example, and also Quebec. (The same dynamic is occurring in Scotland in the nominally non-federal UK).

Thus, federalism may undermine national integration in some cases. This is particularly true in cases in which a territorial cleavage maps directly onto an ethnic one, such as in the Bosnia-Herzegovina and Iraq chapters in this volume. The Dayton Accord resolving the Bosnia conflict married the self-declared Serb Republic with the remainder of Bosnia, refusing to redraw boundaries and essentially creating a tense consociationalism which was self-reinforcing. While consociational solutions may be attractive in situations of violent conflict, they can easily become embedded. (In any case, consociationalism may be less effective than was once thought.[22]) In Iraq, the disadvantaged

[17] See also George Anderson and Sujit Choudhry, *Constitutional Transitions and Territorial Cleavages* (International IDEA 2015) 19.

[18] Zachary Elkins and John Sides, "Can Institutions Build Unity in Multiethnic States?" (2007) 101 (4) American Political Science Review 693.

[19] Philip G Roeder, *Where Nation States Come From: Institutional Change in an Age of Nationalism* (Princeton University Press 2007).

[20] Elkins, Ginsburg, and Melton, *The Endurance of National Constitutions* (n 1) 133.

[21] Dawn Brancati, *Peace by Design: Managing Intrastate Conflict through Decentralization* (Oxford University Press 2009).

[22] Joel Selway and Kharis Templeman, "The Myth of Consociationalism? Conflict Reduction in Divided Societies" (2012) 45 (12) Comparative Political Studies 1542.

status of Kurds in the country's history culminated in the establishment of *de facto* autonomy after 1993 and a fully recognized Kurdish autonomous region in the 2003 Constitution, a *de facto* mini-state with its own military, revenues, and other attributes of statehood. This did not end the pressure for secession, however. A 2017 referendum in which voters overwhelmingly chose secession seems to have led to precisely the opposite result, as Iraqi forces retook the crucial city of Kirkuk. Similar fears of ethnic enclaves have been a factor in the Sinhalese nationalist approach in Sri Lanka, in which demands for federalism have never been accepted.

To be sure, there are some recent counter-examples to the idea that segment states are an *essential* prerequisite of secession: in South Sudan, and arguably Kosovo, secessionist movements succeeded without much prior administrative infrastructure.[23] Secessionist pressures have also arisen in unitary states Sri Lanka, the Philippines and Indonesia, to cite only the examples that emerge from the case studies. Still, the point that federalism can be centrifugal is an important one in the context of enduring cleavages, and help explains why it is not always the best solution. In their chapter on Kenya, for example, Ghai and Cottrell describe how fears of centrifugal pressures after independence led to an abandonment of the *majimbo* idea and the creation of a highly centralized state. Constitutional reform in the 2000s sought to reverse this centralizing trend, but also to avoid exacerbating ethnic tensions: the ultimate design divided the country into forty-seven counties to keep units small. Indeed, this axis of debate about disintegration and attachment is one of the themes of the chapter on Kenya. Another example of how state reorganization and the drawing of boundaries can ameliorate conflict is found in the Nigerian case study by Suberu. There, iterated federalrestructuring under the military from the late 1960s reveals the benefits of opting for a large number of small states (thirty-six at the time of writing) instead of a small number of large states. In this case, creating multiple, relatively small states helped to disperse enmity between large groups, reducing ethnic conflict. At the same time, Nigeria has experienced centralization over time. While the Nigerian *process* has been rather top-down, the outcome has been one of integration and reflects the ability of federalism to accommodate shifts in the locus of powers over time.

Overall, our cases in this volume indicate that federalism need not lead to disintegration, and can be a valuable tool of integration. In Fiseha's account of Ethiopia, the creation of multiple states corresponds to an investment in regional government structures, which employ many people. Although the Constitution provides for a right of secession (to be discussed below) this has not led to centrifugal pressures, largely because of the role of a repressive, dominant political party. While the relative success of this case may be due to the country's long history as a "devolved autocracy," it also shows that national political parties can counteract Roeder's thesis that segment state lead to breakups.

Consider also the case of India, analyzed in the chapter by Bhattacharyya. The debate over the national language became a major issue in India, exacerbating linguistic cleavages that also had a territorial component. The 1956 States Reorganization Act and its successor statutes created several states with one dominant language, but also took into account the cultural boundaries and economic viability of each new region.[24]

[23] In these two cases, the international context was crucial to the successful secession bids, as the international community supported both efforts. To some degree this support was punitive in nature, responding to international frustration with Slobodan Milošević and Omar al-Bashir. This illustrates again that national Constitutions have an international context.

[24] Sujit Choudhry, "Managing Linguistic Nationalism through Constitutional Design: Lessons from South Asia" (2009) 7 (4) International Journal of Constitutional Law 577.

The states, which generally have equal powers, have relative autonomy within the federation. The reorganization has been successful in lessening conflict and securing stability. More demands followed, especially in the northeast, but the creation of new states there reflected tribal and strategic factors more than linguistic differences. Three new states were created in 2000, mainly to address underdeveloped regions, but the most recent creation, Telengana, created a Telugu-speaking state. The 1956 act and its successors, then, seems to have succeeded at minimizing conflicts centered on language differences. In some sense, the cases shows that federalism may play a role in "extending the Republic" as Madison imagined. By creating linguistically and ethnically defined states, in a larger diverse entity, the Indian state reduced the stakes of politics at the center, while ensuring that no one entity or group could dominate the country as a whole.

As in Ethiopia, for much of its history India featured a dominant party that provided channels for representation of regional interests as well. However, the very success of federalism in incentivizing political mobilization and participation at the state level also changed the nature of political competition at the national level. As regional, caste, and linguistic concerns became a basis of political organization, smaller parties were able to challenge the Congress party and weaken it, and it has now been relegated to a second-rank position in Indian politics, at least as at the time of writing.

South Africa's constitutional negotiations have been subject to much scrutiny, but one point that has not been widely recognized is that creation of provinces turned out to be critical in producing the constitutional compromise. (South Africa is not formally a federation, though it is sometimes treated as a federal case.) During the negotiations over the interim Constitution, a particular provision relating to the so-called *Volkstaat* allowed Afrikaner hardliners to join the constitutional bargain. This is an example of how federalism can be used in negotiations to defuse potential spoilers. While the final Constitution did not include any provision for a Volkstaat, as hardliner power had decreased significantly in the years between 1993 and 1996, the proposal of a provincial scheme reassured the white and Zulu minorities that they might at least have some governmental power.

Beyond its utility in facilitating bargaining in a highly charged environment, the South African scheme is the one case in which the "minor league" aspects of federalism seem to be at play. Each province has its own elected executive and legislature. Furthermore, boundaries were drawn in such a way as to undermine the previous Bantustan structures, with their great deprivations. It has functioned decently well, though in a dominant-party system the formal structures are not as important as the party. The African National Congress (ANC) has liberally used a "cadre deployment" system to assign its members to serve in various lower-level bodies, as a way of developing talent.[25] This operates much the same way as it would under a Leninist system, and shows that the existence of multiple levels may be useful even in a context where policy is set rather centrally.[26] (To be sure, cracks are now appearing in ANC dominance.)

An important test case for the virtues and risks of federalism will be the forthcoming experiment in Nepal, described by Malagodi in her case study. After a brutal civil war, the elimination of the monarchy, and an eight-year interim arrangement,

[25] Sujit Choudhry, "'He Had a Mandate' The South African Constitutional Court and the African National Congress in a Dominant Party Democracy" (2009) 2 Constitutional Court Review 1, 2.

[26] Theunis Roux, *The Politics of Principle: The First South African Constitutional Court* (Oxford University Press 2013).

Nepal adopted a new Constitution in 2015 that creates a federal republic out of the prior unitary state. A major challenge is that there are no prior administrative divisions of appropriate scale to draw upon for reference in designing provinces, and there are also demands for previously underrepresented groups to be able to have their names associated with certain provinces. The bargaining has focused on the numbers, names, and boundaries of territorial states, with central elites preferring few sub-units and traditionally marginalized areas preferring more. Federalism in this context is being asked to solve multiple problems at once: a history of exclusion in a context of tremendous ethnic diversity, but in which the geographic configuration is highly asymmetric. For the Madhesi minority that lives in the lowlands bordering India, territorial federalism makes sense as a way of promoting self-governance; however, the delimitation of provinces did not satisfy them and led to violent protests and a reopening of negotiations. Constitutional amendments have not yet met this challenge.

Nepal is an utterly diverse society, with well over 100 languages spoken. For most groups in Nepal, besides the Madhesi, the creation of federal states will recreate local problems of exclusion and inclusion. In short, only one of the major ethnic cleavages in Nepal is primarily *territorial* in nature. Federalism will be challenging in this environment: it may, but probably will not, facilitate more efficient provision of public goods, and may exacerbate rather than resolve the territorial cleavages. Its effect on ethnic cleavage remains to be seen.

Many of the federal case studies in this volume provide stories of centralization, gradual or sudden, of key powers. Examples here include Nigeria, India, and South Africa. Iraq's 2005 Constitution was designed to have a relatively weak center, but the failure of any region to emerge except for Kurdistan meant that there was strong centralization over the Arab parts of the country. South Africa represents a somewhat special case, in which centralization made sense given the vast differences in local capacity in the wake of apartheid, combined with ambitious transformative goals and a dominant political party. This made radical decentralization unattractive when it came to constitutional implementation. Finally, Bolivia reflects a kind of reinforcement of the status quo, after a decentralization program led to centrifugal pressures that were contained.

On the other hand, the cases of Bosnia-Herzegovina, Indonesia, the Philippines, Spain, and Scotland reflect movement in the opposite direction. Each involved asymmetric accommodation of a localized cleavage, which had violent histories (except for Scotland, where violent conflict ended centuries ago). A key factor in explaining whether shifts in the direction of centralization or decentralization concerns the overall heterogeneity of the nation. When a territorial cleavage is quite distinct and limited to one or two discrete regions, it makes sense to decentralize as a means of accommodation and preserving overall unity; but in utterly diverse places, like India, this design strategy invites centrifugal pressures and conflict.

To summarize, federalism—with its myriad variations—is an important part of the toolkit to ameliorate tensions that have led to conflict in the first place. On the other hand, federalism may create new sources of identity formation and tension. In this regard, facilitating sub-unit representation at the center is an important feature for working out shared governance. Issues of timing, with relation to the particular history of grievance and conflict, may be the crucial factor in determining whether federalism reduces the cleavage, stabilizes it, or provides a mere waystation toward disintegration. One recent study finds that the existence of prior conflict is a crucial variable for determining when and whether autonomy helps to ameliorate or exacerbate tensions.[27]

Decentralization and special autonomy

The global trend toward decentralized government through statutory or non-constitutional schemes seeks to leverage some of the general advantages of federalism even within unitary states. Decentralization is argued to advance the efficient and responsive production of public goods, and to facilitate policy competition and experimentation. Decentralization also reduces the stakes of controlling the central government and so can ameliorate latent territorial tensions.

A general program of decentralization is likely to reduce the emergence of territorial cleavages in the first place. Once a cleavage arises, decentralization is surely part of the toolkit. The Philippines and Indonesia cases in this volume provide examples. In the Cordillera region of the Philippines, discussed by Lau, a potential demand for autonomy was ameliorated through the general decentralization. In the Indonesian case, decentralization created local counterweights for dominant groups.

Yet decentralization, by increasing local capacity, may also create the building blocks for future territorial demands, including for more formal federal schemes. The 1994 decentralization law in Bolivia, discussed by Moreno and Molina in their chapter, created new political units and guaranteed each a share of the national budget. This created the basis for a broader mobilization in both the east and west of the country once an economic shock hit. The two sides had very different demands, with politicians in the resource-rich eastern lowlands demanding a strengthening of local autonomy at the departmental level, while those in the western highlands advanced a more centralized but plurinational vision in which revenues were broadly shared. But both utilized the local capacities that had been developed for a very different purpose a decade earlier. When conflict in the Constitution-making process led into violence, departments passed their own autonomy statutes.[28] The principles from these were then incorporated, in much modified form, into the 2009 Constitution.[29] However, President Evo Morales was able to resist the maximal fiscal demands of the lowlands, and so the overall story is one of in which the majority resisted a privileged territorial minority.

Devolution can also function to devolve corruption and rent-seeking. Much of the commentary on devolution in Kenya following the 2010 Constitution has made note of this feature. Instead of providing local public goods, counties are providing local private goods, replicating the venality of the national politicians. Ghai and Cottrell, in their chapter, argue that it is too soon to say whether or not the situation is an improvement. There is some evidence of enhanced local public goods provision, and perhaps a devolution of ethnic tensions as losers in one county may be winners in a neighboring one. Another feature is that the requirement of minority representation at county government level may incentivize groups to cooperate, even if only to carve up the pork.

[27] Lars-Erik Cederman, Simon Huq, Andreas Schadel, and Julian Wucher, "Territorial Autonomy in the Shadow of Conflict: Too Little, Too Late?" (2015) 109 (2) American Political Science Review 354. When divisions are not preceded by conflict, territorial decentralization decreases the probability of future conflict, but there is no such effect in post conflict settings. This suggests that in such contexts, only representation at the central government is likely to be effective.

[28] David Landau, "Constitution-Making Gone Wrong" (2013) 64 (5) Alabama Law Review 923.

[29] Departments became actual political units with elected governors and assemblies, creating a three-tier system of government.

Another design option is special autonomy arrangements, a kind of asymmetric devolution in which one (or more) regions is given authority over certain subjects.[30] As compared with federalism, special autonomy arrangements are relatively flexible in terms of institutional design, and can be tailored to the particular needs of the territorial cleavage. For example, the strategically located Åland Islands of Finland were once the subject of territorial disputes between Russia, Finland, and Sweden. In 1856 these became demilitarized by treaty, and today the islands retain autonomy within Finland. The residents of the islands are exempt from conscription into Finland's military, the islands retain the Swedish language by law, and international agreements carve out some exceptions from EU law to preserve their territorial character. In this way, the arrangements have lowered the stakes of government for the region, defusing a potentially serious cleavage.[31]

Oftentimes, autonomy is used to recognize distinct histories within unitary states. In other circumstances, autonomy is intended to limit centrifugal tendencies. Immediately prior to the failed Scottish referendum on independence in 2014, recounted by Tierney in his chapter, the British government announced that it would create a commission to devolve extensive new powers to the Scottish Parliament in the event voters rejected secession. The Smith Commission recommended that Scotland have the power to set personal income tax, be allowed to borrow, and have extensive control over local political processes. As Tierney notes, Scotland is now one of the most autonomous sub-units in the world, and secured some of these powers as a result of a credible threat of secession.

Many of the other cases in this volume reflect special autonomy arrangements, each of which has seen varying degrees of success. Crimea had special autonomy within the Ukraine for several years before its eventual annexation by Russia.[32] In Indonesia, special autonomy laws were drawn up for both Aceh and Papua in 2001, and again for Aceh in 2006. The 2001 Law on Aceh failed to placate the secessionist movement, partly because of the government's refusal to negotiate or consult popular opinion.[33] In 2006, a new agreement, produced with the help of external mediation from the former president of Finland, led to the passage of a new law. (The external shock of the 2004 tsunami's devastation of Aceh also led to cooperation in the rebuilding effort, which spilled over into the broader political debate.). As Bertrand notes, the success of autonomy in Aceh (as opposed to the failure in Papua) relied on three conditions: negotiation between parties, precision and detail within the new law, and the involvement of an external mediator. In addition, Aceh had a good deal more internal unity, and thus more leverage.

The Philippines case study here is another example of autonomy. The "People Power" Constitution of 1987 sought to resolve long-standing grievances in Mindanao by allowing the creation of autonomous entities, leading to the creation of the Autonomous Region in Muslim Mindanao (ARMM) soon thereafter. Weak capacity issues meant this entity never became effective, and a separate insurgency by the Moro Islamic Liberation Front, led to negotiations over the creation of the Bangsamoro

[30] See Yash Ghai, "Introduction: The Nature and Origins of Autonomy" in Yash Ghai and Sophia Woodman (eds), *Practicing Self-Government: A Comparative Study of Autonomous Regions* (Cambridge University Press 2013).

[31] Sia Spiliopoulou Åkermark, *The Åland Example and Its Components – Relevance for International Conflict Resolution* (The Åland Islands Peace Institute 2011).

[32] Gwendolyn Sasse, "The 'New' Ukraine: A State of Regions" (2001) 11 (3) Regional & Federal Studies 69, 82.

[33] Bertrand, Indonesia case study at 12–13.

Juridical Entity, with a good deal more autonomy (the deal has not been ratified at the time of writing).

Special autonomy may be particularly useful when the population of the unit in question is quite small, as in the Åland case. Larger autonomous units are likely to create larger spillovers into the rest of the polity, and thus be more politically sensitive, as evidenced by the debate in the UK over whether MPs from the devolved regions should vote on laws that do not affect their constituents. Another crucial variable is the presence of minorities within the prospective autonomous regions, which was a major obstacle in the creation of the Bangsomoro in the Philippines; it was resolved by permitting small areas to opt in or out of the arrangement by referendum. That said, where the root of the cleavage is about local self-determination over cultural issues, autonomy may be a viable and indeed attractive option.

One of the general conjectures in the literature is that asymmetric grants of benefits will have knock-on effects, as other units will seek similar treatment. This has surely been the case in Spain, where the expression "coffee for one, coffee for all" captures the spread of devolved powers initially contemplated only for a small number of units.[34] A similar dynamic has been apparent with Scottish devolution, which has led to complex discussions about the other regions of the UK, and the role of dominant England in the Constitution. The secession of East Timor led to increased demands in Aceh and West Papua. But other case studies in this volume do not present much evidence of the knock-on effect. When the beneficiaries of special arrangements are relatively small in number, or when they are the result of distinctive histories as in Jammu and Kashmir in India, the center and other regions may simply not care very much.[35] In short, asymmetry might be a tool that can be wielded more frequently in confronting territorial cleavages.

A final conclusion from reviewing our case studies is that forms of asymmetry seem to be ubiquitous. Setting aside the cases in which the cleavage is essentially bilateral (Cyprus and Sri Lanka), asymmetry has played some role in most of the other systems. Even in South Africa, where constitutional negotiators were unwilling to generate special carve outs for the Zulu leader Chief Buthelezi, gestures toward self-determination helped to reduce territorial pressures from that part of the country. Likewise, the possibility of provincial Constitutions materialized asymmetrically, with KwaZulu-Natal putting forward a draft that was ultimately rejected by the Constitutional Court, and only the Western Cape actually producing a formal document that entered into force. As a normative matter, asymmetry seems to work best in situations in which the beneficiaries are relatively peripheral and small, or else if the grant of asymmetric deviation is minimal in the case of larger units.[36]

Rights, Redistribution, and Representation at the Center

Another set of institutional arrangements to deal with territorial cleavages concerns the center, and can be divided into three subcategories: rights, redistribution, and

[34] The one exception is the Basque country, which has long-standing special fiscal arrangements not available to any other autonomous community.

[35] Note though the current Indian government has raised the issue of Kashmir's special status, embodied in Art. 370 of the Constitution.

[36] Thanks to George Anderson for crystallizing this point.

representation.[37] These are not mutually exclusive, but rather, different tools that can be deployed in different combinations.

Rights refers to the idea that protecting the interests of greatest importance to people will reduce their desire to leave the political system. Protecting the ability of people to practice their religion, speak their language, and engage in communal life means that they will fear government less; even if this does not produce greater attachment to the center or to the country as a whole, it will reduce the felt need to take drastic action with regard to the structure of the state.

Rights, both group and individual, are often a major component of constitutional settlements.[38] Guarantees of communal rights were an important component of the Indian constitutional story, and the South African constitutional bargain put rights at the very center. Yet rights alone are unlikely to be able to resolve territorial cleavages without representation or devolution. As Zahar reports, one trigger for the Bosnia-Herzegovina war was the finding by the Badinter Commission that minorities had communal rights within the territory, but this was also a central element of the ultimate consociational settlement.

Redistribution from rich areas to poor is also a central feature of settlements, though not always guaranteed explicitly in a Constitution. Redistribution concerns the allocation of revenues throughout a territory. Sometimes territorial cleavages are exacerbated by virtue of the presence of valuable resources in one part of the country or another. Providing for mechanisms of fiscal equalization can help to ameliorate some tensions, particularly if the region in question is poorer than the rest of the country.[39] On the other hand, if a region is rich with natural resources, it might seek to minimize the flow of wealth to other regions. Bargaining over redistribution is a central political issue implicating territorial cleavages.

Another institutional mechanism is special representation at the center. Representation in central institutions binds the region to the rest of the polity, ideally giving it a stake in maximizing overall welfare. It thus is a useful tool for managing territorial cleavages. At the same time, representation can generate resentment to the extent that it dilutes the power of the rest of the country.

Representation takes various forms, but one important mode is giving the units a special role in constitutional amendment, either in general or just for specific provisions.[40] Such rules can prevent unilateral modification of the founding bargain. More than 6 percent of all Constitutions in force—accounting for nearly half of countries that are nominally federal or confederal—give at least one territorial unit some role in amendment —.[41] Providing a dual consent requirement for constitutional amendments with regard to territorial arrangements is a way of rendering the territorial arrangements self-enforcing. The Constitution of the USA, for example, does not allow changes

[37] See Daryl J Levinson, "Rights and Votes" (2012) 121 Yale Law Journal 1286.

[38] On group rights see Sujit Choudhry, "Group Rights" in Michel Rosenfeld and Andras Sajo (eds), *Oxford Handbook of Comparative Constitutional Law* (Oxford University Press 2012) 1100–23.

[39] See Pablo Beramendi, *The Political Geography of Inequality: Regions and Redistribution* (Cambridge University Press 2012).

[40] Jonathan Marshfield, "Decentralizing the Amendment Power" (2015) 19 (4) Lewis and Clark Law Review 871.

[41] As of 2014, the list of countries included Brazil, Canada, Colombia, Comoros, Ethiopia, Mexico, Nigeria, Russia, Switzerland, Uganda, and the USA. In Australia, a dual majority is required and several proposed constitutional amendments that won a majority in national referendums nevertheless failed because they were unable to secure the required ratification by a majority of voters in a majority of states. Australia Constitution, s. 218. See Marshfield (n 40) at 984, note 122.

to the equal representation of states in the Senate without their consent, while the Constitution of Malaysia provides Sabah and Sarawak with a veto power over amendments to the provisions governing their entry into the country. Among the case studies in this volume, Ethiopia involves the subnational units in approving all amendments, while South Africa, Nepal, and India include subnational units only for amendments that affect the interests of the sub-units. Conversely, Sri Lanka's Constitution has a special requirement of a referendum for any amendment that would change the unitary character of the state, and this proved to be a barrier to negotiated settlements.[42]

A common means of providing voice to states at the center is through representation in an upper chamber of the legislature. In the USA, each territorial state has equal representation in the Senate, meaning that small states have more political weight influence relative to their population than do large states. Members of the upper house may be directly elected at the level of the sub-unit, or selected by constituent unit executives or legislatures. The jurisdiction of the upper house might focus primarily on legislation that affects federal arrangements. Many of the cases discussed in this volume use such a mechanism. Ethiopia's upper house, elected by the state legislatures, has a role in resolving disputes over federal jurisdiction as well as the budget. Kenya and South Africa have upper houses, but with very limited powers restricted for the most part to issues related to provinces or counties. Spain's upper house was also designed to represent provinces and autonomous communities, but because most of its members are elected by popular vote it does not play a major role in this regard. The Indonesian case is a counter-example, in which, as Bertrand notes, the level of government represented in the upper house is not the same as that to which power has been devolved.

The efficacy of upper houses in managing territorial cleavages depends on the broader system in which they are embedded, and also on the manner of formation. In some systems, such as Germany, delegates are representatives of state governments, while in others such as Ethiopia (and the USA before the adoption of the Seventeenth Amendment), they are elected by state legislatures. Seats may be allocated in proportion to party weights in the state legislature. There are also complex systems that mix delegates and indirect election (e.g. South Africa), and other variations. In parliamentary systems, upper houses often lack power, particularly because the lower house is generally the source of government formation, but in presidential systems upper houses can have extensive powers that give smaller units extra weight in central lawmaking. In some cases, such as in Brazil, this extra weight can be excessive.

Regions can also get designated representation in executive, military, or judicial institutions. In Canada, for example, the culturally distinct province of Quebec is guaranteed three seats on the Supreme Court. Informal arrangements may also be effective in this regard, such as in Nigeria's principle of rotation of the presidency between north and south, or Ukraine's "Faustian bargain," described by Way, which was stable until 2015. Zahar's account of the governance structure of Bosnia-Herzegovina describes a system of mutual vetoes, with a collective presidency and representation in the legislature and courts being explicitly divided among the three major ethnic groups. This is the ultimate form of representation, in which the central machinery of government is carved up to ensure that power is shared.

[42] Sujit Choudhry, "Classical and Post-Conflict Federalism: Implications for Asia" in Rosalind Dixon and Tom Ginsburg (eds), *Comparative Constitutional Law in Asia* (Edward Elgar 2014).

Another important form of representation concerns state institutions. While classical thinking about representation focuses on electoral institutions, appointments in the state bureaucracy, military, judiciary, and regulatory institutions are perhaps more important in contemporary government.[43]

The specific design of territorial representation arrangements implicates the broader debate between consociationalists and integrationists. Consociationalist models emphasize tools such as mutual veto and peak-level bargaining, and are epitomized by the Bosnia-Herzegovina arrangements. Integrationist models focus on techniques to bring together different groups. Some such options may be useful in the context of territorial cleavages, while others are less so. The "republican model" of an integrated unitary state, with a president as a unifying national figure, seems particularly unsuited for enduring territorial cleavages.[44] But many other models may be quite feasible in such situations.

Integrationist approaches to electoral rules can play an important role in ensuring representation. For example, Nigeria's dual threshold requirement for electing the president (an overall majority and at least a minimum vote in each region) seeks to produce candidates that truly represent the nation. In addition, Nigeria bans political parties based on ethnicity, while requiring parties to have representation from multiple different regions to qualify in national elections, with a view to ensuring that each party reflects the country's federal character. National parties, of course, can still be vehicles for a strong regional voice, as was the case with Scotland when it voted heavily for the Labour Party.

Representation is not only about the affirmative ability to voice ones views. A seat at the table can facilitate distribution as well. For example, Way's chapter on Ukraine shows that the period of territorial stability was facilitated by a corrupt bargain between eastern and western interests. Nigeria's requirement that the cabinet reflect the "federal character" of the country not only allows regions a voice in policy, but also a share of the trough of the national budget: pork, not policy, is the goal. However, such representation throughout national institutions can put strain on the merit principle, and distort decision-making. One implication of this point is that resolving territorial cleavages might be associated with poorer quality governance.

Voice can also can be used to articulate protest, refusal, and blockage. The functional key to consociationalism in general and for self-enforcing federal arrangements in particular is that of veto. A veto is the right of a territorial unit to block proposals. While some territorial units may have a right to unilateral veto over general national policy, it is more common to limit vetoes to particular issues. The logic is that assigning territorial units power over issues most important to their constituents will increase their willingness to accede to policies that are less directly relevant. For example, if a group is allowed to speak its own language in its homeland, it will be more willing to accede to central government decisions, on say, the budget for road-building, for example.

There are many examples of territorial cleavages that were exacerbated by the lack of minority veto. The grim history of ethnic relations in Sri Lanka, recounted in this volume by Welikala, is one such example. While there were genuine efforts at accommodation early on, these broke down. Had Tamil citizenship not been restricted and had Tamils retained a veto over important issues such as language policy, history might

[43] Heather Gerken, "Exit, Voice, and Disloyalty" (2013) 62 Duke Law Journal 1349.

[44] John McGarry, Brendan O'Leary, and Richard Simeon, "Integration or Accommodation? The Enduring Debate in Conflict Regulation" in Sujit Choudhry (ed.), *Constitutional Design for Divided Societies: Integration or Accommodation?* (Oxford University Press 2008) 41–88.

have been different. Instead, there was a cycle of ethnic outbidding and the entrenchment of Buddhism in the 1972 and 1978 Constitutions. For several years after the defeat of the Liberation Tigers of Tamil Eelam (LTTE), there was no attempt to secure territorial accommodation, though at this writing there is some hope. Domination within a unitary state framework, rather than decentralization and federalism, has been the result.

Veto provisions, however, also risk creating "hold-up" problems wherein the entire national order is prevented from moving forward because of the concerns of one unit or a subset. Managing cleavages by veto, then, might have uncertain welfare effects for the country as a whole. The consociational solution to Bosnia-Herzegovina, for example, may have stopped the violence but it also rendered governance problematic for the foreseeable future.

In some instances, if a territorial unit cannot block a national policy at the center, it might still be able to undermine it at the local level during implementation, to the extent that it has a role in that stage. Such rejection of central policy is known as "nullification," and may be an underappreciated virtue of federalism in general.[45] Nullification allows subnational units to ignore policies of the center with which they disagree. This tactic was commonplace in the antebellum period in the American South, and later contributed violently to the demise of reconstruction there.[46] More recently, states have resisted federal policies on marijuana and immigration policy.

In short, representation at the center, including the ability to veto, are important policy levers to be considered in trying to manage territorial cleavages, particularly for areas with large populations. (It may be less important for discrete small units that can be dealt with through asymmetric arrangements.) Conversely, the lack of representation and rights at the center was one of the factors that contributed to the failure of Nigeria's first republic. Interestingly, the military in Nigeria drew from all ethnicities and regions, providing a channel for national integration.[47]

There is no guarantee that these mechanisms will be effective, as they can be undermined by political factors. A national political party, for example, can undermine the effectiveness of subnational inclusion at the level of the center. Studies in Brazil and Australia have shown that upper house legislators tend to vote based on national party rather than regional interests in constitutional amendment proposals.[48] The South Africa story, recounted by Steytler in this volume, is one in which territorial differences have largely been attenuated over time, through special accommodations at the outset and the presence of a dominant political party that integrated various interests. Ethiopia, too, has accommodated tremendous diversity in a federal scheme through a dominant (and not particularly democratic) party regime. In such environments, though, there may be a corollary benefit that sub-unit leaders can end up rising through party ranks to become national leaders—the "minor league" rationale for federalism.

[45] Kyle Scott, *Federalism: A Normative Theory and its Political Relevance* (Continuum 2011) 94–115.

[46] South Carolina sought to nullify a tariff put on foreign goods before the civil war, which they thought would end up hurting southern exports to Europe. Through making demands, South Carolina was able to secure a compromise in the form of a reduced tariff in 1833. Later, Vermont confronted the Fugitive Slave Law, which made it mandatory for citizens of any state to return runaway slaves to the south. Vermont passed a Habeas Corpus law making it essentially impossible to enforce the law in the state, ibid. On reformation, see C Vann Woodward, *Origins of the New South 1877–1913* (LSU Press 1951) 1–22.

[47] Samuel Huntington, *Political Order in Divided Societies* (Yale University Press 1968).

[48] Marshfield (n 40), text at notes 254–5.

Exit at the Center: Secession Clauses

A few Constitutions include a right to secession for certain sub-units, or all of them. The wisdom of this approach has been the subject of a central debate within political theory.[49] Some scholars, such as Cass Sunstein, believe that a right to constitutional secession will encourage sub-units to exercise it.[50] Others believe that such clauses will form a kind of pre-commitment on the part of a majority to deal fairly with the sub-unit population, and will thus encourage deliberation.[51] Both sides recognize that secession clauses will give relevant groups substantial bargaining power in everyday politics: if the larger units' actions are unfavorable, they can simply threaten to exercise the right to secession.

Constitutions deal with secession in several ways, and countries are confronting the issue in some way with greater frequency.[52] Many Constitutions explicitly prohibit secession, either directly or by referring to the territorial integrity of the state. Countries that include prohibitory clauses in the Constitution have, with one exception, never experienced a secession. That exception was the 2014 "secession" of the Crimea from Ukraine, with the active support of Russia. While the Ukrainian Constitution had declared Crimea "an inseparable part of Ukraine . . ." constitutional texts can do little about external dismemberment.[53]

A few Constitutions explicitly allow for secession. A feature of Leninist ideology, secession clauses are most common in countries with a history of communism or socialist movements. Interestingly, two of the major countries with secession clauses, the Soviet Union and Yugoslavia, actually did break up during their transitions to democracy. While not a triggering factor for Bosnia-Herzegovina directly, the secession clause of the Yugoslav Federal Constitution forms a part of the context for that chapter (and also played an important role in movements for the independence of Kosovo). The Ethiopia case study shows that secession clauses can be purely symbolic. At the conclusion of Ethiopia's civil war in 1991, the Tigrayan People's Liberation Front, itself a Leninist party that dominated the governing Ethiopian People's Revolutionary Democratic Front, believed that the Oromo, the largest ethnic group in Ethiopia, would not join the transitional government without a right to secede.[54] In addition, the smaller ethnic groups that were part of the coalition valued the idea of internal autonomy. The Constitution includes the right of "any Nation, Nationality or People to form its own state."[55] This was actually observed to some extent in facilitating the creation of new local or district governments. Yet the other integrative forces in Ethiopia's

[49] David Haljan, *Constitutionalizing Secession* (Hart Studies in Comparative Public Law Book 4, Hart 2014); Daniel Weinstock, "Constitutionalising the Right to Secede" (2001) 9 (2) Journal of Political Philosophy 182; Scott (n 45) 134–69.

[50] Cass Sunstein, "Constitutionalism and Secession" (1991) 58 (2) University of Chicago Law Review 633.

[51] Scott (n 45).

[52] For an empirical summary see Tom Ginsburg and Mila Versteeg, *From Catalonia to California: Secession in the World's Constitutions* (Forthcoming, Alabama Law Review, 2019). Ginsburg and Versteeg show that some right to secession was found in only 1 percent of Constitutions before 1900, but is found in roughly 8 percent written after 1989. 29 percent of Constitutions in the latter period explicitly prohibit secession, as compared with 15 percent before 1900.

[53] Constitution of Ukraine (1996, as amended in 2004), art. 134.

[54] Alem Habtu, "Multiethnic Federalism in Ethiopia: A Study of the Secession Clause in the Constitution" (2005) 35 (2) Publius 313, 324; Alemante G Selassie, "Ethnic Federalism: Its Promise and Pitfalls for Africa" (2003) 28 Yale Journal of International Law 51, 64.

[55] Constitution of Ethiopia (1994), art. 47(3).

authoritarian system have been sufficient to prevent this from leading to the disintegration of the country.

Although the UK has no explicit secession clause, Parliament allowed Scotland to cast a referendum on the topic. This turned out to be primarily an episode to enhance Scottish autonomy within the UK, though in the wake of Brexit one senses that the last chapter has not been written. In contrast, Iraq and Cyprus resisted formal consideration of secession in Kurdistan or Northern Cyprus, even though facts on the ground might be characterized as exhibiting very high degrees of independence in those regions.

A third design option is simply to remain silent. Vicky Jackson argues that Constitutions ought to remain silent on secession, drawing on the moral hazard argument about risks.[56] But historically, secessionist movements do sometimes develop even when there is silence on the matter. In the USA, the lack of a clear clause about secession generated constitutional confusion and political crises for the decades in the early nineteenth century, and eventually led to the Civil War. Secession in one region might also trigger a domino effect of similar movements in other regions, leading to more general centrifugal pressures on the state.[57] Many of these theoretical debates hinge on empirical assumptions, for which the evidence is mainly anecdotal.

Even if one decides to include a secession clause, there are subsidiary design decisions that must be made. First, is there a predicate for secession? Ideally it ought to be a last resort, not a routine threat. Second, who must approve the secession decision? Is it only the sub-unit seeking to secede or must the entire country vote on a change to the territorial integrity of the state? Ukraine's Constitution noted that alterations to the territory of the state were to be resolved exclusively by an all-Ukrainian referendum,[58] thus rendering unconstitutional the 2014 referendum held in Crimea alone, according to many. Third, who resolves disputes about secession? Constitutional courts in Spain and Canada have found themselves confronted with questions of secession, and come to very different conclusions, in part because of their different constitutional structures.[59]

Guarantors and Dispute Resolution

All agreements must incorporate mechanisms for monitoring and enforcement. In the case of territorial cleavages, these roles may fall to a constitutional court. Indeed, disputes over territorial authority have played a major role in the jurisprudence of the German Constitutional Court, the US Supreme Court, and others. South Africa's Constitutional Court had to certify the Constitutions of provinces for conformity with the Constitution, and rejected the proposed Constitution of KwaZulu Natal.[60]

[56] Vicki Jackson, "Secession, Transnational Precedents, and Constitutional Silences" in Sanford Levinson (ed.), *Nullification and Secession in Modern Constitutional Thought* (University of Kansas Press 2016).

[57] Barbara F Walter, "Building Reputation: Why Governments Fight Some Separatists but not Others" (2006) 50 (2) American Journal of Political Science 313.

[58] Constitution of Ukraine (1996, as amended to 2004) art. 73.

[59] Tribunal Constitucional, "Nota Informativa No. 26/2014, El TC por Unanimidad Estima Parcialmente el Recurso del Gobierno contra la Declaración Soberanista de Cataluna" (Government of Spain March 25, 2014) <www.tribunalconstitucional.es/NotasDePrensaDocumentos/NP_2014_026/NOTAINFORMATIVANUMERO262014.pdf>; *Reference Re Secession of Quebec* [1998] 2 SCR 217.

[60] Constitution of South Africa (1997), art. 144.

Courts are also players in the process of resolving territorial cleavages, and sometimes serve as voices for national integration, even blocking agreements when necessary. In this sense, external monitors can exacerbate rather than resolve cleavages. In the Philippines, as Lau points out, the Supreme Court ruled unconstitutional an initial agreement to establish an independent juridical authority in the putative Bangsamoro region. In Sri Lanka in 2004, after the government and the LTTE came to an agreement recognizing the latter as a self-governing entity for post-tsunami reconstruction. Opponents of the deal brought a case to the Supreme Court, which ruled the arrangements unconstitutional on the grounds that they undermined parliament's role in spending public funds. This decision led many to think that no deal with the LTTE would ever pass constitutional muster.[61]

On the other hand, the presence of an electoral court and constitutional court became crucial in a situation of deep political division in Bolivia, as both institutions helped to channel political attention to Congress on the question of how to institute departmental autonomy and constitutional reform. The Constitutional Court of Bosnia-Herzegovina, as described by Zahar in her chapter, sought to ensure that the entities in the country did not themselves discriminate against their own minorities, and led to a replication of quota-based governance within each entity. In these cases, neutral institutions were able to refine and advance the values of the territorial settlement. Endowments of prior institutions, such as the presence of a relatively autonomous judiciary in South Africa, may help to make bargains possible that would not otherwise be.[62]

Outside courts and independent institutions, political mechanisms seem to prevail. In Kenya, Ghai and Cottrell note complex procedures for inter-unit dispute resolution that have not been much used. And in Iraq, as Al-Ali notes, the Transitional Administrative Law provided for the collective presidency to appoint arbitrators for inter-regional disputes, with the backstop of the UN Secretary General if the presidency cannot agree.

The Role of International Institutions

International arrangements can play an important role in helping to resolve institutional problems of territorial cleavages. In particular, international actors can play a role in crafting solutions, incentivizing cooperative agreements, monitoring performance of agreements, and even helping to enforce them. Of course, they can also muddy the waters by forcing deals before the parties are fully ready to agree to them, as occurred in Iraq. But all these roles heavily implicate questions of institutional design.

International law forms important background conditions that may incentivize or disincentivize territorial mobilization. The general norm of self-determination plays a role, as do international documents like the UN Declaration of Minority Rights of 1992, or the 1989 International Labor Organization Convention No. 169 on the Rights of Indigenous Peoples. The relatively new legal regime of bilateral investment

[61] Choudhry, "Classical and Post-Conflict Federalism" (n 42).

[62] Jens Meierhenrich, *The Legacies of Law: Long-Run Consequences of Legal Development in South Africa, 1652–2000* (Cambridge University Press 2008).

treaties may also have implications for secession, as it may raise the costs by requiring compensation for unlawful taking of property.[63]

Territorial claims exist in an international legal order that can facilitate or retard threats to leave. This legal order has a bias toward the nation-state as the modal political form. It is expressed in international institutions that play a major role in managing secession, and thus shape the bargaining environment for territorial cleavages. Secessionist claims are unsuccessful if the new entity is unable to secure international recognition, and this is usually selectively granted.

Besides the legal order, the international political and economic environment conditions the viability of independent states.[64] Two crucial factors that shape the costs and benefits of independence are the need for national defense, and the benefits of being in a larger market. That is, in a region or era in which there is a risk of being conquered by a foreign power, remaining within an existing state is more desirable. In contrast, when there are few barriers to trade between states, there may be less benefit of remaining in an existing national market. These stylized facts help explain why the number of independent states in the world has tripled since the end of World War II. In an era of relatively little interstate war and relatively free trade, the costs of independence may be lower. This may also explain why there has been an increase in secessionist movements within Europe in the last generation. Catalonia and northern Italy would suffer little in terms of market access or self-defense were they to leave their respective nation-states, so long as they could remain within the EU. But the referendum in which Britain decided to leave the EU made the question of Scottish secession more complicated.

External states or international organizations can play a helpful role in managing territorial cleavages. The minorities treaties adopted in the interwar period in Eastern Europe provide a model, in which new nation-states received recognition in exchange for promising to treat national minorities well. The external parties to the treaties, the victors in World War I, monitored and guaranteed this good treatment, although the arrangements did not last long enough to be considered successful.[65] As noted by Anderson and Choudhry in the final chapter of this book, the involvement of foreign powers is an important dimension along which the case studies presented here differ from one another. Cyprus and Bosnia-Herzegovina are two examples in which outside involvement was quite significant, both in exacerbating the cleavage and in helping to move toward a resolution. In the initial formation of the Cyprus Constitution after independence, the UK, Turkey, and Greece were all given guarantor rights. While the immediate neighbors exacerbated the conflict, the broader international community was a source of ideas and pressure for resolution, notably in the failed Annan plan of 2004. At the time of writing, there is continued effort and engagement in trying to find a formula for reunification of a divided country. Welikala's chapter on Sri Lanka highlights the role of Norway, and before that India, as attempting to broker a solution. The failure of these efforts was followed by an intensification of conflict and the ultimate defeat of the Tamil Tigers, and to date no institutional solution of the underlying grievances that gave rise to that conflict in the first place. In other cases, particularly the Aceh agreement discussed above, external mediation was critical.

[63] Thomas Grant, "International Dispute Settlement in Respond to Unlawful Seizure of Territory: Three Mechanisms" (2015) 16 (1) Chicago Journal of International Law 1.

[64] Alberto Alesina, *The Size of Nations* (Harvard University Press 2003).

[65] See Susan Pedersen, *The Guardians: The League of Nations and the Crisis of Empire* (Oxford University Press 2015).

In Bosnia, the Dayton Accords effectively harnessed intense international pressure to resolve a war, and effectively did so. They also put in place an elaborate monitoring regime, including the presence of internationals on the constitutional court (an approach later adopted in Kosovo). However, peace came at the cost of entrenching a rigid consociational arrangement that has frozen the ethno-territorial cleavages in place. While such arrangements are subject to being re-opened by outside forces, there are few incentives to do so long as the armed conflict remains resolved. In the case of Bosnia, the European Court of Human Rights put pressure on the Bosnian arrangement with its 2009 decision in the case of *Sejdić and Finci v. Bosnia*, which found in favor of two applicants who challenged the provision of the Bosnian Constitution restricting certain political offices to three "constituent peoples."[66] The Court was roundly criticized by advocates of consociationalism.[67] An alternative view though, is that such a court decision might be thought of as a useful example of an external body putting pressure on a consociational arrangement to become more integrationist over time. Only such dynamic shifts over time can ultimately "resolve" a cleavage, be it territorial or otherwise.

Finally, it is worth noting the Ukraine case discussed by Way, in which a dominant outside power, Russia, essentially severed an autonomous region by unilateral intervention. Along with the Cyprus case, in which the Turkish invasion was triggered by a Greek-sponsored coup d'état, this suggests that the close neighbors who are best situated to act as guarantors of a territorial accommodation may in fact have the least incentive to play that role. More systematic monitoring and enforcement mechanisms from the international community would be desirable, but have to be incentive-compatible.

Conclusion

The institutional options for managing territorial cleavages are myriad. We have considered the role of territorial assignments of power; rights, redistribution, and representation at the center, as well as veto and secession; and the role of courts and international actors in establishing and guaranteeing bargains. In any particular situation, the precise allocation of institutional options will, of course, be the subject of intense bargaining and may be highly contextual.

Three themes emerge from this review. First, a combination of representation and decentralization may be sufficient to stabilize territorial cleavages. The rights component is actually rather underdeveloped in many of these cases, and even in theory is insufficient on its own to guarantee success. Only a small set of cases—Spain, the UK, Philippines, South Africa, and India—are fully consolidated democracies. So in some sense we can say that voice is prior to rights, at least when it comes to territorial cleavages.

Second, asymmetry is a useful tool. Special autonomy has been useful in many of the cases, especially when the territory in question is small relative to the whole. Knock-on effects in other units have not led to unraveling of the overall territorial bargain in

[66] *Sejdić & Finci v. Bosnia and Herzegovina*. App. Nos 27996/06 and 34836/06 <www.echr.coe.int>; see Marko Milanovic, "Case Note: Sejdić & Finci v. Bosnia and Herzegovina" (2010) 104 American Journal of International Law 636.

[67] Christopher McCrudden and Brendan O'Leary, *Courts and Consociations: Human Rights versus Power-Sharing* (Oxford University Press 2013).

any of the cases, though the UK is under serious pressure at the moment. Yet, as the Crimean example shows, special autonomy will not be enough in the face of a large outside power intent on exploiting territorial cleavages.

Despite its prominence in the theoretical literature, rights to secession do not seem to be a frequent solution to problems of territorial division. While they facilitated the breakup of the large plurinational federations of Yugoslavia and the Soviet Union, rights to exit create too many incentives for secessionist behavior to recommend themselves as a design tool. Voice, it seems, trumps exit.

Finally, the traditional rationales for federalism fit uneasily with the resolution of territorial cleavages. While resolution of a cleavage may reflect concerns about public goods, jurisdictional competition, training of officials, or tyranny, the primary driving force is often distribution of political and material goods, and fights over voice and identity. This means that while resolution of a territorial cleavage may involve resolving a Hobbesian dilemma, and may serve to end conflict, it need not present an optimum set of policies and institutions for the country as a whole. Poor governance may sometimes be the price for peace.

20

Territorial Cleavages and Constitutional Transitions*

Political Mobilization, Constitution-Making Processes, and Constitutional Design

*George Anderson*** and *Sujit Choudhry****

Introduction

The constitutional politics of territorial cleavages—that is, territorially concentrated, politically salient, collective demands for constitutional accommodation—are a pervasive feature of modern political life. These claims arise in very diverse contexts. Claims for territorial constitutional accommodation are being made in the advanced industrial democracies of the global north, such as Spain and the United Kingdom, as well as in some of the poorest countries of the global south, like Yemen. Territorial claims are a central issue in the negotiations over the reunification of Cyprus. In Bosnia-Herzegovina, territorial power-sharing may have ended a civil war but resulted in a dysfunctional democracy. In Nepal, the federal restructuring of the country was a central element of a civil war settlement and is still a fragile work in progress. Territorial claims have also arisen in peripheral regions with insurgencies seeking special autonomy, such as the Bangsmoro in the Philippines and Aceh in Indonesia. Claims for constitutional accommodation of territorial cleavages often arise as part of a broader process of democratization, as is currently occurring in Myanmar.

What precisely is a territorial cleavage? Political cleavages are the principal axes of political mobilization, around which political claims are framed, political parties formed, elections contested, and governments composed. They can also be the basis on which constitutional claims are made and resisted. In countries where political cleavages are territorial, of territory is a central divide around which political argument occurs. Territorial cleavages can also overlap with and incorporate cleavages on the basis of ideology, class, religion, ethnicity, and race. Moreover, diversity among territories within a state does not necessarily become a territorial cleavage; it is only when

* **Acknowledgments**
We thank Sumit Bisarya, Mattias Kumm, and the audience at a session of the Berlin Colloquium on Global and Comparative Law for helpful comments. All remaining errors are ours. A policy manual drawing on this chapter—George Anderson and Sujit Choudhry, *Territory and Power in Constitutional Transitions*—will be jointly published by the Center for Constitutional Transitions, the Forum of Federations and International IDEA in 2018.
** Center for Constitutional Transitions; Center for Democracy and Diversity, Queen's University.
*** Center for Global Constitutionalism, WZB Berlin Social Science Center.

Territory and Power in Constitutional Transitions. First Edition. Edited by Michael Anderson and Sujit Choudhry. Territorial Cleavages and Constitutional Transitions: Political Mobilization, Constitution-Making Processes, and Constitutional Design Published 2019 by Oxford University Press.

territorial differences are activated by political action that are they transformed into grounds for political division.

Constitutional transitions dealing with significant territorial cleavages face political dynamics and challenges that are quite distinct from such transitions where such cleavages are absent. They can involve different Constitution-making processes, sometimes with representatives of territorial groups having a formal or informal role, and certainly different political dynamics, whatever the defined role of territorial groups in the process. Such transitions also involve very different constitutional design options from those in countries in which territorial cleavages have little political salience; some form of federal, quasi-federal, or asymmetric devolution is usually at issue, and sometimes special power-sharing or minority rights protection arrangements are as well. Debates and choices around the procedural and institutional options relating to territorial cleavages can in turn affect the dynamics of conflict—whether peaceful or violent—within a society.

There is a global discourse surrounding the constitutional politics of territorial cleavages, in both the policy and scholarly domains.[1] Thinking across cases, about lessons learned and dangers to be avoided, continues to grow. Claims for the constitutional accommodation of territorial cleavages have generated substantial literatures on political mobilization, Constitution-making, and constitutional design, but there is little work that addresses the intersection of these three strands of research. This project seeks to integrate these three strands of research by posing this overarching question: **how do patterns of territorial political mobilization shape the processes of Constitution-making and the choices of constitutional design?** The anticipated payoff is both analytical and normative. Scholars can deepen their understanding of mobilization, process, and design by studying how these three factors interact. Seasoned practitioners know that political mobilization, process, and design are at play simultaneously, and that coming to grips with how they interact enables order to provide more informed constitutional advice.

This volume answers this question by bringing together analysis of political mobilization, Constitution-making processes, and constitutional design in societies that have very different structures of territorial cleavages and that have opted for very different constitutional designs—including both countries that have opted to accommodate territorial cleavages in their constitutional design and those that have not, even after a long constitutional debate. The seventeen cases chosen are all relatively recent examples of constitutional transitions and they were highly varied in what might be called the political geometry or configurations of territorial and other cleavages around which politics was mobilized. In addition to differing in the structure of their politically salient territorial cleavages, the cases differ in the characteristics of their other political cleavages (ethnic, linguistic, religious, economic), in their past histories of intergroup relations, including experiences of conflict, violence, and democracy, in the relative power of the key political actors, as well as in the levels of economic development, and the geopolitical situations and influences. They provide material for rich comparative analysis.

Within each case, we examine periods in which there has been intense political engagement over how to respond to significant demands for territorial accommodation from one or several regions. We call these periods of heightened political engagement around potential constitutional change "constitutional moments." Some constitutional moments are relatively brief, while others are spread out over years; some bring

[1] George Anderson and Sujit Choudhry, *Constitutional Transitions and Territorial Cleavages* (The Center for Constitutional Transitions and International IDEA 2015).

significant, enduring change, while others change little or nothing in formal constitutional arrangements; some settle constitutional disputes, whereas others do not, leading to further rounds of engagement over future changes. Whitehead has noted that democratization is a "complex, dynamic, long-term and open-ended process" that requires coordinated collective action over generations.[2] Constitutional moments are likewise slices of time in a much longer, and ongoing, story with twists, turns, and even reversals.

Our core argument is as follows. In constitutional moments in which political mobilization around demands for the constitutional accommodation of territorial interests is important, **three** crucial contextual variables shape the structure and dynamics of the constitutional moment:

1. the *political geometry* of territorial (and other) cleavages, which are products of demography and narratives;
2. the *antecedent circumstances* of *peaceful, legal and institutionalized means* or *violent and extra-legal* means used to advance or reject demands for territorial accommodation; and
3. the *relative power of the key actors*, as shaped by *tests of strength* both peaceful and violent.

The configuration of these variables in the lead-up to a constitutional moment shapes its dynamics as well as the agenda for Constitution-making processes and the options for constitutional design. While each constitutional moment is unique, there are patterns in their configuration across cases which show similarities, and which share a presumptive structure. Of course, the configuration of the three variables can alter over time through the dynamics of the constitutional moment—especially through political tests of strength among the leading actors. But thinking in terms of these contextual patterns can help scholars and policy-makers in particular cases to understand the relevant issues, the prospects and possibilities, and the trade-offs among them. While our argument emphasizes the structural constraints within which political actors make their choices, those actors do retain agency so there is no simple determinacy.

Our emphasis is largely on constitutional moments where the relative power of the key actors is divided, and no party is dominant so that the outcome of the constitutional process cannot be dictated by one side. In these constitutional moments, the principal agenda items are to frame a process that engages the key power holders as well as the possible options to deal with claims for territorial accommodation. The constitutional design option being considered, especially by those seeking territorial accommodation, will closely track political geometry, but the actual choice will be influenced by power relations as well. A critical issue will be whether the ensuing constitutional design, with whatever degree of territorial accommodation, can be interpreted, implemented, and adapted in a sustainable way over time. Our cases include both transitions to democracy—of which they are a subset—and transitions within democracies; they also include cases of significant constitutional change and of little or no change. In all cases, the assumption is that democracy is the end goal of constitutional reform.

Violent struggles can lead to a military stalemate, either in a civil war or with a regional insurgency, in which case the key actors must design a process that combines peace negotiations and Constitution-making, which can pull in opposite directions.

[2] Laurence Whitehead, *Democratization: Theory and Experience* (Oxford University Press 2003) 201; North, Wallis, and Weingast also emphasize that there is no one path but bringing the ruler under the law is fundamental in Douglass C North, John Joseph Wallis, and Barry R Weingast, *Violence and Social Orders: A Conceptual Framework for Interpreting Recorded Human History* (Cambridge University Press 2009).

There may have been a collapse of the legal order requiring the invention of a new process and constitutional design, or the government may insist on the existing legal and constitutional order being maintained while seeking to reconcile the combatants to accepting it on revised terms—most notably with respect to peripheral rebellions. Violent struggles can also end in victory by one side or the other, in which case the victor is largely able to determine what process will be adopted regarding constitutional change. By contrast, where the conflict over territorial claims has developed within a peaceful context of competitive politics, political actors address the issues of process and design within a context of constitutional and institutional continuity, which can bring significant constraints especially regarding process. However, on occasions, existing processes for constitutional deliberation and change may lack political legitimacy among one or more actors—perhaps precisely because they do not adequately accommodate the claims of territorial or other actors for change—so there may be a need to negotiate modified or supplementary processes, while preserving legal continuity.

The approach we adopt is one of structured analytical comparisons of different historical cases. It is retrospective or historical, which is consistent with the approach taken by recent work on democratization.[3] The previous work that most compares with this volume is Amoretti and Bermeo's *Federalism and Territorial Cleavages*,[4] which, despite its title, also looked at special autonomy and unitary regimes, but its case studies were not structured around a common template as ours are. Our chosen three main variables (political mobilization, Constitution-making processes, constitutional design) are interdependent and influence each other, in a process where they are all both dependent and independent variables over time. The law itself can be part of the Constitution-making process variable in cases of continuity because it then influences both processes and design. This causal nexus can make it difficult to disentangle the relative importance of factors.

Any consideration of causation in politics necessarily raises the issue of agency. As important as underlying social conditions and major institutional arrangements, may be as determinants, political actors do face choices, even in the most constrained circumstances. Actors in similar situations will make different assessments of their interests, of the possibilities and of the constraints; they may be deemed to be rational or irrational, bold or cautious, visionary or parochial—and their choices will matter. While the choices of political leaders receive particular attention, there is also agency in the polling booth, in the public square and on fields of battle as well. Moreover, O'Donnell and Schmitter have emphasized the enormous uncertainty during transitions from authoritarian rule (which can also apply to other transitional contexts) where there are "insufficient structural or behavioural parameters to guide and predict outcomes" and they argue that the conceptual tools for normal politics are inadequate for periods with a high degree of indeterminacy.[5] We are limited in our ability to generate general theories about constitutional transitions and territorial cleavages; it should steer us more in the direction of probabilities or tendencies rather than deterministic models. We have taken inspiration from Charles Tilly's work. In considering the historiography of state-making in the West, Tilly argued for comparative work that is historical in nature, consistent in its use of terms and units of analysis, clear regarding

[3] Giovanni Capoccia and Daniel Ziblatt, "The Historical Turn in Democratization Studies: A New Research Agenda for Europe and Beyond" (2010) 43 (8–9) Comparative Political Studies 931.

[4] Ugo M Amoretti and Nancy Bermeo, *Federalism and Territorial Cleavages* (Johns Hopkins Press 2004).

[5] Guillermo O'Donnell and Philippe C Schmitter, *Transitions from Authoritarian Rule: Tentative Conclusions about Uncertain Democracies* (Johns Hopkins University Press 1986) 3–5.

what is to be explained (with general development being too broad), and open-ended and prospective in avoiding rigid assertions of determinants and suggesting rather the probability of different paths.[6] We have strived to follow Tilly's counsel.

A final point on method. Large-n statistical studies of political conflict, Constitution-making process, and constitutional design have been increasing in number in recent years. They can be very enlightening regarding how different variables may affect the probabilities of different political phenomena. But they are necessarily limited in what they can achieve given the very large number of variables at play and the restricted number of cases, even if there are scores of them.[7] Moreover, decisions as to how to code data are fundamental to the questions being examined, and even some of the most suggestive studies around ethnic conflict and politics have not factored the territorial dimension into their analysis.[8] Progress in the study of large-scale political phenomena will necessarily be iterative between methodological techniques, where insights and findings arising from one method are tested and refined using alternative techniques.

This chapter is structured as follows. In "Political Mobilization and the Context for Constitutional Moments," we examine some of the three central factors that influence political mobilization, setting up the conditions precedent for constitutional moments. We then proceed to an initial consideration of how these different factors shape the dynamics of constitutional moments, in terms of both the process and design options chosen or considered ("Context and Dynamics of Constitutional Moments"). We then review Constitution-making processes, their importance, the participants, and the stages, all as they relate to the politics of territorial cleavages ("Constitution-Making Processes"). The last major section looks at constitutional design options as they relate to different configurations of our variables, notably political geometry ("Constitutional Design and Territorial Cleavages"). We conclude with some reflections on the forces shaping the dynamics of constitutional moments and what this might mean for principals or advisors and future research ("Conclusion"). Throughout, we draw on our case studies for examples.

Political Mobilization and the Context for Constitutional Moments

Many factors influence the intensity, duration, means, extent, and goals of territorial political mobilization.[9] We group these contextual factors into three categories: (a)

[6] Charles Tilly, "Western State-Making and Theories of Political Transformation" in Charles Tilly (ed), *The Formation of National States in Western Europe* (Princeton University Press 1975).

[7] Martin Ottman and Johannes Vullers, "The Power-Sharing Event Dataset (PSED): A new dataset on the promises and practices of power-sharing in post-conflict countries" (2015) 32 (3) Conflict Management and Peace Science 327; and Pippa Norris, *Driving Democracy: Do Power-Sharing Institutions Work?* (Cambridge University Press 2008) are examples of the suggestiveness of large-n studies. On the limits of such studies, see Stefan Wolff, "Building Democratic States after Conflict: Institutional Design Revisited" (2010) 12 International Studies Review 128.

[8] For example, see Andreas Wimmer, Lars-Erik Cederman, and Brian Min, "Ethnic Politics and Armed Conflict: A Configurational Analysis of a New Global Data Set" (2009) 74 (2) American Sociological Review 316. This study does not distinguish between regionally concentrated and regionally dispersed ethnic populations; this distinction is key to our analysis. See also Andreas Wimmer and Brian Min, "From Empire to Nation-State: Explaining Wars in the Modern World, 1816–2001" (2006) 71 (6) American Sociological Review 867.

[9] From a vast literature, see Benedict Anderson, *Imagined Communities: Reflections on the Origin and Spread of Nationalism* (Verso 1998); Rogers Brubaker, *Ethnicity without Groups* (Harvard University Press 2006); Ernst Gellner, *Nations and Nationalism* (Cornell University Press 1993); Ted Gurr, *Peoples vs. States: Minorities at Risk in the New Century* (United States Institute for Peace 2002);

the *political geometry* of territorial and other salient political cleavages in the country; (b) the antecedent choices of *peaceful, legal, and institutionalized* or *violent, extra-legal means* to advance regional demands for territorial accommodation; and (c) the *relative power of the key actors*, as shaped by *tests of strength* both peaceful and violent. As we illustrate in "Constitution-Making Processes," while each constitutional moment is unique, the configuration of these three factors across cases show patterns and share a presumptive logic around the agendas for Constitution-making processes and constitutional design.

Political geometry: demography and political entrepreneurs

The relative size, number, and character of political cleavages, including their geographic distribution, is what we term a country's political geometry. Understanding variations in political geometry is crucial in coming to grips with important variations in constitutional design and Constitution-making processes. For territorial cleavages, political geometry is a product of the interaction of *demography* and the *narratives* deployed by regional political entrepreneurs.

The interaction of demography and political entrepreneurship shape a country's political geometry through political mobilization.

The cases chosen were all relatively recent examples of constitutional transitions and they were highly varied in the political geometry or configurations of territorial and other cleavages around which politics was mobilized. For the cases under study, we identify *four different patterns of political geometry*:

- First, states characterized by *multiple politically salient territorial cleavages.* Other salient cleavages may be present but the force of claims around territorial accommodation makes the territorial issue central to engagement on the issue of constitutional change, which typically involves the general architecture of the regime, e.g. federal or devolved. Ethiopia, India (with respect to its linguistic groups), Nigeria, and Spain are examples.
- Second, states characterized by *a majority group and one or two territorially based, minority groups of significant size.* The minority group(s) typically raise(s) demands for territorial autonomy, and if large enough it may advocate a constitutional structure of central institutions to reflect a pact or partnership with special power-sharing provisions among these groups. Examples include Cyprus, with a Greek-Cypriot majority and a Turkish-Cypriot minority (18 percent of the country's population); and, Bosnia-Herzegovina, with a Bosniak majority (51 percent) and Serbian (31 percent) and Croatian (15 percent) minorities. Yemen, with its (divided) northern majority and southern minority (20 percent) has some of these characteristics.
- Third, states with *peripheral, politically mobilized regions.* Such regional groups make claims for territorial autonomy, but without demands for power-sharing in the central institutions, given their small size. Examples include the north-east tribes in India (whose many small ethnic groups total less than 1 percent); the Acehnese (2 percent) in Indonesia; the Moro (5 percent) in the Philippines;

Will Kymlicka, *Multicultural Odysseys: Navigating the New International Politics of Diversity* (Oxford University Press 2009); Andreas Wimmer, *Ethnic Boundary Making: Institutions, Power, Networks* (Oxford University Press 2013).

Scotland (8 percent) in the UK; the northern Tamils (5 percent) in Sri Lanka; and the Russophones in Ukraine's Donbas (15 percent).

- Fourth, states characterized by *politically salient cleavages that are both territorial and non-territorial.* In these cases, the issue of territorial accommodation is part of a larger constitutional agenda in which the strength of demands for devolution may be offset by other claims. Examples include Nepal, where ethnicity, indigenous, and even caste identities can be territorially concentrated but are often dispersed; South Africa, where the non-territorial identity of race exists alongside linguistic or tribal differences among blacks which are territorially based; Kenya, where there has been extensive intermingling of ethnic communities that historically were more territorially based; Bolivia, where major differences between the lowlands and highlands are mitigated by divisions within each and by other non-territorial dimensions; and Iraq, where the Kurds (15 percent) are distinct from the Arabs, but where both groups have significant internal divisions.

These four patterns of political geometry are ideal types, and not every country fits neatly into one pattern. For example, Yemen falls into both the second and fourth categories, because it has a major cleavage between the majority in the north and a territorial minority in the south (17 percent), but both north and south are internally fractured by tribes and religion. Moreover, there is no hard-and-fast threshold between categories two and three. Moreover, claims for territorial accommodation don't always fit the expected pattern. For example, while the Tamil-majority region of Sri Lanka might count as a peripheral region, but aside from a demand for secession, it has focused on a restructuring of the state into a decentralized federalism rather than on special autonomy, perhaps because the latter option seemed foreclosed.

Each of these patterns reflects elements of an underlying demography that have been mobilized by political entrepreneurs. But cutting across them all are important variations in the intensity, internal coherence, and durability of group identities, which affect the nature of territorial political mobilization, and subsequently, the agenda for Constitution-making and constitutional design. Consider the contrast between Aceh and Papua in Indonesia. Aceh is relatively internally cohesive, built around a single ethnic identity and a common language—and a shared grievance related to their petroleum resources. By contrast, Papuans have both an overall identity and many local identities, based on tribe, dialect, and geography, while the migration of large numbers of settlers from the rest of Indonesia into Papua has left indigenous Papuans as only a slight majority. Papua's internal heterogeneity has led to less frequent and sustained political mobilization. These differences made Aceh more determined and successful in pursuing its constitutional goals than Papua. Understanding how variations in political geometry shape the negotiating strategies and goals of actors may increase the chances for principals and advisors to successfully frame Constitution-making processes, or at least highlight challenges.

However, demography is not destiny. Demography does not determine political geometry, which can shift over time through political entrepreneurship, in response to changing structural conditions or exogenous or endogenous events. Constitutional process and design must address these changed realities. Bolivia, for example, has gone through three distinct cleavage patterns. Historically, wealth was concentrated in the Andes because of mining, creating a territorial cleavage with the lowlands. Territorial cleavages were replaced by class cleavages in 1952, yielding class-based political parties. Economic policy decisions on infrastructure and gas transformed Bolivia's economic geography and shifted economic power to Santa Cruz, leading to the return of the territorial cleavage, but with relative economic power reversed. At the same time, indigenous communities whose financial support from the state was withdrawn under neo-liberal economic reforms used the democratic opening of the 1980s and 1990s to mobilize on the basis of ethnicity, demanding the plurinational reconfiguration of Bolivia and land rights, and the redistribution of wealth to the Andes.[10] This shift in cleavages led to the collapse of the political party system and its replacement with a new one that tracked these cleavages.

Now we look more closely at political entrepreneurs. A long tradition in political sociology roots territorial political mobilization as a defensive response to central state-led projects of nationalism. In *Imagined Communities*, Benedict Anderson argued that nationalism is a modern phenomenon and that national identity arises in the particular political and economic context of the "nation-state" system.[11] In many countries, nation-building political elites sought to invigorate the power of the central state and to develop a common national identity, often by assimilationist means. The classic liberal, nineteenth-century version of nation-building saw it as a way to promote democratic equality and self-government, to enhance the effectiveness of the state, and to promote national unity. Classic nation-building policies consist of the centralization of political and legal authority, the fashioning of a common identity around a shared culture and history, and usually, the adoption of a single language becomes the official or quasi-official medium for political and economic life.

The content and contexts of nation-building policies vary. Imperial Ethiopia, which was never colonized, sought to build a nation around language and religion, in the manner of European nation-states. In monarchical Nepal, which also was not colonized, central elites fashioned a nation built not just on language and religion but also caste, ethnicity and region. American colonial authorities in the Philippines sought to integrate Mindanao, a historically Muslim island, through internal colonization by Roman Catholic settlers from Luzon. In Iraq, national governments imposed Arabic on the Kurdish-speaking minority.

Constitutions have often been used to centralize political, legal, and economic power and to impose a national language. This happened in the transitions to independence with Indonesia's 1949 Constitution and India's 1950 Constitution. It has also occurred through democratic politics when majority groups seek to impose their language and symbols, as happened in Sri Lanka, with the replacement of the post-independence Soulbury Constitution with the 1972 Constitution. In Nepal, the 1990 constitutional process, which established responsible government and multi-party competitive politics, was designed to confer democratic legitimacy on the nation-building approach of the monarchy.

Nation-building creates winners and losers by redistributing access to cultural, economic, and political power and privileging central elites and the dominant community. When Constitutions have been used as instruments of nation-building, they have often triggered contestation and defensive constitutional politics by minorities, who may seek constitutional change—either through democratic politics or violent means. Indeed, if the principal object of ethnonational contestation is competition over access to state power, then violent conflict should be more likely when groups are excluded from power, and likelier still when groups lose or fear losing power. Cederman et al. have found that ethnic violence is defensive and dynamic: it arises in response to

[10] Deborah J Yashar, "Contesting Citizenship: Indigenous Movements and Democracy in Latin America" (1998) 31 (1) Comparative Politics 23.

[11] Anderson, *Imagined Communities* (n 9).

exclusion, and even more so to a worsening of political status. Since violent conflict arises from the breakdown of politics, the same forces should also lie at the root of non-violent territorial political mobilization.[12]

But exclusion or discrimination does not necessarily produce political mobilization. Our approach follows the constructivist tradition in political sociology, which argues that political entrepreneurs are critical to the success of political mobilization, by framing a case, developing strategies, and marshaling resources.[13] Political entrepreneurs typically form elite coalitions drawing from various sectors, and the composition of these coalitions can change over time. Indeed, there may be political competition among different regional elite coalitions contending for power. Moreover, territorially based populations, even when they are distinct minorities nationally, may not have a high level of internal political cohesion, which underlines the importance of political entrepreneurs.

To be successful, subnational political entrepreneurs must construct narratives regarding the past and present that resonate with a population's sense of grievance and of its rights. Such narratives often focus on lost political and legal status compared to an earlier period, as well as on past and ongoing cultural, economic, and political discrimination. History is particularly useful if a group once enjoyed political autonomy or even independent statehood: this can support arguments about the group's right to new arrangements (rooted in the right to self-determination) and the practical viability of the arrangements they seek. Past arrangements can also provide a natural benchmark for assessing the adequacy of current offers, which may be condemned as falling short.

There are many contemporary examples where political entrepreneurs have deployed past memories to promote current demands for greater autonomy or independence. For example, the Moro areas of Mindanao were independent sultanates before the Spanish arrived, and Spanish colonial authorities did not assert practical control over the area. It was only after the United States acquired control of the Philippines in the late nineteenth century that the Moro were brought under central authority. In Spain, Catalonia was a county that was part of an independent kingdom (Aragon) through the Middle Ages, with its own laws and legal system operating in Catalan, which survived the unification of Spain in the late fifteenth century. At the beginning of the eighteenth century, the Spanish monarchy abolished Catalonia's separate institutions in favor of a highly centralized structure. In Indonesia, Aceh had been an independent sultanate from 1511 until it was conquered by the Dutch in 1871. In Yemen, it was only in 1990 that South Yemen united with the North. If self-governing territories were incorporated by consent conditioned on certain substantive or procedural commitments which have been breached, this vitiates the original consent on the basis of a retained right to self-determination. Scottish nationalism has invoked the argument that the terms of the 1707 Act of Union, which abolished the Scottish Parliament, have not been respected. Papua was integrated into Indonesia under a United Nations-brokered agreement requiring the holding of a referendum to put this issue to the population, which has never been held.

Even without a past history of independence, subnational political entrepreneurs can build narratives around historical grievances. For example, in Cyprus, attempts to unite Cyprus and Greece—*enosis*—coupled with massacres and the fear of genocide, are

[12] Lars-Erik Cederman, Andreas Wimmer, and Brian Min, "Why Do Ethnic Groups Rebel? New Data and Analysis" (2010) 62 (1) World Politics 87.

[13] See the works by Anderson *Imagined Communities* (n 9); Brubaker (n 9); Gellner (n 9); Wimmer (n 9).

still deployed by political leaders in the Turkish Cypriot part of the island. Grievances can also be rooted in fears of a future that has not yet materialized. Serb political leaders in Bosnia-Herzegovina interpreted a decision of the Badinter Commission that recognized Bosnian Serbs as a national minority as downgrading them from their status as a constituent people and placing them in physical danger. The Bosnian Serbs then armed themselves with Serb support and engaged in ethnic cleansing with a view to securing control of certain territories and secession to join neighboring Serbia. These anxieties were also fed by Croatia's failure to guarantee minority rights to its Serb minority, which created the fear Croats would do the same in Bosnia-Herzegovina.

The framing of narratives is an important tool for political entrepreneurs seeking to shape the mobilization of a group. For ethnic relations, Loizides defines framing as "the conscious strategic effort to shape shared understandings about an ethnic group, its recent memories, grievances and boundaries (identity or physical), particularly with regard to its perceived territorial entitlements."[14] Frames link past experiences with contemporary policy dilemmas and transform abstract grievances into specific courses of action. The choice of frame affects the nature and strength of claims, as well as the ability to accept possible trade-offs. For example, the internal migration and resettlement of majority populations in areas of minorities have been encouraged by many states as a nation-building policy, but this has often been framed by regional political entrepreneurs as a form of internal colonialism. The charge of colonialism admits of no compromise because it delegitimizes the central state, and justifies calls for constitutional autonomy or even secession. Moreover, it puts the question of property—ownership, restitution, and compensation—on the constitutional agenda. Political entrepreneurs in Kenya, Iraq, the Philippines, Cyprus, Indonesia, and Sri Lanka have used this frame. But in states where ethnic intermixing occurred through labor migration but not internal settlement policies, such as Nepal and Bosnia-Herzegovina, this frame is unavailable.

Because frames can help mobilize political constituencies and shape constitutional agendas, they can be deeply contested. Often, two populations are attached to diametrically opposed narratives in a true dialogue of the deaf. In Cyprus, Greek Cypriot leaders have framed their claims through justice and rights discourses, which have led them to demand a right of return for displaced persons to their properties in the Turkish zone of control. Turkish Cypriot leaders have offered a counter-framing to justify the new realities on the ground, built around persecution by the Greeks which led to the mass movement of population, the property rights of current users, and security concerns to counter a right of return. Underlying this disagreement is a more fundamental one over how to frame the possible reunification of the island: Greek Cypriots see it as a "holding together" of the existing Cyprus while Turkish Cypriots argue that it would be a "coming together" of two states to form a federation, to adopt Al Stepan's terminology.[15] These radically different frames have implications not only for constitutional design, but also for structuring the process of Constitution-making so that parties with such incompatible frames can engage and potentially reach agreement.

While claims for territorial accommodation are often framed in terms of group identity and cultural difference, they may be driven by an underlying economic dispute even if there are minimal differences in territorial identity. Such disputes may be

[14] Neophytos Loizides, *Designing Peace: Cyprus and Institutional Innovations in Divided Societies* (University of Pennsylvania Press 2016) 54.

[15] Alfred Stepan, "Federalism and Democracy: Beyond the U.S. Model" (1999) 10 (4) Journal of Democracy 19.

rooted in the structure of the economy, the distribution of natural resources revenues, decisions regarding public sector expenditure, the rules governing public sector employment, or the allocation of public debt, among other issues. These situations are all characterized by political claims for territorial accommodation over the distribution of material resources. In Bolivia, the new wealth from natural gas of the eastern lowlands sparked political battles over sharing the benefits, with the lowlands seeking more autonomy, and the highlands and indigenous groups favoring greater central control and redistribution. In India, one major outcome of the creation of linguistic states was the development of state-level bureaucracies that would operate in regional languages, thereby opening public sector employment more broadly to regional populations. In Ukraine, a trigger for territorial mobilization was the breakdown of a Faustian bargain in which both eastern oligarchs, who had obtained state subsidies for their industries from Kiev, and nation-building parties from western and central Ukraine both had favored centralization. The demand for autonomy for the east by Russophiles has fluctuated depending on whether eastern interests could obtain power, and material benefits, at the center.

Natural resources play a role in many conflicts, sometimes as the principal object of the conflict, at other times as a contributing factor.[16] Paul Collier and Anke Hoeffler have identified possible links or "channels of causation" between natural resources and conflict. These include resources being "honeypots" over which people fight; giving secessionist movements credibility about future wealth; and financing rebel groups.[17] All of these were evident in the secessionist movements in Aceh, Nigeria, and South Yemen, whereas in Mindanao it was the prospect of yet-to-be-developed resources that were a motivation for the rebels. Resources were also a key part of the political conflict between the Kurds and Arabs in Iraq, and that between the highlands and lowlands of Bolivia.

Existing regional institutions of self-government provide important resources for territorial political mobilization. They can be used to promote territorial political identity around culture, history, and language, to provide institutional resources in political contests or negotiations with the central government, and to provide embryonic institutions which can serve as a foundation for more extensive forms of territorial self-government. Democratically elected regional institutions can provide the benefits of incumbency for regional political parties that can mobilize support. Spain and the UK show how existing institutions of regional self-government, and regional political parties, have been key resources for territorial political mobilization. However, they also illustrate how Constitutions simultaneously empower and constrain. Both regional governments could not hold referendums within the existing constitutional framework. In the UK, the central government and Scotland negotiated the terms of the referendum, especially on the question to be posed. In Spain, there was no such negotiation with Catalonia, and as a result, the central government and the Spanish Constitutional Court declared a regional referendum in Catalonia to be illegal. In Bolivia, the administrative structure of departments became a focus for territorial empowerment, even before elected officials had much voice within departments;

[16] Edward Aspinall, "The Construction of Grievance: Natural Resources and Identity in a Separatist Conflict" (2007) 51 (6) Journal of Conflict Resolution 950; Nicholas Sambanis and Branko Milanovic, "Explaining Regional Autonomy Differences in Decentralized Countries" (2014) 47 (13) Comparative Political Studies 1830.

[17] Paul Collier and Anke Hoeffler, "High-value Natural Resources, Development, and Conflict: Channels of Causation" in Paivi Lujala and Siri Aas Rustad (eds), *High-Value Natural Resources and Post-Conflict Peacebuilding* (Routledge 2011).

departmental political power then increased dramatically once department heads were elected.

Even *de facto* self-governing powers can be a vital institutional resource. This was certainly the case in Iraq, where after the 1991 Gulf War, the Kurdish region enjoyed *de facto* independence. The existence of a government in the Kurdish region was a central reality in the constitutional processes after the Iraq War. While the Kurdish region failed to secure constitutional recognition of its independence, it achieved extensive autonomy that would have been highly unlikely otherwise. Similarly, the extensive *de facto* autonomy enjoyed by the LTTE in northeast Sri Lanka in 2001–09 increased the LTTE's leverage in ceasefire and peace negotiations. The decisive defeat of the LTTE by the Sri Lankan government illustrates that the ultimate foundation for *de facto* autonomy is armed force—and that if it is overwhelmed by force of arms, there is no legal recourse domestically or internationally.

The example of institutionalized territorial self-government arrangements in one part of a country can create a constitutional logic for claims for their replication. In India, the creation of a single state on linguistic lines—Andhra Pradesh, in 1953—led to the formation of the States Organization Commission and the eventual redrawing of India's entire political map along linguistic lines over the next several years. In addition, an arrangement for one unit can serve as the basis for a presumption of symmetric treatment, in terms of powers and status, for other units. In Spain, when autonomous communities were created in the 1978 Constitution, it was expected that the "historic nationalities" would have significantly more devolved powers than the other regions, but every other region said they wanted the same through a process that has come to be known as "café para todos."

Means antecedent to a constitutional moment: peaceful and institutionalized politics or violent and extra-legal

Political entrepreneurs must choose the means to pursue claims for territorial accommodation. On the one hand, they may seek change through peaceful means, working through existing institutional channels and under legal—including constitutional—constraints. Or they may reject the existing constitutional order and decide to work outside of it, extra-legally, through violence. The choice of means is influenced by the nature of the political regime in which political entrepreneurs are operating, by their positions on constitutional options, and by past history or experience in pursuing their goals. While a society may have many underlying tensions that suggest latent territorial cleavages, in an autocracy, or an intolerant and assimilationist majoritarian regime, territorial minorities may find no effective peaceful outlet for debate and mobilization. Thus, the political lid can come off when such regimes liberalize or even break down. Such events often open a major constitutional moment, where territorial and other groups mobilize to promote their objectives. The exact triggers of democratic openings or regime change may be sudden and unexpected. The death of Franco in Spain allowed for the re-emergence of Catalan and other sub-national groups, which mobilized politically. The end of the Cold War led to the democratic transition in South Africa, with claims for territorial accommodation made by Zulu and Afrikaner nationalists; it also triggered the breakup of Yugoslavia. The Asian financial crisis led to the fall of the Suharto regime and a broader process of democratization that created an opening for Achenese and Papuans to demand special autonomy. The First and Second Gulf Wars provided the opportunity for the Kurds to *de facto* establish and then seek to constitutionally entrench their autonomy. The Arab Spring brought the fall of Saleh and an intense period of constitutional dialogue in Yemen.

The choice of means will also be influenced by political leaders' assessments of the substantive distance between themselves and the government or other influential actors and of their political leverage. Regional political parties are often the key instrument for non-violent, mass mobilization around territorial claims through institutionalized channels. The creation of a regional political party reflects an assessment that this is the most effective way to promote regional claims, often because other political parties are indifferent or opposed to accommodating the claims of a territorial group or groups. In Kenya, the Kenya African Democratic Union (KADU) was formed in 1961 as a consortium of medium-sized tribes to lobby for ethnic regionalism, and to protect them from the larger tribes that dominated the Kenya African National Union (KANU) and its agenda of centralization. On other occasions, the leaders of a territorial group may choose to work within a non-regional party, making the contingent judgment that this will maximize their political leverage. It is worth emphasizing that even when there may be a regional party or parties advancing strong territorial claims, regional populations are often not politically unified, and it is not uncommon to see them split their votes among regional and national parties with opposing agendas.

Pursuing constitutional change peacefully occurs in a context of legal and institutional continuity. The procedures for constitutional amendment and ordinary law-making apply, channeling debates over territorial accommodation into existing institutions and rules. These rules determine the leverage that different groups have. They can be highly contested, as they are currently in Spain regarding the drive for Catalan independence. Moreover, legal and institutional continuity is often inherently conservative in terms of substance if there are high hurdles for constitutional change, which may make the amendment of the existing Constitution more likely than the adoption of a new one. However, with a large enough consensus, as in Bolivia and Spain, a new Constitution can be adopted within the rules of its predecessor. Moreover, in certain cases, as in Nepal and South Africa, the new political configuration results in an agreement to prepare a new Constitution under conditions of formal legal continuity long enough to create, through the established (or adapted) procedures, an interim regime with new rules, which reflect the different forces at play and lay the ground for a developing a new Constitution.

Depending on a group's grievances and circumstances, regional political elites may reject normal politics, perhaps because they have failed, and turn to violence. Arguably, violence is the continuation of political mobilization by other means, but it also brings a shift in the character of politics, notably in giving those with guns (both government and rebels) a central role while marginalizing others. Indeed, some leaders of violent action have no experience of normal politics, which has important downstream implications for Constitution-making processes and the objective of developing normal political life. Violent instruments of political action range from small-scale insurgencies, through guerrilla warfare, to full-scale armed conflict and civil war.

Territorial groups who turn to violence typically do so with a deep sense of grievance and frustration with peaceful means. Such a choice is easily understandable in a context of repressive autocracies, but it can happen in democracies, especially fragile democracies or democracies that strongly favor nation-building over the accommodation of differences. This is particularly true in former colonies, where the post-independence political environment was largely one of nation-building and hostility to territorial claims for constitutional accommodation, which were perceived as an existential threat. In many post-colonial states, the legacy of the anti-colonial struggle produces a unitary state mindset. For example, although India has been effectively federal since its inception, its Constitution characterized it as a "Union" and never used the term "federal," given the concern for a strong center. For the same reason the Constitution's drafters initially rejected linguistic states out of the fear that identity-based subunits would undermine national integrity. In Indonesia, the Dutch colonial authorities created a federal republic that was rejected by the independence movement as a divide and conquer strategy. Accordingly, violence in India, the Philippines, and Sri Lanka all took place (or continued) in contexts of reasonably democratic regimes where the demands for territorial accommodation had been refused.

Our cases run the gamut from highly peaceful to murderously violent. They include the civil wars in Nigeria and Sri Lanka, where the governments defeated attempts at secession, as well as the civil war in Bosnia-Herzegovina, which saw ethnic cleansing during a state's breakup. In Ethiopia, a coalition of regional insurgents won a long-running civil war against a brutal, highly centralizing dictatorship. In Nepal, the government and Maoists fought to a standstill. In Cyprus, a breakdown of public order and trust between the two communities led to military intervention by an outside power and the partition of the country. South Africa never experienced full-scale civil war, but its history of armed insurgency and violent suppression by the authorities was critically important to framing the conflict and bringing the parties to the negotiating table. A number of the violent conflicts concerned peripheral regions: the Bangsamoro in the Philippines; Aceh in Indonesia; the Houthis in Yemen; and various tribal communities in northeastern India. Iraq had a unique history, with the Kurdish region achieving effective partition after the Gulf War and then being reunited after the fall of Saddam, in both cases because of foreign military intervention.

Indeed, very few of our cases lacked violence of some kind leading up to the constitutional moment. There had been bloody riots in Kenya, and violent demonstrations in Bolivia. Spain had experienced violent struggle from Basque nationalists and memories of its terrible civil war were still strong when the post-Franco era was under consideration. The UK had faced a long insurgency in Northern Ireland (although Scotland has been entirely peaceful). While Ukraine was peaceful following its independence from the USSR as it entered its constitutional moment, this peace was eventually shattered by uprisings in the capital and Russian incursions in the Crimea and Donbas.

The choices leaders make about whether to work through peaceful, legal, and institutional mechanisms or turn to violence depend in part on political geometry. Does the political constellation provide reasonable prospects for the group to have sufficient leverage for its grievances or aims to be addressed? The answer is contextual. Even a relatively small population in an environment of highly contested politics amongst many political parties may well find that a regionally based party can influence the formation of governments, even join a coalition, and affect the content of legislation and the system's engagement on constitutional change. The power wielded by small regional Indian political parties in national politics for nearly two decades, and of the Catalan and Basque parties on the drafting of Spain's Constitution during a period of minority governments, are examples. By contrast, if a small population is up against a dominant party representing an intransigent majority, it may find that even with overwhelming support in its region, it can achieve little with normal politics and eventually turns to violent means. This was the political trajectory in Sri Lanka, where over the course of fifty years of constitutional politics, the Tamil minority was frustrated by the rejection of their claims by the major Sinhalese parties. Over time its politics became radicalized with the demand for a separate state, and eventually a faction within the community promoted the rise of the LTTE, which then crushed internal dissent using unrestrained violence against moderates and used terrorism against the majority Sinhalese. Sometimes, political entrepreneurs pursuing a territorial claim choose to operate within a national party, where their region's support gives them leverage.

Of course, the frustration of political demands does not necessarily result in secessionist demands or outright violence: groups may have more limited demands and resort to non-violent measures outside of normal politics, such as strikes, mass demonstrations, blockades, and various disturbances. In Nepal, secessionist demands by the Hindi-speaking residents of the Madhesh are still rare, and they have thus far only used disruptive tactics—but no serious violence—to promote their demands for linguistic equality, a fair share of resources, and a single province that would constitute 40 percent of Nepal's population.

Very small, peripheral regional populations present a different context. For them, a regional political party would at best secure minimal representation and leverage in the central legislature. The low returns from such political mobilization may discourage them from forming a political party, especially if their grievances are not too strongly felt. However, if they are deeply aggrieved, leaders may appear who advocate recourse to violence. In Aceh and Papua in Indonesia, and the northeast of India, there was little or no evidence of the mass political mobilization around regional political parties before the rise of insurgencies. However, the fact that electoral politics has only been attempted briefly or not at all before the turn to violence does not mean that it cannot follow from a properly structured constitutional settlement that addresses major grievances (as we explain later).

A dominant majority's insistence on constitutional orthodoxy can also serve as a source of frustration driving political mobilization off the track of legal and institutional continuity into extra-legal action and violence. The established rules can be seen as raising too many procedural and substantive hurdles to the accommodation of the territorial cleavage—for example, as in Sri Lanka, by constitutionally entrenching the commitment to a unitary state and requiring a referendum with a supermajority requirement to amend it, which is politically infeasible. Relatedly, the existing constitutional order may empower "institutional spoilers"—for example, courts, opposition parties, the government backbench, and/or elements of the political executive—to block a territorial accommodation in the name of a vision of a centralized, unitary state (discussed later). As we consider below, a puzzle is how to reconstitute constitutional order in a context where at least one party has rejected legal and institutional continuity.

Tests of strength and relative political power

The third variable that defines constitutional moments is that of the relative power positions of the different political actors, including governments and the leaders of territorially mobilized groups. The issue of constitutional accommodation of territorial demands may have been around for a long time before the key actors decide to actively engage with one another on the question of constitutional change. Government leaders and others who are facing these territorial demands must also consider how to react, both with respect to goals and means. Do they see the claims for territorial accommodation as extreme and constitutionally unthinkable (e.g. secession in many countries) or as reasonable or at least open to discussion and possible political resolution? Where subnational political entrepreneurs have mobilized peacefully, formed regional parties, and contested elections, they have been able to do so because of the space offered by constitutional democracy, thereby creating a political presumption for central governments to respond through peaceful means as well. But even among constitutional democracies, states have set outer boundaries around the domain of constitutional politics. Most Constitutions explicitly or implicitly prohibit the unilateral secession of a region, and some states—for example, Spain—have inferred from this prohibition a series of restrictions on political activity that arguably extend back into ordinary politics. The use of violence by the central state is nearly a certainty when subnational political entrepreneurs have opted for violence themselves.

At the point when actors launch into the process of constitutional reform, they may have had tests of their relative strength, whether through competitive politics or violent clashes. The outcome of such tests of strength can determine when and how a constitutional process is engaged and the relative power of the different actors to influence the outcome. Power positions for territorial leaders are influenced by the size of the territory's population, the political cohesion of that population, and the leverage these assets provide in light of the power positions of other actors—so, for example, others things being equal, a regional movement of a certain size may have more influence in a context where the larger party system is relatively fractured and fluid than in a context where one party has a solid majority of the population.

In democratic politics, the most important tests of strength are electoral. These can permit a group or coalition to capture governmental power, either nationally or (if territorial governments exist) regionally. In the UK, the Scottish National Party was able to form a majority government in Scotland, which put it in a position to push for a referendum. The UK government used its legal powers to negotiate the terms of the referendum, and did so in part because public opinion polls made it confident that there was no majority in Scotland for secession. In Kenya, the results of the election of 2007 were close enough that the opposition contested the result and violence ensued; this led in due course to an internationally mediated agreement for a power-sharing government and a new constitutional process. In Ukraine, the constitutional positions of key politicians from the eastern region shifted according to whether they were in government in Kyiv; there was regular tension between the president and parliament about constitutional reform, with the president having considerable leverage because of his apparent support in public opinion polls. The constitutional agenda in Bolivia was shaped by the confrontation brought on by Morales's election to the presidency, and subsequent electoral tests of strength nationally and in departments as well as through referendums. Spain's constitutional transition was shaped by the fact that no one party had the majority to form a government, so this, plus the broader concern for a broad consensus to ensure a successful transition to democracy, gave significant political leverage to opposition parties, including territorially based parties, in shaping the new regime.

A genuine process of constitutional transition cannot take place during a raging civil war or insurgency. With violent conflicts, the critical issue is whether the two sides have reached the point of a stalemate, with neither being able to defeat the other so they turn to negotiations—or whether a clear victor has emerged. Victors will be in a strong position to determine the substance of constitutional change, including how to deal with the territorial claims that gave rise to the civil war in the first place. Moreover, they are likely to have great control over process. Our main interest regarding post-conflict situations centers on those arising from stalemates. Stalemates led to negotiations with regional groups in India, Indonesia and the Philippines and stalemated civil wars that led to negotiations in Bosnia-Herzegovina, Cyprus, and Nepal. In Sri Lanka, the intractable nature of the conflict led to some, ultimately unsuccessful, efforts to find negotiated solutions. In South Africa, the government concluded that it could not maintain the regime in the face of the insurgency, especially given how the end of the Cold War had weakened its geopolitical situation. For stalemates, conflict theorists refer to a conflict needing to be "ripe" as a precondition for effective bargaining, which means that when both sides see little possibility of outright victory and the cost of continuing as insupportable, they may enter into a ceasefire and then negotiations for a peace agreement and a reunification of the state under a unified constitutional order.

While power relationships at the outset of a constitutional moment weigh heavily in shaping the Constitution-making process and agenda, they can shift significantly once the process has started: different sides can be strengthened or weakened as the process unfolds. In Sri Lanka, after the breakdown of negotiations, the LTTE and the government returned to war and the government ultimately prevailed militarily. The possibility of shifts in power is especially true when elections and referendums occur—as happened in Bolivia, Kenya, Nepal, Scotland, South Africa, Spain, and Ukraine. In Cyprus, a referendum killed a possible agreement. These examples also show that even when constitutional moments emerge from an initial context of violence, elections and referendums can become an important factor in subsequent phases. More generally, negotiations may not reach a successful conclusion; there is no guarantee the parties will agree, and the possibility of violence resuming can affect how negotiations unfold.

In some cases, a decisive component in the power equation is the role and influence of external actors. There is a considerable literature on the important role of external factors in democratic transitions, including diffusion, democracy assistance and promotion, and multilateral conditionality.[18] In Bosnia-Herzegovina, Cyprus, and Iraq, external powers had real power to influence developments directly because of their military interventions.

Context and Dynamics of Constitutional Moments

The actual start of serious engagement on the possibility of constitutional change—a constitutional moment—may be triggered by any number of events, such as the end of or a halt to a conflict, the arrival in office of a new political party, or a decision by power holders to address a major issue of institutional design. But whatever the trigger, the nature, and interrelationships of the crucial variables—political geometry, the choice of peaceful, legal and institutionalized or violent and extra-legal means, and relative political power as determined by tests of strength—will set the agenda for the choice of Constitution-making process and the menu of potential options for constitutional design. Constitutional moments can carry on over extended periods, and during that time there can be developments or shifts in the political geometry and the relative power positions of key actors. There are often major tests of political strength during a constitutional moment that are decisive as to how the political contest is resolved. The situation is evolving and dynamic, not static and pre-determined. There is no simple causal relationship that leads from initial context to eventual outcome.

Table 20.1 locates our different cases in terms of how they relate to the three dimensions of the variables: four categories of political geometry; two regarding the means for the antecedent contest; and two with respect to the power distribution, with

[18] See Steven Levitsky and Lucan A Way, *Competitive Authoritarianism: Hybrid Regimes After the Cold War* (Cambridge University Press 2010) 38–54.

a dominant actor vs. divided or diffuse power arrangement. The table is indicative and not every case fits neatly into a single box. The different structures of these political contexts each presents an inherent logic regarding how the leading political actors set their constitutional goals and pursue them. These variations in contextual factors shape the agenda for process and design for the different constitutional moments.

We note at the outset that not all cases led to a consensual accommodation of a territorial claim within a state: Croatia was a case of unilateral secession; Sri Lanka in 2009 saw a military defeat of the LTTE; Yemen failed to achieve a new Constitution and descended into civil war; Cyprus is still a frozen conflict; and Corsica has had minimal success in achieving its demands for autonomy. In other cases, territorial populations seeking accommodation of their demands have achieved less than they desired. So these factors are more predictive of the characteristics of the process and the constitutional options under consideration than they are of the eventual substantive outcome.

Table 20.1 Antecedent Power Political Context Distribution Geometry[a]

		Multidimensional territorial cleavages	**Majority-minority territorial configuration**	**Small, distinct peripheral regions**	**Mixed territorial and non-territorial cleavages**
Violent	**Victory**	Ethiopia, Nigeria		*Croatia* Sri Lanka (2009)	
	Stalemate		Bosnia-Herzegovina, Cyprus	NE India Aceh/Indonesia Moro/Philippines Sri Lanka (2002)	Nepal S. Africa Iraq
Non-violent	**Dominant**	India (linguistic states)	*Pakistan* (1956)	*Corsica*	*Russia*
	Divided	Spain	*Belgium*	Scotland Ukraine	Bolivia Kenya Yemen

[a]Moreover, our cases do not cover all the boxes or possibilities, so for illustrative purposes we have inserted a few cases (in italics) outside the scope of our study to illustrate other possibilities: Pakistan, where in 1956 the Prime Minister forced through a federal Constitution giving equal power to the West, which was opposed by representatives of the majority in East Pakistan; Russia, where a dominant party in a peaceful, constitutional context has been able to rewrite the Constitution into a very centralized form of federalism; Corsica, where the (mostly) non-violent political push for autonomy has encountered resistance from the dominant national parties in France. We have also included Belgium, whose periodic constitutional moments in a bi-communal and peaceful, constitutional context have resulted in a federal, consociational system. The situation in Sri Lanka changed between 2002, when there were negotiations, and 2009, when the government had prevailed militarily. Finally, Yemen is hard to place: its North-South cleavage suggests it be assigned to the majority-minority column, but both the North and South are themselves very divided, territorially and in other ways, which led to it being placed in the mixed territorial and non-territorial column.

We begin with design, where there is a close correlation between political geometry and the main constitutional option considered during a Constitution transition. In cases of multidimensional territorial cleavages, the design option is generally significantly decentralized symmetrical devolution or federalism combined with a majoritarian central government. For majority-minority territorial configurations, in which the minority is relatively large, the design option is presumptively highly devolved federalism, with a consociational central government. For small, distinct peripheral regions, the design option is typically special, asymmetric autonomy and a central government that is majoritarian. Finally, countries with a mix of territorial and non-territorial cleavages may consider devolution or federalism, which may be quite centralized and perhaps with a large number of units with a majoritarian central government. We elaborate upon these models and link them to political geometry in "Constitutional Design and Territorial Cleavages" below. While our descriptions of these options are necessarily high level, the distinct configurations of political geometry tend to drive the options considered for designing a Constitution that reflects the territorial dimension. The logic of such options is no guarantee that they will be considered or adopted, because depending on the power configuration the majority may be resistant to accommodating territorial claims, or at least to doing so within certain models. The case of Sri Lanka is a case in point, where the only option to the status quo that found even a brief possibility of agreement was federalism, when special autonomy might have been considered a more logical alternative (but was rejected by the majority).

While a constitutional moment that results in change is usually thought to end with an agreement on a new or revised Constitution, it is in reality one step in a longer process, which includes the critical issue of implementation. A territorial accommodation, whether in the form of a constitutional amendment or a statute, launches further processes whereby that accommodation is operationalized in practice, in the course of which it will be interpreted, reviewed, and adapted over time to changing circumstances. Moreover, on many occasions, the very same disagreements that gave rise to the demand for the territorial accommodation in the first place will resurface in debates over how to translate that accommodation into practice. Thus, constitutional territorial accommodations do not necessarily resolve issues. Rather, they may manage them, by establishing some points of consensus and channeling remaining issues into institutional mechanisms and ordinary politics.

Let us now consider process. Arising out of tests of strength, relative political power can be dominant or divided. It is important and interesting that constitutional design to accommodate territorial cleavages can occur under both conditions. If there are dominant actors—as was the case in Ethiopia and Nigeria, with their military victors, and in India in the 1950s, with its dominant Congress Party—they control the process. To the extent there is a political process it may be largely within the army or party of power. Even so, such dominant actors may encourage a constitutional design that responds to territorial claims to enhance legitimacy or regime stability. These cases are not our primary focus, but such dominant actors should consider territorial accommodations as possible mechanisms of cooptation or control, which may be prudent ways to prevent future conflict.

Our main focus is on constitutional moments where the relative power of the key actors is divided, with no party able to dictate the outcome, so that there needs to be some kind of agreement if the issue is to be resolved. The political geometry and power positions of the main actors will be key to determining the nature and character of the constitutional process. The process will also be shaped by whether the constitutional moment arises out of antecedents of peaceful, legal, institutionalized politics or extra-legal, violent conflict.

Where power is divided because of electoral results, political actors address the substantive agenda items in a context of legal and institutional continuity within a constitutional democracy. The existing Constitution provides a procedural framework to debate, adopt, and implement constitutional change, including possible territorial accommodation. In Bolivia, Kenya, Spain, and the UK, the process of constitutional change unfolded within the existing rules of the constitutional framework. However, there may be political reasons to seek a broader consensus, beyond what is required by the Constitution; such a consensus may bring greater political legitimacy to the result than would have happened with a decision that met the minimal constitutional requirements for approval. Thus, in Spain there was an informal political agreement to work for a broad political consensus, while in Kenya, the need for a broad consensus was tied to the constitutional process taking place during a period of a government of national unity. In Bolivia, there was a special mechanism designed for constitutional change that was to supplement the established procedure—a Constituent Assembly—but in the end this failed and the established procedure, relying on Congress, prevailed.[19]

Where there is a military stalemate, the agenda must combine peace negotiations and Constitution-making. These can work at cross-purposes in that a peace agreement is backward-looking and focused on ending violence, while Constitution-making looks forward to creating effective institutions that operate under constitutional democracy and peaceful, legal politics. The question is how to design a peace process among armed parties that can thicken and broaden into a constitutional process among many parties, including the public, with a much broader agenda. The process needs to provide "on ramps" from armed conflict and peace negotiations to peaceful, democratic politics for the armed parties.

A cross-cutting issue for constitutional moments with divided power—regardless of whether the antecedents are violent or peaceful—is the risk of a lack of credible commitment. In the short term, where the constitutional system continues to exist in all or part of the state, it can potentially empower institutional spoilers to prevent the government from implementing any territorial accommodation. This is particularly true in cases of peripheral rebellion, such as in the Philippines and Sri Lanka, where apex courts struck down draft agreements as unconstitutional. In "Constitution-Making Processes," we discuss how negotiators can try to mitigate these risks by involving potential political spoilers, or by working around them—for example, in some cases, by opting for ordinary legislation over constitutional amendment. Credible commitment problems can also occur in the medium-term across multiple electoral cycles because opposition parties can campaign against agreements and proposed constitutional arrangements and may dismantle them if they win power. For example, in Sri Lanka, the Sri Lankan Freedom Party (SFLP) led by Mahindra Rajapaksa campaigned against the LTTE peace process while in opposition, and once in power, formally abrogated the ceasefire agreement and defeated the LTTE militarily. A potential response by negotiators to this risk may be to constitutionally entrench any deal reached against easy repeal—or to create a pluralistic process that provides space for divergent political views, in the hopes of building a broad consensus from an early stage. Finally, just as spoilers within the system may undermine a constitutional commitment, so can excluded political actors. In Nepal, the 1990 constitutional process did not include the Maoists, whose demands for constitutional reform in 1996 were not met, leading to the civil war and ultimately the replacement of the 1990 Constitution.

[19] In this chapter, we use the generic term "constitutional assembly" to refer to elected bodies with a mandate to produce a constitutional text. However, in the case of Bolivia, we refer to that body as the "Constituent Assembly," to accord with its usage in that context.

This brief review gives an initial sense of how the three main variables influence both process and design. The next two sections go into these issues in greater depth.

Constitution-Making Processes

The importance of process

There has been a subtle but clear shift in recent scholarship and practice, away from a nearly exclusive focus on constitutional design, to one where process is given equal attention.[20] Vicki Jackson, for example, sees a need for less emphasis on static constitutional design because "post-conflict situations motivate constitution-making but create conditions unlikely to produce lasting constitutions,"[21] creating a need for a greater focus on staged constitutional or political processes. Andreas Wimmer goes so far as to argue for the primacy of process over design in determining the viability of a Constitution. He suggests that "the best strategy of conflict prevention for institutionally weak states is to encourage a gradual, endogenously sustained process of state formation and nation-building," and expresses deep skepticism about the importance of institutional design, since "formal political institutions either don't influence conflict dynamics in any systematic way, or only show a rather unstable and fragile association with infighting between power-sharing partners."[22] While we disagree with Wimmer, it is nonetheless clear that the process whereby a constitutional settlement—even a provisional one—is reached can have a determining influence on its acceptance by key actors and its sustainability.

Most of the transitions considered in this volume have been from some form of authoritarian or undemocratic rule. O'Donnell and Schmitter have argued that such large-scale transformations often have insufficient structural or behavioral parameters to guide and predict outcomes and that the tools for normal political analysis are inadequate given high degree of indeterminacy, even regarding the roles of key actors.[23] This is a useful caution, but we suggest that attention to political geometry, the means of political contests prior to a constitutional moment, and the power distribution amongst the key players can help reduce the scope of such uncertainty. Nancy Bermeo has pointed to the critical role of elites in democratic transitions, even when there are high levels of popular mobilization.[24]

Saunders helpfully sets out three stages to Constitution-making processes, which we follow: agenda-setting, deliberation, and decision or ratification.

[20] Some examples of the literature include: Andrew Arato, *Post Sovereign Constitution Making* (Oxford University Press 2016); Michele Brandt, Jill Cottrell, Yash Ghai, and Anthony Regan, *Constitution-making and Reform: Options for the Process* (Interpeace 2011); Sujit Choudhry and Tom Ginsburg (eds), *Constitution-Making* (Edward Elgar 2016); Laurel Miller and Louis Aucoin (eds), *Framing the State in Times of Transition: Case Studies in Constitution Making* (United States Institute of Peace Press 2010); Abrak Saati, *The Participation Myth* (Umea University 2015); Stephen Tierney, *Constitutional Referendums: The Theory and Practice of Republican Deliberation* (Oxford University Press 2012).

[21] Vicki C Jackson, "What's in Name? Reflections on Timing, Naming and Constitution-Making" (2008) 49 (4) William and Mary Law Review 1249.

[22] Andreas Wimmer, *Waves of War: Nationalism, State Formation and Ethnic Exclusion in the Modern World* (Cambridge University Press 2013) 196, 177.

[23] Guillermo O'Donnell and Phillippe C Schmitter, *Transitions from Authoritarian Rule: Tentative Conclusions about Uncertain Democracies* (Johns Hopkins University Press 1986) 3–5.

[24] Nancy Bermeo, "Myths of Moderation: Confrontation and Conflict during Democratic Transitions" (1997) 29 (3) Comparative Politics 305, 314–17.

Agenda-setting

The initial phase of constitutional agenda-setting reflects the *scope* of the substantive issues to be addressed—that is, a broad constitutional review or one targeted on a specific territorial question—as well as the *process, participants, and decision-rules* for Constitution-making. Decisions on these matters will be influenced by the political geometry and the power distribution among political actors and they may be constrained by the existing Constitution and law. In situations of deep mistrust after a conflict, the agenda-setting phase may address and resolve some *principles or issues of substance* regarding the ultimate outcome. There is no one formula for this phase, which may be done quickly or over a very extended period. And it can overlap in varying degrees with the ensuing phases of deliberation and ratification. The choices made may be recorded in a formal or informal document. Agenda-setting is typically led by elites, though the representativeness of the elites and their weights at this stage will reflect their relative power positions.

Procedural agenda: The crucial factor is the whether the antecedents to the constitutional moment are legal, peaceful, and institutionalized or violent and extra-legal.

When the antecedents to a constitutional moment are legal, peaceful and institutionalized, established constitutional procedures govern. The procedures may be well established, such as the creation of a constitutional assembly and recourse to a constitutional amending formula. If constitutionalized, these procedures may serve as constraints. These procedures also presumptively designate the constituent actors in the process, which may include national and regional governments, opposition parties, civil society, and (in the case of referendums), the electorate. For example, in the UK, since the adoption of the Scotland Act in 1998, the agenda for discussions around further devolution and the holding of a referendum have been set by bilateral discussions at the cabinet level between Westminster and Holyrood. Ensuing agreements are essentially political in nature, such as a pact, joint statement, or accord, which may then require legislative implementation at both the regional and central level. However, Constitutions often give no direct role to regional governments or legislatures in constitutional change. Thus, in Bolivia in 2006–08, the newly elected departmental prefects had to play on the outside, while it was the elected members of regional parties in Congress—and later, in the Constituent Assembly—who were the main actors in the formal process, which was distinct from the larger political contest. The negotiations to create the Constituent Assembly occurred in Congress and through the steps of the legislative process, including committees, and were reflected in the terms of legislation. Similarly, in Spain and India, the elected heads of the regional governments had no formal role in initiating and determining the process of constitutional change. However, later on, they came to play a role, because in India existing states are asked for their consent to changes to their boundaries (although it is not required), and in Spain the governments of Autonomous Communities negotiated and ratified the quasi-constitutional Statutes of Autonomy, once the 1978 post-Franco Constitution had been approved. In practical terms, depending on circumstances and the political strength of the political parties, this phase may be largely determined by the government alone (e.g. India) but more frequently there is interparty discussion and debate (e.g. Bolivia, Kenya, Spain, Yemen).

Under conditions of legal and institutional continuity, there can still be latitude about various non-constitutional forums, such as special commissions and public consultations. Sometimes a national conference or dialogue outside the normal institutional framework can be important in setting a constitutional agenda. Membership and rules of procedure can depart significantly from normal parliamentary or intergovernmental procedures; indeed, they can be loose and fluid. The participants may include political parties and governments (blending legislative and intergovernmental processes), as well as a much broader range of non-elected actors, including labor, business, organized religion, and other civil society organizations. In Scotland during the 1990s, much of the political elite joined an informal, cross-party Constitutional Convention, which developed a blueprint for evolution in the absence of any elected regional representatives. When the Labour Party came to power in 1997, it endorsed this plan and submitted it to a Scotland-wide referendum before passing the Scotland Act of 1998. In Spain, debates over territorial accommodation had occurred even before the transition to democracy formally started. Several national political parties came together before Franco's death in 1975 to agree on principles of a democratic transition and were joined following his death by the main regional parties. A first step was to legalize all parties and adopt a general political amnesty. The outgoing Francoist parliament approved a law on political reform, which set the framework for a peaceful transition to democracy and a new Constitution. This was approved in a popular referendum. This lead to free election, after which the democratic parties agreed to resolve their differences so that the army or other anti-democratic forces would have no pretext to usurp the transition to democracy. Whatever the exact mix of forums, under conditions of legal and institutional continuity, having political elites (including elected political representatives where possible) participate in agenda-setting is integral to ensuring that the constituencies they represent will accept the legitimacy of the rest of the Constitution-making process, participate in it, accept it, and implement the resulting constitutional settlement.

After violence, if there are winners, they can decide on the agenda, as happened in Ethiopia and Nigeria (and after the defeat of the LTTE in Sri Lanka). However, our main focus is on stalemates. The parties to the conflict normally negotiate to set the agenda and this can be an elaborate and time-consuming process, as in South Africa. The process may be assisted by mediators or external parties, as in Cyprus, Nepal, Indonesia (regarding Aceh), and the Philippines (to deal with the Bangsamoro). Unusually, in Bosnia-Herzegovina and Iraq, outside powers largely set the agenda and the process for negotiations. Very occasionally, as in Cyprus, external powers are direct parties in the conflict and so play a role in agenda-setting.

For stalemates after violent conflicts, the participants in agenda-setting are normally by default the main armed combatants, as happened in Nepal in 2006, though for Bosnia-Herzegovina the Americans largely determined the process and it was the presidents of Serbia and Croatia who were the lead negotiators, rather than local leaders of their communities. In many long-running territorial conflicts, armed combatants have evolved into *de facto* regional governments, as was the case in Sri Lanka with the LTTE. In this context, President Chandrika Kumaratanga decided, prior to the 2002 ceasefire, to lead a constitutional reform process during the Sri Lankan civil war that on paper could have gone some way to meeting the demands of Tamil nationalists; however, the LTTE was excluded from the process and therefore had no stake in the ultimate result, which was one reason for the failure of that effort. In Kurdish Iraq and North Cyprus, regional institutions, with elected assemblies and leaders, asserted sovereign powers, making them state-like entities that have to be central to any constitutional negotiations. The resolution of peripheral rebellions, even without *de facto* regional governments—such as in the Philippines, Indonesia, and northeastern India—has required armed rebels be at the table, with the central government representing the state.

In situations of violence, both the constitutional process and peace process begin with a ceasefire. A ceasefire agreement, in principle, can memorialize agreement on the substantive and procedural constitutional agenda. However, the capacity of a ceasefire agreement to do so must reckon with the legal and institutional context. In some cases, the constitutional order and its institutions have effectively collapsed. The ceasefire and agenda-setting negotiations determine the Constitution-making process, and also set substantive constitutional principles or parameters that must be respected by the ultimate Constitution. This presents both an opportunity—because existing constitutional amending rules and legislative procedures need not constrain the creative crafting of process—and a challenge, because there is no default script for process, which may be contested. The rules of the game would have to be constructed as they are being used. Moreover, as we explain below under deliberation, in cases of state collapse, parties will often create provisional governing arrangements—including constituent assemblies which wield legislative functions as well. In Nepal, for example, the civil war came to end with a twelve-point agreement between seven political parties and the Maoists in 2005; that agreement included key commitments to an interim government including Maoists, and an elected Constituent Assembly. The parties and Maoists created a small, representative commission to prepare an interim Constitution, which took over a year. In 2006, the parties reconvened the 2002 Parliament that had been dissolved in 2005, which then adopted the interim Constitution that designated this body as the Interim Parliament; that body then admitted Maoist members and passed an electoral law for constituent assembly elections.

In other cases of violence prior to a constitutional moment, there may be legal and institutional continuity in most of the state, even if the central state's presence in the regions under conflict may be greatly diminished or barely existent. The state views its constitutional order as extending to areas under armed conflict and as governing the Constitution-making process. The challenge is how to coordinate existing procedures for legislation and constitutional amendment, where armed rebels have no formal role, with bilateral processes in which armed parties and central government are the central participants, growing out of a ceasefire. Institutional spoilers can sometimes raise constitutional objections at the agenda-setting stage, as in Sri Lanka, for example, where the mere fact of the ceasefire agreement with the LTTE was attacked as being unconstitutional because it was built around a line of control that *de facto* accepted the limited reach of the Sri Lankan state. Precisely because of this risk, armed rebels may seek to negotiate assurances regarding these downstream processes during the agenda-setting phase. In Sri Lanka, for example, while the ceasefire agreement did not address constitutional issues, the bilateral dialogue launched by the ceasefire yielded the Oslo Principles, which put down some key markers for the shape of a future constitutional process (an agreement would need to be "acceptable to all parties") as well as for the substance of a constitutional agreement (a federal structure within a united Sri Lanka)—which led Sinhalese hardliners to attack the ceasefire process for arising from an extra-constitutional process, and pursuing unconstitutional ends; their opposition was a reason for why the constitutional process never got off the ground.

This conundrum has been addressed in some cases through hybrid processes which formally comply with the Constitution but work around them to determine both the process and substantive principles of a constitutional transition. A striking example was in South Africa, where there was a stalemate between the African National Congress (ANC), which rejected the existing constitutional system as racist and illegitimate, and the South African government, which insisted on legal and institutional continuity. This process began with years of "talks about talks" before the National

Party government repealed the ban on the ANC and informal negotiations began. This bilateral process culminated in the National Peace Accord, which set the stage for the Convention for a Democratic South Africa (CODESA) among nineteen groups. Because these talks took place outside of formal parliamentary institutions, they could include the ANC, which had no elected representatives, as well as other entities—such as the leadership of Bantustans, especially KwaZulu, as well as the Afrikaaner-nationalist Vryheldsfront—which also lacked parliamentary representation. After CODESA collapsed, it was succeeded by another multiparty forum underpinned by consensus between the ANC and the National Party.

These observations suggest a challenge in the Ukraine at present. Ukraine has launched constitutional reform processes, with a presidentially mandated constitutional commission and other activity centered on the Rada. But since the Russian intervention in Donbas, citizens in the non-government controlled areas have no effective representation in Kyiv. Moreover, the Ukrainian government will not engage with the leaders of the self-proclaimed republics in Donbas. Negotiations on the reintegration of Donbas are occurring within the Minsk process, an international forum where negotiations take place with Russia, an external actor, as well as with Western powers. Thus, the challenge is how to give voice to those in the non-government- controlled areas as the constitutional and Minsk processes proceed.

Substantive agenda: Regardless of whether the antecedent to the constitutional moment is peaceful or violent, agenda-setting agreements can include significant substantive provisions, and can do so in a way that constrains the content of an eventual constitutional settlement. The substantive scope of the constitutional exercise can influence the nature of the process—for example, a process that aims to fundamentally rewrite a whole Constitution should be quite different from one aimed at a far more targeted issue, such as the accommodation of a particular region's territorial claims.

When territorial claims for autonomy are a potential driver of constitutional reform, an important decision during the agenda-setting phase is whether to broaden the scope of the process to include other issues. There are good arguments for doing so. Regional autonomy may be seen as the sole means to diffuse political power and accommodate the country's various cleavages, when other mechanisms might be considered. Including certain rights in the Constitution—such as language rights, especially for education and local government—can reduce the pressure for a proliferation of federal units. Electoral system design at the national level can enhance the prospects of minorities being represented in national institutions. And when the central issue is relations between a majority and a large minority, the prospect of some power-sharing in central institutions may be potentially valuable and lessen the degree of regional autonomy needed. In Nepal, for example, a provision in the interim Constitution stated that the "restructuring of the state . . . by eliminating the centralized and unitary form of the state" would be a tool to address all forms of social exclusion, including those that are non-territorial, such as caste, class, religion, and gender. In addition, it is important to offset the centrifugal pressures created by self-rule with arrangements for shared rule designed to support the viability and functioning of the shared state. The idea of power-sharing in central institutions was entirely absent from the 2003–08 Sri Lankan peace process, when federalism was briefly considered, thus creating legitimate concerns about the long-term viability of any such settlement (but the fact that the northern Tamils represent only 5 percent of the population would have put considerable limits on power-sharing as well). Finally, having many possible instruments for addressing territorial and minority concerns on the constitutional agenda can permit trade-offs and bargaining among them, facilitating agreement.

The scope for broadening the constitutional agenda also depends on the relative importance of the territorial issue. In India and the UK, the pressures from peaceful large regional movements made addressing the territorial issue central to the constitutional moments on state reorganization or Scottish autonomy. However, in Spain and Bolivia, where the territorial issue was fundamental, the constitutional agenda was much broader and encompassed the whole constitution; this was also true in countries such as Kenya, Nepal, South Africa, and Ukraine, where the territorial issue was one among several issues associated with a comprehensive constitutional agenda. Normally, agendas after a broad civil war involve a host of constitutional and non-constitutional issues beyond whatever territorial question might arise: these include issues such as transitional justice, resettlement of displaced populations, property restitution, security arrangements, and rule of law reform. However, the agenda to resolve peripheral rebellions is normally focussed narrowly on the territorial issue.

Placing territorial accommodation on the agenda of a constitutional process does not guarantee a desired outcome if there is no indication as to the expected substantive resolution. In some contexts, its mere inclusion with no substantive constraints may be an insufficiently strong guarantee for armed groups or groups inexperienced with politics. Thus, groups advancing territorial demands may seek guarantees during agenda-setting that bind the process to a certain substantive outcome on key points. In South Africa, for example, a schedule to the Interim Constitution contained thirty-four Constitutional Principles that legally bound the Constitutional Assembly, including one principle that required that the Final Constitution create a multi-tier constitutional system with national, provincial, and local levels of government, and further stipulated that provincial powers "shall not be substantially less than or substantially inferior" to those under the Interim Constitution. The Interim Constitution also provided that the Constitutional Court would have to certify that the Final Constitution complied with these principles for the Constitution to come into force; the Court rejected the first version of the Final Constitution on the basis that it did not, necessitating that the text be amended. Nepal's Interim Constitution also bound the Constitution-making process to require territorial accommodation.

Similarly, in Bolivia those favoring departmental autonomy insisted that the issue not be left to future negotiations. In negotiating the terms of reference of the Constituent Assembly (CA), the parties adopted a law for a referendum on autonomy that obliged the CA to create a regime of departmental autonomy and automatically opted-in those departments where the yes-side in the referendum prevailed. This arrangement constrained the CA, where there would not have been a supermajority in favor of autonomy arrangements. Such an option was possible because institutionally departments already existed so they could conduct referendums.

Deliberation

The deliberation stage is normally distinct from the agenda-setting stage in two respects: participation is more inclusive, and the consideration of substantive issues is much more detailed and concrete. The agenda-setting phase will normally have established some key terms regarding process (participation, forums, decision-rules and timing), but these often require significant elaboration and even modification. A major question at this stage is how to provide for political pluralism on all sides of the constitutional discussions—in order to build a broader political consensus in support of any resulting framework, supporting credible commitment in the short and medium term.

Participants: It is usual that the deliberation stage broadens participation beyond the actors who set the constitutional agenda.

When the antecedents of the constitutional moment are violent and extra-legal, at least one party will be an armed group. The lack of political pluralism can be an acute problem within armed groups, whose leaders are not elected and may in fact oppose an electoral test of their strength. An extreme example was the LTTE in Sri Lanka, which was notorious for its opposition to political pluralism, and ruthless in attacking and even murdering moderates within the Tamil community. To be sure, if a region is internally unified politically behind a single rebel group, that internal coherence can actually drive bargaining success, as occurred in Aceh in Indonesia. But if there are excluded armed groups that command significant support and possess sufficient capacity, they may turn into spoilers that can undermine a settlement, as happened with early agreements with the Moro in the Philippines. When one group has won a civil war, it will be able to determine both the process and the substance of Constitution-making; thus in Ethiopia, there was constitutional convention for the deliberative phase, but its members were decided by the victors, who chose to exclude some former allies. A cautionary tale comes from Bosnia-Herzegovina where the local combatants were completely marginalized. NATO was able to force the belligerents to a constitutional lock-up in Ohio, where the Americans designated the Serbian and Croatian presidents as the representatives of those communities—with the leadership of the Bosnian Croats and Bosnian Serbs reduced to consulting with the two presidents outside the room. The Americans controlled the process and their central objective was peace, not the terms of the new Constitution. The three ethnic communities had no buy-in to the Constitution agreed to under the Dayton Accord, though paradoxically, they were institutionally empowered by it to spoil it from within once it was implemented.

"On ramps" for armed groups to transition from violent conflict to peaceful, multiparty politics provide a way to broaden a constitutional process to promote political pluralism, by enmeshing such groups in a system of electoral competition and political pluralism. In Nepal, for example, the armed Maoist rebels agreed to take seats in an Interim Parliament which then quickly held elections for a CA which they contested with considerable success, winning the greatest number of seats and heading the first post-civil war government. This kind of sequenced approach, from peace negotiations to a democratically elected constituent assembly, was acceptable to the Maoists because they anticipated sufficient representation in the CA to drive their agenda. The CA elections also permitted a broad cross-section of political parties to field candidates and win seats, which had the effect of promoting political pluralism at the deliberation phase. However, these disparate groups could not reach the required degree of consensus after five years of deliberation, so the assembly was dissolved, new elections held, and its successor completed the job.

In India's northeast, this process of an "on ramp" from violent conflict to electoral contestation for rebel groups occurred in a number of stages, and with a focus on regional politics. It converted armed militants into stakeholders in political life as they achieved greater autonomy and promoted political stability. The Nagaland Peace Accord of 1947 carved the Naga Hills out of the state of Assam and made a Union Territory under central control, but with some local autonomy. In 1963, the government and Naga representatives negotiated a sixteen-point agreement that led to the creation of the Nagaland state in which former rebels competed in elections as a political party. While India is basically a symmetric federation (with limited exceptions for Kashmir and Goa), the government acceded to rebel demands for special autonomy on such subjects as religious and social practices, customary law, and ownership of land and resources; these accommodations were uncontroversial at the national level, largely because of the small population and remoteness of these regions. In parallel fashion, Tripura, Manipur, Mizoram, and Arunachal Pradesh acquired status first as Union territories, with little or no autonomy, as a stage before acquiring statehood—as part of a strategy to provide "on ramps" to politics for armed rebels. Meghalaya achieved autonomy within Assam, and then was granted statehood. "On ramps" may require locally specific accommodations for political competition. In Aceh, for example, the peace agreement provided for the right to organize local political parties, which was an exception to an Indonesia law that requires all political parties to have a national outlook; this enabled the Free Aceh Movement to become a political party.

The deliberative phase can also be broadened to promote political pluralism and the legitimacy of the process when there are elected governments—whether the antecedents of the constitutional moment are peaceful or violent; however, this too can pose issues and play out differently according to the institutional arrangements as well as the political context. In parliamentary systems, which operate on the basis of simple majorities, opposition parties could be excluded or marginalized if the government controls the legislature. To counteract this risk, most parliamentary constitutions require a supermajority for constitutional amendments, potentially giving opposition parties leverage. Semi-presidential regimes may have cohabitation, in which the President and the government hail from different political parties. While in principle cohabitation provides an opportunity for political pluralism, its potential to do so depends on political culture. In Sri Lanka during the 2003–08 process, notwithstanding cohabitation, the hyper-partisan nature of Sri Lanka's political party system acted as an impediment to building a cross-party consensus on the peace negotiations. The exclusion of the People's Alliance (PA) President Chandrika Kumaratanga from the negotiations conducted by United National Party (UNP) Prime Minister Ranil Wickremsinghe led her to dismiss three cabinet ministers and trigger early elections, which led to the collapse of the talks. Presidential systems present a genuinely hard case. In the Philippines, control of the Presidency and the Senate by different political parties has blocked the implementation of commitments made at the negotiating table—as occurred in 2015—even though the Bangsamoro agreed to this route because they thought the President could secure passage in the Senate. There is no easy solution to this difficulty.

Political leadership can be a major driver of inclusion and pluralism in deliberative processes when there is competitive, pluralistic politics. In Spain, given the objective of a successful transition to democracy, the outgoing Francoist parliament approved a democratic law on political reform, while a broad-cross section of parties, including those that had been excluded from politics, developed a broad consensus that kept the lid on partisanship during the critical transitional phase. By contrast, in Yemen, there was an absence of leadership in the wake of the fall of Saleh. The national dialogue, which conducted extensive consultations to address the Constitution did not engage the real power-holders in serious negotiations: Saleh was excluded in order to mark a sharp break from the past, and southern separatists boycotted the meetings; the Houthis played only a marginal role. Political tests of strength during a constitutional process, whether through elections or referendums, can create provide an occasion for greater inclusion in the debate and potentially shift the power positions of the players. In Bolivia, for example, the population was mobilized by elections, referendums, and street demonstrations in repeated tests of strength, which in turn shaped negotiating dynamics to the favor of Morales.

Forums and decision-rules: The options available for the forum for constitutional deliberations are a function of the nature of the constitutional moment—including political geometry, and whether the antecedents have been peaceful and legal or violent and extra-legal. Legal and institutional continuity can determine or constrain choices of forums as well as the decision-rules, whereas with rupture everything is to be decided.

Under legal and institutional continuity, the consideration of territorial claims occurs within existing provisions regarding constitutional amendment and the forum for deliberation. Most constitutions leave the power of constitutional amendment with the legislature voting with a supermajority, impliedly making it the deliberative body though some required ratification by referendum (and several federations require some level of approval by the legislatures or populations of the federal units). However, these legal rules rarely foreclose the creation of supplementary deliberative bodies, such as the constitutional commissions in Kenya or the state reorganization commission in India. In Bolivia, while Congress possessed the formal authority over constitutional amendment, it passed a law creating the Constituent Assembly (though in the end the process reverted to Congress).

While supermajorities are the norm for constitutional change, the UK is very much the outlier in requiring no more than a simple majority as part of the ordinary legislative process. Regional devolution occurred through ordinary statute, but there were political decisions to incorporate non-binding referendums into the process—first prior to the creation of the Scottish Parliament, and more recently on the question of Scottish independence. The threshold is also low in India; although a constitutional amendment is required to alter state boundaries and create new states, it can be enacted through a simple majority in the parliament (a state whose borders are changed is consulted but has no veto). In the other cases of legal continuity under study, Kenya required a double simple majority (legislative and referendum), and Spain required a supermajority in parliament and a simple majority in a referendum. In Bolivia, Congress had the power to amend the constitution, but there was a political agreement to hold a referendum to ratify.

When the antecedent of a constitutional moment is a stalemate in a regional insurgency or rebellion, the government will assert legal continuity for constitutional change, but this may channel deliberations into fora, such as the national parliament, where elected representatives representing the rebels would be too small to have any weight. In bilateral peace negotiations between rebels and the government, the failure to address this issue carefully may undermine the ratification or success of an agreement. In Indonesia, for example, the central government initially had the parliament, where representatives from Aceh and Papua had a minimal presence, enact autonomy laws unilaterally. These laws were unsuccessful in stemming armed struggle—even though for Aceh, the laws had some favorable terms, especially on resource revenues. By contrast, the 2006 Aceh autonomy law has been largely successful because its terms were spelled out in the negotiated peace agreement of 2005. So too in the Philippines, non-consensual, unilateral change has been unsuccessful. The adoption of the 1987 Constitution authorized Congress to enact legislation to create the autonomous regions, which it did in 1989 through a law setting up the Autonomous Region in Muslim Mindanao (ARMM). It did this over the objections of the Moro National Liberation Front (MNLF). The legislation required a referendum to determine the geographic scope of the ARMM, and the two big cities voted to stay out. Although the smaller region with limited powers won the support of some Moro politicians, it failed to satisfy Moro insurgents, and did not succeed. In 1996, there was a peace agreement with the MNLF, but in 2001 Congress acted unilaterally to enact legislation that only partially implemented it. Moreover, the government ousted the head of the

MNLF, which led the organization to split, and to a new round of violence. A later stage in the Philippines process illustrates a creative institutional solution for linking peace negotiations and the ordinary legislative process, providing a role to both regional minorities and to a broader set of statewide political elites within an overarching framework of legality. As part of the 2012 Framework Agreement on the Bangsamoro, the negotiating parties agreed to create the Bangsamoro Transition Commission, a hybrid body with 50/50 membership from the Moro Islamic Liberation Front (MILF) and the government which drafted legislation to implement the peace agreement to be adopted by Congress.

The initial and central forum for resolving a territorial insurgency becomes a bilateral table, government, and rebels, to negotiate peace and a constitutional settlement. But a single focus on the bilateral peace negotiations risks failure downstream in the process, when the normal procedures for constitutional review and deliberation and ratification must apply. There is a need, especially for governments, to consider how they will address all stages of the process. In the Philippines, the Supreme Court ruled that the 2008 Memorandum of Agreement on Ancestral Domain, negotiated by the government and MILF, was ruled unconstitutional by the Supreme Court because its terms promised to adopt any necessary constitutional amendments to implement it, whereas the power of constitutional amendment rested exclusively with Congress. In due course, the MILF entered into new negotiations and reluctantly opted to proceed by ordinary statute to avoid the difficulty in getting a constitutional amendment approved, given the very high threshold required. A hybrid body, with 50/50 government/MILF membership, drafted the Bangsamoro Basic Law, but legislative approval, which had seemed highly likely, was derailed in the Senate after a botched and very bloody government anti-terrorist raid.

Another example of the problems posed by institutional spoilers comes from Sri Lanka, where government backbenchers and opposition legislators challenged the constitutionality of an interim governing arrangement for LTTE-controlled areas (the P-TOMS), which was struck down by the Sri Lankan Supreme Court on the basis that the proposed entity's spending powers infringed on parliament's control of public finance. This decision ended any prospect of further cooperation between the parties. The different reactions of the LTTE and MILF to the respective court rulings—in Sri Lanka, ending negotiations, whereas in the Philippines, continuing to negotiate and search for alternative implementation mechanisms—may have reflected the very different political contexts: there was much greater polarization between the LTTE and the Sri Lankan political class than there was between the MILF and politicians in Manila. The Bangsamoro Basic Law probably would have passed had the bloody raid not soured the mood. There was never a strong prospect in Sri Lanka of an agreement, let alone one that would pass legal muster.

These examples show the potential challenges during constitutional moments posed by institutional spoilers, who have legitimate interest in the results of negotiations but can upset delicate negotiations because of their late involvement and negative opinions. The question is how to mitigate this risk. Legislators who must eventually implement an agreement could be brought into the negotiating process in some ways at the agenda-setting or deliberative stages, but this is a highly tactical matter that requires subtle political management. In the case of the courts, this is much harder, because they cannot be parties to negotiations. But the South African transition, which occurred under legal continuity, developed a creative option whereby the Interim Constitution created a new Constitutional Court, and an appointments procedure which ensured a court with judges acceptable to the major political parties. The

Constitutional Court was assigned the task of assessing the final constitutional text for compliance with the thirty-four Constitutional Principles agreed to by a multiparty consensus. The Constitutional Court was therefore an external judicial check on the constitutional process, and indeed, it found parts of the constitutional draft unconstitutional. However, because the Court was an institution of the transition, it conceived of its role as facilitating the adoption of a new constitutional order, a striking contrast to the regime-preserving mindsets of the Sri Lankan and Philippine courts. Of course, it may be more possible to adopt such a mechanism as part of a total constitutional overhaul than in dealing with a peripheral rebellion.

When a Constitution is being considered in a situation of complete legal and institutional rupture, as after large-scale civil wars, there may be no legal constraint on the choice of forums and decision-rules. The Dayton Peace Accord's constitutional premise was one of a complete break with the previous constitution, which opened the way for the Accords to be produced by a unique constitutional process, in which armed parties negotiated with direct international participation and yielded an agreement that simultaneously ended armed conflict and adopted a new Constitution within three weeks. Cyprus, where fighting stopped long ago in its "frozen conflict," resembles Bosnia-Herzegovina in that negotiations over a formal end to the civil war are tied to those for a new constitutional settlement, though they have had to deal creatively with the Greek Cypriot view that there is continuity of the state (not of the constitution) and the Turkish Cypriot view that two sovereignties are being brought together.

In most civil wars, the transition from civil war, to ceasefire, peace agreement, and Constitution takes place over an extended period. If the previous state has collapsed or the government lacks any effective presence and/or legitimacy, there is often a need to create provisional governing arrangements during the period in which longer-term Constitution-making process can occur. These provisional arrangements, whose negotiation will have been largely elite led, may be set out in an interim Constitution or other document that creates transitional governing institutions, determines their membership, defines decision-making procedures and establishes a Constitution-making process. Interim constitutions may set out these provisional arrangements in situations where at least the form of legal continuity is maintained, but where the existing regime is so tainted and weakened that it cannot continue even during an interim period. In such cases, interim constitutions occupy a middle ground between legal continuity and discontinuity. In South Africa, the transition from the old order to an interim Constitution preserved legal continuity but fundamentally changed the regime by providing for universal suffrage elections to a Constitutional Assembly and a power-sharing executive that would have carriage of the constitutional process. The story was similar in Nepal.

Interim constitutions can create path dependencies, substantive and procedural, for the shape of a more permanent constitution. Substantively, they can provide substantive baselines for negotiations over the final constitution. The right to self-determination in Ethiopia's Charter carried over to Article 39 of the 1995 constitution. Iraq's Transitional Administrative Law recognized Kurdish autonomy and created a procedure for ratifying a new Constitution by referendum that effectively gave the Kurdish region a veto, and thus set a baseline for Kurdish autonomy under the permanent constitution.

Procedurally, interim government arrangements that are inclusive can generate buy-in to the Constitution-making process and build trust among political opponents. Ethiopia illustrates the risks of rejecting an inclusive interim government. The victors in the civil war were a coalition led by the Ethiopian People's Revolutionary Democratic

Front (EPDRF) that included other parties, such as the Oromo Liberation Front (OLF). These parties formed the power-sharing Transitional Government of Ethiopia (TGE). However, the TGE ended with a disagreement over the timing of elections, with the EPRDF for early elections while the OLF demanded a delay to prepare. The elections proceeded, which led the OLF to withdraw and relaunch the civil war. The drafting of the Constitution was largely determined by the inner circle of EPDRF leaders, with a compliant constitutional convention providing formal review and ratification. The OLF did not support the constitution, and while weakened militarily it continued a low-level insurgency that has ended only very recently, with the new openness of the Ethiopian government to opposition groups. Conversely, South Africa illustrates the value of a power-sharing interim government for the success of a constitution-making process. Both the National Party and the Inkatha Freedom Party (representing Zulus) were represented in the cabinet, participated in the constitutional process, and supported the final constitutional text even though they were not able to achieve all of their goals.

Constitutional assemblies: Elected constitutional assemblies are often central to major Constitution-making processes. They are two kinds of constitutional assemblies. First, there are specialist constitutional assemblies with no ordinary legislative responsibilities which are elected as part of a specific constitutional reform process, at the end of which they permanently dissolve. Their appeal largely lies in the theory, which is questionable, that they may be put above ordinary politics and beyond the control of political parties (e.g., if political parties are expressly excluded from fielding candidates). Second, there are dual-purpose elected constitutional assemblies that simultaneously serve as legislatures. These bodies are also created as part of a specific constitutional reform process and are almost always elected in a public campaign where the constitutional agenda is the main or a central issue. Political parties openly field candidates and operate according to the conventions of government and opposition (though there may be a broad-based government). After the Constitution comes into force, this body may become an ordinary legislature exercising power under the constitution. (And, indeed, in many countries the legislature is a kind of standing constitutional assembly, *sans le nom*.)

A specialist constitutional assembly was elected in Bolivia (alongside the existing legislature, and named the Constituent Assembly) and dual-purpose constitutional assemblies were elected in India (as part of the lead-up to independence), Iraq, Nepal, South Africa, and Spain. There can also be alternatives to elected or fully elected constitutional assemblies. The Bomas process in Kenya used a hybrid body that brought together parliamentarians with non-politicians. A constitutional assembly has been proposed by some civil society organizations for Nigeria. Yemen opted for a national dialogue, which had many of the features of a specialist constitutional assembly in that it was meant to draft guidelines for a new constitution. As these examples illustrate, constitutional assemblies may be used in cases of regional movements mobilizing non-violently through institutionalized channels (India, Spain) and politically salient cleavages that are both territorial and non-territorial (Bolivia, Iraq, Kenya, Nepal, South Africa, Yemen). As well, they can be used as part of peaceful democratic politics (Bolivia, Kenya, Spain) or following civil war stalemates (Iraq, Nepal, South Africa), and ethnic political mobilization with both territorial and non-territorial dimensions through non-violent means (Kenya, South Africa). They are not useful for addressing peripheral rebellions, because of the small relative population of the region in question. In Bosnia elite (and foreign) driven peace negotiations and constitutional negotiations occurred simultaneously, which precluded a constitutional assembly, while in Cyprus the negotiations are led by the heads of the two elected governments, with ratification subject to approval in parallel referendums. These latter cases suggest that constituent assemblies may be particularly difficult in dealing with contexts of a majority dealing with a large, territorially based minority.

The main argument made by proponents of specialist constitutional assemblies is to guard against the risks of institutional self-interest and self-replication that may occur in a body that is dominated by political parties.[25] However, there are good reasons to be skeptical of this argument. As a practical matter it is difficult to keep parties out of politics and their buy-in will be necessary for implementation. And comparative experience highlights that the unlimited mandate of constitutional assemblies can fall prey to abuse. As Andrew Arato observes, "[v]ery often . . . the constituent [i.e. constitutional] assembly turned out to be a mere instrument for whatever force was able to convene it."[26] In Latin America and the former Soviet Union, for example, presidents have convened constitutional assemblies for partisan ends, in order to wrest control of the Constitution-making process from legislatures controlled by opposition parties. Urged on by the executive, these constitutional assemblies have also inferred from their unlimited constitution-making powers the authority to exercise plenary power unrestrained by any constitutional limitations. They have seized legislative powers and reconstituted other institutions at will and have expanded executive and shrunk legislative powers. Sometimes, presidents have used plebiscites to ratify a Constitution produced by a constituent assembly to provide democratic legitimacy. Usurpation is motivated by narrow political ends, not high-minded constitutional principle. Venezuela is the most recent illustration of these risks.

These experiences suggest the need for caution regarding the role of specialist constitutional assemblies, especially in the context of territorial cleavages, which are in large part claims for the dispersal of centralized public power. Bolivia is a cautionary tale. The Constituent Assembly (CA) was created by legislation that was the result of a compromise between the Movimiento al Socialismo (MAS), which favored a centralized regime, and Poder Democratico Social (PODEMOS), which advocated regional autonomy. Each party controlled a chamber of Congress, making agreement on regional autonomy and on any broader constitutional reform difficult, so they opted for a CA that could only approve a new Constitution by a two-thirds majority. The CA was obliged to create a framework for regional autonomy, which departments had already opted into via referendum. It was far from non-partisan, and although MAS won a majority in the CA, it fell short of the supermajority. The CA became deadlocked, which led MAS to argue that the CA had unlimited constituent authority to make decisions by a simple majority, and thus to overturn the two-thirds voting requirement. This led PODEMOS to walk out of the CA. MAS then used its control of the CA to draft a Constitution and then attempt to take it to a referendum, but this was blocked when the Electoral Court held that any referendum required Congressional assent. Given the risk of civil war, Bolivia's neighbors intervened with an offer of mediation. The parties went back to the negotiating table, and Congress (not the CA) ultimately approved a new constitution, which passed by 60 percent in a national referendum.

In Ukraine the instrument of usurpation was a constitutional commission. The politics of constitutional reform shifted with President Kuchma's reversal of his former support for federalism, and his attempts to build a coalition of western Ukrainophiles

[25] Jon Elster, "Legislatures as Constituent Assemblies" in Richard Bauman and Tsvi Kahana (eds), *The Least Examined Branch: The Role of Legislatures in the Constitutional State* (Cambridge University Press 2006).

[26] Andrew Arato, "Conventions, Constituent Assemblies, and Round Tables: Models, Principles and Elements of Democratic Constitution-Making" (2012) 1 (1) Global Constitutionalism 173, 183.

and eastern economic interests in favor of strong centralization. He took control of the stalled constitution-making process by creating a commission that would support his views and threatened a consultative referendum on confidence in himself and the unpopular parliament if parliament did not agree. Parliament yielded and approved a temporary constitutional agreement for a year. Kuchma then created yet another commission, even more submissive to him, which produced a draft Constitution that was strongly presidential and widely opposed by political parties. Again, the president threatened to put this draft to a referendum; the parliament buckled in the face of this pressure and approved it by an overwhelming vote in a marathon session.

The purported defect of a dual-purpose constitutional assembly—that it vests a primary role for Constitution-making with the same political parties that will wield power under the constitution—may in fact be a strength. As Nathan Brown has argued, a Constitution-making process that excludes elites may ultimately be counterproductive, because it is those elites who will operate the gears of the constitutional democracy created and can undermine it from within.[27] Conversely, allowing political parties to bargain around self-interest favors the stability of the resulting constitution, whose framework they will see as being more advantageous than the alternatives of force and fraud. Even when a Constitution has been adopted in a referendum, if political leaders do not buy into it, they may not implement it. A vivid example is Iraq, where the hastily drafted and incomplete Constitution was approved by a referendum in October 2005. However, its provisions on federalism are unimplemented because most Arab political leaders, who dominate the central government, felt no ownership of the constitution-making process and resent the extensive autonomy of the Kurdish region, the provisions on federalizing the Arab areas, the call for a referendum on Kirkuk, and the provisions on oil and gas.

The Bomas process established in 2000 in Kenya provides another example of the potential risks of excluding political elites from Constitution-making. Public consultation and the initial preparation of a constitutional draft was overseen by the arm's length and largely non-partisan Constitution of Kenya Review Commission. This draft was then referred to a hybrid body, the National Constitutional Conference (NCC), with members drawn from the legislature, the districts, political parties, and civil society, which was to review, potentially amend and adopt the commission's draft and transmit it to Parliament. Parliament was then to vote on it without amendment, with a two-thirds majority required for approval. This arrangement was not sustainable because the earlier phases had not satisfactorily accommodated the views of the political parties, which used their control of the final, parliamentary step to make substantial revisions to the draft. This draft was rejected in a referendum in 2005 that was in many ways a plebiscite on the president. The subsequent Kenyan constitutional process set up a Committee of Experts in 2008 to work directly with Parliament via a Parliamentary Select Committee; this draft passed in a referendum in 2010. Yemen provides another example of the same problem because the national dialogue failed to engage, at least directly, the most important actors in the country. The members of this large body were in many cases non-partisan, but they were loosely organized and not truly capable of negotiating on difficult subjects. Those who were affiliated with political parties or interests had leaders who were pulling strings from outside and often trying to obstruct agreement. In the absence of elections, it was difficult to determine who could really speak for different parts of the population, but at no point did the major leaders come together with a view to negotiating.

[27] Nathan Brown, "Reason, Interest, Rationality & Passion in Constitution Drafting" (2008) 6 (4) Perspectives on Politics 675.

A crucial issue for regional and political minorities advancing claims in a dual-purpose assembly is to avoid majoritarian decision-making that disregards the wishes of regional minorities. For example, in the context of a civil war stalemate in Iraq, the Constitution Drafting Committee of the National Assembly acted on the basis of a simple majority, which meant that the views of the Kurds who were consistently outvoted. The Americans intervened and took control of the process, which gave the Kurds, who already had a well-established regional government, considerable weight in the final draft constitution. The most obvious and powerful tool for protecting minority interests in a constitutional assembly is to require supermajority agreement—such as through a two-thirds threshold, as was used in Bolivia, Nepal, Spain, and South Africa. But supermajority requirements increase the risk of deadlock, as happened for a time in both Bolivia and Nepal, which can be highly destabilizing in a major transitional context. And minorities may still be outvoted even when there is a super-majority requirement, as happened in Nepal, where the Madhesi and Tharus were marginalized.

There can be mechanisms to overcome deliberative deadlock set down in a Constitution or in an interim agreement. In India, if the upper house rejects a decision of the lower house, it may be resolved by a joint sitting. In Spain, under the post-Franco 1978 Constitution, constitutional amendments normally require 60 percent in both houses, but if the Senate falls short of this threshold, an amendment may be approved by two-thirds in the lower house and a simple majority in the Senate (with a referendum if requested by one tenth of the members of either chamber). For fundamental amendments to the first section of the Constitution, a two-thirds majority is required in each chamber, followed by a mandatory referendum.

South Africa's Interim Constitution provided that in the event the Constituent Assembly could not reach the supermajority of two-thirds, a simple majority in the assembly could submit a draft to referendum with a 60 percent approval threshold; if that referendum failed, there would be elections for a new assembly. In Cyprus, the two sides had trouble agreeing on substance so the UN Secretary General was mandated to prepare a proposal for submission to parallel referendums (which failed in the Greek Cypriot community). In cases where deadlock-breaking mechanisms have not been spelled out in advance, it has fallen to the courts to craft a solution, which may be to turn matters over to the electorate. In Nepal, the Supreme Court dissolved the deadlocked Constituent Assembly after a constitutionally imposed deadline had been extended four times; the new elections changed the composition of the Constituent Assembly, which finally succeed in meeting the two-thirds threshold. In Bolivia, the Electoral Court ruled some proposed referendums unconstitutional, but held that Congress could enact referendum legislation, which it eventually did as part of a constitutional settlement. In effect, the court remanded the issue to Congress, which would have faced the electorate on a fixed timetable had it not resolved the issue.

While there are challenges in Constitution-making processes in achieving a broad-based consensus that includes territorial minorities and other minorities, there can occasionally be risks in the other direction, when somehow a majority has been marginalized in a constitutional settlement. Arguably this happened in Iraq. During the early stages of the process, the minority Kurds were consistently outvoted by simple majority in the Constitution Drafting Committee. However, the National Assembly failed to meet the deadline for an agreed Constitution imposed by the occupying powers, so the Americans short-circuited the legal process and transferred the drafting to an informal body called the "Leadership Council," an opaque group that met at the US Embassy and Kurdish Region's headquarters in Baghdad. The Kurds had outsized influence in this process, which excluded a large segment of Iraq's political class. As a result, Shia political elites have refused to implement many key terms on federalism, as explained earlier.

Scotland offers another example. When the "Yes" side in the Scottish independence referendum appeared to be on the cusp of victory, the leaders of the UK-wide unionist parties made a collective "vow" to implement greater devolution if independence was rejected. The "No" side prevailed, and the British government set up an independent commission, which recommended how to proceed, but with little consultation with either the British or Scottish parliaments or publics. The British government introduced legislation to implement the report, which recommended extensive new powers for Scotland, and this legislation passed but with little deliberation, especially in the UK outside Scotland. A House of Lords committee has described the "haphazard approach to the United Kingdom's constitution" in devolving powers "piecemeal" to Scotland, Wales, and Northern Ireland.[28] The lack of broadly based buy-in from the political majority has left unresolved issues, notably the continuing controversy over the role of Scottish MPs in the British Parliament.

Ratification

The final stage of a constitutional process, ratification, is usually separate in time from agenda-setting and deliberation, though as we have seen, the decision-rules for ratification can very much influence the preceding process. When there is constitutional continuity, the ratification of a constitutional amendment by a legislature typically requires a supermajority, as opposed to the simple majority needed for ordinary legislation. Some ratification procedures end when the national legislature or constitutional assembly has voted in the required numbers (if necessary by recourse to the deadlock breaking mechanisms described above). Other procedures give the final say to the electorate in a referendum: in these cases, the legislature may be able to approve a draft by a simple majority, with final ratification then requiring a majority in the referendum. Several federations also require the consent of some proportion of regional legislatures or populations (by referendum); examples in our cases include Nigeria (two-thirds of state legislatures) and South Africa (two-thirds of provinces for fundamental provisions and changes affecting their boundaries or powers), but these rules were not operative during the constitutional moments examined. For most constitutional amendments (though not changes in state boundaries or the creation of new states) India requires a two-thirds majority in both houses of parliament, of which the upper house is indirectly elected by the states, so the states have an indirect role in amendment through this mechanism, which has applied to the creation of new states.

In both Nepal and South Africa the outgoing regimes wished to maintain legal continuity, but a constitutional process based on the old Constitution was unacceptable to the Maoists and ANC respectively, and the compromise was an interim constitution. A critical issue at the agenda-setting stage was to negotiate the provisions in the interim Constitution for the ratification of a new constitution. In Nepal, the Constituent Assembly could ratify the Constitution by a two-thirds vote, but there was also a constitutional commitment to making decisions by "consensus." In the final stages of the Nepali process, there was major tension over whether ratification could proceed based on a two-thirds vote or whether there should in addition be consensus. Legally, the former was applicable, but the constitutional reference to consensus weakened the

[28] Select Committee on the Constitution, *The Union and Devolution* (HL 2015–16, 149-X) 3.

legitimacy of the two-thirds rule, which was opposed in major demonstrations by the Madhesis and Tharus, who did win some minor concessions. In South Africa, the constitutional assembly could ratify by a two-thirds majority, but failing that, a majority could approve a draft that would then be submitted to referendum, where 60 percent approval would be required. In the event, the ANC, which was short of two-thirds of the votes in the assembly, compromised with the National Party and the Inkatha Freedom Party to get over the two-thirds threshold. South Africa was also unique in the role given to its new Constitutional Court regarding ratification. The Court was empowered to review a draft constitution, which to be put to a final vote was required to conform with the thirty-four fundamental constitutional principles that had been established at the outset of the process; its judgment required important changes to the original draft.

Ratification is a whole different matter when there has been legal rupture, in that those who have the power can decide on the rules. The Nigerian military passed power to civilians through a Constitution that had no approval by an elected legislature or referendum. That is extreme, in that even victors in a civil war normally try to cloak a new Constitution with some kind of popular legitimacy, as the EPDRF did with its pliant Constitutional Assembly in Ethiopia. Another extreme case, also lacking in any normal legitimacy, was the Dayton Agreement, where the Americans basically drove the process and the principals to the negotiation, the presidents of Croatia and Serbia, did not hold office in Bosnia-Herzegovina. The Constitution was an annex to the peace agreement with no further process for ratification. However, even in such cases of arguably illegitimate constitutions, the politicians who are meant operate within the new regime must decide whether or not to respect it or risk system breakdown. In Bosnia-Herzegovina, local politicians have certainly tested the limits of the regime, while in Nigeria the Constitution of 2001 has been respected, despite its perceived illegitimacy—mainly because there is no viable option. The procedure for ratification in Iraq was also essentially imposed by the occupying Americans, and consisted of approval by the transitional National Assembly and then a national referendum vote. Ratification in the referendum required a national majority, but would fail if more than two-thirds of registered voters in more than two governorates voted no. This latter rule was an interesting device, originally designed to protect the Kurdish minority, which in the end voted for the Constitution (partially because they had so much influence over it), but it was the Sunni-majority governorates that almost torpedoed ratification (in two, more than two-thirds voted no, and in one more the threshold was almost met).

A referendum is the most inclusive approach to ratification and it provides the whole public with a chance to pronounce on a draft Constitution (or amendment) prepared by their representatives. A positive result in a referendum can add to the legitimacy of constitutional change, and this was the result in Bolivia and Spain, as well as in Kenya in 2010. However, there are risks to taking this step, especially in polarized situations where the Constitution contains difficult and controversial compromises. For example, in Bolivia, although a statewide majority approved the new Constitution in 2009, majorities within each pro-autonomy department rejected it. In Cyprus, the Annan Plan was subject to two parallel referendums, one in each community, and was rejected by Greek Cypriots, so the frozen conflict continues (with renewed attempts at negotiation). Of course, a negative vote in a referendum may prove salutary. In Kenya, voters in the constitutional referendum in 2005 rejected the draft, partly because of its content, but equally because of opposition to then-president. Most Kenyans would agree the defeat led to a better process and content in 2010, when a Constitution was approved by referendum.

Referendums are sometimes not for formal ratification of a draft Constitution or amendment, but serve as tests of public opinion. This was true in Scotland, where voters rejected independence in a referendum that had no legal status but was accepted as decisive politically. In Bolivia, national and local referendums were used as tests of strength (along with elections) in the contest over the country's constitutional form; these eventually set the context for the final negotiations and the ratification of the new Constitution by referendum. In Ukraine, President Kuchma's threats to hold consultative, non-binding referendums, which public opinion polls suggested he would win, gave him decisive leverage in forcing the Rada to adopt his constitutional proposals. Of course, elections, whether to constitutional assemblies or normal parliaments, are the normal field of political battle in democracies. They can critically influence the course of a constitutional process, as happened in Nepal, when new elections broke the logjam in producing a Constitutional Assembly that was able to reach the two-thirds necessary to ratify a constitution, after the previous Constitutional Assembly could not over many years.

There can also be important post-ratification steps for the full implementation of a constitutional settlement. In Spain, for example, the new Autonomous Communities (AC) had to be created, which in cases of mergers of provinces was done by votes of municipal councilors, and in a few cases by local referendum. Moreover, each AC needed to negotiate its Autonomy Statute, which then was ratified by legislatures both national and regional. A tough negotiating issue in the settlement on Bangsamoro related to the use of referendums at the implementation stage to determine the exact boundaries of the new territory.

While our case studies all involve the possible constitutional accommodation of territorial cleavages in some manner, very few recent Constitutions (in contrast to those in many established federations) give a formal, constitutional role to territorial representatives or populations in ratifying constitutional change. The Iraqi referendum rule stands out as an exception, as does the requirement that both communities in Cyprus ratify a new Constitution by referendum. In South Africa, the Interim Constitution required a two-thirds majority in the Senate (whose members are nominated by provincial legislatures) for changes affecting the powers and boundaries of provinces. The British government's acceptance of the legitimacy of a Scottish referendum on independence as a binding expression of opinion falls short of formal ratification, but certainly gives a decisive voice to the regional population. Similarly, the negotiation of settlements with insurgents in peripheral territories in northeast India, Aceh, and Mindanao gave these representatives a central role on the substance of agreements, but none in their formal ratification (which in the Philippines proved hostage to politics in Congress).

Supermajority rules can sometimes give significant political leverage to territorial minorities around the ratification of a Constitution, as happened in South Africa and Spain. However, these rules are not normally equivalent to a power of veto by a regional minority. In Nepal, the aim to achieve consensus prolonged the process but eventually gave way to a two-thirds majority overriding strong objections, notably from the Madhesis, who vociferously objected to the new provincial map. They eventually got some minor revisions, but far short of their goal. In Yemen, the national dialogue could not resolve the number and boundaries of the new regions, so the president created a mechanism to approve his preferred option, which both the Houthis and the Southern movement rejected. This was a key factor in the outbreak of civil war.

In summary, ratification rules as the end point of a constitutional process are fundamental for shaping the preceding events and for the legitimacy or acceptance of the eventual result. The principal parties may be constrained by the ratification rules, but in cases of state collapse, or even in cases of total regime change within a context of constitutional continuity, the lead actors may be able to determine or shape the rules of ratification. While some constitutions are virtually imposed by victors in a civil war or powerful outside actors, with little concern for popular legitimacy, in most cases there is a process in which elected representatives and possibly the electorate through a referendum are empowered to ratify constitutional change in a specified manner. However, it is rare, even in cases where the territorial issue is central, for a ratification procedure to guarantee territorial minorities a determining role in ratification. It may be that they can use their political leverage to promote their interests, but it is unlikely that the formal ratification procedure will suffice on its own.

Constitutional Design and Territorial Cleavages

Constitutional moments and constitutional design

A key test of constitutional designs or innovations is how well they function, which means how appropriate the design is to the context.[29] Even initially contested designs may come to be accepted if they function well, but this is not a static matter because the underlying politics of a country change with time. And while design does matter, the history of a Constitution-making process can also have lasting effects in terms of how different groups view the legitimacy of the outcome. There are often powerful political imperatives to develop "permanent" Constitutions, not least in conflict-inflicted countries; while the processes of making such Constitutions can take more or less time and be done in different ways, there comes a point when a new Constitution is deemed to be operational and that becomes a fact with its own consequences.

There are three major constitutional design options to respond to claims for the accommodation of territorial cleavages. The applicability of each option has a presumptive logic, most closely related to the underlying political geometry. These logics can be summarized briefly:

- *Symmetrical federalism or devolution with a majoritarian central government*: Symmetrical federalism or devolution is a common form of government covering many varieties and degrees of decentralization, and should be considered carefully in countries whose political geometry is highly territorialized, such as Ethiopia, India, Nigeria, and Spain, but also to those with a mix of territorial and other cleavages, such as Bolivia, Kenya, Nepal, and South Africa. (Moreover, symmetrical federalism may be combined with special autonomy arrangements for smaller units, as discussed below—with the leading example being India.)

[29] In general, see Sujit Choudhry (ed), *Constitutional Design in Divided Societies: Integration or Accommodation?* (Oxford University Press 2008); Yash Ghai and Sophia Woodman (eds), *Practising Self-Government* (Cambridge University Press 2013); Donald Horowitz, *Ethnic Groups in Conflict* 2nd edn (University of California Press, 2000); Arend Lijphart, *Democracy in Plural Societies: A Comparative Exploration* (Yale University Press 1977); John McGarry and Brendan O'Leary, *The Northern Ireland Conflict: Consociational Engagements* (Oxford University Press 2004); Andrew Reynolds (ed), *The Architecture of Democracy: Constitutional Design, Conflict Management and Democracy* (Oxford University Press 2002).

The major design issues include the number and boundaries of the constituent units, the protection of minority rights (nationally and within constituent units), territorial representation within central institution (notably upper houses), the form of the legislature and executive, and the extent of devolution of powers. The political dynamics when there are multiple cleavages can be quite fluid, with governing coalitions varying over time, potentially limiting how often any group or territory is routinely excluded from power. In these circumstances, majoritarian government at the center is broadly accepted, but upper houses often give extra weight to representatives of small territorial units. Iraq and Yemen are hard to place. In principle, Iraq opted for symmetrical federalism, but the design was incoherent and has never been implemented, so the Kurdish region effectively has special autonomy. Yemen failed to agree on a constitution, but the design considered provided symmetrical devolution to six regions and twenty-one governorates, while providing special power-sharing between northern and southern representatives within the legislature.

- *Highly devolved federal government with a consociational central government*: This difficult institutional arrangement is sometimes chosen when the political geometry is of two (or sometimes three, as in Bosnia-Herzegovina) antagonistic and territorially separate communities that must cohabit within a single state. Typically, there is a majority and a minority community and the latter must be of significant size for this option to be considered. Mutual mistrust can push the communities to prefer maximum devolution or self-government for each community, but some important functions inevitably remain with the central government, for which the communities may turn to power-sharing or consociational arrangements. Consociational government is particular form of power-sharing in which the agreement of a majority of representatives of each community is necessary for certain specified, major decisions. Belgium has a highly developed form of consociational federalism. Yemen's regional character led the constitutional drafters to provide for symmetrical devolution to six (not two) regions (plus twenty-one governorates), but its north-south division was accommodated by special power-sharing within the national legislature. In principle, both parties in Cyprus agree on that a solution should have this form, but they have been unable to resolve the details, which shows the difficulties of negotiating such an arrangement, even when it appears necessary.
- *Special autonomy for territories in a federal or non-federal state with a majoritarian central government*: This option is most appropriate in cases where the political geometry includes very small, peripheral territorial populations with a strong sense of distinct identity (and often of grievance). The national majority may resist claims by such groups for special autonomy for ideological reasons, but as a practical matter such arrangements can work well if the population is very small relative to the total population, as in Aceh or northeastern India, or if the extent of special status is not too extensive. Special autonomy can be more problematic, as in Scotland, when the population is relatively large and the devolution very extensive. The Minsk agreement foresees this option for the districts in Donbas that are not government controlled, but this idea is strongly resisted by many from western Ukraine. Special autonomy might have made sense for the northern province in Sri Lanka, but it was never the focus of negotiations and has been foreclosed by the military defeat of the LTTE.

Of course, there are alternatives to these three options, even when a country is highly territorialized or has strong claims for autonomy in some regions. One is a centralized, unitary regime in which there is little or no accommodation of territorial cleavages, and possibly an attempt to assimilate minorities. And another is secession, where the breakup of the state is accepted as preferable to a difficult cohabitation.[30] Secession was the avowed aim of rebels in India, Indonesia, the Philippines, and Sri Lanka, but they were forced to settle for less. Majorities can often favor a strong, indivisible "nation" and resist options for devolving or sharing powers. As well, countries can sometimes have features of more than one of our basic types so that one than one architectural option is at least conceptually possible. Thus, there is no inevitability that the apparently most appropriate model for territorial accommodation will be adopted: that will depend on the details of political geometry and the relative strength and ideologies of the key players. Moreover, when a country is riven by particularly deep, territorially based conflicts, it may be that there is no constitutional design option that will produce relatively functional and sustainable democratic politics.

A common thread to these constitutional models is whether to devolve government—and if so, how. There is no shortage of failed federations, some of which were cobbled together by imperial powers as they exited their colonies[31] and others emerged from the collapse of communism. The more optimistic view is that federalism "does not guarantee 'success', but it is hard to see any form of successful accommodation of multiple nations within a single state that does not include federalism."[32] There is a vast literature on the strengths and possible weaknesses of federalism, as well as the conditions that influence its success or sustainability, which we do not review here. Rather, we address three cross-cutting issues that arise out of our exploration of the nexus between mobilization, process, and design.

First, politics is about power, and devolution or federalism is an important way to diffuse power. Understood this way, while devolution or federalism is the main way to respond to demands for territorial constitutional accommodation, it can also respond to other demands for inclusion. Federalism or devolution, for example, promotes political pluralism and the diffusion of access to power by allowing political parties that lose power in central institutions to contest and potentially win at the subnational level, where they can have executive authority over local matters and the advantages of incumbency to pursue their interests in national politics. As well, devolution or federalism expands the institutional opportunities for citizens to participate in democratic self-government. Democratic theorists since Madison have long argued that federalism promotes democracy, because it brings government closer to the people.

Second, devolution can also pose its own problems or challenges. The devolution of some powers can pose issues for the coherence or effectiveness of governmental policy and for the mobility of citizens, goods, and services. This is why a number of federations, such as South Africa, have opted for German-style federalism, with a heavy emphasis on concurrent powers in which the central government has paramountcy.

[30] Thomas Chapman and Philip G Roeder have found secession emerges as a better solution than the alternatives in avoiding future conflict, in Thomas Chapman and Philip G Roeder, "Partition as a Solution to Wars of Nationalism: The Importance of Institutions" (2007) 101 (4) American Political Science Review 677. Of course, this option is often refused by the international community or a national government.

[31] Ursula Hicks, *Federalism: Failure and Success: A Comparative Study* (Macmillan 1978).

[32] Richard Simeon and Daniel-Patrick Conway, "Federalism and the Management of Conflict in Multinational Societies" in Alain-G Gagnon and James Tully (eds), *Multinational Democracies* (Cambridge University Press 2001) 362. Bermeo argues along the same lines.

However, this can result in federal legislation that is so detailed that it reduces the role of constituent units largely to administration in areas of concurrent jurisdiction. Another risk with federalism, especially when it is largely ethnic or linguistic in the design of the territorial units, is that minorities within these territories may have little effective political voice and be subject to various forms of discrimination. This risk can be mitigated in various ways, including constitutionalizing minority rights, affirmative action, and local autonomy where these minorities form the majority. But such mitigation requires a positive context of goodwill and effective institutions, such as courts, to protect minorities. In sum, there are major issues in the precise design of a devolved or federal system.

There can be bitter debates about the appropriate constitutional model for a country, which can make it difficult to predict the architectural model chosen. Majorities may see options such as devolution and power-sharing as concessions to minorities that weaken national unity, undermine national sovereignty, violate basic principles and symbols, and, potentially threaten territorial integrity by paving the way to secession. Proponents of these options may counter that concessions are the only way to secure national unity. Moreover, when a country is riven by particularly deep territorially based conflicts, it may be that there is no constitutional design option that will produce relatively functional and sustainable democratic politics. As Simeon and Conway have observed, "federalism is predicated on the existence of 'nested identities,' the ability to maintain dual loyalties" and its effectiveness is contingent and depends on the interaction between institutions and society.[33] This challenge exists for any institutional model that tries to accommodate deep cleavages and antagonisms within a single country.

Symmetrical federalism or devolution with a majoritarian central government

Most federal and devolved systems are essentially symmetrical in that the territorial sub-units have the same powers and responsibilities and their national institutions are essentially majoritarian in design.[34] This system seems suitable for countries that are highly territorialized with several salient regions, such as India and Spain, and to those where there is a mix of territorial and non-territorial cleavages, such as Kenya or South Africa. Key design issues within this model are the number and boundaries of the constituent units, the type of central legislature and executive, the upper house, the electoral system, and the allocation of powers and fiscal resources between orders of government.

Of these design issues, the determination of the number and boundaries of the constituent units was a major issue in several of our cases (though in some cases this is essentially an historic given),[35] notably Bosnia-Herzegovina, Ethiopia, India, Kenya, Nepal, Nigeria, South Africa, Spain, and Yemen. The criteria for forming sub-units can include historic boundaries, sociocultural identities, economics, administrative efficiency, geographic features such as rivers and mountains, the desired number or size

[33] ibid 339, 361.

[34] Of course, at the municipal level this is not true: there are often quite different powers assigned to municipalities depending on their size. Similarly, in a few federations there are still territories with very small populations that have lesser powers.

[35] See George Anderson, *Creation of Constituent Units in Federal Systems* ("Meeting the Challenges of Emerging Constitutional Democracy" Working Paper Series, Center for Constitutional Transitions 2014) <www.constitutionaltransitions.org/publications/creation-of-constituent-units-in-federal-systems/>.

of units, and, inevitably, political pressure. In Spain and South Africa, the approaches to creating units was largely successful. The redesign of the political maps of India and Nigeria has also been positive for stability and political dynamics, but there are still pressures for more states. In Nepal, the strong dissatisfaction among the Madhesi over their failure to get a single province poses a significant political challenge, but a single Madhesi province with 40 percent of the population could prove even more destabilizing. In Yemen the proposed regional boundaries in the north were a virtual *casus belli* for the Houthis, while the Southern Movement was hostile to the proposal for two regions in the south.

Most highly territorialized countries have more than one level of territorial cleavages—for example, the territories of big confederated tribes versus smaller sub-tribes—and this can provide an element of choice in drawing the political map, especially in relation to dealing with sociocultural identities, such as ethnicity, language, and religion, which are all potentially very symbolic and politically volatile. Ethiopia, India, Nigeria, and Spain are sometimes viewed as "ethno-federations," because territorially based ethnic political mobilization has been at the root of demands for constitutional accommodation and has been important in determining unit boundaries. However, these countries have taken different approaches. In some cases, ethnic boundaries largely align with subunit boundaries. In India, the leaders of the independence movement feared for its unity and put off addressing the call for linguistically based states. But within a few years India proceeded with a fundamental state reorganization, which largely ceded to the call for linguistically defined states and this has progressed further over time. To be sure, with more than 100 languages, twenty-two of which are listed in a schedule to the Constitution, India has not created a state for every territorially concentrated linguistic group. But the earlier fears of linguistically based states proved largely unfounded in India; their creation helped bring government closer to the population and the dynamics of national politics remained fluid in terms of political alignments given that there were several states. In Spain, virtually everyone can speak the national language, but the three "historic nationalities," which have their own languages and represent over a quarter of the population, harbored strong grievances about their treatment under the Franco regime. These regions led the push for major devolution, but the view was that the fifty provinces were too numerous to be the principal units of a quasi-federal regime based on Autonomous Communities (ACs). So the historic nationalities were guaranteed AC status, whereas most Spanish-speaking provinces of the mainland were required to amalgamate to reduce the total number of units to 17.

By contrast, in Nigeria, sub-unit boundaries have been designed to break up the major cleavages. Nigeria's original three federal states each embraced a major tribe and language—Hausa, Yoruba, and Igbo—as well as many smaller tribes and sub-tribes. The political dynamics were dysfunctional, especially because the northern state had a majority of the population. After the army coup and war in Biafra, the generals, who showed themselves very sensitive to the politics of state creation, moved to restructure the federation into an eventual thirty-six states. Most of these have a dominant tribe and language, but this sub-unit design has tried to breakup the cleavages among the three major populations that were so destabilizing for the country's politics. The chosen design of Kenya's new devolution is somewhat similar. Kenya has some forty to sixty ethnic groups and three or four major tribes. Its politics have been heavily tribal, especially around the few large tribes, but there is no neat territorial division, especially among its largest tribes. Given the history of tribal rivalry and conflict, politicians feared a political map that would reinforce tribal tensions. In its constitutional debate, the issue of the main units of devolution and their powers became hugely contentious, but tribal cleavages were not a significant issue. The centralizers preferred a presidential regime with many, weak districts, while others wanted larger, more powerful units. In the end, the former largely prevailed. Many of the forty-seven counties have a majority tribe, which has posed issues for local minorities, but devolution has enabled some groups in opposition nationally to form regional governments, thereby diffusing power.

The risk of discrimination against minorities within constituent units is a frequent challenge of devolution. In India, for example, linguistic minorities within states are disadvantaged with respect to public employment, political representation, and public services. In Nigeria, such discrimination has even given rise to the constitutional claim that those classified as "indigenes" have more rights—for example, to state employment and some educational programs—than "settlers" whose historic roots lie outside the state, even if their families have been in the state for generations. Some federal constitutions protect the rights of internal minorities in constituent units—notably rights to education and public services in a minority language as well as the protection of basic minority rights—but in practice such protections are often weak because politically, central governments can find intervening on behalf of a minority can alienate the majority.[36] So marginalized minorities within federal states may turn to civil unrest and, where a minority is regionally concentrated, may demand a new constituent unit, as has happened in India—although there is a limit to such logic. Sometimes minorities suffering discrimination within constituent units align with those in power nationally, which can provide some protection for them.

Not all devolved or federal regimes are in countries with a highly territorialized political geometry. There are strong arguments for federalism, as Ginsburg discusses in his chapter, which have nothing to do with territorial cleavages. Thus, federalism or devolution can be debated in a constitutional transition for several reasons, but even countries whose political geometry is a mix of non-territorial and territorial cleavages will tend to give careful attention to the territorial dimension in considering the design of its devolved arrangements. This has certainly been the case in Nepal. It is a country of astonishing diversity, with 125 recognized caste and ethnic groups, and a history of political dominance by the upper-caste Chetri and Bahuns, who form less than 30 percent of the population. While the country's deep cleavages became evident in the People's War, Nepal is not highly territorialized in that groups are territorially intermingled, with only fifteen of seventy-five districts having a single group as the majority. A key demand of the Maoists, who became the largest party in the first constitutional assembly, was for "ethnic federalism." This was highly contentious, both because of the initial resistance of the old-line parties to federalism, but also because there were almost no natural ethnic units. Eventually, a consensus was reached on a form of federalism where provinces typically have at least two significant population groups. But, the Madhesi and Tharu argued that that the federal map was designed to disempower them, and this issue continues to fester.

South Africa is also a highly diverse country, with eleven official languages, but the African National Congress deeply resented the bantustans of the *apartheid* regime, and it, along with the white minority National Party, was determined, as Steytler writes, "to unmake the political salience of these manufactured territorial cleavages . . . (and

[36] George Anderson and Sujit Choudhry with David Vitale, *Minority Rights in Culturally Diverse Societies* ("Meeting the Challenges of Emerging Constitutional Democracy" Working Paper Series, Center for Constitutional Transitions 2014) <www.constitutionaltransitions.org/publications/minority-rights-in-culturally-diverse-societies/>.

create) a new narrative of a non-racial, non-ethnicity society and thereby undercut the salience of territory."[37] The interim Constitution created nine new provinces to replace the four previous provinces and ten bantustans. These provinces were largely based on past economic development regions, not ethnic or linguistic criteria. The provinces were to have an essentially subordinate role to the central government, although Chief Buthelezi who headed the Inkatha Freedom Party managed to get some strengthening of provincial powers in the interim Constitution and a guarantee they would not be less in the final Constitution. South Africa's new devolved structure has brought some pluralism into its politics, including within the ANC, but "territorial cleavages" are relatively minor politically, though the prospect of abolishing the provinces, which once was mooted, now seems remote.

Nepal and South Africa illustrate how even in regimes where territorial cleavages have not been central to the debate on Constitution reform, the fact of such cleavages has been given careful consideration in the design of federal subunits. This may not always accommodate the demands of some territorially based groups, as in Nepal, but such cleavages have been a salient issue in the design of the new arrangements, if only on occasion to contain them or to break them up.[38]

While countries with multidimensional territorial cleavages or a mix of territorial and other cleavages tend not to have anything resembling power-sharing within their central institutions, they can nonetheless have arrangements that are designed to promote balance in terms of territorial interests and to reduce political confrontation between regions. Nigeria, with its concern to undermine regional cleavages, requires parties that compete in national politics to have a national character, which means a certain level of membership and candidates across the country. In a similar vein, to be elected president in Nigeria, a candidate must win not just a majority in the country, but also at least one-quarter of the vote in two-thirds of the states. Nigeria's cabinet must have a member from each state, and the composition of the civil service must reflect the country's "federal character." These arrangements have helped mitigate the country's political divisions.

Most federations have upper houses in their parliaments and these serve as the "regional chamber." Of our cases that have opted for new Constitutions with symmetrical federalism or devolution, Bolivia, Ethiopia, Kenya, Nepal, Nigeria, and South Africa all opted for such bodies. Most have equal representation of constituent units in the upper house, though their method of selection (e.g. direct vs. indirect election) and terms of office vary. The powers of upper houses in congressional systems is usually greater than in parliamentary systems, where the lower house is the confidence chamber and also controls finances. The upper houses in Ethiopia, Kenya, and South Africa are largely empowered to deal with issues relating to the territorial units, while the upper house in Nepal is essentially an advisory body (as is the one in South Africa on national issues). It is perhaps telling that Spain put off the reform of its Senate, while Iraq's Constitution provides for an upper house to be determined in due course. The experience with upper houses is that their members vote more along party than regional lines, thus limiting their regional role.[39] To the extent that they rebalance political weight compared to popularly elected lower houses this

[37] Nico Styteler, this volume.

[38] For a fuller discussion see Anderson, *Creation of Constituent Units in Federal Systems* (n 35).

[39] Ronald L Watts, *Federal Second Chambers Compared* (Working Paper 2008-02, Institute of Intergovernmental Relations Queen's University 2008).

favors smaller constituent units, so their role in accommodating major territorial cleavages is highly contextual and usually incidental to the design. The design of upper houses was a secondary issue in the constitutional transitions under study and this underlines the majoritarian character of central institutions in most federal and devolved regimes.

By contrast, the choice of the type of executive and legislature was highly contentious in many cases, though this was not always debated directly in relation to the issue of territorial cleavages. Bolivia, Kenya, and Nigeria opted for presidential-congressional arrangements, while Ethiopia, Nepal, South Africa, and Spain opted for parliamentary systems with responsible governments. The debate was central to Kenya's transition, where the opposition parties tended to favor a parliamentary regime on the basis that it was more likely to lead to coalitions and power-sharing, where they might have access to office, while the stronger parties preferred the winner-take-all approach of a strong presidency. There is a large literature on the respective strengths and weaknesses of presidential versus parliamentary regimes (and of hybrid semi-presidential regimes), but in practice the choice between them in our cases seemed little informed by such analysis and more influenced by past history of institutions or the preferences of the more powerful.[40]

Nigeria's constitutional prohibition on regional parties is unusual, but it points to the potential importance of electoral laws for translating territorial and other cleavages into electoral representation and the party system. In a highly territorialized system, first-past-the-post systems, which favor largest parties within ridings, can give a distorted representation of local sentiment (Scotland is an extreme example, where the Scottish National Party won 4 percent of seats with 22.5 percent of votes in the 1992 UK election and then 95 percent of seats with 50 percent of the vote in 2015.) Proportional representation systems limit these distortions and give a better sense of support for national and regional parties and so can limit the potentially destabilizing over-representation of regional parties. Constitutions may be silent on the choice of electoral system or, as in South Africa, indicate what kind of law should apply, while leaving the details to legislation. Brancati has argued that the effectiveness of decentralization hinges on the shape of the party system and the balance between statewide and regional parties: it is least successful when regional parties are in control, but it can be undermined as well if statewide parties fail to integrate regional interests.[41]

Finally, the allocation of powers and finances between the central government and the constituent unit governments is a critical issue, in that regimes that have a federal

[40] For example, see John M Carey and Mathew S Shugart, *Presidents and Assemblies: Constitutional Design and Electoral Dynamics* (Cambridge University Press 1992); José A Cheibub, Zachary Elkins, and Tom Ginsburg, "Beyond Presidentialism and Parliamentarism" (2014) 44 (3) British Journal of Political Science 515; Arend Lijphart, *Patterns of Democracy: Government Forms and Performance in 36 Countries* (Yale University Press 1999); Juan J Linz and Arturo Valenzuela (eds), *The Failure of Presidential Democracy* (Johns Hopkins Press 1994); Pippa Norris, *Driving Democracy: Do Power-sharing Institutions Work?* (Cambridge University Press 2009); José Cheibub, *Presidentialism, Parliamentarism, and Democracy* (Cambridge University Press 2007); Alfred Stepan and Cindy Skach, "Constitutional Frameworks and Democratic Consolidation: Parliamentarism and Presidentialism" (1993) 46 (1) World Politics 1.

[41] Dawn Brancati, *Peace by Design: Managing Intrastate Conflict through Decentralization* (Oxford University Press 2009); also see David Lublin, *Minority Rules: Electoral Systems, Decentralization, and Ethnoregional Party Success* (Oxford University Press 2014).

or devolved structure vary considerably in the extent of true devolution of powers. Thus, South Africa opted for a centralized form of federalism, based on the German model, with extensive concurrency with the federal government having paramountcy. In Bolivia, a good part of the conflict was over revenue allocation, where the central government emerged strengthened while the gas-producing departments still retained significant advantages. In Iraq, the hurried effort to draft a Constitution led to a draft with significant ambiguity regarding the allocation of powers, nowhere more glaringly than on the critical issue of powers over petroleum resources. Of the countries in our cases writing new Constitutions, Spain probably created the most devolved regime, which reflects the depth of its territorial cleavages. In principle, Ethiopia and Nigeria, which are also highly territorialized, might have been expected to opt for major devolution, but in practice the control that the military and the EPDRF had, respectively, over the transitions resulted in centralized outcomes (though on its face the Ethiopian Constitution, with its openness to secession, appears highly accommodating to territorial claims).

Highly devolved federalism with a consociational central government

Countries whose political geometry is characterized by two or three major and highly territorialized communities that are antagonistic to one another may consider the option of a highly devolved federal structure combined with formal power-sharing or consociational arrangements at the center. While such arrangements can have a strong underlying logic, they are difficult to design and manage and they risk reifying political divisions in the country. They may be especially difficult if the regional populations are significantly different in size.

A number of federations that had only two or three units broke up after a relatively brief existence (Pakistan in 1971, Czechoslovakia in 1992, Sudan in 2011), while Nigeria was fundamentally restructured to escape its dysfunctional three-state structure that aggravated north–south relations and contributed to civil war. None of these bi-polar federations had effective power-sharing in the central government, although Sudan was meant to have. Belgium, which was initially a unitary country, has become the one example of a democracy that has developed a federal system with a constitutionalized, consociational government at the center.[42]

As difficult as such federal-cum-consociational arrangements can be, their logic arises from two (or three) communities finding that they are forced to cohabit within one country, often because of international pressure; the populations are territorially largely separated—perhaps after regional homogenization following conflict, as in Bosnia and Cyprus—so it is possible to create territorially defined sub-national governments for the respective communities that can assume important powers. At the same time, it is inevitable that some decisions must be made by the central government; since the population of the smaller community or communities (Bosnia-Herzegovina) rejects majoritarian decision-making, which it fears would disempower it, arrangements for power-sharing at the center become essential for an accord. This logic led to the imposed settlement in the Dayton Accord, and still underlies negotiations regarding a possible settlement in Cyprus. There has been some very creative thinking about how

[42] Switzerland also has some consociational features within its collective executive. As well, the fact that a set number citizens can require by petition referendums on controversial questions has proven an important incentive for politicians to work for broad consensus.

to improve the design of such consociational arrangements,[43] but given its difficulties this model should be considered only in exceptional circumstances.[44]

While the consociational power-sharing in Bosnia-Herzegovina has brought peace, it is widely recognized to have created a deeply problematic government. It has hardened ethnic identities, so that despite international support for free and fair elections and incentives for multi-ethnic and moderate parties and constraints on ethnonationalist parties, multi-ethnic parties have fared poorly and moderate ethnic parties have been drawn to more extreme positions. The reason is that the Constitution organizes politics around ethnicity, giving rise to a system of (as Zahar puts it) "monoethnic non-competitive electoral competition"[45] with outbidding within ethnic communities. Moreover, because ethnic appeals occur across multiple offices simultaneously, there is a coattail effect of campaign appeals to hard-line ethnic positions even at the level of the constituent entities, where there should be space for greater political pluralism. The system of ethnic parties has become the basis of a political economy of patronage. The mechanism for corruption is the requirement that government appointments be ethnically representative, coupled with government ownership of a large percentage of the economy. This has led ethnic parties to reward their supporters and themselves via concessions, procurement, and financing. There has been great difficulty getting effective decision-making at the center because of mutual vetoes. For a long time, the system relied on the internationally appointed High Representative to break deadlocks.

The Annan Plan for Cyprus was based on the idea of a bizonal, bicommunal federation, with consociational arrangements in the central government. The plan was rejected by the Greek population by referendum in 2004, but this model remained the basis for the negotiations that failed to reach an agreement in 2017 and is the likely basis for future negotiations. While there are many difficult issues in the negotiations, including security, rights of return, property, and territorial adjustment, the possible governance arrangements have proven to be very difficult. Since the Turkish population is only 15 to 20 percent of the population on the island (depending on how it is counted), the Greek community has understandable concerns about equal power-sharing, while the Turkish community feel the need for it to avoid Greek dominance. The Senate proposed in the Annan Plan would have had equal representatives from both communities, while the Chamber of Deputies would have no less than 25 percent of its members from the Turkish Cypriot community. Special voting arrangements would have meant that a significant minority of members from both communities would have had to approve the appointment of the executive and other issues of vital interest. As in Bosnia-Herzegovina, the Supreme Court would have had an equal number of judges from each community plus foreign judges to avoid deadlocks.

Two of the most successful consociational (albeit non-federal) arrangements have been in Belgium and Northern Ireland, but in these cases the ratio of majority to minority is close to 60 to 40 or 55 to 45, which makes power-sharing difficult but potentially manageable.[46] Similarly, in Bosnia the minority Serbs and Croats represent

[43] See Loizides (n 14) 74–126. In most cases of power-sharing, the largest population group is between 60 and 45 percent of the total population, while in Cyprus the Greek constitute about 80 percent of the population, which makes power-sharing more difficult.

[44] And the breakdown of consociational government in Northern Ireland at the time of writing underlines this point. While based on a unitary model because the populations are so intermingled, this case had been widely seen as a model. It may still be the least bad option for Northern Ireland.

[45] Marie-Joelle Zahar, this volume.

[46] Brendan O'Leary suggests that to work consociationalism requires mutual commitments to cohabit a state and not try to assimilate the other and leaders must have the autonomy to make compromises, which may only be practicable in moderately divided societies. He does not mention

31 percent and 16 percent of the population compared to 51 percent for the Bosniaks. By contrast, in Cyprus, the Turkish population constitutes less than a fifth of the total. The constitutional deliberations in Yemen's national dialogue were driven toward a federal system, but the south's preferred option of two regions was rejected; the accommodation of the south was meant to come through significant power-sharing in the central legislature (but not in the presidency or the courts). In this case the focus was on giving southern representatives in the parliament vetoes on matters touching their interests, yet with southerners standing at only about 20 percent of the population, it was unclear how viable this arrangement would be. The already difficult challenges of consociational arrangements are much greater when the minority is relatively small—analogous to how peripheral regions cannot plausibly make claims about the structure of central institutions. Indeed, for that reason, consociationalism has never been seriously considered in Iraq, where the Kurds are around 15 to 20 percent of the national population, or in Sri Lanka, where the Tamil-majority northern province represents around 5 percent.

While consociationalism is rare and difficult to achieve as a longer-term constitutional design, this type of power-sharing has been used quite effectively on an interim basis for a period of transitional government during a constitutional transition in which longer-term arrangements are to be worked out.[47] This strategy worked well in South Africa, and reasonably well in Kenya, but it was clear in both cases that the longer-term arrangements would be majoritarian—though with important constitutionalized protections for the formerly dominant minority in South Africa.

An apparent alternative to a complex federal-cum-consociational structure for two territorially distinct and mutually hostile populations would be partition and the creation of new independent countries. Circumstances matter greatly when it comes to breakup. The international community has been prepared to sanction mutually agreed breakups, as it did in several post-Communist countries, and has even set the stage for potential breakup, as it did in mediating the peace agreement in Sudan in 2005. By contrast, the international community is extremely reluctant to reward military intervention, as in Cyprus, or ethnic cleansing, as in Bosnia-Herzegovina; moreover, the majority population in these cases is still not prepared to let the minority Turks and Serbs secede. The international community is even reluctant to support more democratic attempts at promoting secession, as can be seen in the isolation of the Catalan and regional Kurdish governments following their attempts to force independence through referendums. In his chapter, Ginsburg discusses alternative constitutional treatments of secession, where few federations provide a right, or even a conditional right to secede. At the same time, there is some quantitative evidence that partition as a solution to nationalist wars is more likely to promote post-conflict peace and democracy that the alternatives of unitary government or regional autonomy, though this may depend on context.[48]

the respective sizes of populations. Brendan O'Leary, "The Elements of Right-sizing and Right-peopling the State" in Brendan O'Leary, Ian Lustick, and Thomas Callaghy (eds), *Right-sizing the State: The Politics of Moving Borders* (Oxford University Press 2001) 43–4.

[47] See Wolff (n 7).

[48] Chapman and Roeder (n 30); see also Lars-Erik Cederman, Simon Hug, Andreas Schädel, and Julian Wucherpfennig, "Territorial Autonomy in the Shadow of Conflict: Too Little, Too Late?" (2015) 109 (2) American Political Science Review 354–70.

Special autonomy for small territories and a majoritarian central government

Countries with one or more peripheral regions that are highly territorialized relative to the rest of the country should consider special autonomy arrangements for these territories, especially if the population of the territory is small relative to the rest of the country. Such arrangements may be considered following a stalemated secessionist insurrection and/or in a liberal democratic country that is not doctrinaire about centralized sovereignty. Given their small size, peripheral territories with special autonomy are not accorded power-sharing arrangements at the center.

This option is one of asymmetric autonomy. It has been suggested that asymmetric autonomy "remains the tool of choice in the settlement of ethno-political and self-determination conflicts,"[49] but this is an overstatement. In our case studies, such demands for asymmetric treatment arose in Indonesia, for Aceh and Papua; in the Philippines, for the Muslims of Mindanao; in India, notably in the northeastern tribal areas; and in the UK for Scotland. (There are also special fiscal arrangements in Spain's Basque country and Navarre, but this represents an historic arrangement.) In most of these cases in which special autonomy has been granted, the relevant territorial population is very small relative to the national population: Aceh, 2 percent; Bangsamoro, 5 percent; and in India's northeast, the three new states carved out of Assam (Meghalaya, Mizoram, and Nagaland) together account for 1 percent of India's population. This practice is consistent with other comparable cases, such as the Aland Islands, 0.5 percent; Jammu and Kashmir, 1 percent; and Zanzibar, 2 percent. There is a strong logic to special autonomy being largely restricted to territories with relatively small populations. Small peripheral populations do not expect or demand power-sharing in the central government. They can maintain their normal representation in central institutions and their representatives can even vote on matters that do not affect them because they are such marginal players. And in federations, the larger constituent units are more likely to accept special autonomy for a very small, very distinct territory than they would for a large constituent unit, which they would see as their equivalent.

The small relative size of most regions with special autonomy helps to explain the constitutional dynamics surrounding devolution for Scotland. Devolution in the UK is asymmetric, both because there is no devolution to England (and so nothing resembling federalism) and because the three devolved regions each have different arrangements. The three regions total 15 percent of the UK's population, 8 percent of which is in Scotland. Thus, Scotland has the largest relative population of the territorial units in our cases having a special autonomy arrangement—and it also has exceptionally extensive devolved powers. This arrangement has posed the still unresolved structural issue of the role of MPs from Scotland and the other devolved regions voting on legislation that applies only to England. This is an especially acute question in a parliamentary regime in which the House of Commons is the confidence chamber for the government, for which there is no neat solution. The UK example shows the risks of special autonomy if it applies to a significant part of the country and to a wide range of powers. The Kurdish region in Iraq, with about 15 percent of the country's population,

[49] Marc Weller, "Conclusion" in Marc Weller and Katherine Nobbs (eds), *Asymmetric Autonomy and the Settlement of Ethnic Conflict* (University of Pennsylvania Press 2010) 298–306; Ferran Requejo would let 100 flowers bloom in terms of asymmetry and rights to secession: Ferran Requejo, "Value Pluralism and Multinational Federalism" in Alain-G Gagnon, Montserrat Guibernau, and Francois Rocher (eds), *The Conditions of Diversity in Multinational Democracies* (Institute for Research on Public Policy 2003).

effectively has very extensive special autonomy so this may pose similar issues about the role of its representatives in the national government longer term.

While special autonomy can function well in cases of small minorities, majorities can strongly object to special autonomy, even for very small and peripheral regions, often for symbolic reasons or out of fear of facilitating eventual secession. There has been frequent opposition to special autonomy for the Muslims of Mindanao from the Philippine majority, which reared its head again in the final year of the Aquino administration. Aquino's successor, President Duterte, however, supported the peace agreements and in mid-2018 Congress passed a bill that enshrined the major provisions of the peace deal in domestic law. But what special autonomy would mean within a federal Philippines that President Duterte is proposing is unclear and could be closer to state status. The idea of special autonomy for the Tamil's in northern Sri Lanka never found its way onto the agenda, perhaps because it would have been unacceptable to the Sinhalese majority, but in principle the population in question (especially if the eastern province were excluded) was small enough that such an arrangement might not have been destabilizing. So structural indicators favorable to special autonomy are no guarantee it will be adopted. It may be that on occasion symmetric devolution across the whole country prepares the way for special autonomy in some region or regions. In Indonesia, for example, there were the 1999 and 2004 decentralization laws for all 292 regencies, prior to the special autonomy law in Aceh. The general decentralization law changed the political baseline and made Aceh's special autonomy more acceptable across Indonesia.

Conclusion

This chapter has argued that three crucial variables shape the structure and dynamics of constitutional moments when claims for territorial accommodation are important. These contextual variables set the stage for a period of engagement by leading political actors on constitutional change, including, potentially, changes that address claims coming from politically mobilized, territorially concentrated, populations. The three variables are: the political geometry; the antecedent means of political engagement, whether peaceful, legal and institutionalized, or violent and extra-legal; and the relative power positions of key actors.

This volume has looked at seventeen very different case studies of constitutional moments, emerging from different contexts, developing through different processes and endings (to the extent that they have ended) with very different designs and outcomes. Part of the originality of this volume is to consider the constitutional transitions in which very different political geometries put very different potential constitutional options on the table. Thus, at the highest, architectural, level, our cases include symmetric federalism or devolution combined with majoritarian government at the center, bi-communal federalism combined with consociational power-sharing at the center, and asymmetric devolution, which combines with majoritarian decision-making at the center. Bringing these different cases together helps highlight how each architectural alternative is likely to be the presumptive option for constitutional revision in distinct contexts of political geometry. Political geometry captures the state of political mobilization in a country as defined by the cleavage pattern in terms of territorial and other groups.

Countries with multiple, salient territorial cleavages or with a mix of territorial and non-territorial cleavages are likely to consider some form of federalism or devolution, with the central institutions of government being largely majoritarian in design. Highly territorialized countries may opt for a greater degree of devolution than those that are less territorialized or that are characterized by a mix of territorial and non-territorial cleavages. Countries in which there are two (or perhaps three) highly territorialized and antagonistic communities are likely to consider a very devolved form of federalism, but with power-sharing arrangements at the center. This is a very challenging architectural option, especially if there is a major disparity in the relative sizes of the communities because the majority may then be more resistant to power-sharing. Territorially concentrated, peripheral communities that are relatively small within a national context are more likely to campaign for special autonomy and this can function quite well if the community's population is not too large and the extent of devolved powers not too great; if these are large and great, this can pose potentially destabilizing issues regarding the role of the region's elected representatives at the center on laws that would not apply to their region. There is no guarantee these indicated options will be adopted or even considered. Sometimes majorities (and even minorities) foreclose options that may have seemed prospective.

Political geometry can also influence the shape of constitution-making processes, notably whether advocates of territorial accommodation are given voice as significant participants. Such processes are also shaped by the context preceding the initiation of a constitutional moment, notably whether it has been peaceful or violent, and this can be tied to political geometry. Violent conflict, whether a civil war or a regional insurgency, can end in victory for one party or a stalemate. If there is a victor, the victor will typically tightly control both the process and substance of constitution-making; that said, the underlying political geometry can still strongly influence the constitutional design chosen. However, our main interest in cases of violent conflict is when it has led to a military stalemate, which requires a process that combines peace negotiations with constitution-making, often in a situation where the constitutional order has collapsed or has been rejected by armed rebels. A constitutional moment in such cases starts when the fighting stops; violence has been fundamental to precipitating the constitutional moment and it also strongly colors the power distribution, where typically it is the leaders of the formerly fighting parties (typically the government is one) who sit down to negotiate. The first phase of negotiations, which may extend over a considerable period, sets the agenda for the subsequent Constitution-making process, but often it also establishes fundamental substantive features that must be part of any final constitution.

This volume and our analysis join a growing body of work that draws links between Constitution-making processes and conflict resolution, which until recently existed in intellectual and policy silos.[50] The former is backward-looking, is focused on ending violence among armed combatants, is oriented around negotiations for ceasefires and DDR (disarmament, demobilization, and reintegration) and it relies on mediation. The latter is future-oriented and directed at creating the institutions of constitutional democracy and peaceful political contestation; it draws in expertise from law and political science. The relationship between conflict resolution and Constitution-making has, for the most part, been viewed sequentially—that is, conflict resolution is prior to, and the condition for, Constitution-making. But the link between the two is actually conceptual, because ceasefires and initial peace agreement can be rich in constitutional content, in that they can determine the decision-making process for the future

[50] See, for example, Christine Bell and Kimana Zulueta-Fülscher, *Sequencing Peace Agreements and Constitutions in the Political Settlement Process* (Policy Paper No 13, International IDEA 2016).

Constitution and stipulate key substantive terms.[51] This project has highlighted how conflict resolution and Constitution-making interpenetrate each other and both can aim to create a pathway toward ordinary politics. Peace agreements can create "on ramps" for armed groups to become political parties and participate in Constitution-making processes.

When a territorial conflict has been between a central government and a peripheral territorial rebel group, the framework for peace-making and Constitution-making is normally that of legal continuity within the existing Constitution (federal or unitary). Thus, the Constitution will constrain the parties, both in terms of the rules for any constitutional amendments and the possible compliance of any non-constitutional arrangement with the constitution. The scope of any constitutional negotiations in such a context will normally be limited to certain special autonomy arrangements for the territory in question. Indeed, the changes under consideration may not even be "constitutional" in the strict sense, especially if the politics of constitutional change are too difficult; a special law complying with the Constitution may be the chosen instrument. Our cases also show that when post-conflict negotiations take place within constitutional continuity, the way may be opened for "institutional spoilers" to undo what has been agreed at the negotiating table. This poses the problem of the government negotiators being able to provide credible commitments that the deal reached at the table will be implemented. Potential institutional spoilers may be the courts or politicians whose opinions or assent are required for ratification or longer-term implementation of a settlement; they are legitimate actors under the Constitution and a challenge for the negotiators, especially government negotiators, is to anticipate this risk and develop mitigating strategies.

The situation is quite different when there has been a wider conflict, a civil war, perhaps with major powers intervening, and where there are significant territorial (and perhaps other) cleavages; the issue is the re-founding of a state with a new Constitution. In these cases of post-conflict, a new Constitution is often drafted with a rupture in constitutional continuity, where the negotiating parties (which may include outside powers) face a constitutional tabula rasa and develop their own understanding on the process for considering and ratifying a new Constitution. In such a post-conflict environment, the parties may even maintain the form of legal continuity, but effectively put aside the old Constitution with an interim substitute that has been agreed by them (very rarely a peace agreement and new Constitution are negotiated and ratified simultaneously, with no interim arrangements). Designing interim and transitional arrangements can provide the first step in developing "on ramps" for former armed combatants to switch their engagement to democratic politics. Such general, post-conflict Constitution-making processes are typically negotiated by the relevant elites at the agenda-setting stage, but they can become more inclusive during the deliberative stage, with the introduction of competitive elections to new constitutional assemblies. Such large bodies can sometimes have difficulty resolving critical issues unless leaders are actively engaged and in some cases the deliberative stage is entirely elite controlled, even if there are broader deliberative forums. The final stage, ratification, can be the most inclusive if it requires approval by referendum (perhaps with a special voting requirement), but this carries obvious risks in upsetting delicately balanced settlements.

The dynamics of drafting a new Constitution when the preceding context was peaceful is different, in that it is constrained by the existing rules of constitutional

[51] Sujit Choudhry, "Civil War, Ceasefire, Constitution: Some Preliminary Notes" (2012) 33 Cardozo Law Review 1907.

amendment. But when there are significant territorial and other cleavages, the issue is similar to a post-conflict situation in that at its core it is about political negotiations that must take account of the power balance of key factions. Assuming they have proven themselves in political tests of strength, the negotiations include leaders of movements or parties asserting claims for the accommodation of territorial claims in the new regime. Because they are constrained by the existing rules, typically the elites have limited say at the agenda-setting stage over at least some aspects of the process. They may also have limited ability to impose substantive guidance as to what the new Constitution shall contain. In these contexts, the existing Constitution will stipulate a process relating to its amendment where elected representatives play a central role, but there is often room for creative use of consultative and advisory bodies in enlarging that deliberative phase that are not constitutionally mandated. There may also be a political understanding, beyond the minimum required for constitutional amendment, that a settlement should seek to achieve some kind of understanding with key factions around a new balance in the territorial provisions of the Constitution. An existing Constitution will specify the procedure for ratification, whether by a supermajority in the legislature or constitutional assembly or by popular referendum.

These brief outlines show how in analyzing political processes around claims for constitutional territorial accommodation we have sought to integrate the literatures on mobilization, process, and design in the context of concrete examples of constitutional moments. In this conclusion, we offer further reflections on the potential contributions to those bodies of scholarship arising from this intellectual encounter and suggest possibilities for future research.

This volume and our analysis brings the law, especially Constitutions and constitutional argumentation, into the heart of the literature on territorial political mobilization. That literature is rooted in political sociology and comparative politics. Although such mobilization has constitutional change at its center—both in demands for change and resistance to it—the role of Constitution-making processes and constitutional design have not been very closely studied in most work on territorially based challenges to regime design.[52] In earlier work, one of us argued that concrete debates over constitutional interpretation and design were arenas for debates around competing conceptions of political community, and that careful analysis of competing positions could sharpen our understanding of these phenomena for both political sociology and comparative politics.[53] This research project highlights the role of law and legal institutional frameworks within the constitutional politics of claims for territorial accommodation. When there is no constitutional rupture, these institutions both empower and constrain through their conferral (or non-conferral) of power on different actors and through the requirement that any decision must comply with the Constitution. Thus, the design of existing Constitutions and their deliberative institutions give rise to strategic behavior in constitutional transitions under legal continuity. However, a critical issue at the agenda-setting stage for a constitutional moment regarding a wholesale constitutional revision is whether or not legal continuity will be maintained—and if it is to be maintained, whether the existing institutions need to be replaced by interim arrangements that reflect the new power balance between the parties. If the existing

[52] An important exception is Stephen Tierney, *Constitutional Law and National Pluralism* (Oxford University Press 2004).

[53] Sujit Choudhry, "Constitutional Politics and Crisis in Sri Lanka" in Jacques Bertrand and André Laliberté (eds), *Multination States in Asia: Accommodation or Resistance* (Cambridge University Press 2010).

institutions are seen as favoring a status quo that is unacceptable to a least some key actors, then those actors, who may be advocates of territorial accommodation, may propose or insist on interim arrangements that will function during the transitional period. Paying close attention to the law at the outset of a constitutional moment can help us to better understand the opportunities, constraints faced, and choices made, by political actors. This volume and our analysis broadens debate over how constitutional design can accommodate territorial cleavages. The constitutional accommodation of territorial claims does not resolve these conflicts; rather, it provides an institutional framework within which to manage them through politics. We have shown how different architectural frameworks have a logical relationship with different configurations of political geometry.

We end with a final observation. The constitutional accommodation of territorial cleavages occurs within a broad framework of constitutional democracy and institutional architecture. How these accommodations function within an institutional framework depends on how the arrangements designed to accommodate territorial claims interact with other features of the constitutional structure, such as electoral laws, bureaucracies, and the courts, but also non-governmental institutions, especially those in civil society important to territorial or other communities. Of particular importance is the idea that all constitutional democracies share the goal of creating a framework for bounded pluralist partisan contestation among political parties.[54] Thus constitutional design has the potential to create conditions for fluid and cross-cutting coalitions through appropriate territorial accommodations. These may be part of a broader project of creating institutional arrangements for political pluralism.

[54] Sujit Choudhry, "Will Democracy die in Darkness? Calling Autocracy by its Name" in Mark Graber, Sandford Levinson, and Mark Tushnet (eds), *Constitutional Democracies in Crisis?* (Oxford University Press, 2018) 571–84; and Sujit Choudhry, "Resisting Democratic Backsliding: An Essay on Weimar, Self-Enforcing Constitutions, and the Frankfurt School" (2018) 7 (1) Global Constitutionalism 54.

Index

Abad, Fundacion Manuel Gimenez xv
Abdullah, Zaini 134–35
Abiy Ahmed (Ethiopian Prime Minister) 77–78, 79–80
Abu Sayyaf Group, Philippines 207, 210
Aceh, Indonesia 128, 138, 374, 382, 388
central government challenges 126
compared with Papua 123–24, 380
constitutional transition 120
destruction of capital, Banda Aceh 130
external mediation 139
Free Aceh Movement (GAM) 124, 129–31, 134–35, 138, 400–1
grievances 119–20, 123, 128, 129–30, 135
Helsinki peace negotiations 130, 131
Henry Dunant Centre 130, 139
Law on Aceh (2006) 119–20, 124–25, 130, 131, 134, 135, 138, 362
mobilization in 122, 128
phases to conflict in 124, 128–29
special autonomy laws 129, 348, 385, 402–3, 424
as a Special Operations Zone 129
unity 120
see also **Indonesia; Papua, Indonesia**
Addis Ababa, Ethiopia 61–62, 65, 66, 67–68, 73–74
Council 74–75
Africa *see* **Ethiopia; Kenya; Nigeria; South Africa**
African National Congress (ANC), and South Africa 219, 220, 222, 223, 224–25, 227–28, 229, 230–33, 235–36, 328, 341–42, 359, 397–98, 417–18
deal with National Party (1993) 225
agency 377–78
agenda setting 340, 394, 395
procedural agenda 395–98
substantive agenda 398–99
Aguiyi-Ironsi, Johnson 186
Ahmar, Sheikh Sadiq al- 322–23
Ahmed, Abiy (Ethiopian Prime Minister) 77–78, 79–80
Akinci, Mustafa 55–56, 58–59
Ali, S. Fazl 87
All Amhara People's Organization, Ethiopia 66–67, 69
Alliance of Independent Social Democrats (SNSD), Bosnia and Herzegovina 37–38
Al-Qaeda 312–13, 323
ambiguity of constitutions 348
Ambrosini, Mario 230
Amhara, Ethiopia 72–73, 76–77
Amhara National Democratic Movement (ANDM) 64
Anandi Devi (Nepalese political party) 166
Anastasiades, Nicos 48–49, 55–56
Anastasiades-Eroğlu Joint Declaration (February 2014) 57
ANC *see* **African National Congress (ANC), and South Africa**
Anderson, Benedict
Imagined Communities 381
Andhra Pradesh, India 86–87, 88, 385
Annan, Kofi (UN Secretary General) 43–44
Annan Plan (2002–04), Cyprus 43, 421
adoptability problems 44
assumed political structure if successful 51–52
and background to conflict in Cyprus 44
drafters 58
endorsement by Turkish Cypriots (2004) 43–44, 54, 56
five iterations 43–44
internal constituent state citizenship principle 52
lessons learned 44–45
cross-learning 58
negotiations 47
outcome of process 54
overview of case 43
permitting of Turkish and Greek troops in Cyprus 53
power-sharing arrangements v, 45, 53, 58
Presidency Conclusions (1999) 54
promise of 49
proposed Chamber of Deputies 51–52
proposed Presidential Council 51–52
proposed Senate 51, 52
proposed Supreme Court 52
referendums 44, 54–55, 56, 58, 410–11
rejection by Greek Cypriots 43–44, 51, 53, 54–55, 57–58, 59, 345
secrecy allegations 58
significance of 43–44
unilateral intervention rights 53
and United Nations 43–44, 47, 49, 51, 54, 56
see also **Cyprus; Greece; Greek Cypriot communities; Turkey; Turkish Cypriot communities**
apartheid, South Africa 219, 220, 222, 223, 224, 225, 226, 334–35, 360, 417–18
Aquino, Corazon (Filipino President) 204, 209
Aquino III, Benigno 209, 212, 214–16
Arato, Andrew 406
Arbitration Commission of the Conference on Yugoslavia 24–25
Arroyo, Gloria Macapagal (Filipino President) 207, 208–9
Artisaari, Martti (Finnish President) 130
Arunachal Pradesh, India 92–93, 95, 400–1
Asian financial crisis (late 1990s) 4–5, 124–25, 385
Asmal, Kader 233, 236
Assam, India 89, 90, 91, 92, 95, 400–1

asymmetrical arrangements
asymmetrical forms 335–36, 363, 372–73
constitutional design and territorial cleavages 355, 360, 363
devolution 335–36, 362, 375, 423–24
Indonesia 120, 139
Philippines 210
Scotland 266, 277–78, 286
South Africa 219, 233, 234
Spain 249–50
systems 233, 277–78
asymmetrical autonomy 217, 391–92, 423
Austin, Granville 84
Australia 342
Autonomous Region in Muslim Mindanao (ARMM), Philippines 205, 206–8, 209–11, 213, 362–63, 402–3
autonomy 349
asymmetrical 217, 391–92, 423
compared with federalism 362, 380, 391–92, 412–13
constitutional arrangements 426
and decentralization 361, 362
and federalism 362, 413
Indonesia 119–20, 126, 128–29, 130, 131, 132–33, 135, 136–37, 138–39, 355–56, 361, 362, 374, 385–86, 424
with a majoritarian central government 413
Philippines 202–3, 204, 205–6, 207, 210–11, 212, 213, 217
Scotland 413
size of units 363, 372–73, 423–25
for small territories and a majoritarian central government 423
Sri Lanka 255–57, 258–59, 266–67, 271, 424
Statutes of Autonomy, Spain 247, 248, 250–51, 252
Ukraine 362, 372–73
United Kingdom 423–24
see also **special autonomy laws under specific countries**
Azikiwe, Nnamdi (Nigerian President) 184

Baath Party, Iraq 102, 103
Babangida, Ibrahim 186
Baby, Sophie 239
Bachelet, Michelle 14–15
Badinter Arbitration Committee *see* **Arbitration Commission of the Conference on Yugoslavia**
Badinter Commission 382–83
Bahah, Khaled 327
Balasingham, Anton 265, 266
Balewa, Tafawa (Nigerian Prime Minister) 184
Balfour, Sebastian 239
Basque Country, Spain 237–38, 240, 241–42, 244, 245–46, 248, 249, 250, 253, 356–57, 387–88, 423
Basque Nationalist Party (PNV) 240, 241, 243
compared with Catalonia 241–42
ETA (Basque Homeland and Freedom), terrorist group 239, 241–42, 243, 247
nationalism 240, 241–42, 243, 247, 250, 387
provinces 241–42
radicalism 241–42
Statute of Autonomy 247
see also **Catalonia region, Spain; Spain**
Belfast Agreement (1998) 57
Benomar, Jamal 314–15, 318–19, 322
Berlin Wall, fall of (1989) 222
Bhattarai, Baburam 170, 174–75
BiH *see* **Bosnia-Herzegovina (BiH)**
Bihar, India 88, 92–93
bizonality principle 47, 52, 421
BJP (Hindu-based Indian party) 89–90, 92–93, 94–95
Blanco, Carrero 241
Bolivia 1, 402, 410–11
administrative structure 384–85
ADN (*Accion Democratica Nacionalista*) 4–5
and Asian financial crisis (1990s) 4–5
Autonomous Charter, drafting of 2, 9, 11–12, 19–20
citizen organization 5–6
civic committees 3, 5, 6, 7, 9
civil society 3, 5
cleavages 2, 3, 15–16
Cochabamba meetings (2008) 15
collapse of party system (2005) 6
Constituent Assembly *see* **Constituent Assembly (CA), Bolivia**
constitutional change 21
constitutional reform 392–93
background to events 2
compromise agreement (2008) 15
Constitution of 2009 (Oruro) 12, 13–14, 15, 19–20, 361
constitutional amendment (2004) 5–6
constitutional engagement period 1
Constitutional Tribunal 1, 2, 16, 19, 20
rationale for 20–21
transition (2006–08) 1, 20–21
constitutional transition 331, 333–34
decentralization 3–4, 6, 15
Administrative Decentralization Law 17
Framework Law on Autonomies and Decentralization (FLAD), 21 15, 16–17, 18–19
Democratic National Council (CONALDE) 12, 13–14
demonstrations and protests 6, 7, 9, 10, 11, 13–15, 18, 19
eastern lowlands 1, 2, 5, 6
energy prices, effect of decrease 18–19
Framework Law on Autonomies and Decentralization (FLAD), 21 15, 16–17, 18–19
gas rents struggle 18
half moon (media luna) *see* ***half moon* departments, Bolivia (media luna, area of opposition to Morales)**
history 1

hydrocarbons sector 2, 5–6, 17, 18
Hydrocarbons Code 17
instability and uncertainty in 5, 10
institutional reforms (2004) 6–7
January Agenda (2005) 6, 8
La Paz 11–12, 15
Law of Jurisdictional Demarcation (LJD), 2010 16
lessons learned 19
low levels of territorialization xvi
MAS-IPSP *see* **MAS-IPSP (*Movimiento al Socialismo–Instrumento Político por la Soberanía de los Pueblos*), Bolivia**
megafields 18
MIP (*Movimiento Indigena Pachakuti*) 4–5
MNR (*Movimiento Nacionalista Revolucionario*) 2, 4, 11
multiparty democracy (1980s and 1990s) 3
municipal structure 17
National Revolution of 1952 1, 2, 3–4, 20
October Agenda (2003) 5–6, 8
outcome of process 15
oversight committees 3–4
Pando 6, 13–14
pipelines to Brazil 2, 13–14
Plurinational Constitutional Tribunal 1, 16, 19, 20
as a plurinational state 3–5, 6, 16, 20–21
PODEMOS (*Poder Democrático y Social*) movement *see* **PODEMOS (*Poder Democrático y Social*) movement, Bolivia**
political legitimacy 15
political mobilization 1
political violence, Pando (2008) 1
Popular Participation Law (PPL) 3–4, 17
prefects 6, 7–8, 13
Proposed Law Calling for a Constituent Assembly (LCCA) (26) 7, 9, 11
referendums 7–8, 9, 10, 11–12, 13, 408
referendum of 2009 on new Constitution 1, 15
Santa Cruz 2, 3, 5
"second-tier" institutions 1
self-determination 5
social class issues 2
social conflict 10
sub-national party systems 5–6
Sucre, status of 10–12
Tarija 2, 6, 13, 17–18
territorial cleavages 331
territorialization
into 311 municipalities (1994) 3–4
dynamics 1
Unity Pact (UP) 7–8, 9, 12
violence 1, 10, 13, 14–15, 18–19
western highlands 1, 5, 6
Bomas process, Kenya 145–46, 154, 160, 405–6, 407
Bombay, India 82–83, 88, 96
Bombay Reorganization Act 1960 89
Borger, Julian 41
Bosnia and Herzegovina (BiH)
ethnic concerns 24
Bosnia-Herzegovina (BiH) 22, 400, 420–21
Assembly of the Serb People of Bosnia and Herzegovina 23–24
background to events 22
Badinter Commission 382–83
Bonn Powers 33
"Bosnian Spring" (2014) 39
Brčko (Bosnian-majority strategic municipality), international arbitration of 33–34
canonization principle 28, 29
citizenship issue 29, 31, 33–34
citizens' loyalties 39
civil war 387, 389–90
compared with Cyprus 404
complex structure 30–31, 32
consociationalism 22, 367
Constituency of Peoples 34
Constitution 29–30, 31–32, 34, 35, 37, 38
Preamble 34
constitutional change/transition 331, 332–33, 337–39
Constitutional Court 30, 33, 34–35, 370
Constituency of Peoples decision (2000) 35
constitutional design and territorial cleavages 360, 365, 371, 372
constitutional engagement period 25
constitutional process 25, 29–30
Council of Europe membership (2002) 35
Council of Peoples 35
declaration of independence (1992) 23–24, 29
demonstrations and protests 39
discrimination case law 35
disintegration of SFRY, effect on 23–24
Election law 35
elections 36, 39–40
ethnic concerns 387
ethnic civil war 26
ethnic cleansing 22, 24–25, 26, 27, 31, 32, 387
ethnonationalist parties 37–38, 40
mono-ethnic non-competitive electoral competition 37, 40
European Union
European Court of Human Rights (ECtHR) case law 35, 372
impact of 33
Stabilisation and Association Agreement, ratification (2008) 35
federalism 357–58, 415–16
General Framework for Peace (GFAP) *see* **Dayton Peace Agreement (DPA), Bosnia & Herzegovina**
greater than the sum of its parts, whether 30
highly territorialized region xvi
individual and collective rights 34–35
institutional structure 29, 30–31, 34–35
international institutions, role of 371
legal continuity 29
lessons learned 36
as model or cautionary tale 41
Muslims 24–25, 27, 41
nationalism 26–27, 37, 40–41
Office of High Representative (OHR) 33–35
outcome of process 32

Bosnia-Herzegovina (BiH) (*cont.*)
Parliamentary Assembly 30–31, 32, 33, 35
partition plans 26–27, 34, 40–41
Peace Implementation Council 33
political elites 39
power-sharing arrangements 421
public assemblies 39
reorganization of Bosnia as a consociational federation 22
secession/secessionist movements 24–25, 29, 41
Sejdić (Dervo) & Finci (Jakob) v. Bosnia & Herzegovina 35, 372
self-determination 24–25, 27
Šestorka (sextet), informal coalition 38–39
sovereignty, declaration of (1991) 23–24
Stabilisation and Association Agreement with the EU, ratification (2008) 35
state capture 36
Statement of Principles for New Constitutional Arrangements 26–27
status of "Others" in 34–35
territorial cleavages 331, 360, 365, 371, 372
territorial restructuring 22, 29
and centrality of territory 26
cleavages 36
Dayton Peace Agreement (DPA) 22, 26, 29
lessons learned 36
overview of territorial reorganization 22
role of territory at Dayton 26
as state comprising two Entities 22, 30–32, 34–35, 40–41
US involvement 22, 28, 29
violence 41, 332–33, 367
war in 24, 25, 26, 28
Dayton Peace Agreement *see* **Dayton Peace Agreement (DPA), Bosnia & Herzegovina**
origins of 25
siege of Sarajevo (1992) 25, 26
Vance-Owen Peace Plan (VOPP) 27
youth unemployment 40–41
Brancati, Dawn 357
Brčko (Bosnian-majority strategic municipality), international arbitration of 33–34
Brexit referendum, UK (2016) 276, 288
Brezhnev, Leonid 293
British Cabinet Mission Plan (1946), India 84
Brown, Nathan 407
BRR (Agency for Rehabilitation and Reconstruction), Indonesia 135
Buhari, Muhammadu 196–97
Buthelezi, Mangosothu 220, 224, 228, 229, 232, 233, 234, 236

CA1 (first Constituent Assembly), Nepal *see under* **Constituent Assembly, Nepal**
CA2 (second Constituent Assembly), Nepal *see under* **Constituent Assembly, Nepal**
Campbell, David 26–27
Canada 365
Caputto, Dante 14–15
Carlos, Juan 242–43
Carras, Costa 55
Catalonia region, Spain 237–38, 239–41, 242, 243, 245–47, 248, 250–51, 252, 253, 357, 371, 382, 384–85
Assemblea de Catalunya 240–41
compared with Basque Country 241–42
crisis of 2017–18 251, 252
historical nationalities 240, 249–50
nationalism 240, 241–42, 243, 244, 245–46, 247
Statute of Autonomy 250–51, 252
Unified Socialist Party of Catalonia (PSUC) 240–41, 244
see also **Basque Country, Spain; Spain**
ceasefires 385, 389–90, 396, 425–26
agreements 393, 397
Philippines 204, 207
Sri Lanka 259, 260–61, 264, 268–69, 273–74
Chamber of Regional Representatives (DPD), Indonesia 127–28, 138, 139
Chaudhary, Rukmini 177
Chautari, Martin 170
Choudhry, Sujit 356
Christofias, Demetris 55, 58
citizenship
Bolivia 5–6
Bosnia-Herzegovina (BiH) 29, 31, 33–34
citizens' loyalties 39
Cyprus, internal constituent state citizenship principle 52
Civic Committee, Santa Cruz (Bolivia) 3, 5, 7
Enough! (communiqué of 2003) 5
civil war
Bosnia-Herzegovina (BiH) 387, 389–90
Cyprus 389–90
duration 404
Ethiopia 368–69, 387
ethnic 26
India 389–90
Indonesia 389–90
Iraq 102
Nepal 389–90, 397
Nigeria 181, 387
Philippines 389–90
Spain 237, 238
Sri Lanka 387, 396
Yemen 328
see also **demonstrations and protests; rebellions; violence**
Clerides, Glafcos Ioannou (Cypriot President) 48–49
Coalition for Unity and Democracy (CUD), Ethiopia 74–75
Coalition of Ethiopian Democratic Forces 66
Coalition Provisional Authority (CPA), Iraq 104–5
Governing Council 103–4
Property Claims Commission established by (2004) 105–6
Cohen, Herman 65
Collier, Paul 384

Communist Party of Nepal (UML) 161–62, 166, 167, 169, 170, 172, 173–74, 175–76, 177–78
CONALDE (Democratic National Council), Bolivia 12, 13–14
Concerned South Africans Group (COSAG) 225
consociationalism 331, 366, 420–22
  Bosnia-Herzegovina (BiH) 22, 367
  constitutional design and territorial cleavages 364, 366, 367, 372
  Cyprus 44, 45, 58–59
  highly devolved federalism with a consocialized central government 413, 420
  South Africa 222, 223
  Sri Lanka 262
  Ukraine 310
  Yemen 324–25
Constituent Assembly (CA), Bolivia 5, 395, 399, 402, 405–6
  Congress approval 8
  demand for 4–5, 7
  gridlock 10
  as plenipotentiary 9
  procedural paradoxes facing 9
  proposals regarding 8–9
  and Sucre, status of 10–12
  see also **Bolivia**
Constituent Assembly, Nepal 167, 168, 174, 176–77, 400, 405–6
  first Constituent Assembly (CA1) 161–62, 167, 169, 171, 174, 175, 178, 180
    actors and decision-making 169
    Caucuses 171
    Committees 171–73
    context and background 167
    dissolution of (2012) 161–62, 174, 175, 178, 408
    elections 168–69
    institutional structure 171
    Party Whips 171, 176
    Rules of Procedure 171
  second Constituent Assembly (CA2) 161–62, 168–69, 175–76, 180
Constitution Drafting Committees (CDCs)
  Iraq 107–8, 116, 408–9
  Yemen 312, 320–23
Constitution of Kenya Review Commission (CKRC) 144, 145–46, 147–48, 152, 153, 154, 158
  Commissioners 152, 158–59
  Constituency Constitutional Forums set up by 145
  establishment (2000) 143
  legislation 159
  mandate 157
  proposals 148, 151–52
  Task Force 149–50
constitutional assemblies 405–9
  Cyprus 405–6
  dual-purpose 407
  Ethiopia 68–69
  India 405–6
  Iraq 405–6
  Kenya 405–6
  Nigeria 191–92, 405–6
  South Africa 404, 405–6
  Spain 405–6
  Sri Lanka 256, 257, 258–59, 262
  see also **Constituent Assembly (CA), Bolivia; Constituent Assembly, Nepal**
constitutional bargaining 353
constitutional change 340–41, 342, 375–77, 379, 381–82, 386, 387–89, 390, 402–3, 410–11, 412, 424, 426, 427–28
  Bolivia 21
  Bosnia-Herzegovina (BiH) 38
  India 81, 86, 94
  Indonesia 137
  Kenya 143
  Nepal 180
  Nigeria 196, 197, 198–99, 201
  Philippines 208–9, 214–15, 217
  Scotland/UK 275, 276, 281, 286, 289, 291
  Sri Lanka 265, 333–34
  see also **constitutional transition**
constitutional design and territorial cleavages 352, 412
  asymmetrical arrangements 355, 360, 363
  and constitutional moments 412
  constitutional moments 412
  decentralization and special autonomy 361
  federalism 353–61
  guarantors and dispute resolution 369
  international institutions, role of 370
  nullification 367
  Philippines 370
  political geometry 391–92
  redistribution 364
  representation at the centre 364–67
  rights 364
  secession clauses 368
  special autonomy 361, 423
  symmetrical federalism 412–13
  violence 353, 361, 367
  see also **territorial cleavages**
constitutional engagement period
  Bolivia 6
  Bosnia-Herzegovina (BiH) 25
  Cyprus 49
constitutional federalism 353
constitutional moments 402
  and constitutional design 412
  context 378, 390
  with divided power 393
  dynamics 376, 390
  India 81
  means antecedent to 385
  Nepal 167, 176
  Philippines 209
  and political mobilization 378
  relative power of key actors 376, 388, 391, 392
  violence prior to 397
constitutional processes
  Bosnia-Herzegovina (BiH) 25, 29–30
  South Africa 224

constitutional processes (*cont.*)
Yemen
framing 317
progression 318
see also **Constitution-making**
constitutional reform
Bolivia
background to events 2
compromise agreement (2008) 15
Constitution of 2009 (Oruro) 12, 13–14, 15, 19–20
constitutional amendment (2004) 5–6
constitutional engagement period 1
Constitutional Tribunal 1, 2, 16, 19, 20
rationale for 20–21
transition (2006–08) 1, 20–21
Kenya 140
Nigeria 183, 197, 198, 201
see also **constitutional change; constitutional design and territorial cleavages; constitutional moments; constitutional transition**
constitutional transition 330
agenda setting 340, 395
Bolivia 333–34, 392–93
background to events 2
compromise agreement (2008) 15
Constitution of 2009 (Oruro) 12, 13–14, 15, 19–20
constitutional amendment (2004) 5–6
constitutional engagement period 6
Constitutional Tribunal 1, 16, 19, 20
rationale for 20–21
transition (2006–08) 1, 20–21
Bosnia-Herzegovina (BiH) 25, 332–33, 337–39
constitutional engagement period 25
challenges confronting statehood 336
and civil war 389–90
context 332, 350
Cyprus 332–33, 335, 337–38, 340, 348
deliberation and ratification 342
dimensions of process 339
Ethiopia 334–35, 337, 340
federalism 349–50, 351
geopolitical context 338–39
implementation and related matters 345, 351
India 81, 86, 94, 333–34, 335–39, 340, 349
Indonesia 119–20, 333–34, 335–36, 346, 348
international advisers 346–47
international involvement 337, 339
Iraq 334, 337, 348, 349
Kenya 143, 335–36, 337–38, 346, 392–93
Kurdistan Region 335, 341, 349–50
legal and institutional continuity 386, 401–2
nature of 332
Nepal 332–33, 334, 335–36, 337–39, 340, 349–50
Nigeria 181, 193, 195, 199–200, 201, 331, 334–36, 337–38, 340
phases 339
Philippines 332–33, 335–36, 337, 340, 342, 345
and political mobilization 86
postponements 347
process 330–32, 333–34, 335–37, 342
dimensions of 339
phases 339
public participation 346
referendums 344–45
refusal to deal with combatants 333
Scotland 332–33, 335, 341
South Africa 333–34, 335, 337, 341–42, 343–44, 345, 348
Spain 237, 252, 335, 337, 338–39, 341, 392–93
Sri Lanka 255–56, 274, 331, 333–34, 335–36, 342
territorial cleavages *see* **territorial cleavages**
Ukraine 337, 338–39
United Kingdom 337, 338–39, 340, 392–93
United Nations 339
Yemen 326
see also **constitutional change; constitutional reform**
Constitution-making process xv, 343, 378, 394, 425–26
consensus requirement 344–45, 408–9
constitutional design 412
constitutional transition 334, 343, 347–48
deliberation 399
exclusion from 407
importance 326, 394
in military stalemate 393
Nepal 334
Nigeria 186, 197
political mobilization patterns shaping 375
ratification 409
South Africa 334
continuity, legal and institutional 386, 402
Convention for a Democratic South Africa (CODESA) 224–25, 397–98
Cordillera People's Liberation Army (CPLA)
Philippines 205–6
Costas, Ruben 8–9, 13
Crimea 293, 297
Autonomous Republic of Crimea 340
see also **Soviet Union, Former; Ukraine**
Croatia
failure to provide minority rights guarantees 24
Serbian population 24–25
Croatian Democratic Union *see* **HDZ (Hrvatska Demokratska Zajednica), Croatia**
Croats 400
and 1974 Constitution of SFRY 22–23
non-involvement of Bosnian Croats in Dayton Peace talks 26
Vance-Owen Peace Plan (VOPP), acceptance by Bosnian Croats 27
Cruywagen, Dennis 235–36
Cuellar, Ruben Dario 11
Cutileiro, José 26–27
Cyprus 43, 383, 396, 410–11

Anastasiades-Eroğlu Joint Declaration (February 2014) 57
background to conflict in 44
bailout plan (2013) 55–56
civil society organizations 49
civil war 389–90
"coming together" versus "holding together" federation issue 47, 383
compared with Bosnia-Herzegovina 404
compromise of 1959 45
compromise of 2010 55, 58
Constitution of 1960 44, 45, 51–52
Constitutional Assembly 405–6
constitutional design and territorial cleavages 371, 372
constitutional engagement period 49
constitutional transition 331, 332–33, 335, 337–38, 340, 348
Copenhagen European Council summit (2002) 54
de facto division into north (Turkish controlled) and south (government controlled), 1974 46–47
political equality principle 51
EU accession 44, 47–49, 53–54, 56–57
federalization proposals 47–49
Greek Cypriot communities *see* **Greek Cypriot communities**
Helsinki European Council meeting (1999) 48
"High-Level" agreements between Greek Cypriot and Turkish Cypriot leaders (1977 and 1979) 47–48
highly territorialized region xvi
independence from United Kingdom (1960) 44–45
intercommunal violence 44–45
international institutions, role of 371, 372
loss of territory in 1974 46
Luxembourg European Council meeting (1997) 48
negotiations on problem of 47
Northern Cyprus 46, 47, 48–49, 54–55
opposition to peace process 48–49
political elites 22
political parties 48–49, 55, 58–59
presidential system 45
property rights disputes 47, 52
referendums 44, 54–55, 56, 58, 410–11
Republic of 46–48, 53–55, 56
right of return for displaced persons, demand for 47, 49, 52
secession/secessionist movements 47, 53
sovereignty issue 47
territorial cleavages 331, 335, 371, 372
Treaty of Establishment (1960) 45
Turkish Cypriot communities *see* **Turkish Cypriot communities**
Turkish invasion (1974) 46–47
violence 44–45, 59
see also **Greek Cypriot communities; Turkish Cypriot communities**

Dahal, Pushpa Kamal 170
Dar Commission, India (1948) 85, 87, 96
Darul Islam movement, Indonesia 121–22, 124
Dayton Peace Agreement (DPA), Bosnia & Herzegovina 400, 404, 410, 420–21
complex structure created by 30–31, 32
constitutional design and territorial cleavages 357–58, 372
and Cyprus 52
enactment of BiH Constitution 25, 30
ethno-territorial nature of arrangement 30, 34, 38
evaluation of achievements 26, 40
and Federation of Bosnia and Herzegovina (FBiH) 28
international engagement in the implementation of 33
non-involvement of Bosnian Serbs and Croats in the talks 26
parties involved 25
signing of 29–30, 31
statehood, challenges confronting 337–38
territorial restructuring 22, 26, 29
see also **Bosnia-Herzegovina (BiH); Federal Republic of Yugoslavia (FRY); Federation of Bosnia and Herzegovina (FBiH); Republika Srpska (RS), Bosnia; Socialist Federal Republic of Yugoslavia (SFRY)**
De Klerk, FW (South African President) 222, 228, 234
de Soto, Alvaro 49
decentralization 331
Bolivia 3–4, 6, 15
Administrative Decentralization Law 17
Framework Law on Autonomies and Decentralization (FLAD), 21 15, 16–17, 18–19
Indonesia 126–27, 129, 133, 134, 135, 137, 138
Scotland 275, 284–85
Spain 237, 240, 243, 245–46, 248–50, 252, 253
and special autonomy 361, 362
Ukraine 297–98, 307, 308–9
deliberation 399
constitutional assemblies 405–9
forums and decision-rules 401–5
participants 400–1
"on ramps" process 400–1
and ratification 342
democracy
Bolivia 3
Coalition for Unity and Democracy (CUD), Ethiopia 74–75
Movement for Social Democracy (EDEK), Cyprus 48–49
Scottish constitutional democracy 276, 290, 291
South Africa 219, 224, 226–27, 231, 232–33, 234
democratic transition 385
Spain 237, 238, 241, 252

Democratic National Council (CONALDE), Bolivia 12, 13–14
Democratic Nationalist Action (ADN), Bolivia 4–5
Democratic Party (DIKO), Cyprus 48–49
Democratic Party (DP), Northern Cyprus 48–49, 55
Democratic Party of Indonesia for the Struggle (PDI-P) 125–26, 127–28, 137
Democratic Rally (DISY), Greek Cypriot party 48–49
demography and political entrepreneurs 379
demonstrations and protests
 Bolivia 6, 7, 9, 10, 11
 Bosnia-Herzegovina (BiH) 39
 Ethiopia 76–77
 India 89
 Indonesia 125
 Ukraine 305, 307, 309–10, 387
 Yemen 313
 see also **rebellions; violence**
Denktaş, Rauf 48–49
***Derg* (Military Junta in Ethiopia, 1974–91)** 63, 65
Desmukh, CD 89
devolution 414
 asymmetrical arrangements 335–36, 423–24
 and federalism 353–61
  highly devolved federalism with a consocialized central government 420
 Kenya 140–41, 144, 145, 147–48, 150, 151, 156, 159, 361, 416–17
  coming into force 154–55
  Compromise Proposal for Devolution 151–52
  consequences 159–60
  cooperative 156
  debates 147
  design 160
  districts 148, 149, 153
  legislation 148–49
  levels 148, 151
  NCC, discussion in 149
  objectives 148, 155
  political mobilization for 142
  proposals/recommendations 149–50, 151–52, 154, 158
  site 160
  support for 156, 157
  terminology 143–44
 with a majoritarian central government 412–13, 415
 Northern Ireland 277–78
 Scotland 275, 276, 277–78, 280–81, 285, 286, 287, 288, 363, 402
  administrative devolution 279
 Spain 248, 253, 254
 Wales 277–78
 whether to devolve 414
 see also **federalism**
devolved autocracy, Ethiopia 61
displaced persons
 Cyprus 47, 49, 52
 Kenya 142
Dixit, Kanak Mani 174
DPA *see* **Dayton Peace Agreement (DPA), Bosnia & Herzegovina**
Duterte, Rodrigo Roa (Filipino President) 216–17, 424

East Timor 119–20, 123, 126–27, 128–29, 130, 138, 363
elites
 economic 2, 298
 ethnic 195
 governing/ruling *see* **ruling elites**
 local 79, 357
 national 72
 negotiations 252
 new 248, 252
 old/traditional 70, 252
 political *see* **political elites**
 regional 81, 386
 religious 167–68
 Tigrayan 64
Elster, Jon 343–44
EOKA (National Organization of Cypriot Fighters) 44–45
EPLF (Eritrean People's Liberation Front) 65
EPRDF (Ethiopian People's Revolutionary Democratic Front) 64–65, 66–69, 70, 73, 74–77, 78–79, 404–5, 410
 Council 77–78
Erdoğan, Recep Tayyip (Turkish President) 49, 57
Eritrean People's Liberation Front (EPLF) 65
Eroğlu, Derviş 55–57
 Anastasiades-Eroğlu Joint Declaration (February 2014) 57
ESM (Ethiopian Student Movement) 60, 63
ETA (Basque Homeland and Freedom), terrorist group 239, 241–42, 243, 247
Ethiopia 60, 266–67, 393, 396, 400, 404
 Addis Ababa 61–62, 65, 66, 67–68, 73–75
 All Amhara People's Organization 66–67, 69
 Amhara 72–73, 76–77
 Axumite invention/innovation 64
 background to events 61
 Boundary Commission 67–68, 349
 centers of power 61
 centralization process 61–62
 Charter 65, 66–69, 70–71, 404
 civil war 368–69, 387
 Coalition for Unity and Democracy (CUD) 74–75
 Coalition of Ethiopian Democratic Forces 66
 collapse of socialist dictatorship 60–61
 Constitution of 1995 66–68, 69–71, 72, 73, 74
 Constitutional Assembly 68–69
 constitutional design and territorial cleavages 358, 359, 365
 constitutional engagement period 65
 constitutional transition 331, 334–35, 337, 340
 "controlled freedom" policy 75–76
 Council of Representatives (CoR) 65, 67–68
 democratization process 75–76

Derg (Military Junta, 1974–91) 63, 65
devolved autocracy 61
elites 69
  national 72
  political 63–64, 65, 66, 69, 72–73, 74
  ruling 60, 61–62, 63–64, 69, 78
  Tigrayan 64
emergence of modern state 60
Eritrean People's Liberation Front (EPLF) 65
"Ethiopia first" 69
Ethiopian People's Revolutionary Democratic Front (EPRDF) 64–65, 66–69, 70, 73, 74–77, 78–79, 404–5, 410
  Council 77–78
Ethiopian People's Revolutionary Party (EPRP) 63
Ethiopian Student Movement (ESM) 60, 63
ethnic federalism 69–70, 74–75, 77–78, 79
ethnonationalism 60–62, 64, 67, 69, 71–73
failed "nation building" 62–64
federal system 60–61, 67–69, 70–72, 73–74, 76–80
  ethnic federalism 69–70, 74–75, 77–78, 79
federalism 415–16
Flag Day (September) 72
Forum (*Medrek*) 74–75
"Greater Ethiopia" perspective 69
highly territorialized region xvi
"Horn of Conflicts" 78
Institute for the Study of Ethiopian Nationalities (ISEN) 67–68
language 61–62, 71
lessons learned 78
Marxism–Leninism 70
MEISON (Ethiopian Socialist Movement) 63
militant political culture 63
minorities 72–73
Muslims 61–62
nation building 61–62
"National Liberation Fronts" agenda 66, 70, 72
nationalism/'nationality question' 60, 61–62, 63, 67, 70
Oromia 71–74, 76–77
Oromo Liberation Front (OLF) 65, 66–67, 68–69, 404–5
Oromo People's Democratic Organization (OPDO) 64, 65, 66–67, 73–74
outcome of process 70
overview of case 61
peasant rebellions 62
pluralism, political 60–61, 66–67, 79–80
political elites 63–64, 69, 72–73, 74
  centralizing 66, 69
  centrist 65, 66
political legitimacy 63
political mobilization 60–61, 69, 79–80
political pluralism 79–80
protests 76–77
rebellions 62
regional forces 61
religion 61–62
secession/secessionist movements 69–71, 74–75, 77–79
self-determination 67, 68–69, 70–71, 72, 404
Showa (historical region) 61–62
"socialist" regime (1974–91) 63
and Southern Nations, Nationalities and Peoples Regional State (SNNPRS) 67–68, 71–72
state structure, transformation 61–62
territorial cleavages 331
Tigray People Liberation Front (TPLF), Ethiopia 61, 64, 65
Transitional Government of Ethiopia (TGE) 65, 66–69, 404–5
upper house 365, 418–19
violence 66, 396
Workers Party of Ethiopia 66
ethnic concerns, Bosnia & Herzegovina 24
  ethnic civil war 26
  ethnic cleansing 22, 24–25, 26, 27, 31, 32, 387
  ethnonationalist parties 37–38, 40
  mono-ethnic non-competitive electoral competition 37, 40
ethnic federalism
  Ethiopia 69–70, 74–75, 77–78, 79
  Nepal 79, 161–62, 164–65, 167, 174, 175, 179
  South Africa 219, 220, 222, 223, 226, 228–29, 231, 232–33
ethno-linguistic cleavages
  India 81, 82–83, 89, 95–96
  South Africa 220
  Ukraine 292–93
ethnonationalism
  Bosnia-Herzegovina (BiH) 37–38, 40
  Ethiopia 60–62, 64, 67, 69, 71–73
ethno-territorial cleavages
  Dayton Peace Agreement (DPA), Bosnia & Herzegovina 30, 34, 38, 85
  India 83, 85–86
  Sri Lanka 269, 271, 372
"Euromaidan" protests, Ukraine 304, 307, 309–10
European Community Conference on the Former Yugoslavia
  Working Group on Bosnia 26–27
European Court of Human Rights (ECtHR)
  Bosnia-Herzegovina (BiH) 35
  Cyprus 47
European Union
  accession of Cyprus 44, 47–49, 53–54, 56–57
  Bosnia-Herzegovina (BiH)
    European Court of Human Rights (ECtHR) case law 35
    impact on 33
    Stabilisation and Association Agreement, ratification (2008) 35
  Committee of Regions xv
  External Action Service xv
  failures in Southern Europe 57
Eurozone debt crisis 55–56
Exit, Voice and Loyalty framework (Hirschmann) 353

Famagusta, Cyprus 51, 54–55
Faustian bargain, Ukraine 295–96, 300–1, 303, 304, 310–11, 365, 383–84
  breakdown 303

FBiH *see* Federation of Bosnia and Herzegovina (FBiH)
Federal Party, Sri Lanka 258–60, 261, 262
Federal Republic of Yugoslavia (FRY) 24–25, 29
  genocide, abetting 29
  see also Bosnia-Herzegovina (BiH); Federation of Bosnia and Herzegovina (FBiH); Milošević, Slobodan (FRY President); Socialist Federal Republic of Yugoslavia (SFRY)
federalism
  benefits 354–55
  Bosnia-Herzegovina (BiH) 357–58, 415–16
  "coming together" versus "holding together" federation 47, 70–71, 288–89, 342, 352–53, 383
  compared with special autonomy arrangements 362, 380, 391–92, 412–13
  constitutional 353
  constitutional transition 349–50
  and devolution 353–61
  Ethiopia 60–61, 67–69, 70–72, 73–74, 76–80, 415–16
    ethnic federalism 69–70, 74–75, 77–78, 79
  ethno-federations 416
  failed federations 414
  highly devolved 391–92
    with a consocialized central government 413, 420
  India 93, 94, 415–16
  Indonesia 121, 137
  Iraq 103–4, 110–11, 116, 117
  Kenya 415–16
  Nepal 161, 168, 172, 173–74, 177–78, 415–16
    debates 172
    ethnic federalism 161–62, 164–65, 167, 174, 175, 179
    federal restructuring 161–62, 167, 168–69, 171–74, 176–77, 178, 179, 374
  Nigeria 183–84, 358, 416
    presidential federalism 181, 183, 186, 190–91, 194, 195, 198, 200–1
  political mobilization 357
  rationales 355–56
  risks 414–15
  Scotland 288–89
  South Africa 414–16
  Spain 415–16
  and special autonomy arrangements 362
  subsidiarity principle 355
  symmetrical 412–13, 415
  Ukraine 292–93, 295, 296–97, 298, 299–300, 307, 310
  United States 355–56
  Yemen 324–25, 415–16
  see also devolution
Federation of Bosnia and Herzegovina (FBiH) 28, 34
  Bosniak population 40
  and division of BiH into two Entities 22, 30–32, 34–35, 40–41
  see also Bosnia-Herzegovina (BiH); Federal Republic of Yugoslavia (FRY); Socialist Federal Republic of Yugoslavia (SFRY)
Fernandez, Leopoldo 14
Fernández-Miranda, Torcuato 242–43
Fessha, Yonatan 232
first Constituent Assembly (CAI), Nepal *see* CAI (first Constituent Assembly), Nepal
forums and decision-rules 401–9
Franco, General Francisco 237, 238–39, 240–42, 246, 252, 355, 385–86, 387, 395–96, 401, 408
  death (1975) 240, 241–42, 395–96
  Francoism 237, 238–39, 240, 246
  regime of 240–43, 355, 416
Free Aceh Movement (GAM) 124, 129–31, 134–35, 138, 400–1
Freedom Front, South Africa 228, 232, 234–35
Friends of Cyprus 55
Friends of Yemen 315

Galicia, Spain 238–39, 240, 246–47, 248, 249
Gandhi, Mahatma 82, 95
Georgia
  Rose Revolution 74–75
Ghai, Yash 145, 151–52
Glorieta Palace, Bolivia 11–12
Goa, India 92–93, 400–1
governing elites *see* ruling elites
Granic, Mate 28
Greece
  financial and political meltdown 56–57
  relations with Turkey 45, 46, 48
  see also Cyprus; Greek Cypriot communities
Greek Cypriot communities 383
  Annan Plan submitted for ratification 43–44
  constitutional transition 337
  electoral roll 45
  fear of "imposed settlement" 44
  forced eviction by Turkish military 46
  foreign policy advantages 57
  "High-Level" agreements between Greek Cypriot and Turkish Cypriot leaders (1977 and 1979) 47–48
  nationalism 53
  power-sharing arrangements with Turkish Cypriots 45, 53, 58
  rejection of Annan Plan 43–44, 51, 53, 54–55, 57–58, 59, 345
  right of return for displaced persons, demand for 47
  sovereignty issue 47
  statehood, challenges confronting 337
  statistics 51, 55
  union with Greece, desire for 44–45
  see also Annan Plan (2002–04), Cyprus; Cyprus
Greenfield, Richard 61
Greer, Scott L. 240–41
Gujarat, India 82–83, 89, 93, 96
Gulf Cooperation Council (GCC)/GCC Initiative, Yemen 313–16, 320, 323
  Implementation Mechanism 314–15, 326

Habibie, Bacharuddin Jusuf (Indonesian President) 126–27
Hadi, Abd Rabbuh Mansur al- (Yemeni President) 313, 314–15, 316, 317–18, 320, 324, 325–26
Haile Mariam Desalegn (Ethiopian Prime Minister) 76–77, 79–80
Haile Selassie (Ethiopian Emperor) 61–62
***half moon* departments, Bolivia (media luna, area of opposition to Morales)** 9, 11–12, 15–16
  civic committees 7–8
  prefects 7–8, 18–19
  pro-autonomy segments 17
  protests organized by (2006) 9, 10
Hatt, Mohammad 120–21
HDZ (Hrvatska Demokratska Zajednica), Croatia 23–24
Hellmann-Rajanayagam, Dagmar 261
Hirak (secessionist Southern movement), Yemen 312–13, 315–16, 320–21, 327
Hirschmann, Albert 353
Hoare, Marko Attila 41
Hoeffler, Anke 384
Holbrooke, Richard 25, 26, 29
Hornsby, Charles 141, 144
Horowitz, Donald 51–52
House of Peoples, Parliamentary Assembly of Bosnia and Herzegovina 30, 32, 33, 35
House of Representatives, Parliamentary Assembly of Bosnia and Herzegovina 30
Houthi, Abd-al-Khaliq al- 322
Houthi, Abd-al-Khaliq Badr-al-Din al- 322
Houthis (Islamic armed movement), Yemen 315–16, 317–18, 319–21, 322–23, 324, 325–26, 327–28, 387, 411, 415–16
Hryniov, Volodymyr 296
Hulsey, John 37, 40
Hume, Nathan 356
Hussein, Faisal bin 100–1
Hussein, Saddam 102
Hyderabad, India 88

identity politics
  Nepal 164–66, 167, 178
Ihedioha, Emeka 195–96
India 402
India 81, 381, 399
  background to events 81
  Bengalis 82–83
  Bombay Presidency 82–83
  British colonial regime 82–83, 90
  civil war 389–90
  Commissioner for Linguistic Minorities 97–98
  composite nationalism 82–83
  Congress 82–83, 85, 86, 87, 94–95
    Anti-Congress opposition parties 89
    Nagpur Secession (1920) 86
    Provincial Committees 82, 86, 95
  Constituent Assembly 82, 84–86
    JVP Report (1948) 87
  Constitution 82, 86, 91, 95, 97–98
    quasi-federal nature of 81, 85–86
  constitutional change/transition 81, 86, 94, 331, 333–34, 335–39, 340, 349
  constitutional design and territorial cleavages 358–59, 360
  constitutional engagement period 84
  constitutional moment 81
  Dar Commission (1948) 85, 87, 96
  decolonialization 336–37
  elections 82, 84, 94–95
  ethnic peace 81, 91–92
  ethno-linguistic cleavages 81, 82–83, 89, 95–96
  ethno-regional nationalities 82–83
  ethno-territorial cleavages 83, 85–86
  federal system 93, 94
  federalism 415–16
  Government of India Act 1935 84
  Gujrati people 88, 89
  highly territorialized region xvi
  Hindi-speaking states 88
  independence (1947) 81, 84
  Interim Government (1946–49) 84
  lessons learned 96
  linguistic homogeneity 87–88
  linguistic minorities 88
  majoritarian political principle 97–98
  Marathi people 88, 89
  micro-minorities 97–98
  Motilal Nehru Report (1928) 82
  neo-liberal reforms 81, 98
  North-East region 90, 92, 96, 97, 98, 400–1
    Autonomous Tribal District Councils 97
  outcome of process 93
  overview of case 81
  Partition with Pakistan (1947) 82, 83, 86
  political elites 81, 82–83, 96
  political mobilization 86, 92, 96
  postponements 349
  presidencies (colonial regime) 82–83
  protests 89
  religious cleavages
    Hindus 82, 83, 84, 89–90
    Muslims 82, 83, 84
    Sikhs 89–90, 93–94, 96
  secession/secessionist movements 414
  self-determination 82–83, 85, 92
  Special Category States 97
  state creation 89, 94–95, 96, 97
  states reorganization 81, 89, 93, 95, 98
    State Reorganization Commission (SRC) 87–90, 97, 385
    States Reorganization Act 1956 88–89, 358–59
  subnational autonomy 81, 85
    units 95
  subnational units 81
  territorial cleavages 331, 335–36
  territorial reorganization/restructuring 81, 85
  Twelve Point Agreement (2005) 167
  violence 82, 86–87, 89, 92, 386–87
  see also specific ***states, such as Punjab, India***

India National Congress 82
Indian Peace Keeping Force (IPKF), Sri Lanka 259
Indonesia 119, 381, 383, 396
Agency for Rehabilitation and Reconstruction (BRR) 135
asymmetrical arrangements 120, 139
background to events 120
central-regional relations 126
Chamber of Regional Representatives (DPD) 127–28, 138, 139
civil war 389–90
Constitution of 1945 121, 122
return to 121, 122
constitutional amendments 119–20, 121, 124–27, 137, 333–34
constitutional change 137
constitutional engagement period 124–31
constitutional transition 119–20, 124–25, 126, 331, 333–34, 335–36, 346, 348, 349
Darul Islam movement 121–22, 124
decentralization 126–27, 129, 133, 134, 135, 137, 138, 361
deconcentration 126
Democratic Party of Indonesia for the Struggle (PDI-P) 125–26, 127–28, 137
demonstrations 125
diversity of 119–20, 121, 126
Dutch control 120–21, 122–23, 386–87
and East Timor 119–20
federalism 121, 137
Fretilin (political party) 123
Golkar (party of New Order regime) 125–26, 127, 137
grievances 119–20, 123, 128, 129–30, 135
highly territorialized peripheral regions xvi
"imagined community" 120–21
Law on Aceh (2006) 119–20, 124–25, 130, 131, 134, 135, 138, 362
Laws No. 22 and 25, 1999 127
Laws No. 32 and 33, 2004 127
lessons learned 137
Masyumi party 120–21
Military Operations Zones 123, 124
New Order regime (Suharto) 123, 124–25, 126–27
outcome of process 133
overview of case 119
Pancasila (five principles affirming basis of) 121–22, 125
parliament 127–28
People's Consultative Assembly (MPR) 119–20, 124–26
political elites 121–22
political mobilization 122
postponements 349
rebellions 121–22, 124
regional organization 126
Revolutionary Government of the Republic of Indonesia (PRRI) 122
secession/secessionist movements 120, 121–22, 126, 132, 135–36, 137, 414
special autonomy laws 119–20, 126, 128–29, 130, 132–33, 136–37, 138–39, 355–56, 361, 362, 374, 385–86, 402–3
Special Autonomy Law 120, 131, 132–33, 134, 135–36, 348
territorial cleavages 119, 133, 134, 136, 137, 138, 139, 331, 335–36
unitary state principle 120, 121–22, 125
violence 119, 124, 125, 128, 129, 130, 134, 136, 138, 139
see also **Aceh, Indonesia; Papua, Indonesia**
Inkatha Freedom Party (IFP), South Africa 224, 228, 230, 233–35, 404–5, 409–10
Institute for the Study of Ethiopian Nationalities (ISEN) 67–68
Inter-American Convention on Human Rights 19
interim constitutions 397, 398, 399, 403–4, 408, 409–10, 411, 417–18
constitutional design and territorial cleavages 359
constitutional transition 334, 339–40, 342, 344
Ethiopia 76–77
Iraq 99, 101–2, 104–5, 118
Nepal 168–69, 170–72, 174–75, 176–77, 179–80
South Africa 225, 227, 228–29, 230–31, 233, 234–35, 236, 408, 411, 417–18
International Arbitral Tribunal for Brčko 33–34
International Conference on the Former Socialist Federal Republic of Yugoslavia (ICFY) 27–28
international institutions, role of 370
International Labor Organization Convention on the Rights of Indigenous Peoples, 1989 370–71
International Peace Conference on Yugoslavia 24–25
Iran
conflict with Iraq 102
Iraq 99, 383
Arabs 99–100, 104, 106–7, 380, 384
Baath Party 102, 103
background to events 99
Baghdad 101, 103, 104, 107–10, 111–14, 115
British control 100–1
civil war 102
Coalition Provisional Authority (CPA) 103–6
Constitution 99–100, 101, 103–5, 106, 107–10, 111, 112–13, 114
Article 112 109–10
Article 115 109
Article 117 109
Article 118 109–10
Article 140 112
draft 99, 103, 107–8, 419–20
final (2005 Constitution) 108–11, 112–13, 114, 115, 116, 360, 407
interim constitutions 99, 101–2, 104–5, 118
objectives 115–16
vague nature of 116–17

Constitution Drafting Committee (CDC) 107–8, 116, 408–9
constitutional engagement period 103
constitutional rupture 334
constitutional transition 331, 334, 337, 348, 349
corruption 111–12
elites
political 115–16
ruling 117
federalism 99, 103–4, 110–11, 116, 117
guerrilla war 101–2
Gulf War, 1991 102, 385
Gulf War, 2003 103, 385
history 100
interim parliament 99
Iran, conflict with 102
Iraqi Islamic Party 104
Islamic State of Iraq and Syria (ISIS) 112, 113–14
Kirkuk province 101–2, 105–6, 110, 115
Kurdish population 99, 100, 101, 102, 105, 110, 357–58, 380, 384, 385–86
displacement 101–2
Kurdistan Alliance 104–5, 106–8, 109, 117
Kurdistan Democratic Party (KDP) 102
Kurdistan Region 100, 101–2, 104, 105, 107, 109–10, 111–15, 117
Kurdistan Regional Government (KRG) 112–15
Leadership Council 107–8, 109, 110–11, 408–9
lessons learned 115
majoritarianism 99, 115–16
minoritarianism 116
multiculturalism 101
Muslims 99–100, 104
National Assembly 408–9
"no-fly zone" 102
oil and gas resources 109–11, 112–13
outcome of process 110
overview of case 99
Patriotic Union of Kurdistan (PUK) 102, 103–4
postponements 349
referendums 411
Supreme Court 114–15
territorial cleavages 99, 110–11, 331, 336
Transitional Administrative Law (TAL) 104–8, 110, 112, 404
Transitional Government 106
Transitional National Assembly (TNA) 106–8
United Iraqi Alliance 106–7
United Nations Assistance Mission to Iraq (UNAMI) 112
violence 101–2, 106–7, 108
voluntary union status 114
Islamic State of Iraq and Syria (ISIS) 112, 113–14
Ivanic, Mladen 39–40
Izetbegović, Alija 25, 34

Jackson, Vicky 369, 394
James, Alan 44
Jammu, India 82, 88, 89
Jan Sangh (BJP, Hindu-based Indian party) 89–90, 92–93, 94–95
Janatha Vimukthi Peramuna (JVP) 268
January Agenda (2005), Bolivia 6, 8
Justice and Development Party (AKP), Turkey 49, 57

Kadirgamar, Lakshman 268–69
KADU (Kenya African Democratic Union) 142, 143, 386
Kalla, Jusuf (Indonesian Vice-President) 130
Kangu, Mutakha 149–50
KANU (Kenya African National Union) 142, 143, 144, 146, 386
Kashmir, India 82, 88, 89, 91, 355, 400–1
Kaufman, Chaim 26
Keating, Michael 279–80
Kenya 140, 383, 402
background to events 141–42
Bomas process 145–46, 154, 160, 405–6, 407
boundary drawing 141
commissioners 144, 145, 146
of CKRC 152, 158–59
Constitution 158, 159, 160, 345
CoE process 154
Committee of Experts 154, 407
Constitution of Kenya Review Act (1997) 143–44
draft 140, 143–44, 145–46, 149–50, 153, 154, 157–58
independence 143
new 140–41, 142, 143–44, 145, 146–47, 152, 158, 159
original 143–44, 146, 147
Wako draft 153, 157
Wanjiku consensus 152
Constitution of Kenya Review Commission (CKRC) 144, 145–46, 147–48, 152, 153, 154, 158, 159
Commissioners 152, 158–59
Constituency Constitutional Forums set up by 145
establishment (2000) 143
legislation 159
mandate 157
proposals 148, 151–52
Task Force 149–50
Constitutional Assembly 405–6
constitutional change/transition 143, 331, 333–34, 335–36, 337–38, 346, 392–93
constitutional design and territorial cleavages 365
constitutional engagement period 145–52
adoption process 152
devolution discussion 147–49
constitutional reform 140–41, 143–44, 154, 155, 158
corruption 155–56
devolution 140–41, 144, 145, 147–48, 150, 151, 156, 159, 361, 416–17
coming into force 154–55
Compromise Proposal for 151–52

Kenya (*cont.*)
devolution (*cont.*)
consequences 159–60
cooperative 156
debates 147
design 160
districts 148, 149, 153
legislation 148–49
levels 148, 151
NCC, discussion in 149
objectives 148, 155
political mobilization for 142
proposals/recommendations 149–50, 151–52, 154, 158
site 160
support for 156, 157
terminology 143–44
displaced persons 142
elections 143, 144
of 2002 146, 157
of 2007 140–41
of 2013 154–55, 157
of 2017 156
federalism 415–16
independence (1962) 140, 141–42
KADU (Kenya African Democratic Union) 142, 143, 386
KANU (Kenya African National Union) 142, 143, 144, 146, 386
lessons learned 157–59
low levels of territorialization xvi
multi-partyism 143
Muslims 151
National Accord 154
National Assembly 147, 156, 158
Working Group 154–55, 156–57
National Constitutional Conference (NCC) 140, 143, 145–46, 147, 150, 151–53
devolution discussion 149
Steering Committee 151
Technical Committee 150–51
National Rainbow Alliance (NARC) 146
Orange Democratic Movement (ODM) 153–54
outcome of process 153
overview of case 140
Parliamentary Committee on the Constitution (PRC) 152
Parliamentary Select Commission 154
political mobilization for devolution 142
power-sharing arrangements 147
Provincial Administration 144, 149, 153
referendums 140–41, 147, 153–55, 159, 410–11
secession/secessionist movements 141–42, 159
Senate
Committee 155–56
territorial cleavages 142, 331, 335–36
upper house 365, 418–19
violence 140–41, 143, 154, 159
and Zanzibar 141–42
Kenyatta, Jomo 143
Kenyatta, Uhuru 146
Kerala, India 88
Khamal, Jhalanath 170
Khrushchev, Nikita 293
Kibaki, Mwai (Kenyan Vice-President) 74, 146–47, 151, 153–54, 158
Kissinger, Henry 229
Koirala, Sushil 170
Koljević, Nikola 26
Komšić, Ivo 28
Krajišnik, Momcilo 26
Kravchuk, Leonid 295–96, 297–98, 308
Kuchma, Leonid (Ukrainian President) 293, 295, 296–97, 298–301, 302, 406–7
Kumaratanga, Chandrika (Sri Lankan President) 260–61, 263–64, 267–69, 272, 396, 401
Kunzru, H.N. 87
Kurdish population, Iraq 99, 100, 101, 102, 105, 110, 357–58, 380, 384, 385–86
dialect 100
displacement 101–2
Kurdistan Democratic Party (KDP) 102
Kurdistan Alliance 104–5, 106–8, 109, 117
Kurdistan Region 100, 101–2, 104, 105, 107, 109–10, 111–15, 117
constitutional transition 335, 341, 349–50
Patriotic Union of Kurdistan (PUK) 102, 103–4
territorial cleavages 335
Kurdistan Regional Government (KRG) 112–15
KwaZulu-Natal, South Africa 228–29, 356, 362–63, 364–65, 366, 368, 369, 397–98

La Paz, Bolivia 11–12, 15
Latin America
constitutional assemblies 406
LCCA (Proposed Law Calling for a Constituent Assembly), Bolivia 7, 9, 11
Liberation Tigers of Tamil Eelam (LTTE), Sri Lanka 255–56, 258, 259–61, 263–64, 265, 266–70, 271–74, 366–67, 371, 387–88, 393, 396, 400, 403
ceasefire agreement with 397
Lijphart, Arend 200–1
Linera, Garcia 11, 13
Lippman, Peter 36, 38, 41
Loizides, Neophytos 382–83
Lyman, Nathan 226–27, 228

Madhesi People's Rights Forum (MJAF), Nepal 169
Madhya Pradesh, India 88, 92–93
Madison, James 355, 358–59
Madras Presidency, India 82–83
Maharashtra, India 85, 89, 93, 96
Mahmud, Syamsuddin (Indonesian governor) 128–29
majoritarianism 343, 415, 423
India 97–98
Iraq 99, 115–16
supermajorities 343–44, 402, 408, 411
territorial representation 342

Makarios III, Archbishop and President of Cyprus 44, 46
al-Maliki, Nouri 113–14
Mandela, Nelson 222, 226–27, 228
Manipur, India 91–92, 95, 400–1
Marinkovic, Branko 11
MAS-IPSP (*Movimiento al Socialismo–Instrumento Político por la Soberanía de los Pueblos*), Bolivia 1, 7, 8, 12, 14, 15, 17, 19–20, 406
on the CA 9, 10
composition of 17–18
elections 6, 7–9, 16–17
Framework Law on Autonomies and Decentralization (FLAD), 21 15, 16–17, 18–19
hegemony 6–7, 16–17
and National Council for Change (CONALCAM) 12, 13–14
and Sucre, status of 11–12
see also **Bolivia; Morales, Evo (Bolivian President); PODEMOS (*Poder Democrático y Social*) movement, Bolivia**
Mbeki, Thabo (President of South Africa) 228, 232
Megawati Soekarnoputri (Indonesian President) 125–26, 132
MEISON (Ethiopian Socialist Movement) 63
Meles Zenawi (Ethiopian Prime Minister) 64, 70, 76–77
Mengistu Haile Mariam (Ethiopian President) 65
Menlik II, Emperor of Ethiopia 60, 61–62, 65
Mesa, Carlos (Bolivian President) 5–6, 17
resignation (2005) 6
Meyer, Roelf 235
Milošević, Slobodan (FRY President) 24, 25, 26
Mindanao, Philippines 202–4, 205–6, 207, 208–10, 211, 212, 213–18, 362–63, 381, 382, 384, 411, 423, 424
MIP (*Movimiento Indigena Pachakuti*), Bolivia 4–5
Mizoram, India 91–93, 400–1
Mizo National Front 94–95
MNR (*Movimiento Nacionalista Revolucionario*), Bolivia 2, 4, 11
Modi, Narendra 95
Mohammed, Maalim 148
Mohammed, Murtala 186
Moi, Daniel arap (Kenyan President) 74, 76–77, 143, 145, 152, 153–54
Morales, Evo (Bolivian President) 361, 401
commitment of MAS to 19
and CONALDE 12, 13–14
elections 2, 13, 15
landslide victory (Dec 2005) 1, 6–7, 18
opposition to 7, 9
Proposed Law Calling for a Constituent Assembly (LCCA) (26) 7, 9, 11
reform obstacles 7
see also **MAS-IPSP (*Movimiento al Socialismo–Instrumento Político por la Soberanía de los Pueblos*)**
Morgan-Jones, Edward 41
Moro National Liberation Front (MNLF), Philippines 202, 203, 204, 208, 209, 210–11, 212, 214–17, 402–3
Morris-Jones, W.H. 93
Movement for Social Democracy (EDEK), Cyprus 48–49
Movement for Socialism–Political Instrument for the Sovereignty of the Peoples, Bolivia *see* **MAS-IPSP (*Movimiento al Socialismo–Instrumento Político por la Soberanía de los Pueblos*)**
Mubarak, Ahmad Awad bin 313, 318, 322–23
Muslim Brotherhood 313–14
Muslim League, India 84
Muslims
Bosnia-Herzegovina (BiH) 24–25, 27, 41
Ethiopia 61–62
India 82, 83, 84
Iraq 99–100, 104
Kenya 151
Nigeria 197
Philippines 202, 203–4, 206–7, 214–15, 423
Shia 99–100, 104, 408–9
Sri Lanka 257–58, 265
Sunni 99–100, 104
Mysore, India 88

Naga Council, India 91
Naga-Akbar Hydari Accord (1947, Kohima) 91
Nagaland, India 92
Framework Agreement (2015) 95
National Socialist Council 95
Peace Accord, 1947 400–1
Sixteen Point Agreement (1960) 91
narratives, framing of 383
National Constitutional Conference (NCC), Kenya 140, 143, 145–46, 147, 150, 151–53, 407
devolution discussion 149
Steering Committee 151
Technical Committee 150–51
National Council for Change (CONALCAM), Bolivia 12, 13–14
National Democratic Alliance, India 92–93
National Dialogue (ND), Yemen 312, 314–15, 316, 317, 401, 405–6, 407, 411, 421–22
National Dialogue Conference (NDC) 315, 316, 317, 318–22, 323, 324, 325–26, 327, 328–29
National Body for Monitoring the Implementation of the Outcomes 321
Presidium 318
National Party (NP), South Africa 219, 220, 223, 224–25, 228, 229, 230, 231, 232–33, 328, 345, 397–98, 404–5, 409–10, 417–18
deal with ANC (1993) 225
National Rainbow Alliance (NARC), Kenya 146
National Revolution of 1952, Bolivia 1, 2, 20
ideological framework 3–4

National Unity Party (UBP), Northern Cyprus 48–49, 55
nationalism/nationalists
Bosnia-Herzegovina (BiH) 26–27, 37, 40–41
clerical nationalism 40–41
composite nationalism, India 82–83
Ethiopia 60, 61–62, 63, 67, 70
ethnonationalism 45, 236
Greek Cypriot communities 53
Philippines 203, 208, 213, 217
resource nationalism, Nigeria 194
Scotland 276–77, 279, 280–81, 288–89, 290, 382
Spain 244
Basque Country 240, 241–42, 243, 247, 250, 387
Catalonia region 240, 241–42, 243, 244, 245–46, 247
Sri Lanka 256–57, 258, 260, 261, 262–63, 270, 271
Ukraine 293, 294, 295–96, 302, 305
Zulu nationalism, South Africa 219, 222, 228, 231, 232, 234, 236, 385–86
recognizing 228
natural resources 384
Navarre region, Spain 246–48, 249–50, 423
Nehru, Jawaharlal 84, 85, 87
Nemwang, Subhash Chandra 171
Nepal 161, 178, 381, 396, 399, 409–10
administrative structure 163–64
background to events 162–66
civil war 389–90, 397
Committee on State Restructuring and Distribution of State Power 172–73
Congress 161–62, 166, 167, 169, 170, 172, 174, 175–76, 177–78
Constituent Assembly 161–62, 167, 168, 174, 176–77, 400
actors and decision-making 169
context and background 167
first Constituent Assembly (CA1) 161–62, 167, 169, 171, 174, 175, 178, 180, 408
institutional set-up 171
second Constituent Assembly (CA2) 161–62, 168–69, 175–76, 180
Constitution Drafting Committee (CDC) 176–77
constitutional change/transition 180, 331, 332–33, 334, 335–36, 337–39, 340, 349–50
Constitutional Court 176
constitutional design and territorial cleavages 359–60
constitutional engagement period 167–74
federalism and political actors 172
constitutional moment 167, 176
constitutional rupture 334
Constitution-making 334
Constitutions 161–62, 164, 167–68, 174, 175–76, 177
of 1990 161, 162, 164–65, 166, 168, 179
of 2015 177–78, 179–80, 359–60
draft 177–78
Interim Constitution 168–69, 170–72, 174–75, 176–77, 179–80, 398
discrimination 162–63
earthquakes of 2015 176
emergency rule 162
ethnic federalism 79, 161–62, 164–65, 167, 174, 175, 179
federalism 161, 168, 172, 173–74, 177–78, 415–16
debates 172
ethnic 161–62, 164–65, 167, 174, 175, 179
federal restructuring 161–62, 167, 168–69, 171–74, 176–77, 178, 179, 374
first Constituent Assembly (CA1) 180
actors and decision-making 169
Caucuses 171
Committees 171–73
context and background 167
dissolution of (2012) 161–62, 174, 175, 178, 408
elections 168–69
institutional structure 171
Party Whips 171, 176
Rules of Procedure 171
Gorkhali sovereignty 163
grievances 165
High Level Political Committee (HLPC) 171–72
High Level State Restructuring Commission 173–74
Hinduism 163, 167–68
identity politics 164–66, 167, 178
Indigenous and Tribal People's Convention 165–66
Interim Parliament 168, 400
lessons learned 178
Local Self-Governance Act, 1999 164, 179
low levels of territorialization xvi
Madhesi rights activists 164–65, 166, 167, 178, 411
Madhesi People's Rights Forum (MJAF) 169
mainstream political parties and elites 166
Maoists 161–62, 165–67, 168–69, 171, 172, 174, 175–76, 178, 179, 387, 393, 397, 400, 409–10, 417
National Democratic Parties (RPP) 161–62
National Foundation for the Development of Indigenous Nationalities (NFDIN) Act, 2002 164
Nepal Federation of Indigenous Nationalities (NEFIN) 165–66
outcome of process 175
overview of case 161
Panchayat arrangements 163–64
Party Whips 171, 176
"People's War" (1996–2006) 161, 162, 165
perceived threat to physical integrity of 337
political elites 166, 176
political mobilization 165–66
political opposition to regime 165
political parties 161–62, 166, 167, 169, 170–72, 174–75
mainstream 166, 167

power-sharing arrangements 179–80
re-democratization of 1990 162, 164
secession/secessionist movements 166, 172, 178, 388
second Constituent Assembly (CA2) 161–62, 168–69, 175–76, 180
self-determination 165–66
social exclusion 162–63
social inclusion 164, 167, 179
Supreme Court 176–77, 408
territorial cleavages 331, 335–36
territorial restructuring 165, 172, 175–76, 178
Thematic Committees 171–73
violence 162, 168, 172, 175, 177–78, 332–33
Nepal, Madhav Kumar 170
Nigeria 181, 396, 409, 419
agencies of restraint 183, 193, 194
background to events 181
backlash against military's restructuring 193
centralization 189, 194, 358
of constitutional functions and fiscal resources 189
civil war 181, 183, 387
Committee on State and Local Government Creation 188–89
Constituent Assembly 191–92, 405–6
Constitution review bodies 186
constitutional change 196, 197, 198–99, 201
Constitutional Conference (1994/95) 190
constitutional design and territorial cleavages 360, 365, 366
constitutional engagement period 185–93
agencies of restraint 193
centralization of constitutional functions and fiscal resources 189
presidentialism 191
territorial reorganization 187
constitutional reform 183, 197, 198, 201
constitutional transition 181, 193, 195, 199–200, 201, 331, 334–36, 337–38, 340
Constitution-making process 186, 197
Constitutions
of 1963 189, 193
of 1979 186, 189, 192, 193
of 1999 192, 193, 195–96
post-military 187
Eastern Region 188
Electoral Reform Committee (ERC) 198
electoral rules 366
federalism 183–84, 358, 416
presidential 181, 183, 186, 190–91, 194, 195, 198, 200–1
Federation Account 190
First Republic (1960–66) 181, 183, 184–85, 188, 191–92
highly territorialized region xvi
independence (1960) 181, 183
lessons learned 199
Local Council Development Areas (LCDAs) 199
Mid-West 188
military rule 181, 183, 199–200
backlash against restructuring 193
and constitutional reform 185
constitutional sovereignty, preserving 187
elaboration of vision by civilian technocrats 186
flagship decree 189
post-military era 195, 197–98, 201
representative assemblies, legitimizing vision through 186–87
rigid constitutional entrenchment and irreversibility of institutional legacy 187
Muslims 183, 197, 199
National Assembly 189–90, 196–97, 199
National Judicial Council (NJC) 193
Northern Region 183
outcomes 193
overview of case 181
power-sharing arrangements 194, 195
presidential system 181, 183, 186, 190–91, 194, 195, 198, 200–1
resource nationalism 194
secession/secessionist movements 183, 188, 193–94, 199–200
Second Republic (1979–83) 181, 186, 195
Sovereign National Conference (SNC) 197
taxation policy 189, 356–57
territorial cleavages 331, 335–36, 416–17
territorial restructuring 181, 187, 188, 193, 195–97, 201
reorganizations 187
unambiguous centrist constitutional vision, articulating 186
violence 184–85, 396
Northern Cyprus 46, 48–49, 54–55
transfer of Turkish Cypriots to 46, 47
see also **Cyprus**; **Republic of Cyprus (Greek Cypriots)**; **Turkish Cypriot communities**
Northern Ireland
Belfast Agreement (1998) 57
consociationialism 421–22
devolution 277–78
proportional sequential (PS) coalition 58
and Scotland 276
UK membership 278
violence 387
nullification 367

OAS (Organization of American States) 14–15
October Agenda (2003), Bolivia 5–6, 8
Odinga, Raila 146, 147, 153–54
ODPO (Oromo People's Democratic Organization), Ethiopia 64, 66–67, 73–74, 77
Office of High Representative (OHR), Bosnia-Herzegovina (BiH) 33–35
Okondo, Peter Habenga 143–44
OLF (Oromo Liberation Front), Ethiopia 65, 66–67, 68–69, 404–5
Orange Democratic Movement (ODM), Kenya 153–54
Organization of American States (OAS) 14–15

Oromia, Ethiopia 71–74, 76–77
Oromo Liberation Front (OLF), Ethiopia 65, 66–67, 68–69
Oromo People's Democratic Organization (OPDO), Ethiopia 64, 65, 66–67, 73–74, 77, 404–5
Oruro Constitution, Bolivia 12, 13–14, 15
Oslo Principles 397
oversight committees, Bolivia 3–4
Owen, Lord David
  Owen-Stoltenberg Peace Plan 27–28, 29
  Vance-Owen Peace Plan (VOPP) 27
Owens, Robert 33–34

Pando, Bolivia 6, 13–14
Panikkar, K.M. 87
Papadopoulos, Tassos 44, 48–49, 53, 57–58
Papua, Indonesia 131, 388
  Act of Free Choice (1969) 123, 131–32, 136, 139
  central government challenges 126
  compared with Aceh 123–24, 380
  constitutional transition 120
  Free Papua Organization (OPM) 123, 124
  grievances 119–20, 123, 128
  indigenous groups 132–33
  mobilization in 122
  Papuan Customary Council (DAP) 135, 136
  Papuan People's Assembly (MRP) 132–33, 139
  Presidium of the People's Congress (PDP) 132, 133
  provincial legislature (DPRP) 132–33
  Special Autonomy Law (OTSUS) 120, 131, 132–33, 134, 135–36, 348, 385, 402–3
  see also **Aceh, Indonesia; Indonesia**
Parliamentary Assembly of Bosnia and Herzegovina 30, 32, 33, 35
Party for Bosnia and Herzegovina (SBiH) 37–38
Party of Democratic Action, Bosnia *see* **SDA (Stranka Demokratske Akeije), Bosnia**
Pasic, Lena 39
Patel, Vallabbhai 85
Payne, Stanley G 241–42
Peiris, G.L. 265, 266
People's Alliance (PA), Sri Lanka 260, 401
People's Consultative Assembly (MPR), Indonesia 119–20, 124–26
PEPSU (Punjab and East Patiala States Union) 88, 89–90
peripheral rebellions 376–77, 393, 396, 399, 402–3, 404, 405–6
  see also **rebellions**
Philippines 202, 381, 383, 396
  asymmetrical arrangements 210
  Autonomous Region in Muslim Mindanao (ARMM) 205, 206–8, 209–11, 213, 362–63, 402–3
  autonomy 202–3, 204, 205–6, 207, 210–11, 212, 213, 217
  background to events 203
  Bangsamoro region 209–11, 213–14, 345, 363, 370, 374, 387, 396, 411
    Bangsamoro Basic Law 212, 214–17, 403
    Bangsamoro Framework Agreement (2012) 402–3
    Bangsamoro Juridical Entity 208, 209, 213–14, 362–63, 370
    Bangsamoro Transition Commission 212, 213–14, 216–17, 218, 402–3
    conflict 387, 396
    Islamic Freedom Fighters 215
  ceasefires 204, 207
  civil war 389–90
  Congress 402–3
  constitutional change/transition 208–9, 214–15, 217, 331, 332–33, 335–36, 337, 340, 342, 345
  constitutional design and territorial cleavages 370
  constitutional engagement period 209
  Constitutions
    Constitution of 1973 204
    Constitution of 1987 (People Power) 202–3, 204, 205–6, 207, 209, 211, 212, 214, 217, 218, 362–63, 402–3
  Cordillera People's Liberation Army (CPLA) 205–6
  decentralization 205, 361
  highly territorialized peripheral regions xvi
  International Contact Group 213–14, 215–16, 218
  Jabidah massacre (1968) 203–4
  lessons learned 217
  Mamasapano incident (2015) 215–16
  Manila 210–11
  Memorandum of Agreement on Ancestral Domain (2008) 403
  Mindanao 202–4, 205–6, 207, 208–10, 211, 212, 213–18, 362–63, 381, 382, 384, 411, 423, 424
  Moro National Liberation Front (MNLF) 202, 203, 204, 207–8, 209, 210–11, 212, 214–18, 402–3
  Muslim insurgency 202, 203–4, 206–7, 214–15, 423
  nationalism 203, 208, 213, 217
  outcome of process 215
  overview of case 202
  peace talks 207, 211, 215, 217, 218
  perceived threat to physical integrity of 337
  presidential system 401
  rebellions 202, 203–4, 205–6, 217, 393
  secession/secessionist movements 414
  self-determination 203
  special autonomy laws 361
  statehood, challenges confronting 337
  Supreme Court 213, 403
  territorial cleavages 202–3, 214, 217, 218, 331, 335–36, 370
  Tripoli Agreement, 1976 203, 204, 206, 217
  US control 382
  violence 203–4, 210, 332–33, 386–87, 402–3
pluralism, political 272, 399, 400–1, 414, 421, 428
  Ethiopia 60–61, 66–67, 79–80
  Sri Lanka 267, 272

Plurinational Constitutional Tribunal, Bolivia 1, 2, 16, 19, 20
plurinationalism
Bolivia 3–5, 6, 16, 20–21
United Kingdom 277–78
PODEMOS (*Poder Democrático y Social*) movement, Bolivia 6–7, 11, 406
dissolution of 15
elections 6, 7–9
national leadership 12
protests organized by (2006) 9
see also **Bolivia; MAS-IPSP (*Movimiento al Socialismo–Instrumento Político por la Soberanía de los Pueblos*), Bolivia**
political elites
Bosnia-Herzegovina (BiH) 39
Cyprus 22
Ethiopia 63–64, 69, 72–73, 74
centralizing elites 66, 69
centrist elites 65, 66
exclusion from Constitution-making 407
India 81, 82–83, 96
Indonesia 121–22
Iraq 115–16
Nepal 166, 176
Scotland 280–81, 289–90, 395–96
Shia 408–9
South Africa 232–33
Sri Lanka 273
statewide 402–3
political entrepreneurs, and demography 379
political geometry xv–xvi, 375, 376, 378–79, 380–81, 387–88, 390–92, 394, 395, 401–2, 412–14, 417, 420, 424, 425
demography and political entrepreneurs 379
patterns 379–80
Yemen 325
political legitimacy 376–77, 392–93
Bolivia 15
Ethiopia 63
Scotland 288
Yemen 326
political mobilization 359, 374–75, 376, 377, 378, 386, 388
Bolivia 1
constitutional design and territorial cleavages 357
and constitutional transition 86
context for constitutional moments 378
Ethiopia 60–61, 69, 79–80
ethnic-political 405–6, 416, 424
federalism 357
India 86, 92, 96
Indonesia 122, 128
Kenya 142
Nepal 165–66
patterns, shaping Constitution-making 375
Philippines 217–18
Spain 239
Sri Lanka 263
territorial 375, 380, 381, 384–85, 427–28
political pluralism *see* **pluralism, political**
Popular Participation Law (PPL), Bolivia (1994) 3–4, 17
Post-Tsunami Operational Management Structure (P-TOMS) 268
power-sharing arrangements xvi
Annan Plan (2002–04), Cyprus v, vi, xv, 45, 53, 58
Bosnia-Herzegovina (BiH) 421
Ethiopia 71–72, 78
Kenya 147
Nepal 179–80
Nigeria 194, 195
South Africa 223, 225
Sri Lanka 255, 260, 265, 267–68, 270–71
Yemen 318–19, 324–25
Prabhakaran, Velupillai 259–60
prefects (departmental executive authorities), Bolivia 6, 7, 13
half moon 7–8, 18–19
Progressive Party of Working People (AKEL), Cyprus 48–49, 55
proportional sequential (PS) coalition
Northern Ireland 58
protests *see* **demonstrations, protests and rebellions**
public participation
constitutional transition 346
Punjab, India 85, 88, 89–90, 93, 96
language 89–90, 96
Punjabi Suba movement 89–90
reorganization 89–90
SAD Party 94–95
Putin, Vladimir Vladimirovich 306, 307

Qatar 313–14, 317, 329

Rajapaksa, Mahinda (Sri Lankan President) 268–71, 272, 393
Rajasthan, India 88, 89
Ramalu, Sri Potti 86–87
Ramaphosa, Cyril 229
Ramos, Fidel V. (Philippines President) 206
ratification process 43–44
and deliberation 342
referendums 410–11
Stabilisation and Association Agreement, Bosnia-Herzegovina 43–44
rebellions
Ethiopia 62
Indonesia 121–22, 124
peripheral 376–77, 393, 396, 399, 402–3, 405–6
Philippines 202, 203–4, 205–6, 217, 393
Sri Lanka 270, 393
Ukraine 306
see also **civil war; demonstrations and protests; violence**
referendums
Bolivia 7–8, 9, 10, 11–12, 13, 408, 410–11
referendum of 2009 on new Constitution 1, 15
Brexit referendum, UK (2016) 276, 288
constitutional transition 334–35, 344–45
Cyprus 410–11
Cyprus, Annan Plan (2002–04) 44, 54–55, 56, 58
Iraq 411

referendums (*cont.*)
Kenya 140–41, 147, 153–55, 159, 410–11
ratification process 410–11
Scotland 280–82, 334–35
independence referendum, 2014 275–76, 277–78, 283, 284, 285, 289, 409
South Africa 224–25, 411
Spain 251
United Kingdom 276
Renwick, Robin 226–27
Republic of Cyprus (Greek Cypriots) 46–47, 53, 54–55
EU accession 47–48, 53–54, 56
see also **Cyprus; Greek Cypriot communities; Northern Cyprus**
Republican Turkish Party (CTP), Northern Cyprus 48–49
Republika Srpska (RS), Bosnia 26, 29, 34, 41
Army 24–25
and division of BiH into two Entities 22, 30–32, 34–35, 40–41
Revolutionary Government of the Republic of Indonesia (PRRI) 122
Revolutionary Movement of the Left (MIR), Bolivia 2, 4
Reyes Villa, Manafred 10
risks
federalism 414–15
Roeder, Philip 357
RS *see* **Republika Srpska (RS), Bosnia**
ruling elites
Ethiopia 60, 61–62, 63–64, 69, 78
Iraq 117
South Africa 224

Salamat, Hashim 204
Saleh, Ali Abdullah (Yemeni President) 312–16, 322, 323, 326–27
Samjuka Maharasthra Samity 89
Sánchez de Lozada, Gonzalo (Bolivian President) 2, 4
opposition to 5–6
resignation (2003) 5
Santa Cruz, Bolivia 2
Assembly 5
Cabildo (demonstration) 6, 9
Civic Committee 3, 5, 7
civil society organizations and elites 3, 5
demonstrations in 6
opposition parties 16–17
pro-autonomy segments 17–18
see also **Bolivia**
SBiH (Stranka za Bosnu i Herzegovinu), Bosnia and Herzegovina 37–38
Scotland 275
Act of Union, 1707 276–77, 278–79, 382
asymmetrical arrangements 266, 277–78, 286
background to events 276
Calman Commission 281
Campaign for a Scottish Assembly (CSA), 1985 280–81
constitutional change/transition 275, 276, 281, 286, 289, 291, 331, 332–33, 335, 341
Constitutional Convention 395–96
constitutional democracy 276, 291, 425, 428
constitutional engagement period 281
decentralization 275, 284–85
devolution 275, 276, 277–78, 280–81, 285, 286, 287, 288, 363
administrative 279
Edinburgh Agreement (2012) 282–83
federalism 288–89
lessons learned 289
nationalism 276–77, 279, 280–81, 288–89, 290, 382
and Northern Ireland 276
outcome of process 284
overview of case 275
parliamentary elections 275, 276, 277, 289
political elites 280–81, 289–90, 395–96
political legitimacy 288
referendums 280–82, 334–35
independence referendum, 2014 275–76, 277–78, 283, 284, 285, 289, 409
Scotland Act, 1998 277, 278–79, 280–82, 286–87, 395–96
Scotland Act, 2012 277–78, 286–87
Scotland Act, 2016 275, 281, 284–85, 286–87
Scottish National Party (SNP) 275, 276, 277, 279–82, 283–84, 288–89, 290–91, 389, 419
Scottish Parliament 275, 277–78, 281, 283–84
secession/secessionist movements 278–79, 283, 289, 290–91
Secretary of State 279
Smith Commission 285–86, 288, 362
sovereignty 280–81
special autonomy 413
territorial cleavages 331, 335
and United Kingdom 275, 276–86, 287, 288–91, 334–35, 355, 409
see also **United Kingdom**
SDA (Stranka Demokratske Akeije), Bosnia 23–24
secession/secessionist movements 380, 382–83, 384, 387, 388–89, 391, 414, 415, 419–20, 422, 423, 424
Bosnia-Herzegovina (BiH) 24–25, 29, 41
clauses 368
constitutional design and territorial cleavages 353, 356, 357–58, 362, 368–69, 370–71, 372, 373
constitutional transition 337, 338–39, 341–42
Cyprus 47, 53
Ethiopia 69–71, 74–75, 77–79
India 414
Indonesia 120, 121–22, 126, 132, 135–36, 137, 414
Kenya 141–42, 159
Nepal 166, 172, 178, 388
Nigeria 183, 188, 193–94, 199–200
Philippines 414
Scotland 278–79, 283, 289, 290–91
Spain 237–38, 247, 250, 251

Sri Lanka 262, 266–67, 271, 414
territorial cleavages and constitutional design 363
Ukraine 306, 308–9
self-determination 227–28, 382, 404
Bolivia 5
Bosnia-Herzegovina (BiH) 24–25, 27
constitutional design and territorial cleavages 363, 370–71
Ethiopia 67, 68–69, 70–71, 72, 404
external 266–67
India 82–83, 85, 92
internal 265, 266
international institutions, role of 370–71
local 363
national 82–83, 92
Nepal 165–66
Philippines 203
South Africa 220, 223–24, 225, 226, 227–28, 235–36
Spain 246, 251
Sri Lanka 258, 265–67
Serbian Republic of Bosnia and Herzegovina, establishment (1992) 23–24
see also **Bosnia-Herzegovina (BiH)**
Serbs 400
and 1974 Constitution of SFRY 22–23
in Croatia 24–25, 382–83
failure to guarantee minority rights to 382–83
non-involvement of Bosnian Serbs in Dayton Peace talks 26
political preferences of Bosnian Serbs 31
rejection of Stoltenberg-Owen Peace Plan 27–28
rejection of Vance-Owen Peace Plan 27
Šestorka informal coalition, Bosnia and Herzegovina 38–39
SFRY *see* **Socialist Federal Republic of Yugoslavia (SFRY)**
Shagari, Shehu (Nigerian President) 191
Showa (historical region of Ethiopia) 61–62
Silajdžić, Haris (Bosnian Prime Minister) 25, 28
Singh, Khuswant 93
Sinhalese, Sri Lanka 255, 256, 257, 258, 261, 262–63, 270, 357–58, 387–88, 397, 424
Sirisena, Maithripala (Sri Lankan President) 270–72
Sitaramayya, Pattabhi 85
Slovo, Joe 235
Smith Commission 362
SNP (Scottish National Party) 275, 276, 277, 279–82, 283–84, 288–89, 290–91
SNSD (Stranka Nezavisnih Socijal Demokrata), Bosnia and Herzegovina 37–38
Social Democratic Power, Bolivia *see* **PODEMOS (*Poder Democrático y Social*) movement, Bolivia**
Socialist Federal Republic of Yugoslavia (SFRY)
Arbitration Commission of the Conference on Yugoslavia 24–25
and Bosnian Serbs 31
Constitution of 1974 22–23
constitutional federalism 357
Croatia, departure of (1991) 23–24
Croats 22–23
disintegration of 23–24
European Community Conference on the Former Yugoslavia 26–27
International Conference on the Former Socialist Federal Republic of Yugoslavia (ICFY) 27–28
Kosovo, recognition of status (1974) 22–23
Macedonians, recognition 22–23
Montenegrins, recognition 22–23
nationalist parties 23–24
Serbs 22–23
Slovenia, departure of (1991) 23–24
Vojvodina, recognition of status (1974) 22–23
Yugoslav Census (1991) 23–24
Yugoslav National Army (JNA) 23–24
see also **Bosnia-Herzegovina (BiH)**
Soekarno, Indonesian President 120–22, 125
Soekarnoputri, Megawati (Indonesian President) 125–26, 132
South Africa 219, 222, 223–24, 399, 409
and African National Congress (ANC) 219, 220, 222, 223, 224–25, 227–28, 229, 230–33, 235–36, 328, 341–42, 359, 397–98, 417–18
deal with National Party (1993) 225
Afrikaner People's Front (AVF) 225, 226–27
Afrikaner Resistance Movement 223–24
Afrikaners, right wing 219, 220, 223–24, 225, 231, 233, 236
apartheid 219, 220, 222, 223, 224, 225, 226, 334–35, 360, 417–18
asymmetrical arrangements 219, 233, 234
background to events 220
Colored Representative Council 221
Concerned South Africans Group (COSAG) 225
Constitutional Assembly 235–36, 404, 405–6
Constitutional Court 226, 363, 399, 403–4
constitutional design and territorial cleavages 359, 360, 363, 365
constitutional engagement period 222–30
ANC/NP deal 225
constitutional process, trajectory 224
Interim Constitution of December 1993 225, 343, 344
players 223
self-determination 226
Constitutional Principles 227–28
constitutional settlement 219, 233
constitutional transition 333–34, 335, 337, 341–42, 343–44, 345, 348
Constitution-making process 231, 334
Constitutions
Constitution of 1983 222, 224–25, 226, 227, 228–29
Constitution of 1996 230
Interim Constitution 225, 227, 228–29, 230–31, 233, 234–35, 236

South Africa (*cont.*)
Convention for a Democratic South Africa (CODESA) 224–25, 397–98
democracy 219, 224, 226–27, 231, 232–33, 234
democratic transition 385
Democratic Alliance 232
Eastern Cape 226
ethnic federalism 219, 220, 222, 223, 226, 228–29, 231, 232–33
ethno-linguistic cleavages 220
federalism 414–16
Freedom Charter 220
Freedom Front 228, 232, 234–35
indigenous and customary law 228–29
Inkatha Freedom Party (IFP) 224, 228, 230, 233–35, 404–5, 409–10
KwaZulu-Natal 228–29, 356, 362–63, 364, 365, 366, 368, 369, 397–98
lessons learned 233
low levels of territorialization xvi
Multi-Party Negotiating Process (MPNP) 225
Natal 226, 228–29
National Party (NP) 219, 220, 223, 224–25, 228, 229, 230, 231, 232–33, 328, 345, 397–98, 404–5, 409–10, 417–18
deal with ANC (1993) 225
National Peace Accord 397–98
Northern Cape 223, 226
Orange Free State 226
outcome of process 231
overview of case 219
political elites 232–33
power-sharing arrangements 223, 225
Record of Understanding (ANC and NP) 225
referendums 224–25, 411
ruling elites 224
self-determination 220, 223–24, 225, 226, 227–28, 235–36
South Africa Police (SAP) 223–24, 228
South African Communist Party (SACP) 222, 223–24
South African Defense Force (SADF) 223–24, 226–27, 228
territorial cleavages 219, 330–31, 341–42, 359, 360, 363, 365
territorial politics 219, 233, 234, 236
Transvaal Province 226
upper house 365, 418–19
violence 224–25, 226–27, 231–32, 233, 234, 236
volkstaat (expression of right in own territory) 223–24, 227, 231–32, 233, 235–36
Volkstaatraad (People's State Council) 227, 231
Western Cape 223, 226
Xhosa Nostra 232
Zulu nationalism 219, 222, 231, 232, 234, 236, 385–86
recognizing 228
Southern Ethiopia People's Democratic Movement (SEPDM) 64
Southern Nations, Nationalities and Peoples Regional State (SNNPRS), Ethiopia 67–68, 71–72
Soviet Union, Former
collapse of (1991) 292, 293, 297
Communist Party 296
constitutional assemblies 406
constitutional federalism 357
see also **Crimea; Ukraine**
Spain 237, 374, 382, 384–85, 399
asymmetrical arrangements 249–50
Autonomous Communities (AC) 237, 248, 253, 385, 395, 411, 416
Autonomy Pacts 243–44, 249–50
background to events 238
Basque Country 237–38, 240, 241–42, 244, 245–46, 248, 249, 250, 253, 356–57, 387–88, 423
Basque Nationalist Party (PNV) 240, 241, 243
ETA (Basque Homeland and Freedom), terrorist group 239, 241–42, 243, 247
nationalism 240, 241–42, 243, 247, 250, 387
Catalonia region 237–38, 239–42, 243, 245–47, 248, 249–51, 252, 253, 357, 371, 382, 384–85
Assemblea de Catalunya 240–41
compared with Basque Country 241–42
crisis of 2017–18 251, 252
historical nationalities 240, 249–50
nationalism 240, 241–42, 243, 244, 245–46, 247
Statute of Autonomy 250–51, 252
Unified Socialist Party of Catalonia (PSUC) 240–41, 244
see also **Basque Country, Spain; Spain**
Charter 245–46, 247, 250
civil war 237, 238
Constitution of 1931 (Republican) 238
Constitution of 1978 237–38, 243, 244, 245, 246–47, 248–49, 252, 278, 355, 385, 408
Title VIII 248–49
Constitutional Assembly 405–6
Constitutional Committee 244–45, 246
Constitutional Court 248–51
constitutional engagement period 242
constitutional transition 237, 252, 335, 337, 338–39, 341, 392–93
decentralization 237, 240, 243, 245–46, 248–50, 252, 253
democracy 237, 252, 389, 395
devolution 248, 253, 254
elections 237–38, 242–43, 251, 252, 253
federalism 415–16
Galicia 238–39, 240, 246–47, 248, 249
highly territorialized region xvi
Junta Democrática (JD) 240
Law of Political Reform, 1976 241–43
lessons learned 252
Navarre region 246–48, 249–50, 423
Organic Law of the State 238–39
outcome of process 248
overview of case 237

Pactos de la Moncloa 243–44
perceived threat to physical integrity of 337
Plataforma de Convergencia Democrática (PCD) 240
Plataforma de Organizaciones Democráticas (POD) 240
political violence 237, 241, 243
referendums 251
secession/secessionist movements 237–38, 247, 250, 251
Second Republic 238, 242–43
self-determination 246, 251
Spanish Communist Party (PCE) 240, 244, 246
Spanish Socialist Party (PSOE) 240, 246, 248
Statutes of Autonomy 247, 248, 250–51, 252
territorial cleavages 335
territories 237, 240, 243, 247
Union of the Democratic Centre (UCD) 244, 245–46, 247, 248
violence 237–38, 239, 241–42, 250, 387
voluntariness principle 248
Workers' Commissions 239
see also **Franco, General Francisco**
Sparks, Allister 231–32
Sri Lanka 255, 263–64, 383, 396, 401, 428
All Party Representative Commission (APRC) 270
autonomy 255–57, 258–59, 266–67, 271
background to events 256
Bandaranaike-Chelvanayakam Pact, 1958 258–59
ceasefires 259, 260–61, 264, 268–69, 273–74
civil war 387, 396
constitutional amendments 333–34
Constitutional Assembly 256, 257, 258–59, 262, 271–72
constitutional change/transition 255–56, 265, 274, 331, 333–34, 335–36, 342
constitutional design and territorial cleavages 353, 370
constitutional engagement period 263
constitutional politics 255–56, 271–72
Constitutions 259, 381
Donoughmore Constitution, 1931 261, 262–63
ethno-territorial cleavages 269, 271, 372
Federal Party 258–60, 261, 262
highly territorialized peripheral regions xvi
Indo-Lanka Accord 269
Interim Self-Governing Authority (ISGA), LTTE proposals for 267
lessons learned 271
Lessons Learnt and Reconciliation Commission (LLRC) 270
Liberation Tigers of Tamil Eelam (LTTE) 255–56, 258, 259–61, 263–64, 265, 266–70, 271–74, 366–67, 371, 387–88, 393, 396, 397, 400, 403
Muslims 257–58, 265
nationalism 256–57, 258, 260, 261, 262–63, 270, 271
North-Eastern Provincial Council (NEPC) 259
Oslo Comminiqué (2002) 256, 266–67, 271
outcome of process 269
overview of case 255
party politics 260–61, 271–72
peace process 255–56, 260–61, 264, 267–69, 271–72, 273–74
People's Alliance (PA) 260, 401
pluralism, political 267, 272
political elites 273
political parties 401
power-sharing arrangements 255, 260, 265, 267–68, 270–71
rebellions 270, 393
refusal to deal with combatants 333
secession/secessionist movements 262, 266–67, 271, 414
self-determination 258, 265–67
"Sinhala Only Act," 1956 257, 258
Sinhala-Buddhist majority 255
chauvinism 271, 273–74
nationalism 256–57, 258, 260, 261, 262–63, 270, 271
Sinhalese 255, 256, 257, 258, 261, 262–63, 270, 357–58, 387–88, 397, 424
Soulbury Constitution 381
special autonomy 424
Sri Lanka Freedom Party (SLFP) 272
Sri Lanka Monitoring Mission (SLMM) 264
Sri Lanka Muslim Congress (SLMC) 265
sub-committees 265, 266
Supreme Court 269, 403
Tamils 255, 257–58, 261–63, 266–67, 270, 272–73, 366–67, 379–80, 398
territorial cleavages 331, 335–36, 370, 388
United National Front (UNF) 260
United National Party (UNP) 272
United People's Freedom Front (UPFA) 267–68
violence 259–60, 270, 273–74, 386–87, 396
state capture
Bosnia-Herzegovina (BiH) 36
State Reorganization Commission (SRC), India 87–90, 97, 385
balanced approach 87
proposals 88–89
Stepan, Alfred 352–53, 383
Stetskiv, Taras 302
Stoltenberg, Thorvald 27–28
strength and relative political power, tests of 388, 392, 401
Suarez, Adolfo 242–43
Subianto, Prabawo 133–34
subsidiarity principle 355
Sucre, Bolivia 10–12
Suharto, Indonesian President 119–20, 122, 385
New Order regime 123, 124–25
Sunstein, Cass 368
supermajorities 343–44, 402, 408, 411
Surco, Fidel 14
Svoboda Party, Ukraine 305
symmetrical federalism 412–13, 415
Szasz, Paul 30

Talat, Mehmet Ali (Cypriot President) 48–49, 55, 56–57, 58
Tamil United Liberation Front (TULF) 262
Tamils, Sri Lanka 255, 257–58, 261–63, 266–67, 270, 272–73, 366–67, 379–80, 398
Tarija, Bolivia 2, 6, 7, 13
opposition parties 16–17
pro-autonomy segments 17–18
Tatars, Crimean 293
Telangana, India 88, 92–93, 94
Terai Madhes Loktantrik Party, Nepal 169
territorial cleavages
Bolivia 2, 3, 15–16, 331
Bosnia-Herzegovina (BiH) 331, 360, 365
and constitutional design 352
constitutional design 366–67
constitutional politics 374, 375
constitutional transitions dealing with 331, 335–36, 337, 339–42, 343–44, 345, 346, 350, 374, 375
context and dynamics of constitutional moments 390
Cyprus 331, 335
defining 374–75
demography and political entrepreneurs 379
Ethiopia 331, 358, 359, 365
India 331, 335–36, 358–59, 360
Indonesia 119, 133, 134, 136, 137, 138, 139, 331, 335–36
Iraq 99, 110–11, 331, 336
Kenya 142, 331, 335–36, 365
Kurdistan Region 335
multidimensional 418
nature 335
Nepal 331, 335–36, 359–60
Nigeria 331, 335–36, 360, 365, 366, 416–17
peaceful and institutionalized or violent and extra-legal politics 376, 385
Philippines 202–3, 214, 217, 218, 331, 335–36
political geometry 376, 378–79
political mobilization and context for constitutional moments 378
ratification process 411
Scotland 331, 335
South Africa 219, 330–31, 341–42, 359, 360, 363, 365
Spain 335
spatial dimensions 335–36
Sri Lanka 331, 335–36, 388
strength, tests of and relative political power 388, 392
Ukraine 331, 365
upper houses 365, 418–19
territorial constitutional accommodation, claims for 374, 383–84, 391
territorial restructuring
Bosnia-Herzegovina (BiH) 22, 29
and centrality of territory 26
cleavages 36
Dayton Peace Agreement (DPA) 22, 26, 29
lessons learned 36
overview of territorial reorganization 22
role of territory at Dayton 26
as state comprising two Entities 22, 30–32, 34–35, 40–41
India 81
Nepal 165, 172, 175–76, 178
Nigeria 181, 187, 188, 193, 195–97, 201
"thick nations" 95–96
Threlfall, Monica 239
Tierney, Stephen 337
Tigray People Liberation Front (TPLF), Ethiopia 64, 65
Tito, Josip Broz (former Yugoslavian President) 22–23
Tolimir, General Zdravko 26
Transitional Administrative Law (TAL), Iraq 104–8, 404
Article 58 110
Article 58(c) 112
Transitional Government of Ethiopia (TGE) 65, 66–69, 404–5
Transitional National Assembly (TNA), Iraq 106–8
Tripura, India 91–92, 400–1
Truth and Reconciliation Commission 225
Tudjman, Franjo (Croatian President) 25, 26
Turchynov, Oleksandr 306
Turkey
accession talks (2006) 54–55
coup of July 2016 56–57
earthquakes of August 1999 48
elections 49
foreign policy 57
and rejection by Greek Cypriots of Annan Plan 53
relations with Greece 45, 46, 48
see also **Cyprus; Turkish Cypriot communities**
Turkish Cypriot communities 383
Annan Plan submitted for ratification 43–44
and bizonality principle 47, 52, 421
constitutional transition 337
electoral roll 45
endorsement of Annan Plan (2004) 43–44, 54, 56
forced to move to northern Cyprus after 1974 46, 47
"High-Level" agreements between Greek Cypriot and Turkish Cypriot leaders (1977 and 1979) 47–48
non-recognition of jurisdiction of Cyprus by other states 46
partition of Cyprus, desire for 44–45
power-sharing arrangements with Greek Cypriots 45, 53, 58
on right of return for displaced persons 47
sovereignty issue 47
statehood, challenges confronting 337
statistics 51, 55

UCD (Union of the Democratic Centre), Spain 244, 245–46, 247, 248
Ukraine 292, 398, 399
background to events 292
Constitution 292, 293, 295, 297, 298–301, 368

Constitutional Commission 299, 406–7
constitutional design and territorial cleavages 365, 372
constitutional engagement period 295
constitutional transition 331, 337, 338–39
decentralization 297–98, 307, 308–9
demonstrations and protests 305, 307, 309–10, 387
Donbas region (eastern Ukraine) 293
Faustian bargain 295–96, 300–1, 303, 304, 310–11, 365, 383–84
breakdown 303
federalism 292–93, 295, 296–97, 298, 299–300, 307, 310
future of 307
highly territorialized peripheral regions xvi
independence 295
international institutions, role of 372
Interregional Block for Reforms (IBR) 296–97
lessons learned 310
Minsk agreements (2014 and 2015) 307–8
nationalists 293, 294, 295–96, 302, 305
Opposition Bloc 307, 309–11
Orange Revolution 74–75, 302, 303, 305
"Our Ukraine" coalition 302
outcome of process 300–7
overview of case 292
perceived threat to physical integrity of 337
rebellions 306
Russophiles 292, 294, 307, 309–11, 383–84
secession/secessionist movements 306, 308–9
split pyramid bargain 302
Svoboda Party 305
territorial cleavages 331, 372
Ukrainianization 296
Ukrainophiles 292, 294, 295, 298, 300, 301, 302, 307, 406–7
violent conflict 292, 293, 303–4
West, East and Center 292
Yanukovych, collapse of 304
developments following 307
see also **Crimea; Kravchuk, Leonid; Soviet Union, Former; Yanukovych, Viktor**
UNF (United National Front), Sri Lanka 260
Union of South American Nations (UNASUR) 1, 14–15
United Iraqi Alliance 106–7
United Kingdom 374, 384–85, 395–96, 399, 402
Act of Union, 1707 276–77, 278–79, 382
Conservative Party 281, 284–85
Constitution 278, 280–81, 288–89
House of Lords Select Committee 286
constitutional change/transition 275, 276, 281, 286, 289, 291, 331, 332–33, 335, 337, 338–39, 340, 341, 392–93
constitutional federalism 355
Cyprus, independence from (1960) 44–45
English votes for English laws (EVEL) 287
federalism 288–89
highly territorialized peripheral regions xvi
India, colonial regime 82–83, 90
Iraq, control of 100–1
Labour Party 280–81, 284–85
Liberal Democratic Party 280–81, 284–85
Northern Ireland membership 278
parliamentary sovereignty doctrine 287
perceived threat to physical integrity of 337
plurinational 277–78
referendums 276, 280–82, 283, 334–35
Brexit referendum, UK (2016) 276, 288
independence referendum, 2014 276
Scottish independence referendum, 2014 275–76, 277–78, 283, 284, 285, 289, 409
retention of "sovereign" bases in Cyprus under 1960 Treaty 45
and Scotland 275, 276–86, 287, 288–91, 334–35, 355, 409
Scottish National Party (SNP) 389
Scottish referendum 334–35
special autonomy 423–24
see also **Northern Ireland; Scotland**
United National Party (UNP), Sri Lanka 272, 401
United Nations
and Annan Plan 43–44, 47, 49, 51, 54, 56
constitutional transition 339
Declaration of Minority Rights (1992) 370–71
peacekeeping force in Cyprus 46
Secretary General 106, 314, 370, 408
and Cyprus 43–44, 49, 54
Security Council 314, 322, 326–27
UN Decade for Indigenous People 179
UN Development Programme (UNDP) 10
UN Protection Force (UNPROFOR) 28
United Nations Assistance Mission to Iraq (UNAMI) 112
United People's Freedom Front (UPFA), Sri Lanka 267–68
United States 342
Constitution 364–65
federalism 355–56
founding fathers 355
Philippines, control over 382
secession clauses 369
state representation in Senate 365
Unity Pact (UP), Bolivia 7–8, 9, 12
upper houses
Ethiopia 365, 418–19
Kenya 365, 418–19
South Africa 365, 418–19
uprisings *see* **demonstrations and protests; rebellions**
USSR *see* **Soviet Union, Former**
Uttar Pradesh, India 88, 92–93, 97

Vance, Cyrus
replacement by Stoltenberg 27–28
Vance-Owen Peace Plan (VOPP) 27
Varosha (Famagusta), Cyprus 51, 54–55
veto, right of 366–67
Viljoen, Constand 226–27, 228, 234, 235–36
violence/violent conflict 329, 357–58, 360, 381–82, 400
Bolivia 1, 10, 13, 14–15, 18–19
Bosnia-Herzegovina (BiH) 41, 332–33, 367

violence/violent conflict (*cont.*)
ceasefires 259
constitutional design and territorial cleavages 353, 361, 367
constitutional moments, prior to 397
constitutional transition, nature 332–33
Cyprus 44–45, 59
ending 393, 425–26
Ethiopia 66, 396
ethnic 92, 381–82
India 82, 86–87, 89, 92, 386–87
Indonesia 119, 124, 125, 128, 129, 130, 134, 136, 138, 139
intercommunal 44–45
Iraq 101–2, 106–7, 108
Kenya 140–41, 143, 154, 159
memory of 333
Nepal 162, 168, 172, 175, 177–78, 332–33
Nigeria 184–85, 396
Northern Ireland 387
peaceful and institutionalized or violent and extra-legal politics 376
Philippines 203–4, 210, 332–33, 386–87, 402–3
political 1, 162, 184–85, 237, 241, 243
prior to a constitutional moment 397
rationale for turning to 386–87
South Africa 224–25, 226–27, 231–32, 233, 234, 236
Spain 237–38, 239, 241–42, 250, 387
Sri Lanka 259–60, 270, 273–74, 386–87, 396
Ukraine 292, 303–4
Yemen 313, 314, 322
see also **civil war; demonstrations and protests; rebellions**
***volkstaat* (expression of right in own territory), South Africa** 223–24, 227, 231–32, 233, 235–36
***Volkstaatraad* (People's State Council), South Africa** 227, 231

Wahid, Abdurrahman (Indonesian President) 125–26, 130, 132
War of Independence, 1948 46
Welsh, David 235
West New Guinea 122, 123
Wickremesinghe, Ranil (Sri Lankan Prime Minister) 268–69, 270–72, 401
Widodo, Joko 133–34
Wilson, Andrew 298
Wimmer, Andreas 394
Wodajo, Kifle 68, 69–70
Woldeyesys, Asrat 69
Workers Party of Ethiopia 66
World Bank
HIPC II initiative 17

Yanukovych, Viktor 300–1, 302, 303, 304, 306, 310–11
collapse of 304
developments following 307
Yemen 312–13, 374, 382, 401
Aden region 313, 314, 320
AQAP (terrorist group) 322, 327–28
and Arab Spring 312–13, 385
Azal region 320
background to events 312
central institutions, representation in 319
civil war 312–14, 317, 322–23, 324, 325, 328
Constitution 314–15, 317, 320–21, 322–23, 324, 325, 327–29, 391
Constitution Drafting Commission (CDC) 312, 320–23
constitutional process
in constitutional transition 326
framing 317
integrated approach to transitions 328
progression 318
8+8 forum 320, 328
federalism 324–25, 415–16
highly territorialized region xvi
Hirak (secessionist Southern movement) 312–13, 315–16, 317–18, 320–21
Houthis (Islamic armed movement) 312–13, 315–16, 317–18, 319–21, 322–23, 324, 325–26, 327–28, 387, 411, 415–16
Joint Meeting Parties (JMP) 313, 314, 315–16, 320
lessons learned 324–28
National Dialogue (ND) 312, 314–15, 317, 401, 405–6, 407, 411, 421–22
National Dialogue Conference (NDC) 315, 316, 317, 318–22, 323, 324, 325–26, 327, 328–29
National Body for Monitoring the Implementation of the Outcomes 321
Presidium 318
oil and gas resources 319
outcome of process 323
overview of case 312
political legitimacy 326
power-sharing arrangements 318–19, 324–25
regional structure 319
Sana'a region 320, 322–23
sub-national governance 324
Technical Preparatory Committee 317
violence 313, 314, 322
Working Groups 321
see also **Gulf Cooperation Council (GCC)/GCC Initiative, Yemen**
Yudhoyono, Bambang 135
Yugoslavia *see* **Socialist Federal Republic of Yugoslavia (SFRY)**
Yushchenko, Viktor (Ukrainian Prime Minister) 302, 303, 305

Zeleke, Admasu 68–69
Zenawi, Meles (Ethiopian Prime Minister) 64, 70, 76–77
Zulu nationalism, South Africa *see* **South Africa**
Zuma, Jacob 232
Zvyahilsky, Efim 297
Zwelentini, South African King 232